Gregory Freeze is Associate Professor of History at Brandeis University and the author of *The Russian Levites: Parish Clergy in the Eighteenth Century* (Harvard).

The Parish Clergy in
Nineteenth-Century Russia

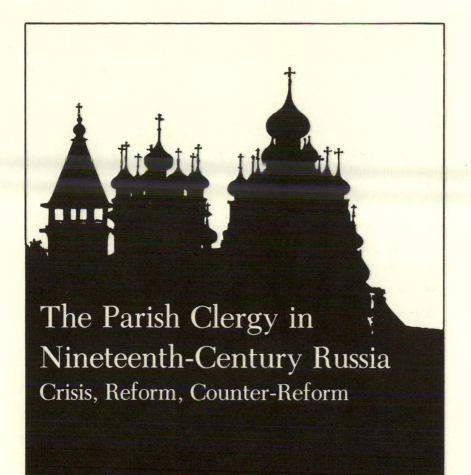

The Parish Clergy in Nineteenth-Century Russia

Crisis, Reform, Counter-Reform

Gregory L. Freeze

PRINCETON UNIVERSITY PRESS
PRINCETON, NEW JERSEY

Copyright © 1983 by Princeton University Press
Published by Princeton University Press, 41 William Street,
Princeton, New Jersey 08540
In the United Kingdom: Princeton University Press, Guildford, Surrey

Library of Congress Cataloging in Publication Data will be
found on the last printed page of this book

This book has been composed in Caledonia

Clothbound editions of Princeton University Press books
are printed on acid-free paper, and binding materials are
chosen for strength and durability. Paperbacks, while satisfactory
for personal collections, are not usually suitable for library rebinding.

Printed in the United States of America by Princeton University
Press Princeton, New Jersey

TO
Katherine
and
Christopher

CONTENTS

CONTENTS

ILLUSTRATIONS

Following page 50

Archpriest G. P. Pavskii. *Russkie deiateli v portretakh* (St. Petersburg,
    1882), p. 137.
The Marriage Ceremony. Gravure by Czech traveler in the 1860s. *Život na
    Rusi* (Prague, 1869).
Funeral Procession in a Russian Village. Stephen Graham, *Undiscovered
    Russia* (New York: John Lane Co., 1914), p. 178.
Icon Procession. Rothay Reynolds, *My Russian Year* (London: Mills and
    Boon, Ltd., 1913), p. 215.
Peasants and Clergy in Icon Procession for Rain. D. W. Wallace, *Russia:
    Its History and Condition to 1877* (Boston: J. B. Millet Co., 1910).
Parish School Serving a non-Russian Minority (Votiaki or Udmurty). V. P.
    Semenov, *Rossiia: polnoe geograficheskoe opisanie*, vol. 6 (St.
    Petersburg, 1901), p. 135.
Russian Priest at Spasskii Church (a mining-camp parish). Herbert Bury,
    Russian Life To-Day (London: A. R. Mowbray and Co., Ltd., 1915), p.
    90.

TABLES

PREFACE

Notwithstanding its manifest importance, the Russian Orthodox clergy has not been the subject of serious scholarly research—in marked contrast to most other social groups in imperial Russia. This volume aims to fill that gap, at once treating the social history of the clergy, the repeated attempts to reform it, and the impact of these reforms upon the structure and *mentalité* of parish clergy. Thus at one level this book is social history, a systematic analysis of the clergy's origins, educational level, career patterns, service order, and economic condition. At the same time, the reader will find here a close inquiry into the inner workings of Church and state administration, both in St. Petersburg and at lower levels; the task is to elucidate how these institutions functioned and interacted (in actuality, not merely as formal law dictated they should act), how they collaborated—and clashed—in planning and executing reform. But perhaps the most important goal here is to explore the changing political and social attitudes of parish clergy, and to assay the regime's success in transforming the clergy from a traditional service estate (*soslovie*) into a modern corps of professional pastors. All that makes for extraordinary complexity; the novelty of the subject, the freshness of the source base (virtually none of which has been previously explored), and the chronological and thematic scope of this inquiry have all combined to make a rather long volume. But I hope that the reader, whether Russianist, social historian, or general Church historian, will be rewarded with a new picture of the Russian clergy, the Orthodox Church, and the problems of social and institutional reform in prerevolutionary Russia.

This work owes much to the support of several institutions: the American Council of Learned Societies, the Fulbright Faculty Research Program, the Russian Research Center of Harvard University, and the John S. Guggenheim Foundation. I am particularly indebted to the International Research and Exchanges Board, which has sponsored multiple research trips to the Soviet Union, making it possible for me virtually to exhaust the rich bank of archival and printed sources. Suffice it to say that, whereas even very good Western monographs on Russia normally use a few score, at most a few hundred, archival files, I have been able to work systematically through some four thousand archival files, drawn not only from central depositories but from six provincial archives as well. That advantage would have been impossible without the support of the above institutions and, in no less degree, the generous and intelligent collaboration of the host institutions and archives in the Soviet Union.

My work has also profited much from the strictures and suggestions of colleagues. I am particularly indebted to Marc Raeff, whose erudition and broad European perspective have substantially enriched the final manuscript, and to S. S. Dmitriev, whose integrity and generosity are a model for any young, aspiring scholar. Harley Balzer, Daniel Field, Nancy Frieden, Norman Naimark, Daniel Orlovsky, and Donald Treadgold read the manuscript in whole or in part; all offered stimulating criticism and suggestions on matters of style and substance. Karen Freeze has been an indefatigable editor, spotting infelicities and spurring me to more lucid prose.

I am grateful for permission to use (in revised form) material from my articles already published elsewhere: "P. A. Valuyev and the Politics of Church Reform, 1861–62," *Slavonic and East European Review,* 56 (1978): 68–87; "Caste and Emancipation: The Changing Status of Clerical Families in the Great Reforms," in *The Family in Imperial Russia* (Urbana: University of Illinois Press, 1978), pp. 124–50; and "Revolt from Below: A Priest's Manifesto on the Crisis in Russian Orthodoxy," in *Russian Orthodoxy under the Old Regime* (Minneapolis: University of Minnesota Press, 1978), pp. 90–124. Archival materials from the Kilgour collection at Harvard University have been used and cited with the permission of the Houghton Library.

A note on technical matters. For transliteration I have followed the Library of Congress system; the only exceptions are names already well-known in an Anglicized form (for example, the names of Russian emperors). The archaic spellings of nineteenth-century names and titles have been partially modified to conform with modern orthography. Dates follow the Julian ("old style") calendar, which lagged behind the Gregorian calendar of the West (twelve days in the nineteenth century; thirteen days in the twentieth century). The footnotes, where appropriate, provide the date of a given document (as day/month/year). A full list of abbreviations is given at the front of this book; the title of individual *fond* numbers of each archive is provided in the first section of the bibliography. Unless indicated otherwise, the text and tables refer only to the Russian Orthodox clergy, not the servitors of other confessions.

The research for this book has not been without great personal cost: to my wife and two children, I can only express my profound gratitude for their forbearance and good-natured acceptance of my archival peregrinations abroad and nocturnal habits at home.

ABBREVIATIONS

AHR	American Historical Review
Astrakhanskie EV	*Astrakhanskie eparkhial'nye vedomosti*
BS	Bibliothèque slave, Paris
BV	*Bogoslovskii vestnik*
ChOIDR	*Chteniia v Obshchestve istorii i drevnostei rossiiskikh*
ChOLDP	*Chteniia v Obshchestve liubitelei dukhovnogo prosveshcheniia*
DV	*Dukhovnyi vestnik*
FDA	*Freiburger Diözesan-Archiv*
Filaret, *PSR*	Filaret (Drozdov), *Polnoe sobranie rezoliutsii*
Filaret, *SMO*	Filaret (Drozdov), *Sobranie mnenii i otzyvov*
GA Irkutskoi obl.	Gosudarstvennyi arkhiv Irkutskoi oblasti, Irkutsk
GA Kalininskoi obl.	Gosudarstvennyi arkhiv Kalininskoi oblasti, Kalinin
GA Kurskoi obl.	Gosudarstvennyi arkhiv Kurskoi oblasti, Kursk
GA Tomskoi obl.	Gosudarstvennyi arkhiv Tomskoi oblasti, Tomsk
GBL	Gosudarstvennaia biblioteka im. V. I. Lenina, Moscow
GPB	Gosudarstvennaia publichnaia biblioteka im. M. E. Saltykova-Shchedrina, Leningrad
Iaroslavskie EV	*Iaroslavskie eparkhial'nye vedomosti*
IRLI	Institut russkoi literatury (Pushkinskii dom), Leningrad
IVO [year]	*Izvlecheniia iz vsepoddanneishego otcheta ober-prokurora*
IZ	*Istoricheskie zapiski*
JBKG	*Jahrbücher für brandenburgische Kirchengeschichte*
JEH	*Journal of Ecclesiastical History*
JGO	*Jahrbücher für Geschichte Osteuropas*
KA	*Krasnyi arkhiv*
Kaluzhskie EV	*Kaluzhskie eparkhial'nye vedomosti*
KhCh	*Khristianskoe chtenie*
Kievskie EV	*Kievskie eparkhial'nye vedomosti*
Kolosov, *ITDS*	V. Kolosov, *Istoriia Tverskoi dukhovnoi seminarii*
Kurskie EV	*Kurskie eparkhial'nye vedomosti*
Lagovskii, *IPDS*	I. Lagovskii, *Istoriia Permskoi dukhovnoi seminarii*

Litovskie EV	*Litovskie eparkhial'nye vedomosti*
LOII	Leningradskoe otdelenie instituta istorii, Leningrad
Malitskii, *IVDS*	N. Malitskii, *Istoriia Vladimirskoi dukhovnoi seminarii*
Moskovskie EV	*Moskovskie eparkhial'nye vedomosti*
Nadezhdin, *ISDS*	A. Nadezhdin, *Istoriia S.-Peterburgskoi pravoslavnoi dukhovnoi seminarii, 1801–84 gg.*
Nikol'skii, *IVDS*	P. Nikol'skii, *Istoriia Voronezhskoi dukhovnoi seminarii*
OR GBL	Otdel rukopisei. Gosudarstvennaia biblioteka im. V. I. Lenina, Moscow
OR GPB	Otdel rukopisei. Gosudarstvennaia publichnaia biblioteka im. M. E. Saltykova-Shchedrina, Leningrad
PO	*Pravoslavnoe obozrenie*
Poltavskie EV	*Poltavskie eparkhial'nye vedomosti*
Prib. TSO	*Pribavleniia k Tvoreniiam Sviatykh Otets*
PS	*Pravoslavnyi sobesednik*
PSPR	*Polnoe sobranie postanovlenii i rasporiazhenii po vedomstvu pravoslavnogo ispovedaniia. Tsarstvovanie Imp. Nikolaia Pavlovicha.*
PSZ (1)	*Polnoe sobranie zakonov Rossiiskoi imperii. 1-aia seriia.*
PSZ (2)	*Polnoe sobranie zakonov Rossiiskoi imperii. 2-aia seriia.*
PSZ (3)	*Polnoe sobranie zakonov Rossiiskoi imperii. 3-aia seriia.*
RA	*Russkii arkhiv*
Riazanskie EV	*Riazanskie eparkhial'nye vedomosti*
RS	*Russkaia starina*
RSP	*Rukovodstvo dlia sel'skikh pastyrei*
Samarskie EV	*Samarskie eparkhial'nye vedomosti*
Saratovskie EV	*Saratovskie eparkhial'nye vedomosti*
SEER	*Slavonic and East European Review*
SIRIO	*Sbornik Imperatorskogo russkogo istoricheskogo obshchestva*
SL	*Sovremennyi listok*
Smirnov, *IMDA*	S. K. Smirnov, *Istoriia Moskovskoi dukhovnoi akademii*
Smolenskie EV	*Smolenskie eparkhial'nye vedomosti*
Speranskii, *OISS*	I. Speranskii, *Ocherk istorii Smolenskoi dukhovnoi seminarii*
Str	*Strannik*

SZ	*Svod zakonov*
TKDA	*Trudy Kievskoi dukhovnoi akademii*
TsGALI	Tsentral'nyi gosudarstvennyi arkhiv literatury i iskus-stva, Moscow
TsGAOR	Tsentral'nyi gosudarstvennyi arkhiv Oktiabr'skoi Revoliutsii, Moscow
TsGIAgM	Tsentral'nyi gosudarstvennyi istoricheskii arkhiv g. Moskvy, Moscow
TsGIA SSSR	Tsentral'nyi gosudarstvennyi istoricheskii arkhiv SSSR, Leningrad
TsGIA UkrSSR	Tsentral'nyi gosudarstvennyi istoricheskii arkhiv Ukrainskoi SSR, Kiev
TsOV	*Tserkovno-obshchestvennyi vestnik*
Tul'skie EV	*Tul'skie eparkhial'nye vedomosti*
Viatskie EV	*Viatskie eparkhial'nye vedomosti*
Vladimirskie EV	*Vladimirskie eparkhial'nye vedomosti*
VR	*Vera i razum*

Archival notation follows the accepted Soviet form of abbreviation.

f.	*fond* (collection)	
op.	*opis'* (inventory)	
g.	*god* (year)	
otd.	*otdelenie* (division)	
st.	*stol* (department)	
r.	*razdel* (section)	
sv.	*sviazka* (sheaf)	
k.	*karton* (box)	
d.	*delo* (file)	
l., ll.	*list, listy* (leaf; leaves)	
ob.	*oborot* (verso)	
ch.	*chast'* (part)	

To expose and reveal our shortcomings is easier than to correct them. The tragedy of our time is that the number of wrongs and errors, having accumulated for more than a century, almost exceeds [our] powers and means to correct them.

Metropolitan Filaret to Bishop Innokentii (1857)

Commissions, committees—all that is marvelous; opinions, deliberations in journals—all that is marvelous too. But are not journal opinions and all the rest just words, words, words?

Father I. S. Belliustin to M. P. Pogodin (1858)

INTRODUCTION

In 1839 Ioann S. Belliustin, just graduating from the seminary in Tver, faced an agonizing decision: either to enter the St. Petersburg Academy for further study, or to accept the proposal of a rural priest to assume his position in the village of Vasilino. At a time when clerical positions were virtually unobtainable, with hundreds of youths idle in the diocese, the priest's proposition was tempting indeed. The parish was a rather large one, including some 1,500 serfs and a wealthy landlord; the parish church possessed slightly more than the usual amount of land (nearly 100 acres) and yielded a "fair income" from parishioners for the ministration of religious rites. The retiring priest, sixty-seven years of age, had an eighteen-year-old daughter, Anna; if the seminarian agreed to marry the girl and provide for the priest and his family, the position was his, together with the family's small wooden house built on church land. The offer proved irresistible. On 17 September Belliustin married Anna, on 12 October he was ordained, and on 27 October he performed his first mass in the Church. Born himself into the clergy, married to a priest's daughter, educated entirely in Church schools, he now bore the Church's mission to the very heart of rural Russia.[1]

"The years 1840–1842," Belliustin later wrote, "were the worst years of my life."[2] As a rural priest he earned his support mainly by performing rites for small fees and by conducting processions on great holidays to the parishioners' homes, collecting eggs, flour, and a few kopecks at each stop. On one Christmas Eve he wrote a friend that "tomorrow begins one of the things I detest most of all—the beggarly wandering about the parish under a seemly pretext—to glorify Christ." But everyone, "myself included," knows that "the purpose of my wandering is a three-kopeck piece, a half-bushel of oats."[3] Still worse was the field labor, a vital part of the rural priest's economy. "Rural life," Belliustin wrote, "with its exhausting labor, petty concerns, with its filth, endless needs, useless and often futile labor, was anything

---

[1] Belliustin, "Semeinye zametki," Gosudarstvennyi arkhiv Kalininskoi oblasti [hereafter GA Kalininskoi obl.], f. 103 (Tverskaia uchenaia arkhivnaia komissiia), op. 1, d. 1291, ll. 144–49; information on Vasilino is taken from the service registers for 1830 and 1860 in ibid., f. 160 (Tverskaia dukhovnaia konsistoriia), op. 1, dd. 16272, 16298. For abbreviations and archival notation, see the list of abbreviations at the front of this volume.

[2] GA Kalininskoi obl., f. 103, op. 1, d. 1291, l. 149 ob. (Belliustin, "Semeinye zametki").

[3] Institut russkoi literatury [hereafter IRLI], f. 616 (A. D. Zheltukhin), d. 6, l. 41 (I. S. Belliustin to A. D. Zheltukhin, 24.12.1858).

but pleasant and joyous." After twelve years in church schools and the seminary, he knew nothing of agriculture and "simply did not know how to go about much of this." His formal schooling, where he mastered classical languages and the fine points of theological issues, proved useless: "Twelve years of study gave absolutely nothing, or almost nothing, for this [rural pastorship]. What is the use of memorizing ancient languages? . . . I was very well versed in the literature of Greeks and Romans, but what was the point? . . . To read the Church Fathers? But where would you find [copies to read]?"[4]

His religious service proved even more discouraging. Despite claims in the salons of Moscow about "Orthodox Rus'" and the spiritual treasury in peasant hamlets, Belliustin found the people virtually ignorant of the faith. "The people are called Orthodox—Lord, what an evil, venomous mockery!"[5] "Orthodox Rus'—every time we hear this word, our entire soul is overwhelmed by feelings of sorrow, irritation, indignation, and intolerable pain." Though his parishioners had some attachment to the externals of religion, "they do not have the slightest conception of the faith, the true path to salvation, or the basic tenets of [Orthodoxy]."[6] His parishioners would never dream of consuming milk products during Lent, but they regarded adultery and dishonesty lightly; perhaps two in a thousand knew prayers or the Ten Commandments; for many the "Trinity is God, Virgin Mary, and St. Nicholas," the latter so popular that some believed that "when God dies, Nicholas will take his place."[7]

Young and energetic, Belliustin threw himself into the task of "converting" these dark masses to true Orthodoxy. But missionary zeal was no equal to serfdom: the local serfowner (a rich Dolgorukov) refused to open a parish school and left little time for her serfs to indulge in religion. "They work six days a week for the serfowner, on the seventh for themselves, and they visit the Church only on main holidays. . . . As a result, they are without the slightest grasp of the faith, the Ten Commandments, or morality. . . ."[8] The priest also had to stand by idly as serfowners maltreated their chattel, exploiting the men, abusing the women, and subjecting those who resisted to the knout.[9]

---

[4]GA Kalininskoi obl., f. 103, op. 1, d. 1291, l. 149 ob. (Belliustin, "Semeinye zametki"); d. 1307, l. 1 ob. (Belliustin, "Iz zametok o proshlom").

[5]IRLI, f. 34 (S. O. Burachek), op. 1, d. 62, l. 3 ob. (I. S. Belliustin to S. O. Burachek, 20.3.1858); Otdel rukopisei, Gosudarstvennaia biblioteka im. V. I. Lenina [hereafter OR GBL], f. 231/II (M. P. Pogodin), k. 1, d. 66, l. 36 ob. (I. S. Belliustin, "Pravoslavnaia Rus'").

[6]GA Kalininskoi obl., f. 103, op. 1, d. 1307, l. 2 ob. ("Iz zametok").

[7]IRLI, f. 34, op. 1, d. 62, ll. 3 ob.-4 (Belliustin to Burachek, 20.3.1858).

[8]GA Kalininskoi obl., f. 103, op. 1, d. 1307, ll. 2 ob.-3 ("Iz zametok"); IRLI, f. 34, op. 1, d. 62, ll. 3 ob.-4 (Belliustin to Burachek, 20.3.1858).

[9]In a diary entry of 3 Sept. 1847, Belliustin described ministering last rites to peasants due to receive punishment for murdering their landlord, a scapegrace who mercilessly abused his

Nor could he turn to fellow clergy for support. His subordinates at the church were barely educated, his superintendent casually plundered local churches, and the other priests in the district lacked his zeal: "There was not the slightest possibility of getting close to them, for they were absolutely alien to all that is called scholarship and literature, even of a spiritual sort."[10] Holdovers from older times, their learning minimal or long since forgotten amidst the toil and cares of rural life, his fellow clergy met only to feast and drink, not to consider the spiritual needs of their flocks.[11] As for the young priest's superiors—monastic clergy who ruled the Church as bishops of dioceses and rectors of schools—they too gave him little support. Venality reigned freely here, as elsewhere in contemporary Russia, determining appointments and favors. Frustrated and angry, the priest confided to his diary in 1849, "The white clergy is governed by the monks—what an anomaly! Can a monk understand the conditions, needs, and demands of family life? Can he sympathize with the invariably bitter condition of the priest living on 200 to 300 rubles [trying] to support and educate sons, to provide his daughters with a dowry?" Rejected and humiliated, he cried, "O Monks—an evil more terrible than any other evil, Pharisees and Hypocrites—*quousque tandem abutere* with your rights?"[12]

Exhausted by field labor, ignored by peasants, oppressed by landlords, abused by superiors, the priest grew profoundly despondent. "The clergy," he wrote, "is now a [mere] apparition, a shadow. . . . Humiliated, depressed, beaten down, it itself is already losing consciousness of its own significance."[13] From his own travels and wide network of acquaintances, he knew the problem was hardly unique to his village, his diocese: "Everywhere, in all corners and parts of Orthodox Russia, it is all the same! Oppressed and trampled, mired in a hopeless and ruinous swamp—such is the lot of our clergy in the north and the south, in the east and the west."[14] He dreaded that his sons would become priests and decried his inability to send them elsewhere; it is terrible, he wrote, "to know that my own children must follow this ruinous

---

serfs. The peasants, he wrote, had earlier appealed to authorities, but to no avail, and finally defended themselves: "The serfowners investigated and judged this case; could one expect any mercy from this scourge of mankind, from these vicious beasts, this incurable ulcer of every government?" (GA Kalininskoi obl., f. 103, op. 1, d. 1291, ll. 7 ob.-8). Later, as emancipation drew near, he wrote his acquaintances that all are "ready to rise up against the nobility, from the soldier to the peasant, from the priest to the sacristan" (IRLI, f. 616, op. 1, d. 6, l. 29 [Belliustin to Zheltukhin, 27.10.1858]).

[10] GA Kalininskoi obl., f. 103, op. 1, d. 1307, l. 6 ("Iz zametok").

[11] In the service registers for Belliustin's district in 1830, 28 percent of the priests lacked a seminary degree—even though the standard in his diocese, as we shall see, was among the highest in the empire (GA Kalininskoi obl., f. 160, op. 1, d. 16272).

[12] GA Kalininskoi obl., f. 103, op. 1, d. 1291, ll. 107–8 (Belliustin, "Dnevnik").

[13] Ibid., l. 34 ob.

[14] OR GBL, f. 231/II, k. 3, d. 49/6, l. 6 (Belliustin to Pogodin, 2.4.1857).

path and to see no means to guide them onto some other path."[15] Though he dreamed of "tearing himself free of this fatal environment, known as the 'clerical rank,'" he could not overcome the harsh penalties imposed for voluntary defrocking and thus remained a priest, albeit unwillingly.[16] To his son he wrote, "What is the result [of my life]? Not a single happy day to this very moment."[17]

In language rich in poignancy and pathos, Belliustin's diaries and letters convey the sense of acute anxiety widely shared by Orthodox clergy in the nineteenth century. The Church, as Belliustin's personal experience shows, suffered from serious deficiencies—in the seminary, in diocesan administration, and in the daily service of parish priests. The Church's condition seemed perilously weak, especially when compared with its status in medieval Muscovy, when it wielded immense wealth and power, commanding obeisance from the man with a scepter no less than from the man with a scythe. But in modern times the Church suffered a steady attrition of resources and power, even as it faced mounting challenges on all sides— unbelief among Westernized elites, Old Belief among commoners, other belief among minorities, or new belief among sectarians.[18] To combat these challenges, Russian authorities—ecclesiastical and secular—were ineluctably drawn to improve the condition and performance of the Church's front-line troops, the secular clergy. The primary task, as they came to realize, was to transform the traditional service estate into a more professional class of servitors, armed with the requisite education, status, and zeal to carry the Church's mission to society.

Bleak as the Russian Church's plight may seem, it was hardly alone. Churches all across Europe faced awesome challenges in the nineteenth century—growing strains in their relationship to the secular state, mortal threats from modern science, and alarming evidence of dechristianization among the lower classes.[19] The response was continuing reformism, making the

---

[15] Ibid., d. 49/4, l. 1 (Belliustin to Pogodin, 26.11.1855).

[16] OR GBL, f. 327/II (Cherkasskie), k. 5, d. 31, l. 3 (Belliustin to E. A. Cherkasskaia, 29.3.1860).

[17] Leningradskoe otdelenie instituta istorii [hereafter LOII], f. 115 (Kollektsiia rukopisnykh knig), d. 1217, no. 18 (unpaginated letter of Jan. 1860 from I. S. Belliustin to N. I. Belliustin).

[18] For an excellent introduction to the problem of the Old Belief (a popular movement opposed to the liturgical reforms of the mid-seventeenth century), see Robert O. Crummey, *Old Believers and the World of Anti-Christ* (Madison, 1967); for the later, but powerful, movement of sectarians, see F. C. Conybeare, *Russian Dissenters* (Cambridge, 1921).

[19] Evidence of dechristianization mounted steadily and was sometimes quantified, as in the 1851 religious census in Britain (see K. S. Inglis, "Patterns of Religious Worship in 1851," *Journal of Ecclesiastical History* [hereafter *JEH*], 11 [1960]: 74–86). By the early twentieth century such investigations showed massive indifference to the Church, as in Germany, where a survey of 1913–1914 found that less than 1 to 4 percent of church members attended a given

nineteenth century an age of vital reform for the church no less than for secular society. In England, for example, authorities began to attack such old vices as pluralism and absenteeism, to shift resources from the depopulated countryside to the teeming cities, and to experiment with more popular forms of open-air evangelism.[20] And throughout Europe the clerical econ- omy became a sensitive issue, as laymen protested such traditional levies as the tithe and the clergy complained of a decline in real income.[21] Most important, churches struggled to raise the quality of parish clergy—to pro- vide them with more specialized training, to modernize and emphasize pas- toral theology, and to inspire them to more zealous service through periodic assemblies and synods.[22] Such tasks seemed particularly great in France, where the Church had to rebuild a clergy decimated by the Revolution and Civil Constitution; by mid-century authorities had succeeded in recruiting and training an aggressive new priesthood, so aggressive in fact that it helped

---

service (A. M. Horowitz, "Prussian State and Protestant Church in the Reign of Wilhelm II" [Ph.D. diss., Yale University, 1976], p. 38). For general discussions, see such works as R. Currie et al., *Churches and Churchgoers* (Oxford, 1977); Yves-Marie Hilaire, *Une Chrétienté au XIXe siècle? La vie religieuse des populations du diocèse d'Arras (1840-1914)*, 2 vols. (Paris, 1977); and John McManners, *Church and State in France, 1870-1914* (New York, 1972), pp. 7–9. For sage warnings about the idea of dechristianization, see Gabriel LeBras, "Déchristian- isation: mot fallacieux," *Social Compass*, 10 (1963): 445–52; on the difficulties of applying such concepts as secularization, see L. Shiner, "The Concept of Secularization in Empirical Research," *Journal for the Scientific Study of Religion*, 6 (1967): 207–20.

[20]Besides such contemporary works as R. Henley, *A Plan for Church Reform* (3rd ed.; London, 1832), and John Wade, *The Black Book* (rev. ed.; London, 1835), see the older study by W. L. Mathieson, *English Church Reform, 1815-1840* (London, 1923), and the more thor- ough analysis by G. F. A. Best, *Temporal Pillars* (Cambridge, 1964).

[21]In Sweden, for example, agitation against the tithe finally led to its abolition in 1862 (see Sten Alsne, *Från prästtionden till reglerad lön. Pastoraliekonventionerna i Uppsala Ärke- stift, 1810-1862* [Uppsala, 1966]). The tithe was also a major source of tension in England; see E. J. Evans, "Some Reasons for the General Growth of English Rural Anticlericalism, c. 1750- c.1830," *Past and Present*, 66 (1975): 85–94. Contrast the attitudes of an earlier time, as described in G. Constable, "Resistance to Tithes in the Middle Ages," *JEH*, 13 (1962): 172– 85. For the economic issue elsewhere, see the accounts of nineteenth-century France (A. Dan- sette, *Histoire religieuse de la France contemporaine* [2nd. ed; Paris, 1965], pp. 378–79, and C. Marcilhacy, *Le diocèse d'Orléans au milieu du XIXe siècle* [Paris, 1964], pp. 125–28) and the United States (W. C. Bonifield, "The Economics of the Ministry: An Analysis of the Demand and Supply of Protestant Clergy" [Ph.D. diss., University of Minnesota, 1968]).

[22]For the interest in clerical assemblies, which gained momentum from the mid-nineteenth century, see Owen Chadwick, *The Victorian Church*, 2 vols. (London, 1966–70), 2: 359–60; Hilaire, *Une Chrétienté*, 1: 227–79; B. Bligny, ed., *Le diocèse de Grenoble* (Paris, 1979), 200– 1; H. Werdermann, *Der evangelische Pfarrer in Geschichte und Gegenwart* (Leipzig, 1925), pp. 90, 124; Horowitz, "Prussian State and Protestant Church," pp. 50–53. For the changing conception of pastoral theology, see such accounts as that in E. Keller, "Das Priesterseminar Meersburg zur Zeit Wessenbergs (1801–27)," *Freiburger Diözesan-Archiv* [hereafter *FDA*], 97 (1977): 108–207.

to precipitate a virulent wave of anticlericalism.[23] Elsewhere too authorities labored to uplift the secular clergy, to make them into better preachers, catechists, and teachers and to increase their skill and diligence in performing sacraments.[24] Although the parish clergy did not form a modern profession in the strictest sense, they did seek to become "more professional," that is, more proficient and specialized in the performance of their spiritual and temporal duties.[25]

The Russian Church shared in this process of reform. Although some attention was given to the problems of monastic clergy, the Church focused most of its efforts upon the secular clergy, seeking to make them more effective in proselytizing the Word to illiterate peasants, freethinking nobles, and dissenting schismatics. The magnitude of the task hardly bears underestimation; the sheer size of the Russian parish clergy—three times that of France, seven times that of England, and seventeen times that of *Vormärz* Prussia—posed a social problem of staggering proportions.[26] In financial terms alone the Russian Empire, so economically backward, could ill afford to assume major new financial burdens. Even the state's own apparatus was seriously undermanned and unprofessional, especially at lower levels, primarily for lack of funds; it would be no easy matter for the state to find a substitute for the traditional emoluments and clerical agriculture that Belliustin so forcefully castigated. Nor would it be easy to involve society in the task of solving such economic problems. Quite apart from the educated classes, wont to regard parish priests with contempt, the lower strata of the population—given their illiteracy, religious ignorance, even proclivity to deviation—made laicization exceedingly difficult and dangerous.

Yet the prospects for reform were not entirely bleak, especially when compared with the far more dynamic patterns of social and religious change

[23]See the accounts in F. Boulard, *Essor ou déclin du clergé français?* (Paris, 1950); P. Huot-Pleuroux, *Le recrutement sacerdotal dans le diocèse de Besançon de 1801 à 1960* (Paris, 1966). On French anticlericalism, see R. Rémond, *L'anticléricalisme en France de 1815 à nos jours* (Paris, 1976).

[24]See Dianna McClatchey, *Oxfordshire Clergy, 1777–1868* (Oxford, 1960), a pioneering piece of research. For two recent works drawing upon clerical instruction manuals, see Anthony Russell, *The Clerical Profession* (London, 1980), and Brian Heeney, *A Different Kind of Gentleman: Parish Clergy as Professional Men in Early and Mid-Victorian England* (Hamden, Conn., 1976).

[25]See P. Jarvis, "The Parish Ministry as a Semi-Profession," *Sociological Review*, n.s., 23 (1975): 911–22.

[26]Whereas Russia had 108,916 full-time parish clergy in 1824, France had only 40,500 parish priests (in 1829), England 14,613 parsons (in 1841), and *Vormärz* Prussia just 5,714 ministers (in 1822). Tsentral'nyi gosudarstvennyi istoricheskii arkhiv SSSR [hereafter TsGIA SSSR], f. 797 (Kantseliariia ober-prokurora), op. 96, d. 5, ll. 1 ob.-2; Dansette, *Histoire religieuse*, pp. 199–200; R. M. Bigler, *The Politics of German Protestantism: The Rise of the Protestant Church Elite in Prussia, 1815–1848* (Berkeley, 1972), pp. 55–56; Chadwick, *Victorian Church*, 2: 244. For per capita ratios, see below, Chapter 2.

faced by Western churches. Perhaps the Russian Church's greatest asset was the piety of its adherents: however ignorant and superstitious they might be, the laity—still overwhelmingly peasant, with only a negligible urban and working-class component—remained intensely pious, manifesting little of the irreligion then threatening churches in the West. Although radical intellectuals tended to deny popular religiousness, citing the high degree of superstition and overt disrespect for clergy, most evidence suggests an extraordinarily high level of piety right to the 1917 Revolution. Data on confession and communion, for example, show that most church members observed these duties, with only a modest decline coming in the first decade of the twentieth century.[27] Although these data are highly imperfect (in terms both of significance and even of statistical reliability), they conform closely to the analysis given by contemporary officials, bishops, and priests. The bishops' annual reports, even to the eve of the 1905 Revolution, consistently stress that "ancient piety, reverence, and respect for the Holy Church are preserved in the people."[28] Indeed, in the judgment of the clergy, the laity's main failing—namely, their blind devotion to ritual, their ignorance of dogma and prayers—only served to reinforce the indispensability of the priest. Significantly, in marked contrast to the anticlericalism then surging in the West, the popular classes in nineteenth-century Russia sought more, not fewer, clergy for their parish church, primarily to enrich the aesthetics of the liturgy and to assure easy accessibility to the vital rites of passage.[29]

Church and state authorities, as the following pages make abundantly clear, were plainly determined to pursue reform in the Church. Although they differed on specific prescriptions, both bishops and bureaucrats concurred on the urgency of reform and called loudly for immediate steps to improve the clergy's condition and performance. Interest in church reform, moreover, drew upon a broader reformist spirit in nineteenth-century Russia, as the *ancien régime* discerned flaws in the old order and labored inces-

---

[27] Though Soviet historians cite selected data to show spot increases in the absolute numbers missing confession or communion in the early twentieth century, such parishioners represented a small proportion of the parish. Observance remained surprisingly high, even in such areas as Tomsk, a Siberian diocese greatly affected by the institutional weakness of the Church and the corrosive effect of Old Believer agitation: by 1916 only 12 percent missed confession and communion, a slight increase from the 9 percent reported in 1784 (TsGIA SSSR, f. 796 [Kantseliariia Sv. Sinoda], op. 63, g. 1782, d. 123, ll. 2–3; L. I. Emeliakh, *Istoricheskie predposylki preodoleniia religii v sovetskoi derevne* [Leningrad, 1975], p. 123).

[28] TsGIA SSSR, f. 796, op. 132, g. 1851, d. 2357, l. 68.

[29] Significantly, even amidst the economic distress of the late nineteenth century, peasants in Voronezh still spent an average of 9.2 percent of their budgets on the Church, and even as much as 13.8 percent in the case of poorer peasants (V. N. Dunaev, "Vystuplenie krest'ian Voronezhskoi gubernii protiv reaktsionnykh deistvii dukhovenstva (mart-oktiabr' 1917 g.)," *Sbornik rabot aspirantov Voronezhskogo Gosudarstvennogo Universiteta*, 1 (1965): 143. See also my "A Case of Stunted Anticlericalism: Clergy and Society in Imperial Russia," forthcoming in *European Studies Review*.

santly to repair or renovate whole institutions.[30] Reform, in fact, was a continual process. Though conventionally divided into three periods—the "prereforms" under Nicholas I (1825–1855), the "Great Reforms" under Alexander II (1855–1881), and "Counter-reform" under Alexander III (1881–1894)—these reforms constituted an ongoing attempt to rebuild the empire's basic social and institutional order. If only because the Church formed an integral component of that old order, it was certain to be drawn ineluctably into the general process of reform.[31]

Nor was the Church wholly deficient in resources. Though stripped of its lands and peasants in 1764, it still wielded considerable reserves in influence, manpower, and institutional strength. Even if vulnerable to the willfulness of tsars and the machinations of bureaucrats, the Church was not without influence: it remained the official state church; its views still prevailed in religious questions like divorce; and its importance as the linchpin of the old order was duly recognized by both sovereign and officialdom. The Church also had a wealth of manpower. For all its shortcomings, the traditional clerical estate, formed as part of a larger system of hereditary estates, assured an ample supply of candidates: the clergy's sons *had* to study in the seminary. As a result, the seminaries produced a steady stream of new candidates; in fact, by the 1830s and 1840s they produced far more graduates than the Church could absorb—a far cry from the situation a few decades earlier, when priests with a seminary degree were few and far between. If some Western churches faced periodic and increasingly severe difficulties in recruitment, the Church in prereform Russia had a great abundance of talent at its disposal. The task was to transform, not to create *ab ovo*, a more effective pastorate out of the traditional clerical estate. As Belliustin's very protest suggests, that kind of transformation promised to evoke enthusiastic support in the generation of younger, better-educated clergy.

That transformation of the clergy from a hereditary status to an occupational profession came to embrace four main issues. One was the structure of the clerical estate, especially its hereditary order, which tended to encum-

[30]See A. K. Tolstoi's classic description of Russian history as a series of futile attempts at reform: "Russkaia istoriia ot Gostomysla s IX po XIX v.," *Polnoe sobranie sochinenii*, 4 vols. (St. Petersburg, 1907–08), 1: 465–77.

[31]The main monograph on the prerevolutionary clergy is P. V. Znamenskii's *Prikhodskoe dukhovenstvo v Rossii so vremeni Petra Velikogo* (Kazan, 1873), and there are some specialized works—most notably, N. Runovskii's summary of legislation (*Tserkovno-grazhdanskoe zakonopolozhenie otnositel'no pravoslavnogo dukhovenstva v tsarstvovanie imp. Aleksandra II* [Kazan, 1898]), A. A. Papkov's essays on journalistic opinion (*Tserkovno-obshchestvennye voprosy v epokhu Tsaria-Osvoboditelia* [1855–70 gg.] [St. Petersburg, 1902]), and a large number of lesser monographs and essays. Though not without value, this literature suffers from an exceedingly narrow source base (with little or no use of archives), the severe limits of censorship existing before 1905, and an impressionistic methodology. For a discussion of the sources used here, see Appendix I.

ber appointments with family claims and to produce a surfeit of candidates. Here the main task was to abolish the hereditary estate (*soslovie*), to reconstitute the clergy into an open social group, and to free appointments from the fetters of family claims. A second issue was clerical education: to provide (2) better-trained priests, it was essential that the seminary expunge the stultifying scholasticism of eighteenth-century schools, reinvigorate the curriculum with modern subjects and practical preparation, and give more effective training to enable the clergy to preach, teach, and catechize to their unschooled flocks. A third focus of reform was the system of clerical service, (3) especially its economic support. Most authorities shared Belliustin's condemnation of emoluments and clerical agriculture and concurred that professional priests required more ample, more respectable support. The fourth (4) issue involved Church administration. At first focused upon corruption and abuse, reform eventually expanded to include the question of the clergy's corporate organization. Conciliarism derived not from Western models but from tradition, Slavophile publicists, and even the precedents accorded other social groups. Its purpose, whether applied to bishops or priests, was to mobilize their energies, pool their experiences, and help them to plot a more effective campaign against the Old Belief, sectarianism, and intellectual atheism. Why Nicholas's piecemeal reforms failed and why the old order commanded more fundamental reform are the subjects of Part One in this book.

Part Two explores the ambitious attempt in the 1860s to rebuild the clergy, aiming to elucidate the politics of reform and, more broadly, the regime's capacity to pursue reform. At one level this reform raised important questions of Church-state relations, not only mutual tensions and conflict but also the Church's ability to function as an interest group in the new system of bureaucratic politics. This experiment in Church reform, moreover, offers a useful case study for the viability of the *ancien régime*, its capacity for problem solving and its willingness to bear the costs and risks of radical change. Historians have written much about the structural weaknesses in Russian autocracy, stressing the limits of reform and attributing inept reformism to the clumsy and overly centralized administration, to ministerial conflict and competition, to the underdeveloped provincial administration, and to capricious meddling by the man in the Winter Palace. A study of reform at the grass roots—the transformation of a social estate like the clergy and the reordering of relationships in a community organization like the parish—can suggest larger insights into the feasibility and quandaries of reform.

The third part of this book explores the impact of reform. Did it succeed in reconstituting the clergy into a professional service group? At the most elemental level that is a question of the reforms' effectiveness in reshaping the clergy's education, economy, social profile, and capacity for more zealous service. No less important, however, are the political repercussions of reform on a traditional service soslovie, which looked primarily to the state to "emancipate" it from its low status and to assist it to become more effective in performing its high mission. In its final decades the *ancien régime* faced mounting disaffection and opposition, as large segments of society—workers, peasants, intellectuals, and even the nobility and bourgeoisie—lost faith in the regime's willingness and ability to solve their particular problems. The last section of this book will shed some light on how reform affected the clergy's willingness and ability to come to the defense of autocracy in its final hours of crisis.

PART ONE

Church and Clergy in Prereform Russia

Nicholas I looms as an archvillain in the accounts of contemporaries and prerevolutionary historians, who have castigated him as "the gendarme of Europe," the autocrat who crushed the Decembrist uprising, the master obscurantist who persecuted all men of good will and liberal thought.[1] For contemporary Europeans, who watched his armies smash the Polish Rebellion in 1830–1831 and the Hungarian revolution in 1849, no attack seemed too vitriolic or unjust. Inside Russia educated society (*obshchestvo*) steadily grew apart from the regime, coming to share the disdain of Nicholas's most inveterate critics.[2] Though official reports routinely depicted an empire of strength, stability, and good government, the reality was far different: in the celebrated phrase of one official, it was all "glitter on top, rot on the bottom."[3] The empire's problems were myriad and fundamental—economic backwardness, a venal and inept administration, a brutal serfdom that threatened to explode in *jacquerie*.

Unbeknownst to contemporaries, Nicholas's regime was actually one of intensive, persistent reformism, for in fact it did attempt to address the empire's problems. The emperor, even if uneasy about industrialization and the creation of a proletariat, did seek to stimulate economic and social development by moderating his financial policies, building the first railroad, and also taking steps to turn state peasants into more industrious, productive citizens.[4] Even the powder keg of serfdom did not escape Nicholas's reformism. To consider this problem, the emperor created ten separate committees, and he told the State Council in 1842 that "there is no doubt that serfdom, in the form we presently possess, is manifestly and obviously bad for all."[5] Although such complex problems as serfdom eluded resolution, Nicholas's government did achieve reforms in other areas. Even where reform stalled, without yielding concrete results, it nonetheless provided a springboard for reform in the

[1] Standard accounts of the Nikolaevan period include M. A. Polievktov, *Nikolai I* (Moscow, 1918), and, as a statement of more recent scholarship, W. B. Lincoln, *Nicholas I* (Bloomington, 1978).

[2] Here see, especially, N. V. Riasanovsky, *A Parting of Ways* (Oxford, 1976).

[3] P. A. Valuev, "Duma russkogo," *Russkaia starina* [hereafter *RS*], 70 (1891), no. 5: 354.

[4] See N. M. Druzhinin, *Gosudarstvennye krest'iane i reforma P. D. Kiseleva*, 2 vols. (Moscow-Leningrad, 1946–58), and W. Pintner, *Russian Economic Policy under Nicholas I* (Ithaca, 1967).

[5] *Gosudarstvennyi sovet, 1801–1901* (St. Petersburg, 1901), p. 64.

1860s. The data it collected, the experts it trained, the proposals it drafted—all served to facilitate the reform process under Alexander II.[6]

Nikolaevan reformism had its own ambience, however. Above all, it placed a high priority on gradualism, deliberately eschewing decisive measures and promises to solve a problem once and for all. Nicholas enunciated this tactic in his coronation manifesto of 1826 when he vowed to solve the empire's problems—not, however, "by bold and rash dreams, which are always destructive," but rather "gradually and from above."[7] That approach, he later declared, was essential in the case of serfdom, where "everything should be done gradually and ought not—indeed cannot—be done at once or suddenly."[8] Moreover, when promising reform "from above," Nicholas actually meant that it would emanate from *outside* the regular bureaucracy and represent the prized handiwork of personal absolutism, partly because of his disdain for his own bureaucracy,[9] but primarily because of his desire to reaffirm the role of personal autocrat. Significantly, Nicholas deliberately tried to emulate and identify with Peter the Great. Concretely, he created a plethora of secret, extrabureaucratic committees under his personal supervision, and in the regular conduct of government as well he assumed an enormous personal role.[10] Perhaps still more striking was another trait of Nikolaevan reformism: its reliance upon outdated cameralist principles, reflected in attempts to mobilize all groups to serve, to address issues of general welfare for state ends, and to make the secret police (the Third Section) function as the moral physician of the state. All such attempts were fully consonant with the goals of the eighteenth-century *Polizeistaat*.[11]

That kind of reformism entailed considerable costs. Above all, it depended primarily upon the emperor for momentum and direction. Yet, even a dili-

---

[6]See, for example, Richard S. Wortman, *The Development of a Russian Legal Consciousness* (Chicago, 1976); W. B. Lincoln, "The Genesis of an 'Enlightened' Bureaucracy in Russia, 1825–1856," *Jahrbücher für Geschichte Osteuropas* [hereafter *JGO*], 20 (1972): 321–30.

[7]A. A. Kornilov, *Kurs russkoi istorii*, 3 vols. (2nd ed.; Petrograd, 1918), 2: 18.

[8]*Gosudarstvennyi sovet*, p. 64.

[9]Such distrust of the bureaucracy was fostered by reports from the Third Section, which declared that "one seldom encounters honest people among [officials]—plunder, fraud, and perverse interpretation of the law are their stock in trade" (see "Graf A. Kh. Benkendorf o Rossii v 1827–30 gg.," *Krasnyi arkhiv* [hereafter *KA*], 37 [1929]: 150).

[10]As Nicholas's chief secretary later complained, "amidst matters of first-rate importance, which required the Sovereign's attention, he was mired down in a mass of petty details" (M. A. Korf, "Iz zapisok," *RS*, 102 [1900]: 272). Nicholas could show an astounding concern for minutiae, as in 1827, when he approved the use of a dark green uniform for the Church's lay clerks, but with the qualification that the uniforms have "not dull, but shiny buttons with a coat of arms" (TsGIA SSSR, f. 796, op. 108, g. 1827, d. 1216, ll. 1–24).

[11]For the *Polizeistaat* traditions in Russian statecraft, see Marc Raeff, "The Well-Ordered Police State and the Development of Modernity in Seventeenth- and Eighteenth-Century Europe," *American Historical Review* [hereafter *AHR*], 80 (1975): 1221–43.

gent ruler could not control and master all the details of his vast empire and administration. Typically, a single sensational incident came to Nicholas's attention, triggering an imperious command for action; rarely did reform spring from the regular processes of administration. It was impossible for Nicholas to direct all affairs of state, and, once his hand left the throttle, reform tended to stall.[12] Moreover, Nicholas's penchant for secret reform (concealed from many high officials) left educated society unaware of reform, made the regime's policies appear as reactionary as its rhetoric, and sometimes provoked misunderstandings about the intent of reform.[13] It also deprived reform of a supporting consensus capable of sustaining and inform- ing the efforts of Petersburg commissions and committees. Although secrecy simplified the reform process, permitting authorities to operate free from the pressure of outside interest groups, it precluded a public opinion that could help to push the sluggish bureaucracy to complete its plans for reform.

So far as the Church was concerned, Nicholas displayed a continuing interest in its welfare and in the cause of reform. His interest derived partly from genuine religious piety, which—unlike the Voltairism of his grand- mother Catherine or the mystical pietism of his brother Alexander—took a conventional form, anchored in the traditional institutional Church. Signifi- cantly, Nicholas greatly distrusted mysticism and radical sectarianism, insist- ing that religion be bound to the Church. That notion led him to oppose translation of the Slavonic Bible into vernacular Russian for popular use, spe- cifically on the grounds that the study of religious texts and their elucidation was properly the duty of clergy, not laity.[14] For the same reason he demanded a competent priesthood capable of providing religious instruction for the people, delivering sermons in simple language, and teaching cate- chism to the unlettered peasantry.[15] At bottom here rested the idea that "good, educated and well-intentioned priests" are "virtually the sole means for the elimination of evil" among peasants.[16]

That interest in good clergy, moreover, embodied a more modern concep- tion of priesthood—less liturgical, more pastoral in its focus. This shift in emphasis appeared first in eighteenth-century Europe, where both Protestant and Catholic churches began to redefine the clergy's role, partly in order to

---

[12]See, for example, his recurrent intervention in parish reform in the late 1820s (below, Chapter 2).

[13]For example, in 1849 the emperor restricted admissions to the university in an effort to drive the nobility's sons into military service, but educated society interpreted this as merely an attack on the universities. See M. A. Korf, "Iz zapisok," *RS*, 102 (1900): 44–45.

[14]See "Dva pis'ma Serafima k gr. N. A. Protasovu," *Russkii arkhiv* [hereafter *RA*], 1878, no. 12: 522–23.

[15]See below, Chapter 3.

[16]Quotation from report of 1841 by the governor of Vologda (TsGIA SSSR, f. 796, op. 123, g. 1842, d. 239, l. 2 ob.).

blunt Enlightenment criticism of "useless clergy" and harmful "superstition" and partly to satisfy state demands for public service from the established Church.[17] Concretely, churches set less value on purely ritualistic functions and attached new importance to pastoral theology, sermons, and catechization.[18] The Russian Church began to emulate this shift in the late eighteenth century, commanding priests to deliver sermons and to catechize, but it had achieved little success before Nicholas ascended the throne in 1825. Much of the problem rested with the seminary; like the old Western models upon which it was based, the seminary treated homiletics as a form of rhetoric (preferably embellished with classical allusions), not as a form of mass communication.[19] More to the point, by 1825 relatively few priests as yet had a full seminary education; most knew little of such exotica as dogmatic theology and delivered only two or three sermons a year—and those cribbed from a manuscript miscellany or even read straight from a printed collection.[20] A primary goal of the Nikolaevan regime was to reorder the Church—its seminary curriculum, service system, and the clerical soslovie itself—so that the parish priest would have the training, zeal, and sheer time to perform the new pastoral role as well as the more traditional sacramental one.

Like his predecessors, however, Nicholas evinced more interest in the clergy's temporal role than in their spiritual one. His guiding leitmotif here was eighteenth-century cameralist ideas that the clergy should seek "through their teachings to form not only good Christians, but also to form good citizens for the state."[21] Specifically, that meant ascribing to them sundry tem-

[17]See, especially, John M. Stroup, "The Struggle for Identity in the Clerical Estate: Northwest German Protestant Opposition to Absolutist Policy in the Eighteenth Century" (Ph.D. diss., Yale University, 1980).

[18]See, for example, discussions of the change in England (Russell, *Clerical Profession*, pp. 53–99; McClatchey, *Oxfordshire Clergy*, pp. 80–97); Catholic Germany (Keller, "Priesterseminar," pp. 177–78) and Austria (A. Zschokke, *Die theologischen Studien und Anstalten der katholischen Kirche in Österreich* [Vienna, 1894], pp. 51–54); and Protestant Germany (Werdermann, *Der evangelische Pfarrer*, pp. 129–32).

[19]For the English case, where the sermon as rhetorical exercise and literary form gave way to the sermon as a means of popular communication, see Heeney, *Different Kind of Gentleman*, pp. 40–41; McClatchey, *Oxfordshire Clergy*, p. 82; and Russell, *Clerical Profession*, pp. 85–99.

[20]That is evident from the service lists for 1830, which show that the parish priests without seminary degrees invariably used printed collections (see, for example, the service registers for Tver diocese in GA Kalininskoi obl., f. 160, op. l, dd. 16272, 16298). Printed sermons had, to be sure, prevailed in the West too, but by the early nineteenth century they were gradually dying out (see Russell, *Clerical Profession*, pp. 85–99; Heeney, *Different Kind of Gentleman*, p. 44).

[21]Quotation from a 1778 manuscript by the influential S. Rautenstrauch (published in J. Müller, *Der pastoraltheologisch-didaktische Ansatz in Franz Stephan Rautenstrauchs "Entwurf zur Einrichtung der theologischen Schulen,"* Wiener Beiträge zur Theologie, vol. 24 [Vienna, 1969], pp. 39–40). For a classic example of such ideas, see C. F. Bahrdt, *Ueber das theologische Studium auf Universitäten* (Berlin, 1785).

poral functions—some, like teaching, consistent with their spiritual role; others, purely administrative and political, tangential, if not contradictory, to pastorship.[22] Emulating Western models, the Russian state had attempted to use the clergy as a spiritual arm of the state, requiring them to report on schismatics, compile vital statistics, read state laws aloud in Church, even violate the confidence of confession if a parishioner revealed "evil intentions."[23] Nicholas, who demanded that "all serve the state," fully embraced such policies and made a determined effort to augment the priest's set of "this-worldly"duties.

Upon one duty—that of checking peasant rebelliousness—Nicholas laid special emphasis. Though the duty to exhort subjects and dissuade them from revolt was not new,[24] Nicholas showed a particularly keen interest in using parish clergy to quell peasant insubordination. He had good cause for such concern, for his reign faced a steady rise in the number of rural disorders, and police reports of a new "mentality" among the serf population heightened the import of such incidents.[25] To the emperor's dismay, at his very accession he encountered evidence that the clergy had not only failed to stop peasant disorders but had even abetted them.[26] Not long afterwards he received an alarming report from the Third Section that "in general the clergy is poorly governed and filled with a harmful spirit" and that "the priests disseminate unpleasant news and spread the idea of freedom among the people."[27] The Third Section tended to overdramatize and exaggerate its sparse data, but such warnings gained credibility as individual cases came to the authorities' attention. Though rare, such incidents included priests who failed to calm their parishioners, penned protests on their behalf, or even engaged in agitation. One deacon in Polotsk diocese, for example, urged serfs

[22] For clerical opposition to such changes, see Stroup, "Struggle for Identity," pp. 82–133, 139–62, 197–242.

[23] For the Russian case, see Gregory L. Freeze, *The Russian Levites: Parish Clergy in the Eighteenth Century* (Cambridge, Mass., 1977), chap. 2.

[24] Ibid., pp. 179–83.

[25] Recent Soviet data, crude but indicative, show 651 disorders and 368 written peasant protests in 1801–1825, then 1,247 disorders and 1,071 written protests in 1826–1855 (see N. M. Druzhinin and V. A. Fedorov, "Krest'ianskoe dvizhenie v Rossii v XIX v.," *Istoriia SSSR*, 1977, no. 4: 107–8). The Third Section (the political police) summed up the peasants' new mood in terrifying (and exaggerated) terms: "The idea of liberation of the peasants is spreading ceaselessly among [them]. These dark ideas of the *muzhiki* are becoming more and more widespread and betoken something awful" (*Krest'ianskoe dvizhenie, 1827–69 gg.*, pt. 1 [Moscow-Leningrad, 1931], p. 32).

[26] For Nicholas's complaint, see below, pp. 65–66. Typical of such disorders was the case of a sacristan in Orel who interpreted one manifesto of 1826 as a summons to disobey the squires (TsGIA SSSR, f. 796, op. 107, g. 1826, d. 310, l. 3), and the file on a cleric in Nizhnii Novgorod who administered an oath of unity to rebellious peasants (*Polnoe sobranie postanovlenii i rasporiazhenii po vedomstvu pravoslavnogo ispovedaniia. Tsarstvovanie Imp. Nikolaia Pavlovicha* [St. Petersburg, 1915], no. 36 [hereafter *PSPR*]).

[27] "Graf Benkendorf," p. 152.

to "disobey their owners and, without the slightest doubt or delay, to leave with their families from their homes."[28] As Nicholas made clear in one of his first communications to the Synod, he sought clerical reform first and foremost to ensure the appointment of reliable clergy.[29]

Nicholas's political interest in clerical reform was most transparent with regard to the western provinces, a hotbed of nationalist and revolutionary ferment. The Poles, who had rebelled in 1830-1831 and smoldered with discontent thereafter, had a disturbing influence upon the entire western region, where the elite—Polonized and Catholic—proved a cause of great concern for St. Petersburg, provoking repeated demands for Russification.[30] Because much of the local peasantry was Orthodox or Uniate rather than Catholic, authorities hoped to use the parish clergy to secure stability and defend Russian culture. Thus, in addition to measures to paralyze the Catholic Church[31] and to incorporate the Uniates into the Orthodox Church,[32] Russian authorities adopted specific measures to improve the education and performance of Orthodox clergy. In part, they sought to do so within the existing system; for instance, they ordered seminaries in central Russia to train clergy for the western provinces,[33] and they prescribed that the clergy go beyond a narrow liturgical role and deliver "sermons in a simple, comprehensible language,

---

[28]TsGIA SSSR, f. 796, op. 128, g. 1847, d. 864. For cases where clergy wrote peasant petitions, see the file of a Saratov cleric who earned 10 rubles for this service in 1842 (ibid., op. 123, g. 1842, d. 539) and that of a Rzhev cleric who received 5 rubles for the same service (GA Kalininskoi obl., f. 160, op. 1, d. 15844, l. 129).

[29]PSPR, no. 56.

[30]Reports from the Third Section fueled such concern. In 1854, for example, it informed the emperor that "the [Crimean] War has aroused criminal feelings and dreams among the inhabitants of the Kingdom of Poland. They hope that Russia will not withstand the struggle (in their view, an unequal one) with the European powers and dream of the reestablishment of the former Poland" (Tsentral'nyi gosudarstvennyi arkhiv Oktiabr'skoi Revoliutsii [hereafter TsGAOR], f. 109 [Third Section], op. 223 [85], d. 19, ll. 1 ob.-2).

[31]For example, a decree of 1832 placed all elementary education under Orthodox control. As Nicholas candidly explained, "only thus will it be possible for the lower class of people (who, by origin, are Russian) to break free from the grip of the clergy of the Western [Catholic] Church" (Polnoe sobranie zakonov Rossiiskoi imperii [thereafter PSZ], 2aia seriia, 55 vols. [St. Petersburg, 1830–84], 7: 5518).

[32]The archival files on the Uniate question are in TsGIA SSSR, f. 797, op. 6; for an overview, see W. Lencyk, "The Eastern Catholic Church under Nicholas I" (Ph.D. diss., Fordham University, 1961).

[33]PSPR, no. 408. The metropolitan of Moscow warned that students brought from western dioceses to study in central seminaries would not return home and recommended instead that the Church appoint there "bishops of purely Russian origin and with Great-Russian education," who, together with civil officials, could help establish Russian dominance (Filaret, Perepiska Filareta mitropolita moskovskogo s S. D. Nechaevym [St. Petersburg, 1895], pp. 257–58 [note of 18.2.1832]). Local governors persevered in seeking Russian education for local clergy; see, for instance, the 1836 request from the governor-general in Polotsk in TsGIA SSSR, f. 797, op. 5, d. 18403.

or give informal talks in the form of conversations about the catechism" for the benefit of the common people.[34] For decades to come, concern about the western provinces—narrowly political in its primary purpose—would be a major spur to clerical reform.

Eudaemonistic principles were most manifest in the use of clergy to promote development among the backward peasantry, a policy strikingly similar to eighteenth-century cameralism. Most characteristic was the concerted attempt, from 1840 onward, to require that seminarians study medicine and agriculture, with the explicit hope that they could help to fill the peasants' acute need for doctors and agronomists.[35] The clergy were also ordered to propagandize the value of potatoes, to transmit new agricultural knowledge, even to help inoculate distrustful peasants.[36] More conventional by Western standards, but new for Russia, was the regime's attempt to give the parish clergy a primary role in popular education, both by designating priests to teach in the small network of state schools and by encouraging clergy to open parish schools.[37] The shift from past policies that forbade clergy to teach, for fear of competition with state schools,[38] derived partly from the belief that "literacy without morality for the common people is the same as a knife in the hands of a willful child."[39] Although parish schools suffered serious deficiencies (inadequate financing, peasant opposition to the loss of child labor,

[34] TsGIA SSSR, f. 796, op. 120, g. 1839, d. 1654, l. 1 (instruction from Nicholas I on 16.12.1839, communicated to the Synod by the chief procurator).

[35] See below, Chapter 3.

[36] For the state's appeal to clergy to popularize the potato, see TsGIA SSSR, f. 796, op. 122, g. 1841, d. 889 (Ministry of State Domains proposal, 1841), and op. 123, g. 1842, d. 444. For the dissemination of agricultural books and newspapers among parish clergy, see the efforts by the Ministry of Finance and the Free Economic Society in the late 1830s and early 1840s (in ibid., f. 797, op. 5, d. 18361; op. 13, d. 31803). On the clergy's role in inoculations, see ibid., f. 796, op. 133, g. 1852, d. 2213.

[37] The main breakthrough was a decree, confirmed by Nicholas on 29 Oct. 1836, that obliged the clergy to teach reading, writing, arithmetic, and religion. A main focus was Old Believers. To entice them to school their children, priests were authorized to use Old Believers' books for purposes of instruction, and, simultaneously, they were warned not to offend the Old Believers with "harsh reproofs." Because of these concessions to the Old Belief, the decree remained secret; see the copy in Filaret's collected works (*Sobranie mnenii i otzyvov Filareta, mitropolita moskovskogo i kolomenskogo, po uchebnym i tserkovno-gosudarstvennym voprosam*, 5 vols. in 6 pts. [Moscow, 1885–88], 3: 358–69; hereafter Filaret, *SMO*) or the Synodal archive (TsGIA SSSR, f. 796, op. 131, g. 1850, d. 189, ll. 43–44). For a scheme by the Ministry of State Domains to establish parish schools to train village clerks *(pisari)*, see the correspondence between the ministry and Church, 1838–1841, in ibid., op. 119, g. 1838, d. 1178; op. 122, g. 1841, d. 1446.

[38] Reversing a policy initiated in the 1780s, Nicholas's government removed various restrictions on the establishment of parish schools, most notably in a decree of 1831 (TsGIA SSSR, f. 796, op. 110, g. 1829, d. 678; *PSPR*, no. 359).

[39] Memorandum of the 1840s by Innokentii (I. P. Barsukov, *Innokentii, mitropolit moskovskii i kolomenskii* [Moscow, 1883], p. 232).

diffidence on the part of clergy),[40] the new policy laid the foundations for the proliferation of parish schools after mid-century.

In order for the parish clergy to discharge effectively these sundry roles, temporal and spiritual, it became increasingly apparent both to Church and to state authorities that the ecclesiastical domain required fundamental reform. Part One will examine the "clerical question" and the regime's attempt to treat its four main components: Church administration, the system of clerical service, seminary education, and the soslovie structure of the white clergy. In presenting a systematic sketch of the Church and of Nicholas's reform measures, these first chapters will suggest several broad themes. One is the growing contradiction between the old ecclesiastical order and the new pastorate. Precisely because of the dramatic rise in clerical standards (especially in education), the parish clergy became increasingly resentful of their traditional status, which left them subject to the whims of bishops and shamefully dependent upon their parishioners. This phenomenon was not uncommon in central and eastern Europe: fostered by the state, professional groups—in the name of more effective service—demanded state action to emancipate them from their traditional status. A second theme here is the new awareness of the disjuncture between the interests of the institution and those of the soslovie. Cognizant of the urgent need to husband the Church's limited resources, authorities, especially in the final years of Nicholas's reign, evinced a new willingness to abrogate the traditional rights of the clerical soslovie, primarily for the sake of higher standards in the clergy. Most striking was the incipient shift in social policy, reflected in the decision to restrict the automatic matriculation of clerical sons in church schools and to admit only enough students to satisfy the Church's modest needs. A third major theme concerns the abrasive politics of the Nikolaevan reforms, which left a legacy of bitter resentment in the episcopate and, inadvertently, served to provoke high expectations among parish clergy. Ultimately, the Nikolaevan reforms did less to set the stage for subsequent reform than to polarize church politics—bishops against bureaucrats, priests against bishops.

[40] TsGIA SSSR, f. 796, op. 127, g. 1846, d. 954, ll. 92-92 ob., 94 (explanations for declining enrollments, citing, *inter alia*, the peasants' view that "because of their poverty, their children are needed for work" and hence cannot attend school). See also the complaints from the Ministry of State Domains in 1850 in ibid., op. 131, g. 1851, d. 189, ll. 2-6.

CHAPTER 1

Dual Power,
Dual Conflict

"Sire! [Chief procurator] Protasov has made himself a serf-master over the bishops, who have all become servile slaves of the chief procurator and his suite."[1]

T hat plaintive cry to the emperor was followed shortly afterwards by another, but from a radically different perspective: "The relationship between priests and bishops is like that between Negroes and plantation owners."[2] These appeals to the emperor, contained in two memoranda (*zapiski*) in the mid-1850s, dramatically reveal the main lines of conflict inside the Orthodox Church—prelates against procurators, priests against bishops. The two conflicts, to be sure, long antedated the Nikolaevan era; from medieval times bishops had clashed with lay officials, and priests had been at odds with their ecclesiastical superiors. But the traditional antagonism acquired new forms and new intensity in the reign of Nicholas I, setting the stage for the ecclesiastical politics of the Great Reforms. Although conventionally treated as a total bureaucratization of the Church and its reduction to an impotent arm of the state, the Nikolaevan era actually represented much more than a simple attempt by power-hungry procurators to seize control of the Church.[3] This chapter will examine the problems facing

---

[1] [A. N. Murav'ev], "O prichinakh bedstvennogo polozheniia pravoslavnoi kafolicheskoi tserkvi v Rossii," OR GBL, f. 304 (Troitse-Sergeevskaia lavrav, Sobranie), r. 2, d. 259, l. 51 ob.

[2] [I. S. Belliustin], *Opisanie sel'skogo dukhovenstva* (Paris [Leipzig], 1858), p. 112.

[3] For a conventional statement, see D. W. Edwards, "Orthodoxy during the Reign of Nicholas I: A Study in Church-State Relations" (Ph.D. diss., Kansas State University, 1967), and F. V. Blagovidov, *Ober-prokurory Sv. Sinoda v XVIII i pervoi polovine XIX st.* (2nd ed.; Kazan, 1900).

prereform Church administration, the regime's attempts at reform, and the exacerbation of tensions that ensued.

Synod and Procurator

When Peter established the Synod as a collegial body of bishops to govern the Church in 1721, he intended it to rule the whole "ecclesiastical domain" (*dukhovnoe vedomstvo*), representing the "spiritual" counterpart to the Senate in the civil domain.[4] Originally composed of eleven bishops (with the metropolitan of St. Petersburg presiding), the Synod wielded considerable authority and operational autonomy in the eighteenth century, supervising administration in the subordinate dioceses and controlling diverse spheres of Church affairs—justice, censorship, schools, and finances. To be sure, it had to contend with the presence of the chief procurator (*ober-prokuror*), a lay overseer charged with ensuring legality and good administration in the Church; with few exceptions, however, most eighteenth-century procurators played only a minor role in Synodal affairs.[5] By resorting to clever bureaucratic subterfuges, even by overt opposition, the Synod managed to stall or deflect most of the state's attempts to violate Church interests. However, when the issue was truly central and vital, as in the sequestration of monastic lands and peasants, the material interests were so clear and the theology so thin that the state's will ineluctably prevailed. But in most routine matters the government left the Church to its arcane tradition and its labyrinth of canon law, for the state had neither the expertise nor the incentive to meddle in purely ecclesiastical matters.[6]

This relationship changed significantly in the nineteenth century, as the chief procurator acquired substantial, though by no means dictatorial, power over the Church. The Synod formally retained sole authority to set ecclesiastical policy, but it surrendered day-to-day control to a lay bureaucracy subject to the procurator's control. That development was of great significance, for operational autonomy had been the very essence of the Synod's power. Though traditionally regarded as the evil machinations of power-hungry procurators, the state's intrusion into Church affairs had far more

---

[4]On the Petrine reforms, see the classic by P. V. Verkhovskoi, *Uchrezhdenie dukhovnoi kollegii i dukhovnyi reglament*, 2 vols. (Rostov-na-Donu, 1916).

[5]Freeze, *Russian Levites*, chap. 2.

[6]For Soviet recognition of the Synod's autonomy, at least until the 1760s, see: I. A. Bulygin, "Tserkovnaia reforma Petra I," *Voprosy istorii*, 1974, no. 5: 74–93; N. N. Pokrovskii, *Antifeodal'nyi protest uralo-sibirskikh staroobriadtsev v XVIII v.* (Novosibirsk, 1974), pp. 8–10 passim; and N. D. Zol'nikova, *Soslovnye problemy vo vzaimootnosheniiakh tserkvi i gosudarstva v Sibiri (XVIII v.)* (Novosibirsk, 1981), chap. 1.

important goals, namely, to realign the Church to state institutions and to integrate the Church into the evolving system of secular administration.

In part, the state's invasion of Church prerogative resulted from dissatisfaction with ecclesiastical administration. From the very outset of his reign, Nicholas complained of irregularities and soon came to doubt that the Church and bishops were capable of vouchsafing the good order and the good priests that he demanded. In February 1827, for example, Nicholas learned about the case of an archpriest in Kursk who had maintained suspicious liaisons with peasant women and yet eluded punishment; the angry emperor had the cleric summarily defrocked and rebuked the bishop for laxness.[7] The following year, when he learned about a scandal involving an inebriated priest who had dropped the Holy Elements, Nicholas again berated bishops for undue leniency: "Once more I repeat that this serves as new proof of how little local ecclesiastical authorities perform their duty, and I reiterate that priests of dubious conduct are absolutely not to be tolerated."[8] Not long afterwards Nicholas ordered a general purge of clergy with tainted records, and, after receiving data on the large number previously or currently under investigation, he found "new proof" of the bishops' nonfeasance and incompetence in supervising diocesan clergy.[9] His patience was plainly exhausted by 1830, when another case of leniency came to his attention: "Give the bishop a most severe reprimand for his unjustified decision [not to defrock an errant cleric], and at the same time [admonish him] that at the first [reoccurence] he shall be stripped of his diocese and his rank."[10]

Although Nicholas vented his wrath first and foremost upon individual bishops, he ultimately put responsibility upon the Church's central administration. Indeed, at the very outset of his reign, the emperor gave consideration to an anonymous memorandum ("Some Comments and Proposals for Improving Church Affairs") that challenged the Synod's capacity to govern effectively. As Metropolitan Filaret (Drozdov) of Moscow later recalled, the memorandum said "much unfavorable about the current state of affairs in the Russian Church—for instance, that the Synod itself does not know the condition of the Russian Church, that it makes no inspections whatsoever of

[7] *PSPR*, no. 107.

[8] Ibid., no. 216.

[9] TsGIA SSSR, f. 796, op. 110, g. 1829, d. 509, l. 89 (3.11.1829).

[10] *PSPR*, no. 330. The monastic clergy were another source of the emperor's displeasure. In 1841, for example, after learning from the Third Section that several monks had raped a twelve-year-old girl, Nicholas ordered a full investigation and complained that "this disgrace has resulted from the careless acceptance of people into the monastery as novices and from the tonsure of people without testing their commitment to [monastic vows]" (TsGIA SSSR, f. 796, op. 122, g. 1841, d. 32, ll. 7–7 ob. [Nicholas's comment of 15.3.1841]; TsGAOR, f. 109, op. 221, d. 79, ll. 182–86 [Third Section report of 12.12.1840]). See also Nicholas's vexed comments on an 1850 case in TsGIA SSSR, f. 796, op. 131, g. 1850, d. 546, l. 44 ob.

the dioceses, and that the Synod only reviews incoming matters [initiating nothing of its own accord]."[11] The note argued that such nonfeasance was inevitable, since the small number of Synod members had to govern their own dioceses as well as handle the glut of routine Synodal business. The memorandum therefore proposed the creation of a "provisional ecclesiastical council" (*vremennyi dukhovnyi sovet*) to assist the Synod. Asked to comment on the proposal, Metropolitan Filaret categorically rejected the whole idea. If the new council consisted entirely of bishops, he warned, it would suffer the same weaknesses of the Synod: the additional bishops, like present Synod members, would still have to attend simultaneously to the task of managing their home dioceses. If, as Filaret suspected, the author intended to include laymen on the council, that innovation could undermine the whole political order:

> The hierarchy (based on the canons of the Holy Apostles, Holy Councils, and Church Fathers) and a reform or transformation are mutually exclusive conceptions. The establishment of a council to improve Church administration will strike many as a body [convoked] to transform or reform; it is debatable whether this organ will do more good to create order than to provoke an agitation of minds.[12]

Deftly exploiting Nicholas's fear of an "agitation of minds," Filaret succeeded in burying the proposal once and for all.[13] Still, the very appearance and serious consideration given to schemes for "an expanded consistory" with lay and clerical members bore witness to the government's strong dissatisfaction with Church administration.

More important, though, than dissatisfaction with maladministration was the evolution of state bureaucracy, which had a profound impact upon the status and structure of the central Church administration. Most broadly, as the Petrine system changed in its structure and distribution of power, the reference points fixing the Synod's status and power shifted as well. Thus, as the Senate gradually declined from a policy-making organ to a court of high judicial review, the Synod's status vis-à-vis civil administration grew dangerously ambiguous. Still more important was the formation of ministries in 1802, which replaced the old administrative colleges and left the Synod (originally titled "ecclesiastical college") as an anomalous vestige of Peter's collegial system. That new ministerial order gradually made itself felt within the Church, for the entire system presupposed single ministerial heads capable of attending the new Committee of Ministers (and, later, State Council)

[11] A. V. Gorskii, *Dnevnik* (Moscow, 1885), pp. 81–82.
[12] Filaret, *SMO*, 4: 217 (memorandum of 9.8.1827).
[13] Gorskii, *Dnevnik*, p. 82.

to defend the interests of their particular institution. Of more concrete significance was the development of new ministerial organs to augment the minister's authority and enable him to manage his own bureaucracy as an autonomous organization. All these innovations slowly intruded into the Church: the procurator represented the Church at the State Council or Committee of Ministers, emulated the ministerial model for internal organization, and formed a lay bureaucracy under his own personal control.

The first hint of procuratorial pretensions came in the reign of Alexander I (1801–1825). The pioneer was A. A. Iakovlev, who held the post briefly in 1803 and unabashedly sought to expand his authority, primarily in the name of tight finances and good administration. On these grounds Iakovlev demanded that all the Synod's mail go through his office (not that of the St. Petersburg metropolitan), that diocesan secretaries be subordinate to him (not to local bishops), and even that "procurators" be appointed to oversee each diocesan consistory. Iakovlev's encroachments touched off a furor in the Synod, which eventually persuaded the emperor to remove the abrasive and ambitious procurator.[14] Although his immediate successor, A. N. Golitsyn, an agnostic, seemed unlikely to meddle in ecclesiastical affairs, he in fact proved a diligent overseer, determined to make administration more efficient and to excoriate fiscal abuse. Thus, with an eye to developments in secular administration, Golitsyn placed the Synod's chancellery on a more orderly basis, adopted the new procedures and rules of state offices, and took steps to tighten supervision over diocesan authorities.[15] Eventually Golitsyn broadened his role as procurator, first in the seminary reforms of 1808–1814 and later as Minister of Ecclesiastical Affairs and Education, overseeing not only the Orthodox Church but public schools and other confessions as well.[16] Although Golitsyn's power should not be exaggerated (the Synod's routine functions remained intact, with senior prelates clearly dominant), his attempt to create an ecclesiastical ministry parallel to similar institutions in

[14]Blagovidov, *Ober-prokurory*, pp. 325–46; A. A. Iakovlev, "Zapiski A. A. Iakovleva," *Pamiatniki novoi russkoi istorii*, 3 (1873): 87–112; TsGIA SSSR, f. 796, op. 84, g. 1803, d. 799.

[15]Blagovidov, *Ober-prokurory*, pp. 347–91.

[16]On the seminary reform, see B. V. Titlinov, *Dukhovnaia shkola v Rossii v XIX st.*, 2 vols. (Vil'na, 1908–09), 1: 23–53. The Synod's membership also changed, not only declining in numbers (from 11 to 7) but also becoming partly transient: a decree of 1805 divided its members into permanent appointees (*chleny*) and temporary appointees (*prisutstvuiushchie*), Though the rule was ostensibly intended to familiarize the emperor with provincial bishops (who would, in turn, come to Petersburg as temporary appointees), its main effect was to weaken the Synod's cohesion and even to admit a manipulation of policy through the appointment of younger, more malleable bishops. Moreover, from the early nineteenth century, the emperor also designated some court priests (his confessor and chief chaplain of the army) as members of the Synod. *PSZ (1)*, 28: 21790, 36: 27872; S. T. Barsov, *Sbornik deistvuiushchikh i rukovodstvennykh tserkovnykh i tserkovno-grazhdanskikh postanovlenii po vedomstvu pravoslavnogo ispovedaniia* (St. Petersburg, 1885), pp. 8–9.

the West and consonant with the new ministerial structure in Russia adumbrated the primary lines of subsequent development.[17]

As the Synod's power had waxed and waned in the eighteenth century, so too did it in the nineteenth, and Nicholas's accession to the throne brought a resurgence in the Synod's power that lasted into the first decade of his reign. Thus Golitsyn's successor, P. S. Meshcherskii, dealt circumspectly with the bishops, affording due respect to their traditional prerogatives and privileges.[18] That respect diminished noticeably under his successor, S. D. Nechaev (1833–1836), a former military officer eager to dominate ecclesiastical administration. According to critical foes, he spared little to subdue the hierarchs. He allegedly instigated anonymous denunciations of bishops and even dared to "change the resolutions and decisions of the Holy Synod, either through sheer persistence or legerdemain."[19] Whatever the veracity of such claims, more important were his efforts to restructure Church administration into an integrated system, primarily through schemes "to limit the power of [diocesan] bishops and to give more authority to the consistories."[20] The bishops, however, were no pliant tools; they tenaciously resisted his plans and, during the procurator's absence from the capital, prevailed upon Nicholas to appoint a new official to his post. With considerable relief they greeted his replacement, N. A. Protasov (1836–1855), another military officer, but one who vowed to respect Church privilege. In a congratulatory note to the new procurator, Metropolitan Filaret wrote that "your appointment is received with complete sympathy, satisfaction, and high hopes."[21]

Those hopes were soon dashed, for Protasov proved far more domineering than any of his predecessors. His power derived not from law or consecration but from the implicit trust of the emperor, who believed that, through the like-minded Protasov, "I will govern the Church myself."[22] In the first instance Protasov justified a more active procuracy by the demands of

---

[17]On the establishment of a separate Ministerium der geistlichen Angelegenheiten und des Unterrichts in Prussia, see Ernst R. Huber, ed., Staat und Kirche in 19. und 20. Jahrhundert, 2 vols. (Berlin, 1973), 1: 118; PSZ (1), 34: 27106.

[18]Blagovidov, Ober-prokurory, pp. 391–99.

[19]F. Ismailov, "Iz vospominanii sekretaria pri Sv. Sinode F. F. Ismailova (1829–1840 gg.)," Strannik [hereafter Str.], 1882, no. 9: 77–78.

[20]Ibid., p. 78.

[21]I. A. Chistovich, Rukovodiashchie deiateli dukhovnogo prosveshcheniia v Rossii v pervoi polovine tekushchego stoletiia (St. Petersburg, 1894), p. 316. See similar comments by A. N. Murav'ev (subsequently Protasov's inveterate critic) that "it would have been impossible to have made a happier choice" and that "all the prelates, including the [metropolitans of] St. Petersburg and Moscow, are very satisfied" with Protasov's appointment ("Iz bumag S. D. Nechaeva," RA, 1893, no. 5: 149). The contemporary spelling of the procurator's name was Pratasov. It was subsequently modified to Protasov in the historical literature, and that later form will be observed here.

[22]"Iz zapisnoi knizhki," RA, 1908, no. 2: 249–50.

administrative efficiency—or, to quote a hostile contemporary, he acted "under the pretext that various kinds of matters in the Synod were too numerous."[23] But Protasov was more than a mere zealot for administrative efficiency, for he shared the emperor's views on the need for Church reform. Protasov was especially critical of the educated elite who dominated the Church, warning that their scholastic education—derived from Western models and attracted to such fields as biblical criticism and hermeneutics— might erode religious conviction and eventually lead to political revolution. In his view Western hermeneutics only encouraged "rationalist principles" that "offend the sensibilities of our pious forefathers on the authenticity, veracity, and divine spirituality of the books of the Holy Scripture." Such inquiries, he claimed, had the aim of "founding faith on reasoned conviction or, what is the same thing, putting reason in the place of [faith]."[24] Instead, Protasov sought more practical, utilitarian education for clergy, such as med- icine and agronomy, even at the cost of diminished instruction in philosophy and theology.[25] Desire to tighten Church administration, commitment to these utilitarian principles, and determination to realign ecclesiastical admin- istration with that of the state impelled Protasov to seek an unprecedented role in routine Church administration.[26]

To the bishops' dismay, Protasov hastened to establish firm control over the Synod's lay chancellery, transforming its staff into his own subordinates and leaving the Synod disarmed and dependent. As one Synodal official later wrote, "*all the lay employees* serving in the Synod are appointed, removed, and promoted by the Synod at the procurator's recommendation, by the pro- curator himself, or by the emperor at the procurator's recommendation. . . . Hence he is the chief of all: to him all direct their gaze; he is the one that every clerk wishes to please and serve."[27] As a result, Protasov acquired the power to control the flow of documents, set the agenda, summon or suppress information, and formulate and even pigeonhole the Synod's resolutions. In 1840 Metropolitan Filaret complained privately that "lay [officials] in the Synod are taking liberties and even annul decisions of the Synod."[28] Because the Synod had lost control over implementation, its resolutions remained powerless until the procurator deigned to write "Implement." In the Synod's

[23] Ismailov, "Iz vospominanii," *Str.*, 1882, no. 9: 78–81.

[24] TsGIA SSSR, f. 797, op. 12, d. 29882, l. 14 (Protasov's report to Nicholas on the Pavskii affair, 7.3.1842).

[25] See below, pp. 125–27.

[26] Murav'ev rightly describes the Protasov tenure as a major revolution in Church-state rela- tions; see his "O prichinakh bedstvennogo polozheniia," OR GBL, f. 304, r. 2, d. 259, ll. 27– 56.

[27] Ibid., l. 34.

[28] Nikodim, "O Filarete," *Chteniia v Obshchestve istorii i drevnostei rossiiskikh* [hereafter *ChOIDR*], 101 (1877), kn. 2, chast' 2: 69.

external relations with the state, Protasov's dominance was total. He controlled all correspondence with the ministries and exercised an all-important power in autocratic politics: he alone—not the Synod—"represented the condition of the Church, clergy, and bishops" to the emperor.[29]

To complement that power within the Synod's chancellery, Protasov built a separate apparatus under his personal control. Significantly, one of his first measures was to establish, with Nicholas's approval, a "special chancellery" for the chief procurator that was organizationally and physically separate from the Synod's chancellery. At first limited to some twenty clerks, the procurator's chancellery grew rapidly and in time came to rival that of the Synod in its number of staff and volume of business.[30] Its archives mirror that ascendancy: ten volumes of inventory encompass the entire holdings of the chief procurator from 1721 to 1840, but thereafter one volume appeared each year to keep pace with his chancellery's rising workload. The creation of this chancellery, though characteristic of the new ministerial bureaucracy,[31] marked a major change for the Church: it gave the chief procurator a modest base of power, not only for purposes of patronage but also for ensuring his independence from the Synod and his ability to check the performance of bishops, whatever their rank and stature. In 1836, still his first year, Protasov also gained control of the Church's fiscal administration, persuading Nicholas to establish a special Fiscal Committee (*Khoziaistvennyi komitet*), with the procurator holding authority to resolve matters "in the event of disagreement among [the committee's] members."[32] Three years later Protasov engineered a similar change in the administration of Church schools. The Commission of Ecclesiastical Schools, dominated by clergy, was replaced by a new organ, the Bureau of Ecclesiastical Education, composed of lay and clerical members and directly under Protasov's control.[33] Thus, without revising the Ecclesiastical Regulation of 1721 (which, until 1917, remained the institutional charter of the Orthodox Church), Protasov significantly altered the balance of power in his own favor.

His power derived as well from changes in the composition of the Synod. No doubt the most significant changes occurred in 1842, when Protasov deprived the Synod of its two more powerful figures, Metropolitan Filaret (Drozdov) of Moscow and Metropolitan Filaret (Amfiteatrov) of Kiev.[34] The

[29] Murav'ev, "O prichinakh bedstvennogo polozheniia," OR GBL, f. 304, r. 2, d. 259, l. 33.

[30] TsGIA SSSR, f. 796, op. 117, g. 1836, d. 1097 (formation of chancellery).

[31] Daniel T. Orlovsky, *The Limits of Reform: The Ministry of Interior, 1802–1881* (Cambridge, 1981), pp. 13–37.

[32] TsGIA SSSR, f. 796, op. 1836, d. 1503 (formation of Fiscal Committee).

[33] See below, pp. 141–42.

[34] Although several prelates bore the monastic name Filaret, unless otherwise indicated, reference throughout will be to Filaret (Drozdov), metropolitan of Moscow.

immediate cause was the "Pavskii affair," involving the unauthorized translation of books from the Old Testament into modern Russian. Both metropolitans disavowed the particular translation but in principle favored the publication of a Bible in modern Russian—a view that Nicholas categorically rejected. Whether Protasov provoked the crisis and manipulated documents (as ranking prelates claimed) is a moot point. The effect was the same: both Filarets were "permitted to withdraw to their dioceses, neither ever returning to the Synod.[35] Most important was the departure of Filaret Drozdov, a central figure in the Synod who had often been entrusted with drafting key memoranda and resolutions. As one prelate recalled, only after Filaret's departure did the lay officials take full command of Church affairs, some even daring to treat the Synod with unveiled contempt.[36] Protasov himself openly dominated the Synod, whose members were too low in rank and too deficient in courage to contest the will of Nicholas's imperious procurator.

Besides Protasov's rising ascendancy in daily administration, the Synod's power suffered as well from the incursions of the ad hoc committees so characteristic of Nikolaevan bureaucracy. Though extraordinary committees had appeared before (most notably, the commission on seminary reform in 1808–1814), such organs became a salient element of the new, aspiring procuracy. Their principal effect was to divert power from the Synod to irregular bodies, usually joint Church-state organs with a heavy lay representation. The change, and its import, is perhaps best illustrated by comparing the procedures used for Nicholas's two parish reforms: that of 1829 was the handiwork of the Synod, that of 1842 the product of several joint committees.[37] Such committees, especially when the issue was even remotely sensitive, tended to be secret, not only from the public and diocesan clergy but from many bishops as well. The prelates justly feared such joint committees. Even prior to Protasov's appointment, for example, Metropolitan Filaret protested plans to convoke a joint lay-clerical committee to consider existing marital law: "I fear the committee on marriages. One clerical member and three laymen—what will they do? And will it not be said that laymen have become lawmakers in ecclesiastical affairs?"[38] Although such committees always had a clergyman as chairman, he was usually of junior rank (suffragan bishop or mere archimandrite) and had to contend with several state officials, including a special deputy of the chief procurator himself. The result was erosion

[35]TsGIA SSSR, f. 797, op. 12, d. 29882, ll. 7–14, 17–18 ob., 22–23; Filaret, SMO, 3: 54–61; A. Kotovich, Dukhovnaia tsenzura v Rossii, 1799–1855 gg. (St. Petersburg, 1909), pp. 160–62, 177–84.

[36]Nikodim, "O Filarete," pp. 68–69; see also I. S. Markov, "Neizdannaia stat'ia ep. Nikodima Kazantseva o M. M. Filarete," RS, 161 (1915): 96.

[37]See below, pp. 65–97.

[38]Filaret, Perepiska s Nechaevym, p. 135 (letter of 18.8.1833).

of initiative and authority in the Synod: the power to impose change, as well as to supervise, had shifted to irregular organs vulnerable to state control and manipulation.

The Synod became primarily a consultative and supervisory organ, a passive board of trustees, not the collegial command center envisioned by Peter the Great, formulating policy and overseeing its implementation. As one contemporary wrote with some exaggeration, "the chief representatives of the Church retained only judicial authority, while Church administration shifted into the hands of laymen, the Synod having only a consultative voice."[39] Not that the Synod ceased to act. Each year its archivist amassed some two thousand files, from judicial appeals to inquiries from state officials; its resolutions continued to deal with broad and important issues, from the substance of reform statutes to the problems of their implementation. Nevertheless, as the Synod's archival inventory shows, it squandered much time on mere formalities, such as perfunctory reviews of judicial sentences and petitions to take monastic vows. The Synod's chancellery dutifully filed away voluminous reports (directly from bishops as well as from Protasov's sundry organs), yet rarely did these require—or seek—action by the Synod itself.

Protasov's power should not be exaggerated, however. It was, after all, informal and individual. its basis was the emperor's personal trust, not formal law, for the Ecclesiastical Regulation of 1721 remained unrevised. Thus the procurator's power was vulnerable and extrainstitutional. A new emperor, a new procurator—and Russia got both in 1855—would have to redefine the interrelationship between Synod and procurator. Moreover, Protasov's authority was especially restricted with regard to diocesan affairs; his sole link was the diocesan secretary, and canon law unequivocally accorded the bishop monocratic authority. Nor did Protasov control these bishops; he was no state minister empowered to discharge, transfer, or promote at will. In extreme cases involving demonstrable malfeasance, Protasov could seek to force retirement; he could also influence promotions, but by no means did he have a free hand in dealing with obstreperous prelates. Nor did the influence of the two Filarets evaporate with their departure from St. Petersburg, as contemporaries were wont to believe. Metropolitan Filaret of Moscow, in particular, remained active in Church policy making, as his file of memoranda—solicited by Protasov on major issues in the late 1840s and 1850s—clearly attests.[40]

Though not the lay patriarch that his foes liked to depict, Protasov had made the procurator more a director than a simple overseer of the Synod. It was, as the bishops painfully realized, a fundamental break with the old Petrine system: Peter made the Church part of the state; Protasov made the

[39] Ismailov, "Iz vospominanii," *Str.*, 1883, no. 5: 81.
[40] See Filaret's memoranda of 1842–1855 in volume 3 of *SMO*.

state part of the Church—an altogether different set of propositions. The difference was not lost upon the prelates. Their hostility toward Protasov knew no bounds, as the exaggerated description of his power, venomous talk about his "Jesuitical education," and accusations of corruption and deceit all attest. However much the bishops had internalized the Petrine bureaucratic ethos (in the view of many clergy, they now acted more like chief administrators than chief priests), the episcopate did not submissively acquiesce in state domination—and state exploitation—of the Church. But under the imperious Nicholas they could do no more than seethe with resentment, castigating Protasov for violation of the Petrine system and fellow bishops for pusillanimity. As the metropolitan of Kiev complained, "the only sound coming from Petersburg is the rattling of the chief procurator's sword—the men of the Church have fallen silent."[41] And with power went blame: bishops held the procurator personally responsible for the Church's problems and the failure to resolve them. After Protasov's death in 1855, the bishops would seek to recover their former authority—in their view the first essential step in reform.

The conflict between hierarchs and procurators, which would overshadow Synodal politics right to 1917, meant a highly unstable structure of power, a peculiar kind of "dual power" at the very top of the Church. That dual power was fraught with significant consequences. One was its impact upon the Church's role in the larger system of bureaucratic politics, where ministries came to act as interest groups representing specific institutions and social groups.[42] For that kind of politics the Church was ill-prepared to compete. Although structurally the chief procurator acted as the Synod's spokesman, articulating ecclesiastical interests vis-à-vis state ministries (and Protasov, like his successors, in fact did this),[43] he suffered severe handicaps in comparison with the ministers. Quite apart from his exclusion from such organs as the Committee of Ministers,[44] he lacked the powers of patronage and internal dominance that gave the state ministers such influence. Procurators, from Protasov to Sabler, had to fight a war on two fronts—with other ministers and with their partner the Synod as well. That made the procurator and his program, whether conservative or liberal, doubly vulnerable. The second consequence of dual power, episcopal disgruntlement, was no less important

---

[41]"Pis'ma Arseniia mitr. kievskogo," *Trudy Kievskoi dukhovnoi akademii* [hereafter *TKDA*], 1884, no. 8: 584 (Arsenii to Innokentii, 9.4.1840).

[42]On the emergence of bureaucratic interest-group politics, see S. F. Starr, *Decentralization and Self-Government in Russia, 1830–1870* (Princeton, 1972).

[43]See, for example, Protasov's role in resisting state control of the Church budget and proposals to conduct a conscription among excess clerical sons (below, pp. 49, 169–70).

[44]Though invited for special matters, the procurator did not become a formal member of the Committee of Ministers until 1880, when K. P. Pobedonostsev became a regular member representing Church interests.

and was reflected in mounting tensions and conflict, even with procurators (such as A. P. Tolstoi and K. P. Pobedonostsev) who initially promised to respect and even to enlarge episcopal prerogatives. That conflict was built into the very structure of Church government. Exacerbated by institutional crisis and the need for reform, it at first stirred episcopal aspirations to restore the Petrine system and, later, provoked demands for conciliarism (*sobornost'*) and restoration of the patriarchate.

Bishops and Priests

Operating under the general supervision of the Synod and chief procurator, the bishop in each diocese bore personal responsibility for the conduct of day-to-day ecclesiastical administration. The hierarch's rank (bishop, archbishop, or metropolitan) was a personal status, though the higher ranks tended to go with the more populous, prestigious dioceses.[45] Assisted by a minuscule diocesan bureaucracy (in the larger dioceses, sometimes by a suffragan bishop), the hierarch held primary responsibility for a broad spectrum of business: the establishment of churches, ordination of priests, supervision of both white and black clergy, exercise of ecclesiastical justice, and compilation of sundry data for authorities in St. Petersburg. In most cases, the territory he governed was a sprawling diocese of immense proportions, comprising several hundred churches (sometimes over a thousand), several thousand parish clergy, and several hundred thousand laymen, all scattered over vast areas.[46] Recruited exclusively from the monastic clergy in accordance with Russian custom, not canon law, the hierarchs found it exceedingly difficult to govern their dioceses effectively. Their monastic status, together with the shortcomings of diocesan administration, proved a central dynamic in the rising tension between the Church hierarchy at the top and the parish clergy below.

The Prereform Episcopate: Leaders and Profile

The Church's ranking prelates were the metropolitans of St. Petersburg, Moscow, and Kiev, all promoted to their positions on the basis of service,

[45] The title of metropolitan was once extended to the prelate of Lithuania (Iosif [Semashko], 1839–1868); otherwise, it was limited to the occupants of the sees of Moscow, St. Petersburg, and Kiev.

[46] For data on the number of churches and clergy in each diocese from 1836, see the chief procurator's annual reports, *Izvlecheniia iz vsepoddanneishego otcheta ober-prokurora* [hereafter, *IVO (year)*], appearing under varying titles in St. Petersburg, 1837–1914. The original source of the data is the Synodal archive, listed annually as "Vedomosti o tserkvakh i o dukhovenstve."

seniority, and (at times) personal connections. Formally most influential was the metropolitan of St. Petersburg, who presided over the Synod and, potentially, could exercise a dominant influence in Church affairs. For the first part of Nicholas's reign that post belonged to Serafim Glagolevskii (metropolitan of St. Petersburg from 1821 to 1843), an archconservative jealous of Church power, but one whose advanced age and ill health deprived him of the ability to provide effective leadership. His successors—Antonii Rafal'skii (1843–1848) and Nikanor Klement'evskii (1848–1856)—were passive, anemic creatures incapable of restraining Protasov and providing leadership in the Synod. More influential and active were the metropolitans of Kiev, Evgenii Bolkhovitinov (1822–1837) and Filaret Amfiteatrov (1837–1857). Evgenii aided in the seminary reforms of 1808–1814 and thereafter remained a prominent figure in Church affairs. Filaret, a more conservative figure, generally opposed change in the Church, declaring that "Christ's Church in the beginning appeared in all its spiritual perfection. . . . All who introduce innovations and reforms in the Church, under the pretext of improving things, are extremely harmful, pretentious, and deceptive."[47] Such statements concisely show why he opposed Protasov's assertiveness, but the Pavskii affair in 1842 ended in his departure from the Synod, essentially shutting him off from Synodal politics.

Without question, the most influential prelate in prereform Russia was Metropolitan Filaret (Drozdov) of Moscow. Born in the small town of Kolomna (Moscow province) in 1782, Filaret first attracted attention through his energetic activities as the administrator of reforms at the St. Petersburg Ecclesiastical Academy in 1810–1814. After a brief term in Tver, Filaret became archbishop of Moscow in 1821 and four years later rose to the rank of metropolitan, a position he occupied until his death in 1867. He was a towering intellectual figure and a principal architect of Church policy, at least until the Pavskii affair caused his departure from the Synod. He was, as well, an extremely complex figure, one who defies such conventional categories as conservative or liberal. In contrast to the archconservative Serafim, for example, Filaret held relatively liberal views on *religious* reform, consistently favoring the translation of the Bible into modern Russian and reform in the seminary curriculum—all in the name of abetting popular religiousness.

On the question of institutional reform, however, Filaret tended to be much more conservative, fearful that change would only erode the Church's power and yield little palpable benefit. That belief derived partly from the notion that the principal problem was moral regeneration, not institutional change. As he wrote of one reform scheme in 1832, "it is tedious how people see only disorder and abuse in everything, and—because of the misdeeds of

---

[47]"Pis'ma Filareta, mitr. kievskogo," *TKDA*, 1884, no. 4: 624.

one person in one place—want to reorder the whole world." The task, he held, was to change people, not institutions.[48] In practice, however, that view tended to degenerate into a sterile negativism that infuriated foes and dismayed admirers. As one close associate wrote, Filaret sought to "freeze" development in the Church, seeking not to discover things new or to make things better but only to ward off things harmful.[49] One intellectual, whom Filaret drove from Moscow Academy for excessively liberal views on the Old Believers, described the prelate as "a cobra, who drains a man of everything and then casts him aside as something unneeded."[50] From the 1840s, Filaret grew increasingly cautious, as he warned of dangers from female education, defended the virtues of corporal punishment, castigated "democratic principles," and cast suspicion on any change, whatever its goal. Even admirers lost patience with the venerable metropolitan. As one vexed layman (who hoped to steel episcopal demands for greater autonomy) wrote to Filaret, "thirty years of work in a difficult field in the last reign has made you too cautious."[51] Still, Filaret elicited begrudging admiration from many (even the radical intellectual Alexander Herzen) and bequeathed a school of likeminded bishops, known as the "Filaretovtsy."[52]

Beneath this elite core of metropolitans stood the diocesan bishops.[53] In social background virtually all came from the clergy, usually from the families of priests and archpriests, sometimes from those of deacons and sacristans, only rarely from lay status groups. Although bishops were chosen exclusively from the ranks of monastic clergy, they included a few former parish priests—men who had been widowed, taken monastic vows, and risen later in the hierarchy. Coming almost entirely from the homes of white clergy and educated in the same schools as future recruits for the priesthood, the bishops on the face of it should have been closely tied to the clerical estate, forming with it a cohesive "clerical" party. At least potentially, that social homogeneity promised to avoid the kind of social tension found in Western

[48]Filaret, *Perepiska s Nechaevym*, p. 70 (letter of 14.6.1832). Besides Filaret's multivolume collection of memoranda on general church questions *(SMO)*, his resolutions on diocesan matters have been published as *Polnoe sobranie rezoliutsii Filareta* [hereafter Filaret, *PSR*], 3 vols. (Moscow, 1905).

[49]A.V., "Iz otzyvov i vospominanii P. S. Kazanskogo o mitr. moskovskom Filarete," *Pravoslavnoe obozrenie* [hereafter *PO*], 1882, no. 8: 724, 732.

[50]"Pis'ma k P. I. Bartenevu," *RA*, 1912, no. 6: 312 (N. P. Giliarov-Platonov).

[51]A. N. L'vov, *Pis'ma dukhovnykh i svetskikh lits k mitropolitu moskovskomu Filaretu* (St. Petersburg, 1900), p. 283 (A. N. Murav'ev to Filaret, 22.3.1857).

[52]A. Gertsen, *Sochineniia*, 8 vols. (Moscow, 1956–58), 4: 131–33; for the literature on Filaret, see Igor Smolitsch, *Geschichte der russischen Kirche 1700–1917* (Leiden, 1964), pp. xxxvii, 288–99.

[53]Data here are derived from an analysis of *Spisok arkhiereev i ierarkhov vserossiiskikh i arkheograficheskikh kafedr so vremeni uchrezhdeniia Sv. Sinoda (1721–1895 gg.)* (St. Petersburg, 1896).

churches, as in prerevolutionary France, where parish priests disliked bishops as much for their aristocratic blood as for their episcopal power.[54]

In fact, however, Russian bishops belonged to a world quite alien to that of the parish clergy, divided by profound differences in educational levels, career patterns, and expectations. Most striking was the bishops' high level of education. Although most eighteenth-century prelates had acquired a respectable education for the time, their successors in the nineteenth could boast of truly elite learning, with advanced degrees (master's and doctor's) from the ecclesiastical academies.[55] That set them radically apart from most parish clergy, who rarely held more than a seminary degree, and even from the regular monastic clergy, which included large numbers of uneducated, even illiterate, monks.[56] The bishops' elite status made them highly visible as the "learned monks" who dominated ecclesiastical schools and the hierarchy, where they came into sustained contact with members of the parish clergy. Although formal education was also concurrently reshaping the profile of other status groups (most notably, the civil service), it had an unusually great impact upon the episcopate, which was relatively free of the patronage and aristocratic ties that could override educational criteria in secular society. Indeed, formal education became virtually the sole determinant in episcopal careers: the academy degree became a de facto prerequisite for elevation to the hierarchy.

And that elevation came early: after a brief tenure in the seminary or academy as a rector, the learned monk—still in his thirties—became a "venerable bishop" of the Church, barely a decade after he had completed his studies at the academy. His meteoric career did not stop with consecration. Although some bishops served for decades in a single diocese, most held several successive appointments, transferring often and far. Hence the death of a bishop could trigger a burst of transfers, as in the case of musical chairs that followed the death of one bishop in 1838: "His position is assigned to the bishop of Irkutsk, Innokentii; the bishop of Viatka, Nil, is transferred to

---

[54] On the suggestive parallels in the French Church, see: Ruth Necheles, "The Curés in the Estates General of 1789," *Journal of Modern History*, 46 (1974): 425–44; Timothy Tackett, *Priest and Parish in Eighteenth-Century France* (Princeton, 1977), pp. 241–68; Hilaire, *Une Chrétienté*, 1: 153; E. T. Gargan, "The Priestly Culture in Modern France," *Catholic Historical Review*, 57 (1971): 5–7; and M. G. Hutt, "The Curés and the Third Estate," *JEH*, 8 (1957): 74–92.

[55] By 1855, virtually all bishops had some form of higher education: 88 percent had advanced degrees from the academy, 6 percent had some other form of elite education, and only 6 percent (mostly ex-Uniate prelates) had inferior education (calculated from *Spisok arkhiereev*).

[56] On Russian monasticism, the object of abundant but mostly unscholarly research, see Igor Smolitsch, *Russisches Mönchtum: Entstehung, Entwicklung und Wesen, 988–1917* (Würzburg, 1953).

Irkutsk diocese; the suffragan bishop of Tver diocese, Neofit, is appointed
to the post [in Viatka]."[57] Such transfers, though not an innovation under
Nicholas, sharply increased during his reign: the average number of prior
appointments nearly doubled, and the number of bishops without prior
appointment declined from 39 percent in 1825 to 17 percent in 1855. The
motives for transfer were diverse: some dioceses had larger budgets; older
and more venerable dioceses carried greater prestige; some dioceses (especially those in Siberia or borderland areas) posed great difficulties because of
the presence of other confessions or the shortcomings of the local clergy.[58]
Although transfer served some positive functions, providing a reward for
good performance and giving bishops a more "global," less provincial perspective on Church problems, it clashed sharply with canon law, which presumed all appointments to be permanent.

More important, the bishops' high mobility directly impinged upon their
relations with parish clergy, who, with increasing frequency and vehemence,
complained of their prelates' "careerism" and the erosion of traditional
"paternalistic" ties.[59] Their complaints were not unfounded. Indeed, bishops
moved so often (every seven years, on the average) that they had little time
to develop a close familiarity with either their diocese or the parish clergy
in their charge. As a result, the bishops came to rely heavily upon administrative aides or the diocesan elite—the archpriests who served in the capital.
Although the prelates' distance and "formalism" derived partly from the
sheer press of other business, their high rate of mobility was a major contrib-
uting cause. The leading prelates were well aware of the problem. Metropolitan Filaret, for example, complained in 1832 that "it is true that bishops
are moved too often," but he declared that the Synod seemed unable to curtail the practice: "They agree with this comment in the Synod, but when it
comes to a choice, they follow previous examples [of relocating bishops]."[60]
That mobility was fraught with other dangers as well, such as manipulation
by the procurator, yet the Synod declined to abandon this method of reward-
ing and punishing bishops.

Celibate, armed with elite education, often graced with ties to local notables, highly mobile, the new "learned monks" of Nikolaevan Russia had relatively little in common with the mass of parish clergy under their rule. Significantly, that social distance—rooted not only in differences of rank but
also in differences of career—was reflected in the white clergy's tendency to

[57] *IVO (1838)*, p. 5.

[58] On the budgetary differentials, see below, pp. 332–33.

[59] See, for example, the complaints by clergy in the mid-1830s, late 1850s, and 1916 (below,
pp. 32–33, 209–10, 457).

[60] "Materialy dlia biografii mitr. Filareta," *Chteniia v Obshchestve liubitelei dukhovnogo
prosveshcheniia* [hereafter *ChOLDP*], 8 (1869): 69 (letter of 1832).

distinguish between ordinary bishops and those who had previously been white clergy (and, as widowers, took monastic vows and became prelates). To quote one instance of hope engendered by the appointment of a former priest to the diocese: "From whom else could one expect more aid and defense than from him—who himself (and quite recently at that) was persecuted and oppressed by the enemies of white clergy and without cause?"[61] The differences in status and career, which widened steadily as the learned monks took a more prominent role in Church administration, weighed heavily upon intraclerical relations in the Church.

Order and Disorder in Diocesan Administration

To aid in the conduct of diocesan business, each bishop had a modest apparatus of clerical and lay assistants. His principal aid was the consistory (*konsistoriia*),[62] a collegial board of clergy that functioned as the wheelhouse of diocesan administration, examining each case, compiling a synopsis, and drafting a resolution for the bishop to confirm, amend, or reject. The consistory ordinarily comprised five to seven clergy, who, like the bishop, usually held an advanced degree from the academy.[63] Significantly, white clergy dominated the consistory: whereas monks had composed a numerical majority in the late eighteenth century, by 1861 parish clergy made up 78 percent of all consistory members.[64] These parish clergy were not village priests but the diocesan elite, whose superior education assured them choice appointments in the diocesan capital. Only white clergy who merited such positions could reside in the capital and thus be available for appointment to the consistory. Once appointed, they ordinarily became permanent fixtures, remaining there until death, even in cases of infirmity and virtual incapacity.[65]

Because the consistory members simultaneously held full-time clerical appointments and in fact received no remuneration or special training for their consistory duties, much of the actual administrative work devolved

---

[61]"Iz peterburgskikh pisem M. I. Muretova," *ChOIDR*, 231 (1910), 3: 24.

[62]In 1832 the Synod standardized the term *konsistoriia*, prohibiting the term *dikasteriia* still used in some western dioceses; see *PSZ (2)*, 7: 5380.

[63]In 1860, 52 percent of the consistory members held an academy degree, something virtually unknown among the parish clergy (TsGIA SSSR, f. 796, op. 142, g. 1861, d. 1999, ch. 1–2).

[64]The consistories were composed of monastic clergy (22 percent), archpriests (53 percent), and priests (25 percent); for the eighteenth-century monastic domination, see Freeze, *Russian Levites*, pp. 53, 245.

[65]Significantly, the consistory members were older: their average age was 49.4 years, compared with 40–41 for clergy in most dioceses (TsGIA SSSR, f. 796, op. 142, g. 1861, d. 1999, ch. 1–2).

upon the lay employees of the diocesan chancellery. Most of these chancell-erists were impecunious scribes appointed from the ranks of poor seminari-ans whose bad record—or bad conduct—denied them hope of a parish appointment. Different in origin and status was the diocesan secretary, head of this administrative apparatus; chosen from lay ranks, he wielded consid-erable power in the consistory as the bishop's chief aide and direct manager of the consistory's paperwork. No doubt the importance of this position impelled procurators, from Iakovlev to Protasov, to seek control over such appointments and thus to turn the secretary into their own special agent in the diocese.[66]

Outside the diocesan capital the bishop relied upon two organs to exercise his control over parishes and clergy. At the intermediate level was the district board (*dukhovnoe pravlenie*), composed of two or three clerics and serving as a transmission belt between the bishop and two or three outlying dis-tricts.[67] More important was the local ecclesiastical superintendent (*blago-chinnyi*), an archpriest or priest appointed by the bishop to oversee ten to fifteen neighboring parishes. Earlier this office had been an elective one; called the "clerical elder" (*popovskii starosta*), he was primarily responsible for the delivery of various church levies to the bishop. From the late eigh-teenth century, however, prelates replaced the elder with superintendents, who bore no fiscal duties and instead had to supervise subordinate clergy and provide good order (*blagochinie*) in the parish. Though numerous, especially if compared with the weak infrastructure of state administration, the super-intendents simultaneously held regular clerical appointments, drew no salary for their work, and provided only intermittent supervision, mainly through biannual visits to each parish.[68]

Assisted by these organs, the bishop had to discharge a host of complex responsibilities. One was to authorize the creation of new parishes—a diffi-cult task, since parishioners were wont to construct new churches (an exercise designed to display their piety and earn God's grace) even when there was no legitimate need and no means to maintain the church or to support its clergy. Beginning with Peter the Great, authorities employed tight regula-tions to stop the proliferation of "useless" churches, requiring that the bishop investigate each petition carefully and submit the case to the Synod for

[66]Murav'ev, "O prichinakh bedstvennogo polozheniia," OR GBL, f. 304, r. 2, d. 259, ll. 27–56.

[67]Each district board had responsibility over some 20 to 100 churches, depending upon the diocese (full data for 1829 are in TsGIA SSSR, f. 796, op. 110, g. 1829, d. 770, ll. 87–98 ob.). Because the boards were convenient but not essential units, bishops gradually closed about a third of them in the 1840s and early 1850s, diverting their budgets to cover the more urgent needs at the consistory. See *IVO (1841)*, p. 9; *IVO (1855)*, pp. 6–7.

[68]On the replacement of clerical elders by superintendents, see Freeze, *Russian Levites*, pp. 50–51, 54–55.

approval. In addition, the bishop had to oversee the spiritual well-being of laymen in his diocese, protecting Orthodox folk from apostasy and ensuring good morality. Though the Church's authority over the laity had atrophied in modern times, bishops still had the power to punish promiscuity and apostasy by imposing various forms of penance, even incarceration in monasteries. Most important, they retained primary responsibility in deciding divorce cases.

The bishop's chief duty, however, was to govern the clerical population in his diocese, namely, the clergy and their families. One major task was to appoint and ordain clergy, a matter where the bishop came to exercise ever greater discretion, primarily because of the larger number of qualified candidates at his disposal. The right of parishioners to nominate candidates, still in force in the eighteenth century, declined swiftly in the first decades of the nineteenth century, especially in the central dioceses; given the large number of seminarians (with their abilities and morality attested by seminary officials), the bishop had no need to rely upon parish nominations or their testimonials about the candidates' merits.[69] Even so, appointment remained a complex task. Thus the bishops sometimes did pay heed to parish recommendations, especially in the case of serf villages, where they ordinarily took pains not to offend the sensibility or traditional prerogatives of the local squire. They also had to provide welfare for the retired priest or his family, giving preference to a candidate willing to wed into (or, at least, financially support) the family of his predecessor. It was plainly a complex task, especially when the prelate had to weigh qualifications, parish wish, and the need for clerical welfare.

Still more difficult was the dispensation of ecclesiastical justice, the supervision and punishment of clergy for malfeasance and misconduct. However remote the parish, the bishop had ample means for discovering misdeeds, the denunciations coming from the superintendents, outraged laymen, or fellow clergy on the parish staff. Most cases involved relatively minor matters, such as unauthorized absences or drunken misconduct, but a few concerned serious offenses, such as solicitation of excessive emoluments or illegal mar-

---

[69] Parish claims still persisted in some areas; see, for example, the complaint in 1826 from the bishop of Smolensk about the parishioners' control over the selection of priests in his diocese (TsGIA SSSR, f. 796, op. 107, g. 1826, d. 460, ll. 93–93 ob.). Though the explosion of seminary enrollments in the 1820s and 1830s ended any practical need for prelates to rely upon nominations in most dioceses, the hierarchs in practice did give due attention to parish wish, especially when the parish belonged to an influential landowner. As an official report of 1863 correctly noted: "In practice it often happens that, in making the appointment of priests and deacons, one takes into account (or at least does not deem it superfluous to obtain) parish approval for the candidates." See "Zametka otnositel'no uchastiia mirian v izbranie sviashchennikov i d'iakonov," TsGIA SSSR, f. 804 (Osoboe prisutstvie po delam pravoslavnogo dukhovenstva), op. 1, r. 1, d. 11, l. 179.

riages.[70] Once the consistory had investigated the case, the bishop had broad discretion in setting punishment, for the Church had no detailed code of laws.[71] In minor matters the bishop usually meted out light punishment, including small fines, prostrations, or mere verbal reprimands, but in serious cases of immorality or malfeasance he prescribed more severe penalties, such as several months' incarceration in a monastery, suspension from service, forcible relocation to an inferior parish, and demotion from priest to sacristan (either temporarily or permanently). Probably the harshest punishment, short of defrocking, was forcible relocation. Dictated by the gravity of the offense and irredeemable loss of respect in the parish, such transfer was ruinous for the cleric, who had not only to find a vacant position but also to bear the high costs of relocation.[72]

Ultimately, however, when the crime was grave and the record bad, the bishop ordered the supreme punishment: defrocking and expulsion from the clergy. Still, defrockings were rare, as most bishops—to Nicholas's consternation—displayed amazing patience toward chronic offenders. For example, the service record of one demoted priest in Tomsk showed twenty eight offenses in twenty one years of service.[73] Sometimes defrocking was a fairly simple decision, as in the case of a priest in Nizhnii Novgorod: "Exerting a corrupting influence on parishioners, [he has been dwelling] in the house of a peasant woman Agafinia Koz'mina, with whom fifteen years ago he had had an adulterous relationship, and to the disgrace of the clergy, he has worked as a nurse for her young children, washed their diapers, and cleaned her livestock as well."[74] Nor did the Synod question the decision to expel a sacristan from the same diocese in 1828. The man drank with abandon, chanted so badly that parishioners laughed, and after one wedding ran outside the church, displayed "his private member, then chased after the

---

[70]TsGIA SSSR, f. 796, op. 132, g. 1851, d. 2354, ll. 185–185 ob. This file from Nizhnii Novgorod shows that 112 clergymen were involved in judicial cases: 24 for alleged drunkenness, 16 for insulting various laymen or clergy, 54 for unauthorized absences from their parishes, 10 for unseemly behavior, 5 for solicitation, and 4 for illegal marriages.

[71]The arbitrary determination of punishment, with special harshness for sacristans, is evident from judicial files. For one of many such examples, see the case of a Moscow clergymen in Tsentral'nyi gosudarstvennyi istoricheskii arkhiv g. Moskvy [hereafter TsGIAgM], f. 203 (Moskovskoe dukhovnoe pravlenie), op. 552, d. 157, l. 1.

[72]Forcible translation had long been a favored form of punishment; see criticism of the practice below, p. 317. Bishops in France also used this device, evoking considerable opposition among the parish clergy; see, especially, the protest of two brothers in 1839 (C. Allignol and A. Allignol, *De l'état actuel du clergé en France et en particulier des curés ruraux appelés desservans* [Paris, 1839]), and the account in Marcilhacy, *Le diocèse d'Orléans*, pp. 270–72.

[73]Gosudarstvennyi arkhiv Tomskoi oblasti [hereafter GA Tomskoi obl.], f. 170 (Tomskaia dukhovnaia konsistoriia), op. 1, d. 265, ll. 20–23.

[74]TsGIA SSSR, f. 796, op. 107, g. 1826, d. 874, l. 3 (Nizhnii Novgorod case).

women, grabbed their breasts and. . . ."[75] Once the Synod approved the decision to defrock, the bishop dispatched the cleric to civil authorities for inscription into the poll-tax population as a state peasant or townsman and sometimes for deportation to underpopulated regions of the empire.[76]

Perhaps the most striking feature of diocesan administration was the high frequency with which it intervened in the lives of ordinary clergy. A vast number of them, usually for some trivial matter, fell into the tentacles of diocesan justice. One investigation of the late 1820s revealed that over ten thousand priests (roughly 30 percent of the group) had been subject to judicial inquiry or formal trial at some point in their careers.[77] Rates varied sharply from one diocese to the next, reflecting the moral state of local clergy and the efficiency of diocesan administration; proportions were high in Nizhnii Novgorod (51 percent) but relatively low in Moscow (23 percent) and Irkutsk (16 percent). To Nicholas these data proved that bishops were permissive: such tainted clergy, in his view, should long ago have been expelled from the clergy.[78] In fact, the data were inflated, since 95 percent of the "offenses" involved minor service errors that entailed only light punishment.[79] What the data do show is the high degree of contact between white clergy and diocesan justice. The bishop and consistory were not some distant and forgotten abstraction; rather, they embodied an institution—fraught with serious shortcomings—that lay heavily upon ordinary parish clergy.

And these shortcomings were many. So far as central authorities were concerned, the main problem was the ineptness of diocesan administration. Thus not only Nicholas but also the Synod decried the bishops' lack of good supervision over the clergy. In the Synod's view, clerical misconduct resulted from nothing other than "weak supervision" and the failure to take measures to eradicate vices in the clergy.[80] Of greater concern to parish clergy, however, were the problems of injustice and bribery. Though hardly unique in Nikolaevan bureaucracy, such abuses seemed all the more reprehensible when they flourished in the Church and under the direct hand of the bishop himself. Central authorities were not unaware of the problem. In 1828, for exam-

[75] Ibid., op. 109, g. 1828, d. 598, ll. 16–16 ob. (Nizhnii Novgorod case).

[76] For exile to remote areas, see PSZ (2), 10: 8139; 12: 8750a.

[77] TsGIA SSSR, f. 796, op. 111, g. 1830, d. 509, l. 3 ob.

[78] Ibid., ll. 7–7 ob. Areas with higher rates included Kiev (33 percent), Kazan (36 percent), and Chernigov (41 percent); dioceses with low rates included Novgorod (14 percent) and Perm (17 percent).

[79] Ibid. Typical was the pattern in Moscow, where the bishop found only 57 of the 299 clergy guilty of serious offenses meriting expulsion. Similar are data for England in the early eighteenth century: of nearly 1,000 clergymen in one area, 22 percent had some judicial troubles, though most of these were for lesser offenses (J. H. Pruett, Parish Clergy under the Late Stuarts [Urbana, 1978], pp. 128–32).

[80] PSPR, nos. 176, 216.

ple, the chief procurator complained of receiving numerous reports that "some [lay] employees of our consistories and ecclesiastical boards, forgetting the respect due the clerical rank, treat the church's servitors in an unseemly fashion and with insolence."[81] "In many dioceses," he also reported, "bribery abuses occur when the parish registers are submitted to the consistory and ecclesiastical boards" by the clergy.[82] The Third Section made similar disclosures, complaining, for example, that the bishop of Kostroma appointed tainted clerics as ecclesiastical superintendents and tolerated a consistory where "affairs are conducted with bias and great delays."[83] Similar complaints appeared in various memoranda to the Synod. One submitted in the early 1830s declared that "the elected church elders serve poorly, the ecclesiastical superintendents supervise poorly, [and] the consistory operates poorly (and its powers are unlimited)."[84]

The most trenchant critique appeared in a memorandum sent in 1836 from a priest in Kaluga province, Ioann Pokrovskii.[85] The memorandum, adorned with literary flourishes, was cast in the form of correspondence between a newly ordained priest and a more experienced colleague, who tried to dissuade the young priest from needless entanglements with diocesan authorities. But the young priest, determined to make his parish a model of piety, resolved to improve the behavior of his subordinates on the parish staff: "The sacristan is drunk every day, [and] the deacon is both drunk and rowdy"—conduct common for these lowly ranks and a bane of the Church and clergy. He thus ignored his colleague's counsel and complained to his diocesan superiors, asking that the sacristan be removed. Soon, however, the young priest discovered the rank injustice pervading diocesan administration. Corruption took its toll: the sacristan escaped unharmed, while the priest was fined and reprimanded for filing "a false complaint." Still determined to obtain justice, the priest journeyed to the consistory to see the bishop personally, but found his path barred:

> My eyes were opened. I became convinced that the bishop is heavily burdened with many matters and that he lacks the time to become involved and inspect all judicial matters properly. His offices are almost always overflowing; members of the diocesan consistory and ecclesiastical boards, superintendents, seminary administrators, important gentlemen and citizens; the consistory secretary appears with great heaps of paper—one after

[81] TsGIA SSSR, f. 796, op. 109, g. 1828, d. 225, l. 1 (chief procurator to diocesan secretaries, 13.2.1828).

[82] Ibid., d. 122, l. 1 (procurator to Synod, 1828).

[83] Ibid., op. 111, g. 1830, d. 786, ll. 6–6 ob. (Third Section report).

[84] "Mnenie prikhozhanina ob otbiraemykh dlia khraneniia i prirashcheniia na pol'zu tserkvi svechnykh dokhodov" (published in Filaret, Perepiska s Nechaevym, p. 71).

[85] TsGIA SSSR, f. 796, op. 117, g. 1836, d. 1777 (zapiska).

the other, and often jointly, they keep the bishop preoccupied until 2 p.m. almost every day. In addition, [the bishop] supervises a flock with up to 1,000 priests, 2,000 lower-ranking clergy, ten ecclesiastical boards, and so many bureaus and superintendents who constantly distract him with various reports and complaints, true or otherwise.

Though the Synod spurned the memorandum ("as a work without foundation, it merits no attention"), Pokrovskii raised issues that would become stock themes in the reformist literature of the 1860s.

The causes of maladministration were many. One major problem was excessive centralization at both the Synodal and the diocesan level. So much authority resided in Petersburg that local bishops found it extremely difficult to resolve promptly even the most urgent business. For example, the bishop needed prior authorization from Petersburg to make any substantial expenditures, to fill teaching vacancies at the seminary, or even to authorize the opening of a new parish in some isolated hamlet. Such centralization, deemed essential because local authorities were unreliable and corrupt, impeded efficiency, obliging officials to wait long periods for approval and routinizing procrastination and lethargy in the conduct of administration. The memoirs of one chancellerist offer a memorable example: a consistory for decades sought permission to rebuild its offices and repeatedly found belated authorizations lagging behind inflation.[86] A parallel problem existed at the diocesan level, where the bishop and his staff handled virtually all matters, however petty, and delegated no independent authority to the lower organs of their administration. The result was a crushing volume of business. Characteristic was the case of Bishop Parfenii of Vladimir, who was rebuked for failing to submit a much-needed report to the Synod. Parfenii explained that he had intended to handle the matter personally rather than entrust it to his consistory, but "because of the mass of current diocesan business, I could not take the time to fulfill my intention." Similarly, in 1852 the bishop of Tula wrote that "the great number of cases is a heavy burden," and many of his colleagues voiced the same complaint.[87]

Centralization accorded ill with the underdevelopment of diocesan administration, creating a sharp contradiction between the bishops' responsibilities and the apparatus actually at their disposal. The Synod was aware of the problem and candidly attributed the failures of diocesan administration to "the vast [territorial] expanses and dense population of dioceses and the consequent difficulties of close control and supervision."[88] For instance,

[86]Ismailov, "Iz vospominaniia," *Str.*, 1883, no. 6: 237–43.
[87]TsGIA SSSR, f. 797, op. 8, d. 24145, ll. 2–2 ob. (Parfenii to Synod, 28.2.1838); "Pis'ma Dmitriia, arkhiepiskopa khersonskogo," *TKDA*, 1884, no. 8: 598 (letter of 9.9.1852).
[88]*PSPR*, no. 176.

bishops were expected to make annual visitations to parish churches, but in practice they found it possible to visit only a small segment of their dioceses each year, try as they might.[89] In 1855, for example, bishops in forty dioceses inspected 3,353 churches—about 10 percent of all churches in the empire.[90] Even then, the visitations were perfunctory; the schedule left no time for serious inquiry into parish affairs or clerical performance. The bishops' travel logs typically show that although they did occasionally uncover some problems (decrepit churches, incompetent sacristans, and angry parishioners), the chief effect of the trip was to exhaust the bishop and distract him from regular administrative duties.[91] As one bishop wrote in 1827:

> What did we see during the visitation? I rode all over Kursk diocese but could not eradicate abuses by doing so. What can one see in an hour's time? In the meantime the consistory does as it pleases during our trips. The queen bee does not leave the hive; cases come to us on their own account, and it is easy to tell what each person is worth. It is useful to visit the diocese once (to become acquainted with the area), but [annual] visitations are mere escapades, not business.[92]

Most of the time, of course, authorities ruled from their nest in the diocesan capital—in itself no easy task in a domain with thousands of clergy scattered over several thousand square miles, isolated by the notoriously poor communications of nineteenth-century Russia.

The imperious style of some prelates only aggravated tensions, suggesting that bishops were simply clerical bureaucrats, not paternalistic heads of their dioceses. Although few prelates escaped accusations of cruelty and heartlessness, perhaps the pronouncements of one, Innokentii (Borisov), can give some sense of their manner. Thus when one sacristan sought promotion to a higher rank, Innokentii thundered in anger: "Deprive him of his sacristan's position until he has learned what he is supposed to know (or, if he likes, release him into secular society)"—no doubt a shocking resolution for the cleric who had sought promotion. In another case Innokentii ordered a sacristan suspended until he learned to read and sing well, or "throw him out of the clerical estate." When another sought a sacristan's position, citing family needs, Innokentii wrote: "What do such fools need to get married for? He should have studied first! Otherwise, the path would lead straight for [consignment

---

[89] For the injunction to make visitations, see ibid., no. 621.

[90] *IVO (1855)*, pp. 6–7. Western bishops systematically visited all their parishes every two or three years and ordinarily collected data beforehand in the form of surveys. See, for example, the case of France as described in Hilaire, *Une Chrétienté*, 1: 271–72, and Bligny, *Le diocèse de Grenoble*, p. 179.

[91] TsGIA SSSR, f. 796, op. 112, g. 1831, d. 833, ll. 1–5 ob., 12–14 ob., 48–49 ob. (travel logs for 1830 from bishops in Podolia, Olonets, and Kursk).

[92] "Materialy dlia istorii russkoi tserkvi," *ChOLDP*, 1874, no. 11: 58.

into] the peasantry." Significantly, Innokentii's decisions were reasonable, designed to raise standards in the clergy; it was his style, his disrespect for parish clergy that was so abrasive.[93]

Poor administration was also due to the minuscule budgets alloted for the support of diocesan clerks. Ever since the state secularized Church property in 1764, the lay scribes of the consistory depended upon a state budget for support. That budget, however, was small and rarely increased, leaving the Church's administration undermanned and underpaid, incapable of processing the glut of paperwork so routine in Nikolaevan Russia. Civil administration, significantly, experienced explosive growth under Nicholas, as it tried to keep pace with the spiraling red tape.[94] The Church had much the same volume of paperwork (preparing audits and submitting to the emperor's insatiable demand for reports and data), yet it lacked the independent resources to expand and improve its clerical staff.[95] As one overworked bishop exclaimed: "How numerous indeed are the new staff lists of officials and appointments [in civil service]! If they would only give [us] poor bishops just a single copyist for [our] own use in the [coming] new year! You have to write out everything yourself, yet there are [constantly] new demands, reports, exactions—without end."[96] Thus the Nikolaevan bureaucratization exerted extraordinary strains on the Church's apparatus, expanding its tasks but not the manpower to perform them.

Inadequate funding meant not only few clerks but also bad ones.[97] Most apparent to all was the widespread bribery: lay clerks received a mere pittance (literally a few rubles per month), manifestly inadequate to sustain life, and were obliged to seek "gifts" from clergy who came to the consistory on business.[98] Whether termed gifts or bribes, such tribute was a prerequisite for prompt and satisfactory treatment of suits, unquestioning approval of periodic reports or parish registers, special consideration in appointments,

---

[93] T. Butkevich, "Arkhiepiskop Innokentii Borisov," *Vera i razum* [hereafter *VR*], 1 (1884), tom 1: 941–42, 943, 950; tom 2: 253.

[94] The civil service numbered about 38,000 officials in 1800 but grew rapidly during Nicholas's reign, reaching 114,000 in 1857 (Walter Pintner, "Evolution of Civil Officials," in W. Pintner and D. Rowney, eds., *Russian Officialdom: The Bureaucratization of Russian Society from the Seventeenth to the Twentieth Centuries* (Chapel Hill, 1980), p. 183.

[95] For comparable problems in the judicial administration, see Wortman, *Russian Legal Consciousness*, p. 238.

[96] N. M. Vostokov, "Innokentii, arkhiepiskop Khersonskii," *RS*, 23 (1878): 371.

[97] The inferior quality and dubious ethics of diocesan chancellerists were recurring themes in bishops' correspondence; see, for example, F. I. Titov, ed., "Perepiska moskovskogo mitropolita Makariia Bulgakova," *TKDA*, 1907, no. 1: 56–57; S. Karpov, "Evgenii Bolkhovitinov," ibid., 1913, no. 9: 136–51.

[98] For comparable patterns in the civil service (at least in its lower divisions), see P. A. Zaionchkovskii, *Pravitel'stvennyi apparat samoderzhavnoi Rossii v XIX v.* (Moscow, 1978), pp. 66–68.

and the like. Though some bishops fought extortion, most recognized the necessity of modest fees even while regretting their inability to convert such assessments into a regular diocesan levy.[99] Hence they tolerated venality or even resorted to dubious devices like that employed in Tambov, where the bishop—like a medieval tsar of Muscovy—dispatched diocesan clerks periodically into the diocese for "feeding" (*kormlenie*), the collection of tribute from parish clergy.[100] Moreover, because the clerk's lot was a hard one, the Church lost its best staff. As the bishop of Arkhangel'sk complained in 1850, the "extremely small sums" available for chancellerist salaries meant a constant drain in staffs, for the clerks "use every opportunity to transfer to government service and they do so in spite of every effort by diocesan administration to restrain them."[101] Without competent staff, diocesan administration at times completely broke down, as in Tomsk in the mid-1850s, where the consistory had a backlog of five thousand unfinished files.[102]

Diocesan administration also suffered from "lawlessness," the lack of a unified law code giving clear prescriptions on administrative and judicial process. Actually, this lawlessness was due to the excess of laws, a maze so complex and contradictory that it made arbitrariness inevitable and abuse easy. Although that description applied in some measure as well to civil administration, the problem was more pronounced in the Church, which had a plethora of legal guides—Holy Scripture, canon law, the Ecclesiastical Regulation of 1721, and reams of government and Synodal decrees over the past century. Which law applied or had precedence remained unclear; traditional laws were often vague and ambiguous, more recent ones contradictory and unsystematic. As in secular administration, legal ambiguity abetted manipulation by underpaid clerks and consistory boards given to peculation and extortion.[103]

When abuse became intolerable, parish clergy could appeal to the Synod for justice, and in fact each year a small number did just that.[104] Ordinarily, the Synod—if the appeals met the legal requirements (proper form, statute of limitations, and the like)—immediately ordered the bishop to investigate and submit a full abstract of the case. It did not dispatch special investigators but used the report to determine whether procedures were proper and judgments fair. The petitioner's prior record played a crucial role in such appeals. Those with long case histories of misconduct received scant attention, as evidenced by the case of a sacristan in Orel who accused the consistory of

---

[99] For earlier periods, see Freeze, *Russian Levites*, pp. 64–65.

[100] V. F. Pevnitskii, "Zapiski," *RS*, 123 (1905): 144.

[101] TsGIA SSSR, f. 796, op. 132, g. 1851, d. 2357, l. 3.

[102] A. A. Misiurov, *Kratkii istoriko-statisticheskii ocherk Tomskoi eparkhii* (Tomsk, 1897), p. 12.

[103] I. Listovskii, "Filaret, arkhiepiskop chernigovskii," *RA*, 1887, no. 11: 322.

[104] For Synod judicial data, see *IVO (1840)*, p. 54.

"coercing" him to resign his position. The Synod summarily rejected his petition once the bishop filed a report cataloguing the sacristan's many misdeeds.[105] Often, however, the Synod did modify a bishop's verdict, either to correct a faulty judgment or, more often, to display "compassion." For instance, when one sacristan contested his bishop's decision to expel him from the clergy, the Synod concluded that the cleric was guilty but that, "in consideration of his advanced age and quite large family," he should be left as a watchguard in a parish church.[106] At times the Synod exposed and corrected injustice. In 1828, for example, it reversed one bishop's decision against a sacristan and sternly rebuked the consistory for its improper handling of the case.[107] In 1836 the Synod exonerated a superintendent who had been summarily punished without formal investigation and rebuked diocesan authorities for mishandling the case.[108] Most petitions were less fortunate, with the Synod finding no reason to overturn a decision or even refusing to consider the appeal for technical reasons.[109] Such rejections only reinforced a longstanding suspicion among parish clergy that the Synod, composed mostly of bishops, was little inclined to condemn a fellow prelate or, especially, one of its own members.[110]

Reform in Diocesan Administration

Well aware of these problems, authorities made diverse attempts during Nicholas's reign to improve diocesan administration—not far-reaching changes that would redistribute power, but measures that would make this system work somewhat more efficiently. One device, an old one, was to increase the number of dioceses, making them smaller and more managea-

---

[105]TsGIA SSSR, f. 796, op. 109, g. 1828, d. 550, ll. 1–10.

[106]Ibid., op. 123, g. 1842, d. 1129.

[107]Ibid., op. 109, g. 1828, d. 450.

[108]Ibid., op. 117, g. 1836, d. 689, ll. 1–80.

[109]Thus the Synod refused to consider a petition from a cleric in Kaluga because the statute of limitations for appeals had lapsed (ibid., op. 109, g. 1828, d. 536); likewise, it rejected petitions from clergy in Kaluga and Viatka because they had used improper (not embossed) paper (ibid., op. 123, g. 1842, d. 1058; op. 131, g. 1850, d. 487).

[110]Occasionally, clergy flouted both Synodal and episcopal authority, as in the case of a priest in Orel diocese, Ivan Filippov, who had previously been decorated for meritorious service. When he became entangled in an investigation of theft, he vehemently protested his innocence and refused to acknowledge his guilt. In response to the Synod's inquiry into the case, the local bishop recounted the priest's feats of incalcitrance, impelling the Synod to wonder "whether there is real damage to his brain, or is all this stubbornness against his superiors' demands just the result of a difficult, hardened personality?" The case simmered on for an entire decade, with Filippov refusing to heed (or even hear) directives from the bishop or the Synod, all the while claiming "headaches" and "terrible noises in his head" (ibid., op. 109, g. 1828, d. 309, ll. 1–216).

ble. Nicholas in fact actively supported this idea, increasing the number of dioceses by one-third during his reign.[111] The emperor also increased the number of suffragan bishops, who were "to ease the work of diocesan hierarchs in supervising the clergy, instructing the laity, and training candidates for diocesan positions."[112] Petersburg also made some attempt to improve its supervision of diocesan administration, primarily by emulating the government's system of annual reports (*otchety*), with detailed comments upon specific matters, including the condition of local administration (for example, the number of backlogged cases), the moral and economic condition of parish clergy and monks in the diocese, and the state of religious sentiment among parishioners. Protasov prepared this new formula in 1844 and three years later put the new system into effect, providing the Synod and procurator with regular, systematic information on each diocese.[113] The Synod also required that each consistory maintain "complaint books"—here too emulating a new practice in civil government—as a further check on the performance of local authorities.[114] With these enhanced controls, even a powerful figure like Metropolitan Filaret declined to evade Synod orders: "If I was strict, it is because the Synod's decree was very strict, and I feared to deviate much from it."[115] Authorities also entertained plans to have outside bishops visit and inspect diocesan administration; though the scheme eventually foundered on opposition by bishops, it underscored Petersburg's growing interest in closer control.[116]

Nicholas also made a modest attempt to alleviate the budgetary problems of Church administration. In 1827 his government agreed to increase the Church's budget, in effect doubling the sums allotted for salaries. That amount was considerably less than the Synod's request for a *sevenfold* increase, but it did make a significant improvement, with some vague promises of further increases later.[117] To the Synod's dismay, however, that increase was the first and last in Nicholas's reign; not until four decades later

---

[111]See the procurator's twenty-five-year report for 1825–1850 in *Sbornik Imperatorskogo russkogo istoricheskogo obshchestva* [hereafter *SIRIO*], 148 vols. (St. Petersburg, 1866–1916), 98: 457–60.

[112]*PSZ (2)*, 11: 8928.

[113]TsGIA SSSR, f. 796, op. 125, g. 1844, d. 1616, ll. 1–64. Not all were pleased about the innovations; Metropolitan Filaret, for example, sardonically observed that "now people are keen on annual reports" (Gorskii, *Dnevnik*, pp. 70–71).

[114]*PSPR*, no. 422.

[115]"Materialy dlia istorii russkoi tserkvi," *ChOLDP*, 1877, no. 12: 174.

[116]Filaret, *SMO*, 3: 64–68.

[117]Though unwilling to grant the Synod's proposal to increase the Church budget from 88,953.80 to 583,760 rubles (*PSPR*, no. 93), the state nonetheless doubled its budget (ibid., no. 166).

did the state authorize new increases—after galloping inflation had long since annulled the increase of 1827. Moreover, the chief procurator's new administrative organs prospered at Church expense, for they were financed by revenues from the sale of candles.[118] As these revenues were already inadequate for their primary purpose of supporting Church schools, the Church had no interest in tapping them further to alleviate the needs of diocesan administration. As a result, by mid century most diocesan clerks had minuscule incomes, and most clerical officials—members of consistory boards, superintendents—received no supplementary allowances for their toil or even funds to cover travel expenses. The poverty of diocesan administration was all the more painful when compared with the swollen budgets of the central Church administration. The chief procurator, for example, received eight thousand rubles per year, more than the budgets for most diocesan chancelleries. Thus in the end the state did little to ease the Church's fiscal problems, refusing to divert the substantial sums needed to modernize and strengthen the diocesan bureaucracy.[119]

Nicholas's government also professed an interest in eliminating useless paperwork, not so much through decentralization as through the trimming of documentation. There was much to trim—such as the customary reports of the late 1820s "on the condition of dioceses," vapid statements of no value to central authorities.[120] In 1828–1831, after the minister of finance outlined plans to give local officials more discretion on petty cases, Nicholas's government decided to extend this change to other ministries and domains. Significantly, the Church showed great interest in decentralization, which would in effect greatly enhance the authority of individual bishops. Thus the original draft placed before the Synod not only eliminated "useless paperwork" but also shifted final authority to diocesan bishops for many important matters (such as divorce and defrockings) and even proposed to confer authority on local superintendents for lesser matters (to reduce intradiocesan paperwork). That proposal, however, failed to pass the Synod, where the ranking prelate, Serafim Glagolevskii, showed little comprehension or sympathy for decentralization, writing that "it is easy to shift a heavy burden onto someone else's shoulders and call this a reduction in [paper]work."[121] The Synod drastically modified the original draft, deleting the main proposals for decen-

[118]Murav'ev, "O prichinakh bedstvennogo polozheniia," OR GBL, f. 304, r. 2, d. 259, ll. 27–54.

[119]For summary data, see Smolitsch, Geschichte, p. 700.

[120]See, for example, "otchety o blagosostoianii eparkhii" in TsGIA SSSR, f. 796, op. 110, g. 1828, d. 1182.

[121]Ibid., op. 112, g. 1831, d. 226, l. 18 ob. ("O merakh k sokrashcheniiu deloproizvodstva po dukhovnoi chasti").

tralization, including the enhanced authority for superintendents. Still, even in its final, emasculated form the law shifted some functions to the diocesan level and abolished some categories of periodic reports.[122]

Nicholas's government, as in the civil domain, took an interest in improving the Church's legal system. The state, under the direction of M. M. Speranskii, had already completed its own legal reforms, first publishing the complete collection of laws in 1830, then issuing a systematic digest of these in 1833. Speranskii thereupon persuaded Nicholas to publish a parallel collection for the Church.[123] Interestingly, Speranskii planned to publish only modern Church law (as he had done for the civil domain), that is, Synodal and civil decrees since 1721, not earlier ecclesiastical law, "because all previous laws do not have force and equal value in administrative affairs."[124] Although Speranskii's staff actually had one volume ready for publication in 1836, the Church suddenly canceled the project on post-Petrine law, complaining that it had "certain defects," and instead began to prepare an edition of canon law. In a note to the emperor, Protasov explained that republication of the post-1721 laws was "dangerous," since they contained many contradictory elements, even on strictly theological matters: "Is it necessary to list all the baneful effects that one might fear from such [renewed] controversies in the Church? In the West the theological principle of free investigation of dogma led to the political principle [that one can make] the same kind of inquiry into autocratic rights, and ultimately that led to popular sovereignty."[125] It was a disgrace, he added, not to have canon law readily available in translation, particularly since the most commonly used source (the *Kormchaia kniga*) was unreliable. Speranskii acceded to this abrupt change, and in 1839 the authorities published the new volume.[126]

Of far greater significance—and more consonant with Protasov's interest in aligning the Church to state institutions—was the Statute of Diocesan Consistories, formally adopted in 1841. Although consistories had steadily grown in importance and competence, they had no detailed set of rules to govern their functions, legal authority, and procedures. The result, complained Protasov, was legal chaos that left petitioners ignorant and defenseless.[127] A Synodal committee drafted a preliminary statute in 1838, which

[122] Ibid., ll. 55–58 ob.; *PSPR*, no. 445. For similar discussions in 1853, see *IVO (1853)*, pp. 46–47; for the general phenomenon, see A. Violette, "The Grand Duke Konstantin Nikolayevich and the Reform of Naval Administration, 1855–70," *Slavonic and East European Review* [hereafter *SEER*], 52 (1974): 586.

[123] TsGIA SSSR, f. 797, op. 5, d. 21345, l. 6 (Speranskii to Nechaev, 1.6.1835); see also Nechaev's letter in "K biografii Innokentiia," *RA*, 1911, no. 10: 172.

[124] TsGIA SSSR, f. 797, op. 5, d. 21345, ll. 7–13 ob.

[125] Ibid., op. 8, d. 23511, ll. 1–121 (quotation from l. 2 ob.).

[126] Ibid., ll. 20–20 ob.

[127] *IVO (1838)*, pp. 36–38; *IVO (1839)*, p. 47.

was experimentally applied in selected dioceses and then revised in the light
of bishops' commentaries.[128] Finally promulgated in 1841, the statute provided the first detailed handbook of local diocesan administration, fixing such
matters as the consistory's composition, the procedures for various kinds of
cases, the forms for annual reports, and the consistory's relationship to the
bishop, parish clergy, and Synod. Although the statute brought some
improvement and regularity to diocesan administration, it grew increasingly
archaic and, more fundamentally, represented a mere digest, not a coherent
code of old law.[129]

All these measures had some effect, but they did little to solve the major
problems in diocesan rule: even as bureaucratic responsibilities proliferated,
diocesan administration remained undermanned and underfinanced. Extortion became so acute that one prelate, Elpidifor of Podolia, ingenuously
announced that "if the [parish] clergy wish to make a contribution to members of [my] suite (in accordance with custom), they should not use funds
belonging to the parish church for this purpose but their own."[130] The metropolitan of Lithuania, Iosif, graphically described the crisis overtaking his
administration:

> Service in the Lithuanian consistory is extremely difficult indeed. Each
> year up to fifteen thousand documents go out of it. If one compares that
> with the local provincial board, the number of outgoing documents is
> almost one-half, whereas [the consistory] has but one-fifth the number of
> clerks. Furthermore, the cases in the [government office] are almost exclu-
> sively of an executive character, whereas all kinds of cases are concen-
> trated in the consistory—the most confused in substance, especially given
> the local conditions.[131]

Overcentralized and understaffed, the Church's administrative apparatus
was unable to handle the volume of business and seemed all the more backward by the inescapable comparison with the burgeoning administration of
the state.

---

[128]The archival file is in neither the Synodal nor the chief procurator's collection from the
period 1839–1841; one diocesan opinion, favorable to the statute and making only minor comments, was published as "Mnenie Saratovskoi dukhovnoi konsistorii i Saratovskogo preosvia-
shchenstva na proekt Ustava dukhovnykh konsistorii," Saratovskie eparkhial'nye vedomosti
[hereafter Saratovskie EV], 1878, no. 2: 37–40.

[129]IVO (1841), p. 43; PSZ (2), 16: 14409. See Filaret's tone of resignation ("it seems to me
that [this article in the draft] is tolerable, since objections to it would not make it any better")
in "Materialy dlia istorii russkoi tserkvi," ChOLDP, 1877, kn. 11, otd. 3: 122–23. For a perceptive critique of the statute, see T. V. Barsov, "O sobranii dukhovnykh zakonov," Khristianskoe chtenie [hereafter KhCh], 1897, 2: 281–319, 754–84.

[130]TsGIA SSSR, f. 796, op. 131, g. 1850, d. 205.

[131]Ibid., f. 797, op. 21, d. 46016, l. 44 (letter of 8.9.1855).

Although authorities made no attempt to restructure Church administration, such schemes were already in circulation in Nikolaevan Russia, laying the groundwork for reform aspirations and discussions in the 1860s. One very suggestive memorandum from the mid-1820s propounded a scheme that would attract growing support among the episcopate: decentralization of Church administration, essentially by "grouping dioceses into regions and giving each region a metropolitan, as a kind of governor-general."[132] Such metropolitanates would at once insulate bishops from state encroachment (as in the Synod) and enable senior prelates to share experience and oversee the work of younger prelates. On the other hand, some parish clergy groped toward a different solution to maladministration: self-government by parish clergy. Especially interesting was an anonymous memorandum from Pskov in 1843, which argued that the Church's administrative problems could be solved only by giving parish clergy a greater voice in diocesan affairs. The author embellished his argument with a comparative note on the clergy's relative status: "Every estate enjoys the right to select from its midst its own administrators and defenders, who are periodically replaced by others, and hence each of the electors may someday hope to be elected himself for the general welfare. . . . Only the clergy do not exercise this right," in contrast to the nobles' marshals and the peasants' elders. Complaining that all diocesan officials in the consistory and the superintendents are appointed by the bishop and ordinarily serve for life, the memorandum argued that even the best-intentioned bishop could "not know each individual as well as the local clergy do—his private life, his suitability for a given position." The memorandum therefore proposed to permit parish clergy to elect members of the consistory, superintendents, and other officers for three- or six-year terms.[133] Though that proposal, so antithetical to episcopal authority, received short shrift in the Synod, it hinted at broader aspirations among the clergy for administrative reform and enhancement of their own role, as much for the sake of relative status as for the need to eliminate administrative disorders. Such aspirations emerged in the 1860s as a major component of the clerical liberalism that sought a broad shift in authority and responsibility from the monastic episcopate to the white clergy.

Ecclesiastical Censorship

In Russia, as in Western Europe, institutional censorship took shape only when the printing press became important. Whereas both the printing press

[132] L'vov, Pis'ma, p. 84.
[133] TsGIA SSSR, f. 797, op. 13, d. 31862, ll. 4–4 ob. (note of 15.9.1843).

and censorship became fixtures of Western Europe in the sixteenth century, they did not come to Russia until the eighteenth. The Ecclesiastical Regulation of 1721 made the Synod responsible for religious publications, but only at the end of the century, when *private* presses appeared, did Church censorship acquire distinct institutional form. The crucial year was 1787, when the Synod ordered that all clergy submit manuscripts to Church authorities before having them published. In 1796, at the very close of her reign, Catherine formed clerical-lay committees to examine publications, and the following year her heir, Paul, outlined an ambitious system of censorship, with a special Moscow Censorship Committee as its chief organ. In 1814 that system was augmented by the creation of special faculty conferences at the reformed academies, charged with the task of overseeing religious publications under the presumption that religious writings would be closely connected with these elite schools. As a result, by the early nineteenth century the Church possessed several overlapping censorship organs with vaguely defined competence, which presented a source of constant conflict and oversights.[134]

To resolve these problems, Nicholas promulgated a new censorship statute for both the state and the Church in 1828.[135] The primary goal was to impose an orderly structure: committees at the four academies bore responsibility for regular ecclesiastical censorship, and the Synod remained the supreme supervisory organ, with responsibility for liturgical books. The statute also delineated a new kind of active censorship, enjoined not merely to interdict "harmful and dangerous" writings but also to evaluate works in terms of the "importance and truth of the ideas (consistent with the teachings of the Church), the purity of style, the clarity and accuracy of exposition." Such imprecise guidelines invited arbitrariness, especially in an institution that suffered a high turnover in censorship staffs. Hence it was difficult for the Church to fix clear standards, for censors to enforce them, and for authors to heed them.[136] Naturally, it was far safer for censors to err on the side of excessive vigilance. As a result, ecclesiastical censorship seemed not merely repressive but arbitrary, provoking even Metropolitan Filaret to complain: "Strange is the fate of books here. Sometimes harmful books are not perse-

---

[134]The classic work, Kotovich's *Dukhovnaia tsenzura*, is based on extensive archival research.

[135]Filaret, *SMO*, 2: 8–22; *PSZ (2)*, 3: 1981.

[136]In 1828, in response to Filaret's complaints of censorship oversights in the journal *Khristianskoe chtenie*, the Synod rebuked the responsible censors (Filaret, *SMO*, 2: 248–49; *PSPR*, no. 220). In 1830 the Synod once more reproved the censorship committee in Petersburg for misfeasance (*PSPR*, no. 290), and in 1845 it urged all committees to "examine such works [on dogma] with greater vigilance" (*Sbornik zakonopolozhenii i rasporiazhenii po dukhovnoi tsenzure vedomstva pravoslavnogo ispovedaniia s 1720 po 1870 god* [St. Petersburg, 1870], p. 122).

cuted, while they harshly persecute that which is not harmful, if not entirely correct and pleasant."[137]

The censorship archives in fact abound with eloquent testimony in support of Filaret's complaint. Rejection of manuscripts was no rarity; in 1847, for example, censors forbade publication of 40 percent of the manuscripts submitted that year (437 of 1,086).[138] Heeding the statute, censors banned works that in no way offended the faith or seemed dangerous. For example, the Petersburg committee in 1829 gave this explanation for a decision to forbid publication of a volume translated from Greek: "[This work] is not approved for publication, because the translation is too literal, because there is neither purity in style nor clarity in thought, and because there are ungrammatical expressions of the wildest sort."[139] The Petersburg committee also rejected a well-intentioned manuscript called "The Triumphal Messenger of Zion": "[This work] is not approved because the author: (a) tries to repudiate false opinions, not by means of demonstrated truths, but by means of strange declarations and vulgar, barnyard profanities; (2) distorts the texts of the Scriptures; (3) presents his ideas in a pompous style."[140] Sometimes the censors also adduced substantive objections. In 1841, for example, the Petersburg committee rejected a work because, "contrary to the true teachings of Christian morality, the author attempts at many points to persuade people to live for the present and in the present. . . ."[141] In 1839 the Moscow committee reviewed the manuscript of an archpriest, Matvei Gumilevskii, entitled "The Apocalypse, or the Prophetic History of the Church of Jesus Christ." The committee complained of the author's needless digressions and prolixity but primarily objected to his thesis: "Excessively bold and decisive prophecies of hardship for our fatherland, with the time of these [precisely] fixed, will seem bizarre in the judgment of educated people, while at the same time can terrify and disturb the hearts of simple, uneducated folk."[142] At work here, as in parallel secular censorship, was the conception of the "positive" state, content not merely to quash harmful phenomena but to tolerate and stimulate only the good in "the beautiful autocracy."

The *cause célèbre* of Nikolaevan censorship was the Pavskii affair of the early 1840s, involving the lithograph of an unauthorized translation of Old Testament books into modern Russian (not Slavonic). G. P. Pavskii, a professor at the St. Petersburg Ecclesiastical Academy, sought to learn the meaning

---

[137] Filaret, *Pis'ma kolomenskogo i moskovskogo mitropolita Filareta k Gavriilu, arkhiepiskopu riazanskomu* (Moscow, 1868), p. 70 (letter of 19.2.1846).

[138] *IVO (1847)*, p. 44.

[139] TsGIA SSSR, f. 796, op. 111, g. 1830, d. 54, l. 4 (1829 otchet).

[140] Ibid., l. 6.

[141] Ibid., op. 123, g. 1842, d. 103, l. 8 (1841 otchet).

[142] Ibid., op. 121, g. 1840, d. 937, ll. 4–4 ob. (1839 otchet); see the rejection of a similar apocalyptical piece in 1841 (ibid., op. 123, d. 103, l. 12).

of the Old Testament books by returning to the original Hebrew texts, disregarding the Greek texts used for the Church Slavonic Bible. His immediate goal was to provide his students with a Russian translation of the original texts, a decision novel both for the choice of Hebrew texts and the use of modern Russian; yet his purpose was strictly pedagogical—to make the original texts available for classroom use. The translations, however, were lithographed by the students (in fact, three times—1838, 1840, and 1841) and, as a contemporary cleric noted, Pavskii's work provoked intense interest throughout the Church:

> When news of Pavskii's lithographed translation spread through the seminaries, I immediately ordered a copy through a friend (a student in the XIII class of the Petersburg Academy); the rector of our [Tobol'sk] seminary, Archimandrite Venedikt, ordered a copy for himself through [another student]. More than once my copy found its way not only into the hands of colleagues [teaching at the seminary] but also into those of the venerable bishop of Tobol'sk, Afanasii.[143]

Unfortunately, a junior instructor at the Moscow Academy, Agafangel (later a fairly prominent prelate), chose to report the matter through an anonymous note to the chief procurator. Though his purpose was to thwart dissemination of a corrupt translation, Agafangel unwittingly gave the whole matter a dangerous political hue.[144] The result was a long, intensive investigation with major repercussions, including the exclusion of both the Kievan and Moscow metropolitans from active participation in Synodal affairs. The Synod eventually exonerated Pavskii but ordered all copies of the translation destroyed.[145] Perhaps the most important consequence of the affair was its crippling effect upon intellectual life in the Church, forcing ecclesiastics not only to abandon plans for a Russian translation of the Bible but also to limit scholarly research on the Bible. The case traumatized censors; even the mere inclusion of a Russian-language paraphrase of a biblical text could doom a manuscript. Appalled by the heavy-handed treatment of the whole incident, Bishop Innokentii (Borisov) exclaimed that "they only take things away from us—what do they [ever] give us in their stead?"[146]

Not only clerics but also lay authors who broached religious subjects had difficulties, even if they had high connections and "good intentions." Illus-

[143] Kotovich, *Dukhovnaia tsenzura*, pp. 160–62.

[144] In 1843 Innokentii complained that the affair was poorly handled and had needlessly "brought disgrace upon [Moscow] Academy" (N. M. Vostokov, "Innokentii, arkhiepiskop khersonskii," *RS*, 24 [1879]: 660–61).

[145] Kotovich, *Dukhovnaia tsenzura*, pp. 160–62, 177–84, 245; N. I. Barsov, "Prot. G. P. Pavskii," *RS*, 27 (1880): 111–28, 269–88, 495–510, 705–30, 28 (1880): 116–24, 219–32.

[146] Vostokov, "Innokentii," *RS*, 24 (1879): 661.

trative is the case of A. N. Murav'ev, a former official in the Synodal chancellery and subsequently a prolific and popular religious writer. He was in fact so popular that in 1839 the minister of foreign affairs, Nesselrode, proposed to combat the activity of American missionaries in Athens by distributing free copies of Murav'ev's works. That proposal triggered a formal review of his writings by the metropolitan of Kiev, Filaret, who conceded Murav'ev's good intentions but concluded that "the author makes a rather significant number of mistakes in [this work]." He therefore concluded that "it seems to me inappropriate to send this work to Greece for so important a matter." Murav'ev filed a testy reply to each of Filaret's criticisms, but the metropolitan did not deign to respond.[147] Even the writer Nikolai Gogol, in preparing his controversial *Selected Passages from Correspondence with Friends*, which celebrated serfdom and the knout, encountered difficulties over his chapter on the Church.[148] The Synod ultimately agreed to publication, but only after requiring massive excisions.

Besides restricting the flow of religious literature, church censors discouraged the proliferation of religious periodicals, just at a time when "thick journals" were capturing a preponderant place in secular literature and culture. In October 1845 the bishop of Saratov requested permission to establish a diocesan journal to be called *Saratovskii dukhovnyi zhurnal*, but the Synod rejected his request on the grounds that the journal would be an unnecessary burden for the superintendents (who were supposed to distribute the paper), prove an expensive drain on Church revenues, and merely duplicate materials already available in the journals of the theological academies.[149] In another case the Synod formally spurned a proposal to found diocesan newspapers (*eparkhial'nye vedomosti*) as ecclesiastical counterparts to those already published by the secular government (*gubernskie vedomosti*).[150] As a result, not until the 1860s would the Church acquire a network of periodicals, especially diocesan papers, to compete actively in the marketplace of ideas.

It was an era of stultifying silence. As M. P. Pogodin confided in his diary in 1825, "a book describing our theology is absolutely necessary," for ordinary laymen know almost nothing about Orthodoxy—"the mass is a hieroglyph for us."[151] Though the Church made some progress over the next three decades, it generally failed to provide suitable literature for either the cul-

---

[147] TsGIA SSSR, f. 797, op. 8, d. 24571, ll. 1–1 ob., 59–61 ob., 62–76.

[148] Ibid., op. 16, d. 37414, ll. 1–9.

[149] A. Pravdin, "Predpolozhenie ob izdanii dukhovnogo zhurnala v Saratove," *Saratovskie EV*, 1878, no. 8: 147–52.

[150] TsGIA SSSR, f. 797, op. 13, d. 31802.

[151] N. P. Barsukov, *Zhizn' i trudy M. P. Pogodina*, 22 vols. (St. Petersburg, 1888–1906), 1: 303–4, 168.

tural elite or the popular masses. In 1843 an anonymous memorandum urged the Synod to publish an Orthodox encyclopedia as an antidote to the consuming ignorance of educated society: "Russians of all estates who presently receive education remain in absolute ignorance or [have only] extremely limited knowledge of the divine Orthodox religion."[152] The dearth of popular literature for lower groups spurred the creation of special committees in the 1840s that were supposed to publish religious literature—mainly reprints of traditional texts—for popular consumption at inexpensive prices. None of the committees, however, in fact accomplished much, despite great plans and prickly reprimands from Nicholas.[153] As one perceptive contemporary observed in 1838, "[secular] literature already exists as a commercial affair, but there is [still] no moral or spiritual [literature]—and it does not seem likely that such will appear in the immediate future."[154]

From the late 1840s, in reaction to the revolutionary convulsions in Europe, authorities made censorship still more repressive, establishing special secret committees to tighten controls over the press.[155] Indicative of the new spirit was a complaint from the Church that a booklet published by the Ministry of State Domains contained "democratic elements."[156] The iron hand of censorship even fell upon authors of prominence and influence. Baron August Haxthausen, who enjoyed Nicholas's personal patronage, encountered serious problems of censorship over the third volume of his *Studies on the Interior of Russia,* because Church censors protested his negative portrait of the Russian clergy and "extremely prejudiced [favorable] view of the Old Believers."[157] Nor did the vigilant censors spare the "learned monks," even bishops. Thus Bishop Filaret (Gumilevskii) of Khar'kov, dismayed by the censor's cavilling criticism of his history of the Russian Church, exclaimed in exasperation: "To listen to and accept the arrogant comments [of a young censor], at times in total ignorance of the subject matter, is something that is extremely difficult to endure."[158] Of the learned monks, one bishop later

---

[152]TsGIA SSSR, f. 797, op. 13, d. 31793, ll. 1–2 ("zapiska").

[153]On the Moscow committee and its work, see ibid., op. 17, d. 39239, and Filaret, *SMO,* 3: 99–101, 142, 210–11; on a similar committee in Mogilev, see TsGIA SSSR, f. 797, op. 17, d. 41114. In 1850, after the minister of education reported that the committees were inert, Nicholas chided them to be more diligent (ibid., f. 796, op. 131, g. 1850, d. 818).

[154]Kotovich, *Dukhovnaia tsenzura,* p. 159.

[155]On the formation of a new supreme censorship committee, see TsGIA SSSR, f. 797, op. 21, d. 46054, ll. 1–29. For an instance of its action, see ibid., d. 46056, ll. 3-3 ob.; for its first year's journals, see ibid., f. 796, op. 132, g. 1851, d. 826/a.

[156]Filaret, *SMO,* 3: 358–69.

[157]TsGIA SSSR, f. 797, op. 22, otd. 1, st. 2, d. 157, l. 56. Significantly, in transmitting the volume, Nicholas ordered the Synod not to engage in "detailed" censorship but only to indicate "large errors," clearly hinting that he wanted prompt approval (ibid., ll. 1–2). See his earlier order that the Church assemble data for Haxthausen's work (ibid., op. 17, d. 39253).

[158]Kotovich, *Dukhovnaia tsenzura,* pp. 414–17.

wrote: "Look at the monks—those who wrote and published anything have suffered to the very last man."[159] Matters stood still worse for parish clergy, now totally subordinate to ecclesiastical censorship: a Synodal decree of 1850 instructed priests to obtain permission from Church censors before publishing sermons in secular papers, and this requirement was later extended to manuscripts on any subject. The few who braved this censorship suffered painful humiliations—not merely rejection of manuscripts but also contemptuous notes to the diocesan bishop about the hapless author.[160]

Repressive as it was, tight censorship had larger implications: it effectively thwarted discussion of the "clerical question" and therefore deprived reform of public support and comment. For some, it also reinforced suspicions that bishops, not bureaucrats, were collaborating to block reform.[161] In addition, censorship proved especially chafing for educated priests, denying them an outlet for their hard-earned education and blocking their attempts to emulate "learned monks" and advance their careers through publications. The unshackling of the press in 1855 would have as profound an impact upon both the clergy and the larger process of Church reform as it did upon secular society as a whole.

Tensions in the Church

The final years of Nicholas's reign served only to intensify the prelates' abiding concerns about the state's willingness to violate the Church's most vital interests. Even provincial officials dared to transgress the authority of the Church, causing Metropolitan Filaret to complain that "the secular governor conducts investigations [of accused monks] and thereby precludes the possibility of ecclesiastical authorities acting to establish order."[162] The bishops were particularly disturbed by the government's plan to assume control of Church finances through a uniform system of public finance, leading,

---

[159] Nikanor (Brovkovich), *Biograficheskie materialy* (Odessa, 1900), pp. 156, 187.

[160] *Sbornik zakonopolozhenii po tsenzure*, pp. 131–32, 136. For a case of censorship, see Gregory L. Freeze, "Revolt from Below: A Priest's Manifesto on the Crisis in Russian Orthodoxy," in Theofanis Stavrou and Robert Nichols, eds., *Russian Orthodoxy under the Old Regime* (Minneapolis, 1978), p. 95.

[161] By the 1860s moderate journals like *Pravoslavnoe obozrenie* would also argue that censorship had been a primary cause of stultification in the development of Orthodox theology and culture: "No doubt one of the main reasons for the weak development of our spiritual literature so far was precisely the status of religious writers with respect to ecclesiastical censorship, whose demands extend even to the very quality of the prose" ("Nuzhno li preobrazovanie dukhovnoi tsenzury?" *PO*, 1862, no. 3: 97–105). Such views became predominant in later discussion of censorship reform; see below, pp. 338–39.

[162] "Materialy dlia istorii russkoi tserkvi," *ChOLDP*, 1877, no. 12: 158.

inter alia, to the appropriation of funds unspent at the end of the fiscal year. Though controls had previously existed for monies paid out of the state budget, the government was now seeking to control *all* Church revenues, including those raised by the Church itself (for example, income from the sale of candles).[163] The Synod fiercely resisted such encroachments and, with Protasov's support, succeeded in turning back the challenge.[164] The state also raised questions about the right of the Church (and, especially, monasteries) to acquire real estate; though the Church turned back such inquiries, the whole debate only fueled anxieties among leading prelates.[165] Understandably, once the government took up such issues as Catholics and Old Believers, some bishops responded with alarm, suspecting concessions to these inveterate foes of the Church.[166] Altogether, these issues—coming at a time of an apparent eclipse in the Synod's authority—left ranking prelates with an acute sense of weakness and vulnerability. Indicative of the mood was Filaret's admonition to the Synod not to raise even legitimate issues with the state for fear of provoking new encroachments.[167]

Ripples of discontent also appeared among the parish clergy, but here the adversary was bishops, not bureaucrats.[168] To be sure, such discontent was

---

[163] Earlier, when state authorities sought to audit monastery budgets, Filaret exploded: "What can an auditor's controls save from a monk's salary of twenty-four rubles [per year]?" (Filaret, *Perepiska s Nechaevym*, p. 189).

[164] See the retrospective account in A. P. Tolstoi's memoranda (OR GBL, f. 214 [Optina pustyn'], d. 63, ll. 40–44; TsGIA SSSR, f. 832 [Filaret], op. 1, d. 27, ll. 4–8).

[165] TsGIA SSSR, f. 797, op. 21, d. 46042, ll. 3–17 ob. ("Mysli o voprose, polezno li v tserkovnom i gosudarstvennom otnoshenii, chtoby tserkvi i monastyri vladeli nedvizhimymi imeniiami"); reprinted in Filaret, *SMO*, 3: 433–40; draft text in TsGIA SSSR, f. 832, op. 1, d. 85, ll. 52–63. On the monks' right to inherit property, see Filaret, *SMO*, 4: 186–203.

[166] Russian clergyman circulated copies of a speech by Pope Pius IX in 1848 that boasted of concessions from the Russian government ("Rech' v tainoi konsistorii 3 iiunia 1848 g. o peregovorakh s predstaviteliami Rossii o polozhenii Katolicheskoi tserkvi v Rossii i Pol'she," in OR GBL, f. 302 [A. P. Tolstoi], k. 3, d. 21, ll. 1–10). See also "Zapiska Innokentiia o eparkhii rimsko-katolicheskoi v Khersone," *RA*, 1868, no. 3: 412–35. Predictably, Nicholas did not treat the Catholic Church so generously; see the complaint by one Catholic that the Concordat was being systematically violated (Abbé Jacunski to Jean Gagarin, 17.12.1850, in Bibliothèque slave [hereafter BS], f. Gagarine, IX [Polonais au P. Gagarine]).

[167] See Filaret, *SMO*, 3: 445–48.

[168] Cases of political disaffection were exceedingly rare. One involved a priest implicated in the Decembrist uprising, during which he allegedly told the people that "there should be no earthly tsars and it is required that they be mentioned in the Church [services] solely to deceive the people" (*PSPR*, no. 43). More striking still was the protest by a priest in Orenburg, Petr Levashev, who denounced the "immorality in our fatherland," where "the rules of the faith no longer have any force: from the highest government posts to the lowliest judicial positions, they are drinking the blood of the people; and taxes and assessments have so risen that the peasants are no longer able to bear the burden." Levashev even accused the emperor himself of great transgressions, in particular, "the subjugation of the Church to your laws" (TsGAOR, f. 109, op. 221, d. 121, ll. 3–4 ob.).

muted: the parish clergy had no assemblies or press to express grievances, and most were no doubt too inured to the old order to challenge episcopal authority. Still, as occasional memoranda, diaries, and random anecdotes attest, they nourished strong grievances toward the bishop who ruled and, seemingly, tolerated abuses among his subordinates.

The most eloquent statement of such antiepiscopal and antimonastic sentiments appears in the diary of I. S. Belliustin, the provincial priest who appeared on the first pages of this book and who rose to become the leading exponent of clerical liberalism during the Great Reforms. If prelates looked askance at the state, priests like Belliustin despised bishops and monks who "trample law and justice," who "promote and award distinctions to those who have the means" to bribe them, and who "persecute and destroy the poor." His animus toward the black clergy knew no bounds:

> The present monks are divided into two classes: the learned and the unlearned; the former are the superiors in the monastery and dioceses, the latter are unskilled labor. The former live according to these rules: (1) the diocese or monastery is an estate, from which one can extract whatever is good and valuable; (2) given the impossibility of having one wife, one can have two or three "nieces" as the circumstances allow; (3) to avoid needless worries in administering the diocese, delegate all authority to the clerk, and in the monastery, [do the same] with a nephew; (4) permit subordinate monks to do anything, and if one commits something truly horrendous (for example, knifes and strangles his lover), then as far as possible conceal this and with all your might defend him before justice; (5) persecute and destroy anyone who dares to have the insolence not to live according to these rules; (6) spare no money to rise from archimandrite to bishop, and then to become a member of the Synod; (7) to reach this goal, it is possible to become a [Free-]mason, a communist—whatever, just so as to reach this goal as soon as possible. . . .[169]

Such explosive, venomous comments surely did not characterize the feeling of most priests and sacristans, who remained scattered among tiny villages, concerned more about the next harvest and gratuity than the heartlessness of bishops. But Belliustin, first in his diary and later in the press, articulated a set of major concerns for parish clergy and in the end would draw many around his banner of clerical liberalism.

---

[169]GA Kalininskoi obl., f. 103, op. 1, d. 1291, ll. 108–9 (Belliustin, "Zametki i dnevnik," entries of 26.8.1849 and 27.8.1849).

Archpriest G. P. Pavskii

The Marriage Ceremony.
Gravure by a Czech traveler in the 1860s.

Funeral Procession in a Russian Village

Icon Procession

Peasants and Clergy in Icon Procession for Rain

Parish School Serving a Non-Russian Minority
(Votiaki or Udmurty)

Russian Priest at Spasskii Church
(a mining-camp parish)

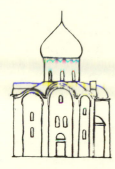

CHAPTER 2

The Structure
and Economics of
Parish Service

A s Bishop Amvrosii of Tver examined the service files of clergy from Kaliazin district in 1830, he must have been struck by the kaleidoscopic diversity among its sixty-six parishes.[1] At the very top of the file was the report from clergy at the cathedral in Kaliazin, the district capital; a relatively old parish (established in 1694), it had eleven clergymen (including an archpriest), served nearly 5,000 laymen, and yielded 4,400 rubles per year in emoluments. As he leafed through the reports, the bishop also found some relatively prosperous rural parishes, such as the village of Ushanovo, where a priest and three subordinates ministered to some 1,200 state peasants, "cultivate the [thirty-three dessiatines] of land themselves," and wrote that their income from emoluments—321 rubles in 1830—"is satisfactory." Although the average parish had nearly 1,400 parishioners and yielded 482 rubles in fees, many parishes fell far below that line, causing their clergy to complain that the support is "scanty" (*skudno*) or "inadequate" (*nedostatochno*). Pathetic indeed was the plight of clergy in the village of Novgorotskoe. Serving a mere 120 serfs and their master, the clergy had access to just twenty-five dessiatines of land and earned only 80 rubles in 1830—small resources for three married clerics and their twelve dependents.[2] However, all the clergy in the district did have some things in com-

---

[1] GA Kalininskoi obl., f. 160, op. 1, d. 16272 (klirovye vedomosti, 1830).

[2] Such diversity characterized all the dioceses. Thus the superintendency of Belgorod showed several parishes with substantial incomes (Tavolzhanka, for example, had 1,500 parishioners and yielded an income of 500 rubles); other parishes, like Izbitskaia, provided "an extremely scanty" income from its 500 parishioners (Gosudarstvennnyi arkhiv Kurskoi oblasti [hereafter GA Kurskoi obl.], f. 20 [Kurskaia dukhovnaia konsistoriia], op. 2, d. 10, ll. 1–70).

mon: none enjoyed parsonages (all possessed "their own wooden houses built on church land"), tithes, or substantial support other than land and emoluments. At bottom, each parish formed a world unto itself, unique in its social composition, size of staff, parish population, and resources.[3]

This diversity was rooted in the status of the parish as a community organization just beyond the reach of Church and state. Although authorities had intruded ever more frequently into parish affairs, especially since Peter the Great, they left it to the immediate parish to construct the church and support the clergy who served in it. Thus the economy of each parish was unique: without central regulation or support, each church and its clergy depended entirely upon the local community for support, drawing no income from either the Church or the state.[4] Each parish, as a result, varied radically in its resources—the quantity and quality of land, the prosperity and piety of parishioners. The spectrum in clerical economies was consequently broad, from the wealthy archpriest in a sumptuous cathedral to an impecunious sacristan in some dilapidated rural chapel with a leaking roof, ragged vestments, and handful of destitute serfs for parishioners. At the foundation of such diversity lay the particularism of the traditional parish, which formed a self-enclosed unit largely free of outside interference until more modern times.

In the nineteenth century that parish economy became the central focus of reforms that sought to improve both the amounts and forms of material support for members of the white clergy. It was a complex task, involving vast numbers of clergy and reaching down to the grass-roots parish level; yet, as bishops and bureaucrats concurred, it was vitally important to rebuild this traditional economy. Why they thought so, how they changed it, and what they achieved by 1855 are all important questions, casting light on the quandaries of reform and the significance of the Nikolaevan prereforms.

A Half-Regulated Service Order

In 1825 the Russian Church had over one hundred thousand clergy serving in its parishes, but that clergy was a complex order, consisting not only of priests but of a whole range of sundry ranks. Formally, the secular clergy

[3]Only 4 of the 66 parishes had capital endowments, the largest being that of the village Kashinskoe Ust'e, which provided 150 rubles in annual income. The parish had only 500 parishioners, and the endowment served as a supplement to a minuscule income from emoluments (112 rubles).

[4]The exception was the cathedral. Ever since secularization in 1764, cathedrals in provincial and district capitals received small sums from the state; see Freeze, *Russian Levites*, pp. 121–24.

TABLE 1

The Structure of Clerical Ranks

Ordained clergy (*sviashchennosluzhiteli*)
    Archpriest (*protoierei*)
    Priest (*ierei; sviashchennik*)
    Deacon (*diakon*)

Sacristans (*tserkovnosluzhiteli, prichetniki*)
    Diachok (reader, chanter)
    Ponomar (reader, chanter)
    Psalomshchik (reader, chanter)

comprised two distinct strata: ordained clergy (*sviashchennosluzhiteli*) and sacristans (*tserkovnosluzhiteli*), each subdivided into specific ranks (see table 1). Ordained clergy had all received holy orders through the sacrament of ordination; in ecclesiastical and social terms, they composed the upper strata of the white clergy. Whereas the title of archpriest was largely honorific, confined to a dozen or so clerics in a diocese with several thousand clergy, the ranking cleric in most parishes was the priest. Constituting fewer than one-third of the white clergy, priests bore primary responsibility in the parish for administering sacraments, performing private prayer services, overseeing subordinate clergy, and filing varied documents with their superiors in the Church (see table 2). About half of the parishes also had a deacon. Though not required for the liturgy or rites, deacons were immensely popular among parishioners for improving the aesthetics of the service, and, consequently, they were often chosen more for their voices than for their intelligence or morals. The bottom stratum of the clergy—the other half of the secular clergy—were the sacristans, who held the ranks of diachok and ponomar. Installed rather than ordained, the sacristans could not administer sacraments but merely assisted the priest, mainly by reading and singing various parts of the service. They also discharged sundry menial duties, such as cleaning the church, ringing the bells, silencing boisterous parishioners, and locking up when services were over. As the very structure of ranks suggests, the secular clergy was in composition and numbers oriented primarily toward serving the sacramental, ritualistic needs of the flock, traditionally regarded as the primary (if not sole) interest of the Church.

Ever since Peter the Great, however, authorities had endeavored to regulate the size and distribution of clergy, primarily in the hope of preventing the proliferation of poor churches and poor clergy. In addition to limiting the bishops' right to open new parishes, central authorities also attempted to restrict the number of clergy at any given parish. They did so through the

TABLE 2

Secular Clergy and Parishes in 1824

Parish Clergy		
Priests, archpriests	34, 095	(31%)
Deacons	15,081	(14%)
Sacristans	59,740	(55%)
Parishes		
Number of parishes	27,492	
Parishioners (males)	17,186,862	
Average parish (males)	625	

SOURCE: TsGIA SSSR, f. 797, op. 96, d. 5, ll. 1 ob.-2

clerical *shtat* (table of organization), first issued in 1722 and slightly revised in 1778. Its aim was to relate parish size to numbers of clergy, setting for the smallest parishes (one hundred households) the minimum clerical staff: one priest and two sacristans. By establishing a rough proportion between numbers of parishioners and numbers of clergy, authorities hoped to satisfy the laity's need for services *and* to create a viable parish economy for the clergy. Although not easily implemented, the new shtat gradually took effect, and, by the end of the eighteenth century, it firmly regulated parish service.[5]

Authorities also made some attempt to reconstruct the traditional parish economy based upon emoluments and land, but here their efforts achieved considerably less. In the 1720s and again, more seriously, in the 1780s, the state discussed the possibility of a parish tithe and state salaries but in both cases retreated before the complexities and costs of such reform. More important was the state's attempt, from the mid-eighteenth century, to provide each parish church with a minimum land allotment. Forming part of a general land survey, this measure required local officials to mark off a standard allotment (thirty-three dessiatines) of land, cultivable and easily accessible to the parish clergy. But the survey was slow (not reaching some portions of the empire until a century later) and vulnerable to local deviations, with many clergy failing to receive the prescribed allotment. The only other significant intervention in the parish economy was characteristically bureaucratic: a tariff of regulatory rates issued in 1765 set the sums due for the main sacraments. Although the tariff did not preclude higher donations or, indeed, even require any payment, it set a norm to guide these "voluntary contributions," primarily in an attempt to discourage extortion and solicitation by the parish clergy. The state's most radical reform, an attempt in 1797 to

---

[5] For the eighteenth-century shtat, see ibid., pp. 114–17.

require that parishioners cultivate the clergy's land, provoked such furious opposition from below that it had to be revoked four years later.[6]

By the time of Nicholas's accession in 1825, the parish clergy still depended entirely upon their traditional sources of support: emoluments, holiday collections, and cultivation of parish-church land. A few churches enjoyed some other forms of support: cathedrals had small subsidies from the state, and some urban churches had small capital endowments or rent from real estate bequeathed by parishioners.[7] In very rare instances the clergy too enjoyed fixed support—mainly in kind and known as *ruga*—usually provided in lieu of land or because of the parish's small size.[8] In most parishes, however, the clergy enjoyed no such support and had to depend on the traditional emoluments and parish land for sustenance. That support, as both Church and state authorities agreed, showed major weaknesses.

To begin with, the monetary income from emoluments was simply inadequate. The clergy themselves, in their annual service reports, often described the income from gratuities as "scanty," occasionally as "average," very rarely as "satisfactory."[9] The clergy's superiors, like the bishop of Penza, confirmed such negative assessments: "The parish clergy receive no more than one hundred rubles in the very best parishes [here] as monetary income, and on the average they receive no more than fifty rubles, or even thirty rubles, per annum."[10] Paid a few kopecks for the main rites and at most a few rubles for marrying well-to-do parishioners, the priest earned a small pittance, which he then had to share with the rest of his staff. As one cleric

---

[6]Ibid., pp. 117–20, 164–68; "Pis'ma mitr. Evgeniia," *RA*, 1889, no. 5: 46.

[7]Capital endowments and income-producing real estate were much more common in urban parishes, especially Moscow. Thus the Kos'mo-damianskaia Church in Kadashev supported its clergy with 50 rubles per annum from capital endowments and 350 rubles per annum from business properties (TsGIAgM, f. 203, op. 766, d. 315, ll. 1–5); the Kazanskaia Church near the Kaluga Gates also provided 77 rubles from rents and 615 rubles from business properties, enabling the clergy to report that their "income is satisfactory" (ibid., d. 294, l. 1).

[8]Thus 2 of the 15 parishes in one Kursk superintendency reported that the local squire provided annual stipends (GA Kurskoi obl., f. 20, d. 10, ll. 1–70). Reports of ruga also occur among some parishes in Kiev diocese, though, again, only among a handful of parishes (Tsentral'nyi gosudarstvennyi istoricheskii arkhiv Ukrainskoi SSR [hereafter TsGIA UkrSSR], f. 127 [Kievskaia dukhovnaia konsistoriia], op. 1009, dd. 275–76). Parishes in Siberia, where distances and dispersion of parishioners made emoluments a highly unsatisfactory form of income, generally received some form of regular parish support in money or kind; however, as the service files for 1830 make clear, the parish clergy found their ruga "extremely scanty" (Gosudarstvennyi arkhiv Irkutskoi oblasti [hereafter GA Irkutskoi obl.], f. 50 [Irkutskaia dukhovnaia konsistoriia], op. 1, d. 3840, ll. 1–170).

[9]For example, only 4 of the 66 parishes in Kaliazin district in 1830 found their income "satisfactory" or "sufficient"; the rest chose more negative terms: "average," "mediocre," or even "scanty" (GA Kalininskoi obl., f. 160, op. 1, d. 16272).

[10]TsGIA SSSR, f. 796, op. 112, g. 1831, d. 957, ch. 57 (prilozhenie), ll. 1 ob.–2 (report to Synod, 3.11.1831).

recalled from his childhood in the mid-nineteenth century, "payment [for performing rites] was insignificant and played a small role in the family budget—everything was in [our] land and what it yielded."[11] However hard the lot of priests, that of sacristans was considerably worse, for they received but a fraction of the priest's share of land and emoluments. Even by mid-century the bishop of Tambov wrote that the sacristans' "own labor and fees from parishioners provide them with no more than fifteen to thirty silver rubles per year, on which they must support families consisting of five to ten people."[12] Their lot in fact palpably deteriorated in Nicholas's reign, as the Synod reduced the sacristan's share from one-half to one-quarter of the priest's income. As a group of sacristans wrote in a petition to the chief procurator, "we have become so impoverished that we not only cannot afford to support our sons at the seminary for the full course of study (as our parental duty obliges us to do), but we do not even have the means to feed ourselves."[13]

Why was the income from emoluments so small? No doubt one major reason was the social composition of parishes, where parishioners were often too poor and too few to provide sufficient support for the three local clerics and their families. Notwithstanding the state's efforts to increase the average size of parishes, many in fact remained exceedingly small because geography, low population density, and poor communications defeated attempts to combine them. Moreover, the backward economy and weight of serfdom left little surplus in the countryside either for clergy seeking "voluntary contributions" or for the hard-hearted tax collectors of the state, as the data on arrears constantly attest. Finally, argued many priests, the emoluments were small because the normative tariffs promulgated in 1765 fixed minuscule sums and strictly forbade clergy to solicit more. Although revised upward in 1801, the tariffs actually prescribed amounts below the current rates and, worse still, declined in real terms as a result of inflation. As one archpriest fumed in 1829, "the amounts fixed are so low that it is a disgrace even to talk about this."[14] An official tabulation a few years earlier confirmed such complaints, showing that, if observed strictly, the tariffs yielded a mere 10.81

[11]OR GBL, f. 356 (A. B. Derman), k. 3, d. 43, l. 7 (S. Ia. Elpat'evskii, "Vospominaniia").

[12]TsGIA SSSR, f. 796, op. 132, g. 1851, d. 2357, l. 305 (Tambov); see also ibid., l. 368 (Minsk).

[13]Ibid., op. 121, g. 1840, d. 1343, ll. 2-2 ob. (petition from 32 sacristans in Kostroma to the chief procurator, 1840). Earlier, in 1827, the Synod ruled that, in the event of disputes over income distribution in any diocese, it would apply the rules used in Moscow, which prescribed that the sacristan receive one-quarter of the priest's share. For earlier cases, see the files on Tver diocese (ibid., op. 119, g. 1838, d. 554) and Riazan (*PSPR*, no. 555); for the eighteenth-century background, see Freeze, *Russian Levites*, pp. 136–38.

[14]TsGIA SSSR, f. 796, op. 107, g. 1826, d. 460, l. 199.

rubles per staff—well below the amounts actually received.[15] As the clergy complained, the tariffs held down the natural inflation of rates and clerical income, and provided parishioners with legal grounds to refuse to pay larger and (in the clergy's view) "fairer" sums.

Emoluments were not only deficient in amount but pernicious in form as well. Above all, they proved a source of constant tension, as parish priests struggled to collect more generous sums, as parishioners resisted and resented such importunity. In Western churches emoluments of far lesser significance were nevertheless a significant source of anticlerical sentiment; one can well imagine their effect in Russia, where they constituted virtually the sole form of monetary income for clergy.[16] Some clergy even withheld services until properly remunerated. As one landowner complained to the Synod, the local priest demands "excessive payments" and "does not give the rites to anyone who is unable or unwilling to satisfy [his demands]—that is, deceased people are left for a long time without burial, people [have to] cohabit without marital rites, etc."[17] Accusations of solicitation blotted the record of many parish clergy, clogged the dockets of diocesan justice, and gave rise to such anticlerical saws as "who takes from the living and the dead?"[18]

Moreover, emoluments left the clergy dangerously dependent upon their parishioners: with no tithe or other fixed income, priests could oppose parish demands only at great risk. In religious matters that dependence made the priest reluctant to chasten his parishioners and to combat moral or religious deviance. The priest who violated parish wish by declining some uncanonical

---

[15] The calculation (based upon the numbers of births, marriages, and deaths and the fees permitted under the 1801 rates) showed a significant increase from a similar calculation in 1784 (showing just 3.69 rubles per parish each year). The rise reflected both demographic growth (births, for instance, increased from 737,419 to 1,546,224) and the doubling of rates for emoluments in 1801 (ibid., f. 797, op. 96, d. 5, ll. 1 ob.–2).

[16] As a French priest wrote in 1765, such emoluments constitute "a disgrace for the minister and the ministry . . . an impediment to the work of God, destroying the parishioners' confidence in the curés" (Tackett, *Priest and Parish*, p. 186). See also Hilaire, *Une Chrétienté*, 1: 189; Bligny, *Le diocèse de Grenoble*, pp. 171–72; E. Weber, *Peasants into Frenchmen* (Stanford, 1976), pp. 357–59. For attempts to limit conflict over emoluments by regulating the rates, see Tackett, *Priest and Parish*, pp. 130–31, and P. Loupès, "Le casuel dans le diocèse de Bordeaux aux XVIIe et XVIIIe siècles," *Revue d'Histoire de l'Église de France*, 58 (1972): 19–52.

[17] TsGIA SSSR, f. 796, op. 56, g. 1775, d. 50, l. 10 ob.

[18] Punishment for solicitation, though not common, is recorded in the service files of clergy; typical was a priest in Tomsk diocese who "was sent for two months to the Alekseev Monastery in Tomsk for obedience and labor [as punishment] for extorting illegal fees from parishioners for rites" (GA Tomskoi obl., f. 170, op. 1, d. 279, l. 28 [klirovye vedomosti, 1860]). For the close tie between emoluments and anticlerical saws, see the complaints by clergy in their reports of 1863: TsGIA SSSR, f. 804, op. 1, r. 3, d. 34, ll. 71–71 ob. (Kursk priest); d. 316, ll. 114 ob.–16 (Riazan priest).

custom (of which there were many, from superstitious pagan rites to gross marital irregularities)[19] or waxed too zealous in matters of moral purity risked becoming an outcast—and a hungry one at that.[20] The effect of such dependence was a matter of great concern to Church hierarchs. As the archbishop of Iaroslavl wrote in 1826, "dependent upon the arbitrary assistance of parishioners and [living] in straitened circumstances, [the parish clergy] are often obliged to satisfy parish wish and to violate the canons, thereby invoking criticism and forfeiting the veneration due from the people."[21] State authorities, such as Nicholas's political police, made similar observations but stressed more worldly implications:

> The young priest, sent into the countryside, is dependent upon [local] society, goes to seed, and acquires the visage, character, and even the habits of the *muzhiki* [peasants] around him. In thoughts and feelings, he merges with that soslovie which provides him his sustenance. Poverty and dependence upon the peasantry forces him to encourage the [social] aspirations and passionate desires of his flock; hence the government cannot rely upon parish clergy until it is given a secure existence.[22]

Such concerns impelled one prelate to write at the outset of Nicholas's reign that "we shall not have an honorable clergy until it has adequate support and the emoluments have been eliminated."[23]

The sheer variability in emoluments, moreover, served to erode the clergy's stability and cohesiveness. For one thing, the income in any given parish fluctuated wildly from one year to the next. As the priest at a church in Kiev wrote in 1831, "payments for rites are not bad in some years (depending upon the parishioners' economic condition), but in other years they are niggardly."[24] Such variability, complained the clergy, made it impossible to budget their resources and made them liable to the full ravages of famine or depression, with no reserves to cushion the impact.[25] More important, the

---

[19] Though clergy evidently managed to conceal illegal marriages and only rarely were exposed for such misdeeds (see above, pp. 29–30), it nevertheless was a major source of tensions and, no doubt, bribes. For a brief description of the kinds of illegal marriages (kinship and age being the main issues), see Freeze, *Russian Levites*, pp. 177–78.

[20] See Belliustin, *Opisanie*, pp. 69–73.

[21] TsGIA SSSR, f. 796, op. 107, g. 1826, d. 460, l. 84.

[22] "Graf Benkendorf," p. 152.

[23] "Materialy dlia istorii russkoi tserkvi," *ChOLDP*, 1874, no. 11/3: 69 (Evgenii to Kirill, 1829).

[24] TsGIA UkrSSR, f. 127, op. 1009, d. 293, l. 126 (klirovye vedomosti, Kiev district, 1830).

[25] For the impact of famine, see the plight of clergy in central Russia in the early 1840s: in Kaluga (*Istoricheskaia zapiska ob uchrezhdenii i sostoianii Kaluzhskoi eparkhii za stoletnii period ee sushchestvovaniia* [Kaluga, 1900], p. 21), Vladimir (TsGIA SSSR, f. 796, op. 123, g. 1842, d. 546), and Moscow ("Piat' pisem moskovskogo mitropolita Filareta," *TKDA*, 1868, no. 4: 194).

high disparity in resources from one parish to the next encouraged a high rate of mobility, as priests sought to transfer to more prosperous positions. Thus, according to service files for 1830, nearly half of the priests had served in other parishes prior to their current appointment—an extraordinarily high rate of mobility for such a "traditional" society.[26] Relocation, however, entailed costs: given the lack of parsonages, the priest had to buy and sell homes, set up housekeeping anew, and no doubt grease a few wheels at the consistory to effect the transfer—all at considerable expense.[27] Although authorities used translation as a device to reward good priests and to punish bad ones, transfers, like those of bishops, ran contrary to canons and customs, sundered strong spiritual ties between priest and parish, and reinforced lay suspicions that the priest's sole interest was material, not spiritual. In addition, this system also fostered much intraclerical conflict. As a reform memorandum of 1843 rightly observed, "priests envy each other for rich parishes, try to dislodge their fellow clerics in order to obtain their positions (because of avarice). There is no end to such petitions for transfer or to complaints against [each other]."[28] Some prelates tried—but with little success—to discourage voluntary transfers.[29]

Use of church land, the other main form of subsistence, also failed to provide adequate support. For one thing, many parishes, despite state law, failed to provide the minimum allotment of thirty-three dessiatines, especially in areas still awaiting the general land survey.[30] More important, even where the clergy nominally possessed the required amount, they found the land unsatisfactory or unusable, complaining that it was clayish or sandy, distant or inaccessible, or hopelessly entangled with small strips of peasant land. Typical was the complaint from a priest in Kursk that most of his plot was useless because "the soil was sandy and covered with underbrush."[31] Moreover, the law on parish land provided for only a small amount of hay land

[26]In 1830, for example, 41 percent of the priests in Kaliazin had served earlier in other parishes, and 31 percent of the priests in Tver had given prior service elsewhere (GA Kalininskoi obl., f. 160, op. 1, dd. 16272, 16515).

[27]These expenses became fully evident in the 1840s and 1870s, when authorities tried to relocate surplus clergy (see below, pp. 91–97, 377–78).

[28]TsGIA SSSR, f. 796, op. 124, g. 1843, d. 213 (Amfilogii, "Zapiska"); see similar comments in the annual report from Tver in 1850 (ibid., op. 132, g. 1851, d. 2357, l. 223 ob.). For an example of such conflict, see the protest from a staff in Tver objecting to the bishop's decision to appoint more clergy to join them (ibid., op. 119, g. 1838, d. 47, ll. 1–16).

[29]See A. Pravdin, "Rezoliutsii Saratovskogo preosv. Iakova," Saratovskie EV, 1878, no. 4: 73–74.

[30]For later data on landholdings, see below, pp. 262–63.

[31]GA Kurskoi obl., f. 20, op. 2, d. 10, l. 13 (klirovye vedomosti, Belgorod superintendency, 1840). A staff in Borisoglebskii pogost (Rzhev district) emphasized the vital importance of agriculture to their economy but complained that their "support, mainly because of the unsuitability of the land, is scanty" (GA Kalininskoi obl., f. 160, op. 1, d. 15811, ll. 66–67).

and pasture (vaguely prescribing three dessiatines), too little to support a vital complement of livestock.[32] As one priest wrote later, "the clergy cannot maintain [sufficient] livestock and, consequently, the cultivable land, being poorly fertilized, steadily declines in productivity."[33]

Even if blessed with good land, the clergy found it exceedingly difficult to extract much profit from its use. That was certainly true if the priest used hired labor; given the marginal utility of the land and the high costs of free labor, most clergy found that their "land can only bring profit if cultivated by the priest himself."[34] In many parishes, it is true, the priest still relied upon voluntary parish assistance (*pomoch'*, derived from the word *pomoshch'*, "aid"). Parishioners gathered on a Sunday or holiday and, after the priest had supplied ample food and drink, proceeded to help him work his fields or harvest his crops. Such *pomoch'*, complained the clergy, only reinforced their dependence upon the parish (like emoluments, *pomoch'* was voluntary) and obliged the priest to indulge that great scourge of Russia—drunkenness.[35]

Even with such help, priests still had to do much of the field toil themselves, something they undertook with great difficulty and even greater reluctance. It was, at one level, difficult for the cleric to be an efficient farmer, for he frequently had to abandon his fieldwork to perform various rites (some, like baptism or extreme unction, being undeferable). As one priest explained: "Because of our [spiritual] duties, we are constantly distracted from our work in the fields. Hence the planting is late, and the harvest—from lack of time—is quite slow." The outcome was marginal profit: "Because our planting is not completed at the right time, our yield is one-half that of peasants who cultivate nearby pieces of land; because our harvesting is slow, part of our grain is trampled by [the peasants'] livestock, and part of it rots from the rain."[36] Then, too, many clergy knew little of practical agriculture. After a decade in the seminary, far from home and rural life, they simply did not know how to cultivate the land—to their own despair and to the mirth of neighboring peasants.[37]

More important, many clergy believed that they should *not* know how, arguing that the toil was inconsistent with their rank and mission. In some degree, no doubt, they regarded field toil—the occupation of mere peas-

---

[32]On the legal ambiguities of hay land, see the materials in TsGIA SSSR, f. 804, op. 1, r. 1, d. 90, ll. 90–105.

[33]Ibid., r. 3, d. 20, l. 61 (priest's report from Vladimir diocese, 1863); for another example, see the report from clergy in Kiev (ibid., d. 155, ll. 66–66 ob.).

[34]Ibid., d. 12, l. 99 (Vladimir); see also d. 333, ll. 51, 138 ob. (Riazan). Of the 66 parishes in Kaliazin district in 1830, only one priest (in Arkhangel'skii pogost) "does not use his land . . . [and instead] leases it out" (GA Kalininskoi obl., f. 160, op. 1, d. 16272, l. 49).

[35]For a superb description of *pomoch'*, see Belliustin, *Opisanie*, pp. 73–81.

[36]TsGIA SSSR, f. 804, op. 1, r. 3, d. 328, l. 203 ob. (Riazan, 1863).

[37]See Belliustin, "Zametki," GA Kalininskoi obl., f. 103, op. 1, d. 1291, l. 149 ob.

ants—as demeaning; in the words of one archpriest, "it is indecent for ordained clergy to be occupied with agriculture, for this is unbecoming their rank and station."[38] More interesting, and of greater weight to authorities, was the argument that agricultural toil distracted the cleric from his essential spiritual duties and left him no opportunity to preach, catechize, and teach. To quote the bishop of Vladimir: "Many of the priests, to alleviate their poverty, devote all their time and all their energy to agricultural toil, which has deprived them of the opportunity to pay proper attention to the [religious] instruction of their parishioners." As a result, he complained, the people remain sunken in religious ignorance, and "the Old Belief not only does not decline but has even grown noticeably stronger."[39] Indeed, noted many, the clergy themselves begin to lose the fruits of their hard-earned knowledge at the seminary. Typical was the view of one prelate that "many of the priests not only have no opportunity to expand the knowledge acquired in educational institutions, but even lose that which they acquired there."[40]

The parish economy—at once so amorphous and inadequate—carried a host of implications for clerical status and roles. Above all, it made the cleric a community employee, subject to the demands of the immediate laity— noble squires, peasants, or townspeople—and reluctant to perform the duties prescribed from above. Little wonder then that the clergy, held firmly in the grasp of popular control, shrank from aggressive attempts to reshape popular culture, to expose immorality and persecute the deviant. The clergy's social dependence goes far to explain the weakness of anticlericalism in Russia, and it served as well to blunt the Church's efforts to improve morality and vanquish the Old Belief.[41] Nor indeed could the priest easily attend to such tasks even if he were so inclined: the size of his parish, the multiplicity of liturgical and sacramental duties, and the demands of his own fields left him little time for such pastoral duties as preaching, catechizing, and ministering to the spiritual needs of his flock. Moreover, economic dependence and low income were directly responsible for the clergy's low social status, a fact routinely attested by authorities and decried by clergy.[42] Although at first glance that low status seems contradictory to the proverbial ritualism of popular religion in Russia, it in fact rested upon a distinction between the man and his office: the priest administered the sacraments; his personal qualities had no effect upon their worth. As a result, wrote a clergyman at mid-century, the popular

[38] TsGIA SSSR, f. 796, op. 107, g. 1826, d. 460, l. 199.

[39] Ibid., op. 440, d. 1139, l. 32 ob.

[40] Ibid., op. 442, d. 43, l. 17 ob. Likewise, the bishop of Penza observed that, "by earning their support from agriculture through their own toil, [the priests] are greatly distracted from scholarly activities, so necessary for priests, especially those with a seminary education" (ibid., op. 132, g. 1851, d. 2357, l. 149).

[41] See Freeze, "Stunted Anticlericalism."

[42] That dependence formed a central theme in the clerical replies to a reform commission in 1863; see below, Chapter 6.

classes believe that "the person performing [the rites] can sometimes have few [good] personal qualities" and that "in his rank alone he is something without value, importance or meaning."[43] First authorities, later parish clergy would come to believe that only by "emancipation" from local control could the clergy perform their high mission—liturgical and pastoral, spiritual and temporal. Until that happened, however, the clergy remained a thin, vulnerable wedge into the dark masses, in no condition to fulfill the duties prescribed by Church or state.[44]

The special problems of the Russian clergy are best illuminated by comparison with their peers in the West. Significantly, most European clergy enjoyed a combination of tithes, benefices, salaries, and parsonages. Though by no means free of problems, such resources afforded the clergy a modicum of reliable support and, of particular moment, greater independence from the immediate parish.[45] Moreover, Western churches customarily found some mechanism to satisfy the needs of poor parishes; the special subsidies in England (Queen Anne's Bounty), for example, provided assistance for parishes with incomes below £50 per annum.[46] Although established churches everywhere had great diversity in incomes, none was as particularistic as the Russian Church, which remained wholly dependent upon local resources and lacked the auxiliary wealth to assist poor parishes and poor clergy.[47] The

[43] TsGIA SSSR, f. 832, op. 1, d. 85, l. 11 ("Pravoslavnoe dukhovenstvo est' li kasta?").

[44] The clergy's awkward status—seeking to perform duties assigned from above, yet dependent upon the community from below—bears a striking similarity to the status of emerging professions in central Europe, where absolutist regimes called them into existence yet had great difficulty assuming financial responsibility for their support. For a highly suggestive comparison, see the plight of schoolteachers as a special Berufsstand (Anthony LaVopa, Prussian Schoolteachers: Profession and Office, 1763–1848 [Chapel Hill, 1980]); for a more general discussion of this problem, see Lenore O'Boyle, "The Middle Class in Western Europe, 1815–48," AHR, 71 (1966): 826–45.

[45] For example, in contrast to Russia, where housing constituted one of the clergy's major expenses, churches in Europe almost invariably provided free parsonages. For England, see Pruett, Parish Clergy, pp. 136–53, and McClatchey, Oxfordshire Clergy, pp. 19–29; for France, see Marcilhacy, Le diocèse d'Orléans, pp. 130–31, and Hilaire, Une Chrétienté, 1: 191–92, 270–72; for Sweden, see Alsne, Från prästtionden, p. 445; and for Germany, see H. Werdermann, "Pfarrerstand und Pfarramt in Zeitalter der Orthodoxie in der Mark Brandenburg," Jahrbücher für brandenburgische Kirchengeschichte [hereafter JBKG], 23 (1928): 71.

[46] For discussions of Queen Anne's Bounty, see Best, Temporal Pillars, and McClatchey, Oxfordshire Clergy, chap. 2. For a specific example, the diocese of Exeter provided supplementary aid to about one-fifth of its parishes (M. Cook, ed., The Diocese of Exeter: Bishop Carey's Replies to Queries before Visitation, 2 pts. [Exeter, 1958–60], 2: xiii).

[47] Though most Western clergy had a modicum of support in parsonages, land, tithes, or state salaries, they showed immense diversity in incomes. See, for example, descriptions of the clergy in England (M. R. Austin, ed., The Church in Derbyshire in 1823–24: The Parochial Visitation of the Reverend Samuel Butler [Derby, 1972], p. 13) and Germany (R. M. Bigler, "The Social Status and Political Role of the Protestant Clergy in Pre-March Prussia," in Hans-Ulrich Wehler, ed., Sozialgeschichte Heute [Göttingen, 1974], p. 175).

Russian cleric's two main forms of support, emoluments and land, also existed in the West, but there they bore an entirely different character. Thus both German pastors and English parsons relied heavily upon land for their support, but, compared with their counterparts in Russia, they derived far more profit from such land because of the higher population density, land values, enclosures, and the agricultural revolution.[48] Similarly, although emoluments were known in the West (as "surplice fees" in England, *casuel* in France, and *Kasualien* in Germany), they ordinarily constituted only a minor component of the clerical economy—not the sole source of monetary income, as in Russia.[49]

More significant still, the unique structure of the clerical soslovie in Russia, which imposed an extraordinarily high "clerical overhead" upon lay society, was unlike anything in the West. As a total group of servitors (including sacristans as well as priests), the Russian clergy were exceedingly numerous in proportion to the general population—comparable only to the Catholic clergy (see table 3). In contrast to the Catholic clergy, however, the Russian clergy were married and had a multitude of dependents to support and educate. Nor could the Russian clergy be compared with the Protestant clergy, who, though married, served in relatively large parishes. In brief, if measured in clergy and dependents, the clerical soslovie of Russia was many times more numerous than its counterparts in the West.[50] And to make matters worse, it sought support in a country that was economically backward, from a Church that had no capital base (endowments and the like) from medieval times.

Paradoxically, if measured in terms of *priests*, not total clerical servitors, the Russian Church was seriously undermanned, for two-thirds of its ranks consisted of deacons and sacristans—men of little education, men of little relevance to many pastoral or even sacramental functions. As a result, the Russian priest had great difficulties even attending to his traditional liturgical roles, not to mention new pastoral duties, for he had to serve a parish population roughly proportional to that of Protestant ministers, not Catholic

[48] On the English case, where enclosure and high land values produced the "squarson" phenomenon of the early nineteenth century, see McClatchey, *Oxfordshire Clergy*, pp. 1–79.

[49] In France, where the clergy received salaries, the emolument—with the exception of a few large urban parishes—generally had little significance; see Marcilhacy, *Le diocèse d'Orléans*, p. 124, Dansette, *Histoire religieuse*, pp. 378–79, and Hilaire, *Une Chrétienté*, 1: 189. In England the surplice fees, save for the poorest parishes, were of small importance before the end of the nineteenth century; see Russell, *Clerical Profession*, pp. 76–84, and Austin, *The Church in Derbyshire*, pp. 13–19. On the German case, see Otto Fischer, "Bilder aus der Vergangenheit des evangelischen Pfarrhauses," *JBKG*, 21 (1926): 14.

[50] Appreciation of the different service structures and estates did not appear before the Great Reforms; for the first statement, based upon a comparison of Orthodox and Catholic clergy in the western dioceses of Russia, see the memorandum by P. N. Batiushkov (below, p. 228).

TABLE 3

Parishioner-Clergy Ratios in Russia and Europe, 1815–1850

Church and Area	Ratio	(Year)
Catholic		
Augsburg	295	(1816)
Baden	822	(1836)
France	777	(1830)
Württemberg	839	(1835)
Protestant		
Bavaria	1,250	(1840)
Denmark	1,099	(1835)
England	1,101	(1841)
Finland	1,469	(1840)
Germany (entire)	1,429	(1840)
Norway	2,632	(1835)
Prussia	1,050	(1822)
Sweden	901	(1840)
Württemberg	1,220	(1840)
Orthodox		
Russia		
(total clergy)	316	(1824)
(priests only)	1,008	(1824)

SOURCES: Bigler, *Politics of German Protestantism*, pp. 55–56;
Chadwick, *The Victorian Church*, 2: 244; Dahm, *Beruf: Pfarrer*, pp.
78–79; Harms, "Die örtliche Herkunft," pp. 364–70; Hartmann,
"Geistlichen der Diözese Augsburg," p. 27; H. Jedin, ed., *Handbuch
der Kirchengeschichte*, 7 vols. (Freiburg, 1962–1979), 6 (1): 353;
Mannsåker, *Det norske presteskapet*, p. 76; Neher, *Geistlichkeit
Württembergs*, p. 44; TsGIA SSSR, f. 797, op. 96, d. 5, ll. 1 ob.-2.

NOTE: Parishioners include all formal church members, not the total
population of a country. Clergy include full-time clerics who have
been formally installed.

priests. Yet, unlike Protestant clergy, the Russian priest had to perform a
plethora of rites and sacraments, often in the parishioner's home, and it was
just physically impossible to minister to the ritual needs of overly large parishes. As one bishop pointed out in 1847 while expressing opposition to reductions in clerical positions, "the Lutherans have few rites—unlike the Orthodox"—and hence cannot provide a model for priest-parishioner

proportions.[51] Even without further reductions in clergy and corresponding increases in parish sizes, the Russian priest was responsible to a population several times the size of that served by his Catholic counterpart. And the task in Russia was further complicated by the low population density; often a parish consisted of many hamlets scattered all over the surrounding country-side. Thus Russian priests found it difficult to perform even essential sacra-ments, and they sometimes resorted to such dubious methods as hearing confession "from two, three, or more adults at the same time" to handle their immense workload.[52]

Catholic in its liturgical functions, Protestant in the density of priests, Rus-sian in total population and form of support—the Orthodox clergy posed a stupendous task of reform. Whatever the good will of parishioners and authorities, reform would have to overcome such basic structural problems as the particularism of parish economies, the dearth of resources, and the immense size of the clerical soslovie requiring support and assistance. Although Nicholas tackled this question with determination, his state budget was already strained to the limit and could hardly close the gap between current resources and needs. Authorities would have to seek a gradual solu-tion, an approach well-suited to the Nikolaevan method.

The Parish Reform of 1829

Like his father, Paul, Nicholas first became interested in clerical reform because of the clergy's apparent complicity in peasant disorders at the outset of his reign. In June 1826 Nicholas's aide informed the procurator that "His Majesty, with regret, has deigned to note that in many places priests have encouraged and led peasants in these acts of disobedience." Eighteenth-cen-tury authorities attributed such malfeasance to "simplicity" and lack of edu-cation, but the rapid growth of seminaries in the early decades of the nine-teenth century made that explanation no longer tenable. Expressing astonishment that such disloyalty had occurred in spite of major improve-ments in ecclesiastical education, Nicholas ordered the Synod to consider measures to improve its schools further, to ensure the ordination of more worthy candidates, and to require that all seminary graduates become priests. As the ideal model of a priest, Nicholas held up the example of Father Fedor Filimonov, who "by pastoral exhortations and even by [the use of] spiritual penance on the more refractory members of his flock, aided in

[51] N. I. Barsov, ed., "K biografii Innokentiia, arkhiepiskopa khersonskogo," *KhCh*, 1884, tom 2: 107.

[52] Butkevich, "Arkhiepiskop Innoktenii Borisov," *VR*, 1884, tom 2: 386.

restoring tranquillity, order, and obedience of the peasants toward their landlords."[53] Although Nicholas reaffirmed his earlier conviction that "educated priests" were less vulnerable to popular pressure, he also recognized the important connection between malfeasance and inadequate material support. That hinted at a fundamental shift in perspective, from the earlier preoccupation with "insufficient education" and "simplicity" to a new concern about the parish economy.[54]

Church Bishops and Parish Reform

After distributing Nicholas's order for the clergy to quell peasant unrest and emulate the example of Filimonov, the Synod took up the emperor's request for proposals to improve the clergy's support.[55] In addition to compiling materials on past reforms and data on the clergy's educational level, the Synod also obtained written opinions from its own members.[56] These opinions, composed in November 1826, dealt primarily with the specific issues raised in Nicholas's manifesto, but some ranged further in their analysis. Although diverse in details, reflecting the particular needs of each prelate's diocese and his willingness to violate tradition and custom, all the commentaries concurred on the urgent need for reform.

By far the most conservative views came from the Synod's senior members—the metropolitans of St. Petersburg and Kiev, Serafim (Glagolevskii) and Evgenii (Bolkhovitinov). In general, they did little more than reiterate Nicholas's own demands, including his suggestion that "all graduates be obliged to serve the Church and that they be appointed priest or deacon without first seeking their consent." The two prelates, however, raised one further issue of increasing concern for traditionalists, namely, the relatively new practice of ordaining young seminary graduates as priests. In earlier times, a youth advanced to priesthood gradually, usually after first serving as sacristan in his father's church. But the development of seminaries, especially their rapid expansion from the late eighteenth century, had given seminarians a clear claim to vacant priestly positions without prior service as sacristans. As a result, immediately upon graduation, seminarians well below the canonical minimum age of thirty were ordained as priests. The metro-

---

[53] *PSPR*, no. 56; TsGIA SSSR, f. 797, op. 3. d. 10043, ll. 1–2; ibid., f. 796, op. 107, g. 1826, d. 460, ll. 2–3. Ironically, the priest whom Nicholas so admired did not have any formal schooling; according to his bishop's report, Filimonov "did not study at the seminary" and rose from deacon to priest in 1798, when standards were considerably lower (ibid., ll. 16–16 ob).

[54] For the eighteenth-century approach, see Freeze, *Russian Levites*, p. 80.

[55] TsGIA SSSR, f. 796, op. 107, g. 1826, d. 460, ll. 5–8.

[56] For data on educational levels, see ibid., ll. 29–30 ob.

politans complained that this practice not only violated canon law but also put parishes in the charge of green seminarians who had little experience in worldly matters and who even lacked proper training in the administration of sacraments. Metropolitan Evgenii also noted the tendency among seminary graduates to shun rural appointments (primarily because of the need to pursue agriculture, something "to which they are not accustomed"), and he proposed a state subsidy of 350 to 500 rubles per staff in rural parishes with fewer than one hundred households." Failing that, he recommended an increase in the clergy's land allotment, with a requirement that it be cultivated by "three laborers from the state peasantry."[57]

Much more venturesome and ambitious was the archbishop of Iaroslavl, Avraam (Shumilin). Like the two metropolitans, Avraam denounced the tendency to ordain young seminarians and suggested that all, prior to ordination, be required to serve as aides to experienced priests. More striking was his sharp critique of the whole clerical economy—the emoluments that left the priest dependent and weak, the "field labor [that] constitutes the main basis of sustenance" for rural clergy. His principal proposal for reform was to reorganize parishes into larger units and to require a broad set of fixed parish obligations. Specifically, Avraam proposed to consolidate all parishes with fewer than 150 households, to establish an annual tithe (two rubles per male parishioner per annum), to require parish cultivation of the clergy's allotment, and to demand that parishioners construct parsonages and provide free heating fuel in the winter. All that, of course, represented a radical change in the clerical economy, eliminating both the reliance upon emoluments and the priest's field labor. By combining parishes into larger units, argued Avraam, the total burden on parishioners would not be onerous. In the case of rural parishes that could not be merged for geographical and other reasons, Avraam suggested reducing the staff and, if need be, providing a state subsidy. Avraam, in effect, proposed to rationalize the parish economy, to redraw the parish boundaries, and to eradicate the chaotic particularism in local economies.[58]

Four bishops in central Russia—from Riazan, Vladimir, Kaluga, and Tula—tied their comments more closely to the specific needs of their dioceses.[59] Most striking of all, they categorically rejected Nicholas's suggestion that seminary graduates be conscripted into Church service, not because they were anxious about seminarians' rights, but because their dioceses already had a surfeit of educated candidates and had no need for such com-

---

[57]Ibid., ll. 75–75 ob.; to judge from the handwriting, Evgenii drafted the note, which Serafim then edited.

[58]Ibid., ll. 83–85 ob.

[59]Ibid., ll. 87–88 (Viktor of Riazan), 95–96 (Grigorii of Kaluga), 97–98 (Damaskin of Tula), 99–101 (Parfenii of Vladimir).

pulsory measures.[60] As the bishop of Riazan explained, "even now many graduates are forced to wait a year or more for a priest's position to appear—not merely in urban churches, but even in rural churches."[61] Bishop Grigorii of Kaluga asserted that the surfeit was a widespread problem, averring that "with the exception of extremely few dioceses, [seminary graduates] considerably exceed the number needed [to fill Church positions]." Though Grigorii exaggerated the geographical scope of the problem, the surplus of candidates was indeed pronounced in central dioceses like his own, where the idle graduates included two students from the class of 1822, thirty-four from the class of 1824, and soon an additional fifty-eight from the class of 1826. Ideally, wrote the bishop of Tula, the Church should skim off the very best students and simply release the remainder to pursue secular careers.

All four bishops urged strong measures to assist the parish clergy, but none envisioned an easy resolution of the problem. Like his peers, Bishop Grigorii attributed the clergy's failings to inadequate material support: "Appointees to [impoverished] positions absolutely require proper support, for without this they are so distracted by the necessity of supporting themselves and their families that, almost of necessity, they lose sight of their responsibilities, commit many acts of malfeasance, and acquire various foibles." Nevertheless, Grigorii doubted the feasibility of direct parish subsidies as recommended by Metropolitan Evgenii. He warned that parishes were too unstable to be permanently listed as "poor," often fluctuating in their economic status as the fortunes of the parishioners rose or fell. Instead, Grigorii proposed that the Church provide stipends to educated clerics (not parishes) and then dispatch them to where they were most needed. Interestingly, all four of the prelates from central Russia were cool toward the idea of fundamental parish reform like that offered by Avraam, preferring instead a modest reform to augment, not replace, the existing system of land and emoluments.

The Synod received one comment from a member of the white clergy, Archpriest Muzovskii, the emperor's confessor and a member of the Synod.[62] Like the four bishops from central dioceses, Muzovskii warned of surplus graduates and argued that the principal task was to retain the best graduates, not impress all into Church service. To support youths until they came of age and found suitable positions, Muzovskii suggested a congeries of devices, from state subsidies to appointment as tutors in aristocratic homes. Implicitly articulating the vested interests of the white clergy, Muzovskii defended the system of separate church schools for the sons of clergy and argued that the best method to ease the plight of parish clergy would be for authorities to

---

[60] By contrast, the exarch of Georgia reported an acute shortage of candidates and therefore rejected the mandatory requirement of seminary degrees as unfeasible (ibid., ll. 121–23 ob.).

[61] Ibid., l. 87.

[62] Ibid., ll. 103–6 ob.

assume the full costs of such education, including maintenance. Like most of
the bishops, Muzovskii favored the idea of state subsidies, at least for the
incurably poor parishes, as the sole means to attract qualified candidates to
such positions.

The most elaborate and unusual opinion came from Metropolitan Filaret
of Moscow.[63] On some issues, to be sure, Filaret shared the general view—
for example, that young seminarians should not be ordained, that not all be
conscripted into Church service. On the issue of poor parishes, however,
Filaret took a different tack, seeking to aid all clergy, not just those in poor
parishes, and to do so through a strict requirement that parishes build and
maintain parsonages. Noting that parsonages were virtually unknown in Russia, Filaret proposed that parishes construct them first for priests and then,
as circumstances permitted, for the remainder of the parish staff. Devoted
more to the interests of the Church than to those of the clerical estate, Filaret
argued that this reform would not only aid the clergy by eliminating their
chief expenditure but would also enable the bishop to transfer white clergy
more easily, either for reward or punishment. In contrast to the other bishops, Filaret staunchly defended the traditional system of emoluments—an
opinion that few of his peers, not to say parish clergy, would share. Thus
Filaret regarded the injunctions of Scripture and canon law, which stressed
the voluntary nature of "gifts" to the Church, as immutable and unequivocal, and he categorically rejected suggestions that emoluments be converted
into a fixed levy such as a tithe. The only structural changes he would accept
were an increase in the normative tariffs (badly eroded in real value since
their last issue in 1801) and the establishment of state subsidies to assure
appointment of good ordinands in poor parishes. Like Grigorii, he feared
great practical difficulties in identifying "poor parishes" and preferred to
give stipends directly to seminary graduates, enabling bishops then to assign
them to poor parishes.

These responses are highly revealing about Church authorities' perception
of the clerical question. Most striking was the general consensus that the
existing support was very unsatisfactory, leaving the clergy too impoverished
and dependent to perform their mission effectively. Yet that was essentially
a negative consensus: the Synod's members envisioned very different solutions, reflecting the specific needs of their dioceses as well as their willingness
to deviate from custom and canon. Not surprising for this age of autocracy,
most looked to the state to solve the clerical question, whether through parish
subsidies or stipends to seminary graduates; none, in contrast to later times,
proposed to summon parish initiative or even to consult the opinion of those
below, lay or clerical. Markedly different in substance was Filaret's com-

---

[63] Filaret, *SMO*, 2: 156–70.

mentary, which alone expressed support for gratuities and sought primarily to augment existing income with parsonages and subsidies.

When the Synod formally reviewed these opinions in December 1826, it concurred that the chief problem was not to produce more graduates but to attract them to poor parishes. Its data on the educational level of priests showed that nearly one-half of all urban priests and one-quarter of all rural priests already possessed some advanced seminary education, having either graduated from the seminary or attended its uppermost division.[64] Reaffirming that all priests should hold a seminary degree, the Synod complained that graduates shunned appointment to rural parishes because of the inadequate income and the grim prospects of agricultural toil. However, it rejected Nicholas's suggestion of involuntary consignment; it would be far better, argued the Synod, if seminarians were attracted to poor parishes by a guarantee of good land and a modicum of support. To determine just how many parishes required special assistance, the Synod instructed diocesan bishops to compile a register of "poor parishes," that is, those spurned by seminary graduates. With such data in hand, the Synod could then determine the magnitude of the problem and calculate the costs of a reform proposal.[65]

By the summer of 1827—six months later—most prelates had filed their replies, assessing local needs and offering recommendations to alleviate them.[66] Predictably, the diocesan commentaries varied greatly, reflecting both the special circumstances of each area and the bishop's own general outlook. Most bishops concurred that underpopulation was the principal cause of impoverished parishes, but some adduced other problems, including the poverty of parishioners (especially serfs), the lack of suitable church land, the tendency of parishioners to pay too little for time-consuming rites, and the clergy's inability to exploit parish land effectively because of their liturgical duties and lack of training. To cure these ills the bishops prescribed a broad range of solutions, but they most often emphasized consolidation of small, uneconomic parishes (especially in towns) and state subsidies to poor parishes. A small contingent of prelates suggested such measures as supplementary land grants (in excess of the thirty-three dessiatines prescribed by law), reductions in the clerical shtat (especially the elimination of deacons' positions), the construction of parsonages, and full stipends to cover the cost of educating the clergy's sons. The main point of controversy was parish reor-

[64] A draft of the Synod's resolution contains elaborate data on the clergy's educational level, showing that the number of clergy who had graduated from the seminary or attended its uppermost divisions (theology and philosophy) had risen sharply—from 6,569 in 1805 to 13,769 in 1825. Of the latter, 2,432 served in urban parishes and 10,317 were in rural parishes (TsGIA SSSR, f. 796, op. 107, g. 1826, d. 460, l. 76).

[65] PSPR, no. 91.

[66] TsGIA SSSR, f. 796, op. 108, g. 1827, dd. 1954–55, have most of the responses; a few additional replies were mistakenly filed in ibid., op. 107, g. 1826, d. 460, ll. 135–44.

ganization, which some prelates categorically opposed and others favored. Here, as in later times, the bishops in the western dioceses formed a distinct bloc, adamantly opposing the consolidation of parishes. The Catholic challenge, they argued, was so intense that the government must simply assume the costs of supporting poor Orthodox parishes.[67] By contrast, most of the bishops in central Russia—where churches lay like a thick carpet across the densely populated dioceses—were more amenable to parish reorganization. They argued that a modest level of parish reorganization could create more viable parishes without depriving parishioners of vital services. They recommended the elimination of some 2,000 parishes—approximately 7 percent of all parishes in the empire.[68] Yet even zealous consolidators knew that merger was sometimes impossible, because of unfordable rivers, sheer distance, or the threat of subversion by Old Believers. In such cases the bishops asked that the state provide subsidies (459,615 rubles for 1,812 parishes). Some dioceses (Moscow and several western dioceses) listed hundreds of parishes in need of subsidies, but most advanced more modest claims, in some cases listing as few as 10 parishes requiring assistance.[69] In short, diocesan bishops concurred with the Synod that the parishes required immediate aid and looked primarily, though not exclusively, to the state for a solution.

These deliberations in the Church provoked some state officials to offer their own proposals on parish reform, often considerably more radical than anything discussed by the bishops. Thus the provincial governor of Pskov, with the support of the Third Section, submitted a formal proposal focused primarily on the problem of clerical solicitation. Arguing that solicitation was the primary reason for the Old Belief's success, he proposed to eradicate the practice, by a host of measures—doubling the normative tariff, forcing parishioners to cultivate the clergy's land, and meting out severe punishment to clergy found guilty of solicitation.[70] Another proposal, emanating from the influential Count V. P. Kochubei, rejected emoluments altogether and suggested their replacement by some more regular form of income, such as fixed

[67] Ibid., op. 108, g. 1827, d. 1955, ll. 843–47 ob. (reply from Volhynia); d. 1954, ll. 852–57 (reply from Mogilev).

[68] For example, authorities in Tver proposed to combine 30 percent of the undersized parishes (70 of 240); see ibid., d. 1954, ll. 746–49. Similar proposals came from prelates in Pskov, Kostroma, and Iaroslavl (ibid., d. 1955, l. 598; d. 1954, ll. 287–554, 563).

[69] Ibid., op. 107, g. 1826, d. 460, ll. 237–40 (tabular summary).

[70] PSPR, no. 170; TsGIA SSSR, f. 797, op. 3, d. 10043, ll. 29–30 ob.; f. 796, op. 109, g. 1828, d. 132, ll. 4–6 ob. Apprised of the scheme, Filaret sharply criticized the governor's proposals, especially the demand that parishioners cultivate the priest's land: "[This demand] will meet with the same difficulties [as it did under Paul] and will provoke discontent among the peasants and lead to complaints from the clergy [about noncompliance]" (ibid., f. 832, op. 1, d. 85, l. 29 ob.; Filaret, SMO, 2: 215–16). On the Synod's behalf the procurator reiterated Filaret's critique and insisted that the Synod first review any such schemes to modify the parish economy (ibid., f. 797, op. 3, d. 10043, ll. 32–33).

parish tithes or state salaries.[71] Significantly, both proposals show the government's sensitivity to the problems of emoluments and even its willingness to countenance a radical transformation in the parish economy.

Such proposals elicited a testy rejoinder from Metropolitan Filaret, whom the Synod asked to comment on their substance.[72] As earlier, Filaret defended the traditional emoluments with a litany of Biblical quotations, but he now reinforced them with some practical arguments as well.[73] Thus Filaret candidly declared that emoluments forced the clergy to serve zealously, if only from economic necessity: "The inadequate education of [the clergy] and the difficulties of adjusting to incomes, where there is no material incentive for performing one's duties, could lead to great omissions in service." Although fear that the clergy would become "lazy" about rites was not new,[74] it was hardly a flattering opinion of parish clergy. Filaret further argued that it was simply not feasible to convert the emoluments into regular tithes, for "the people are accustomed to giving the clergy" occasional payments and would refuse to convert these into a regular tax. Even a "mixed system" combining emoluments and subsidies could not work, he warned: once levies were imposed on the clergy's behalf, the parishioners would simply reduce their donations and thereby provoke complaints from disappointed clergy. The metropolitan also regarded a broad clerical tax as "unfair," since prosperous parishes would in effect have to subsidize poor ones—a sure source of resentment among parishioners. Seeking only to increase the tariffs, Filaret was the first to raise the question of popular reaction to reform, revealing both the Church's lack of control over the laity and a deep pessimism about parishioners' willingness to aid the clergy.[75]

As these interminable debates dragged on, Nicholas grew increasingly impatient, and in January 1828 he sent the Synod a brusque reminder to act immediately on his earlier order. Noting that good clergy were vital to a

---

[71]Summarized in Filaret, *SMO*, 2: 207–16.

[72]Ibid.

[73]Curiously, in the draft version of his memorandum Filaret made a telling slip of the pen, which went unrecorded in the published version of the document. He first described emoluments as "fees for performing rites" (*plata za otpravlenie treb*) but then revised this to read "donations" (*daianiia*). The latter was perhaps more canonical, but the former was certainly more realistic (TsGIA SSSR, f. 832, op. 1, d. 85, ll. 26–26 ob.).

[74]In 1815, for example, Metropolitan Evgenii defended emoluments in similar terms: if the clergy were given regular salaries, he warned, they "would become lazy about performing rites, for ours is not the Lutheran Church—[here] most rites are performed in parishioners' homes," at considerable inconvenience to the clergy ("Pis'ma mitr. Evgeniia," *RA*, 1889, no. 5: 46).

[75]The secret Committee of the Sixth of December 1826, formed to assess the problems facing the new regime, reviewed Filaret's memorandum and accepted its main propositions save one: it declined to increase the norms for gratuities ("Bumagi Komiteta 6-ogo dekabria 1826 g.," *SIRIO*, 90: 223).

stable social order and that they required better material support, Nicholas ordered the Synod "to submit without fail the measures it deems necessary" to improve the seminaries and the performance of parish clergy, "especially in poor parishes."[76] In a separate note he commented upon the Kochubei memorandum; while ostensibly accepting Filaret's view on emoluments as firmly embedded in Scripture and canon law, Nicholas still termed the present order unsatisfactory and demanded that the Synod give the matter further reflection. Specifically, he wanted the Church not only to consider increases in the legal rates but also to review "the question of the order for performing these rites and receiving payment" from parishioners.[77] The emperor evidently had in mind the problem of bargaining between priest and parishioner and suggested employing the Petrine demand that payment follow, not precede, the rite to avoid any hint of clerical solicitation.[78]

Spurred by Nicholas's reminder, the Synod finally adopted its formal proposals in April 1828.[79] Its resolution, in fact, followed closely some earlier memoranda by Metropolitan Filaret,[80] an impressive display of his influence in the Synod. Specifically, the Synod ordered bishops to ordain only seminary graduates as priests (preferably not before age thirty), required seminarians to render some service to the Church (but not necessarily as priests, as Nicholas had proposed), and recommended several measures to ease the material needs of clergy, including full land allotments, higher rates for emoluments, and, especially, the construction of parsonages. In the case of poor parishes—defined as those that could not attract candidates—the Synod authorized the local bishop to assign seminarians for a four-year term, for which honor they would enjoy a substantial state stipend (300 to 500 rubles per annum). Because its plan called for state financing, the Synod could not promulgate the reform on its own authority but had to submit the plan to the State Council for review and approval.

Even as the Synod finished drafting its proposals, the State Council transmitted a very different scheme to the Synod, proposing to convert traditional

[76] PSZ (2), 3: 1697; TsGIA SSSR, f. 796, op. 107, g. 1826, d. 460, l. 146.

[77] TsGIA SSSR, f. 832, op. 1, d. 85, ll. 31–32 ob. (undated resolution).

[78] In a marginal note to the Ecclesiastical Regulation of 1721, Peter the Great wrote that the cleric should be paid "not at the time when he performs some rite, but several weeks later" (Verkhovskoi, Uchrezhdenie, 2: 91).

[79] PSPR, no. 184; TsGIA SSSR, f. 796, op. 107, g. 1826, d. 460, ll. 241–60.

[80] For Filaret's earlier memoranda, including a response to the emperor's evident interest in abolishing emoluments, see TsGIA SSSR, f. 796, op. 107, g. 1826, d. 460, ll. 167–90, and Filaret, SMO, 2: 216–17. For favorable comments on his memoranda by the bishop of Riazan and one archpriest serving in the Synod, see TsGIA SSSR, f. 796, op. 107, g. 1826, d. 460, ll. 199–213 ob.). It is worth noting that, whereas Filaret presumed extensive solicitation and proposed measures to curtail it, the archpriest defended the clergy from such accusations, revealing how the white clergy in the Synod, at least on some occasions, could articulate the special interests of their own class.

gratuities into a regular salary either through a parish tithe or state levies.[81] Though cast in general terms, the government's proposal plainly reflected secular dissatisfaction with emoluments and a widespread desire to place the parish economy on very different foundations. Interestingly enough, the Synod rejected this proposal, even though earlier discussions had revealed a keen awareness of the many problems caused by emoluments. The shift in opinion, at least in part, reflected the force of Filaret's memoranda, which combined not only scriptural citations but also practical considerations to defend the traditional system of gratuities. Thus, in its official response to the State Council, the Synod noted that parishioners preferred occasional gratuities to larger annual levies and that payment for individual rites also assured zealous service by the parish clergy. The Synod also argued, somewhat lamely, that donations encouraged the wealthy to give in excess of the legal norm, whereas a fixed tax would preclude such generosity and weigh most heavily upon the poor parishioners. No doubt, however, the Synod's greatest concern was the specific terms of conversion; an arithmetic conversion of legal gratuities could produce paltry terms, far less than the clergy's real income and certain to harm, not improve, their economic condition. Equitable conversion, the Synod calculated, would cost approximately 3.7 million rubles per annum. To cover this expenditure the state would need to impose special levies, which would surely be coercive and only provoke popular resentment toward the clergy. Thus, notwithstanding the weaknesses of the traditional economy, the Synod eschewed a more radical transformation—not, it seems, because of Filaret's scriptural references, but because of fears that conversion would either reduce clerical income or provoke popular anticlericalism.

The State Council, in turn, subjected the Synod's plan to close scrutiny and imposed several major changes.[82] It left unaltered some specific measures, such as the requirement that bishops ordain only seminary graduates (unless such were unavailable, as in outlying dioceses) and the admonition that bishops try not to ordain underaged seminarians as priests. Nor did the State Council mandate that all seminary graduates become clergy, as Nicholas originally suggested, but ruled that they must serve the Church in some capacity for four years (as seminary teacher or diocesan clerk). Instead, it was the Synod's proposals for economic assistance that the State Council subjected to drastic revisions. The most significant change was to reduce cate-

---

[81] TsGIA SSSR, f. 797, op. 3, d. 10043, ll. 14–16 (draft), 17–22 (final copy, dated 29.4.1828). See also the note from Metropolitan Serafim to Kurakin, 28.8.1828 (ibid., f. 1149 [Gosudarstvennyi sovet, Departament zakonov], op. 1, dd. 64/65, ll. 27–31). That Serafim, not the procurator, communicated directly with the state is significant, for under Protasov the procurator's chancellery served as the mediary on all relations with the state bureaucracy.

[82] PSZ (2), 4: 3323; PSPR, no. 269.

gorical imperatives to mere "encouragement" or "whenever possible," a piece of editing that dealt a death blow to such requirements as parsonages, now no longer mandatory but simply "desirable." The State Council also declared supplementary land allotments "desirable" if land in a given region was plentiful; only if the parish church possessed less than the legal norm could the clergy demand additional allotments. On the question of poor parishes, the principal focus of Nicholas's concern, the State Council proved more generous; while urging bishops to consolidate parishes whenever possible, it authorized the 500,000 rubles requested by the Synod. Signed directly into law by Nicholas without further consultation with the Synod, the parish reform of 1829 thus focused primarily upon aid to poor parishes, retreating from the Synod's more ambitious attempt to aid all clergy through parsonages and supplementary land allotments.

The State Council's statute infuriated Metropolitan Filaret. In private correspondence he complained that "the Sovereign displayed compassion toward us, but others have made things difficult." He was particularly incensed that the State Council had promulgated its final statute without first consulting the Synod: "The State Council rose [to consider this matter], but did not deign to ask the humble servitors of the Church about it, the details of which they could not even grasp." As a consequence, the very text of the State Council's statute contained gross errors by copyists (the omission of negatives), poignantly revealing how little the Council understood the issues. With vexation Filaret concluded, "When business is conducted with that kind of attentiveness, just try to compile a statute and govern!"[83] Shortly afterwards, Filaret even drafted a memorandum taking the Council to task for its slovenly treatment of the reform and its baneful effect upon the Synod's carefully crafted proposals.[84] The Synod, however, was unwilling to challenge the State Council for fear of jeopardizing the funds already granted. It therefore tabled Filaret's memorandum and instead turned to the difficult task of implementation.

Implementation

The Synod directed diocesan authorities to compile data on poor parishes once more, and over the next few years it distributed the 500,000 rubles provided by the state. In each case the bishop first submitted a preliminary list of "poor parishes," identifying those that could be merged as well as those that could not (and thus required state subsidies). The Synod, holding special evening sessions, meticulously combed these lists, reducing the number of

---

[83]"Pis'ma mitropolita moskovskogo Filareta," *Pribavleniia k Tvoreniiam Sviatykh Otets* [hereafter *Prib. TSO*], 1872, no. 4: 573.

[84]Filaret, *SMO*, 2: 273–79.

poor parishes and the sums due each.[85] For instance, Archbishop Avraam of Iaroslavl sent a report listing forty-one impoverished parishes, of which he proposed to consolidate seventeen; for the remaining twenty-four parishes he requested a subsidy of 5,450 rubles. The Synod pruned down his request: it sharply reduced the subsidy for some parishes (for example, cutting the subsidy of one parish from 250 to 100 rubles) and rejected entirely requests for some others. In the end it authorized 3,050 rubles for thirteen parishes—about half the bishop's original request.[86] The Synod exercised similar vigilance for other dioceses, particularly for those where the bishop advanced extravagant demands.[87] Most successful by far in soliciting aid was the bishop of the western diocese of Minsk; by citing the large number of Uniates and other non-Orthodox in his diocese, he procured subsidies of 53,950 rubles for 149 parishes. Even so, that amount fell considerably short of the 90,790 rubles he originally requested for 214 parishes in his diocese.[88] The Synod's surgery on budgetary requests made clear from the outset that one-half million rubles, though substantial, did not cover the needs of poor parishes, at least as defined by diocesan authorities.

Apart from insufficient funding, the Synod had difficulty assembling data on the nearly 30,000 parishes in the empire, and as a result it encountered substantial delays in implementing the reform. In 1830, in fact, it allocated only 62,159 rubles for parishes in fourteen dioceses; in 1831 it distributed an additional 12,250 rubles, thereby leaving unspent the great bulk of the 500,000 rubles.[89] Such procrastination irritated Nicholas, who complained to the Synod in August 1831 about the delays.[90] In reply the Synod explained that it lacked preliminary data from many dioceses, and it used the emperor's impatient query to summon prompt action by diocesan authorities.[91] Even so, two years later it was still seeking data from several dioceses and corrected reports from others, not achieving final implementation until the mid-1830s.[92]

Such delays were due not to mere administrative sloth but to the difficulty of identifying "poor parishes." In principle, the determining characteristic—a parish with priestly vacancies that attracted no candidates—should have enabled bishops to identify them. That criterion, however, was future-ori-

---

[85]"Materialy dlia biografii Filareta," ChOLDP, 1869, no. 8: 51 (letter to Nikolai, 4.1.1832).

[86]TsGIA SSSR, f. 796, op. 111, g. 1830, d. 957, ch. 12, ll. 1–57.

[87]Thus Arkhangel'sk received subsidies for 43 of the bishop's 94 requests, and Poltava obtained aid for 26 of its 187 requests (ibid., d. 957, ch. 34, 37).

[88]Ibid., d. 957, ch. 19.

[89]Ibid., op. 107, g. 1826, d. 460, ll. 316–17 ob.

[90]Ibid., l. 366.

[91]Ibid., ll. 369–69 ob. (Synodal resolution, 13.8.1831).

[92]Ibid., l. 507 (Synodal resolution, 18.6.1833); op. 111, g. 1830, d. 957, ch. 20, ll. 26–26 ob. (Synod to bishop of Kishinev, 1832); IVO (1836), pp. 164–65.

ented: many parishes, however poor, currently had a priest (probably an uneducated one) and hence could not qualify for a subsidy until the post fell vacant through death or transfer. In the interim, the treasury refused to transfer the budget to the Synod for temporary expenditures, insisting upon strict observance of the formal statute. Ultimately, the Synod abandoned its "time test" and permitted bishops to designate poor parishes according to apparent need, regardless of vacancies.[93] That opening was virtually a blank check, inviting a flood of inflated claims, even crass falsifications. Metropolitan Filaret, who had originally designed the time test, was highly skeptical of diocesan claims and insisted that bishops personally verify data, not merely transmit the claims of parish clergy and local superintendents. In December 1831 Filaret censured his own diocesan administration, accused his superintendents of filing "manifestly careless and biased" reports, and fined each of them twenty-five rubles for malfeasance.[94] Early the next year he complained to his suffragan bishop that data from their diocese had "deficiencies such as we here [in the Synod] have not encountered in data from other dioceses," adding that it would "be a disgrace to show [our data] to the Synod and impossible not to come away from there without a reprimand." The metropolitan also gave his aide a sharp reproof: "Each part [of the report] was prepared by clerks; the secretary glued all this together; the consistory members, without reading it, signed; you, without looking, wrote 'Agreed.' Wonderful! Now that is the way to handle one of the most important pieces of diocesan business!"[95] Moscow was hardly an exception. In February 1832 Filaret complained that the Synod allocated funds even though diocesan data were grossly unreliable, and thus its "decisions based on [the diocesan reports] are founded more on guesswork than real fact." That carelessness only invited further deception: "Poor churches appeared on the first report and received subsidies. When people saw how complaisant authorities were, still more 'poor' [parishes] were found. One may assume that [all this is just] nominal poverty."[96]

The reform encountered difficulty from still another source: popular opposition to the abolition of parishes. To the laity, consolidation meant abolition of their ancestors' traditional church. It also caused great inconvenience, obliging them to travel further—sometimes ten miles or more across muddy, unsurfaced roads—to attend services or fetch a priest for rites like baptism.

[93]TsGIA SSSR, f. 796, op. 107, g. 1826, d. 460, ll. 353–53 ob.

[94]Ibid., ll. 479–81 ob. (Filaret to Synod, 13.12.1831).

[95]"Materialy dlia biografii Filareta," ChOLDP, 1869, no. 8: 50–51 (Filaret to Nikolai, 1832).

[96]"Pis'ma mitropolita moskovskogo Filareta k S. D. Nechaevu," RA, 1893, no. 2: 139. Filaret also criticized authorities in Kaluga, who first requested aid for just 4 parishes but then demanded aid for 18 the following year (TsGIA SSSR, f. 796, op. 111, g. 1830, d. 957, ch. 24, ll. 1–4, 9–22). Worse still was Minsk, which first sought aid for only 15 parishes but then inflated its request to cover 214 (ibid., d. 19, ll. 2–8, 19–117).

Some parishes appealed to the Synod to countermand orders for consolidation but prevailed only if they agreed to provide additional support for the clergy. In Iaroslavl, for example, several parishes persuaded the authorities to reestablish their churches after the community—usually a wealthy landlord—agreed to provide supplementary land or income.[97] If parishioners refused to provide additional support, however, the Synod summarily rejected their petition and let the bishop's decision stand. In Riazan, for example, the bishop abolished one small parish that had a mere sixty male parishioners. When the local landlord declined to provide more land or income, the Synod upheld the bishop's decision to close the church.[98]

Parish dissatisfaction remained intense, however, and eventually forced Church authorities to retreat, producing a general shift in the bishops' earlier attitudes toward parish reorganization. In contrast to the 1827 reports, when many prelates of central dioceses favored a moderate level of parish consolidation, they now agreed to consolidate relatively few parishes. Few prelates, in fact, were as bold as the bishop of Pskov, who proposed to consolidate 10 percent of the parishes in his diocese, but even that proportion was modest compared with measures taken later in the Great Reforms.[99] Interestingly, even Avraam of Iaroslavl, who had urged far reaching parish reorganization in 1826, merged only twenty-four parishes (3 percent of his diocese).[100] The Synod, once favorably inclined toward consolidation, also lost its former zeal. Reluctance was first apparent in 1832, when it rejected a memorandum from a priest in Smolensk proposing to make a radical reduction in the number of parishes (with two thousand male parishioners set as the minimum, not the current four hundred). The Synod explained that the abolition of many churches, "besides distressing parishioners, is contradictory to the government's intention of strengthening the Christian faith by striving to increase the number of churches, not reduce them."[101] In 1837, after receiving a parish petition opposing the bishop's plans to abolish their church, the Synod reversed his decision and declared that the prelate should first have obtained the Synod's approval before closing the church and "giving the [parishioners] cause to criticize ecclesiastical administration."[102] Three years later the Synod issued a general decree that "henceforth diocesan authorities must adhere strictly to the requirement that decisions to abolish existing parishes,

[97] TsGIA SSSR, f. 796, op. 111, g. 1830, d. 957, ch. 12, ll. 51–57.

[98] Ibid., op. 112, g. 1831, d. 1045 (large unpaginated file, with this protest from Riazan bound together with many others).

[99] Ibid., op. 111, g. 1830, d. 957, ch. 13, ll. 1–4.

[100] Ibid., d. 957, ch. 12, ll. 16–39; op. 107, g. 1826, d. 460, ll. 84–85.

[101] PSPR, no. 429.

[102] TsGIA SSSR, f. 796, op. 116, g. 1835, d. 279, ll. 14–17.

if the parish objects, are not to be implemented without first obtaining the permission of the Holy Synod."[103]

That was a significant retreat, indicating the bishops' growing ambivalence toward parish consolidation. Their attitude became increasingly apparent in official reports, such as that from Moscow, where Filaret expressed fears of excessive mergers. To his suffragan bishop he wrote, "Your committee has designated too many churches for attachment: if nine are [consolidated] in [this] one district, then there will be two hundred in the [whole] diocese. I cannot agree to this. True, the churches are small and close by one another; still, it is an unpleasant job to empty them. Let someone who likes this do it." He concluded that "it is impossible not to merge [some] churches, [but] it is desirable to merge fewer of them."[104] When in 1832 Filaret finally submitted his diocesan proposals for mergers and subsidies to the Synod, he contested his own consistory's plan to make a substantial number of consolidations:

> First, this would produce a very sorrowful impression on many people who perform good deeds and acts for the holy churches. Second, insofar as the people around Moscow, having barely heard matins, often rush to Moscow on Sundays for the morning trade, this inclination to trade on holidays would become even more frequent and harmful if, because of the abolition of many churches, one had to walk a long distance for masses. Third, because of the proximity of large nests of Old Believers (Rogozhskii and Preobrazhenskii cemeteries) and the efforts and cunning there to convert Orthodox folk, it is necessary that a pastor be close at hand in small settlements, defending his spiritual flock from the schismatic wolves.[105]

Even when Filaret agreed that merger was inescapable, he directed that the decision not be implemented until the position fell vacant, at which time the question would be reviewed once again.[106]

Church authorities also encountered difficulties when they tried to implement the rule that all parishes provide the minimum land allotment of thirty-three dessiatines. The Synod actively enforced this demand, ordering bishops to seek swift and full implementation and insisting that state officials cooperate.[107] Evidently, the parish clergy itself did not press this issue: the government reported that there had been few requests for additional state land

---

[103] Ibid., ll. 30–30 ob.
[104] "Materialy dlia biografii Filareta," *ChOLDP*, 1869, no. 8: 73 (letter to Nikolai, 28.3.1832).
[105] TsGIA SSSR, f. 796, op. 111, g. 1830, d. 957, ch. 6, ll. 1–1 ob.
[106] Ibid., ll. 9–11.
[107] Ibid., op. 107, g. 1826, d. 460, ll. 462–70 ob.

and speculated that "this matter is moving so unsuccessfully mainly because the clerical staffs are not petitioning for a land allotment," presumably because they feared antagonizing local parishioners.[108] Whatever the cause, the failure was clearly evident from Synodal data of 1840–1841, which show that many churches still lacked a full complement of land. According to some bishops, state officials were also to blame. For example, the bishop of Smolensk compiled data for 1840 showing that 132 parishes (19 percent of the churches in his diocese) lacked the legal allotment, and he complained that state authorities rebuffed his demands with this claim: "The allotment of supplementary proportions of land to churches on state lands is impossible—partly because of the peasants' land shortage, partly because some churches are [jointly] on [private] landlord estates, with only an insignificant number of state peasants in these parishes."[109]

Nor were the bishops able to ordain exclusively seminary graduates to the priesthood. Central dioceses, given their abundance of graduates, had no difficulty complying with the new rule, but most outlying areas had no such riches of talent and, inevitably, sought exemption. First to appeal was the bishop of Perm, who informed the Synod in March 1830 that he had only 33 candidates for 77 vacancies. The Synod directed him to invite candidates from neighboring dioceses, but when that effort failed, it authorized him to ordain those who had some formal education but lacked a diploma. That remedy too failed to yield sufficient candidates, and the Synod reluctantly authorized the bishop to ordain unschooled deacons, especially after he wrote that "it is extremely dangerous to leave churches without priests, given the great number of schismatics in this diocese."[110] In 1831 the bishop of Poltava obtained a similar exemption, which was later extended as well to the dioceses of Kishinev and Olonets.[111] Even without formal permission, some bishops allegedly ordained nongraduates to the priesthood.[112] Disturbed by reports of such deviations, Nicholas created a special fund in 1832 to assist seminarians in relocating from overpopulated central dioceses to outlying areas where the shortage of candidates was most acute.[113] That measure had only limited success; as a result, each diocese remained largely self-contained, some suffering from surplus candidates, others from acute shortage.

The 1829 reform thus achieved little. The preparation of the statute, lasting over three years, dealt not only with poor parishes but also with larger

[108] Ibid., ll. 473–73 ob.
[109] Ibid., op. 121, g. 1840, d. 1568, l. 42.
[110] Ibid., op. 111, g. 1830, d. 254, ll. 1–10; *PSPR*, nos. 328, 342.
[111] TsGIA SSSR, f. 796, op. 112, g. 1831, d. 624, ll. 1–5; d. 169, ll. 1–7 ob.; d. 740, ll. 1–2 ob.
[112] See, for example, the case described in A. A. Titov, "Orenburgskii arkhierei bylogo vremeni," *RA*, 1904, no. 4: 654.
[113] *PSPR*, no. 441.

disorders in clerical service. The final reform, however, focused mainly upon poor parishes, the only recipients of state aid. In the end such parishes were few, representing only 5 percent of all parishes in the empire, concentrated primarily in the western provinces.[114] Furthermore, even this small-scale reform revealed the fundamental barriers to change in the Church's infrastructure: the parishioners' lack of interest in aiding the clergy, the complexities of even designating poor parishes, state officials' refusal to provide supplementary land, and seminarians' refusal to accept positions in poor parishes or outlying dioceses. The experiment also precipitated new skepticism among Great Russian bishops toward parish reorganization. The ardor for rationalization cooled in the face of peasant refractoriness, gentry complaints, and the Church's inability to mandate compliance. Unable to obtain parsonages or substantial funds from the state, the Synod thus provided only a modicum of aid to the clergy and left the parish question unsolved.

The Second Parish Reform

State authorities raised the clerical question once again in the late 1830s, but this time they pursued very different aims, methods, and tactics—all reflecting the considerable development in Nikolaevan government, both in style and in perspective. The most obvious change was the mechanism of reform: this time it was primarily the state, not the Church, that would formulate and design reform. Of greater importance, the second reform reflected more elaborate, ambitious goals. Whereas the statute of 1829 aimed mainly to make the clergy more politically reliable, that of 1842 aspired to create a clergy that could play a more dynamic role in parish life and social development. It therefore displayed greater willingness to aid *all* clergy, to exact greater demands from parishioners. The result, it hoped, would be a priesthood capable of performing both liturgical roles and newer functions— teacher, paramedic, and agronomist.

The Drafting of Reform

The prime mover of the second reform was the minister of state domains, P. D. Kiselev, the innovative bureaucrat who engineered reform for state peasants and who now sought to employ parish priests in his designs for rural development. In a memorandum of November 1838, Kiselev proposed to improve the "religious education of rural youth," partly by modifying the

---

[114]Only 1,524 of the 28,710 parishes received subsidies by the mid-1830s (*IVO* [*1836*], pp. 164–65; TsGIA SSSR, f. 796, op. 117, g. 1836, d. 1201, ll. 3–6).

seminary curriculum to include practical subjects, such as medicine and agronomy, but also by reforming the parish economy. Kiselev denounced the traditional form of support, especially gratuities, insisting that the clergy required a regular salary: "Provided with a means of existence, the clergy is thereby freed from the necessity to take payments for rites at birth, baptism, confession, marriage, and burial. It is impossible to deny that the payment for sacraments in these cases is inconsistent with the relations that bind the clergy to the people, and that the elimination of [such payments] should raise [the clergy] in the people's opinion, thereby strengthening [the clergy's] moral influence in religious affairs." To replace traditional emoluments, Kiselev proposed a combination of other resources: income from the sale of church candles, land rents from parish property, salaries from teaching in state schools, even a mandatory parish tithe of thirty kopecks per male parishioner. To enable the Church to transfer clergy more easily according to merit and need, Kiselev also proposed to require that each parish provide a parsonage and supply grain for the priest in his first year to facilitate resettlement.[115]

Although the Kiselev note reopened the clerical question, it was but an abstract set of principles, not a detailed plan with costs calculated and terms defined. Acting on behalf of the Synod, the chief procurator obtained Nicholas's approval to convoke a special committee of Church and state officials to consider the scheme in detail and to draft specific proposals. Significantly, reform was not left to the exclusive purview of the Synod itself. Although the ostensible reason was Kiselev's involvement and the ultimate need for state financial assistance, the new procedure reflected both the enhanced role of the chief procurator (Protasov) and the Nikolaevan penchant for interministerial, secret commissions. Chaired by a minor clerical figure (a suffragan bishop, not even a member of the Synod), the committee included several lay officials and even a personal representative of the chief procurator.[116] Apart from augmenting the state's role, the joint committee promised to yield a more concerted reform than that of 1829, when the State Council summarily revised and emasculated the Synod's plans.

Formation of a special committee, moreover, may also have been due to the bishops' cool reaction to Kiselev's note, embodied in a lengthy critique from Metropolitan Filaret. Reaffirming his earlier commitment to the tradition of gratuities, Filaret opposed Kiselev's plan to eliminate these customary payments as contrary to Scripture and canon law.[117] He conceded that solicitation was ubiquitous and harmful but insisted that authorities could eradicate such abuse by thoughtful modification of written law, eliminating

[115]TsGIA SSSR, f. 796, op. 5, d. 21462, ll. 4–7 ob. (Kiselev's note).
[116]Ibid., ll. 13–14 ob.
[117]Filaret, SMO, 2: 435–40.

ambiguities to facilitate prosecution of offenders.[118] The metropolitan also rejected Kiselev's suggestion that other Church revenues (such as income from the sale of candles) be diverted to aid the parish clergy, pointing out that even now these revenues failed to satisfy the Church's most pressing needs.[119] Filaret endorsed the suggestion of salaries for clergy who taught in state schools, but he noted that Kiselev failed to explain how the state could raise such substantial sums. The only new resource identified in the memorandum, complained Filaret, was a parish tithe (the thirty-kopeck levy on all males). Even rough calculations showed that this levy would yield a mere 234 rubles per parish—hardly a substitute for existing gratuities and certainly not an improvement in support.[120] Although no other prelates submitted a formal critique of the Kiselev memorandum, they probably shared Filaret's misgivings, especially about the small tithe, and followed his leadership. The archbishop of Iaroslavl candidly expressed his anxiety about the planned reforms and only hoped that "the new measures not cause more harm than good."[121]

The committee began work in January 1839 and immediately received instructions from Nicholas to give particular attention to the western provinces. Ever since the 1830–1831 Polish Rebellion, Nicholas had attempted to uplift the status of Orthodox clergy in the area, giving them new roles and authority as a bulwark against Catholicism and Polonization.[122] Moreover, authorities gradually took steps to rejoin the Uniates to the Orthodox Church, a policy culminating in the Act of Union in March 1839. It was imperative that the former Uniate clergy receive ample support if they were to be loyal supporters of the new order.[123] Thus at the very first session the chief procurator's delegate transmitted an instruction from Nicholas that "measures for supporting the rural clergy be discussed primarily with regard to the western provinces" and that "the deliberations apply equally to the Uniate clergy," on the verge of formal reunification with the Orthodox Church.[124] Nicholas's directive revealed a baldly political interest in Church reform. Shortly afterwards the emperor sent a further instruction that the committee

---

[118]Ibid., 2: 440–42; TsGIA SSSR, f. 832, op. 1, d. 85, ll. 37–38.

[119]Filaret, SMO, 2: 429–32; TsGIA SSSR, f. 832, op. 1, d. 85, ll. 35–36.

[120]Filaret, SMO, 2: 426–28; TsGIA SSSR, f. 832, op. 1, d. 85, ll. 39–40 ob.

[121]"Materialy dlia istorii russkoi tserkvi," ChOLDP, 1875, no. 2, otd. 2: 13.

[122]See above, pp. 9–10.

[123]See the materials collected in SIRIO, 113: 176–211, and the summary account in W. Lencyk, "The Eastern Catholic Church under Nicholas I" (Ph.D. diss., Fordham University, 1961).

[124]TsGIA SSSR, f. 796, op. 445, d. 88, ll. 4–4 ob. ("Zhurnaly komiteta," 12.1.1839); see also the chief procurator's note to the committee (Otdel rukopisei, Gosudarstvennaia publichnaia biblioteka im. M. E. Saltykova-Shchedrina [hereafter OR GPB], f. 573 [S.-Peterburgskaia dukhovnaia akademiia], op. 1, k. 6, d. 79, ll. 1–1 ob.).

could tap the resources of the Ministry of State Domains to aid the clergy in parishes of state peasants, though the committee should seek "other means" to assist clergy in serf parishes.[125] By the third session (2 February 1839) the committee had outlined its course of action and ordered the Church bureaucracy to compile essential background materials—data on the present conditions in the parish, a summary of canon law on the problem, and information on the methods of material support used in Western churches.[126] As the committee methodically proceeded with its work, Nicholas—no doubt anxious about the Uniate problem—complained of undue delays and reiterated that "it is necessary to speed up this matter, beginning first with the western provinces."[127]

After that imperial nudge, the committee hastened to draft some preliminary proposals for reform in the western provinces. In a memorandum of April 1839 the committee drew a distressing picture of the clergy's plight in the western provinces and concluded that the existing system of support required radical change. Placing primary responsibility upon the parish (not the state), the committee demanded that the parish provide costs for settlement, a parsonage, a full land allotment (including a supplementary twelve dessiatines of hay land), and even a free house servant. The committee also proposed that parishioners cultivate the clergy's land, not as *pomoch'*, but as a regular duty; it argued that, "as something consistent with custom, this can in no way be regarded as burdensome and represents labor of very short duration." Most generous of all, the committee recommended that the state provide each parish with a substantial monetary subsidy—500 rubles for priests and 150 rubles for sacristans (several times the amount distributed to parishes in the 1829 reform and the sum proposed by Kiselev). In exchange for all this support, the committee wanted to abolish gratuities, permitting payments only for special prayer services of an entirely voluntary character. Although this plan failed to explain how the state would finance the enormous subsidies it so generously allotted, the terms were extraordinarily munificent, underscoring the state's determination to improve the material condition of Orthodox clergy in the vital western borderlands. Nicholas approved a preliminary draft of these proposals and wrote "Fair and just" at the top of his copy.[128] The chief procurator solicited comments from dioc-

[125]OR GPB, f. 573, op. 1, k. 6, d. 79, ll. 1–1 ob. (Protasov note to the committee, 18.1.1839).

[126]TsGIA SSSR, f. 796, op. 445, d. 88, ll. 8–13 (zhurnaly komiteta); ibid., f. 797, op. 5, d. 21462, ll. 28–29 ob. (Synodal resolution).

[127]The committee shared Nicholas's apprehensions about the special importance of the western dioceses: "Amidst foreigners and the clergy of other confessions, who enjoy an abundance of means and education, our clergy have incomparably greater needs [there] than do clergy in the internal provinces" (ibid., f. 797, op. 5, d. 21462, ll. 37 ob.–38).

[128]Ibid., ll. 54–60 ob.; see also OR GPB, f. 573, op. 1, k. 6, d. 79, ll. 10–17 ("Zapiska o prikhodskom dukhovenstve").

esan authorities in the western area, and the one extant response (from the bishop of Polotsk diocese) was, predictably, favorable toward these extremely generous terms for the parish reform.[129]

Its guiding principles approved, the committee then labored for nine months to prepare a specific reform project, taking into account resources and expenditures. When it finally completed work in early 1840, it had preserved the principles but changed the details, primarily in an effort to reduce the costs of reform. The main change was the decision to prepare a new shtat in order to strike a better balance between parish resources and the number of clergy and churches. With a higher proportion of laity to clergy, the committee calculated, the new concessions for parish clergy would not weigh so heavily upon individual parishioners. Thus parish reorganization became a key element in the new formula, the committee seeking to eliminate "small parishes" (defined as any with fewer than one hundred male souls) and to limit the number of clergy at each church. Once reorganized into viable units, the parishes should more easily provide the many obligations listed in the original proposal—parsonages, field labor, and the like. In lieu of gratuities, the committee adhered to its earlier promise of substantial salaries (500 rubles for priests and 150 rubles for sacristans), which it hoped to finance through a general levy on the population and through a special tax on entries in parish registers for birth, death, and marriage.[130] Although this formal structure was intended for application throughout the empire, the committee thus far had prepared specific proposals, including a new shtat, only for the western dioceses, as Nicholas had ordered.[131]

Although this detailed proposal earned formal approval from a special conference of high officials and the emperor himself in early 1840, later that year the government shelved the entire plan.[132] The reason was widespread famine and crop failure. Fearful of provoking rural disorders and hostility toward the clergy, the government decided to defer implementation. The delay lasted until late 1841, when Chief Procurator Protasov sent Nicholas

[129]TsGIA SSSR, f. 797, op. 5, d. 21462, ll. 71–76.

[130]OR GPB, f. 573, op. 1, k. 6, d. 79, ll. 18–38 ("Zapiska ob istochnikakh dlia kapitala na zhalovan'e sel'skomu dukhovenstvu i drugie posobiia"), 39–46 ("Kratkii proekt o vzimanii za bumagu upotrebliaemuiu dlia svedeniia, vydavaemykh ot tserkvi v pol'zu prikhodskogo dukhovenstva"). For Filaret's critique of proposals to eliminate gratuities, see his note in TsGIA SSSR, f. 832, op. 1, d. 85, ll. 37–38.

[131]OR GPB, f. 573, op. 1, k. 6, d. 79, ll. 10–17 ob. ("Zapiska ob obespechenii dukhovenstva v zapadnykh guberniiakh"). For an account of this reform committee, the files of which have been poorly preserved (probably because of cannibalization by later reform committees), see the Synod's research note of 1910: [E. Petrovskii], Istoricheskaia spravka kasatel'no sposobov obespecheniia soderzhaniem pravoslavnogo prikhodskogo dukhovenstva v Rossii za sinodal'-nyi period upravleniia russkoiu tserkov'iu ([St. Petersburg, 1910]), p. 16.

[132]Petrovskii, Istoricheskaia spravka, pp. 16–18.

an appeal urging that the reform be applied immediately to the western provinces. Protasov justified his request partly by reference to "the poverty of rural priests in the western area," but his principal argument rested on evidence of acute distress and discontent among the former Uniate clergy: "Having been deprived of all assistance by the local [Catholic] landlords, even suffering covert persecution at the hands of many, [the former Uniate clergy] see that the present fate of themselves and their families is even more onerous than before." To avoid dissatisfaction and tragic consequences, Protasov warned, "the interests of Church and Fatherland require that the reunited [former Uniate] clergy be provided for in an appropriate manner." Since it was impossible to assist only the former Uniate clergy without provoking dissatisfaction among the regular Orthodox clergy, Protasov argued that reform must be extended to both groups. Admitting the financial difficulties involved, he recommended that the government introduce the reform first to the most troublesome areas and in a less ambitious form. Once the minister of finance agreed to the new expenditures, Nicholas promulgated the reform for five of the seven dioceses in the western area: Lithuania, Polotsk, Minsk, Mogilev, and two districts in Volhynia diocese.[133]

The final version of reform differed sharply from the munificent scheme drafted and approved in 1840. The most striking change was the downward revision in salary scales, a decision obviously dictated by fiscal considerations. Thus, in lieu of the 500 rubles for priests and 150 rubles for sacristans promised in 1840, the new scale divided parishes into seven classes according to their size, with the priest's salary ranging from a low of 100 rubles to a maximum of 180 rubles. Based on the premise that the salaries were compensation for abolished gratuities, the scale set larger salaries for the most populous parishes, where priests stood to lose proportionately more.[134] While sharply reducing the state's obligations in money, the formal statute left intact the complex set of obligations in kind (natural'nye povinnosti) due from parishioners—parsonages, free cultivation of parish land, fuel, grain in the first year, and sundry other services. To implement this reform, the government established a special committee in each province (gubernskii komitet), composed of the bishop, the governor, the provincial administrator of state domains, and the marshal of the nobility. After local authorities first drafted an inventory (inventar', a legal contract fixing the precise terms of parish dues), the provincial committee then had to review the draft inventory and determine whether it conformed to the new statute's provisions.[135] Once con-

---

[133] Ibid., p. 18.

[134] PSZ (2), 17: 15470.

[135] Curiously, the state made a similar attempt in the 1840s to regulate the serfs' obligations in the three southwestern provinces, preparing inventories to fix the peasants' dues. For the inventory reform, see I. I. Ignatovich, Pomeshchich'i krest'iane nakanune ikh osvobozhdeniia (3rd ed.; Leningrad, 1925), pp. 191–223.

firmed by the provincial committee, the inventory had the force of a binding legal contract, enabling clergy to invoke government force to obtain compliance from the parish. At the same time, the statute categorically banned clerical demands for gratuities, though it left a loophole for "voluntary" offerings.[136]

The parish reform of 1842, though principally a creation of the state, nevertheless served the interests of Church and clergy. Although the final reform proved far less munificent than earlier drafts, it nevertheless promised substantial benefits for the clergy—granting the parsonages that Filaret sought, freeing priests from onerous field labor, and replacing gratuities with a regular income. The reform, to be sure, violated episcopal authority, reflecting the state's willingness to circumvent the Church and to disregard Filaret's scriptural arguments about voluntary gratuities. Yet the reform aimed to strengthen the Church and especially the clergy's status in the western provinces; if the motive was essentially state interest, the effect was substantial assistance for the clergy. Viability of the reform, however, rested upon its ability to raise the clergy's material income and their status among laity. The statute, after all, placed the principal burden on parishioners. Prelates like Filaret were skeptical of the laity's willingness to accept such changes, and the reform would be a direct test of such pessimistic views.

Parish Reform in Western Dioceses

The new statutes, applied first to five western dioceses and the next year extended to the remaining parts of that area, used the preliminary shtat prepared by the reform committee in 1840.[137] Although the committee in principle favored parish reorganization and slimmer parish staffs, in fact it did not seek radical reductions in the western dioceses, where the government sought to buttress, not weaken, the Church's role and presence. In some areas the Church needed more, not fewer, clergy: in contrast to internal dioceses, areas like Kiev had substantial vacancies in the 1830s, especially in the rank of sacristan and even in the rank of priest.[138] The new shtat, however, caused some reordering as it eliminated deacons or extra sacristans at the smaller parishes, obliging some clergy to retire or relocate. Typical of such clergy was the ponomar Simeon Levitskii, who "had not studied in school," became a deacon in 1837, and then fell prey to the parish reform ("from 1844, because of the policy of shifting clergy, he has remained idle").[139] Most of the clergy's service records, however, show no such misfortune: the reform

[136] *PSZ (2)*, 17: 15872, 15873.

[137] Ibid., 18: 17133.

[138] See below, p. 167.

[139] TsGIA UkrSSR, f. 127, op. 1011, d. 4091, ll. 19 ob.–20 (klirovye vedomosti, Chigirin district, 1860); d. 3875, l. 51 ob. (klirovye vedomosti, Kiev district, 1860).

had little impact upon clerical appointments or parish organization, aiming instead to extract more resources from existing parishes.

That goal provoked critical difficulties as the laity—especially the local elites of Catholic nobility—opposed demands for aid to the parish clergy. The western bishops at first sent glowing reports to St. Petersburg, obviously pleased with the reform's generosity, but within a year they began to discern and bewail resilient opposition to the reform. First to sound the alarm was Archbishop Vasilii (Luzhinskii) of Polotsk, who complained in November 1843 that the local landlords adamantly refused to obey the law and that local officials (especially the marshals of the nobility) had filed draft inventories that patently violated the new parish statute.[140] In 1844 the suffragan bishop of Lithuania filed a report expressing similar concern and frustration.[141] Most insistent, however, was Vasilii, who bluntly accused local authorities of malfeasance and in 1846 declared that, as a result, the statute "is not having the slightest success."[142] His report the next year was still gloomier, asserting that the reform had positively harmed the clergy's condition: "They can no longer insist upon gratuities, yet they still have not received the new forms of support [from the parish]." Vasilii added that, even after five years, authorities had compiled draft inventories only for 35 percent of the parishes and implemented these in only 2 percent. "As a result," he complained, "the clergy cannot cease to demand gratuities from parishioners," even though the statute categorically abolished these and promised to provide other—more ample, more respectable—support.[143] By 1848 the Synod, alarmed by the stymied implementation, sent an urgent request to the minister of interior, asking that he direct his provincial subordinates to implement the statute promptly and precisely.[144]

That appeal achieved little, and in January 1849 the Synod—at Protasov's suggestion—opened a formal inquiry, soliciting comments from each of the western bishops on the progress of reform and the measures needed to accelerate implementation.[145] Significantly, all the bishops of the western provinces pronounced the reform abortive, declaring that, even after seven years, it had achieved only negligible results: formal inventories existed for only a small number of parishes, and of these, only a tiny fraction had been imple-

---

[140] TsGIA SSSR, f. 796, op. 123, g. 1842, d. 1438, ll. 30–32 ob.

[141] Ibid., ll. 55–60.

[142] Ibid., l. 142.

[143] Ibid., ll. 164–68 ob.

[144] Ibid., op. 129, g. 1848, d. 226, ll. 1–3.

[145] The Synod initiated its investigation at Protasov's behest, after the latter received numerous complaints about the nonimplementation of the 1842 statute (see his 1849 memorandum to the Synod in ibid., f. 796, op. 130, g. 1849, d. 137, ll. 1–1 ob.). Even the published annual reports of the procurator, for all their reticence, admit that few inventories had been confirmed; see *IVO (1849)*, p. 36; *IVO (1850)*, p. 42.

mented in full. The bishop of Mogilev voiced despair typical of the replies: "Of the inventories compiled and confirmed by the provincial committee, not one has been implemented precisely in all respects by the district marshals of the nobility or the office of state domains."[146] The data filed by the prelate in Podolia were little better: the provincial committee had confirmed inventories for 42 percent of the parishes in the diocese but had obtained full implementation for only 14 percent of these.[147] Nonimplementation, virtually ubiquitous, had catastrophic effects upon the parish clergy, who had yet to reap the benefit of the new order but who no longer had the right to demand gratuities. Bishop Anatolii emphasized that "the clergy—who have received no gratuities since 1845—support themselves with great difficulty on their [state] salaries alone," small sums intended only to supplement, not replace, parish support.[148] In fact, some bishops tacitly ceased to enforce the prohibition on gratuities, much to the indignation of parishioners and state officials, who opposed the clergy's demands and denounced local bishops for failing to prosecute offenders.[149]

The peculiar religious and social structure of the western borderlands—Polish Catholic landlords astride a largely Orthodox peasant mass—permitted the prelates to blame bureaucrats and nobles for the problems of implementation. Archbishop Vasilii held Catholic gentry directly responsible: "The landlords of Vitebsk province, with the exception of ten Orthodox landlords, are entirely of a different confession and Catholic at that—alien to the ideas, patronage, and acts of benevolence toward Orthodox clergy."[150] Some prelates also placed considerable blame on administrative torpor, especially among the marshals of the nobility, who were chosen from that same class of landlords and who, in the words of Metropolitan Iosif of Lithuania, failed to show "adequate persistence" in implementing the reform.[151] The bishop of Volhynia agreed, writing that "the main cause of the unsuccessful implementation" of reform rests with the marshals of the nobility, who "are preoccupied with their duties, cannot personally attend to these matters," and delegate the task to unreliable aids.[152] Only one bishop conceded that peasants too were hostile to the reform, writing that during one inspection he found

---

[146]TsGIA SSSR, f. 796, op. 130, g. 1849, d. 137, l. 63 ob. (Anatolii of Mogilev to Synod).

[147]Ibid., ll. 59 ob.–60 (report of 1849).

[148]Ibid., l. 65.

[149]See, especially, the complaint from the administrator of state domains in Mogilev (ibid., op. 137, g. 1856, d. 230, l. 74 ob.).

[150]Ibid., op. 130, g. 1849, d. 137, l. 16 (Vasilii to Synod, 24.4.1849).

[151]Ibid., l. 5 ob. (Iosif to Synod, 16.3.1849); see also the replies from Anatolii (ll. 64 ob.–65) and Elpidifor (l. 60 ob.).

[152]Ibid., ll. 48–48 ob. Arsenii added that, when disputes erupted over compliance, state officials declined to assist the clergy and were "more inclined to favor the landowners over the Church and clergy."

that peasants preferred gratuities to the new obligations (which they regarded as "unfounded") and that they performed their new responsibilities poorly, if at all.[153]

To facilitate implementation, the bishops recommended several changes. One was to set specific deadlines for the preparation and implementation of inventories, thereby circumventing opponents' attempts to defer the reform indefinitely. Furthermore, the prelates urged that the state guarantee implementation: if a parish failed to comply (for example, by not providing the parsonage), the government should assume the task and then assess parishioners for the costs incurred.[154] The bishops also suggested that the government assign additional officials to handle the reform and give them precise, unequivocal instructions.[155] Archbishop Vasilii, most aggressive of all, even asked that the government collect "parish arrears," assessing the peasants for past defaulting and thereby compensating the clergy for hardships endured and resources forfeited.[156] Only one bishop, Anatolii of Mogilev, proposed to amend the parish statute. Arguing that the requirement of field labor was "not easily implemented or enforced," Anatolii recommended that it be converted into a monetary payment, collected by the state and disbursed directly to the clergy. Anatolii also proposed a formal legalization of gratuities, which were still being collected, at least until the inventories received full implementation.[157]

The investigation revealed the virtual collapse of reform and provoked new demands from Church and state authorities that local officials act promptly to implement the reform. Spurred by such stern warnings and aided by some streamlining of procedure, the provincial committees quickened the pace of implementation.[158] By 1854 in fact they had confirmed inventories for 96 percent of the parishes, and most parishes had implemented at least part of the obligations.[159] The major difficulty was the parsonage, a capital expenditure beyond the means of many parishes; other obligations, less burdensome, had much higher rates of compliance. Even by 1859, however, committees reported that only a small proportion of the parishes had fully complied (see table 4).

Precisely because implementation now reached a higher level, the reform provoked considerable discontent among parishioners. The first official

---

[153] Ibid., ll. 65–66 (Anatolii).

[154] Ibid., ll. 67 ob. (Anatolii), 17–18 (Vasilii).

[155] Ibid., ll. 17–18 (Vasilii), 60 ob. (Elpidifor), 49–50 (Arsenii).

[156] Ibid., ll. 17 ob.–18 (Vasilii).

[157] Ibid., ll. 66 ob.–68 (Anatolii).

[158] Ibid., ll. 71–71 ob. (Synodal resolution, 31.12.1842), 73 ob. (memorandum from the minister of interior, 31.5.1850).

[159] *IVO (1854)*, p. 42.

TABLE 4

Implementation of the Parish Reform in Western Dioceses, 1859

| | | Inventories | | |
| | Total | Legally | Fully | Parsonage |
Diocese	Parishes	Confirmed	Implemented	Provided
Kiev	1,178	1,174	620	95
Lithuania	453	449	111	212
Minsk	538	538	23	10
Mogilev	518	468	96	84
Podolia	1,326	1,323	308	501
Polotsk	269	256	45	73
Volhynia	1,185	1,170	140	220
Total	5,467	5,378 (98%)	1,343 (25%)	1,195 (22%)

SOURCE: TsGIA SSSR, f. 797, op. 29, otd. 3, st. 1, d. 143, ll. 1–29.

acknowledgment of popular discontent appeared in a report from the governor-general of Vil'na in 1852, who argued that the parish reform, by antagonizing the peasants, tended to weaken, not reinforce, the clergy's influence. The reform, he added, was especially burdensome for small, underpopulated parishes: "Success [in implementing the statute] is impeded exclusively by the destitution of parishioners, who in many places comprise only an insignificant number of people."[160] Later, during the Crimean War, when peasants spurned clerical leadership and even vented their wrath upon men of the cloth, some state authorities discerned still more alarming evidence of the reform's pernicious effect.[161] Although such evidence was thin and inconclusive, the implementation itself—requiring nearly fifteen years to compile inventories, not to say enforce them—suggested the peasantry's lack of interest in reform on the clergy's behalf. Altogether, the experiment confirmed Filaret's fears: the parishioners did not understand or sympathize with ecclesiastical reform from above, particularly when it only escalated their obligations and eliminated their economic leverage on the clergy.

Extension of Reform to the Interior Dioceses

The committee of 1839–1840, though focusing upon the western dioceses, had planned for its design to apply to all other areas as well, and from 1843

[160]TsGIA SSSR, f. 796, op. 130, g. 1849, d. 137, l. 100.
[161]See below, pp. 202–3.

the government gradually extended the statute to some additional dioceses.[162] As in the western dioceses, the state allotted funds for clerical subsidies, which the Synod then distributed to select dioceses, the rates varying in accordance with the economic conditions of the region.[163] In contrast to the western provinces, the form here focused less upon subsidies than upon parish reorganization, eliminating undersized parishes and trimming the size of parish staffs. The reason for the difference was no doubt political: central dioceses raised no concern for political stability, and hence authorities could be much more rigorous in eliminating parishes and, especially, clerical positions. Perhaps because the political stakes were lower, authorities also failed to establish some of the benefits—parsonages, free field labor, and free fuel— imposed in the western dioceses. Then, too, state finances allowed only a gradual extension, a few dioceses each year, reaching less than half the dioceses by Nicholas's death in 1855. Still, the replacement of gratuities with salaries promised a fundamental change in the clerical economy.[164]

To facilitate later extension of the reform, the Synod in 1845 ordered all dioceses to prepare draft shtaty, much as the committee had earlier done for the western dioceses. The goal here was simple: once the government granted new funds, the Synod could act promptly to assign them and to confirm the new parish shtaty. Compilation of such shtaty, however, was a prodigious task. The bishop and consistory had to compile elaborate parish-by-parish lists and decide which parishes to retain or merge, how many clerics they required, and what resources they needed to become economically viable.[165] In contrast to the 1829 reform, authorities now attempted to reduce primarily the size of parish staffs, not the number of parishes. In some dioceses the reductions were immense; in Riazan, for example, the draft shtat projected the elimination of 976 clerical positions, nearly one-quarter of all positions in the diocese.[166] Significantly, however, the Church made reductions not uniformally across all ranks but primarily in the lesser posts of deacon and sacristan. Thus, of all the abolished positions in Riazan diocese, only 12 percent affected priests, the overwhelming majority being in the rank of deacon (42 percent) and sacristan (46 percent).[167] The goal was to minimize

---

[162] For a summary of the extension to other dioceses, see N. Grigorovich, *Obzor obshchikh zakonopolozhenii o soderzhanii pravoslavnogo prikhodskogo dukhovenstva v Rossii so vremeni vvedeniia shtatov po dukhovnomu vedomstvu 1764–1863* (St. Petersburg, 1867).

[163] For a summary of the varying rates, see ibid., pril. IV.

[164] TsGIA SSSR, f. 796, op. 126, g. 1845, d. 117, ll. 22 ob.–23.

[165] Ibid., f. 804, op. 1, r. 3, d. 7, l. 2 (report of 14.4.1845).

[166] The size of reductions varied greatly, from 1,507 in Kostroma to a more modest 797 in Tver (ibid., f. 796, op. 127, g. 1846, d. 1253).

[167] Likewise, few priests' positions were eliminated in Kostroma (where they constituted 17 percent of the abolished positions), Iaroslavl (11 percent), Kaluga (10 percent), Viatka (10 percent), and Tver (11 percent); see ibid., ll. 74–85, 489–89 ob., 491–92 ob., 518–19 ob., 521–21 ob.

the social impact of the reform, keeping most priests and most parishes. That policy derived from several interlocking ideas: the priority of the priest, vital for sacraments; the priest's practical role as teacher, paramedic, and agronomist; and fear of parish opposition, especially to the elimination of churches. Authorities thus deemed the priest indispensable, but the deacon and sacristan expendable.

Such massive reductions, directed against the clergy but for its own benefit (that is, for those who remained), raised serious questions among ranking prelates, long accustomed to their role as paternalistic protector of diocesan clergy. Especially in the central dioceses, with their superabundance of clergy and candidates, the tight shtat guaranteed much hardship for parish clergy. As the bishop of Vladimir wrote when filing his draft registry, "I cannot be silent about the fact that, with the elimination of many positions, it will be extremely difficult for diocesan authorities to find places for those clergy whose positions are abolished (a total of 1,299 individuals) and for those seminarians now entering diocesan service (a total exceeding 500 persons)."[168] Even more acerbic were the comments of Metropolitan Filaret, whose correspondence was laced with criticism of the plans to reduce clergy and parishes.[169] To Archbishop Grigorii he wrote, "The shtaty for clergy are causing difficulties and will continue to do so; as it is, there are now many people without positions and support—what will become of them when the shtat is reduced?" Declaring that the new schedule of one priest and one sacristan per parish makes "it impossible to perform church services" in strict accordance with canon law, Filaret darkly hinted that "I do not think I can persuade myself to submit such a shtat."[170] To another prelate Filaret wrote that "the normal shtat for white clergy will magnify poverty. Of course it must be God's judgment on us—with a surplus of people, the number of positions is reduced."[171] Filaret even praised one bishop for procrastination: "You do well not to rush with the publication of the reduced shtat for rural clergy, so as not to increase rumors and, insofar as possible, to act without undue publicity in implementation."[172] All this, he wrote, is "a visitation for our sins."[173]

Notwithstanding the distress and grumbling, in 1846 the Synod went beyond the call for draft shtaty and ordered bishops to begin gradual application of the shtaty, even before formal confirmation. The purpose was to

---

[168] Ibid., f. 804, op. 1, r. 3, d. 7, l. 2. See also "Pis'ma preosv. Parfeniia," *Vladimirskie eparkhial'nye vedomosti* [hereafter *Vladimirskie EV*], 1880, no. 20: 593; N. Barsov, ed., "Pis'ma Gavriila, arkhiepiskopa riazanskogo," *KhCh*, 1884, tom 1: 640 (letter of 1846 to Innokentii).

[169] "Dva pis'ma blazh. pamiati sviatitelia Filareta," *Str.*, 1873, no. 1, otd. 1: 12; Filaret, *Pis'ma k Gavriilu*, p. 69.

[170] "Materialy dlia istorii russkoi tserkvi," *ChOLDP*, 1877, no. 11, otd. 3: 140–41.

[171] "Pis'ma mitr. mosk. Filareta," ibid., 1870, kn. 13: 35.

[172] "Materialy dlia biografii Filareta," ibid., 1870, kn. 11: 32.

[173] Ibid., p. 35.

cushion the shock of subsequent implementation by reducing the number who would be displaced once the shtat became official. The Synod explained that "in many rural churches the present number of clergy exceeds the actual needs of the parishes" and warned that this surplus would greatly impede subsequent implementation. It therefore ordered bishops "to bear these [draft] shtaty in mind and to be concerned [about this matter] before-hand, gradually using convenient opportunities to adjust the rural clergy to fit this [shtat], through the transfer of excess persons to vacant positions (or those most likely to become vacant)." At the same time, it cautioned prelates to "be completely just and unbiased" in applying the new directive.[174]

That directive, intended to facilitate implementation, inadvertently caused an uproar. Some bishops believed that the Synod demanded full-scale application of the draft shtaty, notwithstanding the qualifications about "caution." Hence they began to institute rigorous implementation, ordering surplus clergy to relocate and refusing to fill vacancies declared supernumerary under the draft shtat. To quell the furor, in November 1846 the Synod issued a supplementary decree, admonishing bishops to exercise more "caution." It also criticized prelates who made the shtat public, stressing that its earlier decrees had specifically said that "these drafts have only been reviewed [by central authorities] and thus have yet to receive confirmation." It was thus patently wrong to publicize the draft shtaty, for "it may be necessary to make some changes [in them] upon further examination of local circumstances, either by enlarging or reducing the number of clergy (according to conditions in the parishes)." The Synod reproved the bishops for lack of caution, reiterating that "in this matter the Synod demands not haste, but measures thought out with due caution and attention to the needs of the clergy and parishes." It directed prelates to leave surplus clergy at their present positions ("until there is the possibility of transferring them to permanent positions conveniently and without harm") and admonished the bishops to exercise "absolute fairness and dispassion" in arranging such transfers, leaving at each church "those people who have acquired the veneration and love of the parishioners, who have not been subject to [judicial] investigation, who have large families, and who have a well-ordered household." In short, the Synod beat a hasty retreat from strict application and tried to blame over-zealous and insensitive bishops for the uproar.[175] The ink on this resolution was barely dry before the Synod received a belated report from distant Simbirsk, where the bishop proudly recounted the stern measures he had taken to implement the first Synodal decree.[176] The Synod did not forgo the opportunity to reprove the bishop. It ordered him to "exercise complete pastoral

---

[174]TsGIA SSSR, f. 796, op. 127, g. 1846, d. 1253, l. 3 (resolution of 30.9.1846).
[175]Ibid., ll. 9–9 ob.
[176]Ibid., ll. 21–23 (Feodotii's report of 31.10.1846).

concern for a gradual, fair implementation" and flatly outlawed his plans for a lottery to determine which clergy had to relocate, declaring that such "a decree could only sow alarm and dissatisfaction among the clergy."[177]

The Synod's second decree worked: diocesan authorities still endeavored to apply the shtaty, but in a more cautious manner. In the first half of 1847, for example, authorities in Ekaterinoslav eliminated 11 percent of the declared redundancies, in Riazan 6 percent, in Orel 0.7 percent, and in Tver 0.9 percent—hardly impressive results.[178] Characteristically, one prelate even petitioned the Synod to increase his shtat, not reduce clergy as the original draft proposed.[179] Archbishop Georgii of Tobol'sk explained that the reform worked special hardships in his Siberian diocese, where "the parishes are underpopulated but dispersed across great territories, making it difficult for the priest to administer rites in parishioners' homes and perform mass." But his other complaints were common to all bishops—the need to appoint seminary graduates, the opposition by parishioners, and the hardships wrought by forcible relocation: "Many clergy, having lived in one place for a number of years, have set up housekeeping and find it difficult and extremely ruinous to move, since they must sell all their housewares and property (acquired at great labor and expense) for a mere pittance."[180] The bishops also emphasized the hardships inflicted upon clerical families. If the shtat abolished a position claimed by a family, a kinsman could not hold the post and hence the family forfeited its claim and its hopes for support.[181] The reform also excited intraclerical conflict, as clergy connived to see that their colleagues, not they, became supernumerary and had to relocate.[182] In the face of such opposition, the Synod became complaisant, tolerating deviation from the shtat when exigency and parish wish required.[183]

Nevertheless, the shtat gradually took its toll, leading to the elimination of scores, even hundreds, of clerical positions in some dioceses. Of the positions declared redundant by draft shtaty, in 1849 authorities in Iaroslavl had eliminated 19 percent, Viatka 17 percent, and Tver 15 percent—a substantial increase over the first two years of implementation.[184] Though more cautious,

[177] Ibid., ll. 24–25 ob.

[178] Ibid., ll. 51–55, 74–85 ob., 164.

[179] Ibid., ll. 112–13 (Perm).

[180] Ibid., ll. 116–17 (Georgii to Synod, 27.11.1857).

[181] Ibid., ll. 259–62 (Evlampii to Synod, 31.2.1848).

[182] G. Khitrov, *Istoriko-statisticheskoe opisanie Tambovskoi eparkhii* (Tambov, 1861), pp. 227–29.

[183] For instances of revision of the shtat, see the files from the late 1840s in TsGIA SSSR, f. 796—for example, those from 1849 for Tver, Iaroslavl, Penza, Minsk, and Vladimir dioceses (op. 130, g. 1849, dd. 1586, 1587, 1575, 375, and 1469). Some requests, however, were rejected; for instance, see the case of a parish in Tambov diocese (ibid., d. 107).

[184] Ibid., op. 132, g. 1851, d. 2357.

that implementation still provoked protests from clergy and warnings from the Synod: "In some dioceses, for which draft shtaty have been prepared, more or less coercive measures to redistribute the clergy (to accord with the shtat) are again being undertaken." The Synod complained that, "among other things, clergy who hold positions subject to later elimination are obliged to sign statements that they will find a regular position within a specified period of time. . . . The performance of this would be difficult under any circumstances, but it is [now] almost impossible, given the reductions in regular positions." It therefore ruled that "these and similar measures impose an extraordinary hardship upon the clergy, something that is absolutely contradictory to the goal and decrees of the Synod."[185]

Although bishops now eschewed open coercion, they continued to apply the shtat, gradually producing a steady attrition in the number of registered positions. Thus by 1852 the elimination of redundant clergy had reached sizeable proportions in some dioceses (for example, 71 percent in Vladimir), more modest dimensions in others (21 percent in Tver, 33 percent in Riazan).[186] Though the tempo had slowed, the reform nevertheless cut a broad swath through the ranks of village clergy, evoking dissatisfaction among laity, priests, and bishops.[187] Although bishops had little choice but to enforce the shtat (mainly by leaving vacant the positions of retiring or deceased clergy), many found the reform positively harmful. The bishop of Arkhangel'sk, for example, complained that "even before the shtat was issued, Arkhangel'sk diocese—given its vast territorial size—had too few churches." But now, he complained, one-third of those churches were closed, with catastrophic results: "The Old Belief has thus grown significantly—in place of the priest, schismatic teachers appear in the village and gradually win over the simple folk, who later begin to observe rites in the Old Belief fashion."[188] The bishop of Vladimir, who had been unusually energetic in applying the reform (having eliminated over 900 clerical positions), also decried a cooling in popular piety: "Because of the reduction in clergy (in accordance with the draft shtat), religious services at many rural churches have begun to be performed less frequently and less reverently, a fact that has unfavorably affected the religious sensibilities of parishioners."[189] Although some bishops

---

[185] Ibid., op. 127, g. 1846, d. 1253, ll. 168–168 ob.

[186] Ibid., op. 133, g. 1852, d. 237, ll. 80 ob. (Vladimir), 90 ob. (Tver), 113 ob. (Riazan).

[187] When parishioners protested to the Synod, it proved unsympathetic, resolving to reestablish parishes or positions only "when [the parishioners] have agreed to establish (in a written contract) adequate funding for [the clergy's] support" (ibid., op. 130, g. 1849, d. 425, l. 3 [Tver]). When parishioners provided such support, the Synod approved their petition; see the Vladimir case in 1849 (ibid., d. 1469).

[188] Ibid., op. 132, g. 1851, d. 2357, ll. 15 ob.–16.

[189] Ibid., ll. 79 ob.–80. The bishop of Olonets complained in 1851 that state subsidies had caused the clergy to shirk their duties, thereby eroding the Church's influence (OR GPB, f. 573, op. 1, k. 5, d. 66, l. 260).

professed belief that the new shtaty would ultimately improve the clergy's material condition, they also granted that the shtaty produced short-run hardship for many clergy and dangerously weakened the parish infrastructure of the Church.[190]

Conclusion

The Nikolaevan reforms clearly failed to resolve the problems of the clerical economy. At best, they yielded a slight amelioration for some clergy in the western dioceses, primarily in those parishes where the 1842 statute achieved fuller implementation. Yet, as we have seen, implementation was most often sporadic, forcing clergy to rely upon traditional emoluments and agriculture for their livelihood. Reform was still less effective in the interior dioceses. Though the state alloted subsidies to about two-fifths of the parishes by 1855, these funds were no substitute for the emoluments they ostensibly replaced. And everywhere the reforms worked great hardships upon the clergy, for the reductions in registered positions entailed forcible relocation or, at least, the loss of a family-controlled position. Nor was the Nikolaevan system for subsidies well conceived: the reform divided parishes into seven classes, with salaries proportionate to the population, but made no allowance for the parishioners' status and prosperity. Hence small parishes with a few wealthy parishioners yielded greater income *before* the reform than afterwards—to the understandable indignation of the clergy.

What went wrong? If Nikolaevan reformism often failed to reach the stage of formal statutes, such was not the case here: the regime did promulgate reforms, but they failed to work. Why? The most obvious reason is the magnitude of the problem: given the size of the clergy and the paucity of state resources, central authorities could do no more than provide tiny subsidies for selected areas. Yet that "gradual improvement," as bishops and priests concurred, was not sufficient to ameliorate the clergy's condition, much less replace the unpopular emoluments. Most perverse of all, the subsidies did not even supplement (much less replace) the emoluments, for parishioners cited the subsidies as grounds for reducing their emoluments, thereby leaving the clergy with less income than before.[191] The ineffectiveness of partial support suggests, more broadly, the peculiar difficulty of "gradual" reform in the Russian parish: if the Anglican Church could use Queen Anne's Bounty to supplement the fixed resources of poorer livings,

---

[190]See, for example, comments in the annual reports for 1850 from bishops in Nizhnii Novgorod, Riazan, Pskov, Saratov, Kursk, and Khar'kov (TsGIA SSSR, f. 796, op. 132, g. 1851, d. 2357, ll. 185 ob.–86, 390, 704, 313, 128–28 ob., 582–89 ob.).

[191]See, for example, the complaint by clergy in Chigirin district, Kiev diocese, in their "opinion" sent to a reform commission in 1863 (ibid., f. 804, op. 1, r. 3, d. 155, l. 141 ob.).

the Russian Church had difficulty not only identifying but even aiding "poor parishes."

Nor did authoritarian reform from above—accompanied by imperious demands that parishioners assume new responsibilities—function well, as the dismal record of the western dioceses suggest. The device employed here—parish inventories with precise obligations—was typical of Nikolaevan reformism: it revealed the belief in reform through central regulation and bore a striking resemblance to parallel attempts at serf reform in the western provinces (which used similar inventories to fix landlord-serf relations). Equally characteristic of Nikolaevan rule was the treatment of local communities: authorities sought enhanced support not by regenerating the parish or seeking local initiative (as the Great Reforms would do), but simply by commanding the laity to assume new obligations, some of which (like parsonages) were quite onerous. As the experience in the western dioceses revealed, that strategy of reform was ineffectual, difficult to implement, and even prone to cause anticlerical sentiments among parishioners.

Almost inevitably, authorities turned to another approach, seeking not to find new resources but to cut costs through a reduction in the numbers of parishes and clergy. One method was to consolidate parishes into larger units, thereby increasing the ratio of parishioners to clergy. But that juggling raised serious difficulties—opposition from laymen, geographical impediments, threats from Old Believers, and substantial hardships for redundant clergy. Bad experiences with reorganization, in fact, left most prelates disenchanted: whereas most bishops favored modest reductions in 1826–1827, few did so in later years. Nevertheless, the average size of parishes increased sharply during Nicholas's reign, continuing a process begun with Peter and reflecting as well a general pattern throughout contemporary Europe (see table 5). But this increased size was achieved primarily through sheer demographic growth, not parish reorganization, and each diocese in fact still had a substantial number of small, undersized parishes.[192]

Given the difficulties of parish consolidation, in the 1840s authorities for the first time began to tamper with the eighteenth-century shtat. As a result, the number of registered positions declined some 4 percent in the empire between 1830 and 1860 (table 6). Although a few dioceses (in outlying areas) showed an increase in clergy, most dioceses recorded substantial reductions—for example, 12 percent in Tver and 14 percent in Vladimir. Perhaps most important, the new shtat aimed not only to reduce clergy but also to

---

[192]Kiev district, for example, increased the average size of its parishes by 30 percent between 1830 and 1860. Nevertheless, the district still had a substantial number of parishes with less than 100 households; their number declined from 45 to 28 percent of all parishes in the area (TsGIA UkrSSR, f. 127, op. 1009, dd. 275–76; op. 1011, dd. 1210, 1275, 1331, 1392, 1429, 1490, 1533).

TABLE 5

Increase in Parishioner-Clergy Ratios in Russia and Europe
(First Half of the Nineteenth Century)

Church and Area	Before Mid-Century		Mid-Century	
	Ratio	(Year)	Ratio	(Year)
Catholic				
Augsburg	295	(1816)	641	(1885)
France	303	(1790)	752	(1848)
Protestant				
Denmark	775	(1800)	1,279	(1855)
England	1,101	(1841)	1,054	(1861)
Finland	1,114	(1800)	1,801	(1860)
Norway	1,884	(1800)	3,164	(1855)
Prussia	1,050	(1822)	1,729	(1847)
Sweden	684	(1800)	1,278	(1860)
Orthodox				
Russia				
(total clergy)	316	(1824)	457	(1860)
(priests only)	1,008	(1824)	1,371	(1860)

SOURCES: Bigler, *Politics of German Protestantism*, pp. 55–56; Chadwick, *The Victorian Church*, 2: 244; Hartmann, "Geistlichen der Diözese Augsburg," p. 27; *IVO (1861)*, prilozhenie; Jedin, *Handbuch*, 6(1): 353; Mannsåker, *Det norske presteskapet*, p. 76; Merkel, "Studien," p. 178; Tacket and Langlois, "Ecclesiastical Structures," pp. 356–57; TsGIA SSSR, f. 797, op. 96, d. 5, ll. 1 ob.–2.

NOTE: Parishioners include all formal church members, not the total population of a country. Clergy include full-time clerics who have been formally installed.

structure its components, concentrating reductions in the less vital ranks of deacon and sacristan.[193] To cite one concrete example, the shtat for Kiev district in 1830–1860 increased the number of priests' positions from 95 to 113 but eliminated many positions for deacons (declining from 38 to 9) and sacristans (reduced from 188 to 172).[194] Such changes reveal that it was immeasurably easier to regulate and change the service estate than to restructure parishes and their economies. The shtat revisions, as we shall see, also precipitated far-reaching changes in social policies toward Church

[193]TsGIA SSSR, f. 796, op. 112, g. 1831, d. 360/b, ll. 3–8; *IVO (1861)*, pril.
[194]TsGIA UkrSSR, f. 127, op. 1009, dd. 275–76; op. 1011, dd. 1210, 1275, 1331, 1392, 1429, 1490, 1533.

TABLE 6

Changes in Registered Positions (Shtat),
1830–1860

Rank	1830	1860	Percent Change
Priest	34,479	37,588	+ 9.0%
Deacon	17,375	12,697	− 26.9%
Sacristan	69,284	66,736	− 3.7%
All	121,138	117,021	− 3.4%

SOURCES: TsGIA SSSR, f. 796, op. 112, g. 1831, d. 360/b, ll. 3–8; *IVO (1861)*, prilozhenie.

schools and the clerical estate, as authorities were driven to relieve the surplus of youths unneeded by the contracting system of service.

Nikolaevan reform had larger implications for subsequent reform. Most directly, it provided concrete experience in reform, which revealed not only the extraordinary complexity of religious change but also the contumacy and residual power of parishioners. Though recent research has tended to suggest the positive effects of Nikolaevan reformism, these experiments also had their negative legacy: they suggested the discouraging complexity of reform, revealed society's apparent indifference to the parish question, and provoked distrust between ranking authorities in the Church and state. More important, for all its presumed secrecy, Nikolaevan reform stirred aspirations in the parish clergy, for state aid, though modest, gave proof of imperial concern and the state's willingness to address the clerical question. The statute of 1842 was less important as law than as precedent, fueling clerical aspirations for fuller implementation and larger subsidies. At the same time, the secrecy of the Nikolaevan reform tended to exacerbate relations between bishops and white clergy: although it was the state that emasculated reform plans in 1829 and 1842, although most bishops favored tithes and salaries over emoluments, some priests believed that the episcopate, not the state, had sabotaged Nicholas's reforms.[195] Thus secret, gradual reform, intended to ensure tranquillity and to avoid unrealizable expectations, had just the contrary effect, unleashing aspirations and hostilities that would come to the fore in the new, more open era of the Great Reforms.

[195] Most notably, see Belliustin, *Opisanie*, pp. 69–70. Given the secrecy of Nikolaevan reformism, such misperception was not surprising; even much later accounts, based upon legislative sources, provide no awareness of the Synod's central role in the 1829 reform. See I. Krechetovich, "Mery k uluchsheniiu sostoianiia dukhovenstva v tsarstvovanie Imperatora Nikolaia I-ogo," *VR*, 1900, tom 1, ch. 1: 421–38.

When Bishop Filofei of Tver examined the service files of Kaliazin district in 1860, he found a picture that had changed but little since his predecessor looked through reports from that district thirty years earlier. Although parishes had increased substantially in size since 1830 (growing by 24 percent), they remained just as diverse in composition and resources. At one end of the spectrum was the cathedral in Kaliazin, which served 5,418 parishioners and yielded some three thousand rubles in emoluments. The bishop still found a number of prosperous churches in the countryside, as in the village Voskresenskoe, encompassing nearly 3,000 parishioners and yielding over eight hundred rubles in emoluments. But, as before, the files located most parishes at the other end of the scale. Typical was Arkhangel'skoe, providing a mere seventy rubles for its three clergymen and their five dependents.[196] Like the priest in N. A. Nekrasov's poem "Who Lives Well in Russia?" most clergy in Kaliazin—and elsewhere in Russia—could truthfully exclaim that "our path is a difficult one."[197]

[196]GA Kalininskoi obl., f. 160, op. 1, d. 16298 (klirovye vedomosti, 1860).

[197]N. A. Nekrasov, *Sochineniia v trekh tomakh*, 3 vols. (Moscow, 1959), 3: 83–94 (Glava I: "Pop").

CHAPTER 3

The Seminary:
Training for the Priesthood
in Russia

"That cad, that pig, that seminarian!"

With this burst of epithets a radical journalist not only anathematized his nemesis, the censor, but also gave vent to a widespread prejudice of his day—hostility toward the seminarian.[1] Nobles had long looked with disfavor upon clerical offspring, resentful of the *parvenus* who frequently penetrated the lower reaches of the civil service.[2] To that was added a cultural moment, the consequence of a special education that gave the seminarian a distinct mien and cast of thought. Cultural tension surfaced in the writings of enlightened noblemen like I. S. Turgenev, who inveighed against "vulgar seminarian principles" and berated those "with soiled collars" who seek "to wipe poetry, fine arts, and all aesthetic pleasures from the face of the earth."[3] With good reason, a "plebeian" writer later wrote that seminarians "are shy in front of lay society, are afraid to talk, knowing that secular society regards the seminarian as a drunken, downtrodden breed."[4]

[1] Belinskii, whose grandfather was a deacon and whose father was very likely once a seminarian, was speaking of A. V. Nikitenko, a famous censor of serf origin (who, of course, never attended a seminary). V. G. Belinskii, *Selected Philosophical Works* (Moscow, 1948), p. 152.

[2] For typical evidence of such hostility, see "Zapiski M. P. Veselovskogo," OR GPB, f. 550 (Osnovnoe sobranie rukopisnykh knig), F.IV, d. 861, l. 385 ob.

[3] A. Ia. Panaeva, *Vospominaniia* (Moscow, 1972), pp. 263–64. Turgenev also put such sentiments into his writings, most notably, *Fathers and Sons*, where the aristocratic uncle (Pavel) contemptuously refers to his antagonist as "a seminary rat" (*Fathers and Sons*, trans. Ralph Matlaw [New York, 1966], p. 121).

[4] F. M. Reshetnikov, "Stavlennik," *Izbrannye proizvedeniia*, 2 vols. (Moscow, 1956), 1: 144.

Such sentiments hardened in the 1860s, partly because of the shocking exposés about the *bursak* (seminarian),[5] partly because of the prominence of some ex-seminarians in the radical movement.[6] Even when compared with the harsh conditions in secular schools, the prereform seminary loomed as a terrifying netherworld—rent by unbelievable poverty and filth, bizarre and ill-taught curriculum, brutal and venal administrators.

This chapter will examine the underlying reasons for that "crisis in the seminary" and the regime's attempts to reconstruct the schools into more effective institutions for training good clergy. The overarching task is to discern the schools' essential weaknesses, which ultimately impelled the state to reconsider the effect of its social policies on the clerical estate.

The Reforms of 1808–1814

The Church operated virtually no institutions of formal education in medieval Russia and only began to construct an educational system in the reign of Peter the Great, in the first quarter of the eighteenth century.[7] At first few in number and limited to a primitive curriculum, by the mid-eighteenth century the seminaries had developed into stable institutions with growing enrollments and a full course of study, from Latin grammar to theology. The development in the late eighteenth century was still more impressive, with sharp increases in student enrollment (from four thousand pupils in the 1760s to twenty thousand by the end of the century) and in the number of schools and seminaries.[8] By the early nineteenth century formal education had become a primary determinant in clerical careers, providing a passkey to the best positions and best parishes, obliging more and more

---

[5]The first exposé was Belliustin's *Opisanie* in 1858, followed by the most famous *bursak* work of all, N. G. Pomialovskii's *Ocherki bursy* (translated by Alfred R. Kuhn as N. G. Pomyalovsky, *Seminary Sketches* [Ithaca, 1973]).

[6]See below, pp. 237–38, 359–61.

[7]On eighteenth-century schools, see Freeze, *Russian Levites*, chap. 4, and the literature cited therein. For the first half of the nineteenth century the published literature is immense, constituting one of the few areas of serious scholarship; besides mountains of memoirs and seminary histories, the two most substantial general accounts are K. Diakonov, *Dukhovnye shkoly v tsarstvovanie Nikolaia I-go.* (Sergiev-Posad, 1907), and B. V. Titlinov, *Dukhovnaia shkola v Rossii v XIX st.*, 2 vols. (Vil'na, 1908–09), which, despite its title, actually reaches only into the sixties. Though Western scholarship on education generally ignores Church schools, some useful material is to be gleaned from the following: Smolitsch, *Geschichte*, pp. 538–690; C. B. Becker, "The Church School in Tsarist Social and Educational Policy from Peter to the Great Reforms" (Ph.D. diss., Harvard University, 1964), pp. 72–199; and D. R. Clayton, "Parish or Publish: The Kiev Ecclesiastical Academy, 1819–69" (Ph.D. diss., University of Minnesota, 1978).

[8]Freeze, *Russian Levites*, p. 88.

youths not only to attend the seminary but also to complete its full course of study.

Yet, however impressive the statistics, the eighteenth-century schools suffered from major deficiencies, some present from the schools' inception, others due to the rapidity of their growth. At the root of most problems was financial weakness: the seminaries' resources were inadequate from the outset, and subsequent funding failed to keep pace with the steady growth. The economic problem became especially acute after 1765, when Catherine forbade the Church to levy taxes on parish clergy and shackled the seminary to a small state budget. Unchanged until the end of the century, the budget was no match for spiraling enrollments and runaway inflation. As a reform committee observed in 1808, "it is impossible to support the school building, the teachers, a library, teaching aids, and up to one thousand pupils on a budget of 8,000 rubles (the maximum sum allotted to any seminary)."[9] Institutional penury meant undernourished pupils, unqualified teachers, minuscule libraries, dilapidated and overcrowded buildings—all severely impeding the educational process.

The schools' curriculum also had major shortcomings. A curriculum based on classical Latin studies, which were already losing favor in European grammar schools, seemed particularly anomalous in Russia, where the clergy served the Eastern Church and drew upon very different traditions. More important, it was irrelevant to the more rudimentary needs of Russia. Given the religious ignorance of the folk and the low cultural level of parish clergy, it was a strange priority to pursue an elitist Latin curriculum and to neglect the more essential subjects. That shortcoming was especially serious in a system with high attrition rates: most students left the school after the first few years, having memorized a smattering of Latin words and phrases but without having studied more pertinent subjects like theology. Moreover, eighteenth-century Church schools borrowed not only the Western curriculum but also its scholasticism—in theory, a method for training the mind, but in practice often no more than a sterile preoccupation with forms and disregard for content. For example, pupils in literature actually read little literature and spent most of their time memorizing "definitions" and "forms." Pedagogy also relied heavily upon rote memorization; although from the 1760s authorities periodically demanded that teachers seek comprehension, not recitation, the old pedagogy proved amazingly hardy, persisting well into the next century. This curriculum, to be sure, was not without merit. It produced some major scholars and laid a prestigious mantle of erudition on all who acquired the classical heritage. The problem was that so few did master this

---

[9] *Opis' dokumentov i del, khraniashchikhsia v arkhive Sv. Pravitel'stvuiushchego Sinoda. Dela Komissii dukhovnykh uchilishch* (St. Petersburg, 1910), p. 6.

curriculum: most pupils abandoned the seminary in the lower classes, and for the graduates that curriculum bore little relevance to the needs of a rural priest.[10]

The schools also suffered from maladministration. In effect, the Church did not really possess an educational system, merely a congeries of independent schools, each existing under the personal patronage and supervision of a diocesan bishop. Although personalized administration was fruitful if the bishop was erudite and industrious, most prelates were too busy to exercise more than ceremonial supervision and left the schools to the diffident control of the consistory. Some prelates, moreover, were simply unfit to manage a seminary. As one reform-minded bishop wrote in 1805, "many diocesan [hierarchs] do not see to it that their schools are successful, dispose of funds arbitrarily, and many do not have the slightest idea whether the people they appoint as instructors are worthy."[11] More important, the seminaries did not constitute a system in intellectual terms: all, whether labeled seminary or academy, had roughly the same curriculum, differing only in standards and material conditions. As a result, the schools failed to meet the diverse, specialized needs of the Church—the kind of education specifically required by sacristans, priests, or scholars.

The Church finally attempted to restructure its schools in the early nineteenth century, partly in response to long-recognized problems, partly in an attempt to emulate parallel reforms in secular schools.[12] The suffragan bishop of St. Petersburg, Evgenii, posed the question of reform in 1803 and the following year obtained the emperor's permission to form a special committee on seminary reform. The Synod nominally designated the metropolitan of St. Petersburg to draft a reform proposal (after consultation with the metropolitans of Moscow and Kiev), but in fact it was Evgenii who wrote the preliminary proposal in 1805.[13] His was a moderate project, aiming primarily to centralize administration, not to make radical changes in curriculum or finance. Yet that very centralization provoked sharp criticism from diocesan bishops, who (in Evgenii's words) resented the prospect that "outsiders"

---

[10] In 1808 nearly a quarter of the students proved unfit for transfer to the reformed schools, showing little evidence of their previous studies. See Titlinov, *Dukhovnaia shkola*, 1: 13–14; N. Malitskii, *Istoriia Vladimirskoi dukhovnoi seminarii* [hereafter Malitskii, *IVDS*], 3 vols. (Moscow, 1900–02), 2: 8.

[11] "Pis'ma mitr. Evgeniia," *RA*, 1870, no. 4/5: 842.

[12] Dissatisfaction with the schools was longstanding; as early as 1762 Catherine the Great, for example, complained that "the diocesan schools have very few worthy and reliable students, a poor course of study, and inadequate support for the students" (*Polnoe sobranie postanovlenii i rasporiazhenii po vedomstvu pravoslavnogo ispovedaniia. Tsarstvovanie Imp. Ekateriny Alekseevy*, 3 vols. [St. Petersburg, 1910–15], 1: 76).

[13] See N. I. Poletaev, "K istorii dukhovno-uchebnoi reformy 1808–14 gg.," *Str.*, 1889, no. 8: 514–41; no. 9: 54–79.

would meddle in the affairs of "their" seminaries.[14] Their opposition succeeded in burying Evgenii's plan, but in November 1807 the chief procurator, Golitsyn, persuaded the emperor to convoke a new committee to redesign the Church's schools.[15] Composed of leading state and Church officials,[16]
the "committee for the improvement of ecclesiastical schools" had a broad
charge not only to reconstruct the schools but also to reconsider the lot of
seminary graduates entering into parish service.

Seeking first to define the guiding principles of reform, the committee
concluded that the specific goal of ecclesiastical schools was to train candidates for the clergy.[17] That purpose, argued the committee, required a thorough transformation of the existing schools. One task was to reform curriculum—to eradicate scholasticism, to reduce the emphasis on Latin, to
emphasize subjects more vital to the Orthodox Church (such as theology,
Greek, and church history). The committee proposed to add some new secular subjects—modern languages, expanded mathematics, geography and
secular history—but its primary aim was to break with the traditional gram-
mar-school curriculum and to provide professional training for future priests.
Moreover, the committee recognized the need for a *system* of learning, an
integrated, hierarchical program of study leading from an elementary school
to advanced studies in elite academies.

The result of the committee's investigations was its plan for a four-tiered
system: township schools (*prikhodskie uchilishcha*), district schools (*uezdnye
uchilishcha*), seminaries (*seminarii*), and academies (*akademii*). That educational structure also provided the skeleton of administration: each academy
was to oversee the seminaries and lower schools, with a central Commission
of Ecclesiastical Schools (*Komissiia dukhovnykh uchilishch*) in St. Petersburg
to govern this whole order. The committee also gave considerable autonomy
to the academy and seminary; although the chief official (the rector) was still
appointed, the reform assigned substantial authority to special faculty conferences. Complex and ambitious, the new system required an immense budget—1.7 million rubles per annum, to be financed by a capital endowment
from the sale of church candles and a state subsidy.[18] Alexander approved
the reform in 1808, and, after experimental application in St. Petersburg,
authorities promulgated a final set of statutes in 1814 that provided the basic
structure of ecclesiastical education until the late 1860s.[19]

[14]"Pis'ma mitr. Evgeniia," *RA*, 1870, no 4/5: 842.

[15]*Opis' dokumentov i del*, pp. 1–7.

[16]For the committee's composition, see Titlinov, *Dukhovnaia shkola*, 1: 23.

[17]*Opis' dokumentov i del*, pp. 1–2, 6–7.

[18]For an able summary of the committee's complicated financial plans, see Titlinov,
Dukhovnaia shkola, 1: 25–27.

[19]*PSZ (1)*, 30: 23122; 32:25673, 25674, 25676, 25678/a. For one detailed case of implementation, see "Svedeniia o preobrazovanii Viatskoi seminarii v 1818 g.," *Viatskie eparkhial'nye
vedomosti* [hereafter *Viatskie EV*], 1868, nos. 20, 23.

Social Policy

The educational reform in 1814 made many significant changes in Church education, but it left intact the earlier social policy: the schools served exclusively the clergy's children. The clergy's sons were required to study only in Church schools, thus ensuring an ample supply of recruits in the future. Though the clergy at first evaded this educational requirement (fathers fearing the expense, sons dreading the schools' harsh regime), by the late eighteenth century most clergy began to comply. As a result, ecclesiastical schools had no need—or even space—for outsiders and thereby constituted an isolated soslovie institution, inaccessible to youths from other social groups.[20] The reform of 1808–1814, in fact, formalized the soslovie character of the school, explicitly ordering the clergy to enroll their sons in Church schools on pain of expulsion into the poll-tax population. Although the statutes of 1814 did not prohibit the matriculation of outsiders, they made no provision for their admission, fiscally or otherwise. Tacitly and uncritically, the Commission of Ecclesiastical Schools accepted this policy of social exclusiveness and sought only to make the Church's schools serve the Church and clergy more efficiently.[21]

At every level, in every school exclusiveness thus remained firmly entrenched, not merely in law, but also in social reality. Although there were some exceptions, primarily in the western provinces and Siberia, only in rare cases and under special circumstances did outsiders find a small place in the seminary. For example, the seminary in St. Petersburg, encircled by a city of bureaucrats, occasionally admitted the son of a local official, but did so rarely and only as a favor to special influence.[22] Somewhat different circumstances obtained in outlying areas, where clerical sons were in short supply, or where diocesan authorities sought youths who spoke the language of non-Russian minorities.[23]

Nor did Church authorities *want* outsiders, as directives from the commission routinely confirmed. In 1819, for example, the commission admonished authorities of overcrowded seminaries not to admit outsiders: "Youths not belonging to the clerical estate are not to be admitted to schools, which [already] have too many pupils from the clerical estate, so that an unnecessary proliferation of pupils not burden the teachers or cause difficulties in instruction."[24] Although the commission permitted outsiders to matriculate in underenrolled schools, it clearly blocked admission to the great majority

---

[20] Freeze, *Russian Levites*, pp. 200–4.

[21] *Opis' dokumentov i del*, pp. 1–7.

[22] A. Nadezhdin, *Istoriia S.-Peterburgskoi pravoslavnoi dukhovnoi seminarii, 1801–84 gg.* [hereafter Nadezhdin, *ISDS*] (St. Petersburg, 1885), p. 243.

[23] On the case of Riga, see below, p. 147.

[24] Diakonov, *Dukhovnye shkoly*, p. 339.

of schools. In 1825 the commission acted to discourage outsiders further by refusing to grant degrees (attestations) to those outsiders who declined to enter Church service.[25] Although the commission rejected proposals to place a categorical ban on outsiders, it reiterated that "the children of laymen should be admitted to the seminary only with the permission of the diocesan bishop, and the number of such pupils should be indicated in annual reports (in a special explanatory note)."[26] Given the surplus of candidates in many dioceses, bishops too had little interest in admitting outsiders. For example, the bishop of Kherson, upon learning that his diocesan schools admitted outsiders, fumed, "Is there any conscience or sense here? Categorically inform all, especially the heads of diocesan schools, to get rid of the [outside] pupils, so that after the vacation there is not a single one left."[27]

The view of the seminary as a special soslovie school not only governed admissions policies but also determined the system of moral training and curriculum. Thus the curriculum of 1814 provided general education only insofar as this abetted the ecclesiastical subjects. In particular, it sought to diminish the pagan elements in classical culture, to limit the attention given to science and mathematics, and to concentrate specifically upon religious problems in such fields as philosophy.[28] The same spirit informed the schools' moral education, which aspired to inculcate a monastic model of conduct, partly because the Church sought to fashion future recruits for monastic orders, but mainly because it regarded monastic norms as the best model for young seminarians. The soslovie policy also applied to the lay faculty, drawn almost exclusively from candidates with clerical backgrounds and clerical schools. Despite their lack of holy orders, such lay teachers formally belonged to the Church's domain (vedomstvo) and were subject to its jurisdiction, rules, and customs. Revealing and characterisitc was the resolution of the bishop of Vologda after discovering that one of the lay teachers in his church school planned to marry a nonclerical girl: "It is bad, very bad, that clerics [sic] pass up their own kind and turn to the laity. This is not to recur."[29]

In 1836, at the very inception of Protasov's tenure as chief procurator, two ministries raised a direct challenge to this system of separate Church schools. One proposal, emanating from the Ministry of Public Education, sought to merge state and ecclesiastical schools. Arguing that it was highly anachronistic to maintain separate estate schools, especially at a time when youths from all estates matriculated at the university, the ministry contended that the major problems, such as a shortage of competent teachers, might best be

[25] Ibid., pp. 339–40.
[26] Ibid., pp. 340–42.
[27] I. Strel'bitskii, Letopis' Odesskoi dukhovnoi seminarii (Odessa, 1913), p. 59.
[28] See Filaret's complaint about secular books, in SMO, 1: 227.
[29] Diakonov, Dukhovnye shkoly, p. 362.

overcome by joining forces.[30] The Ministry of Finance offered a somewhat different proposal, agreeing that the seminary should remain a separate institution, but urging that it incorporate secular courses for professional training—applied chemistry, mechanics, technology, accounting, and agriculture. Although the ministry justified its proposal by the need to provide new outlets for clerical offspring, it primarily had the state's own vested interests in mind, especially the need for technicians and engineers.[31]

The Church quite naturally rejected both proposals. The Synod's reply to the Ministry of Education, penned by Metropolitan Filaret, flatly denied the basic premise that Church schools were in difficulty and required radical changes. Filaret also adduced a host of practical objections, stressing that the educational needs of clergy and laity were quite different: lay youths needed to know Russian, seminarians Slavonic; lay youths needed little of the Latin and Greek that preoccupied seminarians. In addition, wrote Filaret, many pupils currently withdraw from Church school at the lower district level to become sacristans; hence these schools must provide not only general education but also specialized instruction in such subjects as note singing, the typicon, and Slavonic grammar, none of which were necessary for secular students. But the most interesting part of Filaret's comment was his social argument. He warned that it was dangerous to mix secular and clerical youths for fear that the latter would abandon the Church:

> The special orientation [of Church schools] is mandated not only by the special character of Church service but also by the [need for] precautions that pupils . . . not lose their hereditary predisposition toward this. For only hereditary inclination and encouragement toward this service in the Church schools impels pupils to enter [the clergy]. Were they to receive an education in secular schools (and, inevitably, a more secular one), they would be exposed to a strong temptation to prefer—in lieu of poverty, want, and strong dependence in church service—the advantages and brilliant prospects open in other ranks. Church service, already in need of educated priests for the villages, would suffer even more from the lack of [such] people.

Here was a dominant motif in Church policy making: a belief that clerical service was so socially inferior that only coercive policies could assure the Church an ample supply of candidates. It was a telling comment on the bishops' anxieties about the clerical rank and their own commitment to the preservation of a taut soslovie order.[32]

To the proposal by the Ministry of Finance, so baldly interested in turning

[30] Filaret, *SMO*, 2: 386–87.

[31] TsGIA SSSR, f. 796, op. 117, g. 1836, d. 931, ll. 6–8.

[32] Filaret, *SMO*, 2: 386–95; see also Freeze, *Russian Levites*, pp. 203–4.

ecclesiastical schools to state purposes, the Synod responded with a volley of specific objections. It noted, above all, that the existing curriculum was already so complex and demanding that pupils had no time for such extraneous subjects. To the ministry's suggestion that the seminary release unneeded pupils to enter lay professions, the Synod responded that seminarians already had the right to leave the clergy and in fact exercised it, albeit in limited numbers. Moreover, it added, some dioceses suffered from a shortage of candidates, especially educated ones, causing numerous vacancies in certain areas of the empire. Following Filaret, the Synod concluded that these conditions oblige "the ecclesiastical authorities to try to give Church schools an orientation which will predispose more pupils to accept positions in the ecclesiastical domain."[33]

The implicit proposition—that a closed soslovie school was essential for guaranteeing the Church a large pool of qualified candidates—gradually lost its raison d'être in the 1830s and 1840s, when an explosion in seminary enrollments, coupled with the tight new shtat, left the Church with far more candidates than it could effectively use. Some of the bishops in central dioceses had raised the question of excess educated candidates in 1826, though in the early 1830s the number of idle youths remained fairly modest—sixteen in Moscow, five in Tver, and thirty-one in Vladimir.[34] Ten years later, however, those same dioceses reported several times that number—seventy-two in Moscow, thirty-nine in Tver, and eighty in Vladimir.[35] Although authorities had complained of excess clerical sons ever since Peter the Great, the problem was now qualitatively different: dioceses had excess *graduates*, not the hordes of unschooled youths that distressed state officials in the eighteenth century.[36] Worse still was the growing disjuncture between the seminary's resources and the demands placed upon it, a disjuncture that would eventually impel authorities to reconsider the traditional soslovie policy.

[33]TsGIA SSSR, f. 796, op. 117, g. 1836, d. 931, ll. 6–8. According to Synodal data for the mid-1830s, the empire had 3,016 vacant positions for priests, 2,450 for deacons, and 10,933 for sacristans—for the most part, of course, in outlying dioceses or in the poorer parishes of central Russia.

[34]Ibid., op. 111, g. 1830, d. 728, l. 122.

[35]Ibid., op. 122, g. 1841, d. 186, l. 94. In addition to these idle graduates, each diocese had still more unplaced youths without a seminary degree—297 in Moscow diocese, 250 in Tula, and 273 in Vladimir.

[36]See Freeze, *Russian Levites*, pp. 37–41. By mid-century the Catholic Church in France also had surplus candidates (see Hilaire, *Une Chrétienté*, 1: 163–65). Still worse was the situation in Germany; see Fischer, "Bilder," p. 14, and the contemporary account, R. Binder, *Die unglückliche Lage der protestantischen Pfarramts-kandidaten und die verfehlte Stellung der Vikarien in Württemberg* (Ulm, 1841). For a more general statement, see Lenore O'Boyle, "The Problem of an Excess of Educated Men in Western Europe, 1800–1850," *Journal of Modern History*, 42 (1970): 471–90.

TABLE 7

Church School Enrollments, 1819–1838

Year	Seminary	District School	Township School	Total
1819	7,149	14,873	9,198	01,000
1825	10,470	20,790	13,432	44,692
1838	15,830	26,345	19,623	61,798

SOURCE: Titlinov, *Dukhovnaia shkola*, 1: 101. Titlinov's erroneous totals have been recalculated and corrected.

Disjuncture: School and Soslovie

The rise in seminary enrollments after the 1814 reforms was immense and empire-wide, affecting the outer as well as the central dioceses. Authorities had largely completed their implementation of the reform by 1819, thereafter adding few new schools to the basic system.[37] The growth that transpired within the walls of these schools between 1819 and 1838 was spectacular: enrollments rose to sixty thousand pupils, three times what they had been at the outset of the century (see table 7). Although growth occurred at all levels, it was most intense in the seminary, reflecting the very keen competition for clerical positions.[38] Enrollments grew most rapidly in the old dioceses of central Russia—226 percent in Riazan, 280 percent in Nizhnii Novgorod, as much as 333 percent in Tambov. Most grew more slowly, as in Vladimir, where total enrollments rose from 1,984 to 2,985 (an increase of 50 percent). Put it another way, the enrollments in Vladimir in 1838 began to approach those for the whole empire in the 1760s. Paradoxically, enrollments grew most rapidly in dioceses with a surfeit of candidates and most slowly in understaffed or borderland dioceses. That disparity was a direct response to the dynamics of clerical education—the greater the surplus, the greater the pressure to study longer and to graduate—which only perpetuated the manpower disparities in the Church.

Church schools did not enjoy a comparable growth in their financial resources: the elaborate fiscal scheme of 1814 failed to generate the expected income. Not that the reform committee underestimated the financial issue; on the contrary, it declared outright that the principal barrier "to greater

[37] Titlinov, *Dukhovnaia shkola*, 1: 91–104.
[38] For detailed tables, see ibid., 1: 101–2.

success in Church schools always was and now remains the small budget."[39] Its calculations, however, went awry, primarily because of war in 1812, which prevented authorities from amassing a capital endowment and instead forced them to divert an immense sum—3.5 million rubles—from the endowment fund to pay for the reconstruction of buildings damaged in the war.[40] That disaster was compounded by a suspension of state aid in 1817: evidently in response to government wish, the Church "voluntarily" renounced its claim to a state education subsidy of 2 million rubles per year, ostensibly because the Church's financial system was working so well.[41] Nothing could have been further from the truth, for the main source of income— the sale of church candles—proved a great disappointment, yielding less than half the projected revenues.[42] One reason was competition from private vendors, who had long contested the Church's attempt to monopolize the sale of candles and who simply refused to abandon this lucrative trade. Moreover, much of the revenue from the sale of candles in parish churches failed to reach central authorities, for parish finances were managed by lay church elders (*tserkovnye starosty*), who diverted funds for local needs or even lined their own pockets.[43] Despite authorities' repeated attempts to curtail abuses and increase revenues, the income from candle sales rose slowly and unevenly, lagging far behind the needs exacerbated by the mushrooming enrollments in Church schools.

The reform committee misjudged not only potential revenues but also future expenses, for the original budget proved grossly inaccurate and almost immediately evoked calls for substantial increases. As seminary authorities complained and the commission's inspectors confirmed, the original budget greatly underestimated almost every item and, worse still, made no provision for inflation. In 1820 the commission admitted the need for immediate changes and raised the budgets of some schools, essentially by suspending the establishment of additional township schools (*prikhodskie uchilishcha*). As a result, the commission was able to increase its total budget for seminaries

---

[39]"Dokladnaia zapiska," in Poletaev, "K istorii," *Str.*, 1889, no. 8: 521.

[40]Titlinov, *Dukhovnaia shkola*, 1: 293–94.

[41]*PSZ (1)*, 34: 26997.

[42]The commission anticipated an annual income of 3 million rubles from the sale of candles but in fact obtained far less—just 1.2 million rubles in 1825. (Titlinov, *Dukhovnaia shkola*, 1: 293–94).

[43]For the instruction for church elders, see *PSZ (1)*, 30: 22971; see also a commission decree of 1820 that berates local authorities for lax supervision (*PSZ [1]*, 37: 28396). For complaints of peculation, see N. P. Giliarov-Platonov, *Iz perezhitogo*, 2 vols. (Moscow, 1886) 2: 229–31; [I. S. Belliustin], "Zapiska o g. Kaliazine," *Arkhiv istoricheskikh i prakticheskikh svedenii*, 2 (St. Petersburg, 1861): 14.

and academies by 73 percent, the amount varying from one school to the next, but everywhere yielding considerable relief.[44]

That relief was short-lived, however. Again, the chief reason was inflation, an uncontrollable element that mercilessly vitiated the tidy bureaucratic shtat of imperial Russia. Although data varied from diocese to diocese, all reported a steady rise in the cost of living; for example, between 1825 and 1835 in some areas the price of rye flour rose 20 percent and meat 25 percent.[45] Still worse, amidst inadequate funding, local authorities left part of their budget unspent in an effort to demonstrate frugality, hoping thereby to impress their superiors with exemplary management. Consequently, even as seminaries suffered from inadequate financing, authorities amassed several hundred thousand rubles in unexpended funds.[46] To meet the sharp rise in enrollments and costs, authorities modified the budget again in 1836, primarily to increase faculty salaries (50 percent) and the funds for plant upkeep.[47] With that exception, however, the seminary budget of 1820 remained without change right down to the reform of 1867.

As a result, Church schools experienced great economic hardship. One hint was contained in the data on capital endowment, which actually began to decline in the 1840s. Earlier, central authorities had, despite all obstacles, managed to divert current revenues to the capital fund, and between 1815 and 1835 they actually increased the endowment by 14 percent. From the late 1830s, however, they not only ceased to augment the endowment but even had to draw upon this fund, leading to a 9 percent decline between 1840 and 1855.[48] The reversal was due not to lack of zeal but to the widening gap between resources and demands. In fact, the financial state of Church schools was actually worse than these figures suggest, for there were still greater hidden deficits, such as losses due to the failure to maintain physical plants.[49] At the bottom of this crisis lay a disjuncture between swelling enrollments and declining resources.

The schools' ensuing poverty directly affected the educational process, creating intolerable conditions for teaching and learning.[50] Schools lacked

---

[44]Titlinov, *Dukhovnaia shkola*, 1: 295–301.

[45]Nadezhdin, *ISDS*, p. 196; I. Speranskii, *Ocherk istorii Smolenskoi dukhovnoi seminarii* [hereafter Speranskii, *OISS*] (Smolensk, 1892), p. 225n.; P. Nikol'skii, *Istoriia Voronezhskoi dukhovnoi seminarii* [hereafter Nikol'skii, *IVDS*], 2 vols. (Voronezh, 1898–99), 2: 6–8. For statistical data, see Titlinov, *Dukhovnaia shkola*, 1: 314.

[46]Titlinov, *Dukhovnaia shkola*, 1: 357–60.

[47]Ibid., 1: 301–2.

[48]Calculated from data in Diakonov, *Dukhovnye shkoly*, pp. 373–75.

[49]*IVO (1840)*, pril., pp. 74–77; *IVO (1850)*, pril., pp. 74–82; *IVO (1860)*, pril., pp. 108–11; Titlinov, *Dukovnaia shkola*, 2: 193–94.

[50]Titlinov, *Dukhovnaia shkola*, 1: 293–383.

proper libraries, for the small sum budgeted (450 rubles) barely sufficed for textbooks, and usually not even that.[51] An inspection of one school in 1840, showed that the seminary library was "extremely inadequate: there are no Bibles or New Testaments (in Slavonic, Latin or Greek), or any textbooks required by the [seminary] statute."[52] Hence pupils learned Scripture without access to a Bible, explored geography without benefit of maps, and mechanically transcribed notes to compensate for the lack of textbooks. Lack of funds also impelled authorities to maintain a bienniel class system, in which the same teacher and pupils covered a two-year course of study. Though that system reduced the number of faculty (each instructor, in effect, had a two-year cycle of courses), it meant doubly large classes and onerous teaching loads for the faculty.[53] The most shocking evidence of institutional penury was overcrowding, a problem already present at the outset of the 1814 reform. Inspections conducted shortly after the 1814 reform brought warnings that the classes were still unmanageably large. Filaret, for example, inspected the district school in Iaroslavl and wrote that "the excessive number of [pupils] can only impair efforts at a reliable supervision of their efforts and the development of their capabilities. . . . A pupil from one end of the classroom cannot hear and see what the teacher does and says at the other end."[54] The situation grew still worse after the seminaries burst into runaway growth, with ever more pupils trying to squeeze inside their walls. The typical result was evident in an inspector's report on the seminary in Perm in 1829: "The seminary buildings are so crowded that the dormitory and classrooms also serve as a cafeteria. For this reason the pupils receiving stipends, who do not have beds, are obliged each night to move the classroom tables and make their beds upon them."[55] A similar report from Minsk in 1832 revealed that eight pupils crowded into each small room and that "two (or sometimes three) pupils sleep on each bed."[56]

School buildings also suffered from neglect and poor upkeep. Filth was ubiquitous—the characteristic, in fact, that first caught the eye of outsiders,

---

[51] Nadezhdin, *ISDS*, pp. 97–103, 417–22. Even by mid-century the St. Petersburg seminary, according to an official inspection, had a library "almost wholly deficient in works in all fields of scholarship" (ibid., p. 418). Likewise, the seminary library in Voronezh simply ceased to grow after the early nineteenth century, thereafter acquiring only journals, not books (Nikol'-skii, *IVDS*, 2: 169).

[52] Strel'bitskii, *Letopis' Odesskoi dukhovnoi seminarii*, p. 23. Likewise, the seminary in Vladimir reported in 1830 that it had only 24 Bibles for the 800 pupils in the school (Malitskii, *IVDS*, 2: 130).

[53] Titlinov, *Dukovnaia shkola*, 1: 303–5.

[54] Filaret, *SMO*, 1: 217–19.

[55] Diakonov, *Dukhovnye shkoly*, p. 379.

[56] "Iz bumag S. D. Nechaeva," *RA*, 1893, no. 5: 152; see also the 1845 inspection report on Smolensk in Speranskii, *OISS*, pp. 304–5.

the emperor included, in the later reform period.[57] Comtemporary authorities were well aware of the problem. After visiting one seminary in 1836, the inspector wrote that "the classrooms and residential rooms are in extremely poor condition—everywhere the floors are filthy (even in winter), and the walls in places are absolutely covered with soot and dirt."[58] Predictably, the schools were a haven for vermine, lice, and communicable diseases; skin infections were common, deaths of pupils a fact of life.[59] The school buildings were often as hazardous as they were dirty; some were abandoned church properties, and others dated back to the eighteenth century.[60] Sharp-eyed inspectors warned of sagging arches and other structural faults in need of immediate attention.[61] Nor could the tight seminary budget maintain a buildings' interior. A former pupil of the Voronezh seminary recalled that it had "stone walls of immense thickness (covered with green paint), white ceiling arches cracked at various places, a high stove that was never stoked in the winter, black tables carved up by pen knives, worn-down benches, a wide blackboard, damp air like that in a basement, and everything covered by thick layers of dust."[62] In winter, pupils suffered from the bitter cold. An inspector sent to the school in Stavropol even claimed that it became so cold in one room that a pupil froze and had to be taken into the kitchen to be revived.[63] Lacking proper hygienic facilities and even bathhouses, the schools exuded an intolerable stench that left an unforgettable impression on all who chanced to visit them.[64]

Institutional poverty also deprived the schools of good faculty. Despite modest increases in 1820 and 1836, faculty salaries in Church schools were markedly inferior to those for comparable positions in state schools: an academy professor earned only 74 percent of a university professor's salary, a seminary teacher earned but 58 percent of a gymnasium instructor's salary.[65] That great disparity, predictably, caused many of the lay faculty to transfer to state institutions at the first opportunity; for the rest it provided vivid evi-

---

[57]See below, Chapter 5.

[58]TsGIA SSSR, f. 796, op. 130, g. 1849, d. 1313, l. 43 (inspection of Perm in 1850). See also reports on later inspections of the same school, showing no improvement, in I. Lagovskii, *Istoriia Permskoi dukhovnoi seminarii* [hereafter Lagovskii, *IPDS*], 3 vols. (Perm, 1867–77), 3: 449–50.

[59]Speranskii, *OISS*, p. 305; Belliustin, *Opisanie*, pp. 5–10.

[60]Giliarov-Platonov, *Iz perezhitogo*, 1: 39.

[61]Titlinov, *Dukhovnaia shkola*, 1: 325–27; 2: 205–14.

[62]I. S. Nikitin, "Dnevnik seminarista," in *Sochineniia*, 4 vols. (Moscow, 1960), 4: 47.

[63]Diakonov, *Dukovnye shkoly*, p. 433.

[64]Titlinov, *Dukhovnaia shkola*, 1: 366–68; Giliarov-Platonov, *Iz perezhitogo*, 1: 110–11.

[65]Titlinov, *Dukhovnaia shkola*, 1: 307–25. Still lower comparative figures obtained in a report by the chief procurator in 1857: 50.1 percent for academy professors (TsGIA SSSR, f. 832, op. 1, d. 27, ll. 10 ob.-11).

dence of low status and authorities' indifference to their plight.[66] Ecclesiastical schools therefore had to rely heavily upon local clergy, who tried to combine regular parish duties with teaching, and recent seminary graduates who were waiting for a suitable parish position to become available. The consequence was low competence and high turnovers, as in Voronezh, where 85 percent of the faculty served less than ten years (often much less) before leaving.[67] Those who stayed demonstrated neither zeal nor specialized training. Having left the seminary, they taught random courses, lacking preparation in either pedagogy or their subjects of instruction. And on all lay a cloud of ill repute for extortion, as teachers plied parents for bribes on pain of severe hardship for boys unaccompanied by "gifts."[68]

Anemic budgets also meant austerity, if not deprivation, for the young pupils in Church schools. Originally, the Commission of Ecclesiastical Schools planned to give stipends to all pupils, but the collapse of its financial scheme forced it to abandon that dream and strictly limit that expenditure. In the end it gave each seminary about one hundred stipends, obliging most pupils—numbering several hundred in most dioceses—to provide their own support. This obligation, entailing thirty to eighty rubles per year, weighed heavily upon the shoulders of parish clergy.[69] In practice, far fewer than one hundred pupils benefited from full stipends, since seminary authorities regarded these sums as unrestricted funds and diverted some to cover sundry expenses like building repairs or support of the school's clinic.[70] The number of stipends, consequently, was far exceeded by the phalanx of orphans and poor youths in any given diocese. As the bishop of Vladimir wrote to St. Petersburg in 1830, "there are 169 orphans alone in the seminary, and how many poor children are there of retired clergy, how many poor sons of sacristans with large families! . . . Help this terrible poverty!"[71] Given such need, most schools divided the stipends, preferring to give partial support to many

[66]See the censorship case where one author used such data to show the state's neglect of the Church (TsGIA SSSR, f. 797, op. 32, otd. 1, d. 199).

[67]Nikol'skii, IVDS, 2: 78.

[68]See, for example, M. Vruntsevich, "Dukhovnye uchilishcha starykh vremen," RS, 121 (1905): 694; D. I. Rostislavov, "Zapiski," RS, 42 (1884): 506; A. M. Parkhomovich, Stranichka iz zhizni dukhovno-uchebnykh zavedenii Poltavskoi eparkhii v seredine proshlogo XIX st. (Kishinev, 1911), pp. 17–18; D. I. Rostislavov, Ob ustroistve dukhovnykh uchilishch v Rossii, 2 vols. (Leipzig, 1863), 2: 170–83.

[69]In the mid-1850s the clerical publicist Belliustin estimated a seminarian's costs at 80 rubles per year, and a priest of Riazan set 75 rubles as an approximate cost in 1863; sacristans, naturally, paid considerably less, economizing on dress and living quarters (Belliustin, Opisanie, p. 123; TsGIA SSSR, f. 804, op. 1, r. 3, d. 327, l. 97).

[70]Diakonov, Dukhovnye shkoly, p. 412; Titlinov, Dukhovnaia shkola, 1: 339, 2: 214.

[71]Malitskii, IVDS, 2: 22–23.

rather than full support to a few.[72] Most unenviable was the plight of pupils in district schools, where stipends—already few in number and small in amount—were oversubscribed, as authorities gave tiny sums to twice the number of intended recipients. Moreover, the value of stipends steadily dwindled in the 1830s and 1840s, as inflation eroded real income and the number of poor pupils swelled. The inevitable result was great physical privation, gruesomely recorded in the schools' medical records: more than half the pupils were ill at any given time, several of their number died each year (often from "fever"), and all were highly vulnerable to the epidemics that periodically ravaged the empire.[73] At most, authorities sought to alleviate the problem by expelling the chronically ill or mandating the construction of bathhouses, but in the end they could not defeat the combination of malnutrition and unhygienic conditions.[74] The problem in fact reached such proportions that even the Third Section took notice, filing a complaint in 1853 that "the number of ill pupils has proliferated in the Novgorod seminary, and they are receiving very poor care in the seminary and its clinic."[75]

Fiscal crisis, compounded by a shortage of clerical positions, caused enrollments to decline by 4.5 percent in the 1840s (see table 8). Although some areas registered modest growth, by the early 1840s most dioceses reported that their enrollments had ceased to expand, and some even began to contract. Typical was the case in Tula: the seminary grew from 430 to 774 pupils between 1824 and 1838, but by the late 1840s enrollemnt had leveled off at approximately 700 pupils.[76] The cause was not fewer youths or higher transfer rates to secular careers; more than ever the clerical estate had a superabundance of young males seeking a career in the Church. In part, the decline resulted from the introduction of the new shtat in the mid-1840s, which reduced the number of positions and left few openings for the new genera-

---

[72]Titlinov, *Dukovnaia shkola*, 2: 216–20; Diakonov, *Dukhovnye shkoly*, pp. 411–22; Malitskii, *IVDS*, 2: 16–17. The number of stipended students exceeded stipends by 120 percent in Novgorod, 108 percent in Vladimir, and 152 percent in Perm.

[73]With regard to the cholera epidemic in 1830, see the decision to close Vladimir's seminary because of overcrowding and lack of medical care (TsGIA SSSR, f. 796, op. 111, g. 1830, d. 548, ll. 83–86). For the same reasons students were prematurely released in Tver the same year (I. M. Malein, *Moi vospominaniia* [Tver, 1910], p. 123). Cholera actually triggered a rebellion among seminarians in Smolensk after authorities refused to release the pupils (Speranskii, *OISS*, pp. 311–13).

[74]TsGIA SSSR, f. 796, op. 125, g. 1844, d. 1367.

[75]TsGAOR, f. 109, op. 223 (85), d. 18, ll. 44 ob.-45.

[76]TsGIA SSSR, f. 802, op. 5, d. 12986, l. 66. The same file contains detailed data on all dioceses from 1824 to 1850, showing that most followed the pattern in Tula. In most cases the enrollments in seminaries leveled off and declined only slightly; lower schools suffered sharper drops and did so earlier in the decade of the 1840s.

TABLE 8

Church School Enrollments,
1838–1855

Year	Seminary	Lower Schools	Total
1838	15,830	45,968	61,798
1850	16,702	42,872	59,574
1855	13,835	37,180	51,015

SOURCE: Titlinov, *Dukhovnaia shkola*,
1: 101–4; 2: 70–73. Titlinov's erroneous
total for 1838 has been recalculated and
corrected.

tion of candidates. That grim prospect impelled some clergy to lose interest
in their sons' education and to withdraw them from schools at the first opportunity, especially if a sacristan position could be found. A still more important cause of decline was the seminary's economic crisis, which made education for so many youths impossible and forced seminary authorities to
expel marginal, overaged pupils. Notwithstanding this decline, significantly,
most dioceses still had a superabundance of idle youths.[77]

The economic crisis, directly due to enrollments that surpassed Church
needs, eventually impelled authorities to seek a more radical solution to the
seminary's economic difficulties. To be sure, some, like Bishop Innokentii
(Borisov), still hoped for government aid: "Will it be soon that our clergy are
educated with the government's assistance? The need for this is acute, especially in certain areas; without provisions for material support, no reform in
the schools can bear fruit."[78] But by the late 1840s authorities were ready to
strike out in entirely new directions. As happened with the parish reforms,
authorities failed to find new revenues and resolved to reduce costs—in this
case by limiting the number of pupils in Church schools. By adopting a formal shtat for the seminary, geared to the manpower needs of each diocese,
authorities planned to educate only a sufficient number of candidates,
thereby freeing funds to improve conditions and avoiding a surplus of idle
seminarians. The new policy took its toll, causing a 14 percent decline in
enrollments between 1850 and 1855.[79] As we shall see in the next chapter,

[77] See the 1850 otchety in ibid., f. 796, op. 132, g. 1851, d. 2357, and the 1853 data on idle
youths in ibid., f. 802, op. 6, d. 16114, ll. 1–163.

[78] Vostokov, "Innokentii," *RS*, 23 (1878): 383.

[79] *IVO (1850)*, pril.; *IVO (1855)*, pril.

that new seminary shtat reflected a broader shift in state policy that sought to resolve the growing disparities between the clerical soslovie and the institutional Church.

A Seminary Education

Throughout the first half of the nineteenth century authorities sought to reshape the Petrine curriculum and to redirect ecclesiastical education to serve the needs of future pastors. Repeatedly such reform, often emanating from the state, had to overcome opposition from ranking Church prelates, an elite whose own status rested upon the classical school and who generally opposed major changes in that system of learning. Although the statutes of 1814 aspired to adapt the schools more to the needs of parish clergy, they nevertheless retained the basic core of the Petrine school: the classical Latin curriculum. In the late 1830s the state, after overcoming determined opposition from Church hierarchs, modified this curriculum to give it a more practical focus, primarily by adding courses deemed useful for village priests. It was an essential part of the regime's effort to transform the clergy into more useful temporal, not just spiritual, servitors.

The Commission Era (1814–1839)

As the reform committee of 1808 endeavored to reconstruct Church schools, it placed high priority on the task of designing a more comprehensive, systematic curriculum. Its main goal was to eliminate the Protestant scholasticism of the eighteenth-century schools and to develop an educational order firmly rooted in Eastern Orthodoxy. In the words of Filaret (Drozdov), "it is desirable that Russian Church scholarship, which has borrowed so much from foreign scholarship in [its theology] and is now being stimulated, develop its own models in the true spirit of the Apostolic Church."[80] Hence reform was not merely a new list of courses; it entailed the development of a new culture, new books, and new ideas. Moreover, the committee sought a hierarchy of educational establishments, each interlocking, each serving different needs of the Church. Its four-tiered hierarchy of schools aspired to offer more specialization and complexity, not only permitting a logical sequence of study but also satisfying the special needs for parish clergy (lower schools) and Church intellectuals (the academy).

At the base of this system was a new unit: the township school (*prikhodskoe uchilishche*). Although literally called "parish school," in fact such institutions were intended to exist only in some thirty parishes in each diocese

---

[80]Filaret, *SMO*, 1: 141.

(and should not be confused with the "parish school" [*prikhodskaia shkola*] for lay parishioners). The purpose of such township schools was to provide primary instruction, mainly the three Rs and some religious instruction (church singing and catechism).[81] That kind of education, in the eighteenth century, had been provided at home or from a local cleric; indeed, youths could still study that way so long as they showed satisfactory progress in annual examinations. But the township school, in theory, would provide more regular and systematic instruction and be of special value to orphaned children of clergy. In the event, this lower unit (as so often happened with reform in Russia) proved stillborn: the commission established no more than six or seven of the schools in any diocese—not the twenty or thirty originally planned.[82] Precisely because the schools duplicated informal education, the commission, for fiscal reasons, ceased to open such schools after 1819 and made it the parents' responsibility to provide their sons with primary instruction.[83]

More important was the second level: the district school (*dukhovnoe uchilishche*), which usually served two or three administrative districts (*uezdy*).[84] These schools began to proliferate in the late eighteenth century, their main task being to prepare pupils for the seminary and to qualify some for service as sacristans. The reform statute of 1814 retained the broad structure of the old school, especially the heavy stress upon Latin. However, its four-year curriculum also devoted attention to other subjects, some to provide general education (Slavonic, Russian, and geography), others to prepare the youths entering directly into Church service as sacristans (who required knowledge of the expanded catechism and rules on parish recordkeeping).[85]

The third tier in this system was the seminary, a six-year program divided into three forms (*otdeleniia*). The first (lowest) form was rhetoric (*ritorika*), a two-year course in the theory of rhetoric and poetry, with most readings in the classics and some in Russian Slavonic. The main textbook was still J. F. Burgius's *Elementa oratoria* (1776), which had been widely used in eighteenth-century seminaries.[86] The second (middle) form was philosophy (*filosofiia*), which embraced the study of several allied subjects, including logic, metaphysics, moral philosophy, psychology, and philosophical history.[87] The

---

[81] Diakonov, *Dukhovnye shkoly*, pp. 137–39.

[82] Titlinov, *Dukhovnaia shkola*, 1: 99–101, has useful tables here.

[83] Ibid., 1: 98.

[84] For the number of schools per diocese in 1819 and 1830, see ibid., 1: 99–101.

[85] Diakonov, *Dukhovnye shkoly*, pp. 151–74.

[86] F. N. Beliavskii, *O reforme dukhovnoi shkoly*, 2 pts. (St. Petersburg, 1907), 1: 23; Nikol'-skii, *IVDS*, 1: 149; Titlinov, *Dukhovnaia shkola*, 1: 156–65. *Elementa Oratoria*, by Burgius (known in Russia as Io. F. Burgii), was still widely used, despite its age. When the bishop of Vladimir learned in 1834 that it was still in use, he sardonically queried: "Isn't arid old Burgius on pension yet?" (Malitskii, *IVDS*, 2: 129).

[87] Titlinov, *Dukhovnaia shkola*, 1: 144–56.

chief goal of this form, as a syllabus of 1814 declared, was to demonstrate the "limits of reason," to show that man alone could not attain ultimate truth.[88] As in the eighteenth century, pupils derived this insight from a German textbook by F. C. Baumeister, a German Protestant waging battle against Enlightenment rationalism and skepticism.[89] A few schools introduced a more modern volume by F. S. Karpe, but in 1825 the commission pronounced it unworthy and ordered all to use Baumeister.[90] The third (highest) form was theology, which consisted of hermeneutics, dogmatic theology, moral and pastoral theology, "archaeology" (the history of Church liturgy), and the Holy Scriptures. As in the lower forms, instructors relied mainly upon textbooks bequeathed from the eighteenth century, written either by Protestant scholars (J. F. Buddeus and J. J. Rambach) or by Russian prelates (Feofan Prokopovich, Feofilakt Gorskii, and Irinei Fal'kovskii).[91] Although much time was devoted to formal scholarship, the commission did not neglect the Scriptures, which the statute pronounced the "foundation" of the seminary and which later received additional allotments of time.[92] As in the eighteenth century, Latin was to be the primary language of the schools, used in all courses except Scripture, Slavonic literature, and secular subjects. The curriculum also included a smattering of "auxiliary" subjects— Church history, mathematics and physics, secular history, Hebrew, Greek, and modern languages—but the core subjects consumed most of the pupils' classroom time and served as the sole determinants in class rank and promotion. As a result, the auxiliary subjects received only nominal attention from both students and faculty.[93] In brief, the reform essentially retained the classical Latin core but gave the curriculum greater order and coherence, allotted more attention to the Scriptures, and added some new subjects (like hermeneutics).

Standing at the summit of Church education was the academy, an elite four-year institution with a superb library, large budget, gifted teachers, and few students.[94] Although in broad outlines the academy's curriculum was identical to the seminary's upper two forms (philosophy and theology), the

---

[88] Ibid., 1: 146.

[89] Freeze, *Russian Levites*, pp. 94, 259.

[90] Titlinov, *Dukhovnaia shkola*, 1: 61–62.

[91] Beliavskii, *O reforme*, 1: 51.

[92] *PSZ (1)*, 32: 25674.

[93] For the difficulty of teaching such auxiliary subjects, see the memoirs of two former teachers: Malein, *Moi vospominaniia*, pp. 152–53; and F. F. Ismailov, "Iz zapisok starogo professora seminarii," *PO*, 1870, no. 7: 110–11. See also the case of a mathematics teacher in Perm (Lagovskii, *IPDS*, 3:162).

[94] Enrollments in the academy were small but stable: Moscow Academy had 94 students in 1824, 108 in 1838, and 102 in 1850; St. Petersburg had 101 in 1824, 112 in 1838, and 117 in 1850; and Kiev had 71 in 1824, 112 in 1838, and 102 in 1850. Kazan Academy opened only in 1842; it soon leveled off with an enrollment of 60 students in 1850 (TsGIA SSSR, f. 802, op. 5, d. 12986, ll. 58, 72, 93, 190).

four-year academy in fact offered a much more intensive, advanced program of study.[95] It also included some subjects not taught in the seminary; the upper form of theology, for example, included "polemical theology" (*oblichitel'noe bogoslovie*, directed against other confessions and the schism) and formal homiletics (*sobesedovatel'noe bogoslovie*). The academy also devoted more time than the seminary to the study of Scripture, which in fact was a major subject in all four years of the academy. Yet the chief difference was standards; even when faculty used textbooks also found in the seminary, they expected fuller comprehension and supplemented the texts with original lectures. Another major difference was the focus of student work. Here, whatever the subject, the students concentrated primarily on compositions and theses, underscoring the academy's purpose: preparation of future Church scholars, either to teach in ecclesiastical schools or to join the ranks of "learned monks" in the hierarchy.[96]

Although the reform achieved some notable improvements over eighteenth-century schools (especially in the academy), it failed to eradicate major deficiencies in the seminary and the district school. Memoirs, diaries, inspectorate reports—all paint a depressing picture of rote memorization, minimal comprehension and stifling scholasticism, the very things against which the reform committee had protested.[97] Indicative was the result of an inspection in Kazan in 1842, where an inspector from Petersburg found that pupils "read from the catechism without any comprehension, for many gave answers that [actually] pertain to different questions (but which in one word were similar to the [question] posed by the instructor)."[98] Data on the rate of failure and expulsion confirm such verbal accounts: the expulsion rate was 20 to 40 percent in the seminary, 40 to 50 percent in the district schools.[99] Thus, notwithstanding the mushrooming enrollments, most pupils failed to complete their education; graduates in fact represented a small proportion of total enrollments. The number of seminary graduates increased in the first half of the nineteenth century only because total enrollments had increased, not because the schools became more efficient.

Finances, no doubt, were a major cause of such shortcomings. They led to class sizes of staggering proportions—as many as 150 to 200 in a single class.[100] Under such circumstances faculty could hardly cope with their tasks, be it classroom instruction, marking compositions, or administering oral

[95] Diakonov, *Dukovnye shkoly*, pp. 260–302.
[96] Ibid., pp. 295–302; see also "Peterburgskaia dukhovnaia akademiia, 1833–35," *ChOIDR*, 231 (1910), otd. 3: 2–3, and the rich collection of primary materials in *U Troitsy v Akademii, 1814–1914 gg.; iubileinyi sbornik* (Sergiev-Posad, 1914).
[97] Rostislavov, *Ob ustroistve*, 1: 372–436.
[98] Diakonov, *Dukhovnye shkoly*, p. 147.
[99] Titlinov, *Dukhovnaia shkola*, 1: 213–33.
[100] Ibid., 1: 325–37; 2: 50–51, 205–14.

examinations. Hence teachers in both district schools and seminaries relied heavily upon student aides (*avditory*), ostensibly the more capable pupils, who checked their classmates' preparation and performance. Although such aides compensated for the lack of faculty, the practice was pedagogically disastrous, the source of great abuse and neglect.[101] Though teachers sometimes took special interest in particular students (kinsmen or gifted youths), they could not pay heed to the mass of pupils.[102] With good reason more affluent priests sought protection for their sons, ideally by boarding them in the homes of teachers with a broad charge to oversee the youths' studies.[103] Others—the great majority—were not so fortunate. Instructive is the case of A. P. Shchapov, later a brilliant historian, who languished in the back rows of the classroom (reserved for dullards and popularly known as "Kamchatka") until a sympathetic teacher discovered his ability and the cause of his poor performance, namely, abject poverty that denied him books and supplies.[104] Overcrowding also warped the system of oral examinations for promotion and rank. Examiners lacked time to quiz pupils in all subjects, even in annual examinations, and hence only questioned a few students in each subject, little more than a random check on their *avditory*.[105]

The yoke of scholastic traditions also impeded change. As in the eighteenth century, pupils still devoted much of their time to the memorization of "forms" and "definitions," not specific factual knowledge. Thus pupils in rhetoric read little literature, concentrating instead upon the principles, definitions, and categories for analyzing literary works.[106] Although that training ostensibly developed skills of reasoning, it left the pupils without much real knowledge of history, literature, or even vital religious subjects. As one former seminarian from the excellent Vifanskaia Seminary in Moscow diocese recalled, "I definitely came away with little knowledge [from the seminary]. Of course I knew the dogmas of the faith, could discuss them, but I knew little about the history of the Christian Church, and almost everything [I learned] in philosophy flew out of my head. . . . [But] I learned to write freely and with animation, and my thought was rather well-developed."[107] Scholasticism persisted in large part because the existing faculty had been formed in its mold and lacked either the resources or perhaps the ability to teach in

---

[101] See, for example, V. I. Gloriantov, "Vospominaniia," *RA*, 1906, no 2: 211–12.

[102] Diakonov, *Dukhovnye shkoly*, pp. 200–2.

[103] Nikitin, "Dnevnik seminarista," *Sochineniia*, 4: 40–41.

[104] V. Serbov, "Shchapov, A. P.," in *Russkii biograficheskii slovar'*, 25 vols. (Moscow-Petrograd, 1896–1916), 24:1.

[105] Titlinov, *Dukhovnaia shkola*, 1: 242–51.

[106] Nadezhdin, *ISDS*, p. 72; Diakonov, *Dukhovnye shkoly*, pp. 175–81.

[107] A. A. Beliaev, ed., "Professor Moskovskoi dukhovnoi akademii P. S. Kazanskii i ego perepiska s arkhiepiskopom Kostromskim Platonom," *Bogoslovskii vestnik* [hereafter *BV*], 1903, no. 1: 100.

any other way. Burdened with numerous subjects and numerous pupils, none had the time to prepare a whole new system of learning. Nor did the Commission of Ecclesiastical Schools render practical aid. In fact, authorities looked askance at excessive originality, especially in theological questions. That distrust was apparent at the formal examinations in the St. Petersburg Seminary in 1833, when the prelate reproved the rector for training pupils to give reasoned replies rather than a quick recitation from the textbook.[108] More formally, in 1824–1826 the commission, reacting against the spiritualist tendencies in the latter part of Alexander I's reign, forbade instructors to use original lectures and demanded that they adhere strictly to the syllabi promulgated in 1814.[109]

The requirement that Latin be the language of instruction also caused increasing difficulties. The reform committee of 1808 was plainly ambivalent about the role of Latin, at once criticizing earlier preoccupation with this language, yet retaining it as an integral part of the new curriculum. In practice, Latin acquired a highly anomalous status. It remained the language of instruction but received less attention; pupils had little time to develop oral and written skills for practical communication.[110] Consequently, increasing numbers of pupils failed to master Latin and had great difficulty in all other important subjects, which were still conducted in Latin. As one central inspector noted in 1827, "the pupils' success would be still more significant if Latin (in which most lectures are read) were not so difficult for them."[111] In 1819 the commission decided to make Russian the language of instruction but reversed itself in 1824, equating the preference for the vernacular with Protestant tendencies.[112] Nevertheless, authorities found it increasingly difficult to require Latin, because so few pupils had command of the language when they entered the seminary. As Filaret observed in 1838, the decline of Latin "is now more or less universal, differing only in degree."[113] Outside inspectors confirmed that assessment. An investigator to the Odessa seminary, for example, reported in 1840 that even "pupils of the upper division have difficulty answering in Latin the most elementary questions about the most ordinary subjects."[114] Some hierarchs, like Metropolitan Filaret (Amfiteatrov) of Kiev, bemoaned this decline, declaring that Latin was vital for

[108] Nadezhdin, *ISDS*, p. 59.

[109] Chistovich, *Rukovodiashchie deiateli*, pp. 2 6–57.

[110] Nadezhdin, *ISDS*, pp. 54–56; Diakonov, *Dukhovnye shkoly*, pp. 196–97; Titlinov, *Dukhovnaia shkola*, 1: 184–92.

[111] Nadezhdin, *ISDS*, p. 80.

[112] Titlinov, *Dukhovnaia shkola*, 1: 140–42.

[113] Nadezhdin, *ISDS*, p. 412n. This decline was not unique to Russia; see Keller, "Priesterseminar," *FDA*, 98 (1978): 406.

[114] Strel'bitskii, *Letopis' Odesskoi dukhovnoi seminarii*, p. 23.

religious scholarship, especially for studies of the Church Fathers.[115] But
stern commands from Petersburg could not halt the decline, and by 1840
Russian had generally become the language of instruction.[116] Filaret (Drozdov) welcomed this development:

> To make a categorical demand that theology be taught in Latin would, in
> this case, be tantamount to demanding something difficult and, because
> the language is little known, would interrupt the dissemination of theolog-
> ical knowledge. Besides, the fact that Orthodox theology is dominated by
> Latin, once pagan but now papist and protestant, is not a phenomenon
> fully consistent with the spirit and goal of ecclesiastical schools of the East-
> ern Church.[117]

Nevertheless, Filaret and the other prelates still upheld the broad outlines of
the 1814 curriculum, even if they were willing to diminish further the status
of Latin. That curriculum, however, came directly under challenge by the
new procurator, Protasov, who was intent upon giving seminary studies a
still more "practical direction."

The Protasov Reform

The seminary became one of Protasov's major concerns after his appointment as chief procurator in 1836. Under the influence of Kiselev, the minister of state domains, the chief procurator sought major changes in ecclesiastical education. His primary goal was to redirect schools from the purpose
of creating an elite ecclesiastical culture to that of training village priests,
who must primarily combat not the Enlightenment of the West but the darkness of rural Russia. Protasov was especially insistent that clergy learn to
communicate more effectively with their rural parishioners: "Seminary
pupils, after a thorough study of theology, must know how to come down to
the conceptions of the simple people and intelligently discuss with them the

[115]While still serving as archbishop of Riazan, Filaret expressed clearly his views on the
classical curriculum: "Latin, in the opinion of enlightened people, is regarded as the key to
wisdom. In this language people in clerical education can read all that has been written—
books by ancient teachers of the Orthodox Church and by the most recent compilers of theological systems. All the Church Fathers have been translated into Latin; [in fact], many
extremely important writers of the Eastern Church are in Latin, not Greek" (TsGIA SSSR, f.
796, op. 107, g. 1826, d. 460, l. 209). See also N. I. Barsov, ed., "Pis'ma prot. S. Skvortsova,"
TKDA, 1885, no. 7: 480.

[116]See, for example, Malitskii, IVDS, 2: 120, and Titlinov, Dukhovnaia shkola, 1: 152–54,
162–63.

[117]S. K. Smirnov, Istoriia Moskovskoi dukhovnoi akademii do ee preobrazovaniia [hereafter
Smirnov, IMDA] (Moscow, 1879), p. 96.

truths and obligations of Christians." At the same time, Protasov sought to fuse parish clergy and parishioners into a web of mutual interest. He demanded that seminarians acquire knowledge of "auxiliary subjects that they could usefully apply to rural life for both their own sake and that of their future parishioners," thereby strengthening their moral influence over the people.[118]

It was therefore essential, declared Protasov, that the seminary provide proper training to spread the faith. The procurator complained that the present seminary graduate was simply incapable of transmitting or explaining Orthodoxy to his own parishioners, much less carrying the Church's mission to its foes. To a clergyman he once complained that "we do not understand you: your theology is bombastic, your sermons too elevated, [so] we do not understand you. You do not know the language of the people." Furthermore, he complained, for the sake of a false erudition (drawing excessively upon the West), the clergy have neglected the liturgical elements of Orthodoxy most revered by the people: "You shun Church ritual [tserkovnost']—you do not know practical [pastoral] theology and regard it as demeaning to know and study it. As a result, once installed in holy orders, you are at a loss, do not know how to read or sing, and do not know the typicon."[119] On another occasion the chief procurator complained that "the pupils know little of the Church rites and that is a general deficiency in seminarians."[120] The chief procurator therefore insisted that "the seminary must be readjusted to fit rural needs so that pupils, through a fundamental study of theology, know how to reach the minds of the simple people and to discuss the saving Truths of the faith and Christian duties in a simple, intelligible language."[121]

Moreover, Protasov also sought to include "practical" subjects in the curriculum, believing that this would enhance the priest's role and status in the local community. That notion was hardly new. It figured prominently in the religious policies of eighteenth-century Western states and had ample precedent in Russia as well.[122] Protasov revived and expanded such ideas, seeking to add not only medicine but also agronomy to the curriculum, arguing that

[118] *IVO (1840)*, pp. 58–59. Similarly, Protasov's predecessor, Nechaev, wrote that "it is necessary to discard much that is superfluous for rural clergy" ("K biografii Innokentiia," *RA*, 1911, no. 10: 172). See similar concerns in G. Schultz, *Die praktische Ausbildung der Predigtamts-Kandidaten für das evangelische Kirchenamt* (Königsberg, 1844), and O. Dibelius, *Das Königliche Predigerseminar zu Wittenberg, 1817–1917* (Berlin, [1918]), pp. 23–24.

[119] Nikodim, "O Filarete," *ChOIDR*, 1877, kn. 2, ch. 2: 38.

[120] Nadezhdin, *ISDS*, p. 312.

[121] *IVO (1840)*, p. 58. Compare the English situation in Pruett, *Parish Clergy under the Late Stuarts*, pp. 122–23.

[122] For the past attempts, see Freeze, *Russian Levites*, pp. 105, 264. For England, see Heeney, *A Different Kind of Gentleman*, pp. 76–77; McClatchey, *Oxfordshire Clergy*, pp. 165–77; and Russell, *Clerical Profession*, pp. 203–13.

such instruction would bring "profit to the [clergy] themselves and their future parishioners." To make room for such practical subjects, Protasov proposed to reduce some of the existing courses or eliminate them altogether.[123]

Protasov's designs aroused strong opposition among Church hierarchs. Though sensitive to the seminary's failings, they regarded such schemes as inimical to the interests of the Church and designed purely to serve the worldly needs of the state. That view was clearly evident in 1836–1837, when Protasov transmitted proposals to incorporate medicine and agronomy into the curriculum, ideas that the Synod brusquely rejected as unsuitable on practical and pedagogical grounds.[124] In June 1838, however, the Synod did agree to give a more "practical" bent to its religious instruction, prefacing the changes with a ringing critique of scholasticism: "The teaching of all aspects of theology should be adapted for [real] application; as far as possible, it should be free from the arid, unintelligible forms of scholasticism; and it should not be governed by a striving for brilliant, but unfeeling, erudition."[125] The Commission of Ecclesiastical Schools laid new emphasis upon liturgical training: seminary authorities were to make "special efforts so that the spirit of the Church permeates not only the upper division but also the middle and lower divisions (which of necessity are much preoccupied with secular subjects)."[126] Specifically, it directed seminaries to adopt a seventeenth-century catechism, Peter Mohila's Orthodox Confession, as the foundation for theological studies in lieu of the arid textbooks of scholasticism.[127] It also added new courses—patristics and the early history of the Church—and expanded the syllabus for study of the Scriptures.

Such concessions failed to satisfy Protasov, who sought a still more utilitarian focus in the curriculum. Not surprisingly, he warmly supported a proposal in 1838 from Minister of State Domains Kiselev, who urged educational reform to make the parish clergy more "useful."[128] Adopting ideas that were already current in Nikolaevan bureaucracy, Kiselev revived the scheme to add medicine and agriculture to the seminary curriculum, a demand that the Synod had firmly spurned only two years earlier. Leading the opposition now was Metropolitan Filaret, who reiterated views expressed earlier—that seminarians had no time for additional subjects, that the priests were too busy

[123]IVO (1840), p. 59.

[124]TsGIA SSSR, f. 797, op 5, d. 21422, ll. 1-1 ob. (Zapiska); d. 22061, ll. 1-30 (L'vov, "Zapiska"). The Synod's responses are in each of these archival files; for Filaret's views, see Filaret, SMO, 2: 391–95.

[125]Nikol'skii, IVDS, 2: 151–52; Nadezhdin, ISDS, p. 123; Titlinov, Dukhovnaia shkola, 2: 5–6, 1: 129–30.

[126]Diakonov, Dukhovnye shkoly, pp. 46–49; Nadezhdin, ISDS, p. 123.

[127]Titlinov, Dukhovnaia shkola, 2: 6.

[128]This zapiska formed part of Kiselev's broader plan to reform the parishes; see above, Chapter 2.

with religious duties to practice medicine and agronomy, and that such roles interfered with priests' spiritual duties. The metropolitan crowned his argument with the awesome—and erroneous—declaration that such ambitions had not been attempted "even in Europe."[129] The resolute procurator soon surmounted this opposition. He persuaded Nicholas to replace the Commission of Ecclesiastical Schools with a new organ, the Bureau of Ecclesiastical Education, which would be dominated by laymen and directly under his control. Aware that changes were now inevitable, Filaret himself decided to collaborate, warning that "one must now give ground to them in some matters or otherwise they will take away everything."[130] The Synod solicited opinions from local school officials and wove these into a reform statute, finally approved in 1840, that significantly altered the seminary curriculum.

This compromise statute retained the basic curriculum of 1814 but added those subjects now demanded by the state. Thus, in addition to the old curriculum, seminarians had to study agronomy and medicine as well as the requisite background courses in science. To accommodate a curriculum swollen from seventeen to twenty-six subjects, authorities trimmed that course which seemed most superfluous and dangerous in Nikolaevan Russia: philosophy. As a result, the revised curriculum contained some components of the old philosophy (for example, logic) but eliminated such important subjects as metaphysics and the history of philosophy. In the same utilitarian spirit the reform statute attacked the predominance of Latin and formally ordered that courses at all levels of the seminary henceforth be taught in Russian. The statute also downgraded modern foreign languages, reducing them from "obligatory" to "optional" status.[131]

Subsequently, again at Protasov's behest, the Synod augmented this curriculum with still more "practical" subjects, such as icon painting in 1843 and geodesy in 1849.[132] Protasov's justification for geodesy reveals the whole spirit of his reforms: "Upon assuming their positions as priests, [seminarians] can measure church lands for themselves, divide them if necessary into allotments in an economic sense, have some idea of calculations for construction, and oversee the peasants in these matters."[133] In religious subjects, too, the St. Petersburg authorities continued to make significant adjustments. Thus they expanded the time allotted for homiletics (reducing philosophical studies still more), diminished the importance of compositions in Latin, and in 1853 established special missionary courses at selected seminaries.[134]

---

[129] Filaret, SMO, 2: 420–26.

[130] Nikodim, "O Filarete," ChOIDR, 1877, kn. 2, ch. 2: 49.

[131] TsGIA SSSR, f. 797, op 10, d. 26600; see also the circular to diocesan authorities (Lagovskii, IPDS, 3: 1–3).

[132] Nadezhdin, ISDS, pp. 405–9; IVO (1849), p. 47.

[133] IVO (1849), p. 47.

[134] TsGIA SSSR, f. 796, op 126, g. 1845, d. 1367, ll. 1-11; Nadezhdin, ISDS, pp. 371–74, 412–13.

Protasov's final practical reform was the establishment in 1851 of special schools for sacristans, which were intended to provide training more suitable for their specific liturgical functions. In earlier times the sacristan had little or no education, learning the liturgical roles of his rank under apprenticeship to a kinsman. Formal education disrupted that system: the district school and seminary aimed primarily to prepare youths for priesthood and provided little practical training for those expelled and destined to become sacristans. A reform memorandum submitted by an archpriest in the early 1840s argued cogently that the existing curriculum was largely irrelevant to the service of sacristans: "What purpose is served by several years which, as it were, are squandered on Latin and Greek poetry? At the same time, [this means that] the youths receive much fewer lessons on catechism, still less on singing." The author proposed to create special schools for the preparation of sacristans, an experiment actually tried early in the century but abandoned in the ambitious reform of 1814.[135] Although the Synod rejected this memorandum (as it did most other unsolicited advice), it actually created such schools in 1851, forming special sacristan sections (*prichetnicheskie klassy*) in the district schools.[136]

Though a favorite target of criticism, the Protasov reforms nevertheless made some important contributions. One was to place long-overdue stress on subjects neglected by the seminary, such as early church history, Russian church history, and patristics. These innovations, together with the establishment of a special journal to publish translations of the Church Fathers, laid the foundations for the later flowering of Orthodox theology.[137] Important too was the attack on scholasticism, which had resisted decades of formal criticism and only now began to retreat from the schools. The change was apparent in such fields as rhetoric, where students concentrated more on literary texts, not literary definitions.[138] Moreover, Protasov demanded that ecclesiastical scholars prepare new textbooks, and by the end of the 1840s the school system could boast of some important acquisitions, including Makarii Bulgakov's volume on dogmatic theology and Antonii Amfiteatrov's textbook on pastoral theology.[139] The formal rejection of Latin also encour-

---

[135]TsGIA SSSR, f. 796, op 124, g. 1843, d. 1162, ll. 1-16 (Pevnitskii, "Zapiska"). Similar ideas were advanced in 1842 by a minor official in Kherson province (ibid., f. 797, op. 12, d. 29891, ll. 12-20 ob.). Perceptive too was the comment in 1828 by the archbishop of Riazan, Filaret: "Many of those from the district schools, where they fruitlessly are preoccupied with Latin and Greek, upon examination by diocesan authorities prove ignorant of those things necessary for performing the duties of sacristan" (ibid., f. 796, op. 107, g. 1826, d. 460, l. 203).

[136]Titlinov, *Dukhovnaia shkola*, 2: 42–45.

[137]See G. V. Florovskii, *Puti russkogo bogosloviia* (Paris, 1937), chap. 5.

[138]Diakonov, *Dukhovnye shkoly*, pp. 226–28; Beliavskii, *O reforme*, p. 75; Malitskii, *IVDS*, 2: 352.

[139]Makarii Bulgakov, *Pravoslavnoe dogmaticheskoe bogoslovie* (Moscow, 1848); Antonii [Amfiteatrov], *Pastyrskoe bogoslovie* (Moscow, 1851).

aged the development of communication skills in Russian, endowing priests
with an enhanced facility for addressing their audience, whether orally or in
writing. By the 1850s and 1860s priests tended to refocus their sermons from
formal speeches to informal talks (besedy), even impromptu remarks. That
development followed the new spirit in seminary instruction, which required
students to spend less time on "the composition of sermons in accordance
with the rules of rhetorical art" and instead to practice composing "short,
artless talks suitable for understanding by the common people."[140] The
bishop of Vladimir claimed in 1851 that "priests who have completed their
education of late have greater influence upon parishioners than those who
studied earlier, because [the younger priests] try to adapt their homilies to
the ideas of the people, their homilies expressing the truths of the faith in
simple, comprehensible language."[141]

Still, the revised curriculum of the 1840s achieved few of its other goals.
The most striking failure was the addition of such practical subjects as agriculture, medicine, and geodesy. The agriculture courses proved largely the-
oretical, focusing upon the latest advances in Western technology, which
were mostly unsuitable for Russian conditions and at any event irrelevant to
a poor village priest with a small plot of parish-church land. Even the seminary gardens, intended as a model of new methods, did little more than
produce staples for the school's kitchen; in some cases, the authorities surrep-
titiously leased out the garden plots to townspeople.[142] Nor were medical
studies of much value. With only a perfunctory knowledge of natural science, pupils had neither the preparation nor the time to master medicine; at
most, they read through a medical textbook.[143] The grandest farce was geodesy: most seminaries lacked surveying instruments and blithely ignored
orders to teach the subject.[144] Of all Protasov's changes, bishops disliked these
the most and made their repeal a first priority in the Great Reforms.[145]

---

[140] F. I. Titov, Makarii Bulgakov, mitropolit moskovskii i kolomenskii, 2 vols. (Kiev, 1895–
1903), 1: 240.

[141] TsGIA SSSR, f. 796, op 132, g. 1851, d. 2357, l. 79 (otchet for 1850). Given the very slow
turnover in personnel (especially with the shtat frozen and fewer young priests ordained), the
old ornate, scholastic sermons persisted. See, for example, the typical comments in "Propoved'
sel'skogo sviashchennika kak sredstvo narodnogo obrazovaniia," PO, 1861, tom 4: 531–40.

[142] Nikol'skii, IVDS, 2: 156–60. The archbishop of Riazan claimed benefits from agricultural
studies in his annual report for 1850, but the majority opinion was unqualifiedly negative
(TsGIA SSSR, f. 796, op. 132, g. 1851, d. 2357, l. 391). See also the views expressed by committees and sundry authorities from the late 1850s (below, pp. 220–21).

[143] Titlinov, Dukhovnaia shkola, 2: 103–4, cites reports of 43 seminaries in 1856, not one of
which found medical studies progressing satisfactorily.

[144] The rector of the Kiev seminary complained bitterly that "in introducing these new subjects they do not provide more time, resources, books or [teacher's] manuals" ("Pis'ma arkhimandrita Antoniia k Innokentiiu," TKDA, 1884, no. 6: 261–62).

[145] See below, Chapter 5.

Nor did the other subjects, whether old or new, fare well. However useful in principle, even some of the new subjects, such as patristics and polemical theology, existed mainly on paper, adding little to the preparation of seminarians. The main difficulty was the lack of textbooks and sources; without these, faculty in small provincial seminaries could give no more than nominal, perfunctory instruction.[146] At the same time, the various addenda seriously weakened the old curriculum, which now received less attention and declined proportionately.[147] Voicing a complaint that would become routine in the 1850s, one prelate wrote in 1845 that seminarians "have extremely many [subjects], and [these] are almost beyond their powers, if one takes into account both the scope of the subjects and the difficulty in mastering them."[148] Deterioration was most evident in the case of Latin. Although still consuming much time, especially in the district school, "Latin," according to one typical report, "is in decline: the very best pupils barely know it."[149] The tinkering with the curriculum also deprived it of logic and coherence by deleting or shifting prerequisites and arbitrarily dividing fields.[150] In effect, the Protasov reform was a disastrous compromise. In attempting to weld various practical subjects onto the old classical curriculum and in seeking to make the seminary a classical gymnasium and a *Realschule*, it obtained neither goal.

Ideological conservatism also crippled the new order, preventing the preparation of much-needed textbooks and syllabi. The fate of the special Committee for the Review of Syllabi is indicative: it existed for six years (1840–1845) yet failed to approve a single syllabus, all proposals falling victim to caviling criticism.[151] The regular organs of censorship also exerted a baneful influence, especially after the celebrated Pavskii affair, which not only blocked further translations but also paralyzed biblical studies, since, after Pavskii, no one dared to deviate from the Slavonic Bible and use Hebrew texts.[152] The affair also affected the preparation of textbooks, especially in such fields as hermeneutics. Instructive is the fate of a professor who sought

---

[146]Diakonov, *Dukhovnye shkoly*, pp. 210–12, 270–71. To prepare new texts was extraordinarily difficult, as one professor aptly noted: "God alone knows how much work it took to compose this [new work on patristics]," since it meant "taking an uncharted path, walking alone and without any guides" (ibid., p. 271).

[147]In 1845 the Bureau of Ecclesiastical Education, admitting the excess load of courses in the upper division, shifted some subjects to strike a better balance (TsGIA SSSR, f. 796, op. 126, g. 1845, d. 1367).

[148]Ibid., d. 499, l. 1.

[149]Lagovskii, *IPDS*, 3: 172–73; on Moscow, see F. A. Gilarov, "Vospominaniia," *RA*, 1904, no. 5: 105.

[150]Diakonov, *Dukhovnye shkoly*, p. 256; Titlinov, *Dukhovnaia shkola*, 2: 106–17.

[151]Titlinov, *Dukhovnaia shkola*, 2: 93–139.

[152]Diakonov, *Dukhovnye shkoly*, pp. 204–8.

to supply the seminary with a much-needed textbook on hermeneutics: he first submitted the manuscript in 1844, rewrote it twice to incorporate censors' objections, and finally published the volume in 1859—in its *original* form.[153] Under this oppressive atmosphere, faculty and scholars simply avoided the subject of biblical criticism, causing the Church to lag behind Western scholarship in the new fields of contextual, philological, and historical criticism that were fundamentally recasting views on the Scriptures and their meaning.

Furthermore, the Protasov reform failed to address fundamental weaknesses in the system of 1814–1840, especially the material want that underlay many of the schools' difficulties. Although some new textbooks appeared in the late 1840s, faculty still had to rely upon antiquated volumes for most subjects. With good cause the suffragan bishop of Kiev complained that "the most palpable deficiency in education at the seminary is the lack of standard textbooks in almost all subjects."[154] Those that did exist were outdated and ineffective. As one pupil recalled, "reading a seminary textbook is like biting through a thick rope."[155] Texts also remained in short supply, with six to ten pupils sharing a single copy.[156] Seminary libraries, small and primitive, were reluctant to loan books to pupils and had to divert scarce funds to the acquisition of books for new subjects, such as medicine and agronomy. Even the St. Petersburg Seminary suffered from such problems, lacking "recent guides in virtually all branches of scholarship," according to one inspection.[157] Faculty too remained a serious problem. Low salaries and lack of privileges continued to cause frequent turnover, extortion, and widespread faculty discontent.[158] Protasov's reforms also tended to aggravate pedagogical problems, since they multiplied the number of courses without adequately increasing the staff, obliging faculty to teach courses in which they had neither training nor interest.

Thus by the 1850s conditions in the Church schools had seriously deteriorated, exemplified by high rates of failure, expulsion, and voluntary withdrawal. The magnitude of the problems was evident even in the official inspectorate reports, which—as in other parts of the Nikolaevan order—preferred to exalt successes and overlook problems. For example, an inspection in the early 1840s found that pupils in Kazan had little comprehension of Filaret's *Expanded Catechism:* "Pupils either had no knowledge at all of this or had distorted notions of the most simple things. For example, in the upper

---

[153] Nadezhdin, *ISDS*, pp. 357–59.

[154] TsGIA SSSR, f. 796, op. 126, g. 1845, d. 499, ll. 1-1 ob.

[155] Pomyalovsky [Pomialovskii], *Seminary Sketches*, p. 194.

[156] I. U. Palimpsestov, "Volny zhiteiskogo moria," *RA*, 1893, no. 12: 479–80.

[157] Nadezhdin, *ISDS*, p. 418.

[158] TsGIA SSSR, f. 796, op. 124, g. 1843, d. 114; op. 130, g. 1849, d. 281, ll. 1-2; *PSZ (2)*, 23: 22878.

forms of the Church school, some pupils did not know the meaning of these terms—'our debts,' 'spiritual life'; [nor did they know] who the apostles are, what is the assembled church [*sobornaia tserkov'*], what penance is."[159] An investigator of the Iakutsk schools in 1844 found much the same thing: "The pupils, having firmly learned the typicon, have no understanding of it."[160] The attrition rate, as before, remained extraordinarily high in this system of rote memorization. As one priest in Smolensk recalled, "when I graduated from the seminary, I counted the comrades who had studied with me since the second form: of 123 pupils, 7 remained."[161] The jumbled curriculum, aggravated by poor pedagogy and material hardship, would stand at the center of attention in the reforms of the 1850s and 1860s.

Moral Milieu and Upbringing

Moral training (*vospitanie*) was a primary concern of ecclesiastical schools, which, after all, were to train priests, not merely secular professionals. The task of moral education was a dominant theme in law, from the Ecclesiastical Regulation of 1721 to the seminary statutes of 1814, and the subject figured prominently in offical inspections, student ranking, and outsiders' evaluations. The preservation of moral purity, furthermore, was one motive for closed soslovie schools, since bishops believed that it would be easier to isolate pupils from the foibles of the lower class if only the clergy's sons enrolled. However, the schools sought not merely to implant a sense of moral responsibility but also to develop true monastic values, stressing the ascetic ideals of meekness and humility versus urbanity and social graces. Typical of this spirit was the outburst of the rector in Tver, who forbade fashionable dress and railed against students who had "hair like a *barin* [nobleman]."[162] The ideal student was honorable and bright, outwardly pious, meek, and submissive. Yet, however appropriate for monks, such values left the seminarian ill-prepared for life among the laity, especially the upper classes, and severely handicapped those who left the clerical estate for secular life.[163] Coerced

---

[159]Diakonov, *Dukhovnye shkoly*, p. 152. See also the 1854 report on Perm in Lagovskii, *IPDS*, 3: 202, and the account in S. I. Sychugov, "Nechto v rode avtobiografii," *Minuvshie gody*, 1916, no. 1: 122.

[160]Diakonov, *Dukhovnye shkoly*, p. 153

[161]I. D. Briantsev, "Vospominaniia," *Smolenskie eparkhial'nye vedomosti*, [hereafter *Smolenskie EV*], 1890, no 10: 469.

[162]V. Kolosov, *Istoriia Tverskoi dukhovnoi seminarii* [hereafter Kolosov, *ITDS*] (Tver, 1889), p. 328.

[163]See, for example, the summary account of diocesan opinions in *Zapiska po voprosu ob otkrytii detiam sviashchenno-tserkovno-sluzhitelei putei dlia obespecheniia svoego sushchestvovaniia na veskh poprishchakh grazhdanskoi deiatel'nosti* ([St. Petersburg, mid-1860s]).

humility, moreover, easily turned into hypocritical imitation: "To bow low, to quail, to shake with terror at the sight of the rector or inspector, to answer them meekly—these are the hallmarks of this baneful 'virtue.'"[164]

That quasi-monastic atmosphere was most pervasive in the ecclesiastical academies, which primarily sought to train a future ecclesiastical elite. Here the goal was not merely to implant values but to obtain recruits for the monastic orders—learned monks who could then rise to positions of archimandrite, rector, and bishop. Inculcation of such values was by no means easy, especially in Petersburg, Kiev, and Kazan, where the academy competed with all the attractions and diversions of major urban centers. But academy authorities waged a vigorous campaign to win recruits to monastic orders, and, at least until the 1840s, they enjoyed relatively good success.[165] The blandishments of tonsure were many; those who took vows could anticipate favored treatment in the academy and a brilliant career thereafter.[166] Even so, the number of students willing to take vows was small. In fact, in 1852—to the consummate indignation of Metropolitan Filaret—not a single member of the graduating class in the Moscow Academy took monastic vows.[167]

To oversee moral training, the seminary and academy relied upon their second-ranking officer, the inspector, who was to regulate strictly the students' lives, much like an abbot in a monastery. In profuse detail the statute of 1814 fixed a precise regimen—when students were to rise, eat, study, and sleep. It in fact followed closely the regulations so characteristic of the eighteenth-century schools.[168] To enforce these rules, the inspector—invariably a monk—was to oversee pupils closely, visit their living quarters regularly, and submit weekly reports on their behavior to the seminary board. That ambitious level of control, designed when the reformers still hoped to house all youths in dormitories, proved unworkable because most students remained scattered in rented rooms throughout the town. There, as one inspector observed, "the pupils rent from people of low status—factory workers, craftsmen, unskilled laborers, the poor segments of the merchants and townspeople. Association with people of such low rank provides a bad experience,

---

[164]"Zapiski prot. Ioanna Vinogradova," *RS*, 22 (1878): 556.

[165]In 1831–1832 the academies reported that 7.1 percent of the graduating class had taken monastic vows (3 of 35 in Petersburg, 3 of 59 in Moscow, and 3 of 32 in Kiev). That proportion peaked at 10.1 percent in 1839–1840 (3 of 48 in Petersburg, 6 of 59 in Moscow, and 7 of 52 in Kiev). It then declined to 5.9 percent in 1851–1852 (3 of 58 in Petersburg, 0 of 44 in Moscow, 6 of 46 in Kiev, and 1 of 22 in Kazan). TsGIA SSSR, f. 802, op. 8, d. 23638, ll. 10-11 ob.

[166]Rostislavov, *Ob ustroistve*, 1: 99–116. As one pupil recalled, "of some forty students [in the Moscow Academy of the 1830s], those who became monks went furthest of all" (Ia. Milovskii, "Moskovskaia dukhovnaia akademiia," *RA*, 1893, no. 9: 44).

[167]Smirnov, *IMDA*, 167–68.

[168]Freeze, *Russian Levites*, pp. 97–101.

[reflected in] countless incidents in police files, rumors, and reports."[169] Another weakness in the inspectorate was the custom of appointing learned monks to the post of inspector. Destined for higher ranks, they served only briefly, having little time to become acquainted with either the students or the school.[170] In 1830, after a student in Kiev killed a comrade with a knife, the Synod strengthened the apparatus of supervision by appointing assistant inspectors selected from the ranks of the schools' teachers.[171] Ultimately, however, the inspector relied heavily upon student elders (*starshiny*), who were appointed in theory to keep close supervision over their peers and report instances of misconduct.[172] In reality, however, the elders were notoriously unreliable, known not for their moral leadership but for holding their subjects in terror. Recalling this institution, one former seminarian summed up the view of many: "The entire pedagogical system was based upon beatings, tyranny, and verbal abuse."[173] Inside the seminary, authorities tried to shelter pupils from secular influence by withdrawing "harmful" literature from the library, discouraging contact with the low-born and base, and denigrating such secular activities as music and belles-lettres.[174]

For all its ambition, this system of moral education was a dismal failure, regarded by some in fact as the greatest weakness of the prereform school.[175] Almost without exception, memoirists draw a shocking portrait of the school milieu and argue that the school was more likely to corrupt than purify the youth within its fold.[176] As one former seminarian recalled, "if any one of us preserved a spark of goodness, if any good priests came from the midst of our seminary [in Moscow diocese], then he owed this exclusively to his pre-school upbringing, to his parents' prayers, to an act of grace and lessons of life—and not to the care and guardianship of seminary authorities."[177] Brought to the seminary at the age of seven or eight, young boys experienced the harsh, brutal regime of the seminary, a boarding school so overpopulated

[169] Diakonov, *Dukhovnye shkoly*, p. 321. For the lot of those who dwelt among townsmen, see the accounts in such exposé literature as Belliustin (*Opisanie*, pp. 3–15) and the rich memoir literature, such as that of one youth who lived two years with an alcoholic townsman (Almazov memoir in OR GBL, f. 178 [Muzeinoe sobranie], d. 7312, ll. 26-29).

[170] Titlinov, *Dukhovnaia shkola*, 2: 168–72.

[171] Nadezhdin, *ISDS*, pp. 136–37; Malitskii, *IVDS*, 2: 158–61.

[172] For fascinating "instructions" to elders, see those for the St. Petersburg seminary (Nadezhdin, *ISDS*, pp. 130–34), Moscow Academy (Smirnov, *IMDA*, pp. 594–601), and Vladimir (Malitskii, *IVDS*, 2: 161–67).

[173] Vruntsevich, "Dukhovnye uchilishcha," *RS*, 121 (1905): 696.

[174] *PSZ (1)*, 40: 30343; Filaret, *SMO*, 1: 227.

[175] See below, pp. 220–24.

[176] Even official seminary historians, with reluctance, concede that the archival record is overwhelmingly negative and shocking; see Malitskii, *IVDS*, 2: 169.

[177] Beliaev, "Kazanskii i ego perepiska," *BV*, 1903, no. 1: 100–1.

that formal authority was negligible, where real power rested in the hands of older students. Here he learned not the gentle ways of a retiring monk but the brutal ways of the *bursak*, a stock theme in the belles-lettres of the 1860s. Authorities recognized the gravity of the problems but found themselves powerless to correct them. Characteristic is this report on the school in Smolensk: "Many pupils (including both those with and without stipends), at all levels of the seminary, have been exposed for drunkenness, unruly conduct, insolence, and self-willed behavior; some were caught playing cards for money, others were apprehended for theft, and still others were found to be indifferent to services or given to sloth."[178] The conduct reports for the St. Petersburg Seminary reveal a staggering array of misdeeds, with numerous notations like "insolent and cursed the gardener," "clubbed a monastery employee with a bottle," "reads disgusting books," and "frequently goes to taverns."[179] Reports of sexual license and cases of syphilis marred the seminary's reputation.[180] Such escapades sometimes ended in tragedy, not to say scandal: one seminarian in Tula, angered when a prostitute seized his hat for failure to pay, returned to the public house with several friends, and, when the fight was over, one woman lay dead.[181]

Moral disorders in the ecclesiastical schools came to the attention of the government and lay society despite persistent attempts by the Church to keep them secret. In 1847 one alarmed layman sent the Synod an elaborate "Proposal for Correcting the Morality of the Clerical Estate," which gave particular attention to the weak moral supervision in the seminary: "There are few exceptions among the pupils, especially the older ones, who do not smoke or (what is worse) use strong drinks at home."[182] Alongside salacious gossip and general contempt for "seminarians," some shocking scandals became public knowledge and provoked indignant complaints to the Third Section or the emperor. A townsman in Kostroma, for example, sent a petition in 1847 complaining about the local seminarians and accusing them of gross misconduct, "of going through the streets in the middle of the night, bawling out shouts and songs."[183] The Third Section also reported that "pupils of the Perm seminary constantly swim [in public], provoke unseemly attention by their immorality, by their vulgar talk (which is laced with the most indecent and coarse expressions), and by the time spent with women of ill-repute in nearby dwellings, where they give themselves up to various

---

[178]Speranskii, *OISS*, p. 303.

[179]Nadezhdin, *ISDS*, p. 138.

[180]Nikol'skii, *IVDS*, 2: 199–200. See also Kolosov, *ITDS*, pp. 332–33; Malitskii, *IVDS*, 2: 173.

[181]Nikodim, "O Filarete," *ChOIDR*, 1877, kn. 2, ch. 2: 31.

[182]TsGIA SSSR, f. 796, op. 128, g. 1847, d. 1809, ll. 4 ob.-5.

[183]Ibid., d. 144, ll. 1-11.

vices."[184] Reports of seminarians' immorality reached Nicholas himself, who was appalled to discover that nine seminarians recruited for the Main Pedagogical Institute in St. Petersburg were infected with syphilis.[185]

Authorities also encountered faint, but suggestive, flickers of intellectual and political deviance. Such cases, to be sure, were exceedingly rare (as they were in aristocratic society, for that matter), but they foreshadowed the turbulence to follow in the decades ahead.[186] For example, there were some instances of "freethinking" seminarians who expressed skepticism about religious canons. Thus one pupil in the Voronezh Seminary prepared an essay on "Biblical Miracles" and came to the conclusion that such miracles could not be given credence—a heretical conclusion that earned him a prompt expulsion from the seminary and triggered a general investigation of his school by central authorities.[187] Political ideas also began to stir minds in the seminary. Several pupils even dared to send petitions to Nicholas instructing him to reform the empire, an act of impertinence that led to swift punishment and marred careers.[188] Authorities also detected some rare hints of political disaffection, reflected by the favorable reaction to the work of radical intellectuals like V. G. Belinskii. As one seminarian in Voronezh later recalled, "the fiery essays of Belinskii . . . were read feverishly and learned by heart."[189] Inspectors complained regularly of the pernicious reading habits of seminarians but found it virtually impossible to eradicate them.[190]

The persistence of misconduct, even political deviance, testified to the extraordinary weakness of the school's moral education. However zealous the inspector and his aides, it was physically impossible to supervise all the students, most of whom lived not in dormitories but in rented rooms in town, scattered in up to two hundred dwellings.[191] To contain misconduct, the seminary relied upon a bizarre mixture of brutality and tolerance. On the one hand, punishment was brutal. Though prohibited by the 1814 statutes,[192] schools nevertheless made regular use of corporal punishment, especially in the district schools and the lower forms of the seminary. Even "civilized sem-

---

[184]TsGAOR, f. 109, op 221 (86), d. 130, ll. 130-30 ob. These incidents followed an earlier disorder, where students shouted, whistled, and ridiculed local authorities (ibid., ll. 31-55).

[185]Diakonov, *Dukhovnye shkoly*, p. 318; *PSZ (2)*, 4: 2807.

[186]On the small number of political cases in the late Nikolaevan era, see the data in Daniel Brower, "Fathers, Sons and Grandfathers: Social Origins of Radical Intellectuals in Nineteenth-Century Russia," *Journal of Social History*, 2 (1969): 333–55.

[187]Nikol'skii, *IVDS*, 2: 198–99.

[188]Ibid., 2: 199.

[189]Ibid., 2: 176.

[190]TsGIA SSSR, f. 796, op. 121, g. 1840, d. 557, ll. 4-4 ob.; Nikol'skii, *IVDS*, 2: 171.

[191]Diakonov, *Dukhovnye shkoly*, p. 322.

[192]*PSZ (1)*, 32: 25673: "Punishments should be rare, unavoidable, without vengence, without anger, without meanness, and in particular, without humiliation."

inaries" resorted to birch flogging or forced pupils to hold a brick in out-
stretched arms or to kneel for hours—policies that stretch one's credibility
yet were admitted with chagrin by later apologists and local historians.[193]
Punishment sometimes degenerated into sadism, like that described in a
report from the Third Section to Nicholas in 1844: "The instructor in the
Lubensk district school, Khandozhevskii, because of his avarice and severe
personality, permits himself to punish pupils regardless of their [young] ages.
He once flogged a boy so severely that [the boy] died a few days after-
ward."[194] Authorities received a similar report in 1848 about the Arzamas
district school in Vladimir:

> Punishments of pupils in the Arzamas district school are brutal and con-
> stant (daily), with a special day designated each week for the school super-
> intendent and teacher to engage in this activity of punishing with the
> birch rod for several hours. Screams and wailing of the unfortunate pupils
> undergoing punishment is heard not only throughout the [adjoining] mon-
> astery but also in the monastery's church during the liturgy, causing
> embarrassment to the clergy and worshippers.

Similar reports were lodged against a teacher in the Chistopol district school
who allegedly not only birched youths but also "pinched cheeks, grabbed
pupils by the hair and jerked them mercilessly up in the air (sometimes tearing out clumps of hair), or having seized them by the hair, banged their
heads against the wall or desk."[195] In 1848 authorities received complaints
about another teacher who "calls the pupils asses, anathematizes them as
accursed, fixes brutal punishments, and even beats them about the face."[196]
No wonder that, as one inspection report declared in 1842, "students are so
terrified that they sit in class not like children before their fathers, with open
and calm faces, but like slaves, not daring to raise their eyes and trembling
before the gaze [of their teachers]."[197] In 1845, a pupil in Viatka, apprehended while drunk and dispatched to the seminary's detention cell, "out of
terror of punishment with the birch rod, hanged himself on his own under-
pants."[198] As one former pupil observed, "the seminarian with the least bit

---

[193]See, for instance, materials on Viatka (Sychugov, "Nechto," *Minuvshie gody*, 1916, no.
1: 121–24), Riazan (Rostislavov, "Zapiski," *RS*, 34 [1882]: 585–614; 43 [1885]: 87–104), Smolensk (Briantsev, "Vospominaniia," *Smolenskie EV*, 1890, no. 10: 469–70), Volhynia (K. N.
Khranevich, *Pri starykh poriadkakh* [Kiev, 1896], pp. 13–14), and Vladimir (P.S.A., "Iz vospominanii o Vladimirskom dukhovnom uchilishche i dukhovnoi seminarii," *Vladimirskie EV*,
1875, no 10: 493–94, 497).

[194]TsGAOR, f. 109, op. 221, l. 136; for an incident in 1835, see "Pis'mo Filareta," *RA*, 1905,
no. 12: 536–40.

[195]Diakonov, *Dukhovnye shkoly*, p. 333.

[196]Strel'bitskii, *Letopis' Odesskoi dukhovnoi seminarii*, p. 61.

[197]Diakonov, *Dukhovnye shkoly*, p. 333.

[198]Ibid.

of sense always remembers his education with a feeling of horror."[199] Such routinized violence, to say the least, did little to instill high moral values and gentility. As a former pupil in the Volhynia Seminary noted, "seeing cruelty all around, the pupil involuntarily became cruel himself."[200]

Paradoxically, amidst such brutal punishments seminary authorities also exercised leniency in the question of expulsion, however obtuse or obstreperous the student might be. Perhaps because of paternalistic concern, fear of insufficient candidates, protests from parents, or opportune bribes, the rector deferred expulsion as long as possible, permitting overaged and corrupted pupils to exercise an extraordinarily pernicious influence.[201] That policy led to *velikovozrastie*, the practice of retaining older pupils in the same class with younger ones, to the great detriment of the latter. Church authorities periodically complained of such lenience, but took no specific measures to purge the seminaries until the late 1840s. Once the Synod imposed the shtat, seminary authorities had little choice but to trim the schools of the unworthy and unteachable. Only at the very end of the Nikolaevan era did "the law [against] overage [*velikovozrastie*]," in Pomialovskii's phrase, begin to take effect.[202]

Thus Church schools, to the very twilight of Nicholas's reign, remained in an extraordinarily unsatisfactory condition, exposing young pupils to brutal discipline from above and to barbaric exploitation by their own student elders. If good priests emerged from these schools—and many did—it was in spite of, not because of, the seminary and its system of moral training. The better pupils, those with ability or family connections, enjoyed the favor and protection of seminary authorities; discerning parents as well tried to arrange for an instructor (or older pupils) to shepherd their sons and shield them from abuse and temptations. The mass of pupils lacked such privileged treatment, however, and had to endure all the hardship and degradation that pervaded the Church's boarding schools.

Administration

Ecclesiastical school administration proved no match for inadequate finances, academic problems, and weak moral training. Sometimes administrators even compounded the problems through inertia or malfeasance. The offices, to be sure, were not idle: chancelleries bustled with activity, clerks

---

[199] Pomyalovsky [Pomialovskii], *Seminary Sketches*, p. 115.

[200] Khranevich, *Pri starykh poriadkakh*, p. 16; A. M. Parkhomovich, *Stranichka iz zhizni*, pp. 17, 25–27; Gloriantov, "Vospominaniia," *RA*, 1906, no. 2: 210–11; Malein, *Moi vospominaniia*, pp. 61–62.

[201] See, especially, the perceptive account in Giliarov-Platonov's memoir, *Iz perezhitogo*.

[202] Pomyalovsky, [Pomialovskii], *Seminary Sketches*, p. 4.

processed mountains of paper, and the central bureau fired an endless stream of directives and reprimands at subordinates below. Nonetheless, the Church's educational bureaucracy not only failed to correct abuses but even became itself an impediment to the smooth operation of this highly centralized system.

In theory, at least, the administrative structure was neatly symmetrical and rational. At the apex, until 1838, was the Commission of Ecclesiastical Schools, which exercised overall supervision, appointed faculty, reviewed reports, and ordered special inspections of diocesan schools. The next level was the academy, which oversaw seminaries and district schools in its region through a special "external board" of faculty. Internally, both the academy and the seminary had similar forms of organization: an executive board (*pravlenie*, composed of the rector, inspector, and treasurer) and a larger faculty committee, which handled pedagogical matters. Unlike the eighteenth-century system, the 1814 reform gave the bishop only general supervision and strictly forbade his consistory to meddle in school affairs. The underlying goal, implicit in the formation of such faculty organs, was to make the schools into corporate institutions, not mere administrative devices. Only the district school had a more conventional system, which vested most power in the hands of the school superintendent (*smotritel'*), with no provision for faculty participation.

However tidy in theory, this administrative order worked badly in practice. Although the commission's exercise of control was superior to the Synod's (which in fact had left each bishop to his own devices), the commission centralized so much authority that it soon strangled on its own red tape. By the 1830s it was spewing forth seven thousand documents per year—about one document for every eight students in the whole system—yet it failed to keep pace. With rising impatience, seminary authorities complained that the commission responded tardily, if at all, to their requests for teachers, instructions, and funds.[203] Nor did the academies' external boards provide effective supervision of seminaries and district schools, for their faculty had little time for administrative duties and confined their supervision mainly to paperwork. Inspections consisted of infrequent and perfunctory two- or three-day visits that permitted only a superficial glimpse of a school, its faculty, and pupils.[204] Within each school, moreover, the new order failed to function as planned. Provisions for corporate faculty control proved still-born, and real power devolved upon the rector and inspector. To counterbalance their authority, the commission gradually augmented that of the local bishop, a step that undermined the system's organizational logic and clear chain of

---

[203] Diakonov, *Dukhovnye shkoly*, pp. 16–17.

[204] Smirnov, *IMDA*, pp. 69–97; Diakonov, *Dukhovnye shkoly*, pp. 84–97.

command while offering little improvement in routine administration.[205] As a result, power rested primarily with the rector, subject to sporadic intervention by the bishop.

All too often the result was either tyrannical abuse or abject nonfeasance, depending upon the rector's personality. Quite apart from the harmful effect on the schools, such misfeasance had broader social significance, for the rector was invariably a monk, appointed by virtue of his advanced education and destined to rise soon into the hierarchy. That monastic dominance proved a major source of antimonastic sentiments, not only among young boys later to become parish priests but also among the faculty of lay teachers and white clergy, who endured much abuse and who envied the monks' right to rectorships. Significantly, some of the most inveterate enemies of Russian monasticism came from the ranks of the seminary and academy faculty— liberal publicists like D. I. Rostislavov and conservative intellectuals like P. S. Kazanskii.[206] The latter (whose own brother was a prelate) vigorously condemned the appointment of monks as rectors, arguing that this practice not only "absolutely distorts the whole idea of monasticism" but also disrupts school administration: "With the frequent change of rectors [who leave to become bishops], the seminary (which depends entirely upon the rector) cannot be in a good condition. The rector regards himself as a guest and therefore has no incentive to be much concerned with the seminary. [Even] if he did wish to be active, he would not have time to become well acquainted with the needs and wants of the seminary, the teachers, and pupils." "In all my life," Kazanskii concluded, "I have never seen a decent rector: either he is a despot, or a fool, or a capricious egotist interested only in himself and his promotion."[207] In effect, the reform of 1814 dismantled the highly decentralized eighteenth-century system, based upon the bishop's paternalism, and in its stead constructed a highly centralized order, with tenuous links to provincial schools and with much real power vested in monastic rectors appointed for short terms.

Protasov's maneuver to replace the commission with a bureau under his direct control did nothing to improve school administration, and, if anything, only aggravated earlier weaknesses. The new Bureau of Ecclesiastical Education intensified the centralization, as evidenced by the tidal wave of paperwork and scribes: under Protasov the bureau swelled to fifty clerks, who churned out 30,000 documents per year—one for every two students in the

[205]Titlinov, *Dukhovnaia shkola*, 1: 115–19, Diakonov, *Dukhovnye shkoly*, pp. 106–8, 111–17; Nadezhdin, *ISDS*, pp. 15–16; Rostislavov, *Ob ustroistve*, 1: 29–36.

[206]On Rostislavov, see his own memoirs ("Zapiski," *RS*) as well as his two famous assaults on the monastic clergy—*Ob ustroistve dukhovnykh uchilishch* and, especially, *O belom i chernom pravoslavnom dukhovenstve*, 2 vols. (Leipzig, 1866).

[207]Beliaev, "Kazanskii i ego perepiska," *BV*, 1903, no. 9: 23.

system.[208] Much of that paper, significantly, was vapid formalism, such as periodic glowing reports on the idyllic morality of a seminary.[209] As the head of the system grew, the body atrophied: subordinate units fell inert, even ceasing to convene. Inspections became rare and formalistic, impelling the chief procurator at times to invite outsiders to examine schools on his behalf.[210]

Moreover, Protasov's bureaucracy tied up the conduct of school business. Faculty conferences, and especially the academies' external boards, became mere transmission belts, passing on orders from above and requests from below, taking no role themselves in the decisions.[211] Delays grew interminable, obliging schools to wait months for faculty appointments or authorization to patch leaking roofs.[212] In 1844 one prelate chafed at the delays in appointing faculty, despite the abundance of candidates: "What a strange way of acting on the part of the Bureau of Ecclesiastical Education!"[213] Even the influential rector of the academy in Kiev experienced such vexation, exclaiming with exasperation in 1851: "God [alone] knows what this slowness in administration—which is getting worse and worse—will lead to."[214] Although quantitative measures are wanting, the evidence and, especially, contemporary perceptions suggest that Protasov's era witnessed a virtual breakdown in educational administration, permitting abuse, peculation, and misfeasance to reach unprecedented levels. As one prelate observed, "all across Russia, for a long time, the idea has been circulating that our educational administration is not worth a brass farthing. And that is absolutely true: this unprecedented slowness, this neglect of affairs, this disregard for everything knows no analogies." Sooner or later, he warned, "unless this is corrected, it will invite disaster."[215]

This grim portrait of Church schools must be put in perspective: many of these problems were hardly unique to the seminary. The state's schools also suffered from low standards, backward pedagogy, shocking attrition rates, and penurious conditions. After 1855 reformers like N. I. Pirogov would decry major problems in the curriculum, methods, and social policy of secular schools.[216] Serious questions also attended the education of clergy in the West: doubts about the utility of classics, demands that clergy have more

---

[208] Diakonov, *Dukhovnye shkoly*, pp. 61–64.

[209] Titlinov, *Dukhovnaia shkola*, 2: 174–76.

[210] Nadezhdin, *ISDS*, p. 447 (reporting only four inspections for the period 1841–1866).

[211] Diakonov, *Dukhovnye shkoly*, pp. 78–84.

[212] Titlinov, *Dukhovnaia shkola*, 2: 151–72.

[213] Vostokov, "Innokentii," *RS*, 23 (1878): 382.

[214] "Pis'ma arkhimandrita Antoniia," *TKDA*, 1884, no. 6: 264.

[215] "Iz pisem Innokentiia," *RA*, 1907, no. 8: 440.

[216] On Pirogov, see Patrick L. Alston, *Education and the State in Tsarist Russia* (Stanford, 1969), pp. 46–48, 53–58.

"practical" pastoral training, and problems of finances and moral training figured prominently in discussions of clerical education.[217] More important, the prereform seminary managed to produce many excellent priests, whether favored by good teachers, influential fathers, special conditions in some seminaries, or their own sheer intelligence and strong character. Significantly, these seminarians experienced directly the full effect of the shift from scholasticism to pastoral theology and practical training. They left the seminary far better prepared than their predecessors to preach, catechize, and give impromptu religious talks to their parishioners.[218] It was this group, ultimately, that formed the backbone of reformist movements among clergy in the 1850s and 1860s.

Still, conditions in Church schools *were* grim, even if placed on a comparative standard. Their brutality and squalor offered rich fare for the muckraking *littérateurs* of the sixties. Ultimately, as authorities realized by mid-century, the underlying problem in the seminary was its soslovie structure, its attempt to serve primarily the needs of the clerical estate, not merely the more modest personnel needs of the Church. Embedded in state law from 1814 to 1851, that soslovie principle led to a sudden explosion in enrollments *and* a crisis in ecclesiastical schools. Those phenomena—growth and crisis— were inextricably intertwined: excess enrollments denied the schools a proper environment for instruction, dormitories for supervision, well-trained professional faculty, even the most rudimentary supplies and books. This disjuncture between the interests of the soslovie in educating all sons and those of the institution in training a select pool of candidates existed at the outset of Nicholas's reign. But it was only in the late 1840s that authorities finally perceived the issue in these terms. By then they confronted an acute problem of mounting surpluses in seminary graduates, especially in the wake of attempts to rationalize clerical service and reduce the shtat. In the last years of Nicholas's reign authorities were prepared to reconsider the traditional soslovie policy, and as we shall see, to take the first steps toward dismantling the soslovie foundations of the Church.

---

[217] Though Western seminaries had some financial difficulties (see, for example, Keller, "Priesterseminar," *FDA*, 98: 381–82), the main issues were curriculum and moral training. In France, for example, the existing curriculum was sharply criticized for its scholasticism, narrowness, otherworldliness, and polemical spirit (see, for example: Dansette, *Histoire religieuse*, pp. 377–78; McManners, *Church and State in France*, pp. 28–29; Marcilhacy, *Le diocèse d'Orléans*, pp. 227–48). In Germany the education of Lutheran pastors suffered from excessive formalism and inattention to the spiritual development of youths; see, for example, F. Huck, "Gottlieb Christian Baltzer; ein Pfarrleben des 19. Jahrhunderts," *JBKG*, 42 (1967): 134, 138. Similar concerns appeared broadly throughout Europe; see, for instance, the case of Catholic seminaries in Austria (J. Frint, *Bemerkungen über die intellectuelle und moralische Bildung der heranwachsenden Kleriker* [Vienna, 1812], pp. 40–73). See also the collection of sources in W. Herrmann, ed., *Theologische Ausbildung und ihre Reform* (Münster, 1976), pp. 1–58.

[218] TsGIA SSSR, f. 796, op. 132, g. 1851, d. 2357, l. 79 (Vladimir report of 1850).

CHAPTER 4

Service
and Soslovie

S o far we have gradually worked our way backwards from the institution to the social group, moving from administration to parish service to Church schools and, now, to the clerical estate. That regression is not accidental: it follows the actual process of Nikolaevan reform, which sought ways to improve the clergy and ultimately came to question the very structure of the clerical estate. It was not a question lightly raised. Conservative bureaucrats, anxious bishops, and the parish clergy themselves all had a strong interest in perpetuating, even reinforcing the traditional soslovie system. Nevertheless, after fruitless attempts to reform administration, clerical service, and Church schools, authorities began to alter the very structure of the old hereditary order. Why they did so is the primary focus of this chapter, which will consider the structure and resiliency of the clerical estate, the problems this order generated, and the soslovie reforms undertaken in the late 1840s.

The Soslovie Order

In the eighteenth century, as the state reorganized medieval service ranks (*chiny*) into larger social aggregates of estates, its primary purpose was to mobilize society into specialized service orders. Given the state's gargantuan tasks, whether in foreign policy or domestic development, it had to husband its resources and require that all, in one or another capacity, serve the state. It was particularly important to preclude evasion of service, whether it be nobles shirking their military duties or serfs abandoning their fields and their masters. Thus the eighteenth-century state ascribed all to a hereditary service status, obligating each son to follow in his father's footsteps to guarantee ample manpower for that role in the future. To be sure, state fiat was neither absolute nor consistent; the government made exceptions and tolerated violations, whether in response to special needs or opportune bribes. But most men were bound to assume their fathers' rank (*zvanie*). This social order received definitive statement in the first *Digest of Laws* of 1833, which adopted the term *soslovie* and divided all society into four categories: noble, townsman, peasant, and clerical. It was an uncomplicated system, concisely described by a prominent journalist in the late 1850s: "Each estate has its own role to play in the state: the clergy prays; the nobility serves in war and peace; the peasants till the land and feed the people; and the merchants are the mediators who provide what is necessary for each person."[1]

That simple structure, however, proved increasingly contradictory to social reality or even to the state's own needs. Thus even in the eighteenth century it was clear that the soslovie system failed to achieve its primary purpose, its very raison d'être—to assure good servitors for state needs. It was partly a matter of quality: the soslovie could assure abundant recruits but not necessarily men of ability, zeal, and proper training. Largely on those grounds, in fact, the state "emancipated" the nobility in the eighteenth century, not only freeing nobles from obligatory service but also freeing the state to select cadres on criteria of education and achievement, not mere hereditary status.[2] Nor could the soslovie system adequately embrace the complexities and dynamics of a modern society. Even in the eighteenth century the state had to create a juridical catchall—*raznochintsy* ("miscellaneous ranks")—to encompass various groups outside the main status categories.[3] Matters grew steadily more complex in the nineteenth century, for the old soslovie system failed to accommodate and properly acknowledge the special needs and prerogatives of new service groups, especially free professions like doctors and lawyers. And, despite the legal impediments posed by the soslovie boundaries, social and economic development nevertheless proceeded, gradually undermining the soslovie principle and impelling the state to make major adjustments in its legal system.[4] Significantly, just one year before the

---

[1]Statement by M. P. Pogodin in 1859, in N. P. Barsukov, *Pogodin*, 16: 591.

[2]See M. Raeff, "The Domestic Policies of Peter III and His Overthrow," *AHR*, 75 (1970): 1289–1310; Robert E. Jones, *The Emancipation of the Russian Nobility, 1762–1785* (Princeton, 1973).

[3]C. Becker, "*Raznochintsy*: The Development of the Word and the Concept," *American Slavic and East European Review*, 18 (1959): 63–74.

[4]For a case study, see S. I. Smetanin, "Razlozhenie soslovii i formirovanie klassovoi struktury gorodskogo naseleniia Rossii v 1800–1861 gg.," *Istoricheskie zapiski* [hereafter *IZ*], 102 (1978): 153–82.

state formally codified the soslovie system in its *Digest of Laws,* it created a
major new social status—"honored citizen"—outside traditional estate
boundaries, thereby tacitly recognizing the inadequacy of the soslovie order.
Although the state formally adhered to its soslovie conception until the Great
Reforms, in numerous ways it was gradually impelled to make new, larger
loopholes and to deviate significantly from the basic principles of post-
Petrine social policy.[5]

The clergy had been the most rigid, most hereditary of all the eighteenth-
century social estates.[6] Its social bonds were extraordinarily taut, shackling
not only clerics but also their families to the estate, permitting few to leave
and almost none to enter its ranks. The dynamics behind this closed structure
were several, all gaining momentum and force in the eighteenth century:
poll-tax laws, which blocked entrance to the clergy by peasants and townspeople; specialized education, which was available only to clerical sons; and
the clergy's own vested interests, whereby family claims were staked to positions and property. Still, the developments in Nikolaevan Russia—expansion
of secular schools and universities, growth in bureaucracy and professions—
held out the possibility of a significant breakdown in the resiliency of the
clerical estate.

Inward Mobility

Legally, at least, it was possible to enter the clerical estate. Privileged
groups not inscribed in the poll tax (and therefore owing no recruit or tax
obligations) could enter the clergy at will, though few chose to do so, given
the clergy's low status and scanty support. The more probable source of aspi-
rants was the townspeople and peasantry, who were inscribed in the poll-tax
registers and ranked as the clergy's social inferiors. Candidates from both
groups needed a written release from their social collective, which had to
agree not only to allow the departure of this member but also to assume
liability for his tax dues until the next poll-tax census. That policy was a
convenient compromise for Church and state: it upheld the clergy's exemption from personal taxation yet spared the state any loss in tax revenues. The
government first adopted this policy in the early eighteenth century but significantly tightened it in 1826 by requiring that the Church demonstrate
"palpable need" before accepting poll-tax registrants into the clergy. Aware

---

[5]Such changes were a matter of direct concern for contemporaries, especially those with a
conservative cast of mind. See, especially, a memorandum of 1850 protesting the tendency of
soslovie lines to disintegrate: [A. Kamenskii], "O narodnom prosveshchenii i o glavnykh so-
sloviiakh v Rossii," *RS,* 115 (1903): 177–89.

[6]See Freeze, *Russian Levites,* chap. 7.

that the Church had sufficient candidates in most dioceses, the state saw no reason to aggravate that problem by admitting still more.[7]

Despite these obstacles, some outsiders did become clergymen. Thus the service registers for Kiev diocese offer the example of a serf who, "having been freed by his landlord Rzhevskii from serfdom and confirmed in this manumission by the Governor's Council in Kiev, was permitted to enter the clerical estate in 1820."[8] The Senate agreed in 1830 to release a peasant's son for Church service in Siberia, merely stating that such candidates must satisfy the minimum age for clerical appointment.[9] In 1841 the bishop of Minsk reported that he had installed a candidate from the poll-tax population, noting that he was worthy of appointment and possessed a formal release from his social collective.[10] In 1847 the Senate permitted a peasant in Pskov to enter Church service "on condition that the taxes and obligations from him be borne until the next (ninth) revision by the community that released him."[11] That same year the Senate released a peasant in Moscow for clerical service, adding the customary stipulation that his community assume tax and other obligations.[12] Statistically more significant was the large-scale recruitment of outsiders in the Baltic diocese of Riga in the early 1850s, when the bishop consciously sought native sacristans from the Estonian and Latvian peoples, mostly peasants inscribed in the poll-tax registers. In a typical case the bishop first accepted a written application to enter the clergy, obtained confirmation from the governor that the candidate was of good repute and conduct, and then requested the Synod's permission to install him as a sacristan.[13]

Nevertheless, the appointment of outsiders remained exceedingly rare, as the service records from provincial archives make clear. In Tver diocese, for example, not a single outsider appeared on the service lists for the districts of Kaliazin, Tver, or Rzhev in 1830 or 1860: all the clergy came from the clerical estate, the sons of priests, deacons, and sacristans.[14] The available records for Moscow and Kursk, though not systematic, similarly reveal the absence of outsiders. Only in outlying areas, where the soslovie developed belatedly, did the clergy still show the presence of outsiders. The Ukraine, for example, had once known the close intermingling of clergy and nobility but preserved little of that by the nineteenth century. In 1830 outsiders con-

---

[7] *PSZ (2)*, 1: 139; reaffirmed in the Statute of Ecclesiastical Consistories in 1841 (*PSZ [2]*, 16: 14409).

[8] TsGIA UkrSSR, f. 127, op. 1009, d. 238, l. 38 ob.

[9] TsGIA SSSR, f. 796, op. 111, g. 1830, d. 332, ll. 1–4.

[10] Ibid., op. 122, g. 1841, d. 706, ll. 1–8.

[11] Ibid., op. 128, g. 1847, d. 276, ll. 1–2.

[12] Ibid., d. 272, ll. 1–2.

[13] Ibid., op. 131, g. 1850, dd. 1224, 143, 62.

[14] GA Kalininskoi obl., f. 160, op. 1, dd. 16272, 16515, 15811.

stituted only a small proportion of the clergy in Chigirin district (3 percent) and Kiev district (4 percent); by 1860 their number had declined still further (to 0.5 percent in Chigirin district and 2 percent in Kiev district).[15] Nor were outsiders numerous even in Siberian dioceses, long plagued by a dearth of candidates; Nizhneudinsk district in Irkutsk, for example, had only one outsider in 1830, none in 1860.[16] The pattern did not differ among newer candidates: in 1855, amidst several thousand youths who obtained clerical appointment that year, only nineteen came from outside the clerical estate.[17]

The obstacles to entrance, though much the same as in the eighteenth century, became more formidable and evident in all areas of the empire. As before, education was a major barrier. The low standards that had permitted exceptions in the eighteenth century (especially in outlying areas) ceased to be the case in the nineteenth: formal study in Church schools was now a sine qua non for appointment, and, as we have seen, it was accessible only to the clergy's sons. Given the massive illiteracy in prereform Russia, most peasants and townspeople could not even qualify for the lowly rank of sacristan. As in the eighteenth century, the poll-tax registry remained an important obstacle: only if the candidate could persuade his community to assume his tax and recruit obligations could he enter the clergy. In most dioceses, however, the community had no need to do so; the surfeit of candidates meant that a parish could easily find qualified clerical youths eager for appointment. And even where shortages of candidates did exist, as in the Baltic, peasants sometimes refused to release one of their number, explaining that they were simply too poor to assume an additional tax burden.[18] Finally, the clergy itself continued to block entry by outsiders as positions grew scarce (especially after the shtat reform of the 1840s) and as families coveted positions for kinsmen and heirs.[19]

Nor did authorities see any legitimate need to violate soslovie lines: given the abundance of candidates, the chief task was to find positions, not candidates. That surplus underlay the State Council's decree of 1826 requiring evidence of palpable shortages before admitting outsiders, a law that both state and Church authorities strictly enforced. In 1828, for example, the Senate denied a request by the bishop of Chernigov to admit several poll-tax registrants to the clergy on the grounds that there was no demonstrable need.[20] Synodal policy was similar. In 1847, for instance, the Synod con-

---

[15]TsGIA UkrSSR, f. 127, op. 1009, dd. 275–76, 303–4; op. 1011, dd. 1210, 1275, 1331, 1392, 1429, 1490, 1533, 3872, 3875, 3982, 4021, 4068, 4091.

[16]GA Irkutskoi obl., f. 50, op. 1, d. 3840; op. 1, sv. 368, dd. 7337, 7340–41; sv. 369, d. 7368.

[17]IVO (1855), pp. 17, 22.

[18]See TsGIA SSSR, f. 796, op. 131, g. 1850, d. 1895, ll. 1–20.

[19]See above, pp. 95–96.

[20]TsGIA SSSR, f. 796, op. 109, g. 1828, d. 127, ll. 1–2.

firmed one bishop's decision not to admit outsiders with the explanation that "in Mogilev diocese there is no need for people from outside jurisdictions to fill sacristans' positions."[21] In short, the social barriers around the clergy, primarily apparent in the central dioceses in the eighteenth century, hardened and even reached to outlying areas of the empire in the nineteenth.

That taut hereditary structure forms a striking contrast to the Western clergy. Whereas hereditary ties were ipso facto impossible for the celibate Catholic clergy,[22] the married Protestant clergy showed some hereditary tendencies, but nothing on the order of Russia's castelike structure. In England the high status of the parson assured an ample number of recruits from other social groups; the number of parsons from clerical backgrounds, therefore, rose to no more than a quarter or a third of the entire group.[23] Somewhat similar profiles obtained in Sweden and Norway, where some 27 percent of the clergy in 1821–1840 came from pastors' families.[24] Most hereditary of all the Protestant clergy were Lutheran pastors in Germany. In the seventeenth and eighteenth centuries as many as half their number were recruited from the same estate.[25] But by the early nineteenth century that hereditary pull had declined to roughly one-third, similar to the rest of Europe and far below the nearly 100 percent found in Russia.[26]

[21] Ibid., op. 128, g. 1847, d. 407, ll. 1–3.

[22] Still, certain families did have close ties, producing a disproportionate number of clergy; see, for example, Tackett, *Priest and Parish*, pp. 41–71.

[23] One study of the early-eighteenth-century English clergy shows that one-third came from clerical families (Pruett, *Parish Clergy under the Late Stuarts*, pp. 35–36); another, from the late eighteenth century, shows only 23 percent (Mary Ransome, ed., *The State of the Bishopric of Worcester, 1782–1808* [Worcester, 1968], p. 8). For similar figures on New England clergy, see H. S. Stout, "The Great Awakening in New England Reconsidered: The New England Clergy as a Case Study," *Journal of Social History*, 8 (1974–75): 21–47.

[24] Ragnar Norrman, *Från Prästöverflöd till prästbrist. Prästrykryteringen i Uppsala Ärkestift, 1786–1965* (Uppsala, 1970), p. 210; Dagfinn Mannsåker, *Det norske presteskapet i det 19. Hundreåret* (Oslo, 1954), p. 144.

[25] See, for example, data in the following: Gunther Bormann, "Studien zu Berufsbild und Berufswirklichkeit evangelischen Pfarrer in Württemberg. Die Herkunft der Pfarrer," *Social Compass*, 13 (1966): 98; M. Brecht, "Herkunft und Ausbildung der protestantischen Geistlichen des Herzogtums Württemberg im 16. Jahrhundert," *Zeitschrift für Kirchengeschichte*, 80 (1969): 163–75; and the essays on Hesse (by A. Eckhardt) and Saxony-Thüringen (by H. Schieckel) in G. Franz, ed., *Beamtentum und Pfarrerstand, 1400–1800* (Lemburg/Lahn, 1972), pp. 81–120, 149–178.

[26] Proportions of one-third appear for Württemberg, Prussia, and Hesse (A. Neher, *Die katholische und evangelische Geistlichkeit Württembergs, 1817–1901* [Ravensburg, 1904], pp. 36–39; Bigler, "Social Status," p. 178; Werdermann, *Pfarrer*, p. 123). The change is reflected as well in the social composition of students on the theological faculty at universities like Halle, where the proportion of students from clerical families declined steadily—from 41 percent in 1768–1771 to just 20 percent in 1887–1890 (Bormann, "Pfarrer in Württemberg," p. 132). As a result, by 1887–1890, for the whole of Germany, only 20 percent of the clergy came from that class (Karl W. Dahm, *Beruf: Pfarrer. Empirische Aspekte* [Munich, 1971], pp. 86–88).

Exit from the Clerical Estate

The right of clergy to defrock and voluntarily leave the soslovie had been ambiguous in eighteenth-century law, but in practice authorities routinely permitted such departures. Most inclined to depart were widowed priests and deacons. Although the Church no longer incarcerated them in monasteries, it did forbid their remarriage in accordance with canon law, and, to safeguard the clergy's reputation, also prohibited their employment of women housekeepers (save close—and elderly—kinswomen).[27] As a result, a widowed priest faced a grim future, especially if left with young children: not only must he endure "sinful temptations," but he also had to survive without the aid of a wife—an essential component of the family economy as homemaker, tailor, cook, and fieldworker. Aware of such stress, Church authorities dealt leniently with widowed priests, permitting them to defrock voluntarily and transfer to a secular status without penalty or hardship.[28] In 1829, for example, a priest in Tobol'sk diocese, Nikolai Kremlev, citing his "widowhood and youth," obtained permission to leave the clerical estate "for appointment to wherever he is fit."[29]

Nicholas, however, acted to block this unhindered exit by widowed clergy. The question originally arose in the early 1830s, after the Third Section brought to light the case of a hieromonk who had voluntarily defrocked, hastily married, and entered civil service—to the indignation of local society. The Synod imposed stiff penalties on monks who defrocked but resisted attempts to impose similar disabilities on the parish clergy.[30] Nicholas put an end to such leniency in 1839 after learning of a scandal in Voronezh, where an archpriest voluntarily defrocked to avoid prosecution for adultery and promptly obtained a good position in the local civil service. At Nicholas's insistence, the Synod promulgated new rules on voluntary defrocking by white clergy, requiring that they leave their home province and excluding them from civil service for ten years in the case of priests, six years in the

---

[27] By contrast, sacristans could remarry, and their service records show that a handful in each district in fact did so. Because such sacristans could no longer don a surplice *(stikhar')* and perform certain liturgical functions, one bishop in 1827 forbade any further remarriages in his diocese. The Synod, however, found no legal grounds for this order and annulled his resolution; see the file in TsGIA SSSR, f. 796, op. 108, g. 1827, d. 670, ll. 1–11.

[28] Freeze, *Russian Levites*, p. 207.

[29] TsGIA SSSR, f. 796, op. 110, g. 1829, d. 412, ll. 1–8. Likewise, the authorities in Nizhnii Novgorod transmitted the request of a priest in their jurisdiction: "Because of his widowhood, youth, and infirmity of flesh (as a result of which he has lost the strength to resist worldy temptations and attacks by Satan), he has requested that he be removed from the clerical rank and released from the clerical estate to assume a position in imperial civil service" (ibid., op. 109, g. 1828, d. 665, ll. 44–46).

[30] For the new rules on monastic defrocking, see ibid., op. 112, g. 1831, d. 961, ll. 1–61; *PSPR*, nos. 407, 456.

case of deacons.[31] These rules made defrocking so onerous that only a handful voluntarily defrocked over the next two decades, however compelling the
circumstances, however indifferent the cleric might become to his mission
and duties.[32]

Although holy orders formed a natural ecclesiastical constraint against exit
by ordained clergy, that obstacle clearly did not apply to the clergy's sons.
For them, exit was legally possible by obtaining a written release from the
bishop (and also the Synod, if a youth held a seminary degree). In most cases
authorities readily gave such releases;[33] the main exception was outlying
dioceses, where some bishops had too few candidates and sometimes blocked
transfer, especially in the case of graduates. Most prelates, however, were
only too glad to release supernumerary candidates and help ease the pressure
from a great surplus of "idle, unplaced youths." Even the poorly educated
sons of sacristans sought transfer to the poll-tax population, preferring the
status of townsman to that of idle sacristan.[34] Aware of the excess number of
youths, the Synod routinely approved petitions from seminary graduates to
be released from Church service, making no challenge to suspicious claims
of "dizziness" and other mysterious ailments.[35] Consequently, transfer by
clerical progeny was not uncommon: scores of graduates obtained permission
each year to leave the clerical estate, and hundreds more without seminary
degrees also departed for a new secular status.[36]

Still, too few transferred. Whereas in the eighteenth century the Church
had a surfeit of uneducated youths, now it had a surfeit of educated ones as
well. Warnings of such an excess—a major new phenomenon of Nikolaevan
Russia—first appeared in the reform discussions of 1826–1829, and over the
next two decades the Synod compiled data showing a steady growth in the
number of idle youths, educated and otherwise. In 1830, for example, most
dioceses as yet had relatively few unplaced candidates, but within a decade
they reported substantially larger numbers (see table 9). By 1850 the pool of
graduates had doubled in a single decade, surrounded by a still larger num-

[31] *PSZ (2)*, 14: 12148.

[32] See the data in TsGIA SSSR, f. 796, op. 141, g. 1860, d. 1021, l. 17 ("spravka").

[33] For the shifts in earlier policy, see the decrees of 1800, 1801, and 1804 in *PSZ (1)*, 26:
19434, 19897; 28: 21278, 21472.

[34] For example, in 1850 the bishop of Vladimir reported that, whereas 20 percent of the
graduates transferred to secular careers (20 of 99), 61 percent of the expelled pupils left the
clerical estate (159 of 259). TsGIA SSSR, f. 796, op. 132, g. 1851, d. 2357, ll. 81 ob.-82.

[35] For examples of releases on medical grounds, see the petitions of a Penza graduate in 1826
("because of my weak physical condition"), a Moscow graduate in 1830 ("because of the dis-
eased condition of my legs"), and a Vladimir graduate in 1837 ("because of my weak health
and dizziness"). Ibid., op. 107, g. 1826, d. 396, l. 1; op. 111, g. 1830, d. 908, ch. 2, l. 1; op. 118,
g. 1837, d. 252, l. l.

[36] *IVO (1855)*, p. 22.

TABLE 9

Unplaced Seminary Graduates,
1830–1850:
Empire and Representative Dioceses

Diocese	1830	1840	1850
Astrakhan	0	1	3
Iaroslavl	0	23	92
Kiev	4	5	19
Kostroma	4	0	118
Moscow	16	72	44
Novgorod	17	32	101
Tula	36	39	149
Tver	5	39	321
Vladimir	31	80	189
EMPIRE	430	876	2,178

SOURCES: TsGIA SSSR, f. 796, op. 111,
g. 1830, d. 728, l. 122; op. 121, g. 1840, d.
186, l. 94; op. 131, g. 1850, d. 1998, ll. 1–
101.

ber of boys with incomplete educations.[37] The problem was especially acute in central Russia, with dioceses like Kaluga and Vladimir reporting nearly two hundred graduates unable to find clerical positions. Although some clergy in the West experienced a similar surfeit of candidates by mid-century, there the cause was a high status that lured excess candidates, not a low status with exit impeded.[38] Why did so few of the clergy's sons leave the clerical estate in Russia?

The reason, as Church hierarchs conceded, was coercive barriers, not the youths' attachment to the Church or their desire to become priests.[39] Education was a major obstacle: few clergy could afford to educate their sons in

[37] For information on the idle youths, see the diocesan reports for 1830 (TsGIA SSSR, f. 796, op. 111, g. 1830, d. 728, l. 122), for 1840 (ibid., op. 121, g. 1840, d. 186, l. 94), and for 1850 (ibid., op. 131, g. 1850, d. 1998).

[38] For example, in Prussia, where 120 to 150 vacancies appeared annually, the average number of theological students rose steadily, reaching some 1,600 by the 1830s (Bigler, *Politics of German Protestantism*, p. 57). For further references and discussion, see above, p. 110.

[39] See, for example, the 1863 episcopal opinions in TsGIA SSSR, f. 804, op. 1, r. 1 (summarized below, Chapter 6).

secular schools, and in fact after 1814 they had no legal right to do so.[40] All had to study in ecclesiastical schools on pain of inscription in the poll-tax registry. There the curriculum, ambience, and distance from secular ways left youths ill-prepared for worldly careers. Nor did parish clergy have the means to finance other careers for their sons; rare indeed was the cleric with capital to buy land or finance business ventures for his children. Clerical offspring were also dissuaded by the belief that laymen, especially in educated society, were hostile. Quite apart from the justness of that perception—and the evidence was bountiful—it certainly dissuaded many from venturing out of the security of their own soslovie. The clerical soslovie itself also acted to impede and discourage transfers, anxious as it was to have heirs to assume family positions and support elderly clerics and their families in retirement.[41] Au fond the clergy's children feared the worst fate in prereform Russia: descent into the poll-tax population, where they would be subject to taxation and recruit levies and consigned to some collective of townspeople or state peasants.[42]

The greatest impediment, believed some, was the set of discriminatory rules on entrance into state service, an area of booming growth that offered both high status and tempting futures.[43] Policy on this question had oscillated in the late eighteenth and early nineteenth centuries, partly in response to Church attempts to protect its pool of educated candidates, partly in response to the government's mushrooming needs for bureaucrats and scribes. In Nicholas's reign, however, that policy grew increasingly harsh and repressive. The emperor's personal preference became clear in 1826, when he proposed to require all seminary graduates to enter Church service—a suggestion that the bishops tactfully but firmly rejected. Nicholas's view, however, found rapport within the civil bureaucracy, reflecting the elites' longstanding distaste for clerical parvenus in civil service. Even when reaffirming the privileged right of priests' sons to enter civil service, the Senate

---

[40]In 1833, for example, only 150 clerical sons were enrolled in the state gymnasiums, compared with the nearly 60,000 in ecclesiastical schools (A. G. Rashin, "Gramotnost' i narodnoe obrazovanie v Rossii v XIX i nachale XX v.," IZ, 37 [1951]: 72; for data on enrollments in Church schools, see above, p. 110). For the special impact of ecclesiastical education, see the discussion and references in Gregory L. Freeze, "Caste and Emancipation: The Changing Status of Clerical Families in the Great Reforms," in David L. Ransel, ed., The Family in Imperial Russia (Urbana, 1978), pp. 131–132.

[41]One memoirist reports that his father wished to leave the clerical estate for a secular career but that his family insisted that he assume the family's position (S. Ia. Elpat'evskii's memoirs in OR GBL, f. 356, k. 3, d. 43, l. 24).

[42]See above, Chapter 3.

[43]The 1863 diocesan reports claimed that restricted entrance to state service was a major obstacle to clerical transfer; see, for example, the reports summarized in TsGIA SSSR, f. 804, op. 1, r. 1, d. 104(1), ll. 136–50.

in 1828 warned that unqualified or tainted youths from the clergy must not be admitted.[44] The army too spurned clerical offspring, especially the sons of sacristans, declaring that they were too poor and uneducated to enjoy privileges upon enlistment.[45] In 1841 the Ministry of Justice sought to exclude sacristans' sons from civil service, even if they held a seminary diploma, solely on the grounds that such candidates would flood the service.[46]

Although the Church repulsed the more aggressive assaults on the status of clerical sons, the government imposed further restrictions on the right of clerical sons to enter civil service, especially compared with the offspring of the nobility. One major barrier was a strict time limit: priests' sons who failed to find a civil service position within six months or who subsequently suffered discharge from service were consigned to the poll-tax population. Still more restrictive were discriminatory rules on sacristans' sons. For instance, any priest's son with a seminary degree had certain rights for entering civil service, however limited; a sacristan's son, by contrast, had to graduate in the top division of his class (*pervyi razriad*) to qualify, a rule that effectively barred most from state service even as mere copyists.[47] Although clerical offspring sometimes constituted a substantial proportion of provincial officials, the absolute numbers were small—a mere fraction of the fifty or sixty thousand pupils enrolled at any given time. In contrast, clerical sons in the West, especially in Germany, formed a major component of the new professions and secular intelligentsia.[48]

Thus, in social reality as well as in law, the clerical soslovie became more, not less, rigid in the first half of the nineteenth century. That pattern was highly anomalous, contrary to the Western example and even to the modest pace of social change in Nikolaevan Russia. As Nicholas's early manifesto demanding that *all* graduates become priests suggests, the emperor favored this hereditary order, which satisfied the Church's need for candidates and imposed no cost at all upon the state. And, traditionally, bishops staunchly

---

[44] *PSPR*, no. 178; *PSZ (2)*, 3: 1853.

[45] *PSPR*, no. 138; *PSZ (2)*, 2: 1262.

[46] TsGIA SSSR, f. 1149, op. 3, g. 1841, d. 78, ll. 19 ob.-20 (Ministry of Justice), 22–24 (Department of Laws). Significantly, the Church succeeded in blocking this attempt, relying solely upon the argument that education had precedence over birthright. See also James T. Flynn, "Tuition and Social Class in the Russian Universities: S. S. Uvarov and 'Reaction' in the Russia of Nicholas I," *Slavic Review*, 35 (1976): 232–48.

[47] *PSZ (2)*, 3: 2441; 4: 3331; 8: 6107; 11: 9615; 27: 26306.

[48] On Germany, see J. von Schulte's analysis of the *Allgemeine deutsche Biografie*, showing that over half of the 1,600 individuals in that reference work came from clerical families (*Lebenserinerungen*, 3 vols. [Giessen, 1908–09], 3: 271–76). In England, the clergy's impact is reflected in the high proportion of students at Oxford emanating from clerical backgrounds: 3 percent in 1577–1579, rising to 31 percent in 1860 (L. Stone, "The Size and Composition of the Oxford Student Body, 1580–1909," in L. Stone, ed., *The University in Society*, 2 vols. [Princeton, 1974], 1: 38–39, 103). The difference was not lost upon Russians; see the comments by a government official below, p. 311.

defended the integrity of the clerical estate, believing that it was their surest guarantee of an amply supply of ordinands, all educated and reared in the safe cocoon of clerical schools.

Disjuncture: Service and Soslovie

For all its benefits, the clerical soslovie also generated serious dysfunctions and, as authorities increasingly became aware, did not satisfy the special needs of a more modern Church. That discrepancy arose partly from the attempt to transform the priest into a pastor, something more than a liturgical functionary, armed with a full seminary education. As the new standards took effect, it became clear that they affected only the priesthood, not the lower-ranking deacons and sacristans. The old soslovie, moreover, also overproduced ordinands; although surplus clerical sons had been evident in the eighteenth century, the problem became ever more acute in the Nikolaevan era. Finally, the soslovie system entailed extremely high costs for the Church, not only requiring that it divert scarce resources to support sundry kin but also permitting family and welfare claims to encumber clerical positions, directly impeding attempts to raise the clergy's professional level. Let us examine in turn each of these disorders: the widening gap between priests and sacristans, the oversupply of candidates, and the high costs of welfare and family claims.

Priests and Sacristans

Ever since the state defined the white clergy to include both ordained clergy and sacristans, it had placed the latter on a distinctly lower plane. Typically, whenever the state extended new privileges to the clergy, it first conferred them on ordained clergy and only much later granted them to the sacristans.[49] Even while defending the sacristans' status as part of the clerical estate, Church authorities drew a sharp distinction between priests and sacristans, whether in bestowing awards or prescribing punishment.[50] In economic terms, too, the difference between the two categories was immense: priests received four times the income of sacristans, resulting in correspondingly radical differences in their material culture and way of life.[51] The difference in status was so great that in 1837 the chief procurator ordered dioc-

---

[49]For example, in 1835 the state exempted only priests' sons, not the progeny of sacristans, from corporal punishment (*PSZ* [2], 10: 8450; 15: 13268).

[50]See also the legal provisions for this distinction in ibid., 2: 1469; 17: 16376.

[51]For income shares in the eighteenth century, see Freeze, *Russian Levites*, pp. 136–38; for the first half of the nineteenth century, see the Synod's attempt to establish uniform rates in the 1830s and 1840s (above, p. 56).

TABLE 10

Seminary Graduates among Parish Clergy, 1835: Empire and
Representative Dioceses

Diocese	Percent of Clerics with Seminary Degree			
	Priest	Deacon	Sacristan	All
Arkhangel'sk	36.9%	0.0%	0.0%	14.1%
Iaroslavl	58.5	10.7	0.0	18.2
Irkutsk	24.4	0.0	0.0	8.3
Kaluga	61.1	2.0	0.0	17.8
Kiev	28.1	0.3	0.0	12.6
Kursk	73.7	8.3	0.0	21.5
Moscow	73.6	33.6	0.0	26.2
Penza	23.7	0.8	0.0	6.4
Podolia	18.2	0.0	0.0	6.1
St. Petersburg	52.2	22.5	0.0	20.8
Saratov	25.2	0.0	0.0	7.1
Tver	82.8	7.8	0.0	23.5
Vladimir	71.2	6.7	0.0	20.7
Volhynia	42.3	0.0	0.0	14.1
EMPIRE	42.5%	4.2%	0.0%	13.6%

SOURCE: TsGIA SSSR, f. 796, op. 117, g. 1836, d. 1201, ll. 3–6.

esan clerks to specify the precise rank of their fathers on service reports, not
merely indicate "from the clerical estate." Given the vast difference in privilege, such information was essential—and, as the procurator evidently suspected, deliberately obscured.[52]

The rise in clerical educational standards greatly magnified these differences, even serving to divide the two strata into distinct cultural and social
categories. Such distinctions, it should be stressed, were of relatively recent
vintage. In 1800, for example, a full seminary education was still uncommon
for priests, who usually had to demonstrate only some formal education
rather than completion of a full seminary course. A Synod survey of 1805
revealed that only 6,569 priests in the empire—less than 20 percent of the
entire rank—had gone beyond the first form (rhetoric) and studied in the
seminary's upper two forms (philosophy and theology).[53] But the development of the seminary after 1814 soon had a telling effect; by 1825 the num-

[52] TsGIA SSSR, f. 797, op. 8, d. 23987, ll. 1–21.
[53] Ibid., f. 796, op. 107, g. 1826, d. 460, ll. 29–29 ob.

TABLE 11

Educational Level of Clergy: Kaliazin District (1830)

	Priest	Deacon	Sacristan	Total
Academy Graduate	1	0	0	1 (0.4%)
Seminary Graduate	57	6	0	63 (22.7%)
Seminary Attended	18	23	36	77 (27.8%)
District School	3	11	110	124 (44.8%)
No Formal Schooling	0	1	9	10 (3.6%)
Secular Elementary	0	0	2	2 (0.7%)

SOURCE: GA Kalininskoi obl., f. 160, op. 1, d. 16272.

ber of priests with such education had doubled to 13,480.[54] Still more impressive data appeared a decade later, showing that the number of graduates (not merely those who had attended the upper two forms) constituted a majority of priests in central dioceses like Moscow (74 percent) and Tver (83 percent). Although standards were sharply lower in areas like Kiev diocese (28 percent) and Irkutsk (24 percent), the pool of graduates for the whole empire now comprised 43 percent of all priests—a phenomenal increase in just three decades. Significantly, however, this educational revolution did not extend to deacons and sacristans, few of whom, even in such advanced dioceses as Moscow or Petersburg, could boast a seminary degree (see table 10).

The service records of 1830 cast this pattern of education into sharp relief. Kaliazin district, a backwater area of Tver diocese, reported that virtually all its priests had a seminary degree, and one could even boast an academy education (see table 11). The files, to be sure, still list some elderly priests, ordained at the turn of the century, who possessed a distinctly inferior education (three, in fact, went no further than the elementary district school). But the educational profile of deacons and sacristans is radically inferior: none had attended the seminary, and some had even "not studied in schools" (meaning that they had nothing more than home-taught literacy). Predictably, standards were higher in the provincial capital, Tver, where most sacristans had attended the seminary and, no doubt, had taken the sacristan position temporarily until a suitable priest's position became available.[55] In Kiev diocese, although the general level of education was sharply lower, the distinction between priest and sacristan remained firm. In Kiev district, for

[54] Ibid., ll. 30–30 ob. (data for 1825, showing that 3,452 of 6,297 urban priests and deacons had reached the philosophy division or higher and that 10,028 of 42,193 rural priests and deacons had reached the same level).
[55] GA Kalininskoi obl., f. 160, op. 1, d. 16515 (klirovye vedomosti, 1830).

example, relatively few priests had a seminary degree (33 percent), and some (16 percent) lacked any formal education (inscribing "has not studied in the schools" on their service files). The sacristans, however, had still less education: only 16 percent had *any* formal education (usually just a year or two at the district school), and the rest reported that they had "not studied in schools."[56]

With good reason authorities inveighed against the low standards of sacristans, whatever the diocese. In one column of the service registers the local superintendent inserted his assessment of the clerics' religious knowledge, and rarely did he have much good to report in the case of sacristans and deacons. For example, an entry on the service registry for a parish in Kursk diocese reports that "the deacon knows something of the catechism" and the ponomar "knows little of the catechism." In another parish the superintendent reported that the diachok "does not know the catechism" but the ponomar "knows a little of the catechism."[57] To combat such ignorance, bishops sometimes suspended the hopelessly unfit or dispatched them to the diocesan capital for remedial study.[58] Yet the problem was so profound, so ubiquitous, that the bishops achieved little, selecting out only the worst cases during their summer visitations for such special training.

The Synod's aggregate data show that by 1860 the educational revolution was virtually complete for the rank of priest but that it had not even begun for the ranks of deacon and sacristan. As the diocesan reports show (see table 12), most priests in the central provinces now had a full seminary education—95 percent in Tver, to cite one example. Outlying areas, though lagging well behind such high rates, had nevertheless improved dramatically since the beginning of Nicholas's reign. In Kiev diocese, for example, the proportion of priests with diplomas had risen from 28 percent in 1830 to 82 percent in 1860. Even Siberian dioceses like Tobol'sk, which boasted less impressive figures (only two-thirds had a degree in 1860), had improved radically since 1830. Significantly, the change was greater than even these figures suggest, for the overall percentages were pulled down by aged clergy; most new ordinands had a formal degree and conformed to the new standard.[59]

Deacons and sacristans, by contrast, remained on an entirely different

---

[56]TsGIA UkrSSR, f. 127, op. 1009, dd. 275–76 (klirovye vedomosti, 1830).

[57]GA Kurskoi obl., f. 20, op. 2, d. 10, ll. 2–2 ob., 6 ob., 7 ob.-8.

[58]On the enrollment of sacristans in special schools for remedial study, see the occasional notations on service files in Kiev diocese (TsGIA UkrSSR, f. 127, op. 1009, dd. 275–76, 302–3). Sometimes the prelates expelled the unfit; for example, to cite the resolution of a bishop in Penza in 1831, "let him find sustenance in another estate—it is a sin to keep incompetent and lazy sacristans in the Church" (M. I. Satserdotov, "Iz proshlogo Penzenskoi eparkhii," *Istoricheskii vestnik*, 86 [1901]: 656).

[59]*IVO (1860)*, p. 19.

TABLE 12

Seminary Graduates among Parish Clergy, 1860:
Empire and Representative Dioceses

| Diocese | Percent of Clerics with Seminary Degree | | | |
	Priest	Deacon	Sacristan	All
Arkhangel'sk	82.7%	18.4%	0.0%	33.3%
Iaroslavl	95.6	33.9	0.5	35.1
Irkutsk	70.8	5.6	0.2	24.3
Kaluga	97.7	34.5	0.2	35.3
Kiev	82.1	1.4	0.0	31.3
Kursk	97.9	1.8	0.1	29.7
Moscow	97.9	43.0	0.7	36.5
Penza	89.1	17.6	0.2	30.5
Podolia	68.9	0.0	0.0	24.7
St. Petersburg	93.6	50.7	2.1	43.9
Saratov	75.7	1.6	0.3	24.1
Tver	95.1	39.3	0.4	33.9
Vladimir	97.9	36.6	3.3	37.6
Volhynia	94.3	0.0	0.0	37.3
EMPIRE	82.6%	15.6%	0.4%	29.2%

SOURCE: TsGIA SSSR, f. 796, op. 142, g. 1861, d. 2379.

plane. The rank of deacon, to be sure, showed substantial improvement in select dioceses like Moscow (where 43 percent held diplomas). In most cases, however, the deacon was little more than an ill-educated sacristan with a good voice and record, who could rise to the rank of deacon but lacked the requisite education for further advancement. The educational level of sacristans remained abysmally low; rarely did more than 1 percent of the sacristans in any diocese hold a seminary degree. And these, no doubt, were recent graduates waiting for a priest's position or priests demoted to sacristan status for misconduct. As one prelate complained in 1860, the shortage of qualified candidates for sacristan positions was so acute that he still had to install "people whose abilities and knowledge of reading, writing, and singing far from correspond to what is required."[60]

Provincial service lists for 1860 further underscore this radical gap between priests and the lesser ranks: priests' education had improved greatly; that of sacristans remained sharply inferior. In Kaliazin district of Tver dio-

[60]TsGIA SSSR, f. 796, op. 442, d. 40, l. 152 ob. (Polotsk report, 1860).

TABLE 13

Educational Level of Clergy: Kaliazin District (1860)

	Priest	Deacon	Sacristan	Total
Academy Graduate	1	0	0	1 (0.4%)
Seminary Graduate	79	18	0	97 (34.5%)
Seminary Attended	3	15	18	36 (12.8%)
District School	0	9	138	147 (52.3%)
No Formal Schooling	0	0	0	0 (0.0%)

SOURCE: GA Kalininskoi obl., f. 160, op. 1, d. 16298

cese, for example, 95 percent of the priests had a seminary degree; although the sacristans' education had risen slightly since 1830, none possessed a seminary degree, and only 12 percent had studied at all in the seminary, the remainder having gone no further than the elementary district school (see table 13). The gap was still greater in Kiev district: whereas 81 percent of the priests held a seminary degree, over half of the sacristans (53 percent) still had "not studied in the schools."[61] Very broadly, the sacristans' education by 1860 was roughly comparable to that of priests in the late eighteenth century, at least in central dioceses, where *some* education (though not a diploma) was required for appointment. The main point is that the educational revolution had touched exclusively priests and achieved only slight improvements in the lower ranks. The bishop of Saratov summed up the common view of many, writing that most priests had a good education but that "deacons and sacristans—almost without exception—do not know the catechism, and there are even some sacristans who cannot retell [the substance] of the books they read from during the liturgy or the sequence of the religious service."[62] Ultimately, that cleavage in educational and service standards would prompt authorities to consider radical new policies toward the lowly sacristans.

One immediate consequence of the gap between priest and sacristan was the refusal of seminarians to serve as diachki or ponomari, preferring instead to wait for a suitable priest's position. In Kaliazin district, for example, about one-third of the priests in 1830 had begun their careers as deacons or sacristans, but only 11 percent (mostly elderly priests) had done so by 1860. Similar

[61]TsGIA UkrSSR, f. 127, op. 1009, dd. 275–76; op. 1011, dd. 1210, 1275, 1331, 1392, 1429, 1490, 1533. Likewise, in Chigirin district, where most priests had a full seminary education, 69 percent of the sacristans lacked any formal education, and the rest had only a brief exposure to the elementary district schools.

[62]TsGIA SSSR, f. 796, op. 132, g. 1851, d. 2357, l. 311 (Saratov report for 1850).

changes transpired in Kiev district: priests with prior experience constituted 57 percent of the group in 1830, but their number shrank to 16 percent in 1860.[63] A corollary development was the steady drop in age at the time of ordination, already low, to well below the canonical requirement of thirty. Thus, between 1830 and 1860 the average age at ordination fell from 28.1 to 24.1 years in Irkutsk diocese (Nizhneudinsk district), from 29.6 to 25.6 in Kiev diocese (Chigirin district), and from 20.1 to 24.4 in Tver diocese (Kaliazin district).[64] Simultaneously, upward mobility within clerical ranks came to a halt. Ill-educated youths expelled from church school for misconduct or "obtuseness" became sacristans for life, whereas seminary graduates— despite the acute shortage of positions in many dioceses at mid-century— preferred to remain "idle" rather than accept a lowly sacristan appointment, so inferior in rank, status, and material support.

As a result, the "stepladder principle"—giving incentive to those below, experience to those promoted—gradually broke down in the parish clergy. For sacristans, that development no doubt reinforced their unenviable reputation for misbehavior (since hope of promotion was gone) and imprinted an indelible stigma of ignorance and misconduct upon the entire clergy. For priests, this order also created a strong sense of immobility: they achieved priestly status immediately upon graduation, thereafter finding few rewards for good service. That immobility clashed sharply with the clergy's higher level of education and, in the long run, served to fuel the priests' demands for greater power within the Church, even as their service status remained frozen.

Conservative churchmen complained of rather different problems: green seminarians became priests without apprenticeship in ritual, without maturity, without broader experience, and in direct contravention of canon law. The problem of "young priests" had aroused criticism in the reform discussions of 1826–1829 and attracted continual attention thereafter. It was the principal focus of an interesting memorandum by a former Synod clerk, A. N. Murav'ev, submitted to the chief procurator in 1852. Discerning widespread dissatisfaction with the clergy, Murav'ev attributed it to the ordination of young seminarians directly into priesthood. Such priests, he argued, lacked not only broad practical experience but even a working knowledge of the liturgy—the very element of Orthodoxy most prized by the common people. He therefore proposed to require that seminarians first serve as sac-

[63]GA Kalininskoi obl., f. 160, op. 1, d. 16298; TsGIA UkrSSR, f. 127, op. 1011, dd. 1210, 1275, 1331, 1392, 1429, 1490, 1533.

[64]GA Kalininskoi obl., f. 160, op. 1, dd. 12676, 16298; TsGIA UkrSSR, f. 127, op. 1009, dd. 275–76, 303–4; op. 1011, dd. 1210, 1275, 1331, 1392, 1429, 1490, 1533, 2091, 3875, 3972, 4021, 4068; GA Irkutskoi obl., f. 50, op. 1, d. 3870; sv. 368, dd. 7337, 7340–41; sv. 369, d. 7368 (klirovye vedomosti for Kaliazin, Chigirin, and Nizhneudinsk districts in 1830 and 1860).

TABLE 14

Correlation of Fathers' and Sons' Ranks:
Kaliazin District (1830–1860)

	Father's Rank		
Rank of Cleric	Priest	Deacon	Sacristan
1830			
Priest	37 (47%)	16 (20%)	26 (33%)
Deacon	10 (24%)	9 (22%)	22 (54%)
Sacristan	33 (21%)	14 (9%)	110 (70%)
1860			
Priest	41 (49%)	14 (17%)	28 (34%)
Deacon	4 (9%)	7 (17%)	31 (74%)
Sacristan	10 (7%)	16 (10%)	130 (83%)

SOURCE: GA Kalininskoi obl., f. 160. 1, dd. 16272, 16298.

ristans, explaining that "then there would be fewer unsuccessful ordinations, and the ranks of deacon and sacristan would not represent (as they now do) people undeserving the highest rank [of priest] because of their moral deficiencies."[65]

More important, the stratification between priest and sacristan threatened to become hereditary, for the service records show a growing correlation between a cleric's rank and that of his father. This correlation, though not ironclad, is clearly evident in the service lists for Kaliazin district in 1830 and 1860: most priests came from families of ordained clergy, most sacristans came from a sacristan family (see table 14). This pattern derived primarily from the enormous difference in the economic condition of priests and sacristans. The priest, who received four times the income of a sacristan, could far more easily afford to provide his son with a full seminary education, a virtual prerequisite for priesthood. To be sure, some sacristans' sons qualified for stipends, but such scholarships were few (and often only partial) and hence of little assistance to the vast majority of the sacristans' progeny. Less measurable, but no less important, was the disparity in cultural background,

[65] The memorandum, with a cover letter from Murav'ev, is to be found in the archive of the chief procurator (TsGIA SSSR, f. 797, op. 22, otd. 1, st. 2, d. 202, ll. 2–8); a second copy is in Filaret's archive, with a note from the chief procurator soliciting his opinion (ibid., f. 832, op. 1, d. 85, ll. 77–82).

a difference often stressed in memoirists' depictions of the genteel *popovichi* (priests' sons) and the boorish offspring of sacristans.[66]

These differences were well apparent to state authorities, who had sporadically challenged the status of sacristans earlier and who continued to do so. In 1826, for example, the army inquired about the rights of clerical children seeking entrance to military service and pointedly asked whether the sacristans' children enjoyed the privileges of the clerical soslovie. Although the Synod sent back an affirmative reply (the clergy's children "include not only the children of priests and deacons but also the children of sacristans"),[67] the very next year the army tried to deny access for sacristans to the officer corps: "Sacristans . . . compose, as it were, the lower class of people in the ecclesiastical domain, and because of their way of life and poverty, they cannot at all be distinguished from the lower class in other estates, who are admitted to the army only on the general terms of a twenty-five-year enlistment [as ordinary recruits]."[68] Although the state left the sacristans in the clerical soslovie, it showed an increasing willingness to diminish their status and to withhold privileges already granted the upper stratum of the white clergy.

As dissatisfaction with the sacristans' educational level and performance intensified, authorities began to consider some radical proposals for resolving the "sacristan question." One state official recommended in 1832 that the sacristans be converted into "agricultural laborers" for the parish church, supporting not only themselves but also the local priest. He further suggested that this division be made hereditary by excluding all sacristans' sons from Church schools. Arguing that the sacristans only demeaned the clerical rank, he suggested that the schools, like clerical positions, be reserved exclusively for the sons of priests.[69] Such notions appeared first among state authorities, but by the 1840s they began to penetrate the Church as well. In 1847 Protasov raised the issue of policy toward the sacristans' progeny, seeking not to eliminate the current generation of sacristans but at least to forestall the emergence of a new one.[70] The next year he circulated a similar proposal from a provincial priest, who castigated sacristans for their nefarious reputation and urged the Church to eliminate this class of unworthy servitors.[71]

Asked to comment on this last memorandum, Metropolitan Filaret of Mos-

---

[66]For example, see Giliarov-Platonov, *Iz perezhitogo*. Curiously, in 1828 the archbishop of Riazan proposed to regularize this difference, requiring that only the priests educate all their sons in Church schools, permitting sacristans to educate a single son because of their "smaller income" (TsGIA SSSR, f. 796, op. 107, g. 1826, d. 460, l. 204).

[67]*PSPR*, no. 85; see also TsGIA SSSR, f. 796, op. 133, g. 1852, d. 1071, ll. 1–2 ob.

[68]*PSPR*, no 138.

[69]Ibid., no 429.

[70]TsGIA SSSR, f. 797, op. 18, d. 41101, l. 1 (Protasov to Filaret, 1848).

[71]Ibid., ll. 3–10 ob.

cow categorically rejected any scheme to expel sacristans or exclude their sons from Church schools. In Filaret's view, sacristans' sons often made superior candidates for the clergy, for they had been spared the pampering found among more prosperous families of priests. He also denied any hard-and-fast hereditary lines between the two groups, noted that some sacristans' sons became priests, but offered no data to support that contention. Behind all these arguments lay Filaret's real concern: a desire that the Church have the largest possible pool of potential candidates, its only mechanism for raising quality within the old soslovie system.[72] In addition, he noted, the Church needed some sacristans to help perform the liturgy—at least one reader, preferably two, to assist the priest. Yet the Church had little alternative to hereditary sacristans. Few laymen in rural parishes were literate and capable of assisting in services, and few parishes had the wherewithal to employ seminary graduates as sacristans. Those telling objections would long impede any radical attempts to restructure the lower strata of the white clergy.

Demographic Imbalance

Designed to assure an ample flow of candidates, the clerical soslovie had tended to overproduce them ever since its inception. By the 1850s unplaced youths numbered in the thousands and were a major source of concern for both Church and state authorities. A characteristic expression of alarm filled the annual report from Vladimir in 1850:

> Because a great many clerical positions in Vladimir have been eliminated (in accordance with the new draft shtat), the clergy exceed the [number] needed, and the distribution of seminary graduates poses a great burden for diocesan administration. Many of these pupils, because they are orphans or because of their parents' destitution, find themselves in the most pitiable situation. To alleviate their plight in some measure, diocesan administration has consigned some to live in monasteries that have a good income; temporarily, it has permitted others to perform religious rites in positions due to be eliminated under the terms of the draft shtat.[73]

More important, the bishop's statistical data showed that the problem was becoming steadily worse, for each year the seminary added still more names to the list of idle graduates and expelled pupils. The bishop had nearly 600 unplaced seminarians (including 336 graduates), even after applying the quasi-legal measures described above. Several other prelates—in Saratov, Tambov, Viatka, Kursk, Penza, Nizhnii Novgorod, St. Petersburg, even outlying Kishinev—also raised the problem of "surplus youths" in their annual

---

[72] Ibid., op. 19, otd. 1, st. 2, d. 42644, ll. 7–17 ob.
[73] Ibid., f. 796, op. 132, g. 1851, d. 2357, ll. 81–82.

reports for 1850.[74] Metropolitan Filaret, who in theory preferred a large pool of candidates, also became anxious: "The increase in the number of people in dioceses without [vacant] positions, besides increasing poverty, threatens to damage morality and thus requires action by the government."[75] The matter did come to the attention of state officials, just as Filaret had feared. The governor of Kostroma, for example, reported that "the number of pupils and students leaving the schools exceeds by several-fold the number needed to fill all the positions" available in the Church.[76]

Not all dioceses enjoyed such riches of talent. Shortages in graduates were most evident in eastern Russia, especially in the Siberian dioceses, where the vast expanses and extremely low density of population made parishes dispersed, poor, and unattractive. Aware of this personnel problem, the government upon occasion specifically forbade clerical youths to transfer to secular service and permitted the Church to recruit from groups outside clerical ranks. Shortages also affected some outlying areas of European Russia (such as Orenburg, Astrakhan, and Arkhangel'sk) and dioceses in non-Russian areas (such as Riga). Thus in 1850 the bishop of Orenburg wrote that "the shortage (especially of seminary graduates) is very strongly felt," a complaint echoed in several other diocesan reports.[77] The Church had attempted to fill such gaps in 1829, when it required the transfer of surplus candidates from central to outlying areas, but the law had little effect: seminarians refused to abandon hopes for appointment in the home diocese and journey to the desolate wilds of Siberia. Their resistance to such transfer was apparent in 1840, for example, when Irkutsk sought candidates for the 114 priest vacancies in the diocese; bishops in several central dioceses designated candidates, but many petitioned for release on grounds of "ill health" or "family responsibilities."[78] Hence the results were negligible: in 1839, when the number of idle youths exceeded five thousand, the Church managed to relocate only forty to areas outside their home dioceses—less than 1 percent of the surplus seminarians.[79] As a result, the service lists for Irkutsk and Tomsk in 1860 indicate some immigrant priests, but too few to satisfy the manpower needs of Siberia or to offer significant relief for the surplus of candidates in central Russia.[80]

[74] Ibid., ll. 296–97, 305–5 ob., 347, 128 ob., 191 ob.-92, 149 ob., 187–87 ob., 436 ob.-37.

[75] "Materialy dlia biografii Filareta," ChOLDP, 1870, kn. 11: 32–33 (Filaret to Nikolai, 1848).

[76] TsGIA SSSR, f. 797, op. 19, otd. 1, st. 2, d. 42655, l. 2.

[77] Ibid., f. 796, op. 132, g. 1851, d. 2357, ll. 414 ob. (Orenburg), 673–73 ob. (Riga).

[78] Ibid., op. 121, g. 1840, d. 758, ll. 1–134.

[79] IVO (1839), p. 21.

[80] Immigrants, for example, represented a substantial proportion of the clergy in both Irkutsk and Tomsk dioceses; see the files for 1860 in GA Irkutskoi obl., f. 60, op. 1, sv. 368, dd. 7337, 7340–41; sv. 369, d. 7369; GA Tomskoi obl., f. 170, op. 1, d. 234.

TABLE 15

Staffing Proportions, 1830: Empire and Representative Dioceses

	Registered Positions			Actual Clergy			
Diocese	Priest	Deacon	Sacristan	Priest	Deacon	Sacristan	Percent
Astrakhan	79	51	224	81	43	139	74.3%
Iaroslavl	1,016	509	2,061	993	481	2,008	96.8
Irkutsk	445	157	895	440	183	705	88.7
Kiev	1,394	608	2,792	1,295	395	1,591	68.4
Vladimir	1,337	673	2,671	1,320	663	2,625	98.4
EMPIRE	34,479	17,375	69,284	32,001	15,029	57,281	86.1%

SOURCE: TsGIA SSSR, f. 796, op. 112, g. 1831, d. 360/b, ll. 3–8.

One consequence of this surfeit of educated and uneducated youth in most dioceses was a higher rate of staffing in the empire, especially in central dioceses. As table 15 shows, the central dioceses had nearly complete staffing in 1830, not only in the desirable rank of priest but also in the lesser position of sacristan. In fact, full staffing had been achieved by the late eighteenth century in some central dioceses, an old settled area that produced more candidates than the fixed shtat could absorb.[81] Such was not the case in outlying areas, where many positions in the shtat remained vacant (for example, 32 percent in Kiev diocese, 62 percent in Ekaterinoslav). Predictably, most vacancies were in the lowly rank of sacristan; in Kiev district, for example, 93 percent of the priests' positions were filled, but only 58 percent of the deacons, 55 percent of the diachki, and 30 percent of the ponomari. Indeed, only 11 percent of all parishes in that district had a full staff; most had one, sometimes more, vacant positions.[82]

Thirty years later, in 1860, higher rates of staffing existed in most parts of the empire. As table 16 shows, the central dioceses maintained their high level of staffing, and the periphery had begun to catch up (Kiev diocese, for instance, filled 99 percent of its positions, compared with 68 percent in 1830). Behind this change was a push-pull dynamic: the shtat reductions of the 1840s reduced the number of positions, especially in poor parishes, and the soslovie produced ever larger numbers of candidates. As a result, most parishes tended to have a full staff; in Kiev district, for example, the number of fully staffed churches rose from 11 percent (1830) to 96 percent (1860).[83]

[81] Freeze, Russian Levites, pp. 141–42.

[82] TsGIA UkrSSR, f. 127, op. 1009, dd. 275–76 (klirovye vedomosti, Kiev district, 1830).

[83] Ibid., op. 1011, dd. 1210, 1275, 1331, 1392, 1429, 1490, 1533 (klirovye vedomosti, Kiev district, 1860).

TABLE 16

Staffing Proportions, 1860: Empire and Representative Dioceses

	Registered Positions			Actual Clergy			
Diocese	Priest	Deacon	Sacristan	Priest	Deacon	Sacristan	Percent
Astrakhan	148	59	275	145	54	246	92.3
Iaroslavl	1,007	476	2,001	977	372	1,705	87.7
Irkutsk	280	77	840	253	71	434	90.2
Kiev	1,294	70	2,027	1,275	70	2,003	98.7
Vladimir	1,265	508	2,214	1,265	508	2,214	100.0
EMPIRE	37,588	12,697	66,736	37,945	12,444	63,421	97.3%

SOURCE: *IVO (1861)*, prilozhenie no. 4.

Clearly, the Church had reached a critical saturation point in staffing, which implied both greater difficulty in reform (bishops must not only eliminate positions but also dispose of redundant clergy) and greater urgency (the surfeit of youths being certain to rise inexorably and quickly).

The traditional solution since Peter the Great was military conscription (*razbor*), which swept away idle, unlettered, or misbehaving youths and dispatched them to the poll-tax population or the army. Such conscriptions, coming about once a decade in the eighteenth century, wreaked considerable havoc among the clergy, spiriting away intended heirs and exposing the clergy to the humiliation of a recruit levy, previously imposed only upon the lowly commoners, not privileged society. Sensitive to this problem, Alexander I ordered only one conscription during his reign—the levy of 1806, which took sacristans with bad records as well as idle, uneducated sons.[84] Though sacristans and seminarians were permitted to enlist in the army during the war of 1812, Alexander ordered no more conscriptions, partly because he became embroiled in no major foreign war after 1815, the customary trigger for a conscription in the clerical estate.

Nicholas, ever insistent that all serve the state, ordered a new conscription in 1831. The number of unplaced youths had accumulated, and, with the empire's military needs steadily mounting, Nicholas elected to call upon the "Levites" as had his predecessors: "Having recognized the fairness of directing all excess, unneeded people of the clerical domain to the needs of the state, we find that at the present time, when the welfare and glory of Russia demand a necessary strengthening of our armies, this goal can be attained in the best, truest fashion by using these people for military service."[85] An inves-

[84] *PSZ (1)*, 29: 22362.
[85] TsGIA SSSR, f. 796, op. 112, g. 1831, d. 360/b, l. 1.

tigation by the Synod revealed that, alongside numerous vacancies in the empire (11,505 registered positions), there were 45,770 pupils in Church schools, another 66,790 under age fifteen living at home with their parents, and some 7,351 over age fifteen living with their parents. The Synod therefore ruled that diocesan authorities should send idle, unqualified and tainted youths between the ages of fifteen and forty into the army. The primary exception, apart from reserving enough candidates to satisfy the dioceses' current and future needs, was the case of only sons, who were to be exempted from the draft in order to provide for their parents.[86] Metropolitan Filaret of Moscow, in a private letter to the chief procurator, favored even more stringent measures, including the draft of all "expelled pupils," since these were rejected only for good cause, such as obtuseness or immorality.[87] In subsequent months, however, authorities in Petersburg drew back from a rigorous conscription, modifying rules and entirely exempting those dioceses with chronic shortages of candidates.[88]

Nevertheless, the conscription had a severe impact on the remaining dioceses. Those consigned to the army formed a motley group—unschooled youths, expelled seminarians, sacristans with bad records, and redundant employees of diocesan administration. The proportions varied among dioceses, but all were well represented, especially by tainted sacristans. According to later tabulations, the Church dispatched over six thousand youths to the army, which accepted 83 percent of the draftees and returned the balance as unfit. The number drafted, however, varied sharply from one diocese to the next. The largest consignments came from central black-soil provinces (such as Kursk, which yielded 702 draftees), with most other dioceses dispatching one or two hundred.[89]

In the aftermath of this conscription, authorities received hundreds of petitions requesting release from the razbor. In most cases petitioners argued that a son had been wrongly, even illegally, conscripted, that he was urgently needed to fill a registered vacancy at the local parish, or that he was the sole support for aged parents or other dependents.[90] Without question, the conscription provoked widespread opposition and discontent, as many clergy blamed local authorities for their woes and saw themselves as the victims of a corrupt, venal administration.[91] The petitions, which sometimes won the

---

[86] PSPR, no. 369; PSZ (2), 6:4563.

[87] Filaret, Perepiska s Nechaevym, pp. 21–23.

[88] PSPR, nos. 379, 381, 383, 384, 389, 406.

[89] TsGIA SSSR, f. 796, op. 112, g. 1831, d. 360/a, ll. 4, 120–21 obl, 151–52.

[90] For the hundreds of appeals that ensued, see ibid., dd. 1049–51.

[91] For contemporary songs bewailing the conscription, see the materials on Kaluga (Istoricheskaia zapiska ob uchrezhdenii i sostoianii Kaluzhskoi eparkhii za stoletnii period ee sushchestvovaniia [Kaluga, 1900], pp. 30–31) and Penza (Satserdotov, "Iz proshlogo," pp. 663–66). For evidence of the animosity that punctilious bishops could provoke among parish clergy, see A. A. Blagoveshchenskii, "Filaret Amfiteatrov," RS, 42 [1884]: 190–91).

Synod's support and obtained a reversal, persisted well into the 1840s, a major burden on Church administration and a chilling testimony to the hardships wrought by conscription.[92] Nevertheless, the conscription failed to remove significant numbers of youths—six thousand or so versus the tens of thousands captured in eighteenth-century conscriptions. Authorities still focused upon the unworthy (the insufficiently educated or miscreants) and thus tapped a relatively small pool, since the overwhelming majority of youths had attended Church schools and could justly claim exemption. Thus the inapplicability of old principles, not a mere loss of will, made the traditional conscription ineffective and, ultimately, forced authorities to seek some other, radically different solution to the problem.

Still, conventional solutions die hard, and authorities attempted one last draft during the Crimean War. Responding to the army's demand for manpower, Nicholas inquired of the Synod in April 1853 whether it would be "useful at the present time to dispatch to military service the clergy's sons who prove superfluous and exceed the needs of the ecclesiastical domain."[93] On the Synod's behalf Protasov replied that the conscription of 1831 had demonstrated the unfeasibility of conscription, for it had only wrought hardship on the clergy, provoked widespread discontent, and burdened the Synod with a flood of supplications.[94] He noted too that the conscription tended to take the strong and able needed to support the aged and dependents while returning the weak and unfit, themselves in need of support. The chief procurator added that in 1850 the Synod had ordered bishops to make a continuing purge of undesirables. Since fifteen hundred youths had already been removed over the past two years, Protasov expressed doubts that a new conscription would yield many draftees. Warning that a public conscription was degrading for the clergy and useless for the state, Protasov suggested that bishops compile a secret list of unwanted youths, who, after a review by the Synod, could be dispatched to the army. Nicholas approved this proposal, adding, however, that "I hope that this matter is implemented with due scrupulousness and strict equity."[95]

Shortly after Protasov filed this report, Metropolitan Filaret broke ranks with other hierarchs and submitted a memorandum strongly defending the conscription. Not wholly insensitive to the interests of parish clergy, he simply regarded the conscription as preferable to other, more harmful measures already under consideration, such as the expulsion of sacristans or restrictions on seminary enrollments. In Filaret's view, the surplus of youth resulted primarily from the lack of rigorous conscriptions, which not only removed

---

[92]For example, a diachok in Riazan, as late as 1845, obtained his son's release and reappointment (TsGIA SSSR, f. 796, op. 126, g. 1845, d. 1263, ll. 1–14).

[93]Ibid., f. 797, op. 23, otd. 2, st. 2, d. 386, l. 1.

[94]Ibid., ll. 2–5.

[95]Ibid., l. 2.

unworthy youths but also exerted a healthy, sobering effect upon parish clergy, reminding them of the ultimate price for immorality or malfeasance. But Filaret favored the conscription primarily because it enabled the Church to maintain a large pool of candidates, from which bishops could select the most capable and reject the remainder. That represented Filaret's solution to the defects of a closed social order: unable to draw recruits from all social strata, the Church needed to protect its only source—the clerical soslovie. In a word, Filaret welcomed the surfeit: it enabled the Church to choose the gifted and committed, even within the confines of the soslovie order.[96]

Most bishops, however, held the contrary view. In an era when conscription loomed as a great humiliation, clerical conscription wrought great damage to the clergy's status. That view in fact prevailed in the Synod's resolution on the matter in December 1853. Following the main outlines of Protasov's earlier report, the Synod ordered nothing more than a narrow, clandestine purge. Bishops were to compile lists of potential draftees (those deemed unworthy of clerical appointment by reason of education or character), subject to approval by the Synod. Going further than Protasov, the Synod exempted dioceses with a shortage of candidates. Although that resolution provoked protests from the state, the Synod's view—with Protasov's firm support—prevailed.[97]

As state officials rightly suspected, the Synod's purge in fact produced few results. In September 1853, for example, the bishop of Vladimir submitted a list of 271 potential draftees, of which the Synod dispatched just 113 to the army. Elsewhere the numbers were still smaller—14 from Mogilev, 29 from Chernigov, 18 from Novgorod, 43 from Kostroma, and 20 from Polotsk.[98] Most draftees were tainted sacristans, whose misdeeds richly merited expulsion; their departure constituted no great loss to the Church. Thus in the end the conscription had virtually no effect: Church authorities refused to conduct a mass purge of the whole soslovie, leaving intact an immense population of unplaced youths.

Above all, this surplus population overtaxed the Church's meager resources, obliging the Church to support and educate a populace far in excess of its means or even its needs. Overpopulation also worked great hardships on the clergy, who had to educate sons without profit, who even had to support grown sons until a position finally fell vacant. Although that surfeit had some benefits (above all, it assured a rich pool of candidates), by the

[96]Filaret, SMO, 3: 514–17; TsGIA SSSR, f. 797, op. 23, otd. 2, st. 2, d. 386, ll. 11–17.

[97]TsGIA SSSR, f. 797, op. 23, otd. 2, st. 2, d. 386, ll. 35–36; op. 24, otd. 2, st. 2, d. 399, ll. 1–8; OR GBL, f. 316 (Filaret), k. 65, d. 16, ll. 26–27.

[98]TsGIA SSSR, f. 796, op. 135, g. 1854, d. 1098 (Orel); d. 306 (Riga); d. 307 (St. Petersburg); d. 331 (Polotsk); d. 365 (Kostroma); d. 490 (Mogilev); d. 628 (Astrakhan); d. 862 (Novgovod); d. 2284 (Chernigov); d. 2286 (Vladimir).

mid-nineteenth century authorities were no longer willing to conduct the kind of Petrine conscription that this order presupposed. The result was ever larger contingents of youths—educated and otherwise—in the ecclesiastical domain. Unable or unwilling to prune the soslovie as eighteenth-century authorities had done, the Church faced a growing rupture between the soslovie and the institution. The mounting surplus, as we shall see, was the chief precipitant to Nikolaevan reform in the soslovie.

Soslovie and Welfare

Like other institutions in prereform Russia, the Church bore direct responsibility for the population in its domain. That responsibility embraced not just clergy but a multitudinous soslovie of retired clerics, their widows, and orphans—all part of the ecclesiastical domain and entitled to welfare and assistance. This welfare steadily outpaced the Church's growth, especially its resources, and became ever more onerous and complex. The principal problem was the plight of retired clergy and of the families of deceased clerics, who enjoyed neither income from service nor the benefit of personal wealth, pensions, or landholding. If clerical welfare constituted an important problem in the West, it was all the more serious in Russia, given the size of the estate and the dearth of resources.[99] The bishop, to be sure, had some funds at his disposal (income from monasteries, unexpended monies in the diocesan budget, even his own salary), but those sums hardly sufficed to aid the thousands of needy in his charge. As a result, his principal form of welfare was clerical service itself—the dispensation of a position to a kinsman willing to assume an obligation to his predecessor or that man's family. Family claims, moreover, had some valid economic justification: clergy usually constructed their homes on parish-church land, and disposition of the house was simpler in the case of kinsmen. When an outsider was appointed, diocesan authorities had either to mediate the sale or to remove the building so that the new cleric could build his own home. In either event the predecessor was left without a house (if he sold) or without a place to put it. But the primary reason for family claims was welfare: candidates obtained their appointments on con-

---

[99] For the welfare problem in the West, see: Tackett, *Priest and Parish*, pp. 141–43; Fischer, "Bilder," pp. 17–18; and, more generally, the discussion in Georges Dole, *La protection sociale du clergé. Histoire et institutions ecclesiales* (Paris, 1980), pp. 21–45. The Russian clergy's needs, compared with other social groups in Russia, were all the greater because of their greater longevity; one study, for example, showed that 42 percent of all clergy reached the age of seventy, compared with 24 percent of the physicians and 32 percent of the minor civil servants (Nancy M. Frieden, *Russian Physicians in an Era of Reform and Revolution, 1865–1905* [Princeton, 1981], p. 34).

dition that they marry their predecessors' daughters and share income with the retired clerics and their families.[100]

Family ties to positions had long been the subject of criticism by Church and state authorities, especially from the early eighteenth century. Of greatest concern were clannish nests, where a single family placed its members as priest, deacon, and sacristan. The Petrine state objected strongly to such nests, partly because they tended to proliferate appointments beyond actual need, merely to provide for family members, and partly because they seemed likely to conceal the misdeeds of fellow kinsmen. As a result, authorities in the eighteenth century imposed restrictions on family claims, permitting no single family to monopolize parishes and giving education precedence over family rights. Yet that policy left some loopholes: authorities tolerated some family claims, so long as the candidate satisfied the educational norms of that diocese and so long as some outsiders were present in the parish. In effect, eighteenth-century authorities did not abrogate family claims to positions but merely limited them. The right to bequeath a position, especially to a son or son-in-law, through the transfer of positions (*sdacha mest*) provided the principal form of welfare by the early nineteenth century.

Even so, authorities still had good reason to oppose such claims. Above all, this system diminished the role of merit in appointments, inevitably introducing criteria other than education and ability. To be sure, bishops insisted that the kinsman meet the norms prevailing in that diocese for the kind of position and parish he sought. Thus in central dioceses the son or son-in-law seeking a priest's position had to possess a seminary degree; if so, then he could expect precedence over all other claimants for the position. Education, consequently, tended to become merely a qualifying precondition, not the chief criterion in appointments. A low-ranking, even rowdy seminary graduate who struck a deal with a retiring priest (usually involving an agreement to marry his daughter) had precedence over a superior student. As Metropolitan Filaret complained in 1823, the appointment of clergy for purposes of welfare "inhibits the freedom of authorities to select the most worthy and, if used often, will weaken zeal to prepare for service [in the seminary],

---

[100] As Znamenskii wrote after mid-century, "one can say without exaggeration that, of all those entering the white clergy during the last twenty to twenty-five years, hardly more than one-twentieth of them entered upon entirely unencumbered positions—that is, [requiring] no obligations to the family of the previous cleric, or with no requirement that he take [someone's] daughter as his wife" (Znamenskii, *Prikhodskoe dukhovenstvo*, p. 169). The Western churches had little to rival such close family claims; only in Germany did some, less intense, family ties to particular parishes develop. See O. Fischer, "Märkische Pfarrergeschlechter," *JBKG*, 21 (1926): 22–58, 25 (1930): 122–38; and J. Schneider, *Die evangelischen Pfarrer der Markgrafschaft Baden-Durlach in der zweiten Hälfte des achtzehnten Jahrhunderts* (Lahr/Baden, 1936), pp. 27–31.

spreading the idea that one can receive a position through hereditary claims, not merit."[101] Filaret later expressed fears that "if authorities, preoccupied with the noble desire to care for the poor and orphans, pay no heed to the rights of merit and service, then they will often overlook the worthy, who will be left without positions for a long time." Consequently, he warned, "the best seminarians will sometimes transfer to civil administration, and positions withheld from them will be given to inferior [candidates] because of a fiancée."[102]

Beyond lowering the quality of clergy, family control also disrupted prompt staffing of positions. In the case of families where the cleric died young, the position had to remain vacant for a long time—until the cleric's daughter came of marriageable age or the son completed studies at the seminary.[103] Such practices were particularly anathema to Filaret, who complained that "positions reserved for orphans can rarely be left vacant without undermining order in the Church."[104] Although bishops sometimes appointed temporary replacements (who shared the income with the predecessors' families), that solution was hardly satisfactory, since such temporary appointees had no inclination or incentive to develop strong pastoral ties to the parish.

This system of welfare, furthermore, generated serious problems even after the initial appointment. In cases of *mariages de convenance*, though the seminarian inspected the potential spouse beforehand (taking into account her age, looks, and education), he also gave much consideration to the post tendered, the dowry, and the obligations to support her kinsmen. As critics later complained, this bargaining all too often resulted in a match plagued by conflict and tension, hardly a model for parishioners.[105] At the same time, what was welfare to one family was an onus for another: the new cleric found himself bound to support a host of kinsmen, from aged clerics and widows to young boys at the seminary.[106] Sometimes these burdens proved intolerable. Poignant indeed was the petition from a deacon in Riazan, asking permission to abrogate his contract and to relocate to another diocese. The reason, he explained, was the ruinous contract to support his

---

[101] Filaret, *SMO*, 2: 98.

[102] Ibid., 3: 32.

[103] For a typical case of a position reserved for a cleric's daughter, see the service lists for Kiev district in 1860 (TsGIA SSSR, f. 127, op. 1011, d. 1331, l. 124 ob.).

[104] Filaret, *SMO*, 2: 98.

[105] TsGIA SSSR, f. 804, op. 1, r. 1, d. 150 (with comprehensive summary of 1863 reports); for a specific case, see Savva's "examination" of potential brides (Savva [Tikhomirov], *Khronika moei zhizni*, 9 vols. [St. Petersburg, 1897–1911], 1: 172).

[106] The service registries in provincial archives give a graphic picture of this problem in their lists of dependents attached to clerical families; see the lists for Tver in GA Kalininskoi obl., f. 160, op. 1, dd. 15844, 16298.

predecessor: "In the disastrous years [of famine, 1830–1834], I had to sell all my livestock and everything in the house to buy grain for the family of eight" that he was obliged to support.[107] Clerical efforts to renege or renegotiate such contracts clogged the dockets of every diocesan administration.

In the early 1820s authorities attempted to solve the welfare problem by creating special diocesan "welfare boards for poor people in the clerical estate." After Chief Procurator Golitsyn raised this issue in March 1822, the Synod solicited reports and opinions from leading prelates and then promulgated a statute on welfare boards in 1823. It observed that the existing resources were too small to provide adequate welfare and that the appointment of kinsmen for welfare purposes hamstrung bishops' efforts to raise educational and service standards among parish clergy. Although this statute formally authorized some appointments for purposes of welfare (the first time such recognition was accorded in law), it sought primarily to ameliorate the needs of retired clergy and their families by establishing the diocesan welfare boards, financed with 150,000 rubles from the sale of candles. Each board had a specific sum at its disposal, which it was to allot yearly to the most needy and deserving in the soslovie.[108]

Initially, Church authorities seemed determined to restrict family claims. In 1829, for example, the daughter of a deceased priest in Vladimir complained to the Synod that her sister had been unfairly deprived of claims to a family position (with the right to marry a seminarian, who would assume the post). When no member of the top division (*pervyi razriad*) of the graduating class agreed to marry her, the girl made arrangements to marry a lower-ranking student (in the *vtoroi razriad*). To her indignation, the bishop rejected the claim, insisting that such a good position belonged to a student in the first division, and he appointed someone else. The Synod upheld his decision, observing that only the best pupils should hold the coveted positions in city churches and that in any event "appointments to the ordained clergy are made according to merit, not kinship."[109] In another case the Synod formally rebuked a bishop for forcing a seminarian to marry the daughter of his predecessor. Although the bishop had only intended to serve welfare needs, parishioners strongly objected to the appointment and complained to central authorities.[110] Above all, authorities strenuously opposed the formation of clannish nests, insisting that some members of the staff be outsiders. That concern was apparent in a case in Tver diocese, where the bishop

[107] TsGIA SSSR, f. 796, op. 117, g. 1836, d. 499, ll. 1–8.

[108] *PSZ (1)*, 38: 29583; Filaret, *SMO*, 2: 91–107.

[109] TsGIA SSSR, f. 796, op. 110, g. 1829, d. 92, ll. 1–6 ob. Similar cases involved Chernigov diocese in 1831 (ibid., op. 112, g. 1831, d. 18, ll. 3–4) and Riazan diocese in 1836 (ibid., op. 117, g. 1836, d. 922, ll. 1–5).

[110] Ibid., op. 109, g. 1828, d. 46, ll. 1–4 ob.

removed a sacristan "for increasing kinship ties on the staff by concluding a second marriage without his superiors' permission."[111]

Nevertheless, as service records attest, authorities found that they could not enforce such policies and, as before, had to heed claims based on welfare considerations. Although the service lists are incomplete (kinship ties are indicated only for those still living and present in the parish), they reveal a high proportion of parishes with various kinds of family ties—clerics related to each other, to a retired predecessor, or to his kin. In Kaliazin uezd, for example, the files for 1830 show that 56 percent of the parishes had some form of kinship ties; by 1860 the proportion had risen to 73 percent.[112] Such proportions, significantly, are an underestimation: they do not show kinship ties to a deceased cleric or kinsman that determined an earlier appointment. The kinship ties also varied considerably; most often they were marital ties (sons-in-law or brothers-in-law), but sometimes they involved members of the same family (sons and fathers; brothers) serving in the same parish.

Thus family claims held firm in the first half of the nineteenth century, with Church authorities retreating from the restrictive policy of the 1820s. That was true of the Synod itself, which routinely received numerous petitions seeking recognition of family claims and often acted favorably upon them. Although it tended to deny such claims if the petitioner's record was tainted, it usually approved requests from those with long, exemplary service records, declaring that clergy with meritorious service deserved security in their old age.[113] Typical was the case of a deacon in Kaluga diocese, Grigorii Seleznev. In March 1847 Seleznev petitioned the Synod that, after serving forty-seven years, "I intended to give my deacon's position to any pupil in the seminary who earns the approval of diocesan authorities to assume my position, on condition that he take my daughter Ol'ga as his wife." When queried by the Synod, the bishop replied that he had received a flurry of such requests after announcement of the new shtat, which sharply reduced the number of registered positions. In this case, he explained, the deacon was still healthy and the girl, aged twenty-three, should have been married long ago; hence he decided to reject the petition so as not "to increase the number of deacons," a rank greatly reduced under the new shtat. The Synod, however, overturned the bishop's decision: "Direct His Grace, Nikolai, bishop of Kaluga, to retire the deacon . . . Grigorii Seleznev (in accordance with his request), having served in this rank more than forty years without fault, and

[111] GA Kalininskoi obl., f. 160, op. 1, d. 16550, ll. 283–84.

[112] Ibid., dd. 16272, 16298.

[113] For examples of poor records spoiling such requests, see the Synod's refusal to honor a request from a priest in Tver who sought a son-in-law for his daughter with the right to assume his position (TsGIA SSSR, f. 796, op. 130, g. 1849, d. 1207, ll. 1–7).

offer his place to one of the pupils in the seminary who agrees to marry his daughter Ol'ga."[114]

Even the redoubtable Metropolitan Filaret of Moscow acceded to welfare demands. To be sure, he did so reluctantly, warning that excessive preoccupation with welfare could drive the most able seminarians "to transfer to lay ranks" and cause the selection of "poor candidates" merely because of welfare considerations.[115] In a letter of 1828 Filaret conceded that "it is very inconvenient to assign positions according to hereditary claims," but he nonetheless proceeded to order an aide to provide for orphaned daughters by finding a suitable fiancé to occupy the family position.[116] Three years later Filaret still agonized over such cases, as he wrote to fellow prelates: "I have been requested to reserve positions to a daughter for just one year, but I never do this with priests' and deacons' positions, for I think it is a sin against the sacrament of holy orders to leave these to a sex which cannot receive holy orders."[117]

Most bishops, however, were less troubled by welfare appointments and even took steps to reinforce family claims. One measure was to require that candidates for the clergy marry girls only from their own estate, a requirement that turned custom into fiat, all for the purpose of guaranteeing welfare for daughters of deceased clergy. That motive was paramount in eliciting a decree by the bishop of Orenburg in 1850: "So that the clergy's children from their earliest childhood are reared in a spirit appropriate to the clerical estate, and so that girls of the clerical soslovie are provided for, and so that both of these are not a burden to Church authorities upon widowhood, I found it necessary to order that the clergy of Orenburg diocese marry only girls from the clerical estate."[118] Likewise, in the 1840s the bishop of Saratov, Iakov, rejected the petition of one cleric to marry outside his estate ("the petitioner is ordered to marry a girl in the clerical soslovie") and in a second case even ordered the local ecclesiastical superintendent "to find for the petitioner a girl in the clerical estate." When one youth demurred, the bishop thundered that "the petitioner is slandering the clergy: there is nothing on earth better in richness of means and incentive for a virtuous spiritual life," and he ordered the city archpriest to point out local beauties still available.[119]

[114]Ibid., op. 128, g. 1847, d. 478, ll. 1–5. Similar cases are found in ibid., op. 130, g. 1849, d. 424 (Riazan); d. 545 (Tula); dd. 10, 11, 1206 (Riazan); d. 750 (Tver); d. 1129 (Vladimir); op. 131, g. 1850, d. 228 (Tula); d. 230 (Viatka); d. 1583 (Riazan).

[115]Filaret, SMO, 3: 31–33.

[116]"Pis'ma mitr. moskovskogo Filareta," Prib. TSO, 1872, kn. 1: 26.

[117]"Pis'ma mitr. moskovskogo Filareta," RA, 1899, no. 6: 199.

[118]TsGIA SSSR, f. 796, op. 132, g. 1851, d. 2357, l. 424.

[119]A. Pravdin, "Rezoliutsii Saratovskogo preosv. Iakova," Saratovskie EV, 1878, no. 4: 78–79. For similar rules in Kiev diocese, see S. Karpov, "Evgenii Bolkhovitinov kak mitropolit kievskii," TKDA, 1914, no. 1: 96.

Why were hereditary claims, despite their recognized adverse effect upon the clergy's status, so tenacious? The major reason was the Church's inability to devise alternative forms of welfare. The welfare boards simply lacked the resources to provide for the hordes of aged clerics and surviving family members found in each diocese. Each diocesan board in fact dispensed paltry sums, its pensions usually amounting to no more than ten or twenty rubles per year—a fraction of real needs.[120] As one contemporary aptly observed, "these sums are so extremely limited that they can hardly suffice as support for one-third of a year."[121] Diocesan authorities were of course well aware of these problems and in fact made no pretense of meeting the clergy's acute welfare needs. The bishop of Penza, for example, reported in 1850 that "the welfare board for clerical poor, because of the meager amount of resources at its disposal, and because of the great number of people in need, has difficulty satisfying the demands [made upon it]."[122]

Consequently, the Church used for welfare its main resource: disposition of clerical positions. Yet the firm grip of the soslovie on clerical positions was fraught with numerous problems. It obliged new clergy to divert scarce resources to support the soslovie, it blocked entry of outsiders to Church service, and it denied clergy the chance to marry into more prosperous lay families. And, in the end, it still left the clergy virtually without meaningful, effective social security. As one cleric noted in his diary, old age offered little hope: "We [priests] are fed and dressed so long as we have the strength to work. In sickness or old age, we are poorer than anyone—hence we have to be greatly concerned about our future."[123] The clergy's whole economy rested on service—the current income from gratuities and cultivation of parish land (upon which a cleric even built his house). Once the breadwinner retired or died, the clerical family had virtually no income. Particularly unenviable was the plight of widows and orphans. One priest, reflecting upon the misfortunes of his widowed sister, concluded that "in no estate is widowhood and the condition of orphans so oppressive as in ours."[124]

This problem, festering since the eighteenth century, became extraordinarily acute in the 1840s. In addition to crushing overpopulation, the soslovie now endured the squeeze of parish reform, which sought substantial reductions in parish positions and, consequently, eliminated the claims of many families. To forestall that catastrophe, large numbers of clergy sought to

---

[120]See, for instance, the diocesan reports of 1850 in TsGIA SSSR, f. 796, op. 132, g. 1851, d. 2357.

[121]Ibid., f. 797, op. 12, d. 29878, l. 1 (note from Ushakov); see as well the similar comments by Filaret of Riazan (ibid., f. 796, op. 107, g. 1826, d. 460, l. 216 ob.).

[122]Ibid., f. 796, op. 132, g. 1851, d. 2357, l. 145 ob. (Penza report).

[123]"Dnevnik prot. Rodiona Putiatina," *Khristianin*, 1909, no. 9: 123.

[124]GA Kalininskoi obl., f. 103, d. 1291, l. 18 ob. (I. S. Belliustin, "Dnevnik").

retire prematurely, hoping to transfer their positions to kinsmen or heirs before the draft shtaty took effect. Although some bishops resisted these early retirements, the Synod generally proved more tolerant. The result was a sharp increase in the number of retired clergy, a pattern specifically noted by the bishop of Vladimir in 1851: "The number of retired clergy is increasing because many clergy, lacking the means to arrange [marriage] of daughters to men in the clerical rank (because of the dearth of positions), or to men in secular ranks (because they lack the means [for dowries]), are obliged to surrender their positions to pupils who agree to marry their daughters, although many could continue to serve, being in good health at age sixty."[125] The superabundance of retired clergy—12 to 18 percent of the serving clergy in most dioceses—subsisted on the meager income of kinsmen and heirs, adding to the drain on clerical resources.

By the mid-nineteenth century the welfare obligation had broadened in yet another way—a growing belief in the need to educate clerical daughters, not just sons. Female education developed slowly in prereform Russia, and although it had become a prerequisite for the genteel nobility, the quality and substance of that education varied greatly. Despite relatively frequent references in memoir literature on the literacy of clerical wives (who sometimes maintained small parish schools for laity), the service registers for 1830 show that most daughters had "not been taught to read and write," to cite the usual phrase.[126] Ever fearful of lagging behind educated society, however, parish clergy showed growing interest in educating their daughters. As one reform memorandum of the early 1840s noted, "many rural priests bitterly decry the misfortune of having wives without any upbringing and education, who are incapable of being a friend in life or giving their children a [proper] upbringing."[127] In his annual report for 1852 the chief procurator wrote that "everywhere the need to educate daughters is being deeply felt in the clerical class."[128] At the initiative of Nicholas's daughter, the Church in 1843 opened a special school for clerical daughters, which was to prepare women who "are able to provide pleasant company for husbands, to help them keep church buildings in good order, to prepare medicine for the ill, to be occupied with the rearing of their children, and to maintain the household in good order."[129] By 1855 authorities had in fact opened such schools in several dioceses—four under the personal auspices of the empress (Iaro-

---

[125]TsGIA SSSR, f. 796, op. 132, g. 1851, d. 2357, l. 82 ob.

[126]GA Kurskoi obl., f. 20, d. 20, l. 23 (diachok's daughters, aged 13, 15, and 18).

[127]*Ob uchilishchakh devits dukhovnogo zvaniia* (St. Petersburg, 1866), pp. 1–2, quoting a memorandum of 1843 on special schools for clerical daughters.

[128]*IVO (1852)*, p. 56.

[129]*Ob uchilishchakh devits*, pp. 1–3. There was one partial precedent: a special girls' school established in 1832 in Moscow (ibid, p. 9). For an example of the difficulties in establishing such schools, see I. Listovskii, "Filaret, arkhiepiskop chernigovskii," *RA*, 1887, no. 8: 246–48.

slavl, Kazan, Irkutsk, and Tsarskoe Selo), three on the initiative of diocesan authorities (Riazan, Khar'kov, and Tula), and twelve more under the auspices of convents. Still, the number enrolled—a few hundred girls—was minuscule: the Church had only begun to deal with this important new dimension of its welfare responsibilities.[130]

The escalation in welfare problems prompted a repeated—but fruitless— search for solutions. In 1842 a state official, noting the dire plight of clerical dependents, proposed to aid the clerical poor through a tax on parish documents.[131] The next year, for the same purpose, an archimandrite proposed to levy a tax on clergy, calculating that this could provide quite generous pensions for deserving priests and sacristans.[132] Although neither scheme won approval in the Synod,[133] Church authorities formally took up the question in 1851–1852, laying plans to create a capital endowment for clerical pensions. As in the parish reform of 1842, authorities intended to begin with the western provinces, soliciting opinions from local prelates and working up a formal proposal for consideration by the state treasury. In the end, however, the plans collapsed—most likely derailed by the start of the Crimean War.[134] As the Nikolaevan era drew to a close, the Church had made virtually no progress in providing welfare for those in its domain.

The Shift in Soslovie Policy

Fully cognizant of the sundry problems caused by the closed estate, the Church—primarily at the behest of Chief Procurator Protasov—began to reconsider the traditional soslovie policy in the late 1840s. The procurator's personal interest was evident in 1848, when he circulated the reform proposal of a priest in Orel, Iakov Ostromyslenskii, who advocated a radical change in policy toward the clerical soslovie. According to Ostromyslenskii, the problem of surplus candidates had become acute only since the seminary reform of 1814, which firmly wedded the soslovie to the seminary by obliging all the clergy's sons to matriculate in ecclesiastical schools. To alleviate the surplus, Ostromyslenskii proposed to sever the bond, permitting clergy to educate their sons in secular schools without first obtaining a formal release from the Church. The mass of expelled pupils, he urged, should be retrained

[130] Annual reports give a rosy picture of conditions but show that the numbers involved—a mere 120 in the two schools under imperial protection—were negligible (TsGIA SSSR, f. 797, op. 20, d. 44296).

[131] Ibid., op. 12, d. 29878 (memorandum).

[132] Ibid., f. 796, op. 124, g. 1843, d. 213.

[133] Ibid., d. 88; f. 797, op. 12, d. 29878, ll. 14–17 ob.

[134] Ibid., f. 796, op. 132, g. 1851, d. 439/a, ll. 1–16 ob.

as feldshers to serve the rural population, at once liberating the Church from this multitude of unneeded youth and rendering a vital service to society. On the "sacristan question," Ostromyslenskii stopped short of recommending expulsion, but, in view of their "low moral and cultural level," he urged that their sons be schooled separately from priests' sons to avoid contamination. Ultimately, however, he suggested that the Church would have to take decisive measures to free itself of these unreliable, unworthy servitors.[135]

Alarmed by the statistics on surplus candidates, in March 1849 the Synod formed a special committee with lay and clerical members and, to guide the committee's deliberations, solicited an opinion from Metropolitan Filaret of Moscow.[136] Filaret's memorandum, "On the Surfeit of People in the Clerical Rank," conceded the gravity of the problem and reiterated his favorite solution: a periodic, stringent conscription. Sensitive to the crisis facing the soslovie, Filaret proceeded to suggest additional measures to alleviate the surplus, such as special privileges to encourage seminarians to enter civil and military service. Clearly anxious to protect the Church's main reservoir of candidates, Filaret also proposed to add secular vocational training to the Church school curriculum (such as handicrafts and painting), which could prepare surplus youths for alternative careers among townspeople. To encourage outward mobility, Filaret stressed the need to neutralize seminarians' fear of falling into the poll-tax population and recommended that those departing the soslovie be given full exemption from the poll tax and recruit obligations.

But the heart of Filaret's plan was a shtat—normative enrollments—for the seminary. Opposed to the blanket exclusion of sacristans' sons from Church schools, Filaret reiterated his earlier views that sacristan offspring were often superior in diligence and character. The real problem, argued Filaret, was not the surplus of graduates—use could always be found for them, if only as deacons or sacristans—but the mass of dropouts, who were unfit for a career in either the Church or lay society. Rather than impose sanctions on the children of sacristans, the metropolitan proposed to restrict enrollments at the seminary, which should remain at their present size and henceforth admit only the best pupils from elementary Church schools. That proposal, while seeking to accommodate concerns about surplus candidates, nevertheless adhered to Filaret's old ambition to sustain the largest potential pool of candidates, enabling the Church to recruit the best ones for clerical positions.[137]

When the special committee met in March and April 1849, it gave close consideration to the Synod's instructions and Filaret's detailed memoran-

[135] Ibid., f. 797, op. 18, d. 41101, ll. 3–10 ob.
[136] Ibid., f. 796, op. 445, d. 354, ll. 1–2.
[137] Ibid., f. 797, op. 19, otd. 1, st. 2, d. 42644, ll. 7–17 ob. (Filaret, "Zapiska").

dum.[138] On the immediate problem of what to do with the current backlog
of youths, the committee recommended a prompt purge of those found morally unfit, youths with insufficient education, and sacristans with records of
bad conduct. In the case of overpopulated dioceses, it reiterated that bishops
must ordain only seminary graduates and should release immediately any
graduate interested in a lay career. On the long-term problem of how to
prevent surpluses in the future, the committee took a much harsher view
than Filaret, urging a radical change in Church policy toward sacristans and
seminary enrollments. Without commenting upon the worth of sacristans'
sons, the committee observed that few at present completed the course, thus
"in vain" squandering their fathers' small resources. Urging that these youths
apprentice elsewhere and enter lay society, the committee proposed to give
them special legal privileges (such as the tax and recruit exemptions suggested by Filaret) and even land grants of fifteen dessiatines in sparsely populated provinces.[139] More radical still was its scheme to impose a bureaucratic
shtat on seminary enrollments, a rational norm linking enrollments to the
actual manpower needs of a diocese; with enrollment limited, authorities
could both improve the schools and avoid a surfeit of candidates. In fixing
that smaller enrollment, the committee accorded clear preference to the
progeny of ordained clergy: only priests' sons had an unequivocal right to
enter the seminary from elementary district schools; sacristans' sons, by contrast, had to be in the upper division of their class to qualify. That proposal
was of course a compromise, giving priority to the priests' sons (deemed more
cultured), yet leaving the door open to the gifted sons of sacristans (as Filaret
demanded). To diminish further the ponderous weight of soslovie demands
on the Church, the committee sought to annul the requirement that clergy
enroll their sons in ecclesiastical schools only. With these changes, argued the
committee, the Church could simply dispense with conscriptions, which
wrought such havoc and humiliation on the parish clergy. The committee
thus went much further than Filaret, showing less interest in a massive pool
of candidates than in steps to trim the soslovie and maximize the use of
Church resources.[140]

The Synod finally adopted formal proposals a year later, in July and
December 1850. The July decree, largely following the suggestions of the
committee, ordered an immediate purge of unworthy sacristans and youths

[138]Ibid., f. 796, op. 445, d. 354, ll. 3–10 (Zhurnaly komiteta).

[139]In an 1835 case the state ruled that sacristans expelled from the clergy and found unfit
for the army should be dispatched to the "sparsely populated" provinces in the south "for
attachment to communities of state peasants" (PSZ [2], 10: 8139). That rule, to be sure, applied
only to expelled sacristans, but it evidently provided a precedent for the committee's proposal.

[140]By contrast, Filaret flatly denied a gap between sacristans and ordained clergy; in his
view, both were needed to assure a large pool of candidates. See SIRIO, 113: 50–52, and the
unsigned note in OR GBL, f. 214, d. 55, ll. 54–55.

in sixteen of the most populous dioceses (mostly central ones like Moscow and Kursk) and also directed the Bureau of Ecclesiastical Education to draw up suitable proposals for normative enrollments in seminaries.[141] The resolution of December 1850 abolished the clergy's obligation to educate sons only in ecclesiastical schools; hereafter they could matriculate in lay schools, yet return to enter the clergy without prejudice. This resolution also established a mechanism for continual purge: any youth who had not studied in Church schools and did not hold a position was automatically expelled from the soslovie at age seventeen. Although that measure had limited effect (most youths studied, if only briefly, in the schools), juridically it came closer to detaching children from the soslovie.[142]

By the next year the bureau had prepared a normal shtat for the seventeen overpopulated dioceses (see table 17). It projected very sharp reductions— over 50 percent in some dioceses, only somewhat less in most others. By estimating the number of annual openings, both for positions in the parish clergy of each diocese and for admissions to the academies, and by allowing for a certain number of dropouts at each grade (usually on the order of 25 percent), the bureau calculated the size of enrollment each school should have to satisfy local needs.[143] It was an extraordinary attempt to alter Church schools, to reconstruct them from soslovie schools that educated all the clergy's sons to smaller institutions unabashedly seeking to meet the specific manpower needs of the Church.

The shtat encompassed only the seminary, however, not the district school, which still was to educate all the clergy's progeny. That omission of course represented a concession to the clerical soslovie, whose sons would still receive at least four years of elementary education. Yet it was a modest concession; its ultimate purpose, moreover, was to provide a larger pool of candidates for the seminary, tested in their intellectual and moral worth. Most important, this new system merely transferred the disjuncture between soslovie and institutional needs from the seminary to the lower Church school. Authorities simply had to dispose of surplus youths earlier, still an unenviable task. As Bishop Iliodor of Kursk plaintively wrote the Synod, his diocese now had 365 boys completing the Church school but could promote only 140 to the seminary. As for the remaining 225, he wrote, "the question naturally arises: what is to be done with them?"[144] Neither the Synod nor

---

[141] TsGIA SSSR, f. 797, op. 19, otd. 1, st. 2, d. 42644, ll. 36–40; ibid., f. 802, op. 5, d. 12977, ll. 1–7 ob. (Synod resolution, 12.7.1850).

[142] Ibid., f. 797, op. 19, otd. 1, st. 2, d. 42644, ll. 29–32 ob.; ibid., f. 802, op. 5, d. 12977, ll. 27–36 ob. (Synod resolution, 19.12.1850).

[143] Ibid., f. 796, op. 132, g. 1851, d. 1181, ll. 2–13.

[144] Ibid., ll. 65–66. The question—"What is one to do with the surplus?"—also troubled the author of the new scheme, Innokentii. See "Pis'ma Innokentiia," ChOIDR, 68 (1869): 137.

TABLE 17

Normative Enrollments for Seminaries, 1851

Diocese	Average Annual Priests' Vacancies	Normative Shtat Enrollments	Actual Enrollment (1850)	Reduction (%)
Chernigov	62	300	373	19.6
Iaroslavl	94	450	558	19.4
Kaluga	60	280	630	55.6
Kazan	40	190	235	19.1
Kostroma	82	400	468	14.5
Kursk	72	340	536	36.6
Moscow	130	620	852	27.2
Nizhnii Novgorod	54	260	468	44.4
Orel	112	520	660	21.2
Penza	60	280	396	29.3
Riazan	64	300	527	43.1
Simbirsk	50	250	297	15.8
Tambov	70	340	452	24.8
Tula	72	340	704	51.7
Tver	80	370	840	56.0
Viatka	60	280	510	45.1
Vladimir	80	370	717	48.4
TOTAL	1,242	5,890	9,223	36.1

SOURCE: TsGIA SSSR, f. 796, op. 132, g. 1851, d. 1181, ll. 12–13.

Iliodor had an answer to that question, and soon many other bishops lodged similar complaints about the new shtat. Ultimately, authorities agreed the next year to raise the norms by 25 percent; yet a great discrepancy continued between soslovie needs and institutional demand.[145] As Nicholas's reign drew to a close, the normal shtat was just beginning to take effect, and the ponderous demographic dilemma still lay heavily upon the Church.

Yet this whole venture signified a fundamental turn in state policy, a shift from eighteenth-century statecraft, focusing upon the rationalization of institutions, to an attempt to restructure the social estates serving those institutions. In effect, the Nikolaevan regime that first glorified the soslovie system later began to dismantle it. The impetus was the failure of the clerical soslovie, like the others, to answer the more modern requirements of service.

[145]TsGIA SSSR, f. 796, op. 132, g. 1851, d.1181, ll. 133–49.

The soslovie provided a sufficient number of educated candidates (the raison d'être for the soslovie in the first place), but at the price of great disorders. The low, separate status of sacristan; the surplus of candidates; the high costs of welfare—all these disorders exacted a high price on the Church's resources and capabilities. Thus the soslovie order, summoned originally to provide service, became an obstacle to the restructuring of service—the trimming of numbers and the replacement of liturgical functionaries with dynamic pastors who could preach and teach, practice modern medicine and agronomy. Disturbed by the failures of the soslovie and more conscious of the distinction between soslovie and institutional needs, hierarchs and state officials searched for ways to reestablish an equillibrium. Although tempered by some compromises and constrained by the broader soslovie order, authorities in these very first reforms showed a willingness to pursue the interests of the institution, if need be, at the expense of the soslovie.

Conclusions

At the start of Nicholas's reign, the Church suffered from such grave problems that, by common consent, it could ensure neither good clergy nor good parishioners. Its administration, overcentralized and overworked, not only failed to provide effective control over religious life but also caused mounting discontent between priests and parishioners, bishops and bureaucrats. The traditional parish order was too particularistic and impoverished to provide either sufficient or honorable support, making it virtually impossible for rural priests to become effective, full-time pastors. Nor did the Church's schools, despite their spiraling enrollments, assure a better priesthood. As we have seen, the schools' problems—poor moral training, antiquated curriculum, archaic pedagogy, maladministration—undermined the Church's efforts to raise the quality and utility of formal education. Moreover, the hereditary clerical estate, plagued by a surplus of candidates, internal divisions, and enormous welfare needs, was becoming an ever greater burden on the Church. The heart of the Church's crisis, in fact, was the clergy's peculiar castelike structure: that social order caused a widening gap between institution and soslovie, between the Church's needs for fewer, more professional pastors and the estate's own interests for more positions and welfare. The Church, given its inelastic resources and narrower interests, could neither educate nor absorb the populous estate consigned for its use.

The Nikolaevan state made a systematic attempt to address these problems, promulgating a broad set of reforms from the very outset to the very close of Nicholas's reign. The sheer enactment of legislation was a noteworthy achievement. Especially if measured against the dismal record in other areas (for example, police, serfdom, and justice), the volume and scope of Church legislation was impressive. More striking still, the legislative record on Church reform shows a high degree of dynamism and belies the static image conventionally ascribed to Nicholas's regime. Indicative is the difference between the two parish reforms: that of 1829 aimed only to ameliorate conditions in poor parishes; that of 1842 sought to restructure the clerical economy and even to eliminate the baneful emoluments. Noteworthy too was the interest that the reform committee of 1839 showed in Western forms of support for clergy. Such curiosity was unusual for the Nikolaevan regime, which normally abjured Western models and affirmed the uniqueness (*samobytnost'*) of Russian institutions and society. More important, the regime probed ever more deeply into the problems of the Church and, in so doing, underwent a profound evolution in its definition of reform. It began with such issues as maladministration and poor parishes in 1826, shifted focus to questions of education and parish economy in the late 1830s, and toward the very end raised the most elemental and difficult issue of all—the clergy's soslovie order. Significantly, if one looks at the sundry drafts, memoranda, and laws, it is apparent that by 1855 the authorities had already contemplated or even tried most of the solutions used in later reforms.

Yet the volume of legislation was more impressive than its results: by 1855 the Church's condition was worse, not better, than at the outset of Nicholas's reign. Church administration suffered still from the old problems of red tape and venality, made even more intense by the frozen budgets and compounded as well by increased animosity between bishops and procurators, priests and bishops. Nor did the parish reforms have much effect. They failed to improve the clergy's economic condition, provoked anticlerical sentiments (especially in the western provinces, where the terms were most favorable), and wrought much hardship upon the clergy (particularly in central Russia, where the shtat reductions were most extensive). The educational reforms, similarly, failed to address the schools' principal problems, especially their financial weakness; indeed, argued many, the plethora of new subjects only made educational conditions worse, not better, in the schools. As for the issue of the hereditary estate, the regime did nothing to satisfy its welfare needs and left intact its traditional net of family claims and want of pension and aid. Indeed, by abandoning the old device of periodic conscriptions, Nicholas's regime aggravated the demographic imbalance; only in the early 1850s, amidst a swelling population of idle youths, did authorities finally seek to modify earlier policy and help relieve the surfeit of candidates.

Why were Nicholas's reforms so ineffective? The principal obstacle, as was so often the case in prerevolutionary Russia, was financial: the regime clearly recognized the problem of institutional penury but lacked the means to relieve it. That was especially true in this case, where the sheer size of the clerical estate and the magnitude of its institutional problems left the regime with little alternative except to seek palliatives and partial solutions. A policy of "gradualism" not only suited the emperor's conservative outlook but was as well a product of raw necessity: neither the state nor the Church had the wherewithal to solve the problem of poor clerks, poor seminaries, and poor priests. And without compelling evidence of great religious crisis (for example, an acute dearth of qualified candidates, anticlerical riots, or a groundswell of religious deviance or indifference), the regime lacked a sense of urgency that might have driven it to adopt more radical—and more expensive—solutions.

Beyond the financial barrier, Church reform suffered as well from the special modus operandi of Nikolaevan politics. Above all, it relied to a great degree on imperial initiative, which often meant idiosyncratic intervention by the emperor, who then turned the whole matter over to the bureaucracy to resolve. As a consequence, administrative bodies like the Synod tended to await initiative from without and, especially, to repulse proposals from below (witness the regularity and peevishness with which it spurned memoranda from lower clergy or laymen). More important, this process also exposed Church reform to the vicissitudes of autocratic politics, to the influence of ministerial rivalries and ambitions that weighed ever more heavily upon reform. Though institutional rivalry was age-old (with the Synod and Senate in the eighteenth century acting out the traditional conflict between Church and state), in the nineteenth century such conflict became at once more complex and more intense. The development during Nicholas's reign was especially striking, reflected well in the two parish reforms: the State Council sabotaged the statute of 1829, but it was a host of ministerial parties (education, state domains, and finance) that intruded to shape the parish and seminary reforms of the late 1830s. If state interests became more aggressive and defined, such was not the case with the Church: the bishops did not act as a cohesive group but rather held a broad variety of views on such basic issues as parish reorganization and the elimination of sacristans. The only clearly identifiable subgroup was the hierarchs in the western provinces, where the Catholic and Uniate questions provided a decisive influence on their outlook, especially on such matters as reduction of clergy and merger of parishes. Elsewhere the bishops differed sharply in their outlook, age, and status. Dispersed across the dioceses, they did not coalesce into a united interest group shaping policy and repulsing intrusion by state officials.

The most characteristic feature of Nicholas's Church reform was its secrecy: reform came from above, with little or no input from below. At most, authorities solicited comments from diocesan bishops, though even that step was unusual. It goes without saying that reform committees made no attempt to consult common parishioners, educated elites, or even the reform's ostensible beneficiaries, the parish clergy. Nikolaevan reform took place amidst great secrecy and silence; it was like a silent film, with the people and clergy given no opportunity to advise or protest. Fully in the spirit of autocracy, authorities ignored public opinion and imperiously demanded compliance. That indifference to public opinion changed dramatically in 1855. Thereafter reform would involve not only procurators and prelates but ordinary priests and parishioners as well, radically changing the substance and politics of reform.

PART TWO

Great Reforms
in Russian Orthodoxy

With Nicholas's death in February 1855, Russia entered a new era of far-reaching reform. For many contemporaries the humiliating defeat of the Crimean War was not a mere military debacle but a shocking failure of the whole Nikolaevan system, exposing its poor administration, fiscal vulnerability, primitive transport, technical backwardness, and archaic social system—clear proof, argued conservatives and liberals, of the need for fundamental reform.[1] The new sovereign, Alexander II, at first tried to dampen rising expectations by denying plans for reform, but early in 1856, after negotiating an end to the war, he spoke publicly of the need for change, even in the institution of serfdom, and told an audience of stunned noblemen in Moscow that it was far better to make this reform "from above, rather than from below."[2] Although the serf question was central, the emperor recognized the need for a broader reform of the empire's public and social institutions: "Now we face an important task of attempting, with all means, to strengthen the internal system of both military and civil administration."[3] Ultimately, that reform came to encompass not only serf emancipation (1861) but also justice (1864), local self-government (1864), education (1863, 1865), censorship (1865), city government (1870), and a host of measures to improve the army and police.

Though once naively celebrated as "Great Reforms" (more as value-judgment than assessment) and attributed to the heroism of the Tsar-Liberator, the reforms of the 1860s and 1870s were infinitely more complex.[4] The emperor, it turns out, was a reluctant reformer, driven by necessity to accept more fundamental reform, ever fearful of excessive change, intensely protective of his autocratic prerogatives.[5] The dynamics for reform in fact lay

[1] For the burgeoning discontent during the Crimean War, even in conservative circles, see I. N. Kovaleva, "Slavianofily i zapadniki v period Krymskoi voiny," *IZ*, 80 (1967): 181–206; see also D. Beyrau's perceptive comments on the war as a trigger to reform ("Von der Niederlage zur Agrarreform: Leibeigenschaft und Militärverfassung in Russland nach 1855," *JGO*, 23 [1975]: 191–212).

[2] Daniel Field, *The End of Serfdom* (Cambridge, Mass., 1976), p. 62.

[3] Iu. I. Gerasimova, "Krizis pravitel'stvennoi politiki v gody revoliutsionnoi situatsii i Aleksandr II," *Revoliutsionnaia situatsiia v Rossii v 1859–61 gg.*, 2 (Moscow, 1962): 94.

[4] The term "Great Reforms" is used here as a convenient shorthand for the reformist years of the 1850s and 1860s, without the evaluative connotations found in prerevolutionary literature.

[5] See, especially Alexander's notebook-diaries (TsGAOR, f. 678 [Aleksandr II], dd. 312–15, masterfully summarized by Gerasimova, "Krizis") and the analysis of his posture toward political reform provided by V. G. Chernukha (*Vnutrenniaia politika tsarizma s serediny 50-kh do nachala 80-kh gg. XIX v.* [Leningrad, 1978]).

in an enlightened bureaucracy, which steadily broadened the vision of reform from narrow fiscal and manpower concerns to fundamental questions about the social and institutional structure of the *ancien régime*.[6] In large measure the reformers relied upon special expertise as jurists, economists, or educators to secure their dominance over the legislative process.[7] Significant too—and contrasting sharply with the Nikolaevan era—was the overt emulation of Western models. Rarely did a Great Reform proceed without drawing upon Western experience, even adaptation of Western laws, in framing the statutory foundations of the new order.[8]

Yet the most striking element of the Great Reforms was the decision to involve society directly in the reform process. Initially, that meant conscious use of publicity (*glasnost'*), a device to expose bureaucratic pettifoggery and to overcome the inertia that had often proved fatal to Nikolaevan reform.[9] It meant, as well, an attempt to animate official planning with expertise from below, not from mere bureaucrats, but from specialists and professionals who understood the specific problems and actual conditions at the bottom. Involvement of society, or, to be more precise, specific segments of it, had an ulterior purpose as well, for authorities wanted not only advice but also consent—willful acknowledgment of the violation of traditional rights and privileges.[10] Especially in the reforms affecting local society, authorities

---

[6]See the analysis and citations of literature in Beyrau, "Von der Niederlage."

[7]For the summoning of "experts," see the case of the Editorial Commission on serf emancipation (where outside experts composed half its membership) and the preparation of judicial reform (Field, *End of Serfdom*, pp. 233–65; Wortman, *Russian Legal Consciousness*, pp. 142–267).

[8]For the influence of Western models on the reform of serfdom, justice, censorship, local administration, education, city government, police, and labor law, see: S. F. Starr, "Introduction" to August von Haxthausen, *Studies on the Interior of Russia* (Chicago, 1972), pp. xxxv–xl; Wortman, *Russian Legal Consciousness*, pp. 247–49; C. A. Ruud, "The Russian Empire's New Censorship Law of 1865," *Canadian-American Slavic Studies*, 3 (1969); 243; Starr, *Decentralization*, pp. 58–71; W. L. Mathes, "The Struggle for University Autonomy in the Russian Empire during the First Decade of the Reign of Alexander II (1855–66)" (Ph.D. diss., Columbia University, 1966); L. T. Hutton, "The Reform of City Government in Russia, 1860–1870" (Ph.D. diss., University of Illinois, 1972), pp. 34–35; Reginald E. Zelnik, *Labor and Society in Tsarist Russia: The Factory Workers of St. Petersburg, 1855–70* (Stanford, 1971), p. 145; Robert J. Abbott, "Police Reform in Russia, 1858–1878" (Ph.D. diss., Princeton University, 1971), p. 200.

[9]For Grand Duke Konstantin Nikolaevich's tactic of "artificial publicity," see J. W. Kipp, "The Grand Duke Konstantin Nikolaevich and the Epoch of the Great Reforms, 1855–66" (Ph.D. diss., Pennsylvania State University, 1970); Beyrau, "Von der Niederlage," pp. 197–201.

[10]For the tactic of seeking public support, see studies of reform in the police, education, censorship, and judiciary: Abbott, "Police Reform," pp. 61–116; A. Sinel, *The Classroom and the Chancellery: State Educational Reform in Russia under Count Dmitry Tolstoi* (Cambridge, Mass., 1973), pp. 30–31; C. A. Ruud, "A. V. Golovnin and the Liberal Russian Censorship, January–June 1862," *SEER*, 50 (1972): 198–219; Wortman, *Russian Legal Consciousness*, p. 257.

hoped as well to remove the dead hand of bureaucracy and to unfetter social forces, enabling the state to shift some of its massive responsibilities to society.[11] But publicity was a dangerous political game. Ministries appealing to particular social groups ran the risk of pressure from below—as indeed transpired in the case of gentry assemblies and the zemstvo.[12] Though the Great Reforms did not cease in the mid-1800s, those that came later would show a different spirit, less reliant upon society and more reassertive of the traditional hegemony of the state.[13]

How did Church reforms fit into this larger process of reform? In the following three chapters we shall examine the process of Church reform, from the public emergence of the "clerical question" in the late 1850s to the spate of legislation in the late 1860s. One task is to delineate the dynamics and principles of reform, especially the interaction of Church and state in framing the new legislation. That inquiry can shed some light upon the attitudes among the bishops, the role of some prominent secular figures (Alexander II, P. A. Valuev, and D. A. Tolstoi in particular), the willingness to apply Western models, and the modus operandi employed to achieve—or stall—reform. A second task is perhaps even more important: precisely because the Great Reforms involved not just elites in Petersburg but also priests, peasants, and squires in the villages, it is important to "listen" as they articulate their own grievances and aspirations. By turning an attentive ear to these voices, especially in the 1860s, we can learn much about the fundamental problems facing a reformist regime seeking to rebuild its infrastructure from the top down.

[11]On the zemstvo reform, see Starr, *Decentralization*; V. V. Garmiza, *Podgotovka zemskoi reformy 1864 g.* (Moscow, 1964).

[12]On gentry activism, see the accounts in Terence Emmons, *The Russian Landed Gentry and the Peasant Emancipation of 1861* (Cambridge, 1968), and George Fischer, *Russian Liberalism* (Cambridge, Mass., 1958), pp. 3–41.

[13]Though prerevolutionary historians conventionally saw two halves to Alexander's reign (divided by the assassination attempt of 1866, which allegedly precipitated a new era of "reaction"), more recent research has denied such a reform-reaction bifurcation. See Ruud, "Censorship Law," p. 244; Alfred J. Rieber, "Alexander II: A Revisionist View," *Journal of Modern History*, 43 (1971): 42–58. Soviet historians too see the persistence of liberal ("bourgeois") reforms into the eighties; see, for example, N. I. Anan'ich, "K istorii otmeny podushnoi podati v Rossii," *IZ*, 94 (1974): 183–212.

CHAPTER 5

Emergence of
the Clerical Question

B y the late 1850s the "clerical question" that had been buried so
long in Nicholas's secret committees finally came to public attention, joining a long list of other issues in the reformist press. In
contrast to the West, where the clerical question was a matter of pernicious
clericalism and something to be contained, in Russia the question had an
altogether different import: how to aid and uplift the clergy, not suppress it.
In the exciting, dynamic period from the mid-1850s to the early 1860s the
question steadily gained breadth and involved ever larger segments of officialdom and society. Most shared in the consensus on the urgent need for
reform, which, significantly, they described in the same language used to
discuss the emancipation of serfs—"improvement in material condition"
(*uluchshenie byta*). That was heady language, suggesting to many the immi-
nence of a fundamental transformation in the parish clergy. As a provincial
priest wrote to a friend, "You are right, a thousand times right—it is necessary to reform the clergy radically so that it corresponds to the purpose for
which it was created."[1] This chapter will inquire into the initial stage of
reform, examining the evolution of the clerical question, the Synod's first
attempts at reform, and why the state ultimately took charge of the reform
process.

[1]OR GBL, f. 231/II, k. 3, d. 49/4, l. 3 (Belliustin to Pogodin, 25.9.1855); see also Pogodin's
"political letters" of October 1854 (N. P. Barsukov, *Pogodin*, 13:159).

Resurgence of the Synod

N. A. Protasov had wielded formidable power as chief procurator, but his death and that of Nicholas in 1855 enabled Church hierarchs to recover much of their earlier authority and autonomy. Significantly, that restoration was abetted by the new chief procurator, Aleksandr Petrovich Tolstoi, a military officer of conservative religious convictions who believed that the bishops should govern the Church.[2] Hence he acted not only as the sovereign's "eyes and ears" (his official charge) but also as the Synod's spokesman, actively defending the Church's vital interests.[3] He also solicited the counsel of ranking prelates, like Metropolitan Filaret of Moscow, and encouraged the Synod to display more initiative, even in such matters as the appointment and promotion of bishops.[4] When one metropolitan urged that he arrange for the Synod to promote a favorite to the episcopate, Tolstoi summarily refused: "As far as possible, I refrain from taking strong positions in such elections [to the episcopate], so as to preserve here complete objectivity, which is vital in so important a matter."[5] At the diocesan level, too, the procurator sought to refurbish episcopal authority, partly by shifting some functions from the center to the diocese, partly by expanding the bishops' autonomy and power.[6] Revealingly, Tolstoi renounced his predecessors' practice of designating diocesan secretaries, explaining that such a powerful figure in the consistory should be a trusted aide of the bishop, not a factor and spy of the chief procurator. Hence he refused to appoint one prelate's favorite as secretary in another diocese, reiterating that "the bishops should make such appointments according to their own judgment."[7] The procurator's solicitude toward prelates caused one priest to write that, "after an archlascivious life,

[2] For Tolstoi's background, see Chistovich, *Rukovodiashchie deiateli*, p. 359.

[3] The most dramatic case was Tolstoi's spirited opposition to state plans to include the Church in its unified budget, a scheme he regarded as a mortal threat to the Church's fiscal autonomy. Tolstoi stressed that the Church already suffered from insufficient funding (a point he demonstrated by comparing salaries for similar positions in the state and Church) and warned that secular control could have dangerous consequences: "Given the insufficiency of Church resources, there is no possibility for the state to utilize any of this, and all this [new control] would have a harmful moral impact upon the clergy and people, without the slightest gain for for the treasury" ("O poriadke zavedyvaniia dukhovnymi kapitalami," TsGIA SSSR, f. 832, op. 1, d. 27, ll. 4–8). See also his "Zapiska o podchinenii kapitalov dukhovnogo vedomstva grazhdanskomu kontroliu" (copies in ibid., ll. 13–16 ob.; OR GBL, f. 214, d. 63, ll. 28–35; OR GPB, f. 573, no. AI.60, ll. 84–88 ob.).

[4] See the correspondence between Grigorii (Postnikov) and Tolstoi in 1859 on prospective appointments (OR GBL, f. 302, k. 4, d. 31, ll. 1–1 ob.).

[5] Ibid., d. 20, l. 3 (Tolstoi to Filaret [Amfiteatrov]).

[6] For Alexander's effort to curtail red tape, see the files of 1857 in TsGIA SSSR, f. 796, op. 138, g. 1857, d. 2215, ll. 1–25.

[7] OR GBL, f. 302, k. 4, d. 20, ll. 5–6 (Tolstoi to Filaret [Amfiteatrov]).

[Tolstoi] has thrown himself into fanaticism, has become a fanatical admirer of monks, and views everything through their eyes."[8] The procurator's apparent complaisance also disturbed some state officials. In early 1858 the Third Section informed the emperor that, although the chief procurator possesses "excellent qualities of mind and heart" and "sincerely strives to improve that domain entrusted to him," he simply lacks "the strong will needed to overcome the obstacles existing here."[9]

Even as Tolstoi diminished the chief procurator's role, the Protasov order was subjected to a devastating attack in a secret memorandum, appropriately entitled "On the Influence of Lay Authority in Church Affairs."[10] The author was A. N. Murav'ev, a religious writer and former Synodal clerk who had written an earlier memorandum to Protasov.[11] This note, however, vehemently castigated the former procurator, who "became more than a minister, though without possessing this ostentatious title," usurped the Synod's authority, and diverted the Church's scanty resources to feed a bloated and useless lay bureaucracy. The result was a precipitous decline in the Synod's role: "Synod members gradually became accustomed to judging only the matters presented to them—there was no central registry of current business, and they remained wholly ignorant of much (and received no reports on these matters). Nor did they know if what they had decided would be implemented soon." He complained that "they were so accustomed to secular leadership that, even in the chief procurator's absence abroad, they did not fill vacancies in the most important dioceses, for they were not willing to choose bishops without [the procurator]." In Murav'ev's rather exaggerated account, Protasov even gained dominance over diocesan administration, primarily through the appointment of diocesan secretaries, each of whom "became a kind of procurator in the consistory and ceased to be the bishop's subordinate." Murav'ev implored the emperor to revitalize the Synod, to

---

[8]IRLI, f. 616, d. 6, l. 40 (Belliustin to A. Zheltukhin, 24.12.1858). See Tolstoi's attempt to rehabilitate the bishop of Khar'kov (rumored to have spent "two or three nights in a nunnery, thereby arousing doubts about the purity of his relations with the nuns") by appointing him to the Synod as a sign of imperial confidence (TsGAOR, f. 109, op. 223, d. 22, l. 18 [Third Section report, 1857]; OR GBL, 302, k. 4, d. 31 [Tolstoi, "Zapiska"]).

[9]TsGAOR, f. 109, op. 223, d. 22, l. 90 (Third Section report, 1857). Cf. the similarly disparaging reports on the ministers of justice (Wortman, *Russian Legal Consciousness*, pp. 157–58, 179–80). For critical assessments of Tolstoi, see also the letter in Beliaev, "Kazanskii i ego perepiska," *BV*, 1904, no. 3: 572.

[10]"O vliianii svetskoi vlasti na dela tserkovnye" (copies in the "secret section" of the Synodal archive [TsGIA SSSR, f. 796, op. 205, d. 643] and in Metropolitan Isidor's collection of memoranda [OR GPB, f. 573, no. AI.60, ll. 66–75 ob.]). Murav'ev hinted at these problems in another memorandum, which raised questions of Church reform in education, minimum age for ordination, and frequent translation of bishops ("Zapiska A. N. Murav'eva o sostoianii pravoslavnoi tserkvi v Rossii," *RA*, 1883, no. 3, kn. 2: 175–203).

[11]See above, pp. 161–62.

limit the procurator's authority, to reduce his chancellery, and to give the Synod direct control over its agenda and paperwork. Murav'ev also stressed the urgent need to improve diocesan administration—for example, by increasing the number of diocesan clerks and "their income, so that one can demand honest, disinterested service from them." More original and significant for future episcopal ambitions was his proposal for bishops' councils (*pomestnye sobory*) as a complement to the Synod's work: "If diocesan bishops assembled for discussions just once every year or two at the residence of the senior metropolitan [of that region], this would produce much good for the Church and enable the adoption of useful measures against the schism." Although Murav'ev's memorandum failed to stir support from the sovereign, it received "an extremely favorable reply" from Tolstoi, perhaps even inspiring some of his policies described above.[12] More important, Murav'ev had drafted an "episcopal program" that the prelates increasingly came to embrace in the second half of the nineteenth century.

Encouraged by Tolstoi and Murav'ev and chaired by the strong-willed Metropolitan Grigorii (Postnikov) of St. Petersburg, the Synod became more assertive and openly contested state policies at variance with Church interests. Most striking was its staunch opposition to plans to give new rights to Old Believers and Catholics,[13] to infringe the rights of monks and monasteries,[14] and to subject the Church budget to secular control.[15] Ranking prelates like Filaret also took interest in the Murav'ev scheme for episcopal councils; in Filaret's view, the Church should address some major issues, such as the unmanageable size of dioceses, specifically through "special consultations" of bishops.[16] The prelates in fact used the occasion of Alexander's coronation in 1856 to hold a council (*sobor*), which addressed several major issues and—most dramatic of all—overturned the resolution of 1842 on the Pavskii case and laid plans to publish a Russian translation of the Bible.[17]

The bishops' most forceful display of will was their spirited opposition to the state's relaxation of censorship, especially with regard to the Church and

[12]On Tolstoi's favorable reply but failure to act, see Murav'ev's letter to Pogodin of 5 June 1859 (TsGIA SSSR, f. 796, op. 205, d. 603, ll. 1–15). The emperor's lack of sympathy was evident in his curt refusal to approve an award for Murav'ev in 1861 (ibid., f. 797, op. 31, otd. 1, st. 2, d. 65, ll. 17–17 ob.). On Filaret's diffident response, see *Pis'ma Filareta, mitropolita moskovskogo i kolomenskogo, k A. N. Murav'evu* (Kiev, 1869), pp. 509–14; Filaret, *SMO*, 4: 211–16, 223–25; L'vov, *Pis'ma*, pp. 280–81, 283.

[13]On the Old Believer question, see Filaret, *SMO*, 4: 38–47, 55–57, 79–83, 154–66. As an example of toleration sentiments then current in official circles, see "Zapiski Kn. N. A. Orlova," *RS*, 31 (1881): 77–93.

[14]Filaret, *SMO*, 4: 186–203.

[15]OR GBL, f. 304, d. 259, ll. 11–16 ob.; L. N. Iasnopol'skii, *Ocherki russkogo biudzhetnogo prava* (Moscow, 1912), appendixes, pp. 32–34.

[16]Filaret, *SMO*, 4: 116.

[17]Ibid., 4: 116–18, 133–36, 244–62.

religion. Metropolitan Filaret voiced concern as early as 1856 and testily questioned "whether there is not some conspiracy which seeks to debase all that is venerated in society and to shake convictions in faith and morality, so that it will be easier to turn everything into democratic chaos."[18] The bishops' mood was dramatically apparent in a celebrated case in 1857, when an anonymous brochure castigated antireligious tendencies in recent literature and assailed secular authorities for their permissive censorship.[19] When the government protested such insulting accusations and the Church's decision to permit publication, the Synod audaciously defended the brochure: "Given its spirit, purity, and loyal views on faith, given its holy faith in the tsarist throne, the brochure merits complete approval."[20] As the conflict between bishops and state censors grew more heated, in June 1858 Alexander upheld the Church: "Hereafter publication of all articles (or articles with sections) on the Orthodox Church, the Orthodox Church in the East, or the Greek clergy, is not to be authorized without prior permission from ecclesiastical authorities."[21] Although his order did little to stem such open discussion, the whole affair revealed that Church hierarchs were finding it difficult, if not disagreeable, to work admist the new era of "publicity" (*glasnost'*).

Yet it is important to stress that the bishops were not blackguard reactionaries interested only in conserving the status quo and their own authority. On the contrary, like the rest of society, they were swept up by the new reformist spirit, even evincing interest in such secular issues as serf emancipation and judicial reform.[22] Naturally, the prelates were most concerned

---

[18] Ibid., 4: 296–97; see also Filaret's letter of 31.12.1857 to Grigorii ("Materialy dlia istorii russkoi tserkvi," *ChOLDP*, 1877, no. 12, otd. 3: 175). For Filaret's earlier complaints against *Moskovskie vedomosti* and *Biblioteka dlia chteniia*, see Filaret, *SMO*, 4: 83–86, 129–30; TsGIA SSSR, f. 832, op. 1, d. 83, ll. 115–17.

[19] *Sovremennye idei i pravoslavie* (St. Petersburg, 1858).

[20] TsGIA SSSR, f. 797, op. 27, otd. 1, st. 2, d. 151, ll. 1–4 ob. (minister of education to Synod), 7–11 ob. (Synod resolution, 18.5.1857). Church authorities, significantly, knew that state censors had rejected this essay and that permission to publish would surely trigger controversy (OR GBL, f. 302, k. 5, d. 10, ll. 11–12 [letter of K. Serbinovich to A. P. Tolstoi]).

[21] TsGIA SSSR, f. 797, op. 28, otd. 1, st. 2, d. 151, ll. 1–7 (Tolstoi to minister of education); reprinted in *Sbornik rasporiazhenii i postanovlenii po dukhovnoi tsenzure*, pp. 159–61. For an example of Church dissatisfaction with lay censorship in 1858, see Filaret's complaint about an article in *Zemledelie*, which blithely declared that "the word 'seminarian' has become a virtual curseword, expressing disdain" (Filaret, *SMO*, 4: 366–69; see also the case in TsGIA SSSR, f. 796, op. 139, g. 1858, d. 632, ll. 1–6). Bishops also feared journalism on the Bulgarian church issue, where Russia sought to rectify Bulgarian complaints of Greek domination but to avoid an outright schism. See, for instance, Tolstoi's statements on the need for silence so as to avoid stirring false hopes in Bulgaria: TsGIA SSSR, f. 797, op. 27, otd. 1, st. 2, d. 181, l. 75 (Tolstoi to Dmitrii, 7.8.1857); op. 28, otd. 1, st. 2, d. 151, ll. 1–7 (Tolstoi note to Alexander II, 26.5.1858).

[22] The most famous incident was the publication of an essay in the journal of the Kazan Academy. The author declared that "it is clear that Christianity does not support slavery

about the needs of the Church, and from 1856 onwards they began to address some of the main problems facing the Church.

Of these, the most urgent, in their view, was reform in Church schools. In part the bishops were responding to government complaints—not only reports from the Third Section about disorders and lack of discipline, but even reprimands from the imperial family.[23] One incident in 1858 involved the emperor himself: "Upon visiting the seminary in Nizhnii Novgorod the emperor became very dissatisfied with the extreme lack of cleanliness, the dilapidated condition of seminary buildings, the unkempt beds, and the general disorder in the upkeep of the institution."[24] The prelates, of course, had long been aware of the deficiencies in Church schools, especially those emanating from Protasov's curricular reform of 1840. Thus in 1856–1857—well before receiving reprimands from gilded circles—the Synod initiated an inquiry directed especially to the need for "reductions in the number of subjects in the seminary curriculum and the uselessness of medicine and other practical courses."[25] By 1858 reform was in full swing: various prelates drafted secret proposals, Filaret exhumed his old papers on the problem, and the Synod opened a formal investigation.[26] Surprisingly enough, the Synod showed an interest in Western models for reform, directing a Russian arch-

---

[serfdom]," and he denounced "the unlimited personal arbitrariness of the owner, the denial of the slave's human and social rights" (Ioann, "Slovo ob osvobozhdenii krest'ian," *Pravoslavnyi sobesednik* [hereafter *PS*], 1859, no. 4: 334–56). Describing how the essay "immediately caused a storm," the author later denied that he intended to address the serf question so directly (OR GBL, f. 230 [K. P. Pobedonostsev], k. 10802, d. 17, ll. 4 ob.–5 [Ioann to A. P. Akhmatov, 9.8.1862]).

[23]TsGIA SSSR, f. 797, op. 27, otd. 1, st. 2, d. 227. On the disorders in the St. Petersburg Academy (where students rebelled against a new inspector because of his drill-sergeant regime), see G. Polisadov, *Iz vospominanii* (St Petersburg, 1912), pp. 3–5. Prince Oldenburg, a member of the imperial family, visited the seminary in Iaroslavl shortly after Church authorities had filed a glowing report on the school and complained that "the intense smell of tobacco smoke detected during a visit to the dormitory made a most unfavorable impression" (OR GBL, f. 316, k. 67, d. 5, ll. 1–1 ob. [Tolstoi to Filaret, 31.1.1857]). For complaints about rotten meat at the Kiev Academy (and, worst of all, it was being given to Bulgarian students amidst the Balkan religious crisis), see Tolstoi's letter to Serbinovich in OR GBL, f. 302, k. 4, d. 17, ll. 1–2.

[24]TsGIA SSSR, f. 797, op. 28, otd. 1, st. 2, d. 215, ll. 12–12 ob.

[25]"Iz zapisok arkhiepiskopa Leonida," *RA*, 1906, no. 4: 606–8.

[26]I. P. Barsukov, *Innokentii*, pp. 414–18 (on Innokentii's project); OR GBL, f. 302, k. 5, d. 11, ll. 23–23 ob. (Serbinovich to Tolstoi, 25.8.1858, on the bishops' proposals). In early 1857 Filaret searched through his old files for papers on seminary reform and sent them to Petersburg for consideration (Filaret, *Pis'ma Filareta, mitropolita moskovskogo i kolomenskogo, k namestniku Sv. Troitse-sergievoi lavry arkhimandrita Antoniiu, 1831–67 gg.*, 4 vols. [Moscow, 1877–84], 4: 28–29; Filaret, *SMO*, 4: 217–23). In a private letter of September 1857 the procurator's aide referred cryptically to "the file on the transformation of ecclesiastical schools" (OR GBL, f. 302, k. 5, d. 10, ll. 33–33 ob.).

priest in Paris to collect data on Catholic seminaries there and later dispatching an official to make a full study of the schools.[27]

The Synod also took action on several other important problems. Thus it took steps to reduce the surfeit of idle candidates (most notably, by obtaining special privileges for seminarians willing to enter the army as officers)[28] and, notwithstanding the government's postwar fiscal crisis, was successful in obtaining additional allocations for parish subsidies.[29] In addition, the Synod raised the question of diocesan administration, considered ways to decentralize some functions, and solicited the opinion of bishops on potential revenues to augment the salaries of consistory clerks.[30] The Synod also ordered bishops to assemble systematic data on those parish churches lacking a full allotment of land, evidently with the intent of pressing old claims.[31] And, in an open rebuff to the Nikolaevan order, it overturned the 1839 law on voluntary defrocking, primarily in response to its members from the white clergy, who argued that neither canon law nor social necessity justified severe penalties for widowed clergy who defrocked for good cause.[32]

By 1859 the bishops had traveled a considerable distance from the Protasov era. In theory and in fact the Synod had greatly expanded its authority; it had diminished, but not eliminated, the chief procurator's role in Church affairs. More important, the bishops used their new-found authority to embark on Church reform. Their perspective, however, remained narrow, limited to a few issues and in no sense encompassing fundamental institutional and soslovie reform. That recasting of the clerical question would come from without—first from the state, then from the parish clergy, who in succession would give a more radical definition to the question of reform.

The Clerical Question in the Western Provinces

The government's interest in the clerical question, though partly rooted in a longstanding desire for more "useful" clergy, especially amidst the tensions of emancipation, derived primarily from continuing concerns about the western provinces.[33] There, as the Third Section warned, "the Catholic influ-

---

[27] L. K. Brodskii, ed., *Parizhskie pis'ma protoiereia I. V. Vasil'eva* (Petrograd, 1915), pp. 176–79; *IVO (1858)*, p. 52. For the final report, see OR GBL, f. 316, k. 66, d. 28, ll. 1–61.

[28] *PSZ (2)*, 31: 30661; 33: 33532.

[29] TsGIA SSSR, f. 796, op. 140, g. 1859, d. 875, ll. 1–7.

[30] Ibid., op. 445, d. 90, ll. 1–74.

[31] Ibid., op. 121, g. 1840, d. 1568, ll. 91–217.

[32] Ibid., op. 141, g. 1860, d. 1021, ll. 1–16 (memorandum on past legal policy); ibid., f. 832, op. 1, d. 72, ll. 29–40 (Synod resolution, 22.8.1859).

[33] Though the state showed some anxiety that clergy might provoke peasant disorders, it was primarily concerned that priests and sacristans would fail to stem (not cause) troubles in the

ence on affairs has a most hostile cast with regard to the Russian govern-ment," making it all the more urgent that Orthodox clergy there exert a pacifying, stabilizing influence.[34] As local officials warned, however, the par-ish reform of 1842 had not only failed to strengthen the clergy's position but even provoked much popular resentment. The decisive complaint emanated from the governor-general of Kiev, I. I. Vasil'chikov, in his general report of 1856:

> I consider it my duty to inform Your Majesty that one can observe a cool-ing in relations between the peasants and the clergy. Most important in stimulating this development is the requirement [of 1842] that parishioners cultivate parish land [for the priest]. In the peasants' mind, obligatory labor for the priests has acquired the appearance of *barshchina* [serfs' cor-vée labor]. The priests' demand for labor and their use of coercion if the peasants do not comply has sparked frequent discontent among [the peasants] and conflicts between clergy and landowners.

Vasil'chikov therefore proposed to convert the labor duty into a monetary payment, thereby guaranteeing the clergy adequate support, avoiding dis-putes over the labor obligation, and raising the clergy's moral authority among the peasants. Vasil'chikov went on to decry the clergy's low "moral and cultural" level, a problem "especially important in this region, [where] the people are Orthodox but the landlords and gentry, with few exceptions, are Catholic." Hence, he argued, authorities must not only convert the labor duty but also take measures to "raise the material and moral condition of the clergy (especially those in rural parishes) so that they are not only on the

---

village. Indeed, each year there was a handful of reports that clergy had aided rebellious serfs; in one case, for example, the clergy not only failed to pacify serfs but even permitted them to ring the church bells as a tocsin and then spoke on their behalf to local authorities (ibid., f. 796, op. 139, g. 1858, d. 1459). For other cases, see ibid., op. 138, g. 1857, dd. 922, 1433, 1459, 1908, 1966, 2208 (Kursk, Tula, Saratov, Vladimir, and Samara dioceses). To preclude such involvement, the bishop of Samara ordered clergy in his charge "not to enter into conversa-tions on this matter [of serf emancipation], especially with peasants" (ibid., op. 139, g. 1858, d. 922, l. 1 ob.).

[34]TsGAOR, f. 109, op. 223, d. 23, l. 186. See also complaints by A. N. Murav'ev about Jesuit propaganda (letter to Filaret in TsGIA SSSR, f. 832, op. 1, d. 83, ll. 118–19 [January 1857]); censors' efforts to interdict this literature (ibid., f. 779 [Komitet tsenzury inostrannoi], op. 4, g. 1858, d. 38, l. 107 ob.); P. N. Batiushkov's "[Zapiska] o latinskoi propagande na zapade Rossii" (OR GPB, f. 52, d. 29, ll. 1–17); and Filaret's conclusion that "the picture is disturbing, and much has been lost because attention was not aroused in time" (Filaret to Batiushkov, 28.6.1859, in OR GPB, f. 52, d. 244, l. 278). Russian Jesuits in Paris, headed by I. S. Gagarin, were indeed interested in "publishing Russian books—this enterprise is truly ours and . . . will be incredibly useful" (A. Balabine to Gagarin, 23.1.1858, in BS, f. Gagarine, no. 70, rayon 2).

same level with Catholic clergy, but even superior."[35] The emperor endorsed
the conversion proposal but first sent the file to the Synod for further study.[36]

For the next five years, the Synod—piqued by the invasion of its domain,
appalled by the attack on the clergy's "moral level," and fearful of schemes
to emasculate the concessions of 1842—stalled and resisted, using all the
bureaucratic machinations at its disposal to derail state intervention. Its first
step was to solicit the opinion of three bishops in Vasil'chikov's own territory;
predictably, all categorically rejected his assertions and proposals. They flatly
denied that Orthodox clergy were culturally or morally inferior to Catholic
priests and cited data showing the high degree of formal education among
the current generation of priests. The bishops, interestingly, vehemently
opposed changes in the parishioners' labor obligation, arguing that such
duties were neither onerous nor convertible (hired labor being virtually
unavailable at harvest time at any price). As earlier, they placed all blame
for the conflict and noncompliance upon Catholic landlords. who, they
alleged, either forbade their peasants to work for the priest or instigated parish noncompliance. These replies evidently satisfied the Synod, which
regarded the matter closed and took no further action.[37]

Chief Procurator Tolstoi remained unsatisfied, however. In confidential
letters to Vasil'chikov and Metropolitan Filaret of Kiev, Tolstoi recalled hearing during his wartime military service in Kiev that "the introduction of
inventories for labor on behalf of clergy (allegedly) even had the effect of
severing the close creative bond which from ancient times had existed in
those areas between the rural clergy and peasantry, and that this was the
cause of disorders and discontent on the part of the peasants." The cautious
Tolstoi, reluctant to challenge the Synod directly, merely asked Vasil'chikov
and Filaret to comment on this rumor and the general clerical question in
the western provinces.[38]

The two replies proved sharply contradictory, reflecting the authors' differing perceptions and institutional loyalties. Filaret noted the extraordinary
rise in educational standards in recent times (from 20 to 90 percent in the
number of priests with seminary degrees) and warned that abrogation of the
1842 statute would "again deprive the clergy of all their means and leave
them even more impoverished than before"—and hence unable to educate
their sons. Moreover, warned Filaret, conversion would only aggravate par-

---

[35] TsGIA SSSR, f. 796, op. 137, g. 1856, d. 230, ll. 3–5. By contrast, the governor-general of
Vitebsk attributed the reform's problems to the landlords' refusal "to comply with the emper-
or's will" (ibid., f. 797, op. 29, otd. 3, st. 1, d. 148, ll. 99–101).

[36] Ibid., f. 769, op. 137, g. 1856, d. 230, ll. 1–2.

[37] Ibid., ll. 6–26 (replies); the draft version of Arsenii's reply is in ibid., op. 205, d. 312, ll.
1–8.

[38] Ibid., f. 797, op. 26, otd. 3, st. 1, d. 28, ll. 7–9.

ish tensions, for "the collection of money would be difficult for parishioners in places where industry is poorly developed and where it is inconvenient to sell products at the market."[39] The metropolitan admitted that some anticlerical outbursts had occurred recently, but he blamed these on ill-conceived attempts by the state to use local clergy in regulating landlord-serf relations.[40] Although Vasil'chikov did not contravene Filaret's account of the anticlerical disorders, he argued that their very occurrence demonstrated the parishioners' "indifference, discontent, and lack of respect" for the clergy. Reiterating his earlier demands for a "moral improvement," Vasil'chikov put highest priority on conversion, suggesting that it be based on "official" labor rates (far lower than real ones)—clear evidence of his willingness to violate the concessions of 1842 for the sake of greater harmony in the parish.[41]

Although the Synod in effect tabled Vasil'chikov's first report, his successive missives to the emperor—and Alexander's overt support—eventually obliged the Synod to open a formal inquiry into the 1842 reform.[42] But, reflecting its new spirit of independence, the Synod acted with deliberate sluggishness, waiting nine months after the second Vasil'chikov report before taking further action.[43] At last yielding, it solicited comments from the Ministry of State Domains, still an institution of great power and a bureaucracy with substantial responsibilities in the region. No doubt to the Synod's dismay, the minister of state domains, M. N. Murav'ev, not only endorsed the Vasil'chikov report but went on to recommend total revision of the 1842 statute to convert not just labor duties but all obligations in kind (*natural'nye*

[39] The prelate offered other practical arguments as well: "It is impossible to set a fixed amount for field labor, because the labor costs vary in each district and indeed are different in various parts of the same district. Moreover, with the passage of time, money loses in value while that of labor rises; this is particularly evident in Kiev province, where factories become more and more developed with each passing year. To raise the amount collected from time to time would provoke new discontent among parishioners toward their priest" (ibid., l. 19; published also in N. I. Petrov, ed., "Popechitel'nost' kievskogo mitr. Filareta o material'nom obespechenii sel'skogo dukhovenstva Kievskoi eparkhii," *TKDA*, 1885, no. 7: 443–57).

[40] At first the state required priests to examine and certify the new peasant inventories (introduced in 1846–1848 to fix the serfs' obligations to their squires) and to preserve a copy in the parish church, thereby shielding the serfs from new demands. Because of the nobles' protests about clerical "meddling," the government later issued a secret circular abolishing the clergy's role as mediary. When priests subsequently refused to examine inventories at the serfs' request, the latter concluded that the priests had been bribed by landlords and were concealing "the golden manifesto" on emancipation. TsGIA SSSR, f. 797, op. 26, otd. 3, st. 1, d. 28, ll. 16–17.

[41] Ibid., ll. 21–27. The only case known to me of peasant disorders due directly to the 1842 statute occurred in Minsk province in 1857; see *Krest'ianskoe dvizhenie v Rossii za 1857–61 gg.* (Moscow, 1963), pp. 136–37.

[42] TsGIA SSSR, f. 797, op. 26, otd. 3, st. 1, d. 28, ll. 28–29 ob., 38–41.

[43] Ibid., f. 796, op. 137, g. 1856, d. 230, ll. 50–58 (Synod resolution, 28.8.1857).

povinnosti) into monetary payments.[44] He supported that demand with shocking reports from his subordinate officials. According to one:

As the parishioners perform the field-labor obligation for the priests, discontent and conflicts between them are almost ubiquitous. Some priests specify more than ten dessiatines for cultivation (the amount set by the statute) and their gardens as well. Others calculate "workdays" not by days but by hours: when peasants appear later than the specified time, or when the weather is bad, they count several days as one. Some demand that the peasants come to work at times when it is impossible for them to do so—because of family circumstances, because their livestock is weak, or because of other [valid] reasons.[45]

Another subordinate wrote that good priests "are few in number, and the majority must be reproved for their coarse manner of treating parishioners, for their immorality, for their avaricious demands that dispose not only their parishioners but also outsiders to dislike, almost even to detest them."[46] In June 1858, on the strength of such reports, Murav'ev proposed to establish "a special committee of people from the ecclesiastical domain and [the Ministry of] State Domains to discuss this question, so important—especially in its principles [an allusion to *barshchina*]—given the impending reforms in the peasantry."[47]

The Synod, no doubt, derived little satisfaction from such reports, especially the hints of an "inexpensive" conversion rate.[48] Still, it could not disregard the emperor's explicit wish and had to agree to Murav'ev's proposal for a joint Church-state commission. In an apparent effort to procrastinate, it suggested that provincial committees first assemble preliminary data and offer recommendations for the committee in Petersburg.[49] Alexander, however, was no novice in the politics of procrastination: he set a deadline of six months for the collection of this preliminary data and deliberations.[50]

The stage was thus set for a full-scale review of the 1842 statute. As in the preceding reign, the government displayed strong interest in the clerical question, but primarily for secular reasons. Yet its perspective had changed

[44] Ibid., f. 797, op. 26, otd. 3, st. 1, d. 28, ll. 60–63.

[45] Ibid., f. 796, op. 137, g. 1856, d. 230, l. 73.

[46] Ibid., l. 83.

[47] Ibid., f. 797, op. 26, otd. 3, st. 1, d. 28, ll. 74–74 ob.

[48] Ibid., f. 796, op. 137, g. 1856, d. 230, ll. 72–78. Thus the administrator of state domains in Mogilev proposed extremely low rates of conversion—50 rubles for labor, 25 rubles for housing (compared with the several hundred later demanded by the Church).

[49] Ibid., f. 797, op. 26, otd. 3, st. 1, d. 28, ll. 76–77 ob.

[50] Ibid., ll. 108–9 (Tolstoi to Alexander, 27.12.1858).

considerably: reform, in addition to providing the clergy with better support, must do so without provoking parish resentment. Even at this early point, state officials hinted at broader concerns as well, especially the clergy's "low moral level." For their part, the Synod and local bishops clearly opposed a review of the 1842 statute; for all its shortcomings, the statute provided far more than an inexpensive conversion promised to do. Thus the conflict, already emerging in 1858, followed strict institutional lines: churchmen intent on preserving the gains of 1842, bureaucrats determined to diminish those concessions for the sake of social harmony.

The Belliustin Affair

Just as authorities set to work on the 1842 statute, public and official awareness of the clerical question was dramatically reshaped by a sensational exposé published abroad and bearing the innocuous title, *Description of the Rural Clergy* (*Opisanie sel'skogo dukhovenstva*). Written by an obscure priest in Tver diocese, I. S. Belliustin (1819–1890), the book provided contemporary society with its first graphic account of the Church and its problems.[51]

Belliustin, who has already appeared on the opening pages of this book, had a career and background typical for a priest in mid-nineteenth-century Russia.[52] Born to the clerical estate, a graduate of the seminary in Tver, married to a priest's daughter, he first served for four years in a rural parish and then transferred to the cathedral in the district town of Kaliazin, where he was much revered for his diligence and dedication. According to Belliustin's own account, he soon established good rapport with his flock, such that "not a single family matter—from a son's marriage to a daughter's betrothal—took place without prior consultation with me."[53] Testimonials from parishioners confirm both his diligence and popularity, reflected in repeated petitions by parishioners that the bishop elevate Belliustin to the rank of archpriest.[54] One parishioner, for example, testified that "in the name of two hundred peasant souls in the hamlet of Matveikovo [a small community just outside town and attached to the cathedral parish], I declare that our worthy

[51] Paris [Leipzig], 1858. For a more detailed account of the Belliustin affair, see Freeze, "Revolt," pp. 90–124.

[52] Belliustin was the spelling that the priest used for most contact (including publishing) with the secular world; his name was legally spelled Beliustin, a form that appears in all Church records.

[53] GA Kalininskoi obl., f. 103, op. 1, d. 1307, ll. 12 ob.–13 (Belliustin, "Iz zametok").

[54] For the various petitions from 1861, 1866, 1875, and 1879, see TsGIA SSSR, f. 796, op. 160, g. 1879, d. 831, ll. 23–40.

pastor Belliustin, without compensation, [over the years] has taught about 300 boys and girls to read and write as well as the fundamentals of the faith, and that to do this, he had to walk on foot to our hamlet, over two verst [1.2 miles] from town."[55]

Although his cathedral position was superior to a village appointment, Belliustin nonetheless found it extremely dissatisfying. In particular, he complained bitterly of his economic condition, not only because it failed to provide adequately for his large family and, especially, for his sons' education, but also because it exposed him to the degrading task of soliciting emoluments and holiday collections. Penury deprived him of books and journals, prompting him to complain often that he "lacked the opportunity to follow through journals and newspapers the intellectual movements in Russia."[56] Not that his hectic workload—fifteen hundred parishioners and numerous administrative responsibilities—left much time for intellectual endeavors. "It happens," he wrote, "that sometimes a whole week goes by . . . and I do not succeed in taking pen in hand."[57] Frustrated in his attempts to provide adequately for his family, Belliustin asked in despair whether "it is not true that one could lose his sanity under these conditions."[58]

Most frustrating of all, the priest found the path of upward mobility blocked: however zealous he might be, he lacked the formal educational qualification—an academy degree—for a choice appointment in Moscow or even the diocesan capital of Tver. Whatever the reasons for his failure to enter the academy,[59] Belliustin had only a modest seminary degree and, apparently, had reached his maximum career potential—priest in a small provincial town. To overcome that deficiency, he tried to demonstrate achievement in scholarship by composing two works: "Christianity and Science in the Nineteenth Century" (a critique of D. F. Strauss's well-known

[55] OR GBL, f. 344, (P. P. Shibanov) k. 445, d. 10, l. 2 (parish petition of 1875).

[56] GA Kalininskoi obl., f. 103, op. 1, d. 1307, l. 13 (Belliustin, "Iz zametok").

[57] OR GBL, f. 231/II, k. 3, d. 49/2, l. 7 ob. (Belliustin to Pogodin, 25.11.1853).

[58] Ibid., d. 49/4, l. 4 (Belliustin to Pogodin, 25.9.1855).

[59] In earlier writings (such as the above letter to Pogodin), Belliustin explained his decision to forgo the academy by "family and important circumstances"—a plausible explanation, given the shortage of positions and the opportunity presented him at Vasilino. In memoirs published later, he embellished the decision with the claim that early on he realized the uselessness of scholastic learning, having seen numerous specimens among his seminary teachers, and instead preferred to assume practical religious service in the parish ("Iz zametok o perezhitom," *Tserkovno-obshchestvennyi vestnik* [hereafter *TsOV*], 1882, no. 43). However, the seminary rector later claimed that Belliustin *did* intend to enter St. Petersburg Ecclesiastical Academy but was foiled at the last minute by the archbishop of Tver, Grigorii (Postnikov), who attended the final examinations at the seminary and gave Belliustin such a low mark for one answer that it ruined his chances for admission to the academy (I. I. Zav'ialov, communication in *Zhurnal 112-ogo zasedaniia Tverskoi uchenoi arkhivnoi komissii* [Tver, 1912], p. 16).

book, *Das Leben Jesu*) and "Orthodoxy and Catholicism" (a polemical refutation of some unspecified foreign volume).[60] Both efforts suggest familiarity with recent Western scholarship and concern that such works be rebutted, a somewhat surprising phenomenon for an isolated provincial priest, testifying both to his intellectual vitality and to the orthodoxy of his religious views.[61] Both pieces, however, met with a humiliating rebuff from ranking bishops. The archbishop of Tver ignored Belliustin's work, and later Metropolitan Filaret of Moscow dismissed it "as empty philosophizing, which can be of no use whatsoever."[62] Frustrated, Belliustin grew increasingly bitter toward the "learned clergy" who dominated the Church, whether the educated monks who ruled as bishops, rectors, and censors or the academy-trained priests who occupied the best parish positions. Complaining that "I cannot obtain [a position in the capitals]—I do not possess a master's or candidate's degree [from the academy]," Belliustin sarcastically observed that "the academy, which probably possesses some mysterious secret for making all its students into geniuses and consequently deserving of all favors, confers the right to a position in the capitals—not service, however irreproachable, honest, or useful it might be."[63]

As his career in the Church stalled, Belliustin drew closer to the secular world, especially the conservative segment closest to the Church. By far his most important contact was M. P. Pogodin, the well-known historian, publicist, and editor of *The Muscovite*. In part, their ties were professional; Belliustin submitted articles in exchange for a free subscription to Pogodin's journal. They also shared an interest in Russian antiquities, with Belliustin ferreting out old manuscripts and books for Pogodin's vast collection. Yet there was also an important ideological bond, an amorphous blend of Slavophile, anti-Western sentiments. Thus Belliustin castigated the "Europeanism" of the enemy camp, complained that "the Russian spirit" is lacking in their journals, invoked God's wrath upon "Kraevskii & Co. [for] corrupting many souls," and "praised God that Russia still has [in Pogodin] a man of knowledge and erudition, devoted with all his heart to the fatherland."[64] Though that praise of Pogodin appears ingenuous, Belliustin's Slavophilism was founded on despair, not hope: the priest had no illusions about popular

---

[60]Belliustin's diary makes clear his antipathy for Strauss's work, which treated the life of Christ as a myth: "I barely had the strength to complete this tiresome and disgusting insanity by Strauss. The whole work is buried in darkness and obscurity; divine illumination is absent. How much work, scholarship, and erudition was wasted on this!" (GA Kalininskoi obl., f. 103, op. 1, d. 1291, l. 131 ob.).

[61]On the lack of books, see Belliustin, *Opisanie*, pp. 17–19.

[62]OR GBL, f. 231/II, k. 3, d. 49/3, ll. 1–1 ob. (Belliustin to Pogodin, 25.2.1854).

[63]Ibid., d. 49/6, l. 7; 49/4, l. 1 ob. (Belliustin to Pogodin, 1855).

[64]Ibid., d. 49/2, l. 7; d. 49/5, l. 3 ob. (Belliustin to Pogodin, 25.11.1853, 1.5.1856). For Belliustin's literary activities and contacts in high places, see Freeze, "Revolt," pp. 98–99.

religiousness, about the spiritual riches in "Orthodox Rus'." "What a shame
and disgrace," he wrote, "how our Pharisees dare to shout for all to hear that
only in Russia has the faith been preserved inviolable—in Rus', where two-
thirds of the people do not have even the slightest conception of the faith."[65]
That despair, moreover, inspired Belliustin's view that the peasantry
needed emancipation, not only from serfdom, but also from spiritual darkness. Though not insensitive to the material questions of serf emancipation,
Belliustin wrote that "one must think as well about improving the *spiritual*
life of the peasants."[66] At bottom, Belliustin believed this improvement to
mean a fundamental change in Orthodoxy: the sterile "externalism" of traditional "ritualistic Byzantinism," in Belliustin's phrases, must be replaced
by more conscious piety and religious understanding. The most important
change, he believed, was to make the faith directly accessible to the people,
primarily by making the Bible available in the vernacular and in inexpensive
editions, by producing large quantities of popular religious literature, and by
substituting informal talks and readings for the more conventional, pompous
sermons.[67] A corollary to such ideas was Belliustin's interest in public education, which, he argued, should seek to instill good morals and true Christianity, not bare literacy.[68] Above all, these reforms required the revitaliza-
tion of the parish clergy: given the spiritual backwardness of the people, he
wrote, "radical transformation is even more necessary for the entire [clerical]
estate than for the peasants" if the latter were to be truly emancipated.[69]
Pogodin shared these views on Church reform, for he had inspected
Church schools in the 1840s on Protasov's behalf and had a better idea than
most laymen of the serious problems afflicting Orthodoxy. Shortly after
Nicholas's death in 1855, Pogodin persuaded Belliustin to compose a work
"describing the life of the clergy in district towns and villages."[70] The priest
agreed to the idea, vowing to heed Pogodin's imperative "to write only the
truth," without hyperbole and rhetoric. Belliustin deliberately consulted
many other priests for information and ideas, and nearly two years later in
April 1857, sent Pogodin the main text, which was supplemented by a final
installment at the end of the year.[71]

[65] OR GBL, f. 231/II, k. 3, d. 49/6, l. 1 (Belliustin to Pogodin, 22.5.1857).

[66] IRLI, f. 616, op. 1, d. 6, ll. 9–9 ob. (Belliustin to Zheltukhin, 21.6.1858).

[67] Belliustin, "Pravoslavnaia Rus'" (unpublished segment of *Opisanie* in OR GBL, f. 231/
III, k. 1, d. 66, ll. 36 ob.–44 ob.).

[68] IRLI, f. 274 (M. I. Semevskii), op. 1, d. 74, ll. 1–2 ob. (Belliustin to Semevskii, 9.10.1861);
f. 616, d. 32, l. 3 ob. (Belliustin to E. Zheltukhina, 12.1.1861).

[69] Ibid., f. 34, op. 1, d. 62, l. 4 (Belliustin to Burachek, 20.3.1858).

[70] OR GBL, f. 231/II, k. 3, d. 49/4, l. 3 (Belliustin to Pogodin, 25.9.1855).

[71] Ibid., d. 49/6, ll. 5, 13 ob. (Belliustin to Pogodin, 2.4.1857, 26.12.1857). The supplementary sections, which arrived too late for inclusion in the printed *Opisanie*, treat several issues:
voluntary defrocking for widowed priests, the plight of orphans and widows, and (the longest
part) "Orthodox Rus'" (ibid., f. 231/III, k. 1, d. 66, ll. 30–44 ob.).

An untitled note (*zapiska*), Belliustin's essay offered a comprehensive analysis of the Church and its problems as seen "from below" by a parish priest.[72]
Structured as a chronological account of the priest's life and career, from
early schooling to daily service, the essay itemized virtually all the problems
that would preoccupy reformers for the next two decades—Church schools,
parish economy, diocesan administration, and the soslovie order of the
clergy. The opening section on ecclesiastical schools, though drawing heavily
upon Belliustin's personal experience, provided a superb sketch of the schools
and their problems—poor moral environment, venality and incompetence
of the faculty, pedagogical backwardness, and misdirected curriculum (with
a surfeit of courses, though few of practical use to a village priest). Belliustin
was especially critical of the classical curriculum, calling "Latin a dead language, which will be as useful in real life as Sanskrit. . . . A youth exhausts
his talents for six whole years on a language that he will forget in the first
two years of priesthood." Belliustin next analyzed the system of parish service, especially decrying the baneful effect of the hereditary order, both
because it disregarded merit (with positions allotted according to family
claims and bargains) and because it forged highly unsatisfactory marriages
within the white clergy. The essay also drew a shocking portrait of the typical priest's life, revealing the great impediments to effective service—crippling poverty, constant field labor, humiliating gratuities, conflict with insolent sacristans, and maltreatment by parishioners, noble and peasant alike.
To combat such problems, complained Belliustin, the priest found no support
among his superiors in the Church. On the contrary, diocesan authorities—
if not the bishop, then his aides—routinely exacted the "gifts" and "accidental fees" that greased the wheels of Church bureaucracy and justice.

From the first page, Belliustin posed one overarching question: "What is
the cause of all this?" His answer was unequivocal: Church authorities—
specifically, the bishops, who failed to solicit state assistance, who (he alleged)
opposed clerical salaries, who tolerated abuse by diocesan clerks, and who
bowed before the caprice of local squires. Yearning wistfully for more personalized rule and castigating the modern generation of bishops as mere
"administrators," Belliustin proceeded to question the right of monastic
clergy to rule the Russian Church. He accused many prelates of careerism
and claimed that they only became monks in search of high positions and
wealth. Their very vows of withdrawal and ascetisicsm, he argued, should
disqualify them from episcopal or other administrative positions. That was
not an original view; it had been expressed before and would gain wide currency in the decade ahead.[73] More inflammatory still was Belliustin's contention, repeated throughout the essay, that bishops did not even *want* to aid

---

[72] Discussion here follows the printed *Opisanie*, for only the second half of the manuscript
has survived (ibid., f. 231/III, k. 1, d. 66, ll. 1–44).

[73] For such ideas in the late eighteenth century, see Freeze, *Russian Levites*, pp. 74–75.

the parish clergy. It was not canon law or tradition, he argued, but the desire to conserve their own power that caused bishops to leave the parish priest so downtrodden, poor, and weak. Toward the end of his manuscript he suggested the logical consequence of such views, hinting broadly that members of the white clergy—mere priests—should be consecrated bishops of the Russian Church.

That proposal was but one part of a larger plan for reform. Belliustin emphasized, first of all, that the Church must reorder its schools by adopting a more practical curriculum, hiring more professional teachers, and improving the pupils' moral training. The essay also recognized the need to sunder hereditary and family ties to appointments; though not calling for total abolition of the clerical estate (for fear that men of means and education would not voluntarily become priests), Belliustin proposed to make appointment and promotion wholly dependent upon merit, not family claims, not mere formal diplomas.[74] To make service more attractive and to free the priest for full-time pastorship, Belliustin proposed a solution that would dominate clerical aspirations all across the empire in the 1860s: a regular state salary in lieu of emoluments, field labor, and holiday collections. Only a salary, he argued, would liberate the priest from the parishioners' control and enable him to become an independent, dynamic pastor. That spirit of professional pastorship also informed Belliustin's sharp attack on deacons and sacristans. Decrying their lack of education and bad conduct, he proposed to deny them clerical status and to employ them only as hired sextons, subject to replacement for misconduct or poor service. Finally, Belliustin urged various reforms in diocesan administration, most notably, restoration of the clergy's right to elect the local superintendent as a safeguard against venality and injustice.

Significantly, Belliustin looked not to the Church or society but to the state to impose these reforms. Although he repeatedly addressed the bishops in his memorandum (using the second-person pronoun), Belliustin plainly looked to the government—specifically, the emperor—to resolve the Church's problems, to provide the wherewithal for seminary budgets, salaries, and pensions, and to force change upon unwilling bishops. His appeal derived partly from clear precedent—state subsidies in the 1840s, Protasov's role in the Synod—but also from traditional *étatisme*—the belief in the "just tsar" sure to satisfy his subjects' needs. It was also a tactic of necessity. Personal experience persuaded him that parishioners had no desire to grant tithes or salaries, that bishops had no respect for priests and no desire to enhance their status. Altogether, Belliustin's essay offered a devastating portrait of the Church. More radical in tone than in perspective, its diagnosis and prescrip-

---

[74] For Belliustin's warning that the well-born would not agree to become priests, see his 1858 letter to Zheltukhin in IRLI, f. 616, op. 1, d. 6, l. 29 ob.

tion for reform would be echoed again and again in the 1860s by rank-and-file clergy, publicists, and official commissions.[75]

Pogodin was immensely pleased with the essay. He kept a firm editorial hand on the priest, occasionally questioning the veracity of a shocking anecdote or rumor, and then had the manuscript recopied, adding still another zapiska to the many already in circulation.[76] One copy reached Chief Procurator Tolstoi and another V. B. Bazhanov, the emperor's confessor and a member of the Synod.[77] Tolstoi, as marginalia on his copy show, found much to praise in the work, writing "True!" alongside many passages, interspersed with only an occasional objection ("Nonsense!" "He is mistaken!" and "Not so").[78] Pogodin also showed the work to some clerical acquaintances, who affirmed its veracity and added corroborative testimony from their personal experiences.[79] One archpriest wrote that the work "realistically describes the pathetic condition of the clergy," and a bishop declared that "the most zealous defenders of the existing [seminary] find little that is exaggerated" in the work.[80]

Even as the manuscript began to circulate, Pogodin took the audacious step of arranging for it to be published abroad, where it appeared anonymously as *Description of the Rural Clergy* in a series published in Leipzig in 1858.[81] Apprised of Pogodin's action, the priest was petrified with fear: "There is now such chaos in my head," he wrote, "that I cannot put two ideas together sensibly."[82] He had good cause for hysteria. However valid

[75]See, for instance, the findings of an official seminary committee, summarized below, pp. 220–24.

[76]Pogodin deleted excessive references to Tver diocese to help conceal Belliustin's identity (OR GBL, f. 231/III, k. 1, d. 66, ll. 2-2 ob., 6 ob.–7, 9 ob., 10–11). He also struck out some inflammatory assertions—that monks had caused the schism in the seventeenth century, that bishops behaved like serfowning aristocrats (ibid., ll. 7 ob.–8, 14, 15 ob.–18).

[77]N. P. Barsukov, *Pogodin*, 15: 125–26.

[78]Tolstoi warmly agreed with the first section on seminaries—a subject of reform interest in the Synod—but grew more critical as he read on. He sometimes added personal confirmation of Belliustin's comments; for instance, alongside a passage on bribery in the seminary, Tolstoi volunteered confirmation from a clerical acquaintance. The procurator was most critical of Belliustin's acerbic remarks about traditional Church singing, the uselessness of Latin, and the role of peasant pressure in inducing clergy to imbibe (see Tolstoi's marginalia on the manuscript in his archive in OR GBL, f. 302, k. 2, d. 12).

[79]M. P. Pogodin, "Ob"iasnenie," *Russkii vestnik*, 21 (1859), kn. 1, no. 9: 47–48.

[80]Pevnitskii, "Zapiski," *RS*, 123 (1905): 541; I. Barsukov, ed., *Pis'ma Innokentiia, mitropolita moskovskogo i kolomenskogo*, 2 vols. (St. Petersburg, 1897–98), 2: 151, 163–64, 168, 199–200.

[81]Pogodin later claimed that he offered the manuscript for foreign publication spontaneously, but in fact his diary shows a prolonged inner struggle before he surrendered the work for publication abroad; see his diary entries for 9.6.1857, 12.6.1857, and 6.8.1857 in OR GBL, f. 231/I, k. 35, d. 1, ll. 47 ob., 49.

[82]Ibid., f. 231/II, k. 3, d. 50/1, ll. 5-5 ob. (Belliustin to Pogodin, 22.2.1858).

the book's description, however commonplace most of its proposals, Belliustin had penned a manifesto indicting monastic rule in the Church. As he himself observed, "this was originally a private work [not intended for publication], and I did not deem it necessary to indulge in sly circumlocutions."[83] Thus, despite disclaimers in the text that the author does not "despise" monks, the book related scandalous anecdotes about monks and bishops and directly questioned their canonical right to govern the Church. Quite apart from its content, the volume's foreign publication was particularly incriminating: parish clergy could not publish in religious journals without express approval, much less through an underground press in Leipzig. Belliustin wrote later that "my guilt (in their words) does not consist in writing the book, but in [permitting] all Europe to know what is going on here."[84] Not only would the volume provide rich material for the Catholic propagandists whose activities had already alarmed authorities in Petersburg, but it even took its epigraph from the most famous Russian Jesuit of all—I. S. Gagarin.[85] The Catholic connection, if known, was especially dangerous and perhaps provoked Belliustin's furious rebuke to Pogodin: "[My] composition is now in the hands of those who tirelessly seek all opportunities to ridicule that which we revere in the depths of our soul! . . . New food for malice and calumny!"[86]

Once published, the book caused an uproar in Petersburg.[87] Though rare and expensive, the illegal volume quickly circulated in the upper strata of the government, Church, and society. One well-informed diarist recorded the book's appearance on 16 July 1858, observed that "the condition of our clergy does present a horrifying picture," and reported that the metropolitan of St. Petersburg and other prelates "are furious and have called it libel."[88] A few months later Church authorities blamed the *Description* for provoking disorders at the St. Petersburg Ecclesiastical Academy, where students

[83]OR GPB, f. 37 (A. I. Artem'ev), d. 703, ll. 2–2 ob. (Belliustin to P. I. Mel'nikov-Pecherskii, 1859).

[84]OR GBL, f. 231/II, k. 3, d. 50/2, ll. 19–19 ob. (Belliustin to Pogodin, 26.5.1859).

[85]*Opisanie*, p. ii, with a quotation from J. Gagarin's *De l'enseignement de la théologie dans l'Église russe* (Paris, 1856), p. 59. A subsequent volume of *Russkii zagranichnyi sbornik* (fasc. 6) advertised the sale of a Russian translation of Gagarin's book on reunion of the Roman and Eastern churches (*O primirenii russkoi tserkvi s rimskoiu*). The Russian Jesuits in Paris were indeed interested in Bellustin's book. A. Golitsyn wrote Martynov that "je suis occupé dans le moment à faire un article en française de l'*Opisanie sel'skogo dukhovenstva*" (BS, f. Gagarine, no. 70, rayon 4, undated letter).

[86]OR GBL, f. 231/II, k. 3, d. 50/1, l. 13 (Belliustin to Pogodin, 8.7.1858).

[87]Ten years after the affair, one observer compared the sensational effect of Belliustin's book with that of Radishchev's abolitionist volume on serfdom in 1790 ("Vnutrennee obozrenie o noveishikh reformakh dukhovenstva," *Nedelia*, 1868, no. 29: 898). For confirmation of *Opisanie* as an "epochal event," see Giliarov-Platonov, *Iz perezhitogo*, 1: 36.

[88]A. V. Nikitenko, *Dnevnik*, 3 vols. (Moscow, 1955), 2: 31.

protested the oppressive rule of the inspector, urged that none of their number become monks, and attempted to establish ties with students in Kiev.[89]

Predictably, the Synod soon launched a full investigation and by the fall had begun to close in on the unsuspecting priest. The first hint of trouble came in October 1858, when a stranger (who identified himself as Michel de Proudenkoff from "l'Academie de Rome") approached Belliustin and professed an interest in touring the area with him. When the priest warily spurned his requests, Proudenkoff declared: "In vain do you affect such modesty, pretending to be someone who knows and understands nothing; after all, we know who writes what, and for a long time we have known about you."[90] Formal action finally came in January 1859, when a local archimandrite summoned Belliustin to explain his "motives" for writing *A Description of Rural Clergy*, to reveal how and why he "transmitted his work abroad for publication," and to state whether he "regards the information in the composition as just, inoffensive, and harmless." He was reminded that "for confession to the crime, the punishment will be mitigated, but [otherwise] the laws will be applied in all their severity." Incredulous that the Synod had conclusive proof, Belliustin denied culpability by seizing on the technicality that he wrote an untitled memorandum, not a book entitled *Description of the Rural Clergy*. "I not only did not write but also have not even read a work bearing the title *A Description of the Rural Clergy;* having never seen [this work], I do not know whether such a book exists anywhere, in Russia or abroad." If the Church chose to press charges, he wrote Pogodin, "try to see to it that I am able to defend myself before the courts of the civil government [not the Church]."[91]

The denouement was as sensational as the book. The Synod decided to impose an extraordinarily harsh punishment: life exile to "Solovki" (Solovetskii monastery in the barren reaches of the far north) by administrative order, without further investigation or formal trial.[92] With bitter sarcasm Belliustin later wrote that "the *Most Holy* Synod ordered that I be exiled permanently to Solovki—without a trial, without any refutation of my testimony."[93] At the last moment, however, the priest was miraculously saved: Alexander II personally intervened to quash the Synod's decision. In early

[89] TsGIA SSSR, f. 832, op. 1, d. 15, ll. 121 ob.-22 (Isidor to Filaret); L'vov, *Pis'ma*, p. 332; Nikitenko, *Dnevnik*, 2: 38; OR GBL, f. 231/II, k. 3, d. 50/2, l. 2 (Belliustin to Pogodin, 6.1.1859).

[90] OR GBL, f. 231/II, k. 3, d. 50/1, ll. 18–18 ob. (Belliustin to Pogodin, 9.10.1852).

[91] Ibid., d. 50/2, ll. 3–3 ob. (Belliustin to Pogodin, 14.1.1859).

[92] Ibid., l. 7 ob. (Belliustin to Pogodin, 27.1.1859).

[93] OR GPB, f. 37, d. 703, l. 2 ob. (Belliustin to Mel'nikov-Pecherskii, n.d.); IRLI, f. 616, d. 6, ll. 44–45 (Belliustin to Zheltukhin, 27.1.1859). See also "Tekushchaia khronika i osobye proizshestviia. Dnevnik V. G. Odoevskogo," *Literaturnoe nasledstvo*, 22–24 (1935): 94.

January 1859 a friend in Petersburg informed Belliustin that "there are some good people who have taken your side, including (so it is said) the imperial family, which has read your work and found much in it that is true and completely new to them."[94] Some accounts of the emperor's intervention carried tones of high drama: "The Synod had decided to send you [Belliustin] permanently to Solovki, but, before the session had adjourned, the chief procurator received a note bearing the Sovereign's seal. The note expressed His Imperial Majesty's and the imperial family's gratitude for the informative contents of your book and added that the author deserves recognition for the truth [expressed in his book]."[95] Whatever the truth of such stories, the most important element here was the emperor's personal identification with clerical reform. His role in the Belliustin affair was so widely known that by April, Russian Jesuits in Paris had heard of it.[96]

More important, Belliustin's book triggered a debate in the press that for the first time squarely addressed the clerical question. The first reaction to the underground book came from conservative quarters in a polemical brochure by A. N. Murav'ev, who sought to rebut the damaging indictment.[97] Formally approved for publication by Church censors, Murav'ev's brochure accused the *Description* of aiding Catholic propagandists, quoted its more hyperbolic outbursts as proof of "one-sidedness," and somberly concluded that "this harmful and irresponsible book, gradually penetrating into all strata of society, high and low, is causing tragic results everywhere." Significantly, conservatives like Murav'ev did not contest the existence of disorders in the Church. Rather, in contrast to Belliustin, they regarded the secular state as the cause, not the solution, of those disorders.[98] That view reflected the bitter legacy of Protasov's dominance. It was also no doubt an astute judgment of the narrow utilitarian goals of many high officials, already manifested in efforts to retract the generous concessions of the 1842 statute. Predictably, the Murav'ev brochure failed to silence reformist criticism of the Church and only provoked a chorus of caustic rejoinders from people as

[94] GA Kalininskoi obl., f. 103, op. 1, d. 1333, ll. 3 ob.–4 (N. V. Kalachov to Belliustin, 10.1.1859).

[95] IRLI, f. 616, d. 6, l. 44 ob. (Belliustin to Zheltukhin, 27.1.1859).

[96] BS, f. Gagarine, no. 70, rayon 2 (unpaginated letter, Martynov to Gagarin, 15.4.1859). Curiously, the archives hold no trace of the entire affair, either in Church collections (including the separate volumes of "secret resolutions" of the Synod in TsGIA SSSR, f. 796, op. 449, dd. 166–70) or in collections of the various censorship organs (ibid., ff. 779, 807). Evidently, once the emperor forbade punishment, the Synod or chief procurator destroyed whatever file had been assembled.

[97] *Mysli svetskogo cheloveka o knige "Opisanie sel'skogo dukhovenstva"* (St. Petersburg, 1859). On the reputed role of Filaret in preparing this rejoinder, see "Tekushchaia khronika," p. 94; N. P. Barsukov, *Pogodin*, 15: 127–28; L'vov, *Pis'ma*, p. 289.

[98] TsGIA SSSR, f. 796, op. 205, d. 603, ll. 1–15 (Murav'ev to Pogodin, 5.6.1859); a second copy is in ibid., f. 832, op. 1, d. 83, ll. 132–45 ob.

diverse as Pogodin and the radical journalist N. A. Dobroliubov.[99] Although church censors tried to contain the gush of comment and discussion, they could do little to stifle the debate in foreign publications or even in the domestic press.[100] As a moderate church journal observed, "readers (who earlier had never had to consider conditions [in the clergy]) found all this to be very unexpected—this strict analysis of the clergy, of shortcomings in their performance before society, of inadequacies in their education, of the special characteristics of their soslovie."[101]

The result, evident by the fall of 1859, was soaring expectations of fundamental reform in the Church. Perhaps the most powerful stimulus to such hopes was the sovereign's personal involvement in the Belliustin affair, suggesting that Belliustin's appeal to the emperor had not fallen on deaf ears. Indeed, the priest himself had close contacts with the staff of the Synodal chancellery and circulated wild rumors, allegedly emanating from "one of the members of the Synod":

> From the very top [the emperor] the following proposal was submitted in His [Majesty's] hand: "Consider: (1) Is it not useful to convert monasteries into hospitals and monks into feldshers and doctors? (2) Is it not useful to remove the white clergy from the influence of black clergy? (3) Is it not useful to make sacristans into hired laymen? (4) Report on progress made in improving the condition of the rural clergy.

As he had already implied in the *Description*, Belliustin stressed that reform must not be left in the Synod's hands: "Now one must communicate to the very top [the emperor] this idea: 'These questions must not be decided by the Synod, which definitely thinks and acts contrary to the ideas of the emperor and upholds the authority of the monks. Rather, as in the peasant question, experts from all corners of Russia should be chosen.'"[102] A few

---

[99] Pogodin, "Ob"iasnenie," *Russkii vestnik*, 21 (1859), no. 9: 43–50; N. A. Dobroliubov, "[Retsenziia]: *Mysli svetskogo cheloveka*," *Sovremennik*, 75 (1859), no. 6: 340–44.

[100] Most noteworthy was a conservative critique of *Opisanie*, edited by N. Elagin and published abroad under the title *Russkoe dukhovenstvo* (Berlin, 1859); for a summary and discussion of its "illegal" status, see Freeze, "Revolt," pp. 110–12. Other influential pieces included G. Grekov's article, "Dukhovnoe zvanie v Rossii: golos sel'skogo sviashchennika," *Dukhovnaia beseda*, 6 (1859), no. 17: 109–30, which reproved lay society for its neglect of the clergy and urged the conversion of emoluments into more honorable support. Even the Russian Church's official organ in Paris fanned expectations of reform, making exaggerated claims that "an important reform" in the seminary was imminent (*L'Union chrétienne*, 1859, no. 1 [1.11.1859]: 6).

[101] "Obozrenie," *PO*, 1860, no. 1: 239.

[102] OR GBL, f. 231/II, k. 3, d. 50/2, ll. 25–26 (Belliustin to Pogodin, 6.10.1859), I. M. Snegirev, in a diary entry of 17.10.1859, recorded a conversation with Prince N. I. Trubetskoi, who "told me about questions from the Sovereign to the Synod about the clergy" ("Dnevnik," *RA*, 1904, no. 9: 71).

months later the priest jubilantly spread rumors that "V. B. Bazhanov [Alexander's confessor] will soon become the metropolitan of the entire white clergy."[103]

Such rumors, coupled with the alarming candor of the press, proved highly disturbing to the bishops. Some, like Isidor of Kiev, perceived all in the darkest hues and passed on fears of the Church's imminent destruction: "The common people at stations in Khar'kov province are asking whether the noble travelers are telling the truth in saying that soon there will be neither monks nor priests in Russia."[104] Isidor wrote that "the general ferment promises little good: the universities preach that science cannot coexist with faith, that Orthodoxy shackles scientific progress, and that only Lutheranism opens a free path to enlightenment."[105] Murav'ev expressed similar despair in a letter to Metropolitan Grigorii of Petersburg: "What have we come to? In Russia itself a Russian prince [N. B. Golitsyn] preaches union [with Rome] and goes unpunished; a priest in Tver [Belliustin] writes a book on the rural clergy filled with bile and denigrates the episcopal rank and the Church; he gives the manuscript to a journalist [Pogodin], who adds his own share of bile and in that form publishes it abroad. And both of them get off without punishment, even though no one has ever brought such shame upon our Church."[106]

The First Reforms

By the fall of 1859 the Church stood on the very threshold of reform, with special committees formed to study seminary reform and the clerical question in the western dioceses. Despite Belliustin's summons for state domination, power still rested with the Synod and ranking bishops, who had good cause for anxiety about the limits of reform, state intervention, and the more independent spirit now evident among the parish clergy. Such fears were no doubt reinforced by the broader *bouleversement* of the late 1850s and the

---

[103]OR GBL, f. 231/II, k. 3, d. 51/1, l. 2 (Belliustin to Pogodin, 8.1.1860).

[104]TsGIA SSSR, f. 832, op. 1, d. 15, l. 122 (Isidor to Filaret, 25.12.1858).

[105]Houghton Library, Cambridge, Mass., fMS, Russ.50, letter 132 (Isidor to A. M. Fadeev, 25.12.1858). In an undated (but subsequent) letter, Isidor expressed still greater anxiety: "Circumstances are so murky that Church business requires much thought and work. Never was there such intense pressure from the West. Never did the Church have so many enemies inside our Fatherland, ready to cast down every conviction. All talk deleriously about progress, but they themselves have done nothing for the cause of moral improvement. When one considers that at such an unfortunate year, major issues of state are being developed—it is terrifying" (ibid., letter 134).

[106]TsGIA SSSR, f. 797, op. 30, otd. 1, st. 2, d. 224, ll. 10 ob.–11 (Murav'ev to Grigorii, 21.12.1858). On the Golitsyn affair, where a Russian nobleman wrote an essay urging reconciliation and reunion with Rome, see ibid., ll. 1–99; f. 832, op. 1, d. 83, ll. 122–23, 146–54; L'vov, *Pis'ma*, pp. 287–88, 429–30; Filaret, *SMO*, 4: 415–19.

tensions of serf emancipation, student unrest in the universities, and alarming evidence of a steep rise in antireligious sentiments among the educated classes. As the first committees and Synod took up the question of Church reform, it remained to be seen whether they would support or resist the growing demands for a transformation of Church and clergy.

The Status of Widowed Clergy

The first major opposition to reform came not from the bishops but from the chief procurator, A. P. Tolstoi, who had come to office vowing to respect the Synod's prerogatives but now did all in his power to overturn a Synodal resolution. The issue, slight as it might seen, concerned the Synod's resolution in August 1859 to ameliorate the plight of widowed clergy by removing the disabilities on clergy who voluntarily defrocked.[107] In behavior reminiscent of Protasov, the procurator first tabled the Synod's resolution and then dispatched "confidential letters" to the metropolitans of St. Petersburg and Moscow, pronouncing the resolution "inconsistent with those feelings and ideas that throughout my life I have held about 'holy orders.'" He accused the white clergy of "indifference to Church matters and of excessive concern with their own material well-being," faults he attributed to the hereditary structure of the clergy: "Unfortunately, our clergy are forced by marital ties to be concerned with family needs and for the most part to convert the transfer of clerical positions into a device for supporting their children." This peculiarly conservative critique of the soslovie order was offered as evidence not of the need to assist clergy, as liberal reformers argued, but of the need to tighten discipline, even to ordain celibate men to the priesthood. Tolstoi also raised the specter of Protestantism, declaring that Orthodoxy made holy orders "indelible" and that the Synod's resolution therefore represented some kind of "Protestant" deviation.[108]

That attack precipitated a fierce struggle between procurator and Synod that lasted for an entire year. Although Tolstoi won the support of Metropolitan Grigorii, other members of the Synod stood firm, and one, Bazhanov, compiled a formal memorandum refuting Tolstoi's assertions about the "indelible character" of holy orders.[109] As Tolstoi later explained to the

---

[107] TsGIA SSSR, f. 832, op. 1, d. 72, ll. 29–40 (Synod resolution, 22.8.1859).

[108] Ibid., f. 797, op. 29, otd. 1, st. 2, d. 249, ll. 2–4 ob. (Tolstoi to Grigorii, n.d.); f. 832, op. 1, d. 72, ll. 5–6 (Filaret to Tolstoi, 17.1.1860).

[109] Filaret (*Pis'ma Antoniiu*, 4: 215) wrote that the presiding member of the Synod, Grigorii, opposed the rest of the Synod on this issue; hence it was probably Grigorii who authored the critical memorandum on this issue, now found in Tolstoi's archive ("Zapiska neizvestnogo mitropolita po voprosu o sniatii sana sviashchennosluzhitelei," OR GBL, f. 302, k. 3, d. 12, ll. 1–4). A rebuttal, evidently by Bazhanov, is given in "Vzgliad na vopros o neizgladimom kharaktere sviashchenstva i na otnoshenie onogo k tserkovnomu sudu nad sviashchennosluzhiteliami" (TsGIA SSSR, f. 797, op. 29, otd. 1, st. 2, d. 249, ll. 19–22 ob.).

emperor, the Synod could not reach a decision on the matter "because of the disagreement between the bishops and chief priests [archpriests Bazhanov and V. N. Kutnevich]."[110] Actually, not all the prelates sided with Tolstoi. Metropolitan Filaret of Moscow, in particular, rebuked Tolstoi for his unwarranted aspersions on the "canonical validity" of the Synod's resolution. Filaret refused to comment on the substance of the case, testily noting that Tolstoi had failed to send him a copy of the resolution, and he reproved the procurator for gratuitously insulting the Church's ruling body: "By the grace of God a member of the Synod for forty years, I have never encountered such [a deviation from canon law]."[111] Although Tolstoi denied any intention of insulting the Synod and dismissed his "exaggerations" as mere "slips inevitable in any conversation,"[112] Filaret remained skeptical, reminding Tolstoi that he was "called upon to preserve that which was previously despoiled" by his predecessors in the office of chief procurator.[113]

Alexander then enlivened the debate still more by sending an anonymous memorandum, "On the Widowhood of Priests," with a request "to know the Synod's opinion."[114] In fact written by the infamous Belliustin, the memorandum argued that widowhood affected as many as four in ten priests and entailed financial ruin and immoral conduct, especially in the case of young priests in the prime of life. It urged the Church to facilitate voluntary defrocking, at least for widowed clergy, and to demolish the legal barriers that impose "such discouraging, intolerable conditions that it is extremely rare for someone to resort to this means." That reform, argued the memorandum, would free the Church of clergy who "remain priests against their will and desire, fully recognizing their spiritual and even physical inability to observe the necessary purity in body and spirit." In turn, society would gain useful teachers and honest civil servants.[115] That Alexander personally transmitted the memorandum not only bore witness to Belliustin's continuing influence at court but also suggested—misleadingly so—the sovereign's interest in far-reaching reform.

That Belliustin's note offered more consideration to the needs of the clergy than to the canons of the Church infuriated Tolstoi. He flatly declined to

[110]TsGIA SSSR, f. 797, op. 29, otd. 1, st. 2, d. 249, ll. 39–42 ob. (Tolstoi to Alexander, 8.3.1860).

[111]Ibid., f. 832, op. 1, d. 72, ll. 7–11 ob., 5–6 ob. (Filaret, "O vypiske iz zakonov po voprosu o slozhenii sviashchenno-sluzhitel'skogo sana"); f. 797, op. 29, otd. 1, st. 2, d. 249, ll. 15–18 (Filaret to Tolstoi, 22.1.1860), 24–28 ("Zapiska"), 23–23 ob. (Filaret to Tolstoi, 4.2.1860).

[112]Ibid., f. 832, op. 1, d. 72, ll. 27–28 ob. (Tolstoi to Filaret, 12.2.1860).

[113]Ibid., f. 797, op. 29, otd. 1, st. 2, d. 249, ll. 31–32 (Filaret to Tolstoi, 18.2.1860).

[114]Ibid., f. 832, op. 1, d. 72, l. 43 (notation on "Vdovstvo sviashchennikov"). Although none of the participants suspected Belliustin's authorship, the memorandum here is identical to another in Belliustin's hand, which was originally intended as part of the Opisanie but arrived too late for inclusion. See OR GBL, f. 231/III, k. 1, d. 66, ll. 30–35.

[115]TsGIA SSSR, f. 832, op. 1, d. 72, ll. 43–47; f. 797, op. 29, otd. 1, st. 2, d. 249 ll. 34–38 ob. (copies of "Vdovstvo sviashchennikov").

transmit the note to the Synod, as Alexander ordered, and instead sent the emperor a vitriolic critique of the anonymous manuscript:

> Upon reading this memorandum, I found it significant that it makes absolutely no mention of canon law. Instead, it proposes to permit widowed priests to defrock at will and bases all its arguments on human frailties. Hence by severing the sacred bonds that the Church lays on holy orders, it at once undermines not only the sacrament of ordination but also that of marriage. For if infirmity of flesh justifies the violation of the celibate vows of ordination, so much the more does it justify a fourth marriage for laymen or divorce on the grounds of illness by one of the spouses.[116]

Claiming that Filaret favored existing policy, which was not true, Tolstoi asked Alexander to have the metropolitan review the anonymous note before sending it to the Synod, where it would probably become public knowledge: "Once this note is given to the Synod, it will be impossible to keep it secret from the [lay] chancellery, and given the strange contents of this memorandum (and the astounding novelty of [its] blatant violation of the holy canons), rumors about this will fly through the town, and popular talk will distress Orthodox folk and increase the insolence of schismatics."[117]

Tolstoi's will eventually prevailed. Curiously, Metropolitan Filaret, though rejecting the Belliustin note for its "one-sidedness and exaggeration," at first upheld the Synod's resolution and concurred that the penalties for defrocking voluntarily should be reduced.[118] In the end, however, Filaret withdrew his support for reform and agreed to maintain the status quo, primarily to eliminate the sharp conflict that the issue had provoked among members of the Synod.[119] Supported by both Grigorii and Filaret, Tolstoi forced the Synod to retract its original resolution.[120]

---

[116]Tolstoi's comment on the "celibate vows of ordination" refers to the rule that white clergy must be married before ordination and, by canon law, could not remarry afterwards. By voluntarily defrocking, the clergy were, in his view, evading that principle, even if at the cost of leaving the clerical estate.

[117]TsGIA SSSR, f. 832, op. 1, d. 72, ll. 41–42 ob. (Tolstoi to Filaret, 17.3.1860); f. 797, op. 29, otd. 1, st. 2, d. 249, ll. 39–42 ob. (Tolstoi to Alexander, 8.3.1860).

[118]Ibid., f. 832, op. 1, d. 72, ll. 60–80 (draft note, 8.4.1860); f. 796, op. 141, g. 1860, d. 1019, ll. 1–12 ob. (final version); f. 797, op. 29, otd. 1, st. 2, d. 249, ll. 57–58 (Filaret to Tolstoi, 18.4.1864), 59–64 (zapiska "o sniatii sviashchenno-sluzhitel'skogo sana po prosheniiam").

[119]Ibid., f. 797, op. 29, otd. 1, st. 2, d. 249, ll. 99–102 ob. (Filaret, 9.12.1860); f. 832, op. 1, d. 72, ll. 101–2 ob. ("zapiska" of December 1860). For Filaret's anger toward Tolstoi for tabling his earlier notes, see L'vov, Pis'ma, p. 115, and Gorskii, Dnevnik, p. 126.

[120]OR GBL, f. 302, k. 3, d. 12, l. 1 ("Zapiska neizvestnogo mitropolita," with marginal notation in Tolstoi's hand); TsGIA SSSR, f. 796, op. 141, g. 1860, d. 2320, ll. 1–6 (Synod resolution, 16.12.1860). See also the rebuff to the liberal minister of war, D. Miliutin, who had tried to intervene on behalf of a widowed army chaplain (ibid., f. 797, op. 29, otd. 1, st. 2, d. 249, ll. 115–18 ob.).

As a result, reform on voluntary defrocking—a seemingly innocuous issue—proved abortive. The affair underscored the vulnerability of the Synod's new authority; if need be, the procurator could easily reassert his influence and override the will of the Synod, even when it enjoyed the apparent support of the emperor and of influential prelates like Filaret. As the outcome revealed, Tolstoi prevailed because the Synod itself was sharply divided, enabling him to impose his will and bury reform in the name of harmony. Moreover, Tolstoi's admonition that reform threatened to vitiate Orthodoxy with Protestant principles suggested a limitation that would rest heavily upon the Church, almost uniquely so among the Great Reforms: Church reform could not, perhaps dared not, invoke explicit Western precedents and models, save in the most mundane matters. Characteristically, Tolstoi solicited opinions for defrocking policy not from the Russian clergy in Europe but from those in the Near East, whom he asked to report on the policies observed there.[121] Finally, the reform debates occurred in a vacuum; no attempt was made to solicit public, even episcopal, opinion. As we shall see later, most bishops favored reform to ease the lot of widowed clergy. Hence it was a conservative procurator, not conservative prelates, who derailed this first reform attempt in 1859–1860.

Seminary Reform

Like the issue of voluntary defrocking, seminary reform elicited considerable differences among leading bishops and lay officials of the Church: all conceded the urgency of reform, yet each had different ideas on its direction and scope. Most shared the view that Church schools should remain separate and that the curriculum should be purged of Protasov's "practical subjects" (medicine, geodesy, and agronomy). Some, like Filaret, favored only a restoration of the 1814 statute. Metropolitan Grigorii, likewise, wanted to "change everything that was introduced by the late procurator [Protasov]" and "to increase the bishops' influence on the schools (and to weaken—if not eliminate entirely—the influence of the Bureau of Ecclesiastical Education)."[122] Tolstoi had similarly modest designs, declaring that he desired "only to reduce the number of subjects, to give more attention to the physical health of the pupils, and not to eliminate that which is peculiarly spiritual in [the schools], but to preserve it."[123] More ambitious were the plans of Prince S. N. Urusov, director of the Bureau of Ecclesiastical Education and a man

[121] TsGIA SSSR, f. 797, op. 29, otd. 1, st. 2, d. 249, ll. 89–96.

[122] Filaret, Pis'ma Antoniiu, 4: 170–71; Gorskii, "Dnevnik," Prib. TSO, 52 (1885), kn. 1: 201–2, 220–21; OR GBL, f. 316, k. 66, d. 22, ll. 7–7 ob. (Gorskii to Filaret, 29.7.1860); L'vov, Pis'ma, p. 112 (Grigorii to Filaret, 31.5.1860).

[123] Gorskii, "Dnevnik," Prib. TSO, 52 (1885), kn. 1: 201.

with close ties to the court.[124] At the special order of the emperor, Urusov
inspected Church schools in six dioceses in 1860 and visited six more the
following year.[125] Whereas the ranking prelates sought mainly to revise little
more than curriculum, Urusov deemed almost every dimension of the
schools unsatisfactory—the moral environment, the pedagogy, the administration, and, especially, the lack of finances: "Poverty is the chief shortcoming of all the schools in Tula—sometimes it is difficult to sit for any length
of time in the classes because of the stench emitted by the raw sheepskin
coats that cover the pupils [sitting in unheated classrooms]."[126]

To compile a specific proposal, the Synod formed a special committee
under the chairmanship of Archbishop Dmitrii (Muretov) of Kherson.
Reflecting the Synod's dominance, the committee was composed of six clerics
(mostly archimandrites experienced in education) and one representative for
the chief procurator.[127] Earlier, the Synod had obtained detailed reports on
the seminary question from diocesan bishops and seminary rectors, who catalogued the schools' various shortcomings in moral training, pedagogy,
administration, and finances.[128] The principal task of Dmitrii's committee
was to analyze these reports and then compile a draft proposal for reform.

Independent of the reports, however, Dmitrii's own vision of reform went
well beyond mere curriculum. In a special memorandum to the committee,[129] he argued that the chief problem was not curriculum, as the metropolitans believed, and not finances, as Urusov argued, but "inadequate moral
training suitable for clerical youth." In Dmitrii's view the schools were devot-
ing all their attention to scholastic success and ignoring the pupil's moral
development, not from lack of interest, but because most pupils lived with
townspeople, far from proper supervision. To provide such control, he
argued that it was vital for the Church to construct large dormitories, which
would enable school authorities to exercise supervision almost monastic in its
spirit and intensity.[130] At the same time, Dmitrii offered a scheme to deal
with the problem of surplus students and candidates for the clergy. Rather

[124]Urusov, a determined reformer, became a member of the main commission on clerical
reform in 1861 at the emperor's specific instruction (see below, pp. 243–44).

[125]Titlinov, *Dukhovnaia shkola*, 2: 233–34.

[126]OR GBL, f. 302, k. 5, d. 17, l. 2 (Urusov to Tolstoi, 22.1.1861).

[127]TsGIA SSSR, f. 796, op. 141, g. 1860, d. 367, ll. 2–3 (Synod resolution, 25.2.1860/
8.3.1860). Later the Synod invited Filaret to designate a representative, and he chose A. V.
Gorskii, rector at the Moscow Academy (ibid., f. 797, op. 30, otd. 1, st. 2, d. 213, ll. 8–9, 13–
13 ob.).

[128]Titlinov, *Dukhovnaia shkola*, 2: 232–33.

[129]OR GBL, f. 316, k. 66, d. 31 (zapiska, unidentified, but in substance identical to that
described in Gorskii, "Dnevnik," *Prib. TSO*, 52 [1885], kn. 1: 224–25).

[130]Catholic clergy also emphasized the value of separate dormitories for seminarians; see,
for example, a proposal of 1851 for *Knabenkonvikte* (in G. Merkel, "Studien zur Priesternachwuchs der Erzdiözese Freiburg 1870–1914," *FDA*, 94 [1974]: 123–26).

than reduce the number of pupils by excluding sacristans' sons or some such device, Dmitrii proposed to restructure the four-year elementary school and six-year seminary into an entirely new system. The lower part he expanded into an eight-year school, which would combine the general education of the gymnasium with the moral environment of the seminary. That system, he argued, would provide its graduates with learning suitable for lay careers, thus reducing the surfeit of candidates, and the spiritual qualities suitable for an advanced four-year seminary, which would provide the special education needed for priests.

Dmitrii's proposal was an ingenious amalgam of fashionable pedagogical ideas (specifically, N. I. Pirogov's conception of first general, then specialized education) *and* traditional episcopal concerns that the school provide proper spiritual development for future clergy. The scheme presumed massive new resources, however. It aspired to maintain present enrollments, even to prolong education for most pupils, who usually left after the four-year elementary school, and to raise standards through the construction of dormitories to house tens of thousands of pupils. To solve the financial conundrum, Dmitrii proposed to transfer the administration of candle revenues to the diocesan clergy: "Seeing that the means to educate their children depends upon their own zeal, the clergy will become more vigilant in supervising the accurate collection and transmission of income from candles." In essence, Dmitrii aimed to serve the interests of both the Church (in the seminary) and the clerical soslovie (through the eight-year elementary school), primarily by evoking initiative from below to obtain more efficient collection of existing revenues.

The committee commenced work in May 1860 but was soon at loggerheads over basic principles. As one committee member wrote, conflict became so acrimonious that "journals are not even being compiled" to summarize the results of committee deliberations.[131] The procurator's delegate, who had the unenviable duty of keeping these journals, complained to Tolstoi: "Decisions, which were evidently reached in a committee meeting with apparent firmness, are rethought after the meeting, and at the next session these decisions seem unsatisfactory and in need of change and amendment." Consequently, he explained, "not one of the journals that I compiled was signed by the committee's members."[132] The principal issue was Dmitrii's plan, especially questions about its economic feasibility. As one member protested, "His Grace Dmitrii plans reforms without considering the means to realize them, believing that dioceses will supply these resources to the bishops as soon as they act alone."[133] That financial scheme, claimed some, provoked opposition from lay bureaucrats, who "are perhaps frightened by suspicions

[131]Gorskii, "Dnevnik," *Prib. TSO*, 52 (1885), kn. 1: 209.
[132]TsGIA SSSR, f. 797, op. 30, otd. 1, st. 2, d. 213, ll. 29–29 ob.
[133]Gorskii, "Dnevnik," *Prib. TSO*, 52 (1885), kn. 1: 209.

that the goal is to exclude them from controlling the capital of the ecclesiastical domain."[134] Some committee members also feared making the exit to secular careers *too* easy: "If the pupils of Church schools are given equal rights with gymnasium students, will not all our pupils depart before they enter the seminary that provides specifically religious training, and thus will we not be laboring on behalf of others, not the Church?"[135] By the fall of 1860, however, the committee resolved its differences, began drafting reform proposals, and in early 1862 finally submitted these to the Synod for consideration.[136]

Those proposals essentially followed Dmitrii's original memorandum. Hence they attached highest priority to moral education, demanded the construction of dormitories, and restructured Church schools into an eight-year elementary school with general education and a four-year seminary with special theological training. The committee also stressed the need to break down soslovie barriers and proposed to give pupils "the freedom to choose a profession—so necessary for honest, zealous service in any sphere, but especially for the Church." By adopting an open social policy, it declared, "ecclesiastical schools—and the clerical estate more generally—will be free of people who enter it not through free choice but because they were forced to do so by the circumstances of life and hence do not sincerely devote themselves to their calling." The committee also modified the curriculum, eliminating Protasov's practical subjects and reorganizing subjects into a more logical system, with enhanced stress upon Holy Scriptures and patristics. Nevertheless, the committee retained the classical core, partly because of its importance to theological studies, but also because it "promotes a multifaceted development of intellectual abilities." The feasibility of the whole plan depended upon finances, but the committee calculated that diocesan control should increase revenues fivefold—more than enough to support the new system. The committee also emasculated the power of the central Bureau of Ecclesiastical Education (for example, in matters of faculty appointment) and, like the pending reforms in secular education, conferred substantial new power upon the faculty. In one major respect the final proposals went beyond Dmitrii's original plan. To deal with the problems of seminarians ordained prematurely into priesthood, the committee urged that they be required first to serve as sacristans. That duty, it argued, would elevate the lowly rank of sacristan, provide seminarians with a valuable apprenticeship under experienced priests, and supply parishes with inexpensive priests (recent graduates

[134]OR GBL, f. 316, k. 66, d. 22, l. 5 ob. (Gorskii to Filaret, 28.7.1860).

[135]Ibid., l. 2 ob. (Gorskii to Filaret, 21.7.1860).

[136]TsGIA SSSR, f. 797, op. 30, otd. 1, st. 2, d. 213, l. 32 ob. (Filippov to Tolstoi, November 1860); f. 796, op. 141, g. 1860, d. 367, ll. 13–58 (Dmitrii to Synod), 59–254 (Zhurnaly komiteta), 255–437 ("Proekt ustava dukhovnykh seminarii"). A brief summary of the reform is in "Kratkaia zapiska," OR GPB, f. 573, no. AI.82, ll. 319–33.

would not have large families and hence require only minimal support). Though the committee shrank back from mass expulsion of the current generation of ill-educated sacristans, it suggested that those willing to leave be given special privileges and inducements (such as exemption from the poll tax).

Thus the committee's plan was a compromise: it sought both to improve the schools *and* to preserve their special soslovie character, thereby answering the needs of both Church and clergy. Although the tension between such needs had long been evident, the committee's plan drew an explicit distinction between institutional and estate interests even while laboring to maintain a delicate balance between them. The plan also contained a curious mixture of liberal and conservative elements. Thus the stress on moral improvement and plans for monastic seclusion and inspection appeared traditional, whereas the vision of social policy was quite liberal. The plan reflected the new spirit of the sixties in other ways as well—for example, in its plans to augment the authority of faculty, to involve diocesan clergy in supporting the schools, and to give general education priority over professional training.

The committee's grand design never became law. Like many other reforms in the sixties, it foundered on opposition from below. The plan elicited initial criticism in St. Petersburg, especially from lay officials, and the Synod decided to transmit the proposals to diocesan bishops and rectors for review and comment.[137] It required almost two years before all the responses came back, and they proved almost uniformly hostile—liberals castigating the monastic spirit, conservatives the secular curriculum in elementary schools, and virtually all the untested financial scheme.[138] Although none drew the conclusion, it was clear that authorities must either abandon reform, obtain state aid, or—at long last—make the hard choice between institutional and estate interests.

Reform in the Western Provinces

Even as the Synod struggled with the issues of widowed priests and the seminary, it faced still more ominous rumbling on another front: the state's evident determination to erode the 1842 concessions to clergy in the western provinces. The Synod had procrastinated as long as possible, but once the excuses were exhausted and the provincial data were in, it had no choice but

---

[137]TsGIA SSSR, f. 796, op. 141, g. 1860, d. 367, ll. 590–93, 597, 604–11.

[138]The manuscript replies are in ibid., f. 797, op. 36, otd. 1, d. 395, ch. 3, ll. 1–714; they were printed for internal use in a volume entitled *Svod mnenii otnositel'no Ustava dukhovnykh seminarii, proektirovannogo Komitetom 1860–62 gg.* (St. Petersburg, 1866), one copy of which is in the Leningrad Public Library (GPB: 18.199.5.20).

to report that the special committee could now commence its work. The emperor, curiously, permitted the Synod to fix the committee's membership, which predictably was overwhelmingly clerical, with seven clergy (including the suffragan bishop of St. Petersburg, Agafangel, as chairman) and four lay officials (representing the chief procurator, minister of state domains, minister of interior, and minister of finance).[139] The committee held its first meeting in September 1859 and soon adopted its guiding principles, all highly favorable to the clergy: full compensation for the conversion of labor dues and no changes in the other obligations (in kind) of parishioners.[140] Ignoring provincial reports that advocated more radical revision of the statute (for example, conversion of all obligations and transfer of church land to the peasants for compensation), the committee agreed to convert only labor dues (to satisfy Alexander's explicit wish), but on terms highly advantageous to the clergy. The dominant spirit of the committee was evident in its model budget for priests, which set 650 rubles per annum as the norm—perhaps triple the income received by middling priests.[141] Its principles fixed, the committee worked out the details of conversion, using current market rates for labor (not the lower "official" norms) and stipulating that these be revised every five years to account for inflation.[142] Complaining that many parishioners failed to provide parsonages—by far the least observed article of the 1842 statute—the committee advanced a scheme for special state loans, amortized through annual tax levies, to finance their immediate construction.[143] In short, the clerical-dominated committee held reform to a minimum and even used the occasion to augment real aid given the clergy, blithely ignoring government complaints about the clergy's "low moral condition" and popular disgruntlement. By February 1860 the committee had concluded its work and began drafting final proposals for the Synod.[144]

At that point the committee's routine was suddenly shattered by an anonymous memorandum transmitted from the emperor for the committee's consideration.[145] Entitled "On the Moral and Material Improvement of Rural Clergy in the Western Provinces," the note remained secret and its author officially anonymous. Horrified by its contents, chairman Agafangel refused to permit his committee even to consider the document and returned it to Tolstoi: "Since this note speaks of many subjects which the Holy Synod did

---

[139]TsGIA SSSR, f. 797, op. 29, otd. 3, st. 1, d. 148, ch. 1, ll. 5–6 ob. Clerical domination increased further when the committee later added four more archpriests to represent other dioceses in the western region (ibid., ll. 33–35 [Synod resolution, 25.9.1858/30.9.1859]; f. 804, op. 1, r. 1, d. 1, l. 1 ob.).

[140]Ibid., f. 804, op. 1, r. 1, d. 1, ll. 1–1 ob., 3 ob. (zhurnal komiteta).

[141]Ibid., ll. 4–13 (zhurnaly: prilozheniia).

[142]Ibid., ll. 26–93 (zhurnaly, 3.10.1859–11.2.1860).

[143]Ibid., ll. 52–53 ob. (zhurnaly).

[144]Ibid., ll. 96–96 ob. (zhurnal, 13.2.1860).

[145]Ibid., f. 797, op. 29, otd. 3, st. 1, d. 148, ch. 1, l. 60 (note of 5.2.1860).

not have in mind when it fixed the committee's composition [that is, invited lay officials], I most humbly request that Your Excellency petition the Holy Synod for detailed instructions [to guide] the committee in its consideration of the note."[146] Agafangel's allusion to the committee's composition was provocative, implying that the note raised questions of canon law beyond the providence of mere laymen. When Agafangel reported his action to the committee, it did not question his peremptory decision but, in the words of the committee minutes, "received the chairman's words with the utmost respect."[147] Shortly afterwards, Agafangel submitted the committee's "final" report, declaring that "the committee has completed the task delegated to it."[148] No doubt to Agafangel's surprise, the Synod ruled otherwise. It "promoted" him to the post of bishop in Viatka, designated a new committee chairman (Dmitrii of Kherson), and returned the anonymous memorandum to the committee with the vague injunction to follow, "when necessary, the canon law of the Orthodox Church."[149]

The author of the note in fact was a member of the committee: Pompei Nikolaevich Batiushkov, representing the minister of interior.[150] Younger brother of a well-known poet, Batiushkov had specialized in the confessional problems of the western provinces and currently served as vice-director in the Department of Ecclesiastical Affairs of Foreign Confessions. There he showed himself a staunch defender of Orthodox interests, trumpeting the alarm against Catholic influence, urging strict controls on Catholic propaganda, and opposing government plans to open an additional Catholic diocese in central Russia.[151] But Batiushkov tempered religious fervor with bureaucratic caution, as was evident in the debate over policy toward Catholic landlords who failed to construct parish churches for their Orthodox peasants (thereby constraining them to attend Catholic churches). Some Petersburg zealots wanted to confiscate the estates of delinquent landlords, heedless of the turmoil sure to ensue. Batiushkov instead proposed a modest but workable scheme to construct churches with the aid of state loans, amortized by taxes on noble estates—a considerably less incendiary scheme.[152]

[146] Ibid., l. 62 ob. (Agafangel to Tolstoi, 9.2.1860).

[147] Ibid., f. 804, op. 1, r. 1, d. 1, ll. 94–95 (zhurnal komiteta, 13.2.1860).

[148] Ibid., f. 797, op. 29, otd. 3, st. 1, d. 148, ch. 1, ll. 64–64 ob. (Agafangel to Tolstoi, 6.3.1860).

[149] Ibid., ll. 70–75 (Synod resolution, 15.3.1860).

[150] Batiushkov's archives are in OR GPB, f. 52.

[151] OR GPB, f. 52, d. 29, ll. 1–17 ("[Zapiska] o latinskoi propagande na zapade Rossii"); d. 244, l. 278 (Filaret to Batiushkov).

[152] Ibid., d. 14, ll. 1–8 ("Dokladnaia zapiska po voprosu ustroistva pravoslavnykh tserkvei v pomeshch'ikh imeniiakh zapadnogo kraia"); other drafts of his proposal are in ibid., dd. 7, 13. Batiushkov later summarized his achievements in "Zapiska o rezul'tatakh deiatel'nosti po tserkovno-stroitel'nomu delu v zapadnom krae za 1858–61 gg." (ibid., d. 22). For official files, see TsGIA SSSR, f. 797, op. 28, otd. 3, st. 2, d. 28; f. 796, op. 138, g. 1857, d. 935.

Significantly, he also wanted to improve the Orthodox clergy, a better means than coercion to bolster Orthodoxy. Thus in 1858 he had already begun to examine Church files on the clerical question.[153] Hence he earned high praise from church conservatives, who often regarded state officials with apprehension, fearing new enroachments on Church privilege or compromises with confessional foes. In a letter to Filaret Drozdov, Tolstoi reflected this high regard of Batiushkov: "The director of [Batiushkov's] department is now Count [E. K.] Sievers, who, though himself Orthodox, is distinguished by his infinite tolerance toward Protestant countrymen from the Baltic; the entire ministry is extremely well-disposed toward Catholics. Thus Batiushkov is alone, and it is only with great difficulty that he combats tendencies hostile to our Holy Church."[154]

Batiushkov's note put an end to such encomia. Agafangel, who knew of the memorandum before the emperor sent it to his committee, found its contents outrageous and spurned all Batiushkov's attempts to iron away objections. In a letter of 20 February Batiushkov inquired whether Agafangel had really called the author of the note "an enemy of the Church" and asked the bishop to explain his adamant opposition.[155] Agafangel's curt reply stated that he had already expressed his views on the piece. He denied calling its author "an enemy of the Church" but declared that, because of his "health," he could not discuss the matter further.[156] Tolstoi drastically revised his earlier estimate of the vice-director: "This note, as far as it is possible to judge from private information reaching me, was unofficially submitted to the emperor through the efforts of someone known to Your Grace—Actual Counsellor of State, Batiushkov. He belongs to that number of those many active bureaucrats who are eager for improvements but who unfortunately lack a detailed study of the subject, become carried away by their own and others' ideas, and imagine that implementing them is necessary and simple—with [just] good will and a little 'energy' (this word is very fashionable now)."[157]

This uproar was hardly surprising, given the substance of Batiushkov's

---

[153]TsGIA SSSR, f. 797, op. 26, otd. 3, st. 1, d. 28, ll. 100–4 ob. (Batiushkov's correspondence with Tolstoi's chancellery). Significantly, Batiushkov's earlier memorandum on Catholic propaganda stressed the need for reform in Orthodoxy to combat Catholicism: "One should not limit oneself to one-sided measures to preserve things but must adopt measures that can place our faith on firm foundations, and that can be achieved in no other way than by placing our clergy—in education and material support—on a level with the Latin [Catholic] clergy" (OR GPB, f. 52, d. 29, l. 8 ob.).

[154]OR GBL, f. 316, k. 1. d. 24, l. 1 ob. (Tolstoi to Filaret, 10.6.1859).

[155]OR GPB, f. 52, op. 1, d. 97, ll. 1–3 (Batiushkov to Agafangel, 20.2.1860). In a later notation on the letter, Batiushkov wrote that "this concerns my memorandum, transmitted by the Tsar to Count A. P. Tolstoi and sent by him to the committee."

[156]Ibid., d. 119, l. 1 (Agafangel to Batiushkov, 21.2.1860).

[157]TsGIA SSSR, f. 832, op. 1, d. 85, ll. 128–29 ob. (Tolstoi to Filaret, 24.2.1860).

memorandum.[158] His note first postulated that the former Uniate clergy had
lost all moral influence over their parishioners, who not long ago revered
those same priests: "Not twenty years have passed since the unification of the
Uniates [with Orthodoxy], but these very same people have begun to think
of converting to Latinism [Roman Catholicism], which indeed would occur
on a massive scale were the government not obstructing the path of conversion." Most important, Batiushkov regarded the corvée obligation of 1842 as
only a secondary matter. The essential problem, in his view, was the very
structure of the Russian Orthodox clergy, especially its large ballast of deacons and sacristans, who form "an immense estate which the peasants have
to support and provide for together with the priests." The result, he wrote,
is that "the clergy have become impoverished, while discontent has sprung
up among the people," leading to the "conflicts between the pastor and his
flock that have brought disgrace upon the clergy." Thus the task, in Batiushkov's view, was not to increase support for the clergy but to dismantle its
"caste organization." That meant measures "to limit hereditary rights and
privileges (which are incompatible with the present times and the clergy's
special functions)," as well as steps to facilitate movement into and out of
the clergy. In addition, Batiushkov proposed to streamline clerical service by
eliminating deacons, substituting hired laymen for hereditary sacristans, and
authorizing the ordination of celibate priests. To reduce the economic costs
still further, Batiushkov proposed to reorganize parishes into much larger
units that could more easily support the clergy. With these changes in place,
he believed, the committee could simply abolish the obligations in kind: the
remaining clergy could live on current state salaries and the income from
parish lands leased to parishioners at reasonable rates. Given proper support,
the priest could henceforth devote more time to popular education and in
fact should bear primary responsibility in a new system of parish schools.

Despite the removal of Agafangel, this scheme—more radical than Belliustin's celebrated volume—faced certain opposition from the Church. That
fate became immediately apparent in the committee, which turned to a
favorite bureaucratic ruse—solicitation of opinions from lower authorities, in
this case, bishops in the western dioceses. Predictably, they were intensely

---

[158]Copies of the memorandum are in the following: OR GBL, f. 316, k. 65, d. 22; TsGIA
SSSR, f. 796, op. 205, d. 361, ll. 19–26 ob., 27–52. Batiushkov relied not only upon earlier state
papers (such as Vasil'chikov's complaints about the clergy's moral development) but also on
the advice of a Synodal legal expert, K. S. Serbinovich, who read and commented upon various
sections that eventually became part of the memorandum; see "Po predmetu obespecheniia
tserkovnykh prichtov v zapadnykh guberniiakh," with numerous emandations by Serbinovich,
in OR GPB, f. 52, d. 16, ll. 1–9. Batiushkov probably consulted as well some members of the
white clergy, perhaps those on the committee. After first reading the note, Metropolitan Grigorii even speculated that the author was "a priest from the western region" (TsGIA SSSR, f.
832, op. 1, d. 85, l. 128 ob.).

critical.[159] Metropolitan Iosif (Semashko) of Lithuania diocese, who had res-
olutely opposed any modification of the 1842 statute, subjected Batiushkov's
memorandum to scathing criticism. He argued that its economic estimates
(for example, on rents from parish land) were erroneous, that consolidation
of parishes only invited Catholic agitation, and that elimination of deacons
and sacristans violated both canon law and Church custom. Iosif was most
alarmed by the scheme to reorganize parishes and clerical service: "To close
suddenly several hundred parish churches [and] . . . to eliminate the status
and livelihood of the entire sacristan class—all this is to provoke sorrow and
tears among the Orthodox population in the western provinces [and] to compel the suffering to direct their gaze and aspirations toward the exuberant
non-Orthodox." The angry prelate even questioned the anonymous author's
religious integrity: "In general, judging from its content and expressions, the
note was written by someone unfamiliar with [conditions] in the western
provinces or by someone devoted to the convictions of Roman Catholics."
Comments from other prelates were no less vitriolic; all denied Batiushkov's
assertions of a "moral decline" in the clergy or a loss of popular veneration,
blamed Catholic landlords for most parish conflicts, and predicted that to
merge parishes, eliminate deacons, and replace sacristans with hired laymen
would gravely weaken the Church.[160] Significantly, Batiushkov's scheme to
rationalize clerical service derived its urgency from the special political and
confessional problems of the western provinces: yet, precisely on those
grounds, bishops resisted changes that would contract and, in their view,
weaken the Church's parish infrastructure.

The committee, armed with provincial opinions, thus had grounds to
ignore Batiuskhov's scheme and to reaffirm its original set of proposals, which
sought only a narrow, technical conversion of the 1842 statute.[161] Its final set

[159]Only the comment of a Lithuanian prelate, Iosif, is extant from 1859; others survive as
later memoranda, sent in 1863 to reaffirm earlier views. TsGIA SSSR, f. 804, op. 1, r. 1, d. 39,
ll. 84–89; d. 56, ll. 4–37 ob.; d. 53, ll. 110–38; d. 59, ll. 128–42; d. 83, ll. 33–65.

[160]Only the archbishop of Minsk admitted the possibility of eliminating deacons in rural
churches and transforming sacristans into state peasants (ibid., d. 83, ll. 59 ob.–60).

[161]The committee first delayed taking final action, claiming that its data were "inadequate
and unsatisfactory" (ibid., d. 1, ll. 124 ob.–25). It received permission to collect new data in
June 1860, but months passed with no visible progress toward reform. By early 1861, following
the emancipation of serfs and the consequent end to their labor dues, state officials found the
1842 statute absolutely incongruous with the new rural order. As the minister of interior complained, "continuation of the parishioners' obligation to cultivate [church] land will occasion
still more discontent and conflict between the peasants and clergy, and it can lead to a weakening of the parishioners' trust and respect toward the clergy, the preservation of which is
always necessary and especially so at the present time" (S. S. Lanskoi to Tolstoi, 16.4.1861, in
TsGIA SSSR, f. 797, op. 29, otd. 3, st. 1, d. 148, ch. 1. ll. 122–22 ob.). After Alexander gave
the committee until 1 June 1861 to complete its work, it tackled its task with great alacrity
and in June submitted its final proposals (ibid., f. 804, op. 1, r. 1, d. 1, ll. 158–299 ob.).

of draft proposals, submitted in June 1861, painfully reflect the great quandaries of reform in the clerical economy. On the one hand, the committee
reaffirmed the need to realize the promises of 1842 and improve the clergy's
material condition; on the other hand, it had to do this without conveying
"the idea that the state demands this sacrifice [from the parishioners] on the
clergy's behalf." Hence it rejected any direct tax as likely to arouse anticlerical sentiments and simply appealed to the state to assume these costs in the
name of "general state interests." Yet mere conversion, it conceded, would
not improve the clergy's material conditions; it would merely translate existing support into monetary form and yield only two to three hundred rubles
per priest is most areas.[162] As to how the clergy's status might be improved,
the committee had no proposals. It fantasized about an additional state subsidy (five hundred rubles annually for priests) but ruefully admitted that the
cost—nearly two million rubles per year—simply exceeded the government's present financial capabilities. Refusing to countenance more radical
schemes, such as those advocated by Batiushkov,[163] the committee turned
over its files to the Synod and disbanded—two years after beginning work
and with no solution to the "clerical question."

Press and Censorship

As various committees and the Synod labored over all the above reforms,
the Church was experiencing a virtual collapse of its system of censorship—
a far-reaching reform that took place through inaction and required no committees at all. Partly through the influx of underground literature, mainly
through the leniency of state censors, and even through the appearance of
strong reformist currents in ecclesiastical journals, the quality and scope of
comment on Church problems changed dramatically in the years after Belliustin's infamous volume of 1858. The very boldness of the press, as we shall
see, finally impelled the Synod in 1862 to contemplate formal revision of the
old Nikolaevan statute on censorship.

Something clearly had to be done, for the tenor of journalistic comment
had become ever more strident and radical. Predictably, the most candid
discussions appeared in materials published abroad, such as P. V. Dolgorukov's book, *The Truth about Russia*, which offered a compendium of radical
proposals and circulated widely in Russia. Like Belliustin, he accused bishops
of behaving like "omnipotent despots" toward parish clergy, who were mere
"silent slaves," and he urged that bishops be chosen from the white clergy,
not monks: "To appoint bishops from priests would not only correspond completely to religious demands and social propriety but would also provide the

---

[162]The range in (estimated) income after conversion was considerable: 193 to 284 rubles in
Kovno diocese, 253 to 337 in Vitebsk, and 251 to 331 in Kiev (ibid., l. 284 ob.).

[163]Ibid., ll. 154–57 (Batiushkov to Dmitrii, 27.5.1861).

best means for reducing the numbers of people in the monastic estate, an idle and debauched estate, which—next to state officials—is the most harmful social group in Russia." Dolgorukov also proposed to abolish all seminaries, so that future priests would receive their education in secular schools and thus be more likely to come from diverse social orders, not just the clerical soslovie. Interesting too was his support for conservative demands for conciliarism as protection against state interference; however, he expanded the idea to include not just bishops but also representatives of the white clergy.[164]

Secular periodicals inside Russia, though less acerbic, also commented with comparative freedom on the clerical question, becoming increasingly strident after 1860—a measure of the rising impatience with the apparent lack of progress in Church reform.[165] One influential journal, for example, published an overview of the clerical question in 1862 and complained that "while the rest of society has changed, the clergy has not moved forward in the least."[166] Probably the most sensational material appeared in the Slavophile organ *The Day*, which was politically conservative but committed to radical changes to revive the Church. Dismayed by the bishops' inability to achieve reform and anxious to create a more activistic priesthood, in early 1862 it published a controversial essay that, like Dolgorukov's book, challenged monastic domination in the hierarchy and denied any historical or canonical barriers to the consecration of white clergy as bishops.[167] As the surge of critiques made clear, the Church censors were unable to muzzle the secular press or exact vigilance from state censors.[168]

Indeed, even the more controlled ecclesiastical press showed surprisingly liberal, reformist tendencies. One of the most audacious organs was a diocesan serial in Khar'kov, *Clerical Messenger*, which openly advocated democratization of the Church through election of superintendents and judges by parish clergy and election of seminary rectors by faculty.[169] Even so stolid a

---

[164]P. Dolgorukov, *Pravda o Rossii* (Paris, 1861), pp. 188–203.

[165]On the inability of censorship to contain the discussion, see the official memorandum in TsGIA SSSR, f. 797, op. 87, d. 205, ll. 13–49.

[166]F. Ushanets, "O nekotorykh uluchsheniiakh v dukhovnom vedomstve," *Otechestvennye zapiski*, 143 (1862), no. 7: 255–75.

[167]"Byli li u nas v drevnei Rusi episkopy ne monakhi?" *Den'*, 1862, no. 30: 1–3. For other inflammatory pieces, see I. Beliaev, "Gde vziat' uchitelei dlia sel'skikh shkol?" ibid., 1861, no. 9: 4–6; idem, "Zamechanie," ibid., 1862, no. 22: 4–8.

[168]Yet church censors occasionally succeeded in interdicting hostile literature; see, for example, the case of an article entitled "Chto mozhno ozhidat' ot nashego dukhovenstva" (TsGIA SSSR, f. 796, op. 205, d. 645, ll. 1–12; f. 797, op. 31, otd. 1, st. 2, d. 110, ll. 3–4). Still, censors stopped relatively little, causing an exasperated Filaret to exclaim: "If one were to take all that is bad from lay journals and pile it all together, there would be such a stench that it would be difficult to find enough incense to suppress the odor" (Filaret, *Pis'ma Antoniiu*, 4: 322). For the Third Section's similar assessment of the press (on a more general level), see TsGAOR, f. 109, op. 223, d. 26, l. 63.

[169]"Letopisnyi listok," *Dukhovnyi vestnik* [hereafter *DV*], 2 (1862), no. 6: 267–70.

journal as *The Orthodox Review*, published by the Moscow Academy, spoke in favor of moderate reform to give clergy "the means and methods for exerting a beneficial influence upon the people."[170] Specifically, the journal published numerous articles on the need to transform ecclesiastical schools, to overcome the clergy's social isolation, to replace ill-educated sacristans with seminary graduates, and to provide clerical pensions in lieu of family claims.[171] It also lauded the metropolitan of Kiev for permitting local clergy to elect their superintendents, and thereafter it remained an advocate of democratization of Church administration.[172] Such tendencies eventually impelled Metropolitan Filaret, who had hitherto shielded the journal from conservative attack,[173] to warn the editors that "to subject authority to scorn is equivalent to acting on behalf of the destruction of good order."[174]

By 1862 the system of Church censorship had all but collapsed, impelling Church authorities—like their secular counterparts—to entertain censorship reform in the hope of reestablishing, not liberalizing, control over the press.[175] That motive was explicit in a memorandum submitted in May 1862 by a ranking Synod official, T. Filippov. Citing abundant evidence that repeated decrees demanding silence on Church questions "have been regularly violated and are currently being violated (not only by secular censors but also by ecclesiastical censors)," he argued that the Church must rebuild its system of censorship if it were to have any meaningful influence over the press.[176] At the procurator's request, Filippov prepared a more elaborate memorandum on the problem, this time identifying the specific weaknesses of the 1828 statute on censorship. Not only did the statute "leave much to

[170]N. A. Sergievskii, "Po prochtenii manifesta 19-go fevralia," *PO*, 1861, tom 4: 347–54.

[171]I. Beliaev, "Po voprosu o preobrazovanii dukhovnykh uchilishch," *PO*, 1861, tom 4: 193–236; A. Troitskii, "K voprosu ob uluchshenii byta dukhovenstva," *PO*, 1862, tom 1: 102–29; "Pensii zashtatnogo prikhodskogo dukhovenstva," *PO*, 1862, tom 1, zametki: 92–94. The journal also published an essay by the notorious Belliustin on the plight of female orphans in the clergy ("Polozhenie sirot-devits dukhovnogo zvaniia," *PO*, 1862, tom 2: 18–21); see the procurator's complaint about the publication of Belliustin's work in *PO* (L'vov, *Pis'ma*, pp. 583–84).

[172]"Predpolozhenie o naznachenii v dolzhnosti blagochinnykh po vyboru dukhovenstva," *PO*, 1862, tom 1, zametki: 48–49; I. Karelin, "Iz pis'ma v redaktsii: O naznachenii blagochinnykh po vyboru dukhovenstva," *PO*, 1862, tom 2: 42–46.

[173]At issue was the polemical debate between V. Askochenskii (editor of *Domashniaia beseda*) and *PO*, which had published and defended Archimandrite Fedor's "O pravoslavii v otnoshenii k sovremennosti." For a lively, if biased, account, see P. V. Znamenskii, "Bogoslovskaia polemika 1860-kh godov," *PS*, 1902, nos. 4–6, 9–11. For the archival file, see TsGIA SSSR, f. 797, op. 31, otd. 1, st. 2, d. 151.

[174]TsGIA SSSR, f. 797, op. 32, otd. 1, st. 2, d. 301, l. 3.

[175] For the similar motive in state censorship "reform," see Ruud, "Censorship Law," p. 241.

[176]TsGIA SSSR, f. 797, op. 87, d. 205, ll. 13–49 (T. Filippov, "O predelakh dukhovnoi tsenzury," May 1862).

arbitrariness" (the same manuscript could suffer different fates under different censors), it even required that censors enforce "good style"—a curious role, he wryly added, since "there are many passages in the statute itself where one has to guess at the meaning because of errors in grammatical construction." Noting that authorities had issued a mass of circulars since 1828, thereby reducing the whole system to unintelligible chaos, Filippov urged the Church to rebuild its censorship on entirely different principles.[177] When the Synod solicited the opinion of the ecclesiastical academies, which bore primary responsibility for censorship, they expressed unanimous support for such reform. Isidor, now metropolitan of St. Petersburg and presiding member of the Synod, also supported major changes, including some kind of punitive censorship and the elimination of prescriptive standards on style and "usefulness."[178]

These preliminary discussions ended without issue, however, and, in contrast to the state, the Church did nothing to repair its broken gates of censorship. As a result, for the next two decades the press enjoyed surprisingly uninhibited freedom in debating the clerical question. As the Third Section complained in 1863, the press had steadily broadened the scope of its discussion beyond the original problems of seminary education and clerical poverty and now demanded that "the clerical soslovie not be a caste but admit people from all estates who have a calling."[179] Church journalism, moreover, grew rapidly in the 1860s. In addition to central journals and newspapers, a whole new kind of periodical developed—the diocesan serials, which appeared weekly or bi-weekly, reprinted articles on reform from central publications, and offered original pieces of their own.[180] The sheer volume of material, the radical import of its content, and its dissemination among rank-and-file parish clergy—all promised to reshape fundamentally the consciousness of parish clergy, stirring old animosities and new aspirations.

Although Church authorities made some attempt to contain such publicistics, in fact they could do little more than interdict an occasional article.[181]

---

[177] Ibid., ll. 3–13 ob. (T. Filippov, "Zapiska," June 1862). A contemporary state commission on secular censorship transmitted its own journals to the Synod with the request to consider reform but without specific recommendations (ibid., f. 797, op. 32, otd. 1, d. 158, ll. 1–9 ob.).

[178] Ibid., f. 797, op. 32, otd. 1, d. 158, ll. 16–20 ob. (Isidor, note of 10.10.1862). A different, clearly unsympathetic assessment came from Metropolitan Arsenii of Kiev (ibid., ll. 11–12 ob.).

[179] TsGAOR, f. 109, op. 223, d. 30, ll. 56 ob.–57.

[180] For the proliferation of ecclesiastical periodicals, see Julia Oswalt, *Kirchliche Gemeinde und Bauernbefreiung* (Göttingen, 1975), chap. 2. On the optimism generated by diocesan serials, see "Novye dukhovnye periodicheskie izdaniia," *PO*, 1861, tom 4: 344–46.

[181] Among the handful of proscribed articles were essays on the clergy's economic plight, seminaries, and Old Believers; typical was the ban on one article that presented clergy in too negative a light (TsGIA SSSR, f. 807, op. 2, d. 1401, l. 72 ob.; see also ibid., d. 1403, l. 52; d. 1390, l. 47; d. 1398, ll. 188 ob.–89; d. 1401, ll. 22, 120, 127–28 ob.).

And some polemics even circulated with the connivance of state officials. D. I. Rostislavov's sensational volumes on ecclesiastical schools, a vitriolic attack on the schools and the monks who dominated them, originally appeared with government permission for unhindered circulation.[182] Faced with an open assault on hierarchial opinion, even of accepted canons,[183] Church authorities warned that this literature threatened to shatter clerical discipline entirely. To quote the chief procurator in 1863:

> Secular literature, in particular, is rebelling against diocesan authority. While the [parish] clergy are portrayed as oppressed, enslaved victims of episcopal authority, it is not difficult to show that such incitements not only obstruct the Christian spirit of submissiveness and obedience but also the thirty-ninth canon of the Holy Apostles. In addition, this constant assault on bishops, so grievous for pious people, provokes disorders among the superficial, disgruntled members of the [parish] clergy.[184]

Metropolitan Filaret expressed similar concerns, especially over the rising criticism of monasteries. "These articles," he wrote, "unjustly accuse monasteries of parasitic wealth, which provokes avarice in people, like that in those who plundered monasteries in Western states."[185]

A New Machinery for Reform

By the early 1860s Church hierarchs grew understandably anxious about the entire process of reform. In part, their anxiety derived from the general turbulence in contemporary society, especially the emergence of nihilist and atheistic attitudes among the educated youth. In late 1861 Metropolitan Isi-

[182]Of Rostislavov's book, the secular censors wrote: "[This book's] discussion of . . . Church schools is conducted with the utmost tranquillity, without exaggerations or excesses, with a substantive explanation of causes, and it offers evidence at every point" (ibid., f. 797, op. 32, otd. 1, st. 2, d. 326, ll. 1–2 [minister of education to chief procurator, 16.12.1862]). That judgment bore little resemblance to Filaret's view: "Virtually the sole substance of this book is ridicule—for learned monks, teachers, moral education, and administration in Church schools" (OR GBL, f. 316, k. 70, d. 38, l. 1). See also his suffragan's commentary (ibid., k. 77, d. 9) and the Synod's critical resolution (TsGIA SSSR, f. 797, op. 32, otd. 1, st. 2, d. 326, ll. 2a–2a ob.).

[183]See, especially, Urusov's outrage over the publication of an article proposing to permit the remarriage of parish clergy (TsGIA SSSR, f. 797, op. 33, otd. 1, d. 77, ll. 1–3 [Urusov, "Zapiska"]).

[184]Ibid., l. 5 ob.; f. 832, op. 1, d. 83, ll. 171–73 (Akhmatov to Valuev, 12.5.1863).

[185]Ibid., f. 797, op. 33, otd. 1, d. 77, ll. 13–18 (Filaret to Urusov, 13.18.1863).

dor declared that "the contemporary agitation of minds and unbounded striving for reform promises nothing good," and the next year Metropolitan Arsenii of Kiev warned that "we are living in a time of cruel persecution of the sacred faith and the Church."[186] When the Third Section accused Filaret of inserting a special prayer into the mass, pleading that God save Russia from calamity, the metropolitan testily denied the accusation but admitted distributing an unsigned circular to parish churches about "the need for repentance and earnest prayer." That action, he declared, hardly required justification, for "ideas and teachings antithetical to the Church and government have for some time been spreading with particular force in literature (censored and uncensored), in the younger generation, and [all this] is penetrating the lowest strata of society."[187] Worse still, the faithful heard terrifying rumors that "unidentified people are disseminating proclamations to the people 'about the elimination of bishops and priests [popy (a pejorative term)].'"[188] Even the sober-minded Filaret took such rumors seriously: "They are writing from Petersburg of fears that 'the first blow will fall on the higher clergy, monasticism, and the Church.' And this [information] is not written by some mere superficial gossip-monger."[189] Such rumors, incredible as they now seem, appeared quite differently to the senior prelates of the Church in the early 1860s, especially in view of the state's refusal to interdict antimonastic literature, its refusal to finance parish schools,[190] and its continuing attempts to gain control over the Church budget.[191] When state authorities

[186]OR GPB, f. 874 (S. N. Shubinskii), op. 2, d. 201, l. 8 (Isidor to I. M. Snegirev, 1.1.1861); "Pis'ma mitropolita kievskogo Arseniia," RA, 1892, no. 1: 209.

[187]TsGIA SSSR, f. 797, op. 31, otd. 1, st. 2, d. 158, ll. 1–3 (Dolgorukov to Tolstoi), 7–12 (Filaret to Moscow governor-general, 20.12.1861).

[188]Snegirev, "Dnevnik," RA, 1905, no. 1: 122 (entry of 1.10.1861).

[189]Filaret, Pis'ma Antoniiu, 4: 280–81.

[190]For a sound summary, see F. V. Blagovidov. Deiatel'nost' russkogo dukhovenstva v otnoshenii k narodnomu obrazovaniiu v tsarstvovanie imp. Aleksandra II (Kazan, 1891), pp. 8–23. When Alexander created a special committee to discuss the problem of popular education, the Synod's representative (Urusov) reported that, with the exception of Minister of Education Putiatin (an ultraconservative), "I encountered among the members of various ministries little readiness to accord 'main participation' [in popular education] to the clergy," and in fact they all "accuse the clergy of the same thing—'they don't do anything'" (OR GBL, f. 302, k. 5, d. 17, l. 45 ob. [Urusov to Tolstoi, 27.8.1861]). Although Tolstoi published data showing the large number of parish schools recently opened by clergy, it was to no avail: Alexander merely directed the Church and Ministry of Education to "cooperate"—with no provision for state funding of parish schools (IVO [1861], pp. 117–18, 120; "Reshenie voprosa," PO, 1862, no. 9: 37–40; Blagovidov, Deiatel'nost', pp. 27–53).

[191]See TsGIA SSSR, f. 797, op. 32, otd. 1, d. 54, ll. 20–25 (Filaret, "Zapiska," 7.3.1862). After much heated debate, Alexander ordered "further discussion of this matter in the State Council to cease." See the various memoranda and correspondence in OR GBL, f. 302, k. 2, d. 5, ll. 1–18; TsGIA SSSR, f. 797, op. 32, otd. 1, d. 54, l. 19; f. 832, op. 1, d. 27, ll. 20–20 ob.

complained of an essay critical of the state, Filaret defended the piece, adding that many facts "do not lead to the conclusion that service in the Church is encouraged and supported, but rather [cause] one to feel relatively humiliated and a subject of little concern on the part of [secular] authorities."[192]

While some grumbled or just fumed in silent anger, others took up the pen to prepare conservative projects demanding greater autonomy and authority for the Church. Most prolific was A. N. Murav'ev, who wrote several memoranda, including one that perceived a serious decline in the Church's stature *since* Nicholas's death. Once the furious critic of Protasov, Murav'ev now argued that, although Nicholas "worried more about imitation of Europe than preservation of Church canons and statutes," he nevertheless did much for the Church, such as the absorption of the Uniates in 1839, strict measures against Old Believers, and rigorous censorship in literature. Since 1855, however, authorities had violated these policies by bestowing rights on Old Believers, for example, and by permitting the press to "abuse the Church with impunity." Murav'ev appealed to Alexander to emulate his father's defense of the Church.[193] More explosive was a memorandum by Agafangel, the victim of Batiushkov's machinations in 1860. In a veritable manifesto on Church rights and privileges, Agafangel argued that the Church must reestablish the Synod's original authority and eliminate the power of the chief procurator, who "is of no use whatsoever and is a source of great harm." To revitalize the Church and enhance its role in society, Agafangel proposed to decentralize many administrative functions (to overcome sterile bureaucratization) and to admit some bishops to the State Council and Committee of Ministers, a change that would give the Church a direct voice in secular matters.[194]

[192] TsGIA SSSR, f. 797, op. 32, otd. 1, d. 199, l. 8 ob.

[193] OR GBL, f. 214, d. 30, ll. 66–72 ("Ob opasnostiakh, ugrozhaiushchikh pravoslavnoi tserkvi v Rossii" [draft]); f. 302, k. 2, d. 21 (final draft, prepared for Tolstoi and located in his personal archive). Murav'ev also prepared an earlier memorandum free from criticisms of the post-Nikolaevan regime and directed solely against the Protasov order (as in his memorandum of 1856–1857); this second note against Protasov is in ibid., f. 304, r. 2. d. 259, ll. 27–56. Another memorandum, unsigned but very similar to Murav'ev's earlier work, denounces the translation of bishops as contrary to canon law and to resolutions adopted at conferences of Eastern prelates in Constantinople in 1858 and 1860 ("O peremeshchenii episkopov," ibid., f. 214, d. 63, ll. 12–19).

[194] Ibid., f. 573, no. AI.60, ll. 17–38 ob. (the memorandum bore various titles: "Vysshaia administratsiia russkoi tserkvi" and "V chem dolzhno sostoiat' vysshee, vpolne kanonicheskoe upravlenie otechestvennoiu tserkov'iu"). Authorship here is ascribed by Metropolitan Isidor on the cover of his copy of the memorandum. It should be noted that, in contrast to a proposal by P. A. Valuev to include the Synod in the State Council (see below, pp. 241–43), Agafangel wanted only *some* members of the Synod present, presumably so that the Synod would not be wholly absorbed into the state apparatus.

For their part, high state officials were growing increasingly impatient with the Church and clergy. They were especially disappointed by the clergy's lackluster performance during the last, most volatile stages of emancipation. Despite specific measures to restrict the clergy's role, authorities found that most clergy failed to exercise a healthy influence on the peasants and that some even fomented disorders, if inadvertently.[195] As the minister of interior complained in May 1861, "disorders and disturbances occurred among peasants in some places solely because of an incorrect explanation of the [emancipation] manifesto by local priests."[196] Ecclesiastical schools were another source of mounting alarm. These schools now produced some of the most famous leaders among the radical "nihilists," and some schools even showed flashes of political and social radicalism. The most renowed incident occurred in Kazan, where students at the ecclesiastical academy joined peers from the local university in a mass requiem for peasants killed by troops in a local disturbance. At the close of the service, a professor from the academy, A. P. Shchapov, read a short eulogy for the fallen peasants, decried the failure of educated Russia to enlighten and lead them, and even mumbled something about a "constitution."[197] In Perm several seminarians were arrested for participating in revolutionary circles, and even students in the elite aca-

[195] In its annual report for 1861, the Third Section wrote that "after the publication of the statute on peasants, several priests and sacristans in various provinces inspired parishioners with perverse ideas about the law, thereby causing confusion and disorder among them." It reported that 25 priests, 2 deacons, and 10 sacristans had been arrested for such offenses. Though clergy were a small proportion of those detained for inciting revolt, such incidents nevertheless heightened the government's concern (TsGAOR, f. 109, op. 223, g. 1861, d. 26, ll. 107–7 ob.). Unfortunately, the Church's main file on clerical involvement in peasant disorders in 1861 ("Delo o besporiadkakh proiskhodiashchikhsia ot prevratnykh tolkovanii dukhovenstvom manifesta 19-go fevralia") is officially listed as "missing" from the archival inventory (TsGIA SSSR, f. 797, op. 31, g. 1861, otd. 1, st. 2, d. 150, which is registered as a relatively thick file of 206 sheets). For the government's attempt to preclude such clerical malfeasance, see the elaborate steps taken to define the clergy's role in the announcement of the emancipation manifesto: TsGIA SSSR, f. 797, op. 30, otd. 1, st. 2, d. 278 (main archival file); I. Gurskaia, "Tserkov' i reforma 1861 g.," KA, 52 (1935): 182–90; R. Stupperich, "Die russische Kirche bei der Verkündigung der Bauernbefreiung," JGO, 13 (1965): 321–30. For an amazingly confused account of the clergy during emancipation, with errors in the most elementary data, even the name of the procurator, see E. F. Grekulov, "Tserkov' i otmena krepostnogo prava," Voprosy istorii religii i ateizma, 10 (1962): 76–112.

[196] TsGIA SSSR, f. 797, op. 30, otd. 1, st. 2, d. 278, l. 93 (Valuev to Tolstoi, 2.5.1861). See the procurator's circular of 30.4.1861, declaring that "many places have sent complaints about clergy who gave an incorrect explanation of the manifesto, causing some disturbances among peasants" (ibid., l. 91).

[197] Ibid., f. 797, op. 31, otd. 1, st. 2, d. 149; f. 796, op. 142, g. 1861, d. 779, ll. 1–142; see also Daniel Field, Rebels in the Name of the Tsar (Boston, 1976), chap. 2, and the literature cited therein.

demies seemed receptive to radical currents.[198] The Third Section also began to take note of seminarians and former seminarians in the ranks of radicals, and in 1862 it specifically noted that, alongside the customary contingent of students from secular schools, seminarians too had joined the nihilist movement.[199] Finally, and most important, the committee on the western provinces demonstrated that reform could not be left in the hands of the Church. As the new minister of interior, P. A. Valuev, complained, the committee, "limiting itself to a simple conversion of parishioners' obligations in kind to a monetary payment, left unresolved the other questions in its sphere of competence."[200] Even its plan for conversion proved a fiasco, for the minister of finance categorically refused to provide the needed sums.[201] That failure, together with growing alarm about radical sentiments among the rank-and-file clergy, impelled Valuev to campaign for a new mechanism of reform, for a transfer of authority from the Synod to a special mixed commission dominated by state officials.

A career bureaucrat known for his inexhaustible supply of reform projects, Valuev had long nurtured an interest in the clerical question.[202] He had catapulted to prominence in 1855 with a famous memorandum on the deplorable condition of administration and society, and he sustained that momentum with a steady stream of special memoranda to the emperor.[203] He was an early and forthright proponent of religious toleration, strongly opposed to the use of police coercion to subdue the non-Orthodox.[204] Rather than rely

---

[198] On reports that academy students engaged in "nighttime orgies that were insulting to Orthodox religious beliefs in the highest degree," see Leontii, "Moi zametki i vospominaniia," BV, 1914, no. 1: 137–38. On the celebrated affair in Perm, see TsGAOR, f. 109, op. 223, d. 27, ll. 28 ob.-32; IVO (1861), p. 89; OR GPB, f. 573, no. AI.60, ll. 348–57 (report and tracts); OR GBL, f. 316, k. 67, d. 23 (correspondence between Tolstoi and Filaret). Young radicals clearly took an interest in seminarians; see Isidor's (unsigned) report of a revolutionary proclamation posted at the St. Petersburg Academy (TsGIA SSSR, f. 1574 [K. P. Pobedonostsev], op. 1, d. 5).

[199] TsGAOR, f. 109, op. 223, d. 27, ll. 33 ob.-34 (Third Section, report for 1862). In July 1862 the chief procurator sent Alexander a note on the problem of seminary radicalism: "One must, with regret, concede that for some time now former pupils of ecclesiastical schools are among those who, in print or in deed, show disrespect for the basic principles of law and order." Attributing radical tendencies to lax supervision in the seminary, he obtained Alexander's permission to circulate an order to seminary administrators to tighten discipline and control (TsGIA SSSR, f. 797, op. 32, otd. 1, d. 196, ll. 2–5 ob.).

[200] TsGIA SSSR, f. 1275 (Sovet ministrov), op. 93 (1), g. 1861, d. 22, l. 27 ob.

[201] Ibid., f. 804, op. 1, r. 1, d. 470, l. 89.

[202] On Valuev, see the sketch by P. A. Zaionchkovskii (introductory essay to P. A. Valuev, Dnevnik, 2 vols. [Moscow, 1961], 1: 17–44).

[203] Valuev, "Duma russkogo," RS, 70 (1891): 349–59.

[204] See also Valuev's memorandum urging tolerance toward Uniates (TsGIA SSSR, f. 908 [P. A. Valuev], op. 1, d. 112, ll. 1–4) and his proposal to the Council of Ministers, December 1861 (ibid., f. 1275, op. 93, g. 1861, d. 22, ll. 42–78).

upon repression, Valuev urged a rejuvenation of the Church and, especially, the parish clergy.[205] His important *mémoire* on serf emancipation in 1858 also raised questions about the clerical soslovie, urging "an honest and pains-taking examination of the internal structure of our Church."[206] When, shortly after his appointment as minister of interior in 1861, he was called upon to consider the problem of Church reform, he hastened to recast the goals and process of reform.

In August 1861 Valuev submitted a secret note to Alexander, presenting his own ambitious scheme. He attached reports from two provincial officials, one of whom argued that "it is necessary to make the same kind of radical reform in the structure of the Orthodox rural clergy as that now made, through the Sovereign's will, in the peasantry."[207] Noting Alexander's contin-uing interest in the clerical question, Valuev complained that the committee on western provinces offered no hope for either "rapid or significant success" and argued that "it is necessary to pose this question more broadly, to move it from the domain of one or two administrative bodies, and to make it a general problem concerning the whole empire." Although his argument was partly political (the phrase "domain of one or two administrative bodies" referred to the Synod's control of reform), Valuev plainly sympathized with more radical reform (hence his call to pose the question "more broadly"). Then, too, reform involved the very status of the clergy in contemporary society, making isolated reforms for one region impossible. "The Orthodox clergy and Church in the western area," he maintained, "will not assume the status appropriate to their rank so long as this same clergy at the very center of the state remains in their present condition and on their present level." Adding ominously that "conceptions and aspirations contradictory to the state order are beginning to spread through the ranks of the white clergy," the minister surely exaggerated the radical spirit among rank-and-file clergy, probably in a deliberate attempt to play upon the emperor's hypersensitivity to such ideas. Alexander agreed with the main substance of the memoran-dum, authorizing Valuev to prepare a formal report on the matter, but reaf-firmed that he was primarily interested in the western provinces: "Without fail take into account the necessity of providing for clergy in the western provinces before all other segments of the empire."[208] Here, as in other Great Reforms, the emperor would have to be pushed from below into pursuing

---

[205]"Dnevnik gr. P. A. Valueva," *RS*, 71 (1891): 271, 273.

[206]"Riad myslei po povodu krest'ianskogo voprosa," TsGIA SSSR, f. 908, op. 1, d. 102, l. 16.

[207]Ibid., d. 112, ll. 8–9 ob. ("Vsepoddanneishii doklad," 18.8.1861).

[208]Ibid. (Alexander's marginal notation). In his diary Valuev made the remarkable admis-sion that he had submitted "a memorandum on the question of the transformation (or 'improvement,' as it is [euphemistically] ordinarily called) of the clergy's structure"—a telling statement of his intentions (*Dnevnik*, 1: 107).

more radical reform, primarily on the grounds that moderate reform was unworkable and that political stability required drastic, immediate action.[209]

A month later, in late September 1861, Valuev submitted a lengthy report, "On the Present Condition of the Orthodox Church and Clergy."[210] It argued that the Church, despite its privileged position and the severe disabilities on other confessions, had failed to win converts or even to retain the loyalty of its own flock. Instead it "resorts to the display of force and relies primarily upon its ties with civil authorities" to combat other confessions. The paralysis of the Church, argued Valuev, was due to the clergy's low social status, its demoralization, and its "feeling of profound, bitter abasement." Valuev also warned of a major crisis building within clerical ranks "between its component parts—the so-called 'white' and 'black' clergy." That "open rupture" he blamed on the bishops and maladministration:

> Diocesan hierarchs for the most part pursue the life of involuntary recluses [otshel'niki], avoiding the secular world around them, neither understanding nor knowing its needs, not satisfying conditions for a useful interaction with [this world], and they are mainly preoccupied not with the flock entrusted to them, but with the lower clergy subordinated to them. Over the latter [i.e., the priests] they reign with the most cruel despotism, and that despotism is all the more oppressive because it is exerted mainly through the avarice of diocesan chancelleries and consistories.[211]

As a result of such despotism, Valuev claimed, "the white clergy hate the black [clergy], and with the assistance of this hatred, within [its ranks] there is beginning to spread not only democratic and even socialist aspirations but also some predisposition toward Protestantism." In addition to the bishops' failure, Valuev saw a major source of disorder in the clergy's organization as a hereditary soslovie:

> The white clergy is poor, helpless, lacking support for its own existence or the fate of its families. In general, it has a low level of education; it lives in a sphere where it soon loses even the traces of that inadequate education provided in ecclesiastical seminaries and academies. It forms not an organized soslovie in the state, but a caste of Levites, and sees before itself no hope for the betterment of its existence, because with all its great numbers, it cannot count upon significant generosity from the state.

---

[209]Cf. the similar patterns in police and judicial reform (Abbott, "Police Reform," p. 85; Wortman, Russian Legal Consciousness, p. 163).

[210]TsGIA SSSR, f. 1284, op. 241, d. 30, ll. 66–80 (full text of memorandum); an expurgated version, edited for the eyes of Church prelates, is in ibid., f. 908, op. 1, d. 112, ll. 40–47 ob.

[211]This section is in the full text only, not the expurgated version.

Compared with Catholic priests and Protestant pastors, he wrote, the Orthodox clergy were clearly inferior in status, education, economic condition, and
effectiveness.

Valuev's solution comprised two major reforms. The first consisted of measures to "break up the clerical soslovie, to draw it closer to the rest of the
population," and "to satisfy its material needs more generously." Specifically,
Valuev proposed to facilitate the exodus of clerical sons by granting them a
privileged legal status and by ceasing to register them at birth in the clerical
estate; that would encourage sons to leave and admit the possibility of entry
by outsiders. He also emphasized the need to raise the clergy's cultural level
through a "radical transformation of seminaries," but he offered no specific
details. To ameliorate the clergy's economic condition, Valuev proposed to
reduce the number of parishes and clergy, and he spoke vaguely of "expenditures (appropriate for the significance of the matter) by the government,
rural communities, and private landowners." Like Batiushkov, he sought as
well to reduce the number of clergy, primarily on the grounds that this
would significantly reduce the cost of reform. And, to enhance the clergy's
social significance, Valuev proposed to give them a major role in public education, a view not widespread among contemporary officialdom. Sparse on
details, Valuev's proposal followed Batiushkov's formula in its broad outlines—clerical reduction, abolition of the soslovie—but suggested the possibility of more munificent aid, if only in the form of land grants.

Valuev's second reform concerned the Church hierarchy, an issue that he
was the first to raise. Most familiar with the senior and more conservative
bishops, unaware of the more reform-minded attitudes of diocesan bishops,[212] Valuev regarded the prelates as hidebound recluses wholly ignorant
of contemporary needs and currents. That backwardness he would cure by
including Synod members in the State Council:

> This improvement [in the relations between priests and bishops] is hardly
> possible while our hierarchs remain alien to all daily relations, all the civil
> needs of their flock. It is desirable to draw them together, and, for this
> merger, it is quite necessary—at least in certain cases—to give them the
> opportunity of participating in the civic affairs of the country, to show
> them the path by which they can acquire the right to this participation.
> The summoning of several members of the Synod to the State Council,
> with the right to participate in discussions of all matters there, except
> criminal ones, would open up this possibility and show this path to the
> high-ranking members of our clergy.

To orchestrate this transformation of Church and clergy, Valuev proposed
to "establish a special chancellery, on principles similar to those determined

---

[212]See below, Chapter 6.

by Your Imperial Majesty for such a Committee on the Peasant Question."
Alexander approved this report in early October and subsequently autho-
rized Valuev to open discussions on the plan with leading figures in the
Church.[213]

Valuev held his first discussions—also the most difficult and decisive—in
Moscow on 12–13 November with Metropolitan Filaret.[214] Valuev frankly
preferred to give Filaret only an oral explanation of his plans, not a copy of
his candid memorandum to the emperor: "My original memorandum of 22
September, in general, could not be shown to [Filaret], in view of the
thoughts it expressed (with complete candor, for Your Majesty's [personal]
consideration) about the relations between black and white clergy and about
the activities of diocesan authorities." Though preferring an oral discussion,
Valuev nevertheless "prepared, in the event of necessity, the necessary
extracts from [the memorandum]." To his evident relief, "the explanations
took such a turn that there was no need to hand over this extract."[215] Most
important, Filaret approved the plan for broad reform in the parish clergy.
As Valuev reported to the emperor:

> I avoided using the expressions "closed estate" [zamknutoe soslovie] or "to
> break up the estate" [razomknut' soslovie]. Nevertheless, the metropolitan
> obviously grasped the main idea, for he first referred to opening this estate
> to people from other estates; he added that few such are presently admit-
> ted, because "they [the clergy] have difficulty finding places for their own
> people." Then the metropolitan deliberately used the word "caste" in the
> conversation; he opined that the clerical estate does not represent a caste
> and pointed to the fact that his suffragan bishop was by birth a nobleman
> and had been a guard's officer.

Filaret nonetheless raised some objections. He was not enthusiastic about the
possibility of supplementary land grants to the clergy ("the priest does not
have time to be occupied with agriculture") and insisted that seminary
reform remain a matter entirely within the purview of the Synod. His most
strenuous objections, significantly, concerned Valuev's plan to include Synod
members in the State Council. Filaret rejected the idea as "useless," contending that the Petrine solution—joint sessions of the Synod and state officials on extraordinary issues—sufficed. Although the metropolitan expressed
himself circumspectly, he voiced fears that the state would meddle in

---

[213] Valuev, Dnevnik, 1: 118, 126.

[214] TsGIA SSSR, f. 908, op. 1, d. 112, ll. 28–31 ob. (Valuev's note to Alexander, 16.11.1861).

[215] Valuev did have to express two points in writing, though "in extremely cautious phrases":
potential privileges to be given the clergy's children, and the potential reductions in parishes
(ibid.).

Church finances and that the State Council would treat the Synod members with condescension.[216] Filaret's response was characteristic for the period: he was intensely interested in reform for the parish clergy, intensely suspicious of state intentions toward the hierarchy.

Having evidently won the metropolitan's blessing, Valuev proceeded to discuss his plans with other figures in the Church establishment, including Metropolitan Isidor of St. Petersburg, archpriest V. B. Bazhanov, and Chief Procurator A. P. Tolstoi.[217] With Isidor and Bazhanov, the minister quickly reached agreement, but Tolstoi proved intractable.[218] The procurator wrote Filaret to solicit his support against Valuev and attached a note denouncing Valuev's proposal as "a powerful blow against the Church":

> Our bishops are not familar with matters discussed in the State Council and therefore their mute presence, without [real] participation, but with the obligation to sign the minutes, can only lower them in public estimation and in the present circumstances encourage blasphemy. Bishops will share responsibility for matters that will subject them to criticism, a responsibility from which they have hitherto been free.[219]

These conversations about the State Council provoked Filaret to file a lengthy critique of the whole idea. Ultimately, in the face of such determined opposition, Valuev reluctantly shelved that part of his scheme.[220]

He had nevertheless won appeal for his main objective: the formation of a reform commission on the clerical question. After hearing Valuev's report on his negotiations with Church leaders, Alexander formally agreed on 24 November to establish a joint reform commission, and shortly afterwards Valuev and a close aide prepared a draft manifesto.[221] This preliminary text packed the commission with reformers and designated the Grand Duke Konstantin Nikolaevich—the emperor's brother and a renowned reformer—as chairman.[222] Alexander approved this draft on 1 December but added one more member to the commission—Urusov, director of the Bureau of Eccle-

---

[216]Even prior to Valuev's meeting with Filaret, rumors circulated about the inclusion of Synod members in the State Council; see the acrimonious letter described in Gregory L. Freeze, "P. A. Valuyev and the Politics of Church Reform, 1861–62," SEER, 56 (1978): 77–78.

[217]Valuev, Dnevnik, 1: 127.

[218]Ibid., 1: 128.

[219]Filaret, SMO, 5: 173–74; see also Freeze, "Valuyev," pp. 78–79.

[220]For Filaret's determined opposition, see Filaret, SMO, 5: 174–81; Filaret, Pis'ma Antoniiu, 4: 332; Freeze, "Valuyev," pp. 79–80.

[221]Valuev, Dnevnik, 1: 128–29; TsGIA SSSR, f. 908, op. 1, d. 112, ll. 26–26 ob. (Valuev, "Vsepoddanneishii doklad," which summarizes a draft no longer extant).

[222]The commission was to include five lay officials and four clerics; all strongly favored reform, save the chief procurator and (possibly) the prelate to be designated by Filaret.

siastical Education and a known reformer.[223] For tactical reasons, Valuev
sought to publish an imperial manifesto announcing that the commission had
begun work: "The ostentatious publication proposed by me was in itself an
essential part of the whole plan. It was seen as a loud promise, but a promise
seen as a device to elicit the more zealous support of the rural clergy."[224]
That confession is revealing indeed of the minister's new kind of public politics. In contrast to the clandestine activities of Nikolaevan committees, Valuev sought to mobilize rank-and-file clergy and use them as a counterweight
to a conservative Church elite.

Stymied by committee opposition to his plans,[225] Valuev sent the emperor
a new report in January 1862 that reiterated the need for comprehensive
reform in the Church. He contrasted the Russian clergy to their European
counterparts, noting how the latter played an important role in moral
instruction and popular education. The essential problem, he argued, was the
clergy's social organization: "The clergy, concerned about the need for self-
preservation and providing for their own families, have become more and
more isolated from society and more tightly concentrated in themselves,
until in the end they have formed something like a caste." He appended a
new draft manifesto that clearly defined the broad charge of the proposed
commission on reform:

1. Expand the means of material support for the parish clergy.
2. Increase the personal rights and privileges of the ordained clergy.
3. Determine the means to enable the children of ordained clergy and
   sacristans to provide for their livelihood in all spheres of civic activities.
4. Find the means to strengthen and improve the methods of academic
   education for clerical youths.
5. Reorder the number and composition of parish staffs to satisfy the real
   needs of parishes.
6. Give the clergy the means for the maximum possible participation in
   parish and rural schools.
7. Determine the degree and means for parishioners' participation in the
   economic administration of parish-church affairs.

In its definition of competence and composition, this draft represented Valuev's optimal vision of reform. The decree added that the emperor was to
confirm personally all the resolutions of the special commission—an important symbolic gesture, but also a promise of direct action. This draft also

[223]TsGIA SSSR, f. 908, op. 1, d. 112, ll. 26–27 (Valuev's report).

[224]Ibid., ll. 59–60 ob. (Valuev, "Pamiatnaia zapiska").

[225]Even Grand Duke Konstantin Nikolaevich was unenthusiastic about these reform plans,
especially the publicity; see Valuev, Dnevnik, 1: 131–32.

contained a passage instructing the commission to observe canon law strictly, a caveat to reassure conservatives. To ensure state control of the commission, Valuev assigned its administrative work to D. N. Tolstoi and P. N. Batiushkov, both officials in the Ministry of Interior and known to favor fundamental Church reform.[226] Although Isidor was appointed chairman at the insistence of Konstantin Nikolaevich, the commission still had a preponderance of state officials and reform-minded clergy.[227]

Valuev's vision of comprehensive reform was narrowed considerably over the next few months, as strong Church opposition forced him to reduce the commission's authority and recast its membership.[228] The outcome was evident in a new version of the manifesto. Prepared before mid-June, it sharply reduced the commission's competence by eliminating its authority over parish finances and seminary reform, gave the Church a numerical majority by designating the entire Synod as members of the commission, and transferred the commission's chancellery from the jurisdiction of Valuev to that of the new procurator, A. P. Akhmatov.[229] Significantly, Valuev and his critics argued most vehemently over publicity, especially Valuev's call for a "loud public manifesto"; even a special session of the Council of Ministers in June, though approving the substance of the manifesto, failed to resolve the question of its publication.[230] But in this question Valuev's will ultimately prevailed. He won even the Synod's begrudging agreement to publicity *"if in the higher interests of state* it is deemed necessary to make the establishment of this commission generally known."[231] Valuev had thus obtained, if in more modest form, his new machinery for reform and—with the manifesto's publication—a new politics as well, involving far more than a select corps of high-ranking state officials and bishops. It was, in a sense, the end

---

[226] On D. N. Tolstoi's ambitious plans, see his "Iz zapisok gr. Dmitriia Nikolaevicha Tolstogo," *RA*, 1885, no. 2: 47.

[227] TsGIA SSSR, f. 908, op. 1, d. 112, ll. 32–38 ("Doklad po osobennoi kantseliarii MVD," January 1862), 56–57 ("Proekt vysochaishego poveleniia" [January 1862; for dating, see Freeze, "Valuyev," p. 83n.]).

[228] Valuev was also forced to defer action, largely because of the resignation of Tolstoi in December 1861 over Valuev's intrusion into his domain. Though the emperor soon chose a successor, A. P. Akhmatov, formal appointment had to wait until March because of difficulties in finding a suitable replacement for Akhmatov as governor of Khar'kov ("Iz dnevnykh zapisok V. A. Mukhanova," *RA*, 1897, no. 1: 55–56, 60; OR GPB, f. 874, op. 2, d. 201, l. 3 ob. [Isidor to Snegirev, 31.12.1861]).

[229] TsGIA SSSR, f. 908, op. 1, d. 112, ll. 52–53 ob. ("Proekt vysochaishego poveleniia," June 1862).

[230] Ibid., ll. 39–39 ob. ("Vsepoddanneishii doklad"); Valuev, *Dnevnik*, 1: 181. Although documentation is incomplete, the Council of Ministers evidently made one further emandation to the draft manifesto, deleting point 5 ("on reductions of parish clergy") from the commission's charge.

[231] Ibid., f. 1282, op. 2, d. 2017, ll. 4–4 ob.

of Nikolaevan politics and the onset of Great Reform politics in the Church, ultimately embracing not only educated society but rank-and-file clergy as well.

In retrospect, the emergence of the clerical question was a prolonged, difficult process. At the most obvious level, it entailed a steady broadening of definition. The original discussions about curricular reform in the seminary, amelioration of the plight of widowed priests, and modification of the 1842 statute for the western provinces gradually snowballed into a much larger conception of the clerical question—above all, the clergy's organization as a hereditary soslovie. As Church hierarchs failed to achieve reform and spurned more radical definitions of the clerical question, high state officials like Valuev resolved to shift reform from the Church to a new mechanism dominated by the state. That assumption of state leadership, accomplished under the emperor's personal aegis, carried the promise not only of forthright action but also of great risk if the enterprise should fail.

Although it would be foolish to imagine distinct "parties" in this unparliamentary order, it is possible to identify three distinct reform programs that, at least in some sense, represent latent interest groups. One was the episcopal party: though well-disposed to reorder the seminary and assist clergy, its primary goal was to reassert the autonomy of the Church, to defend episcopal power and Church privilege, and perhaps to augment the bishops' authority through regional councils (*pomestnye sobory*). A second party, far more cohesive and dynamic, was state officialdom: high-ranking bureaucrats, from Batiuskhov and Vasil'chikov to M. N. Murav'ev and Valuev, defined the clerical question in much more sweeping terms, aiming ("in a manner corresponding to state needs," to quote Valuev)[232] to transform the Church's fundamental social and institutional order—to rationalize the parish order, to abolish the clerical caste, to imbue even the bishops with a more modern spirit. A third party was the parish clergy, their voice still muted and indistinct, but increasingly aligned behind Belliustin's manifesto of 1858. Their aim, as we shall see, was primarily to improve their material condition and only secondarily to change their status within the Church. As Belliustin's *Description* implied and subsequent events would show, they took a view of soslovie reform altogether different from that emerging within the councils of state. Although parish clergy were as yet only tangentially involved in the reform process, Valuev's manifesto and the burgeoning discussions in the press served to draw them in. Embracing parish clergy as well as ranking bishops and bureaucrats, the politics of reform were now much more complex—triadic rather than diadic; empire-wide rather than confined to elites in the capital.

[232]Ibid., f. 908, op. 1, d. 112, ll. 8–9 ob.

Left out of account here are the common people, who thus far have figured only marginally in the reform process. Yet, in his murky formula of reform, Valuev spoke of aid not only from the state but also from "rural communities and private landowners." In the next few years, in fact, Valuev's commission would—of necessity—turn directly to society for assistance as it searched for the wherewithal to finance Church reform. The fate, and feasibility, of Valuev's original vision would depend upon its response.

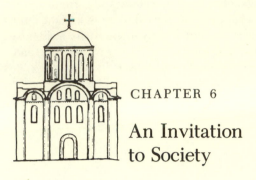

CHAPTER 6

An Invitation
to Society

I n late 1862 reform entered a new phase, moving from a small committee with small goals to a high commission seeking "an improvement in the material condition of parish clergy" throughout the empire. The Special Commission's charge was broad, if not comprehensive, and its composition—Synod members and chief ministers of the realm—implied the authority to take major decisions on behalf of both domains, the state and the Church. As expected, publication of Valuev's manifesto in December 1862 not only made the commission's existence public but also stirred hopes (or fears) of direct involvement by the state, precisely the kind of dynamic autocracy that Russian political culture prescribed and that Belliustin had urged in 1858.[1] Characteristic of the resulting euphoria was an article in an ecclesiastical journal, which reported—wrongly—that "initiative for this institution [the Special Commission] belongs personally to the Sovereign" and in gratitude exclaimed: "Praise be unto God! Praise be to the good Tsar!"[2] Just as foes of publicity had warned, expectations soared. Such hopes, carried aloft by dreams of state salaries and aid, bore little resemblance to the real plans taking shape in St. Petersburg.

---

[1] See, for example, F. Voronov, "Zametka po voprosu o dukhovenstve," *Den'*, 1862, no. 50: 6–7.
[2] N. Stas', "S Kavkaza," *PO*, 1863, no. 3, zametki: 128.

Valuev: A Strategy for Clerical Reform

Jubilant over the news of Valuev's manifesto, few contemporaries—least of all those outside high circles—realized the true limits already implicit in the Special Commission's work. Quite apart from omissions in competence (most conspicuously, reform of diocesan administration and seminaries), the manifesto remained silent on the means to be used in "improving the clergy's material condition." Few were privy to the well-guarded secrets of Batiush- kov's and Valuev's schemes, which sought not to hand over new riches for the clergy but primarily to restructure and streamline the clerical economy through abolition of the caste, elimination of the ballast of surplus sacristans and deacons, and reorganization of parishes. Valuev, it is true, hinted vaguely of some additional government aid in land, but neither the prelim- inary discussions nor the formal manifesto gave concrete aid or even com- mitments. Just how Valuev intended to improve the clergy's economic con- dition remained something of a mystery, even to leading prelates in the Synod. That ignorance and confusion, colored with pessimism, was evident in a letter from Metropolitan Arsenii of Kiev: "We were told beforehand that we should not expect a single kopeck from the Ministry of Finance. Conse- quently, we are obliged to invent the means for improving the clergy's mate- rial condition from our own belly, as the Greeks used to say. As you can see, this task is exceedingly difficult."[3]

The commission, its course as yet uncharted, held its first session in late January 1863, with Metropolitan Isidor of St. Petersburg presiding. Observ- ing that economic support for the clergy had changed "according to the time and development of our state system," Isidor pointed out that the clergy's status varied considerably in different parts of the empire, making reform all the more difficult. To assess properly the clergy's needs, he concluded, it was essential that the commission first assemble comprehensive data on con- ditions at the parish level—tacit recognition that, at least in this area, the Nikolaevan reforms had not amassed sufficient data to facilitate prompt res- olution of the clerical question.[4] More intriguing was the commission's deci- sion on the *kind* of data it would assemble: the clergy in each parish were to compile "opinions" (*mneniia*) on their needs, according to a standard form to be prepared by the commission's staff.[5] Although that decision in part was reasonable, given the diversity of conditions among parishes, it also repre-

[3]"Pis'ma mitropolita kievskogo Arseniia," *RA*, 1892, no. 1: 208.

[4]TsGIA SSSR, f. 804, op. 1, r. 3, d. 470, l. 4 (zhurnal no. 1).

[5]The commission deliberately selected staff with clerical origins. I. Tersinskii was appointed chief clerk because of his experience on the committee for the western provinces and because, "[as someone] coming from the clerical estate and having been educated in Church schools, he has a close familiarity with the means and needs of our clergy from his own experiences in life" (D. Domontovich to Akhmatov, 10.11.1862, ibid., f. 797, op. 33, otd. 1, d. 28, l. 3).

sented a relatively innocuous device for realizing Valuev's publicity and involvement by parish clergy—without, however, running the risks of clerical deputies, a device which had caused such trouble during emancipation among the nobility. Commission members concurred that the clergy should play a major role in parish schools, not only to promote the cause of popular education, but also—if funding proved available—to improve the clergy's well-being. Alexander II approved the commission's first journal but set dates for the submission of the clergy's opinions: "Throughout I have set due dates, so that the matter really moves forward and does not drag on, as so often happens with us, as mere scribbling."[6] The first session pleased Valuev, who jotted in his diary that "nothing was spoiled at the first step—and that's saying a lot."[7] Even so, Valuev sensed the difficulty of Church reform, and he pondered how to publish an announcement of the commission's first resolutions in a way that would neither upset the bishops nor provoke exaggerated hopes among the parish clergy.[8]

The politics of interaction with parish clergy, in fact, proved a major cause of conflict in the commission as it drafted its questionnaire for the clergy's opinions. The original version summoned the clergy to address a broad range of issues and even suggested ideas for their consideration, such as expulsion of sacristans, salaries, and democratization of Church administration.[9] That formula, as Valuev realized, was less a questionnaire than a proclamation. Though a champion of publicity, Valuev was adamant that the commission carefully limit the scope of the questionnaire and avoid stirring unrealizable aspirations among the white clergy. Even a modified redaction of the questionnaire,[10] which struck thirteen of the original fifty-six articles, did not satisfy him. He specifically objected to queries about salaries ("because it would arouse unrealizable hopes," given the condition of state finances), about tax privileges ("this is not the sort of question where the parish clergy can be regarded as competent" to judge), and about civil privileges ("it is inconvenient to raise this question").[11] Valuev's opinion prevailed among the commission, which formally ruled that "matters affecting the expansion of personal rights and privileges in the clerical estate depend exclusively upon state authority and by their very nature can hardly be given over to discussion by private persons (and, especially, the parish clergy, whose very condition

---

[6] Ibid., f. 804, op. 1, r. 3, d. 470, l. 1 (Alexander's marginal notation on the commission's journal, no. 1).

[7] Valuev, *Dnevnik*, 1: 203.

[8] OR GPB, f. 833 (V. A. Tsee), d. 385, l. 203 (Valuev to Tsee, 20.1.1863).

[9] TsGIA SSSR, f. 796, op. 205, d. 361, ll. 2–10 (Voprosy ob obespechenii byta prikhodskogo dukhovenstva s uvelicheniem grazhdanskikh ego prav"). This draft, dated 13.12.1862, bore marginal comments by Metropolitan Arsenii of Kiev, who seemed favorably inclined toward far-reaching reform.

[10] Ibid., ll. 10 ob.–13; f. 804, op. 1, r. 1, d. 9, ll. 17–24 (second draft).

[11] Ibid., f. 804, op. 1, r. 1, d. 9, ll. 17–24 ob. (Valuev's marginalia).

would make it difficult to answer such questions).”[12] That decision had some grounding in sheer practicality. How could rural priests comment on law codes not at their disposal? How could the Commission process prolix replies from thirty-thousand parishes? The elimination of all questions of a controversial variety resulted in an extremely short form that required only partial involvement by parish clergy. Each parish staff was to complete answers to two sections—one on their material condition, the other on parish schools—while each bishop (or his aides) was to comment on the clergy's legal status and the problem of surplus clerical youths.[13]

While waiting for the parish clergy and bishops to submit replies, the commission adumbrated its guiding principles of reform. Here, at last, Valuev unveiled his strategy. Its basic principle was that society, not the state, must assume primary responsibility for improving the clergy's material condition. That proposition was of course central to the Great Reforms. Admitting that autocracy could not bear responsibility for all the manifold needs of modern society, reformist bureaucrats hoped to stir initiative in society and awaken its "vital forces," primarily by devolving responsibilities and authority directly onto society. That idea, most dramatically embodied in the zemstvo reform of 1864, which created new organs of local self-government, also shaped Valuev's strategy for Church reform: unable to tap the treasury for an easy solution, Valuev looked to initiative from below.

These ideas were most fully developed in a commission report of March 1863, representing primarily the work of Valuev. It noted that in the past authorities had focused solely upon needs while disregarding "the resources available for satisfying those needs" and that they had sought instantaneous solutions "everywhere and at once" rather than "gradually and in stages." But the main problem, argued Valuev, was the presumption that responsibility rested primarily with the state rather than the community:

> In searching for means to improve the clergy's condition, attention has been directed almost exclusively toward state resources. However, in view of the aid already provided by the government (and others to be indicated below), the support of clerical staffs and the maintenance of parish churches are primarily the responsibility of parishioners themselves. Further state aid, in general, should have an auxiliary function and be applied to those places where parish means are insufficient and, especially, where the lack of local means is greatest.

Although in certain cases special aid might be provided by the state (as grants from the properties of the State Domain) and the Church (from the capital endowment of seminaries), the primary responsibility rested with the parish. In short, society—not Petersburg—must solve the clerical question. To help

---

[12] Ibid., r. 3, d. 470, l. 12 ob. (zhurnal, no. 3).
[13] Ibid., ll. 12–16.

stimulate the community and ferret out local resources, Valuev proposed to form provincial versions of the Special Commission—provincial commissions (*gubernskie prisutstviia*) composed of the bishop and local state officials, who were to seek local resources, consider the use of state properties (when appropriate and available), and aim toward a "gradual" improvement in the clergy's economic condition.[14] The Special Commission endorsed most of these suggestions in late March and directed diocesan authorities to convoke provincial commissions along the lines described in Valuev's memorandum.[15]

Besides forming provincial commissions to oversee local reform, the Special Commission embraced a still more original device to mobilize Orthodox communities: the parish council (*prikhodskoi sovet*). In one of its first journals the commission noted that such councils had played an important role in the Church and argued that, if revived, they could provide a suitable means to solicit parish support for the clergy. Hence it resolved to give responsibility over "local needs" to parish councils composed of the ordained clergy, lay church elder, and "honored people" chosen by the parish and distinguished by their piety and religious zeal. The commission's interest rested upon a host of interlocking notions—that such councils had historical legitimacy; that lay society would willingly respond to appeals for aid; and that contemporary Russia, so institutionally underdeveloped, required some formal organ to awaken and direct these untapped social forces. Such hopes, moreover, were buoyed by recent experiments in eastern Siberia and some western dioceses, all suggesting that parish councils were at once feasible and popular.[16] Even so, the commission realistically conceded the need for some kind of worldly incentives: "The establishment of obligations alone [to assist the clergy], without any indication of advantages, could hardly evoke public sympathy" for the new councils.[17] But, if properly designed, such councils seemed capable of "arousing and stimulating the independence and autonomous activity of parish communities."[18]

---

[14] Ibid., r. 1, d. 17, ll. 4–15; f. 908, op. 1, d. 112, ll. 67–76.

[15] Ibid., f. 804, op. 1, r. 3, d. 470, ll. 27–53.

[16] First in eastern Siberia (in 1859), then in selected other areas (most notably, Kherson and Kiev dioceses), state and Church authorities established parish councils (*prikhodskie sovety* or *bratstva*) to handle some community functions (charity, schools, and the like) and to aid the clergy. Though initially very favorable to the new organs, the Synod grew somewhat more critical, partly because of adamant opposition from Filaret, but mainly because state officials used the device to encroach on Church prerogatives. Still, by 1862 the councils existed in several dioceses and had attracted much favorable publicity. For pertinent materials, see the commission's archives (TsGIA SSR, f. 804, op. 1, r. 1, d. 11) and Filaret's files (ibid., f. 832, op. 1, d. 88, ll. 1–6). For the background on parish councils, see I. Flerov, *O pravoslavnykh bratstvakh* (St. Petersburg, 1857), and M. Koialevich, *Chteniia o tserkovnykh zapadno-russkikh bratsvakh* (Moscow, 1862).

[17] TsGIA SSSR, f. 804, op. 1, r. 3, d. 470, ll. 9–10 ob. (zhurnal, no. 2).

[18] Ibid., ll. 86–86 ob. (Valuev, "Zapiska ot 10-ogo marta 1863 g.").

When the commission ordered its staff to prepare draft legislation on the councils, it found that it was one thing to posit principles, quite another to translate them into a workable statute. One issue that emerged early in the deliberations was the threat of popular reaction from below. The dark masses, contended some, would reject the new councils as a Western imitation, a deviation from Orthodox traditions and canons. In this respect ecclesiastical reform differed sharply from reform in parallel secular institutions: whereas judicial and educational reform, for example, drew openly upon Western models, the Church felt constrained to disregard Western experience and institutions.[19] In the present case, archconservative bishops like Platon of Kostroma assailed the councils for seeking to "introduce Protestant principles into the structure of the Orthodox Church, [substituting] rule by laymen for that of clergy, to whom the Church was entrusted."[20] Significantly, however, most prelates evinced concern primarily about popular response, not deviation from tradition or canons. They were intensely apprehensive of the peasants' legendary volatility and unpredictability, especially toward changes that directly affected them, as this one did. Such concerns gave Metropolitan Arsenii of Kiev grounds to demand that the commission rename its council, replacing the original term *sovet* (council) with one less likely to suggest foreign imitation, *popechitel'stvo* (council of trustees, or guardians). As Arsenii explained to the other members of the commission:

What is most dangerous here is that some unofficial interpreter, for his own secret purposes, will whisper to the people that this institution and its name are borrowed from churches of another confession. If that happens, no explanations or arguments will have any effect upon the people, who, fearful of becoming contaminated by foreign confessions, will look upon these institutions with a foreign name either indifferently or coldly, or even with hostility.[21]

In Arsenii's view, the term *popechitel'stvo* (long current in Russian law and administration) connoted only trusteeship and tempered the apparent novelty of the reform.[22] The commission approved Arsenii's proposal, thereafter

---

[19]The sole exception was seminary reform, where authorities made a feeble effort to study Catholic seminaries (see above, pp. 199–200).

[20]TsGIA SSSR, f. 804, op. 1, r. 1, d. 54, ll. 2 ob.–3 (1863 report).

[21]Ibid., r. 3, d. 470, ll. 85–85 ob. (Arsenii, "Mnenie").

[22]Privately, Arsenii revealed that he raised this issue rather disingenuously, his real aim being not to change phraseology but to reshape the substance of reform: "In my opinion, confraternities where the priest is chairman are superior to a German Lutheran council *(sovet)*, where the priest has only a consultative vote and everything depends upon the elections and caprice of the [secular] communities" ("Pis'ma mitropolita kievskogo Arseniia," *RA*, 1892, tom 1: 211 [letter of 30.2.1863]).

using the new term in all formal documentation.[23] Still, it was an ill omen if the mere name of the council could cause doubt and unease among commission members.

More animated conflict emerged as soon as the commission addressed the substance of the reform, including the council's authority, its composition, and its relationship to superior Church and state bodies. At bottom the debate sprang from an enervating contradiction in Great Reform politics: the desire to stimulate autonomous social development versus the fear that this initiative might go too far or swerve in an unanticipated, undesirable direction. Despite the desire to awaken "productive initiative" from below, Valuev and his fellow reformers were unwilling to give society their implicit trust. Though willing to let the reins fall slack, they refused to cast them down completely for fear that the troika would bolt off, wildly out of control.[24] Just how taut the reins should be, and who should hold them, provoked sharp debate within the commission, as the bishops and bureaucrats defended the right of their respective institutions to control the new councils.[25]

By late April 1863, the commission had resolved these questions in plenary sessions, and early the next month it formally approved a draft statute and general statement on its proposals.[26] Perhaps most striking in the statement is the leitmotif of uncertainty, the authorities' lack of confidence in either themselves or society, especially the great dark mass of peasantry. On the one hand, the commission's report is imbued with an antibureaucratic ethos, not only decrying the atrophy of the parish in modern times but pointing to excessive bureaucratic control as the very cause of "the parishioners' indif-

---

[23]Significantly, Filaret objected (in vain) to this change, arguing that the term *popechitel'-stvo* connoted peasant trusteeship over the clergy, a notion incongruous with the clergy's status and dignity (TsGIA SSSR, f. 832, op. 1, d. 77, ll. 53–53 ob. ["Nekotorye soobrazheniia o prikhodskikh sovetakh ili popechitel'stvakh"]).

[24]Characteristically, in 1864 Valuev expressed concern about the indefinite status of confraternities, evidently fearful that they lacked proper limits and control from above (ibid., f. 804, op. 1, r. 1, d. 73, ll. 27–29).

[25]The first draft of a statute for the councils, penned by a Synodal employee, gave the councils substantial powers, including taxation, but left them under clear Church control, with the priest as ex officio chairman and with the bishop as primary overseer. That proposal elicited a trenchant critique from Valuev, who strongly opposed clerical hegemony and control. At one level, Valuev was skeptical that parishioners would welcome a summons to aid clergy, especially if forewarned of possible taxes: "People sometimes give willingly, but they do not like it when they are told beforehand that someone will ask money from them." Valuev not only opposed the priest's chairmanship, warning that it would be exceedingly awkward for the priest to lobby for his own benefit, but also saw no reason to give bishops sole jurisdiction, asserting that "the Church has no power over secular affairs" and hence over a parish organization. For the pertinent documentation (the preliminary staff report, draft statute, and Valuev's objections), see ibid., d. 11, ll. 27–36, 141–46, 151–52.

[26]For delays apparently due to disagreements (causing the commission's journals to be redated), see ibid., ll. 129–40 ("Proekt zhurnala").

ference [toward the church]."[27] On the other hand, the commission had little faith in spontaneous reform from below, conceding that the first order of business was to make parishioners sensitive to the "needs of the church and clergy so that they will want to satisfy these [needs] with a sense of moral obligation." Given the social and economic backwardness of the countryside and towns and the exceedingly low level of literacy, the commission saw no alternative but to rely upon a small core of zealous, honorable parishioners, "the best people in the parish." Skeptical of popular willingness to assist, cognizant of the parish's disorganized state, and trusting more in wordly incentive, the commission hoped to enlist the aid of more respectable laymen and to arouse their zeal through various "civil privileges."

In the same spirit the commission drafted only general guidelines for the councils, not the detailed kind of regulations customarily found in prereform legislation. Mindful that initiative from below could not be dictated from above, the commission noted than in earlier times the state had often created social institutions that existed in name only. It therefore admonished diocesan authorities to seek a "gradual, not simultaneous" establishment of councils: "The mere formal establishment of councils, without attracting vital foundations to them, can turn these into a form lacking in content and make them into sterile institutions (like those devised in earlier times)." As a result, the commission left unclear just how and where the councils were to come into existence. Similar motives impelled the commission to allow the parish to determine the council's composition and procedures:

> While upholding the main principles in the draft rules for parish councils, one should not insist upon absolute homogeneity for these institutions but rather should let experience work out those forms which prove useful in real life, depending upon the morality and other circumstances prevailing in a community. One must not lose sight of the fact that what is conveneint in some places often presents difficulties in others.[28]

In that spirit the commission even pronounced its plan an experiment: it proposed to promulgate the statute as a "temporary law," effective only for three years, at the conclusion of which the commission would revise the law in the light of practical experience and needs.

Composed of twelve brief articles, the commission's draft provided nothing more than a general framework for the councils.[29] As in past experiments, the councils were given responsibility for aiding the clergy and for supporting the local church, parish schools, and charity. Although the parish was to

[27] Ibid., r. 3, d. 470, ll. 41–62.

[28] Ibid., ll. 53–53 ob.

[29] "Proekt pravil dlia prikhodskikh popechitel'stv pri pravoslavnykh tserkvakh" (ibid., ll. 63–71).

determine the number of council members, the commission stipulated that they must include the priest, church elder, and "esteemed parishioners" chosen at a general assembly of householders. Hoping to tap the munificence of wealthy parishioners, particularly landed aristocrats and merchants, the commission also provided for an alternative system of a single "honored trustee" (*pochetnyi popechitel'*) who in effect would altogether replace the council. An earlier draft baldly defined the trustee as someone who makes "an annual contribution [in an amount fixed] by the parish council,"[30] but the commission ultimately expunged this passage at the insistence of Valuev, who complained that "it is unseemly to create something akin to the purchase of the rank of trustee." Though the language changed, the purpose remained.[31] On the question of chairmanship, which earlier had provoked sharp disagreement within the commission, a compromise was struck: the draft designated the priest as chairman ex officio (as the bishops had demanded) but stipulated that a layman would preside when the council discussed questions of clerical support (as Valuev demanded). The draft also gave the bishop primary jurisdiction over the councils—another concession to the Church—but carefully circumscribed his authority, leaving much to the discretion of the local council (for example, the council's composition). As for fiscal authority, the council was expected to rely initially upon existing resources from collection urns and the like, but it could levy obligatory assessments if two-thirds of all householders agreed. Finally, to enlist the enthusiastic participation of the "very best parishioners," the draft prescribed various honorific privileges for councilmen, such as special church services and an honorary medal given at the discretion of the local bishop.

In accordance with new procedures adopted in 1862, the commission's draft first had to be reviewed by the emperor's Second Section, and here the proposal received a devastating critique from the section's head, M. A. Korf.[32] In a lengthy memorandum Korf found the commission's plan unsatisfactory, not because it went too far, but because it failed to go far enough. Essentially, Korf rejected the very conception of an elite council composed of "the very best people" and instead urged the government to resuscitate the whole parish by relying upon a broad parish assembly, not a tiny directorate. His explicit aim was to form a new kind of all-class local government.

---

[30]"Nachertanie pravil" (ibid., r. 1, d. 11, l. 141 ob.).

[31]Ibid., l. 151 (Valuev, "Zamechaniia").

[32]For the new role of the Second Section, which, according to an imperial order of 11.5.1862, was to review all legislation prior to submission to the State Council—ostensibly, to assure more overall coherence in the reform process—see P. M. Maikov, *Vtoroe otdelenie Sobstvennogo Ego Imperatorskogo Velichestva Kantseliarii, 1826–1882* (St. Petersburg, 1906), pp. 419–25. For Korf's general perspective and repeated conflict with Valuev over reforms in police, city government, and the zemstvo, see Hutton, "Reform of City Government," pp. 20–21; Abbot, "Police Reform," p. 141; V. V. Garmiza, *Podgotovka zemskoi reformy 1864 goda* (Moscow, 1957), pp. 206–24; Starr, *Decentralization*, pp. 280–86.

In effect, Korf sought to revise the statute on serf emancipation, which excluded nobles from peasant affairs, devised a special township (*volost'*) administration for peasants alone, and thereby left local government divided along estate lines. Korf proposed to reunite social estates in the parish, and he emphasized the need for special measures to entice participation by the nobility, who alone, he believed, could provide the initiative, wherewithal, and leadership to make the new organ function. The commission's project he complained, virtually precluded such participation by nobles, especially by its decision to make the priest council chairman: "At least until such time as differences in estate (soslovie) relations have abated, it is difficult to think that [the landowners] will be interested in a position that obliges them to deal with matters that are mostly petty and insignificant—alongside their former serfs, and under the chairmanship, leadership, and virtual control of the parish priest."[33] Korf also wanted to give the parish greater power, especially in the matter of taxation, urging that a simple majority (not two-thirds, as the commission planned) suffice to levy a mandatory tax on all parishioners. Korf also made two suggestions sure to raise the hackles of Russian prelates: that the council be given the power to arbitrate conflicts between priests and parishioners, not just among parishioners, and that the parish regain the right to select clergy. To leave ample room for spontaneous development, Korf also demanded strict limits on the bishop's supervisory powers.

Korf's memorandum—a manifesto for lay authority in the church and noble dominance in local affairs—provoked scathing criticism from Metropolitan Filaret of Moscow. Though far from ecstatic about the commission's proposal,[34] Filaret found the Korf memorandum highly offensive, even dangerous.[35] Typical were the prelate's comments on the issue of chairmanship: Filaret categorically rejected the selection of laymen as chairmen, even if temporarily (as in the commission scheme), but especially on a permanent basis (as in Korf's proposal). Filaret's comment deserves full quotation, for it vividly expresses a fundamental quandary of reform in the Russian parish:

> Will a peasant chairman place a modest limit to his high position? Here one is concerned not merely about external respect for the priest but also about the correct relations between a pastor and his flock. If the moral and

---

[33] TsGIA SSSR, f. 804, op. 1, r. 3, d. 470, ll. 182–86 ob. (Korf, "Mnenie").

[34] Filaret objected to the commission's excessive enamorment with the confraternities in southwest Russia, arguing that these tended to arrogate power properly belonging to the clergy and in any case provided no model for the rest of the empire. He also opposed the commission's plan to permit a lifetime honorary trustee, warning that such functionaries would become tyrants in the parish and undermine the emperor's desire to grant "freedom to the clergy" ("Nekotorye soobrazheniia o prikhodskikh sovetakh ili popechitel'stvakh," in ibid., f. 832, op. 1, d. 77, ll. 49–66).

[35] Ibid., ll. 49–66 ("Nekotorye soobrazheniia"), 70–73 ob. ("Zamechaniia na predpolozheniia Korfa").

spiritual influence of the priest sometimes now encounters coldness, inattention, disrespect—will there not be a new incentive for such an attitude when the peasant parishioners see someone from their own midst legally placed as the superior to priests in assemblies on church affairs?

Such concerns also inspired Filaret's opposition to the Korf proposal to revive the custom of parish selection of clergy. That scheme, he warned, would wreak havoc on the clergy, undermining efforts begun under Peter the Great to raise the clergy's service and educational standards. Experience had shown, wrote Filaret, that parishioners tended to choose sacristans with strong voices, even though these were invariably ill-qualified and ill-educated; if parish wishes were heeded, the bishop could no longer appoint the most qualified candidates and reward the best seminarians with choice positions. Even as things now stood, emancipation had tended to generate new assertiveness among parishioners, and Korf's scheme could only serve to trigger more "illegal" demands by obdurate parishioners. The vexed metropolitan ended his note with a pointed warning that "the commission was created to improve the clergy's material condition, not to compose new laws or canons on the hierarchy."[36]

Spurning most of Korf's comments, the commission largely reaffirmed its original proposal and in early 1864 transmitted the draft legislation for final review by the State Council.[37] Here the commission—not unlike the Synod in 1829—suffered major revisions in its proposal, primarily along the lines adumbrated by Korf. Thus the State Council, like Korf, wanted to link the parish more firmly to local township (*volost'*) administration and therefore designated officials of the township administration (the *volostnoi starshina* and *volostnoi golova*) ex officio members of the parish council. And like Korf, the State Council doubted that many landlords would agree to serve as ordinary trustees "equal to their former serfs and under the chairmanship of parish priests, who—in education and social status in the parish—generally rank much lower than the landowners." The State Council therefore deleted the requirement that the priest must be chairman and left the question entirely to the descretion of the parish, implicitly assuming that communities would choose their local notables as chairmen. Unlike both Korf and the commission, however, the State Council—composed of superannuated

[36] Reference here is to the commission's charter, which, in an effort to allay popular and perhaps episcopal fears, admonished the commission not to deviate from canon law (*PSZ* [2], 37: 38414).

[37] The commission incorporated Korf's suggestion that the parish assume more responsibility for charity, that it fix its own rules and agenda, and that the statute itself be promulgated as a permanent decree, not something "temporary" and unlikely to win confidence. It vetoed his other suggestions—that the council have a lay chairman, that large parish assemblies be preferred to small councils, and that the parish reassert its traditional right to nominate clerics (TsGIA SSSR, f. 804, op. 1, r. 3, d. 470, ll. 138–52 [zhurnal, no. 11]).

bureaucrats, unmoved by the new Great Reform spirit—severely restricted the council's power of taxation: "Collections for the church may only have the form of voluntary donations. To establish through parish councils new obligatory levies (as obligations and assessments for secular needs) would appear to be unseemly and to be at variance with the prevailing ideas regarding donations to the church, and from the very beginning would induce parishioners to oppose the new institution." The State Council there fore significantly weakened the priest's role and the council's authority even as it left intact the scope of responsibilities, presumably hoping that popular piety or noble initiative would breathe life into the institution. Alexander II accepted the State Council's version without comment and signed it into law on 2 August 1864.[38]

This legislative process lasted some eighteen months and stirred considerable debate between leading clergy and state officials. Although bureaucrats like Valuev provided the main initiative, they generally acquiesced to the clergy's demands, especially in matters of ecclesiastical jurisdiction. It was a significant index of the bishops' residual authority and the difficulty of undermining the status quo with "experts" from the outside. More important, however, the principal issue throughout was less Church-state relations than the conundrum of grass-roots reform: how to design councils so as to inspire community initiative, yet avoid irresponsible behavior by the empire s inexperienced, unlettered peasant masses. The commission's solution was to give the council considerable power but to check abuses through the priest's chairmanship and close supervision by the bishop. For conservative prelates like Filaret, the compromise sacrificed too much Church authority and, perhaps worse still, rested upon unduly optimistic assumptions about popular willingness to aid the clergy. For a noble like Korf, the proposal failed to go far enough: he wanted parish reform to be a capstone to emancipation, reviving the old parish community and reaffirming the natural leadership of the nobility. In the end the State Council short-circuited the whole debate. It drastically revised the commission's proposal, primarily by reducing the clergy's influence and withdrawing the council's power of taxation.[39]

The commission expected to rely primarily upon provincial commissions and parish councils to improve the clergy's lot. But, hoping to exploit the emperor's evident interest in the western provinces, the commission applied

[38]"Vypiski iz mneniia Gosudarstvennogo soveta" (ibid., r. 1, d. 11, ll. 344–46); *PSZ (2)*, 39: 41174.

[39]For the State Council's analogous role in 1861, when it sought to rewrite the terms of emancipation largely to satisfy the nobility's interests, see Field, *End of Serfdom*, pp. 350–54. Curiously, in 1861–1862 Filaret adamantly opposed Valuev's proposal to include Synod members in the State Council, where they might have influenced the outcome of this and other issues (see above, Chapter 5).

to the treasury for special funds to aid clergy in the western dioceses—1.5 million rubles to pay for conversion and 3.6 million to construct parsonages. V. Dolgorukov, a commission member and head of the Third Section, accurately predicted that "satisfaction of this need at the present time will almost certainly meet with difficulties, given the well-known problems of the state treasury."[40] In response to the commission's request, the minister of finance agreed to provide just 200,000 rubles (4 percent of the sums requested) to satisfy the most compelling needs.[41] The Polish Rebellion of 1863, however, provided new urgency to reform. After first installing "collection plates in churches throughout the empire to aid Orthodox churches in the western region," the commission eventually won the emperor's approval to levy assessments on the estates of rebellious Polish nobles. Yielding some 400,000 rubles, the levy enabled the commission to begin conversion of the parish obligations in kind, though at rates far lower than originally envisioned.[42]

The plan for parish councils and provincial commissions, the request for clerical "opinions," the paltry sums allocated for the western provinces—all these efforts did little to resolve the bishops' pessimism about the prospects for effective reform. Metropolitan Filaret wrote the chief procurator in May 1863 that, although "concern for the improvement of the clergy's material condition is entrusted [to us], where are the means?" He observed that to gather the clerical opinions and seek local aid was a slow, complex task and would most likely bring aid to only a few. That prospect "and the other means indicated promise a lot of work and few results." Metropolitan Arsenii of Kiev, though generally sympathetic to broad reform, held similar views: "The proposal for an improvement in the clergy's material condition has given us [bishops] a great task, and, given our utter lack of means, this will rest with all its weight upon the shoulders of the bishops alone."[43] Such pessimism had good cause: Valuev's strategy presumed social initiative from below, but the bishops' long experience in parish affairs gave them little hope for such aid, whatever councils or commissions might be summoned into existence.

Aspirations of Reform: Priests, Bishops, Publicists

In March 1863 the Special Commission disseminated its order for parish clergy to file "opinions" and for diocesan authorities to compose more elab-

[40]TsGIA SSSR, f. 804, op. 1, r. 3, d. 470, l. 21 ob. (zhurnal, no. 4).

[41]Ibid., ll. 89–90 ob. (zhurnal, no. 8).

[42]Ibid., ll. 290–94 ob. (zhurnal, no. 25).

[43]"Pis'ma mitropolita moskovskogo Filareta k Akhmatovu," *RA*, 1890, no. 11: 357; "Pis'ma mitropolita kievskogo Arseniia," *RA*, 1892, tom 1: 214.

orate "considerations," thereby engaging both high and low clergy in the reform process. Although the commission, mainly at Valuev's behest, carefully limited the scope of the questionnaire, the invitation to comment had an electrifying effect, directly touching clergy all across the empire. The parish in most dioceses completed their task in April and May 1863; diocesan authorities took much longer to draft their more comprehensive statements. In late 1863 these documents began pouring into Petersburg and by the following summer comprised some seventy-thousand sheets of "opinions."[44] Some local authorities permitted the opinions or summations of them to be published in diocesan serials, providing a wealth of detailed data to guide public opinion on the reform.[45] The contemporary press, virtually uninhibited by censorship and encouraged by rumors and the commission's public announcements, published voluminous amounts on the clerical question. Nikolaevan secrecy was gone; reform had escaped from the Petersburg chancelleries; and discussions erupted all across the empire as priests made haste to articulate their visions of reform in secular papers, church journals, and diocesan serials. Less public were the views of bishops, who compiled detailed considerations that gave Petersburg its first systematic statement of episcopal opinion. How did these aspirations of priests and bishops mesh with the commission's own conception of reform from below?

Parish Clergy: The Opinions

The opinions provide a graphic portrait of the clergy's condition and their expectations—the only time in imperial Russia when parish clergy all across the empire were summoned to speak to their problems and needs. Their replies ordinarily filled both sides of two sheets of paper and contain a wealth of data about their income, landholding, needs, relations with parishioners, and even the condition of parishioners themselves. In most cases the priest penned the response, which the rest of his staff then signed and which the superintendent subsequently countersigned as confirmation of its veracity. Reflecting the low political and social consciousness of most clergy, the replies usually supplied the data specifically requested but rarely volunteered comments on how to solve the clerical question. Quite apart from the relia-

[44]That vast quantity, in fact, represented only three-quarters of the dioceses hitherto reporting (TsGIA SSSR, f. 804, op. 1, r. 1, d. 33, ll. 72–77 ob.).

[45]For published summaries, see "Koe-chto k slovu o material'nom byte dukhovenstva Poltavskoi eparkhii," *Poltavskie eparkhial'nye vedomosti* [hereafter *Poltavskie EV*], 1864, no. 16: 128–47; the reports in *Iaroslavskie eparkhial'nye vedomosti* [hereafter *Iaroslavskie EV*], 1863, nos. 41–45; "Svedeniia po delam uluchsheniia byta dukhovenstva," *Sovremennyi listok* [hereafter *SL*], 1864, no. 11: 4–6.

bility of the statistical data, especially on income from emoluments,[46] the main deficiency of the opinions is the narrow scope of the questionnaire, which was deliberately framed to preclude the expression of broader aspirations. There is also substantial evidence that diocesan authorities impeded a free expression of ideas. As one priest wrote, "none of the priests in our district expressed their desires frankly and especially on proposals for improving the clergy's material condition, probably fearing that they would be held accountable for such candor."[47] Nonetheless, the replies are richly informative, not only about the clergy's economic condition but also about their fears and hopes for reform.

The statistical data, for all their shortcomings, confirmed what none could doubt—the mind-boggling diversity in parishes, the intense particularism that produced such uneven distributions of wealth, population, and social composition among parishes. The reports show, moreover, that the clergy still depended almost wholly upon emoluments and agriculture, confirming that past reforms had achieved little. Typical are the data on parsonages: despite the 1829 statute, which "encouraged" parishioners to construct parsonages, very few clergy enjoyed free housing.[48] Somewhat fewer than half the parishes in the empire received state subsidies, and everywhere they were still dependent upon the traditional emoluments. Nor had authorities succeeded in improving or expanding the clergy's land allotment; although most parishes provided the minimal amount, some areas reported remarkably high

---

[46] In part, the questionnaire was ambiguous, failing to specify whether the clergy should report only emoluments or include the value of their collections on holiday processions. More important, the whole process invited deliberate falsification of the most unpredictable variety: some clerics might underestimate income, thereby demonstrating need and increasing their chances of aid; others might inflate actual income if they anticipated plans to convert emoluments to a salary. Such uncertainties left the clergy in a quandary. As one memoirist wrote, his local superintendent called the local clergy together to "consider how best to write the income statement—for more or for less" (M. E. Lavrov, *Avtobiografiia sel'skogo sviashchennika* [Vladimir, 1900], p. 47).

[47] P. Rozhdestvenskii, "Po povodu uluchsheniia v byte dukhovenstva," *SL*, 1864, no. 24: 1–3. For other reports, see "S vostochnoi granitsy zavolzhskikh stepei," *Den'*, 1864, no. 17; "Zametka o svobode mnenii v dukhovnom soslovii," ibid., 1864, no. 7 (and the official inquiry about this essay in TsGIA SSSR, f. 796, op. 205, d. 547). For bishops' admissions that they had "corrected" opinions or forced clergy to rewrite them, see the materials on Vologda and Olonets dioceses (TsGIA SSSR, f. 804, op. 1, r. 1, d. 9, ll. 61–62 ob. [Vologda report], 65–66 [Olonets report]; OR GPB, f. 573, op. 1, k. 48, d. 638, ll. 46–47 [Olonets bishop to superintendents]). For press reports of this kind of interference, see "Obozrenie obsuzhdenii voprosa ob uluchshenii byta dukhovenstva, zaiavlennykh v Kh-oi eparkhii," *Rukovodstvo dlia sel'skikh pastyrei* [hereafter *RSP*], 1865, no. 42: 213.

[48] Typical was the situation in Novgorod, where just 34 of the 629 parishes (5 percent) had parsonages, and even then only for part of the three-man parish staffs (TsGIA SSSR, f. 804, op. 1, r. 1, d. 42, ll. 121–238 [my calculation]).

proportions with deficient allotments.[49] More important, even where the clergy did possess the required acreage, they often found the land too poor in quality or inconvenient in location to afford practical use.

As one might expect, the parish clergy were virtually unanimous in judging their income grievously inadequate. Specifically asked to state whether their income was "satisfactory," only a minuscule number found that to be the case—just 2.1 percent of the staffs in Vladimir diocese, 1.6 percent in Saratov, and 0.9 percent in Kursk.[50] To the litany that "our support is unsatisfactory" some clerics volunteered prolix descriptions of their want. A priest in Sudogda uezd (Vladimir), for example, wrote that "even with the most stringent economies, we are barely able to make ends meet," a credible enough statement, considering that his annual income (fifty rubles) was less than that of the lowliest clerk, less than the cost of supporting a single son at the seminary.[51] A priest serving in the Ukraine peered out of his hut and boldly concluded that "no one in the whole world suffers—in absolutely all respects—more than [we] clergy in the village of Kulikovka."[52] Some priests drew particular attention to the plight of the lower-ranking members of their staffs: "Sacristans—in dress, footwear, home furnishings—do not in the least differ from peasants, and some in fact are even worse off."[53] Existing support, wrote clergy from all parts of the empire, was simply insufficient to provide adequately for their families, especially sons requiring education and daughters needing dowries. To quote one priest: "The clergy's sons, because of their parents' poverty, fail to attain their goal and, without completing the seminary, fall into a lamentable condition; because of their parents' poverty, daughters marry mostly into the impoverished classes, while many—for that very same reason—are doomed to become old maids."[54] Little wonder, observed a colleague, that "almost no one from other social estates seeks to become worthy of entering the clerical soslovie or seeks a place in it or . . . that many—one could say the best and most talented—seminarians either

[49]Thus, whereas only 8 percent of the parishes in Saratov lacked legal allotments, far higher proportions appeared in Astrakhan (31 percent), Petersburg (37 percent), and Poltava (62 percent). Ibid., d. 49, l. 276 ob.; d. 35, ll. 3–8; d. 51, ll. 15–20; d. 66, ll. 6 ob.–7.

[50]Ibid., r. 3, dd. 10–22; r. 1, d. 34, ll. 59–64 ob.; d. 51, ll. 6–25. Given the massive volume of these files, I have analyzed only those from selected dioceses: Vladimir (r. 3, dd. 10–22), Kiev (dd. 138–61), Kursk (dd. 181–92), Penza (dd. 266–77), Riazan (dd. 326–37), Riga (dd. 317–25), Saratov (dd. 351–58, 362–66), and Tver (dd. 398–410). For the other dioceses I have relied upon the statistical summaries prepared by diocesan authorities in their "soobrazheniia" (located in ibid., f. 804, op. 1, r. 1).

[51]Ibid., r. 3, d. 22, l. 24 ob. (Vladimir diocese).

[52]Ibid., d. 155, l. 166 ob. (Kiev diocese).

[53]Ibid., d. 327, l. 215 ob. (Riazan diocese).

[54]Ibid., d. 34, l. 83 (Kursk diocese); see also similar statements from clergy in Penza (d. 272, l. 6) and Vladimir (d. 13, l. 147).

enter state service . . . or take monastic vows in hope of attaining a position in the hierarchy."[55]

This discontent, of surprising intensity, is highly suggestive of the clergy's mentality at the outset of the Church reforms. Perhaps most striking is the profound sense of deprivation, an attitude articulated but rarely in the past. Even in the clergy's service reports for 1860, where most regarded their income as mediocre or typical, only a few went so far as to complain that their income was "paltry" (*skudnoe*) or "inadequate" (*nedostatochnoe*).[56] That almost *all* made such claims in 1863 was partly due to the impact of the contemporary press, which had become steadily more vociferous since 1860 and no doubt helped to stir hopes for radical change in the hearts of many clergy.[57] Important too was the vitality of the traditional political culture, with its myth of a just and well-meaning tsar; Alexander's manifesto and personal signature on the commission's journals no doubt helped to fuel expectations.[58] Then, too, the imperial summons to express grievances helped to legitimize such demands, enabling clergy to transcend the ideological barrier—the Church's teachings about otherworldliness and humility—that tended to inhibit Christian clergy in pursuing their economic interests.[59]

More important than complaints about inadequate income was the clergy's argument that the traditional economy directly undermined their spiritual mission. Although such statements served as well to deflect charges of avarice, they suggest the clergy's heightened consciousness of their pastoral role—the fruit of the prereform seminary and contemporary press. The argument that the existing clerical economy was incompatible with true pastorship drew mainly upon practical considerations and paid scant attention to the canons, Scripture, and custom, especially when the latter seemed at variance with practical exigency. This argument appeared in up to half the replies from any given area as part of the attack on the main forms of support—agriculture, emoluments, and holiday collections.

Clerical agriculture, in many replies, loomed as a major barrier to more

[55] Ibid., d. 325, l. 119 ob. (Riga).

[56] Service reports for 1860, for example, show claims of "unsatisfactory" income in only 3 of the 67 parishes in Kaliazin district of Tver diocese (GA Kalininskoi obl., f. 160, op. 1, d. 16298, ll. 319, 478, 531). By contrast, *all* the reports of 1863 pronounced their support unsatisfactory (TsGIA SSSR, f. 804, op. 1, r. 3, d. 402).

[57] For a summary account of the contemporary press, see below, pp. 281–86; for greater detail, see Aleksandr Malakh, "Tserkovnaia reforma v povremennoi pechati tsarstvovaniia Aleksandra II" (partial manuscript, preserved in the archive of St. Petersburg Ecclesiastical Academy in OR GPB, f. 573, k. 33, d. 442, ll. 1–59), and Papkov, *Tserkovno-obshchestvennye voprosy.*

[58] As an "imperially established" body, the Special Commission submitted its journals to the emperor for his personal review and confirmation; the resolutions of the journals were then published under the emperor's signature in the press.

[59] Cf. Bonifield, "Economics of the Ministry," p. 9.

effective service. Although, doubtlessly, a simple wish to be free of exhausting menial toil played a part, the priests criticized clerical agriculture mainly on the grounds that it was incompatible with their primary functions, even the exercise of traditional liturgical roles. As a practical matter, too, the prolonged formal education required for modern priesthood, involving a dozen years study at ecclesiastical boarding schools, left young priests virtually ignorant of practical agriculture and physically unaccustomed from youth to [such hard toil]." The new ordinand was thus more capable of evoking mirth among local peasants than providing food for his family's table.[60] More important, wrote some clergy, agriculture diminished the clergy's spiritual effectiveness. Apart from the undeniable fact that field toil "lowers [the priest's] dignity in the people's estimation," it also "takes up a great deal of valuable time," distracting the priest from preaching, catechizing, or exhorting the people to practice their faith.[61] Agriculture, wrote a priest in Tver diocese, not only denied one the time but even the capacity to be a zealous pastor: "Preoccupied with agriculture by necessity, we (especially priests) not only do not acquire new knowledge, . . . not only do not reinforce and develop our abilities, . . . but virtually forget what we had learned earlier and grow dull in the capacity to think for ourselves."[62]

Nor was there a satisfactory alternative. Hired labor was prohibitively expensive, respondents concurred, and traditional *pomoch'* (voluntary parish aid) directly undermined the priest's spiritual mission.[63] The latter was hardly "free" labor in any case: the priest had to supply abundant food and drink, diminishing the net value of his harvest by nearly half.[64] Worse still were the moral implications of *pomoch'*: the priest personally had to sponsor that great scourge of rural Russia, alcoholism, and "turn his home into something akin to a tavern while the work is being done."[65] But the most insidious effect, they wrote, was to leave the priest hopelessly dependent upon parish good will, reluctant to antagonize parishioners, and driven to ignore moral lapses, religious deviance, and superstition. In the words of one, "the thought of *pomoch'*, which does not abandon the priest all summer, makes the priest dependent upon the people and greatly limits his freedom vis-à-vis the parish, for fear that an angry peasant will not help or will keep others from

[60] TsGIA SSSR, f. 804, op. 1, r. 3, d. 10, l. 50 ob. (Vladimir).

[61] Ibid., d. 18, l. 57 (Vladimir).

[62] Ibid., d. 402, ll. 57 ob.–58 (Tver); see also the collective petition from Ekaterinoslav (ibid., r. 1, d. 74, l. 56).

[63] For a discussion of *pomoch'* (with references), see above, Chapter 2.

[64] The clergy at one parish in Vladimir complained that the priest must spend "half his income on the purchase of wine and other products to host the parishioners who work [for him]" (TsGIA SSSR, f. 804, op. 1, r. 3, d. 13, l. 156 ob). A priest in another district calculated that *pomoch'* cost him 100 rubles per year (ibid., d. 21, l. 25 ob).

[65] Ibid., d. 10, l. 63 (Vladimir).

coming to [perform] this voluntary labor."[66] The clergy was acutely aware that this dependence severely vitiated their social status: "What can be more difficult and sorrowful for a spiritual father, standing with all humility under a peasants' window, than to ask for help and to have to hear from some of them every kind of nonsense because of their coarse, uneducated nature?"[67]

The clergy were still more critical of their other main form of support: emoluments and collections on religious holidays. The most frequent complaint concerned the negligible amount of income, which, in the candid phrase of one priest, simply "does not justify the time and effort."[68] To account for their flocks' failure to pay fairly, some cited the small number of parishioners or the laity's poverty, especially in the case of former serfs.[69] As one priest in Pereslavl wrote, the parishioners are "in no condition to give any aid," partly because "they are so few in number," but mainly "because of their extreme poverty, which overtook them during the time of serfdom."[70] Other clerics complained that parishioners did not *want* to pay a fair sum and craftily found justification in custom and venerable "tradition." One priest complained that the peasants "pay for our work not in accordance with our zeal or the prosperity of a given parishioner but according to the amount paid by their fathers and grandfathers."[71] The clergy also inveighed against the normative rates on emoluments, which set absurdly low standards and gave parishioners a legal basis to refuse more generous payments.[72]

Those traditional and normative sums had declined precipitously in real terms, especially amidst the spiraling inflation that followed the Crimean War.[73] The injustice, wrote the clergy, was that inflation applied only to their expenses, not their income: parishioners held existing rates to be sacred and inviolable but casually raised prices on goods and services required by the clergy. As a priest in Tver wrote, "in early times all the essential commodities were one-half or one-third their present cost, while our income has not increased in the slightest."[74] Anger, disgust, and sarcasm mingled in the

---

[66] Ibid., d. 21, ll. 25–25 ob. (Vladimir).

[67] Ibid., l. 196 ob. (Vladimir).

[68] Complaints about the low rates of emoluments appear on roughly one-quarter of the replies from Vladimir; much higher rates occurred in selected areas, such as Penza district (61 percent) of Penza diocese and Chigirin district (79 percent) of Kiev diocese (ibid., dd. 10–22, 272, 155).

[69] In Vladimir 11 percent of the parishes blamed small emoluments on the shortage of parishioners, and approximately the same proportion cited the parishioners' poverty as the cause (ibid., dd. 10–22).

[70] Ibid., d. 16, l. 199 (Vladimir).

[71] Ibid., d. 402, l. 9 (Tver).

[72] Ibid., d. 327, ll. 60 ob., 65, 68 (Riazan).

[73] In Vladimir diocese 48 percent of the city staffs complained of inflation, compared with just 19 percent of the rural clergy (ibid., dd. 10–22).

[74] Ibid., d. 402, l. 89 (Tver).

report of a priest in Riazan: "What a miracle! We are paid for rites as *in days of yore*, but—for labor and all necessities—people charge us two or three times as much (*to accord with modern ways*), saying that 'everything has become expensive now.'"[75]

Yet, just as the traditional income had declined, the opinions show that consumption patterns—at least for the educated model that clergy aspired to emulate—had risen steadily. A priest in Riazan put it well when he wrote that "payment for rites is now the same as it was in bygone times—but [our] living standards have changed."[76] That change was apparent in the model budgets that some priests offered for the commission's consideration, usually in the range of five hundred to a thousand rubles—that is, several times the current income for a middling priest in central Russia.[77] As one explained, "it is necessary to have decent clothes, to send your sons to the seminary, and to give your daughters a proper upbringing—hence the [current] amount of annual income is far from sufficient for our present needs."[78] Anxiety about family needs and the large number of dependents figures prominently in many of the clerical opinions.[79] Especially onerous was the cost of a year's schooling for sons, estimated at a third or even half the income of most priests. Understandably, then, complaints about the high cost of seminary education pervaded many of the reports, appearing on 40 percent of the opinions from some areas.[80] Amidst such penury, clergy found it difficult to keep abreast of modern culture. As a priest in Riazan noted, "one must now read not only ecclesiastical but also secular journals—and here again money is needed."[81]

Significantly, the clergy's most vitriolic complaints concerned not the *amount* of emoluments but their very form. First of all, noted some clergy, emoluments engendered much conflict between priest and parish that was highly detrimental to the clergy's status and effectiveness. Though relatively few of the replies treat this question, probably for fear that such comments

---

[75] Ibid., d. 328, ll. 75 ob.–76 (Riazan).

[76] Ibid., d. 333, l. 178 ob. (Riazan).

[77] For example, clergy in Chigirin district (Kiev diocese) requested salaries ranging from 500 to 800 rubles (ibid., d. 155, ll. 53, 59, 62 ob., 76); see also the model budget devised by staffs in Riazan (ibid., d. 327, l. 98; d. 329, ll. 140, 198–98 ob.).

[78] Ibid., d. 13, l. 147 ob. (Vladimir).

[79] Six percent of the clergy in Vladimir cited family size as a cause of their distress (ibid., dd. 10–22).

[80] For estimates on the cost of schooling, see replies from Riazan and Kiev (ibid., dd. 329, l. 140; d. 155, ll. 21 ob., 25).

[81] Ibid., d. 327, l. 4 ob. (Riazan); see also similar comments in the reports from Penza (d. 272, ll. 112–13) and Ekaterinoslav (r. 1, d. 74, ll. 56–58). On the attempts to establish parish and district libraries for clergy, see *Kievskie eparkhial'nye vedomosti* [hereafter *Kievskie EV*], 1861, no. 2: 23–24, and "Biblioteki zavodimye dukhovenstvom," *PO*, 1862, no. 9, zametki: 41–42.

would be tantamount to confessions and invite prosecution for "solicitation," some clergy admitted to the temptation to extort ever larger sums.[82] As a priest in Riazan wrote: "Sometimes because of urgent necessity (amidst the constant inflation on everything), it is necessary—if not to extort—then to request and firmly insist upon [larger emoluments]. Often the result is the conflict between pastor and flock that is so unpleasant."[83] A second effect of emoluments loomed much larger in the opinions: such support vitiated the clergy's dignity and honor. Indeed, one of the main refrains running throughout the more articulate opinions is the cry that "reliance upon voluntary donations so demeans the priest that the worst peasant regards himself as superior."[84] Because of the voluntary emoluments, wrote another priest, "parishioners (as everyone knows) regard the clergy for the most part with rude indifference and nourish a certain arrogance and superiority over the clergy."[85] As the priest solicited emoluments or, especially, as he marched through the village collecting gifts on religious holidays, he experienced a profound sense of personal debasement.[86] To quote the poignant cry of a priest in Vladimir: "We are regarded as mere beggars, and [parishioners] contemptuously give us to understand that the only difference between beggars and us is that the former beg from beneath the window outside the house, while we do so from the inside; the former beg in Russian, we in Slavonic."[87] The religious processions on holidays, wrote another, were anything but a joyous occasion: "It is necessary to visit all two hundred households and to subject yourself to open reproofs and scorn (and perhaps secret curses). And for what? For coming to say a blessing on their home!"[88]

Some parish clergy also acknowledged that dependence upon emoluments left them reluctant to assault immorality or religious deviance among parishioners.[89] As in the matter of solicitation, most did not dare to broach the subject for fear of triggering an investigation for misfeasance. A priest in Vladimir, however, declared outright that "to sustain [their] income, clergy are obliged to indulge certain illegal customs, habits, and prejudices of parishioners, for otherwise the parishioners will refuse to give us contribu-

---

[82]Less than 1 percent of the replies from Vladimir admitted to the temptation of solicitation (TsGIA SSSR, f. 804, op. 1, r. 3, dd. 10–22).

[83]Ibid., d. 333, l. 39 (Riazan); see also d. 34, l. 71 (Kursk).

[84]Ibid., d. 18, ll. 3 ob.–4 (Vladimir).

[85]Ibid., d. 10, l. 135 (Vladimir).

[86]Holiday collections ordinarily provided only nominal increments, but there were some important exceptions. One parish in Murom district (Vladimir diocese), for example, reported receiving just 150 rubles in emoluments per annum but derived twice that amount from holiday collections (ibid., d. 11, ll. 118–19 ob.).

[87]Ibid., d. 19, l. 5 ob. (Vladimir).

[88]Ibid., d. 10, l. 20 ob (Vladimir).

[89]See, for example, the striking series of complaints from clergy in Riazan diocese (ibid., d. 334, ll. 22, 50, 60, 62, 150–50 ob., 160, 163).

tions."[90] Another cleric wrote that, "for fear of losing income and indeed in hopes of obtaining still greater rewards for our work, one is sometimes forced to be silent or to indulge rich parishioners or any kind of prosperous peasant, who are swollen with insolence and conceit."[91] As the clergy were well aware, such problems tended to "weaken respect and trust among parishioners toward the priest and to paralyze that positive influence which he should exercise over his flock."[92]

Though all these problems had long been gestating and were implicit in the traditional parish economy, the clergy's difficulties had been substantially aggravated by the emancipation of serfs in 1861. Many nobles moved to the city after emancipation, and of those who stayed, many tended to abjure their special responsibility and patronage for the local priest and church. To quote a priest in Kiev: "After the [serfs'] emancipation, almost all the landlords unanimously responded that they themselves are poor and hence are not obliged to give the clergy anything *gratis*."[93] Likewise, a priest in Riazan wrote that his staff had been accustomed to a subsidy of three hundred rubles per year from the local squire but that in the wake of emancipation "the landlord has refused to give us this salary because of the changes in landlord-serf relations."[94] The loss of the squire's authority was especially apparent in the western provinces, where peasants summarily refused to observe their labor duties under the 1842 statute: "Prior to emancipation, they did not cultivate the priest's plot on time or in a proper fashion, but since then they have categorically refused to do this at all."[95]

As a result, the clergy found themselves more than ever dependent upon peasant parishioners, who simply were "not inclined to give us any kind of additional support."[96] Although some clergy attributed that diffidence to the peasants' own straitened condition after emancipation or to the pernicious influence of Old Believers,[97] most clerics believed that the peasants did not *want* to aid them. The underlying problem, in the clergy's view, was the peasants' inability—or refusal—to appreciate the modern needs of clergy, such as a full education for sons or suitable dowries for daughters. As one

---

[90] Ibid., d. 14, l. 92 (Vladimir).

[91] Ibid., ll. 98 ob.–99 (Vladimir).

[92] Ibid., d. 15, l. 7 (Vladimir).

[93] Ibid., d. 155, l. 87 ob. (Kiev).

[94] Ibid., d. 333, l. 242 (Riazan); see also similar materials on Vladimir diocese (d. 19, l. 151; d. 13, l. 71; d. 16, ll. 69–70).

[95] Ibid., d. 155, l. 85 ob.; also l. 89 ob. (Kiev).

[96] Ibid., d. 11, l. 119 ob. (Vladimir).

[97] A priest in Pereslavl-Zalesskii district wrote that after emancipation parishioners "became more concerned about their own needs than aiding the clergy" (ibid., d. 21, ll. 127 ob.–28). For a case where the onus of responsibility is placed on Old Believers, see ibid., d. 34, l. 124 ob. (Kursk).

priest explained, the peasants "need no special outlays for reading, educating their children, or [purchasing] decent clothes," and hence they simply cannot comprehend that the clergy "must dress decently, support sons in Church schools, and provide daughters with a good dowry befitting our rank and the times."[98] Such arguments also carried overtones of despair and contempt, not unlike educated society's condescending view of the "dark people." To cite a typical remark: "The peasants—our parishioners—have no sympathy for our needs, utterly do not appreciate them, and because of their boorishness and insolence, sometimes do not wish to reward us for our work in administering various rites for them."[99] Dismayed by the peasants' indifference to their new roles as preachers, catechists, and schoolteachers, even the most dedicated priests waxed pessimistic about the prospects of aid from parishioners.[100] In the grim assessment of a priest in Vladimir, "one cannot expect to improve our status through the rural parishioners, for our people—given their lack of education—cannot appreciate the work and deeds of the clergy."[101] Here, in a nutshell, was the major difficulty of religious reform in the sixties: the parishioners, summoned by the commission to aid the clergy, seemed unlikely to appreciate the legitimacy, even the necessity, of such aid.

The questionnaire also charged the clergy to offer their own solution to the clerical question, but most priests proved extremely reticent. Only a minority compiled the laundry list of demands that one might have expected. In Vladimir diocese, for example, roughly half the parishes ended their reports with a complaint that current income was inadequate, but they offered no specific proposals to ameliorate their condition.[102] As one diocesan committee complained after fruitlessly sifting through the massive files, the reports "generally indicate only the clergy's needs, but as for the means to satisfy them, they are generally terse, and one often encounters the phrase 'there are no [local] resources.'"[103] Typical was the report from a clerical staff in Vladimir, which simply listed income, pronounced it unsatisfactory, and affirmed their faith "in the good will of the state to find a solution."[104]

Why such reticence? In part, it reflected the apathy and inertia of many

[98] Ibid., d. 333, l. 243 (Riazan).

[99] Ibid., d. 13, l. 148 ob. (Vladimir).

[100] For the clergy's complaints of peasant resistance to parish schools, one of their main hopes for supplementary salaries and an augmented role in the community, see the summary of official reports in *Nachal'nye narodnye uchilishcha i uchastie v nikh pravoslavnogo dukhovenstva* (St. Petersburg, 1866).

[101] TsGIA SSSR, f. 804, op. 1, r. 3, d. 13, l. 147 (Vladimir).

[102] The rate of no response on this question ranged from two-thirds in backward areas like Arkhangel'sk diocese (ibid., r. 1, d. 6, l. 62) to a more typical 49 percent in Vladimir (ibid., r. 3, dd. 10–22), to a rather unusual rate of one-third in Tambov (ibid., r. 1, d. 38, ll. 3–3 ob.).

[103] Ibid., r. 1, d. 19, l. 33 ob. (Tver).

[104] Ibid., r. 3, d. 11, ll. 114 ob.-15; see also d. 21, ll. 160–61, and d. 20, l. 54 (Vladimir).

rural clerics, especially the older ones, who, while not averse to additional support, were inured to the existing order and distant from the younger clergy, who had sons to educate, complex cultural needs, and a more pastoral conception of their service. Some clergy also feared their parishioners' displeasure. It was not difficult to guess how peasants and landlords would greet demands for more land, parsonages, tithes, and taxes for the clergy's benefit. As the bishop of Kursk observed, "if any staff should ask for land from the surrounding private holdings of land, then of course those landowners would rise up against them."[105] More important still was the clergy's lack of cohesion and unity. Dispersed across the expanses of Russia, immobilized by strict travel restrictions, denied the right of corporate assemblies—the parish clergy had little opportunity to meet and embrace a common set of aggressive demands.[106]

The principal reason for the clergy's taciturnity, however, lay in the commission's demand that they identify *local* resources—a directive intended to dispel fantasies about a state salary.[107] Yet that was precisely the clergy's main aspiration.[108] In the memorable phrase of a priest in Pereslavl district, "to improve the clergy's condition in a material sense, there is no other [suitable] means than a sufficient salary. The clergy have but one desire: Salary!!! Salary!!! Salary!!!"[109] In Vladimir diocese roughly one-quarter of the parishes took no heed of the order to identify local resources only and asked for a state salary: even greater proportions did so in other areas.[110] To be sure, few proposed specific government measures that could finance this vast expenditure, such as a head tax on parishioners or an assessment on land.[111] Whatever the mechanism, they insisted that some government office, whether local or central, collect this revenue and thereby insulate the clergy

---

[105] Ibid., r. 1, d. 34, l. 16 ob. (Kursk).

[106] On the travel restrictions, see the journal of the Special Commission (ibid., r. 3, d. 472, ll. 151 ob.–53). On the isolation, see the typical statement of a priest in Saratov, who wrote in 1862 that "our clergy lead an isolated existence, each parish separated from one another, and they have no place or organ to generalize their interests" ("Pis'mo iz Saratova," *PO*, 1862, no. 2, zametki: 58). Still, in some areas the clergy did consult, at least on the level of the superintendency or neighboring parishes. See, for example, the collective opinion from seven neighboring parishes in Radomysl' district (Kiev diocese) and Ekaterinoslav diocese (TsGIA SSSR, f. 804, r. 3, d. 154, ll. 11–28; r. 1, d. 74, ll. 67–75). Yet such cases were rare; the replies of each area bear only vague similarities, owing more to common concerns than to consultation.

[107] See the commission's special order, issued in June 1863, reaffirming the need for *local* resources and prohibiting requests for salaries (TsGIA SSSR, f. 804, op. 1, r. 3, d. 470, ll. 97 ob.–98).

[108] Even foes of clerical salaries admitted that such was the overwhelming desire of rank-and-file priests ("Ot redaktsii," *PO*, 1863, no. 3: 121).

[109] TsGIA SSSR, f. 804, op. 1, r. 3, d. 13, l. 148 ob. (Vladimir).

[110] The bishop of Saratov reported that 91 percent of the clergy requested a larger state stipend (ibid., r. 1, d. 51, ll. 6–25).

[111] Ibid., r. 3, d. 328, ll. 25 ob., 111–11 ob,; d. 326, l. 257; d. 331, l. 121 (Riazan).

from peasant discontent and arrears.[112] Although some proposals roughly approximated a tithe, the clergy were determined to become salaried officers of the state. As one priest wrote in despair and with finality, "there are absolutely no [local] resources, and all our hopes rest on [receiving] a salary from the state."[113]

That aspiration is highly significant. It was in part a consequence of the Nikolaevan reforms, which provided small salaries in selected areas. Encouraged by the precedent, clergy all across the empire now yearned for the same, though on a scale several times more lavish than Nicholas's modest grants.[114] The desire for salaries, moreover, was a direct expression of the clergy's aversion to their traditional dependence, not only because it eroded their prestige, but also because it impeded their role as more professional pastors. As in the case of the Westernized nobility, the Church's higher cultural standards had at once sharpened the clergy's alienation from the backward peasantry and whetted their appetite for regular support from above. It is significant that the clergy took as their model not foreign clergy but the Russian civil servant, whose salary and perquisites (such as pensions and medals) loomed large in contemporary values.[115] Such attitudes, no doubt, deepened the rift between priest and bishop: ranking prelates feared that the state would swallow the Church; parish clergy had no such compunctions. The clergy's demand for state salaries elicited sharp criticism from conservative quarters, especially from Slavophile publicists, who warned that salaries would transform the clergy into soulless bureaucrats indifferent to the people's needs.[116] To such arguments one priest replied with venomous irony, "Although this [salary] is regarded as 'bureaucratism' by *The Day* [a Slavophile newspaper], it seems that the clergy in the present circumstances are more similar to officials, because—as soon as they perform some rite—they immediately thrust out their hands for a reward."[117]

Still, stark reality and admonitions from above impelled some clergy to suggest alternative or supplementary measures. Despite their abhorrence of

---

[112]Ibid., d. 18, l. 7 ob. (Vladimir).

[113]Ibid., d. 34, l. 4 (Kursk).

[114]Ibid., d. 10, l. 130 (Vladimir); d. 19, ll. 138–38 ob. (Vladimir).

[115]That lack of a foreign reference group markedly distinguishes the clergy from other professional groups, such as doctors or academics (see Nancy Mandelker Frieden, *Russian Physicians in an Era of Reform and Revolution, 1856–1905* [Princeton, 1981], pp. 8–9; Mathes, "University Autonomy," pp. 341–73). Even the sensational *Opisanie* by Belliustin affords only a small comparison with French clergy (pp. 154–55). Instead, some Russian clergy even recommended that they be incorporated into the Table of Ranks for the civil service (see the commentaries from Nizhnii-Novgorod, Mogilev, Kiev, and Riga in TsGIA SSSR, f. 804, op. 1, r. 1, d. 31, ll. 16–17 ob.; d. 55, l. 20 ob.; d. 59, ll. 53–57; r. 3, d. 325, ll. 116–16 ob.).

[116]See, for example, F. Voronov, "Ob ustanovlenii opredelennogo obespecheniia platy za tserkovnye treby," *Den'*, 1862, no. 45: 4–5.

[117]TsGIA SSSR, f. 804, op. 1, r. 3, d. 328, l. 43 (Riazan); see also d. 10, l. 112 ob. (Vladimir).

agriculture, some asked for better land, even double or triple allotments, which would permit them to derive substantial rents or at least to farm more efficiently. More frequent were requests for free parish labor, essentially along the lines of the 1842 statute in the western provinces. In some areas nearly half the clergy advanced this demand, buttressed by several rationales—that poor peasants could more easily provide labor than monetary tithes, that such labor simply regularized customary *pomoch'*, and that statutory obligations would purify *pomoch'* of the expensive, scandalous drinking bouts.[118] Significantly, however, clergy in the western provinces, who had had much experience with coercive labor, preferred to commute the obligation to a regular monetary payment. And perspicacious priests elsewhere foresaw little good from such parish *barshchina*: "The work will not only fail to improve our condition but will provide still more indignation and contempt toward the parish clergy."[119] Perhaps most important of all is what the opinions did *not* suggest, namely, parish councils or reductions in parishes and clerical positions—the very two measures that ultimately formed the main thrust of reform in the 1860s.[120] In sum, the clergy's vision of reform bore little resemblance to the plans being laid in St. Petersburg.

The Bishops: Diocesan Considerations

Reluctant to give the parish clergy full freedom to express their ambitions, the Special Commission assigned primary responsibility for a comprehensive statement to the diocesan bishops. It gave them broad discretion on how their reports might be compiled—alone, or with the assistance of the consistory or a select committee of diocesan clergy. As in all these surveys of provincial opinion, the responses—formally called "considerations" (*soobrazheniia*)— varied greatly, not only in substance but also in length. Some consisted of a few vapid paragraphs; other ran several hundred pages in length and gave a systematic exegesis of law codes. Whatever their structure, the diocesan opinions played a central role in subsequent reform. The commission carefully analyzed and published digest summaries of the reports, which served as a starting point for later reforms in the clergy's status, mobility, and role in parish schools.[121] Their fate was quite different from that of the clergy's

---

[118]Thus 29 percent of the staffs in Vladimir sought to establish obligatory parish labor, with the proportion rising to nearly two-thirds in districts with fertile land (for example, Iur'ev). Ibid., dd. 10–22.

[119]Ibid., d. 16, l. 196 ob. (Vladimir); d. 335, l. 190 (Riazan).

[120]Only 3 percent of the clergy in Vladimir recommended changes in parish organization or reductions in clerical positions (ibid., dd. 10–22); for a similar level of response elsewhere, see the bishops' summaries for the Caucasus (r. 1, d. 68, ll. 9 ob.–11 ob.) and Tomsk (d. 69, l. 9).

[121]See, for example, ibid., r. 1, d. 150, ll. 12–27 ("O pravakh dukhovenstva").

opinions: the latter, an avalanche of material the commission could not digest, a set of demands it could not satisfy, were unceremoniously dumped—unused—into the archives.

Divided into sections on the clerical economy, clerical legal status, the problem of surplus youths, and parish schools, the bishops' reports provide a rich mine of information on the contemporary Church and, especially, on the attitudes and aspirations of diocesan authorities. Compared with the ranking prelates, especially the influential metropolitans Filaret and Isidor, they seemed relatively liberal, not only strongly supportive of clerical demands, but also less anxious about state intervention.

Part I, on the clerical economy, generally concurred with the clergy's desire for salaries but of necessity gave more attention to other forms of support. The bishops agreed that salaries were desirable (indeed, wrote some, this was the "only solution"), and they recommended substantial sums—up to a thousand rubles per annum in one case.[122] More sensitive to the state's inability to provide such funds directly from the treasury, the bishops recommended a special levy on the clergy's behalf, a kind of tithe to be collected and disbursed by the state. A few bishops opposed such taxation, warning that it would only stir anticlerical sentiments: "If one establishes a new and significant monetary levy on the parishioners to support the clergy in lieu of state salaries, this will provoke grumbling among the peasants and refusals [to pay], as often occurs when a few additional kopecks per capita are added to the poll tax or community levies."[123]

In contrast to the parish clergy, the prelates gave considerably more attention to other measures, for by the time the bishops compiled their considerations, the commission had made it absolutely clear that salaries were out of the question.[124] The bishops generally believed that the Church should retain its present system of gratuities and land, at least until adequate alternatives were made available. In the case of emoluments, they proposed such changes as a more precise legal definition of "solicitation" (to facilitate prosecution of offenders and vindication of the innocent) and a significant increase in the normative rates (to remove any excuses for solicitation).[125] As for parish land, the bishops paid due attention to the harmful effects of clerical agriculture, but for practical necessity they argued that the Church should protect, even expand, this kind of resource.[126] The bishop of Arkhangel'sk astutely warned that inflation would erode any monetary settlement, whereas land would

[122] Ibid., d. 83, ll. 6 ob.–7 (Minsk). The recommended amounts varied considerably, from 300 rubles in Astrakhan to 1,000 rubles in Kiev (d. 35, ll. 31–32 ob.; d. 59, l. 19).

[123] Ibid., d. 32, l. 4 (Samara).

[124] Ibid., r. 3, d. 470, ll. 97 ob.–98.

[125] Ibid., r. 1, d. 59, l. 47 (Kiev); d. 71, ll. 3 ob.–5 ob. (Irkutsk); d. 68, ll. 25 ob.–31 ob. (Kavkaz'e); d. 46, l. 4 (Riazan); d. 47, ll. 25 ob.–26 (Tula).

[126] Ibid., d. 59, ll. 15 ob.–16 ob. (Kiev).

probably appreciate over time and thus provide a hedge against inflation.[127] Some prelates, however, cautioned against land grabs, especially in parishes with former serfs, where, in the words of the bishop of Samara, "the peasants are mostly ruined and the landlords refused to give the clergy land or build houses for them." Hence additional land claims would only incite parish protests.[128]

Like the parish clergy, the bishops showed scant enthusiasm for parish councils or parish reorganization. Just a few prelates called the councils "useful," and only one, the veteran reformer, Dmitrii of Kherson, hailed the idea with enthusiasm, even going so far as to submit a draft proposal.[129] The bishops displayed still less interest in parish reorganization, which had caused such difficulty in the 1840s and ran contrary to the clear interests of Church and clergy. At most, they admitted the possibility of highly selective consolidation, primarily in cities. Even the bishop of Vladimir, generally disposed to favor parish mergers, insisted that they be undertaken only if "the villagers agree to it."[130] Most adamantly opposed, as always, were bishops in the borderlands (especially western dioceses) and in areas with substantial populations of Old Believers.[131]

The bishops evinced greater interest in reforming the clerical service structure, for a substantial number favored the elimination of deacons and hereditary sacristans. The bishop of Kaluga, for example, proposed to eliminate deacons in all parishes, even prosperous ones, as simply unessential for religious rites. Authorities in Kursk, by contrast, proposed to keep deacons as teachers in parish schools but to eliminate the ill-educated sacristans.[132] Whatever the method of reduction, the goal was to increase the income shares for remaining staff and to purge the white clergy of its less educated and less venerated strata, thus improving both the material and the moral condition of the clergy. In addition, some bishops tied this reform to the goal of restoring the stepladder, or hierarchical principle, to parish service: by replacing hereditary sacristans with seminary graduates, the Church could

[127] Ibid., d. 6, l. 64 ob.

[128] Ibid., d. 32, l. 4 (Samara).

[129] Ibid., d. 41, ll. 53–61 (Kherson); d. 6, l. 64 ob. (Arkhangel'sk); d. 36, l. 14 (Kaluga); d. 47, l. 25 ob. (Tula); d. 60, ll. 4–4 ob. (Vladimir).

[130] Ibid., d. 60, ll. 4 ob.–6 (Vladimir); see also d. 55, ll. 6 ob.-7 (Mogilev); d. 45, l. 4 (Kostroma); d. 63, l. 26 ob. (Simbirsk); d. 41, ll. 18–22 (Kherson). The most ambitious rationalizer was the bishop of Ekaterinoslav, who proposed not only to combine undersized parishes but also to shift parts of parishes to achieve more even distribution (so that "each parish staff has no less than one thousand souls to support it"). Ibid., d. 74, ll. 30 ob.–31.

[131] For complaints of "too few" churches in the face of dispersion of parishes or threats of other confessions, see the replies from western dioceses (such as Minsk, in ibid., d. 83, ll. 6–6 ob.), from Siberia (e.g., Irkutsk, ibid., d. 71, ll. 2 ob.–3), and even from some central Russian dioceses (e.g., Kostroma, ibid., d. 54, ll. 165–65 ob.).

[132] Ibid., d. 36, ll. 12–12 ob. (Kaluga); d. 34, ll. 5–8 (Kursk).

provide future priests with practical experience and observe canonical rules on minimum age for consecration.[133] Though evidently more inclined than the parish clergy to restructure service, and displaying thereby their loyalty to the institution over the soslovie, most bishops nevertheless took a moderate view of staff reductions, favoring a trimmer shtat but not draconian changes.[134] Perhaps most indicative of episcopal mood was that only a small minority categorically opposed changes on the grounds of custom and aesthetic requirements of the liturgy. Most, by contrast, favored some modest changes to improve the interests of the Church and the condition of the clergy itself.

That reformist attitude was still more evident in Part II of the bishops' replies, devoted to a discussion of the clergy's juridical condition. Highly indicative was the nearly universal demand for changes in the law on voluntary defrocking, a reform, as we have seen, that was blocked in 1860 by the chief procurator. The import of the issue was emphasized by the episcopal committee in St. Petersburg, which wrote that "this law can evoke corrupting ideas and demean the clerical rank, and it can also evoke criticism of Church authorities for brutality."[135] Most of the bishops also denounced a recent decision by the Ministry of Finance to impose a real estate tax on urban property personally owned by the clergy. Apart from the violation of traditional privilege, the prelates acidly noted that the tax was hardly consistent with the government's promise "to improve the clergy's economic well-being."[136] A liberal spirit in the replies was also apparent in demands to abolish the traditional restrictions on commercial activity by the clergy and their families, all in an obvious effort to ameliorate the clergy's economic plight. Such changes, to be sure, did not come easily. Ambivalence was evident in reports like that from the bishop of Eniseisk, who proposed "to permit those who desire to engage in trade and handicrafts (in limited ways and within the realm of decency) to do so."[137]

The most ambitious demands concerned the clergy's civil rights and privileges. Even while reasserting the clergy's special status—demanding, for example, that they be subject exclusively to ecclesiastical courts—the diocesan prelates advanced a number of demands to improve the clergy's legal status. Most striking was their demand that the clergy have the right to hold power of attorney. Previously, the state had expressly forbidden the clergy to represent others in legal matters. Though intended mainly to preclude intercession on behalf of peasants, the law was so categorical that it forbade *any* legal representation, even of fellow clerics. As a result, at considerable

---

[133] Ibid., d. 34, ll. 10–11 ob. (Kursk).
[134] For a more radical view, see the Tomsk report (ibid., d. 69, ll. 11–11 ob.).
[135] Ibid., d. 49, l. 14 (Petersburg).
[136] Ibid., d. 50, ll. 29 ob.–30.
[137] Ibid., d. 70, l. 7 ob. (Eniseisk).

inconvenience and expense, each cleric personally had to go to the provincial capital on all legal matters. Although most bishops referred only to this narrower goal, a few went on to suggest that the clergy be allowed to represent laymen too, thereby perhaps earning popular gratitude for "defending parishioners oppressed by local [state] authorities."[138] In the same spirit some bishops urged that the clergy be given greater authority in community affairs, including the right to participate and vote in the all peasant system of township (*volost'*) government.[139] Most hierarchs also favored changes in the legal status of clerical dependents, who in most cases forfeited their privileges and dropped into the poll-tax population if they left the clerical estate. For example, in the event of remarriage to someone in the lower social orders, clerical widows acquired the social status of the new spouse and all the attendant disabilities.[140] Finally, like the parish clergy, most bishops favored schemes to incorporate the clergy more closely into the secular system of service, even integrating them into the Table of Ranks.[141] Surprising as such schemes might be, the bishops justified them on various practical grounds: inclusion in the Table of Ranks would encourage laymen to pursue Church careers,[142] would inspire "greater [public] respect" toward the clergy,[143] and would provide clergy with the perquisites already afforded civil servants, such as pensions,[144] medals,[145] remuneration for administrative duties,[146] and special funds for travel expenses incurred in official work.[147]

A handful of prelates also broached a more sensitive issue: the role and status of parish clergy in Church administration. Interestingly, a substantial number seemed favorably inclined toward restoring the right of clergy to select their local superintendent. Already introduced in Kiev, the election of superintendents has been demanded in Belliustin's *Description* and apparently enjoyed widespread support among the clergy. Even the relatively cautious bishop of Nizhnii Novgorod voiced support for the innovation:

> Diocesan authorities cannot possibly know well all the priests [in their diocese]. Of course, the consistory, in presenting candidates for vacant superintendent positions, provides detailed reports on them. But official

---

[138] Ibid., d. 50, l. 29 (Tauride); d. 28, ch. 2, ll. 120 ob.–21 ob. (Viatka); d. 39, l. 7 ob. (Lithuania).

[139] Ibid., d. 35, l. 61 (Astrakhan).

[140] Ibid., d. 150, ll. 24 ob–25.

[141] Especially elaborate was the proposal from Kiev, which offered a full scheme for integrating the clergy into the Table of Ranks—archpriests holding rank VI, senior priests rank VIII, sacristans rank XIV (ibid., d. 59, ll. 54–55 ob.).

[142] Ibid., d. 28, ch. 2, ll. 106–8 ob. (Viatka).

[143] Ibid., d. 55, l. 20 ob. (Mogilev).

[144] Ibid., d. 57, l. 11 (Khar'kov).

[145] Ibid., d. 70, ll. 7–8 (Eniseisk).

[146] Ibid., d. 42, ll. 91–92 (Novgorod).

[147] Ibid., d. 41, l. 80 (Kherson).

papers and service records can never give a proper idea of people; one has
to have close, direct, and continuing acquaintance with men to judge accurately their abilities and shortcomings.[148]

Besides this practical argument, bishops were keenly sensitive to threats of
relative denigration, noting that virtually all other groups in society, even the
peasantry, now enjoyed the right to select their immediate superiors as representatives.[149] A few prelates also proposed to create district superintendent
councils, local committees of clergy who would function as courts of lower
instance to resolve minor cases and thus reduce the plethora of petty matters
that clogged the diocesan docket.[150] That, however, was the limit of democratization envisaged by most bishops. Few admitted the possibility of electing members of the consistory; none suggested the consecration of priests to
the episcopate or admission of laity to Church governance. The single radical
proposal emanated from a minority fraction of a diocesan committee in St.
Petersburg. Summoned to advise the prelate on his reply, the Petersburg
priests—the elite of their rank—reflected the heightened consciousness that
one might well expect in the capital, rich in talk and periodicals. This minority urged radical application of the electoral principle for the consistory as
well as for superintendents, proposed the formation of regular diocesan
assemblies—the first such conciliarist demand to emanate from the white
clergy—and even envisaged expanding the Synod by selecting "several additional members from the white clergy . . . [in accordance] with the regulations of Peter the Great."[151] Such radical schemes, obviously, held little
appeal for the bishops. Still, most prelates displayed a willingness to accommodate the new ideas and values gaining currency in the sixties. Indeed, only
one report, from the archconservative bishop of Kostroma, categorically
attacked "democratic principles" and demanded measures to restore "the
rights of bishops."[152]

Most bishops also raised the issue of the hereditary soslovie. Very significantly, the bishops, who were otherwise inclined to support the special interests of the parish clergy, generally favored measures to overturn the hereditary order for the sake of the Church. Family claims and endogamous
marriages, they argued, lacked foundation in canon law or government statute, and, as something unknown to the early Church and appearing belatedly in Russia, this whole order could not even raise the shield of historical
legitimacy. The bishops' primary concern was that marital connections often
obliged the bishop, out of concerns for welfare, to ordain not the most qual-

[148]Ibid., d. 31, ll. 30–31 (Nizhnii Novgorod).
[149]Ibid., d. 26, l. 8 (Orenburg).
[150]Ibid., d. 6, ll. 11–13 (Arkhangel'sk).
[151]Ibid., d. 49, ll. 25 ob.–27 (Petersburg).
[152]Ibid., d. 54, ll. 7–8 ob. (Kostroma).

ified candidate but the one who had reached a private bargain with the previous occupant. *Mariages de convenance*, they added, provided a poor model for parishioners, for they tended to breed feuds and conflict. As some reports noted (especially those where local clergy gave counsel), it was better to allow unrestricted selection of spouses according to mutual attraction—a telling statement of the intrusion of new attitudes toward love and marriage into the clergy.[153] The haggling over positions, the occasional newspaper advertisements, the spectacle of footloose seminarians bargaining with a priest for his position and his daughter—such embarrassments so demeaned the whole clergy that on these grounds alone reform was essential. Some moneywise bishops also pointed out that endogamy deprived the clergy of a chance to "improve their material position through marriage to a well-to-do fiancée."[154] But the main argument against the hereditary claims was the harmful effect upon the clergy's pastoral role. Such claims drove a wedge between the priest and his flock: "Through the loss of this right [to choose freely a spouse from any estate], other estates—seeing that the clergy shuns any kinship ties with them—become estranged from the clergy as a special caste locked inside itself, and such a split produces a coldness between the clergy and other estates and one may even say a certain disdain for [the clergy]."[155] The bishop of Riazan, likewise, declared that endogamous marriages made the clergy "into a caste" and caused "what we now see—the split between the clergy and other estates."[156] Though a handful of prelates defended the endogamous order, mainly on the grounds that it insulated the clergy from the corrupting influences of secular society, most favored giving priests the right to select wives from any estate and to assume a position without "any obligation toward the family of the deceased clergy."[157]

That desire for social openness also informed Part III of the reports, which discussed the problem of surplus candidates and the failure of clerical prog-

---

[153]The rebellion against prereform marriage conventions, though most dramatically expressed among the radical intelligentsia, had broader reverberations across society. Although the history of the Russian family and marriage is still little explored, see the pertinent remarks in Richard Stites, *The Women's Liberation Movement in Russia* (Princeton, 1978), pts. 1–2. The clergy, naturally, did not espouse "free love," but, as the diocesan commentaries show, they did favor the right of priests to select a wife from any estate. See, for example, the statements by the diocesan committee in Nizhnii Novgorod and, more generally, the commission's synopsis (TsGIA SSSR, f. 804, op. 1, r. 1, d. 42, ll. 85 ob.–86; d. 150, ch. 1, ll. 18–19).

[154]TsGIA SSSR, f. 804, op. 1, r. 1, d. 150, ch. 1, l. 18.

[155]Ibid., d. 34, l. 70 ob. (Kursk).

[156]Ibid., d. 46, ll. 21–21 ob. (Riazan).

[157]Ibid., d. 36, l. 24 ob. (Kaluga archpriest, M. Potemkin); see also the files from Orel (d. 43, l. 15) and Tula (d. 47, ll. 30 ob.–31). The authorities in Kostroma and Kaluga dissented from this general view, doubting that few secular women would marry clergy and that, if they did, such unions would only expose the clergy to the corrupting influences of lay society (ibid., d. 54, ll. 12 ob.–18 ob.; d. 36, ll. 17–17 ob.).

eny to leave the estate. Virtually all concurred that too few left, a situation attributed to impediments such as a "natural" attachment to their own so-slovie, the peculiar upbringing and lifestyle of provincial clergy, pressure from their own families, and the impractical education given in the semi-nary.[158] But the principal barrier, wrote the bishops, was the state's wall of discriminatory decrees that barred clerical youths, especially sacristans' sons, from state service. As the bishops pointedly observed, the sons of Lutheran pastors in Russia enjoyed the status of personal nobles in existing law, which placed them on a distinctly higher plane than the sons of Orthodox clergy. Thus, in addition to seminary reform and other measures, the bishops' pri-mary demand was to revise the legal status of the clergy's children, giving them a secular legal status outside the ecclesiastical domain. Most often they defined that status as nobleman (hereditary or personal) for priests' sons, hon-ored citizen (hereditary or personal) for sacristans' sons. That proposal, cast along lines suggested earlier by Batiushkov and Valuev, directly attacked the soslovie order that ascribed a father's status to his children. Legally, at least, the bishops' proposal would transform the clergy from an open soslovie into a profession. Interestingly, the bishops were so concerned about the surfeit of candidates that they did not consider measures to ensure entry by outsid-ers. Nor did they discuss the potential danger that too many seminarians would leave the Church.[159]

Part IV of the reports, concerning parish schools, revealed a predictable desire for clergy to play a dominant role in elementary public education. Though sensitive to accusations that the clergy had done little in prereform Russia to educate the common people and even now often showed diffidence, the bishops laid the blame elsewhere.[160] If Western Europe debated whether the clergy *should* dominate public education, in Russia the issue was whether they *could*, given their many liturgical duties, lack of training, and the like. The bishops attributed the clergy's shortcomings to such problems as med-dling by state officials, who, wrote the bishop of Arkhangel'sk, "make rather caustic remarks about the degree of success and about religious instruction," leaving the priest dispirited and discouraged.[161] The prelates stressed as well the lack of finances, noting that the clergy opened most parish schools on their own initiative, at their own expense, and often in their own home. The schools also suffered from popular indifference, even antipathy, so long as

---

[158] The commission's staff prepared a comprehensive summary of opinion (ibid., d. 104, ch. 1, ll. 117–207). The printed memorandum, with background materials, is available in the Lenin Library as *Zapiska po voprosu ob otkrytii detiam sviashchenno-tserkovno-sluzhitelei putei dlia obespecheniia svoego sushchestvovaniia na vsekh poprishchakh grazhdanskoi deia-tel'nosti* (n.p., n.d.) For a brief overview of the bishops' views, see above, pp. 152–55.

[159] TsGIA SSSR, f. 804, op. 1, r. 1, d. 104, ch. 1, ll. 117–207.

[160] See the summary published by the chief procurator, *Nachal'nye narodnye uchilishcha*, which systematically reviews the bishops' reports of 1863.

[161] TsGIA SSSR, f. 804, op. 1, r. 1, d. 6, l. 51 (Arkhangel'sk).

they promised no clear economic gain and merely entailed the loss of child labor. A few prelates conceded the clergy's own failings, such as their lack of pedagogical training, but argued that these deficiencies could be overcome and that priests could exercise a healthy influence on the lower classes.

With few exceptions, the bishops' reports proved surprisingly liberal, generally inclined to support reform on behalf of the clerical soslovie. Like the parish clergy, they looked primarily to the state for a solution, whether in the form of new taxes, special juridical privileges, or financial aid for parish schools. In two important respects, however, the bishops differed from the white clergy: the prelates placed higher priority on Church, not soslovie, interests (hence the willingness to trim staffs) and seemed willing to admit only a modest level of democratization in Church administration.

Publicists: Lay and Clerical

As the Special Commission sifted through the clerical opinions and episcopal reports, it had one more voice to consider: that of the contemporary press. If only in sheer bulk, the years 1863 and 1864 probably mark the apogee of journalistic comment on the clerical question. As earlier, the press played a major role in pushing back the political horizons, raising issues— such as reform in monasticism and diocesan administration—that received little or no treatment in the Special Commission. The periodicals remain our best insight into the more conscious of the unofficial reformers, those laymen and priests who debated reform and judged its progress. As government authorities were well aware, this new journalism exercised a powerful influence upon contemporary opinion and even shaped government decision making, since reform committees regularly monitored public debates and incorporated synopses of such opinion in their proceedings.[162]

The press, significantly, soon betrayed signs of dissatisfaction with the Special Commission, especially with the decision to solicit opinions rather than to invite deputies to St. Petersburg. Not only liberal organs but also the Slavophile paper *The Day* and the moderate academic journal *The Orthodox Review* urged the commission to summon clerical deputies to Petersburg for consultation. Typical was an article in *The Day*, which urged the commission "to call to St. Petersburg, as elected representatives of the parish clergy, two priests or deacons per diocese (one to represent urban clergy, the other village clergy), with the stipulation that these not be chosen by diocesan authorities but be elected by the clergy themselves."[163] Although evidence is scanty,

[162] Ibid., d. 33, ll. 109–9 ob. (commission's order to compile a digest of press opinions); d. 22 (file of selected articles).

[163] I.B., "Po povodu Osobogo prisutstviia," *Den'*, 1863, no. 4: 8; see also "Osoboe prisutstvie," *PO*, 1863, no. 1, zametki: 1–6.

such proposals seem to have had the support of parish clergy, or at least its more informed and ambitious segments. *The Orthodox Review* published a note from a priest in Moscow diocese who reported an informal conversation among nine local priests, all of whom agreed that "the rural clergy should have their own representatives on the Special Commission."[164] More predictable was the response of thoroughgoing liberals like Belliustin, who sharply rebuked the commission for failing to invite clerical deputies.[165]

After this initial disappointment, the press grew increasingly impatient with the silence and apparent inactivity of the Special Commission. A newspaper published at the St. Petersburg Academy, *The Contemporary Paper*, complained in July 1863 that the Special Commission "is doing its work—if it is doing it—in total silence: God knows what will come of this work, unbeknownst to all."[166] The exceedingly modest form of the questionnaire inspired some to suspect sham reform. Belliustin, for example, wrote that the commission's work "is frankly a jester's comedy: the expansion of rights, the increase of rights, and so forth, but the foundations—culture, education, closed social group—are the same old foundations."[167] Although authorities tolerated much of this criticism, upon occasion they felt obliged to suppress the debate. That was particularly true in the case of measures actually enacted, such as the new statute on parish councils. An article critical of the institution, published in a serial in Kiev in 1864, provoked an angry reproof from Valuev and a stern warning from the chief procurator.[168]

Whether clerical or lay, the liberal press shared some major points of agreement. One was the need to reform diocesan administration, which became a major butt of criticism. Typical was an article by a Petersburg priest, who observed that "the majority of officials [in the consistory], having utterly no education and oppressed by extreme poverty, are guided not by feelings of legality but by gifts and presents." He added that the clerical members of the consistory board were nominally responsible for decisions, which the bishop routinely signed, but that in fact the board's members "have studied the laws little and hence are often guided by the chancellery's [lay] officials."[169] Perhaps the most caustic materials appeared in *The Day*, a Slavophile paper antipathetic in principle to manifestations of bureaucracy in any form, but especially in the Church. Characteristic of the fare it offered

---

[164] V. Rozhdestvenskii, "Sel'skaia beseda po povodu izvestiia o pervom postanovlenii Osobogo prisutstviia," *PO*, 1863, no. 4, zametki: 197.

[165] See the complaint by I. S. Belliustin on the failure to invite "experts" (LOII, f. 115, d. 1215, unpag. letter of I. S. Belliustin to N. I. Belliustin, 29.1.1863).

[166] "Vnutrennie dela," *SL*, 1863, no. 27: 290–97.

[167] OR GBL, f. 231/II, k. 3, d. 51/4, l. 4 ob. (Belliustin to Pogodin, 4.2.1863).

[168] TsGIA SSSR, f. 797, op. 34, otd. 1, d. 349, ll. 1–21 (Valuev to Akhmatov, 22.12.1864).

[169] *SL*, 1864, no. 5: 1–2; see also F. Giliarovskii, "Prakticheskie zamechaniia ob uluchshenii byta dukhovenstva," ibid., 1864, nos. 27–34.

was an unsigned article in April 1863 that attributed all the clergy's moral failings to maladministration, especially endemic corruption and venality, and it documented these charges with tales of shocking injustice.[170] Some clerical writers even discerned maladministration as a major cause of the clergy's poverty, arguing that bribery was so rampant that it drained the clergy's few resources.[171] To combat maladministration and to awaken the "vital forces" of rural clergy, publicists called for democratization of the Church—at a minimum, the election of superintendents, more often the election of consistory members as well.[172] Though less common, the press also published materials on the conflict between white and black clergy, demanding that the white clergy be consecrated to the hierarchy and that the monastic clergy undergo far-reaching reform.[173] Such material became sufficiently common and influential that the suffragan bishop of Moscow declared that the press had become overtly antimonastic, favoring priests over bishops and yearning to expropriate monastic property for the white clergy's benefit. Such literature, he warned, was becoming "an evil influence" in the rank-and-file clergy.[174] To contain such influence, the chief procurator commissioned the rector of the Kazan Academy to write a formal defense of the monastic monopoly over the hierarchy and then had the piece published in a prominent academic journal.[175] That parry had scant effect; given the weakness of censorship, antimonastic and even antiepiscopal sentiments gained ever wider currency in the ranks of lower clergy.

On other substantive issues of reform, however, consensus broke down between clerical and lay publicists. All agreed that improvement of the clergy's material condition was essential, but they disagreed sharply on *how* to reform. To all it was clear what the clergy desired: "Our clergy, utterly exhausted by the dependence and helplessness of their position, are almost

---

[170]"Koe-chto po voprosu ob uluchshenii byta dukhovenstva," *Den'*, 1863, no. 13: 1–2; no. 17: 11–14.

[171] *Ob uluchshenii byta pravoslavnogo dukhovenstva sobstvennymi sredstvami dukhovnogo vedomstva* (St. Petersburg, 1864), pp. 22–24.

[172]V.S., "Kak izbiraetsia v dukhovenstve dukhovnik," *Syn otechestva*, 1863, no. 54; A. Kolosov, "O blagochinnicheskikh vyborakh," *RSP*, 1863, no. 3: 66–81, no. 4: 101–21.

[173]"Ob otnosheniiakh mezhdu dukhovenstvom i nachal'nikami," *Den'*, 1863, no. 40: 6–11; *Ob uluchshenii byta pravoslavnogo dukhovenstva sobstvennymi sredstvami dukhovnogo vedomstva* (proposing to tap monastic wealth to aid the clergy); "O bezbrachii i monashestve po otnosheniiu k izbraniiu v san episkopa," *PO*, 1862, no. 10: 140–50.

[174]OR GPB, f. 531 (A. S. Norov), d. 427, ll. 18 ob.-19 ob. (Leonid [Kavelin] to Norov, December 1862). For an example of demands that monastic property be used to aid the clergy, see "Ob uluchshenii byta pravoslavnogo dukhovenstva," *Russkii vestnik*, 1863, no. 9/10: 461.

[175]"O monashestve episkopov," *PS*, 1863, no. 4: 442–73; no. 5: 99–155; no. 6: 193–342. For the preparation of this manuscript, see the official correspondence (in TsGIA SSSR, f. 797, op. 32, otd. 1, d. 143, ll. 1–135) and the emperor's official expression of gratitude to the author, Ioann (ibid., op. 33, otd. 1, d. 22).

unanimous in wishing to go over to state salaries."[176] That aspiration provoked strong opposition from conservative journalists, especially the Slavophile paper *The Day*. Seeking to revive the medieval parish, with the reformed priest close in spirit and occupation to the people, it categorically rejected salaries as likely to transform the clergy into mere officials dressed in cassocks.[177] The moderate reformist journal *The Orthodox Review* also opposed salaries, warning that "state salaries, if the sole source of support, will further strengthen the hereditary isolation of the clergy and make the clergy into a corporation enrolled in state service and isolated from the people."[178] On the other hand, most periodicals, especially clerical ones, favored state salaries or at least a fixed parish tithe. Thus *The Contemporary Paper*, consciously seeking to articulate the demands of parish clergy, sarcastically attacked the foes of regular salaries: "*The Day* says that it is necessary to give the rural clergy land, which they should cultivate with their own hands. Such support, in the view of *The Day*, will help draw the clergy and people together. Oh, that accursed 'fusion with the people.' How many childish fantasies have we not heard about that! Fusion! Why does the priest need such fusion that will merely make him as poor and boorish as the common peasant?"[179] This latter view, no doubt, comes much closer to the opinion of parish clergy, yet the controversy revealed deep hidden divisions within the reform consensus, all rooted in differing conceptions of the clergy's role and the direction of reform.

More acrimonious still was the debate over parish reorganization and in staffing. Discussed sparingly in the clergy's opinions and the bishops' reports, such ideas enjoyed far greater currency in the press. Some journalists, especially lay writers, showed much greater willingness to merge parishes, especially in the central dioceses, where many small parishes in close proximity made parish consolidation, in theory, relatively feasible.[180] As one might suspect, such suggestions provoked acerbic rejoinders from parish clergy and bishops, not on the grounds that reorganization would cause hardship for clergy, though that unstated motive was surely present, but on the grounds

---

[176]"Ot redaktsii," *PO*, 1863, no. 3: 121.

[177]N.M., "Eshche neskol'ko slov po povodu Osobogo prisutstviia iz dukhovnykh i svetskikh lits dlia izyskaniia sposobov k luchshemu obespecheniiu byta belogo dukhovenstva," *Den'*, 1863, no. 8: 4–5; B., "Neskol'ko slov o voznagrazhdenii dukhovenstva za treby," ibid., no. 19: 10–11.

[178]"Po povodu tolkov ob uluchshenii byta dukhovenstva," *PO*, 1863, no. 4: 368. *Russkii vestnik*, a secular periodical, also held that salaries would violate Scripture and canon law; see "Ob uluchshenii byta pravoslavnogo dukhovenstva," 1863, no. 9/10: 440, 451.

[179]"Vnutrennee obozrenie," *SL*, 1863, no. 14: 136.

[180]For example, see: P. Krasovskii, "Vopros ob uluchshenii byta dukhovenstva," *DV*, 1864, tom 7: 216–19; A. Ivanov, "K zametke o 'Novom razdelenii prikhodov v g. Tule,'" *Tul'skie eparkhial'nye vedomosti* [hereafter *Tul'skie EV*], 1863, no. 11: 684–88; I. Tikhomirov, "Predpolozhenie sel'skogo sviashchennika," *PO*, 1863, no. 4: 190–92.

that reductions would weaken the Church's grip on society.[181] Still more controversial were proposals to replace traditional sacristans with laymen or seminary graduates, an idea that had long been discussed and seemed to enjoy much favor among priests.[182] The most famous exponent of such plans in the 1860s was a priest, P. Krasovskii, who urged authorities to free the Church of its ill-educated sacristans—"a special caste, which has acquired a special kind of life, special mores and ideas, special interests, even special civil rights."[183] Such ideas seemed all the more ominous because of rumored official support, especially after the Church's Parisian paper, *L'Union chrétienne*, reported Valuev's intention not only to reduce clergy and parishes but also "to abolish completely the lower clerical rank of readers and singers [sacristans]."[184]

Yet the most fundamental issue—abolition of the clerical soslovie—failed to elicit debate. Laymen and clergy, liberals and conservatives all held the antisoslovie attitude of the 1860s, believing that the restrictive estates were in principle bad and were especially so in the case of the clergy. Typical was the declaration of *The Contemporary Paper*. Though dedicated to clerical interests, it called for "the elimination of the caste character of the clerical soslovie and the admission to the clerical rank of all those who [so] desire."[185] Indeed, argued a church journal in Kiev, the clergy's problems cannot be overcome until, as in the case of serfs, the state liberates the clergy and their families from the rigid clerical estate.[186] How to do that elicited some muffled debate—whether through educational reform, by opening the seminaries or establishing an integrated Church-state school system, or through more pos-

[181][Vneshnii], "Otvet na stat'iu *Dukhovnogo vestnika*," *SL*, 1864, nos. 44–45.

[182]See above, pp. 179–81, 210.

[183]Krasovskii, "Vopros ob uluchshenii byta dukhovenstva," *DV*, 1864, tom 7; Krasovskii, *Otvet "Sovremennogo listka" na stat'iu "Dukhovnogo vestnika"* (Khar'kov, 1865). See also N.M., "Eshche neskol'ko slov," *Den'*, 1863, no. 8: 5; I. Tikhomirov, "Predpolozhenie sel'skogo sviashchennika," *PO*, 1863, no. 4: 192–96.

[184]*L'Union chrétienne*, 1863, no. 16. Such proposals provoked alarm among sacristans and ignited much public debate. For critical responses, citing the unwillingness of seminarians to become lowly sacristans and the lack of suitable laymen for appointment as sacristans, see "Otvet na stat'iu *Dukhovnogo vestnika*," *SL*, 1864, nos. 49–50; V. Kholminskii, "O prichetnikakh," *Kaluzhskie eparkhial'nye vedomosti* [hereafter *Kaluzhskie EV*], 1864, no. 5: 73–87; I. Dumitrashko, "Neskol'ko myslei ob uluchshenii byta dukhovenstva," *Poltavskie EV*, 1863, no. 10: 398–401; "Po voprosu ob uluchshenii byta dukhovenstva," *Kievskie EV*, 1863, no. 12: 366–73; "Eshche suzhdenie po voprosu o prichetnikakh," *RSP*, 1863, no. 12: 381–92, no. 15: 481–95.

[185]"Ob uchrezhdenii Osobogo prisutstviia," *SL*, 1863, no. 1: 4–5. See also, for comparison, *S.-Peterburgskie vedomosti*, 1863, no. 135; N.M., "Eshche neskol'ko slov," *Den'*, 1863, no. 8: 5; "Ob uluchshenii byta pravoslavnogo dukhovenstva," *Russkii vestnik*, 1863, no. 9/10: 463–80.

[186]"Soslovnost' russkogo belogo dukhovenstva i odno iz ee posledstvii," *RSP*, 1864, no. 47: 458–70; no. 48: 503–10.

itive measures, such as conferring secular legal status on clerical sons or abolishing family rights to positions.[187] Curiously, at least until the latter part of
the 1860s, the clergy did not openly defend their special soslovie rights,
partly because they were preoccupied with the economic issue, but mainly
because they shared the general hostility toward soslovie principles. There
were, to be sure, some exceptions; yet bald statements of soslovie interest—
even if these reflected the sentiment of rank-and-file clergy—enjoyed little
support in the largely reformist contemporary press, which demanded a
thorough transformation of the clergy.[188] Thus even *The Contemporary
Paper*, though sensitive to the needs of the clergy, favored abolition of hereditary rights and urged the Church to devise other forms of welfare.[189]

The press, beyond the points of dispute, projected a far more radical vision
of reform than that countenanced by authorities or the clergy. Its most significant service was to sustain a broad definition of the clerical question,
going beyond the narrow economic issue (virtually the sole focus of the commission's work) and stressing broader issues of soslovie structure and episcopal domination. It is difficult to measure the influence of such journalism
upon regular diocesan clergy. Many, no doubt, shared the views of the priest
in Pereslavl who affirmed "but one desire—Salary!!! Salary!!! Salary!!!" More
important, the contemporary press—contrary to its explicit aim—helped to
reinforce the clergy's identity as a separate soslovie by providing a medium
through which they could unite and by threatening their vested interests in
hereditary positions, closed schools, and special treatment in formal law.

The Experiment in Community Initiative

While priests, bishops, and publicists looked principally to the state to
resolve the clerical question, the Special Commission proceeded on a radically different course, seeking reform "from below" through direct community initiative and aid. Not that the Special Commission had any illusions

[187] For the abolition of separate clerical schools, see P. Dolgorukov, *Pravda o Rossii* (Paris,
1861), pp. 199–200. For the conferral of a secular legal status, see "[Peredovaia]," *SL*, 1863,
no. 47: 526. For the abolition of family rights and claims, see V. Sokolovskii, "O zachislenii
vakantnykh sviashchenno-tserkovno-sluzhitel'skikh mest za sirotstvuiushchimi devitsami
dukhovnogo zvaniia," *DV*, 8 (1864): 268–74; P. Obraztsov, "Neskol'ko slov o domashnem byte
sel'skogo dukhovenstva," *SL*, 1864, no. 16: 1; Nikitinskii, "O tom, kakim obrazom zame-
shchaiutsia sviashchenno-tserkovno-sluzhitel'skie mesta," *Den'*, 1864, no. 19: 1–4, no. 20: 9–
12.

[188] See, for instance, Father Amfiteatrov, "O brakakh v dukhovnom zvanii," *Kaluzhskie EV*,
1863, no. 8: 132–39.

[189] *SL*, 1864, no. 11: 1–5.

about the enormous difficulty of the task before it. As the drafting sessions for parish councils clearly show, the commission was painfully sensitive to the difficulty of summoning and regulating spontaneous action from below. Yet through the stimuli of provincial commissions and parish councils—the institutional structures it created to generate community action—the Special Commission's reform from below went further than a bland, hopeless appeal to society at large.

The provincial commissions, however, proved virtually impotent. Apart from soliciting modest concessions from the Ministry of State Domains,[190] they did little more than amass interesting files of data and opinions. Although the commissions suffered from some organizational problems (especially, absenteeism by the governor) and internal disputes, their main problem was the lack of clear authority. That issue rose to the fore almost immediately, causing the commision in Vladimir to complain that existing decrees "have defined neither the rights, nor the degree of authority, nor the manner of action [appropriate] for provincial commissions."[191] The response from the Special Commission defined the provincial boards as little more than transmission belts. The task of the commissions, it declared, was "to collect data on the condition of clergy and on means to improve their condition; to compose proposals for such improvement by the means they regard as most appropriate for this purpose; present these to the Special Commission for review; and implement these once confirmed." But, it emphasized, local authorities must identify *local* resources, not countenance demands on state resources. The commissions were to serve as provincial arms for the Special Commission in St. Petersburg.[192]

Consequently, most commissions did little more than review the clerical opinions of 1863, confirm the urgency of reform, and draft a list of conventional demands. Typical was the commission in Irkutsk, which rejected the clergy's demands for salaries as manifestly unattainable but urged steps to increase the tariff on emoluments and to encourage the construction of parsonages.[193] At most, the commissions issued appeals to parishioners, exhorting

[190] First to tap the resources of the state domains was the diocese of Kovno, which obtained the income from several state properties (yielding 5,824 rubles per annum) to aid 14 parishes (TsGIA SSSR, f. 804, op. 1, r. 1, d. 39, ll. 58–60. 62–62 ob.). The minister of state domains raised hopes still higher through a circular of November 1863, which ruled that any parish could qualify for claims to state property, even if distant from one another (ibid., d. 17, ll. 245–45 ob.). But the following year the minister took a less magnanimous position, rejecting some requests out of hand while procrastinating on others (often through peremptory demands for "additional data"). See, for example, the fate of a Kursk request for 12 pieces of state property in ibid., d. 19, ll. 12–13, 37–38, 67–68.

[191] Ibid., d. 17, ll. 152–57 (Vladimir commission journal, 20.6.1863).

[192] Ibid., ll. 213–15 ob.

[193] Ibid., d. 71, ll. 12–17, 18–26 (Irkutsk commission journals, 16.10.1863, 21.10.1863).

them to convert traditional emoluments and land into a formal, contractual tithe.[194] A handful of commissions, such as those in Khar'kov and Tver, showed somewhat greater initiative, forming special district committees under the superintendent to agitate among parishioners on behalf of such measures.[195] Most unusual was the ambitious commission in Penza, which not only drafted a specific, quantitative set of demands for supplementary land, free parish labor, and parsonages but backed it with threats to close the churches of recalcitrant parishioners: "Wherever parishioners are not in the highest degree zealous in aiding their parish clergy (who suffer an acute need for support and, especially, for parsonages), the provincial commission of Penza will either reduce the number of parishes (by attaching one to the other, insofar as proximity and communications permit) or will reduce the number of clergy at the church."[196]

But exhortations, even veiled threats, achieved little. Typical was the experience in Pskov, where the commission's appeal to city fathers met with unceremonious rejection: "Almost all the parishioners of churches in the city of Pskov announced that, while agreeing to pay the maximum possible for rites, they categorically refuse to assume the obligation of permanent, fixed contributions or a fixed tax on property to support the clergy."[197] Occasionally, parishes promised to aid the clergy but then reneged. The most famous incident involved the city duma (council) of Odessa, which first earned national praise for promising to levy a voluntary tax but later repudiated this burden on the grounds of "financial difficulties."[198] When the question of a tax was raised in Ekaterinoslav, the duma members slyly stayed home to avoid expressing any opinion, and at the assembly itself the crowd shouted down a clerical speaker with "noise, catcalls, and whistles."[199] Another celebrated case occurred in the town of Tot'ma (Vologda diocese), where parishioners responded to official demands for increased support by cheerfully agreeing to reduce the number of parishes and clergy in the town.[200] Townsmen in Kiev spurned appeals to aid the Church by declaring that "our clergy

---

[194] Ibid., d. 17, ll. 224–24 ob. (Tambov report). Some commissions advanced sundry auxiliary proposals—for additional land, higher tariffs on emoluments, construction of parsonages (through loans from monasteries), and the like. See, for example, the ingenious catalogue of demands from the commission in Kostroma (d. 54, ll. 567–70) and the comparatively radical proposals from the Petersburg commission (d. 49, ll. 263–72).

[195] Ibid., d. 57, ll. 62–63 (Khar'kov report); d. 19, ll. 33–36 (Tver report). See also "K voprosu ob uluchshenii byta dukhovenstva," SL, 1864, no. 24.

[196] TsGIA SSSR, f. 804, op. 1, r. 1, d. 48, ll. 49–49 ob. (Penza report).

[197] Ibid., d. 72, l. 87 ob. (Pskov report, 27.7.1864).

[198] Ibid., d. 41, ll. 62–63, 102–7, 119–22 ob. (Kherson).

[199] F. Mikhalevich, "Reshenie voprosa ob uluchshenii material'nogo byta pravoslavnogo dukhovenstva Ekaterinoslava," RSP, 1865, no. 1: 26–30.

[200] Moskovskie vedomosti, 1864, no. 117; S.A.K., "Opyty obespecheniia dukhovenstva obshchestvami," RSP, 1864, no. 36: 21.

does not need any assistance—they are already rich as it is."[201] Indeed, only one commission, that in Tauride diocese, could boast much success. Yet even there the commission secured agreements from only 19 percent of the parishes after three years of cajolery and threats.[202]

Empowered only to exhort and draft proposals, the provincial commissions had little to show for their effort, and a sense of failure pervades their reports to the Special Commission in Petersburg.[203] Nor was their failure lost upon contemporary observers. To quote one diocesan paper: "The [local] commission's proposal to urban and rural communities that they increase support for the staff in money, salaries, or grants of land, woods, pasture, and the like rarely met with a favorable response."[204] A priest in Tambov, plainly exasperated by the provincial commission's failure, complained in a caustic essay that these bodies had achieved virtually nothing after several years' existence.[205] State authorities, especially those with large concentrations of Old Believers, grew restless and impatient with the provincial commissions' failure, and, like the governor of Arkhangel'sk, filed formal complaints about the lack of concrete achievement.[206] Nor were prelates misled by the stacks of journals and statistical reports. One bishop formally questioned the very logic of the approach. Noting that, "with the extension of liberty in everything, [parishioners] manifest still less concern and regard for the clergy's welfare [than in earlier times]," he argued that the only effective measures would have to come from above: "For a successful conclusion to this, it is absolutely necessary to have—and without delay—direct legal measures from the imperially established Special Commission."[207]

By far the most dramatic defeat of the Valuev strategy came in the effort to create parish councils, which foundered on almost universal indifference that sometimes even turned into open opposition and anticlerical incidents. Most bishops played the mildly benevolent role dictated by the Special Commission's demand for caution and gradualism in implementing the new statute.[208] Typical was the effort by the bishop in Orel, who confined his

[201] P., "Obrazchik sodeistviia gradskikh obshchestv zabotam pravitel'stva ob uluchshenii byta dukhovenstva," *RSP,* 1864, no. 45: 367.

[202] TsGIA SSSR, f. 804, op. 1, r. 1, d. 50, ll. 96–98 (Tauride report, 19.11.1865).

[203] See, for instance, the dismal reports from Vladimir and Kaluga in ibid., dd. 60, 47.

[204] "Prikhodskie popechitel'stva i svedeniia ob otkrytii ikh po eparkhiiam," *Kievskie EV,* 1865, no. 14: 553. For a similar assessment, based upon a reading of reports from all parts of the empire, see "Vopros ob uluchshenii byta dukhovenstva v 1864 g.," ibid., 1865, no. 3: 95–106.

[205] V. Pevnitskii, "Polozhenie voprosa ob uluchshenii byta dukhovenstva v Tambovskoi eparkhii," *PO,* 1866, tom 20: 283–84.

[206] TsGIA SSSR, f. 804, op. 1, r. 1, d. 6, l. 90.

[207] Ibid., d. 65, ll. 8 ob.-9 (Tobol'sk report, 17.9.1863).

[208] See, for example, the reports from Podolia and Samara in 1865 (ibid., d. 11, ll. 492–501, 455–85).

"encouragement" to a proclamation welcoming the new councils and an instruction to priests on how best to win parish support for the venture.[209] Similarly, the bishop in Tula used his diocesan paper to publish an account of some priests' favorable experiences, to make public the annual reports on council activities and membership, and to extol the work of the more zealous councils for others to emulate.[210] But that seemed to be the limit of proper encouragement. The councils presupposed parish initiative, and their viability ultimately depended upon the laity's own interest.[211]

Though authorities in Petersburg kept a close watch on the councils and at least publicly found cause for optimism,[212] it soon became apparent that the reform had badly misfired. Difficulties became evident almost immediately. The bishop of Nizhnii Novgorod, for example, reported that councils seemed suitable for only one-eighth of the parishes in his diocese. The rest, he wrote, would not welcome councils to assist the clergy "because the peasants themselves have small allotments of land and forest, or because the parishioners are infected with the spirit of schism and are cold, even hostile, toward the Church and clergy."[213] The bishop of Kaluga reported that, one year after the statute's promulgation, only 13 parishes out of 665 had established councils, and these had thus far done little of practical significance.[214] In response to such reports the Special Commission's secretary observed that the councils "have been opened in only a few places, and so far as is known, the parish clergy (because of the novelty of this matter) have difficulty proceeding in this."[215] Even where councils had sprung up, they did little for the clergy or schools, instead diverting most of their resources to that traditional popular fetish, church construction.[216] Such reports led contemporaries, save the most determined proponents of reform, to conclude that the

[209]"Vozzvanie k sel'skim zhiteliam preosv. Polikarpa, episkopa Orlovskogo i Sevskogo, po prochtenii Polozheniia o prikhodskikh popechitel'stvakh dlia pravoslavnykh tserkvakh," *Orlovskie eparkhial'nye vedomosti*, 1865, no. 3: 98–104; "Instruktsiia," ibid., pp. 105–10.

[210]For the optimistic report by one parish priest, see I. Liubitskii, "Otkrytie prikhodskikh popechitel'stv," *Tul'skie EV*, 1867, no. 13: 4–21; for typical council resolutions, see ibid., 1867, nos. 3–7. For a survey of the general pattern, see "Prikhodskie popechitel'stva i svedeniia ob otkrytii ikh po eparkhiiam," *Kievskie EV*, 1866, no. 14.

[211]"Raznye izvestiia," *PO*, 1865, no. 2: 100–1.

[212]By 1870 the empire had some 8,000 councils, which had not only raised nearly 1 million rubles but had also—at least in one diocese, Khar'kov—begun to attack drunkenness, superstition, and other of the parishioners' foibles (*IVO [1868]*, pp. 135–36). That gave the procurator grounds to conclude that "the parish councils are increasing [in number] with each passing year, and, as their resources develop, they are expanding their sphere of activity" (*IVO [1870]*, p. 128).

[213]TsGIA SSSR, f. 804, op. 1, r. 1, d. 11, l. 486 ob. (Nizhnii Novgorod).

[214]Ibid., ll. 549–50 (Kaluga).

[215]Ibid., l. 421 (Domontovich to Isidor, 4.5.1865).

[216]Thus, in 1870, 85 percent of the budget was spent on church construction and renovation; see *IVO (1870)*, pril.

councils had failed to achieve their main task of providing assistance for the clergy.[217]

More disturbing still was the clergy's humiliating experience when they tried to persuade parishioners to form councils. Though the local council itself was to consist of the better parishioners, the entire parish first had to agree before the council could be legally constituted. Since most nobles failed to play an active role, the fate of the reform hinged on the interest of ordinary parishioners. Here was the Achilles' heel of the reform: despite the peasants' obvious lack of interest, the authorities devised no clear instrument, lay or clerical, to promote the establishment of councils.[218]

In the end it became principally the parish clergy's unenviable task to promote the councils. As Valuev had warned, the clergy's agitation on their own behalf was bound to be "awkward," not to say provocative. Their efforts to form councils fully bore out his admonition, for they often ended in a devastating, humiliating rebuff. A priest in Arkhangel'sk diocese poignantly recounted the parishioners' reaction to his suggestion that they form a parish council:

"No, No," they all began to say, "we do not need any councils whatsoever. Just let everything remain as it was in the old days." "Yes, let everything remain just as it was before, in the old days," repeated many voices. And that is how my parishioners received the statute on parish councils.[219]

A priest in Podolia diocese had a more shocking experience:

I hesitated and feared to raise the question [of forming a parish council]. And not without cause. What did I not have to listen to and to endure for the sake of opening a council! Hardly had I arrived at the assembly of my parishioners and announced to them the cause of the assembly than all those present began to whisper, mumble, and finally talk aloud. Those who stood closest to me began to laugh ironically and to beat the hem of their outer garment as a sign of shock and astonishment; those standing further away began to make sounds [of discontent]. . . .[220]

[217] *Golos*, 1865, no. 146; Ioann Gorskii, "Vzgliad sel'skogo sviashchennika na prikhodskie popechitel'stva," *SL*, 1865, no. 72: 67; I.S., "Mogut li chto sdelat' tserkovnye popechitel'stva v sel'skikh prikhodakh dlia uluchsheniia byta dukhovenstva i dlia soderzhaniia tserkvei?" ibid.. 1866, nos. 7–8.

[218] See the suggestion by a priest in 1876 that authorities, by fiat, establish councils throughout the empire: N. Nikol'skii, *Ob obshchestvennoi blagotvoritel'nosti i ee organakh—prikhodskikh popechitel'stvakh* (Moscow, 1876).

[219] A. Kolchin, "Golos sel'skogo sviaschennika," *SL*, 1866, no. 17: 5–6.

[220] S.K., "Neskol'ko slov po povodu uchrezhdeniia prikhodskikh popechitel'stv v odnom iz prikhodov podol'skoi gubernii," ibid., 1866, no. 29: 4–5.

One last report, from Orel diocese, described a priest's efforts, as the local superintendent, to encourage parishioners to form councils. In almost every parish he met with determined opposition:

> Having arrived in a given village, I gave a prayer service together with the parish clergy and afterwards read "the [bishop's] appeal" to rural residents [to form councils]. I explained to them what all this is about, what is demanded in the authorities' decree. . . . But alas! . . . I was obliged to hear the kind of exclamations and responses made by parishioners in other dioceses. Those assembled became noisy and rowdy, and everything became confused and muddled. . . . Almost all of them were shouting, drowning out one another's voices. It was possible, however, to discern the more general arguments: "Let things remain as they were! After all, our grandfathers lived that way!" "After all, priests in the old days were no worse than these [and yet required no councils]!"[221]

Such experiences only confirmed the clergy's profound skepticism toward the councils, which, as we have seen, did not elicit much enthusiasm in either the clerical opinions or the bishops' reports of 1863. As one priest in Nizhnii Novgorod dourly concluded, "the formation of councils will not in the least improve the existing forms of support for the clergy, for the peasants— amidst their poverty—envy the present condition of the clergy" and see no reason to pay for improvements.[222]

The campaign to open councils thus stalled, achieving little of its original purpose. In fact, the councils appeared in significant numbers only in those few dioceses where the confraternity tradition provided historic roots, where the authorities had created parish soviets earlier, or where a bishop's pressure caused the formation of numerous councils. But many areas, especially in the central provinces, had relatively few councils, and those represented only a small proportion of the parishes in the diocese (see table 18). Moreover, even where councils did exist, they failed to perform their primary function, namely, to improve the clergy's material condition, ideally by replacing emoluments and land with a more ample, regular income. Instead, most councils devoted almost all their funds to the construction or renovation of churches; only 4 percent of their total revenues were used to assist clergy, amounting to an average of several rubles per three-man staff (see table 19). Both the failure to establish councils and the actual work of those that did exist underscored dramatically the parishioners' refusal to aid the clergy. As one zemstvo assembly in Ekaterinoslav aptly noted in 1868, "the parish coun-

[221] N. Korol'kov, "Zametki o sovremennom byte sel'skogo dukhovenstva," ibid., 1867, no. 72: 5–6.

[222] P. Nadezhdin, "Kak mnogie dumaiut ob otkrytii pri tserkvakh prikhodskikh popechitel'stv," ibid., 1865, no. 41: 6–7.

TABLE 18

Growth of Parish Councils, 1870: Empire and Representative
Dioceses

Diocese	Number of Churches	Number of Councils	Percent with Councils
Arkhangel'sk	363	10	2.8%
Chernigov	1,170	370	31.6
Kaluga	675	33	4.9
Kazan	464	282	60.8
Kostroma	1,046	1	0.1
Moscow	1,437	25	1.7
Samara	680	451	66.3
Tver	1,126	147	13.1
Vladimir	1,155	9	0.8
Voronezh	862	43	5.0
EMPIRE	38,092	8,361	21.9%

SOURCES: *IVO, (1870); IVO (1871)*. Data for Eniseisk, Iakutsk, Perm,
Poltava, Riga, and Tomsk dioceses were lacking for 1870, and the
reports for 1871 have been used instead.

cils arouse little real enthusiasm among the people, because they see in the
regulations of these councils [merely] a new method for obtaining revenues
for the parish clergy."[223]

Perhaps most alarming to authorities, some councils displayed a tendency
common to all new social institutions of the sixties—a willingness to violate
the formal limits on their competence.[224] Parishioners had long resented the
attempt of central ecclesiastical authorities to expropriate local parish revenues for other needs; not surprisingly, some councils made haste to seize or
conceal these funds. The chief procurator complained of this problem in
1868 and reported that the Synod had had to take special measures to curtail
such abuses.[225] Elsewhere some bishops acceded to the councils' pressure, as
in Poltava, where the prelate authorized the council to display the cross and
Gospels at its meetings—implying lay control of the parish church and causing much inconvenience for the clergy who had to deliver and guard this

[223] TsGIA SSSR, f. 804, op. 1, r. 1, d. 11, l. 562 ob.

[224] For characteristic concern about such excesses, see Valuev's early memorandum on the
zemstvos (V. G. Chernukha, "Zapiska P. A. Valueva Aleksandru II o zemskikh uchrezhde-
niiakh," *Sovetskie arkhivy*, 1971, no. 4: 79–87).

[225] *IVO (1868)*, p. 137.

TABLE 19

Effectiveness and Expenditures of Parish Councils, 1870:
Empire and Representative Dioceses

		Allocation		
	Total		Charity	Aid
	Expenditures	Church	and	for
Diocese	(rubles)	Construction	Schools	Clergy
Arkhangel'sk	37	100%	0%	0%
Chernigov	11,865	93	5	2
Kaluga	1,359	31	69	0
Kazan	54,204	96	2	2
Kostroma	0	0	0	0
Moscow	4,727	55	45	0
Samara	84,592	77	5	18
Tver	7,949	54	42	4
Vladimir	4,595	62	26	12
Voronezh	2,605	90	8	2
EMPIRE	927,647	85%	11%	4%

SOURCES: *IVO (1870); IVO (1871)*. Data for Eniseisk, Iakutsk, Perm, Poltava, Riga, and Tomsk dioceses were lacking for 1870, and the reports for 1871 have been used instead.

Church property. The Poltava incident incensed Metropolitan Filaret: "Is it useful to give in to the tendencies of [this] century, which wants to undermine all that is holy and lofty, and to plunge into the murky waters of an excited populace?"[226]

Disillusionment with the councils, though slow to penetrate official reports, quickly swept the contemporary press. Typical was an essay in the secular journal *Beseda*, where an anonymous author used official data to demonstrate that the councils were few and ineffective. "Read the publications and reports of the councils' activities," he wrote, "and you will be amazed by the triviality of their activities: in one place they install a church bell, in another they repair a church fence, and in a third they bought a new shroud of Christ [*plashchanitsa*], and so forth."[227] Clerical journals were equally disparaging. A priest in Tula diocese, for example, wrote in his diocesan weekly that one could expect little good from the councils: "The parish councils in villages,

[226]TsGIA SSSR, f. 832, op. 1, d. 77, l. 75 ob. (Filaret to Synod, 15.2.1867).
[227]N.K., "Vopros o tserkovno-prikhodskikh popechitel'stvakh," *Beseda*, 1872, no. 12: 346.

consisting of landowners as chairmen, generally are ill-disposed toward the clergy, and the peasant members [on the council]—comprehending nothing of all this—sometimes not only fail to fulfill their responsibilities toward the clergy but even act in flagrant violation of their obligations."[228] Although the statute remained in force, the councils existed in name only, springing to life just to renovate the church, sullenly refusing to render aid to either the clergy or the parish schools.[229]

The experiment in parish councils—and, more broadly, community initiative—thus proved extremely disappointing: the new institution formally survived, but it brought few benefits to either the Church or the clergy. Above all, the reform reflected a central quandary of Russian Church reform: how to regulate the grass-roots response to ecclesiastical change. As the legislative discussions on councils showed, authorities were hamstrung less by canon law, tradition, and defense of clerical privilege than by uncertainty about the laity's reaction. Curiously, authorities foresaw two potential responses, polar opposites and both extreme. One was an anti-Western reaction, spurning the councils as a perverse imitation of Protestant models. More important and dominant was the second expectation, that the laity might use the new organ to harm, not help, the clergy. The reform discussions of 1863–1864 concentrated primarily on the latter issue, seeking to strike some compromise that would give the laity room for initiative but not release entirely the reins of authority. These quandaries, though important for their own sake, also suggest broader problems of reform in imperial Russia. Recently, historians have written much about the structural weaknesses in Russia autocracy, attributing inept reformism to clumsy and overly centralized administration, ministerial conflict and competition, underdeveloped infrastructures, and the emperor's wavering commitment to reform. But misfired reform also derived from a paralyzing contradiction in the thinking of enlightened officialdom: it had lost confidence in state tutelage, but as yet it had little faith in the ability of society to assume responsibility.

In the end the debates in St. Petersburg proved irrelevant: parishioners rejected the council, not because they had too much responsibility and too little power, but because they abjured its very purpose—"improvement in

[228] P. Kutepov, "O nedokonchennoi reforme dukhovenstva," *Tul'skie EV*, 1874, no. 14: 60. See also Ia. Novitskii, "K voprosu ob otkrytii tserkovnykh bratstv," *Kurskie eparkhial'nye vedomosti* [hereafter *Kurskie EV*], 1873, no. 5: 208–9.

[229] A survey of Kiev diocese in the late 1870s showed that parish councils had not only stopped growing but had even declined in recent years ("Kievskaia eparkhiia v 1878 g.," *Kievskie EV*, 1879, no. 3: 3). The diocesan paper in Saratov also painted a grim picture of the councils' inertia and suggested that local authorities had even begun to discourage the formation of new councils as a futile exercise (N. Vasil'evskii, "Sel'skie prikhodskie popechitel'-stva," *Saratovskie EV*, 1874, no. 3: 71–80).

the material condition of the clergy." Although some contemporaries put the
blame on parish clergy, claiming that they failed to proselytize for the new
organs, the real problem lay much deeper.[230] As parish priests had warned
publicly and privately, the peasantry failed to appreciate their needs and
remained completely indifferent toward helping them. In a word, peasants
wanted only a liturgical functionary and had no interest in a more professional pastor who had the education and time to catechize, preach, teach,
and perform sundry other tasks as well. As one priest cried out in despair,
"we shall never achieve an improvement in our material condition if this is
left to the will of the parishioners."[231]

Like the *ancien régime* more generally, the Church suffered from the
basic fissure of modern Russian society—a broad gap between educated
elites and the backward population in the countryside. As the bishops' opposition to parish selection of priests illustrates, the prelates opposed laicization
not so much as an encroachment on ecclesiastical privilege but as a threat to
their efforts to improve the clergy and Church. At great cost and hardship
the Church had achieved a veritable revolution in educational standards
among parish priests by the mid-nineteenth century. That achievement stood
in jeopardy if parishioners were given a free hand to choose whomever they
fancied. In a sense, reformers faced a vicious circle: parishioners refused to
provide the means that would enable priests to be true pastors; yet, until such
pastors appeared, the Church had no hope of overcoming attitudes rooted in
a narrow liturgical conception of Orthodoxy. The vicious circle, as contemporaries realized, was implicit in a popular proverb and its inverted parallel:

> "As the priest is, so too is the parish."
> "As the parish is, so too is the priest."

Valuev's invitation to society had failed to break this vicious circle, to overcome the disparity between the traditional Orthodoxy in the village and the
modernizing Orthodoxy of the institutional Church.

That failure was fraught with significance. Above all, it terminated the
state's reliance upon social initiative, precipitating a gradual return to the
prereform notions of state hegemony and tutelage. Symptomatic of the shift
was the thinking of Valuev, primary architect of the Special Commission's
strategy on reform from below. Speaking in 1867 to the more general problems of reform, Valuev was now more sensitive to the dilemmas of "stimu-

---

[230] A subsequent chief procurator, K. P. Pobedonostsev, once claimed that the parish clergy
had deliberately sabotaged the councils because they feared that the new bodies would divert
parish revenues from their own pockets into charity and schools. There is no evidence to support this claim, which primarily reflects Pobedonostsev's low regard for parish clergy. See *IVO*
(1882), p. 118.

[231] Priest M., "Eshche neskol'ko slov," *SL*, 1865, no. 95: 6.

lating social initiative" and declared that "the Russian people, for centuries, have been accustomed to strong authority and its uniform application everywhere." With reluctance but conviction, he concluded that the state must reassert its leadership: "Only government authority, balanced in its weight and with equal, forceful influence upon all the far-flung parts of our state, will be able to guide society to its further development on a true and lawful path."[232] In Church reform itself, by 1865 it was clear that more coercive, radical measures were essential if authorities were to overcome the clergy's manifold problems. Significantly, the provincial commissions—in ever growing numbers—began to suggest that the only way to obtain parish assistance was threats to reduce clergy and close churches wherever the parish failed to supply sufficient additional support.[233]

As far as the parish clergy were concerned, the bright hopes of 1863 soon dulled and disappeared. Dreams of salaries, aspirations of independence, visions of a higher pastoral status—all vanished beneath a blizzard of decrees and proposals that had virtually no effect upon the clergy's economic and social position in the parish. By the summer of 1865, reform had apparently reached a cul-de-sac, with no visible progress on the economic or any other issue of the all-enveloping clerical question. That failure provoked rising impatience and stridency in the contemporary press. As one Petersburg paper observed in May 1865, "It seems that not a single question moves so slowly here as the question of improving the clergy's material condition, although action was begun on this over a year and a half ago."[234] One angry priest even wrote that, amidst all the talk "of improving the condition of the clergy, there in fact has been a positive worsening in their condition."[235] By mid-1865, just as Dmitrii Tolstoi became the new chief procurator, the process of reform seemed to have run its course.

---

[232] Orlovsky, *Limits of Reform*, p. 75, citing a Valuev memorandum of 1867.
[233] See below, pp. 369–72.
[234] "[Peredovaia]," *S.-Peterburgskie vedomosti*, 1864, no. 100.
[235] A. Baratynskii, *O postepennom ukhudshenii byta dukhovenstva i o sovremennykh ego nadezhdakh* (Khar'kov, 1865), reprinted from *DV*.

CHAPTER 7

Great Reforms
in the Church and Clergy

I
n the late 1860s, after a decade of inconclusive talk and ineffectual
decrees, when the momentum of the Great Reforms seemed spent,
authorities in St. Petersburg suddenly promulgated fundamental
reforms in the Church and clergy. The dominant spirit in these changes was
the new procurator, D. A. Tolstoi, who displaced Valuev as the architect of
reform and acted decisively to bring this protracted process to fruition. The
result was a spate of far-reaching decrees and statutes that abolished the
hereditary soslovie, transformed the seminary, reorganized parishes, profes-
sionalized clerical service, and augmented the priest's role in the Church and
community. Still more radical plans were drafted to reform Church censorship and justice, altogether aiming to reestablish harmony between the
Church and contemporary state and society.

This chapter will examine Tolstoi's Great Reforms in Orthodoxy. The primary aim is to elucidate how and why this renowned "reactionary" engineered reform, and especially to see how it differed in method and conception from earlier visions of clerical emancipation. As will become clear, the
second half of the sixties did not mark an end to the Great Reforms but
represented a new kind of reformism that consciously sought to reassert state
authority and institutional interests.

Dmitrii Tolstoi and Church Reform

Tolstoi's long tenure as chief procurator (1865–1880) and minister of education (1866–1880) hardly seems a propitious time for Church reform. Per-

haps only his successor to the post of chief procurator, K. P. Pobedonostsev, could compete for the title of chief reactionary in imperial Russia.[1] After an undistinguished career in the ministries of interior and education, in 1861 Tolstoi became a member of the Senate, where he earned notoriety for a memorandum condemning the emancipation of serfs, mainly on the grounds that in its present form emancipation spelled ruin for the Russian nobility.[2] But Tolstoi's black reputation derives mainly from his later service as minister of education and, in the 1880s, as minister of the interior. In both positions he earned the animosity of genteel society no less than of the revolutionary left for his repressive measures to stifle nihilism and reimpose strong autocratic rule on the universities, zemstvos, and villages. Only in recent years have historians begun to reconsider the traditional view of Tolstoi, derived primarily from prerevolutionary historiography and contemporary publicistic accounts. His role in Church reform will further reinforce the revisionist view of Tolstoi, revealing a bureaucrat of surprising liberality who favored abolition of the soslovie, radical restructuring of Church censorship, democratization of administration, and even corporate assemblies for the parish clergy.

That liberality, however, had its own underlying—and rarely articulated—mainsprings. Above all, Tolstoi remained a *gosudarstvennik*, a bureaucrat who identified with the needs of the state, not his own class (the nobility), and still less with an amorphous "society." Emanating from the circle of state-minded reformers around Grand Duke Konstantin Nikolaevich, Tolstoi, like the other "Konstantinovtsy," placed highest priority on designing reforms to serve broader state or institutional interests, with only secondary concern for their impact upon specific sosloviia and social groups.[3] That statist attitude was reinforced by a highly unflattering conception of the common people. Tolstoi nourished no Slavophile illusions about the hidden virtues of Russia's "dark masses": "In the abstract, when the best traits

[1] The historiography, almost uniformly hostile to Tolstoi, has generated bizarre misrepresentations—that Tolstoi "did very little as procurator" or, without purpose, mindlessly reduced the number of parishes (the quotation is from James Mills, "Dimitrii Tolstoi as Minister of Education in Russia, 1866–1880" [Ph.D. diss., Indiana University, 1967], p. 39). For a revisionist view of Tolstoi as minister of education, see Alston, *Education and the State*, pp. 87–104, and, especially, Sinel, *The Classroom and the Chancellery*.

[2] OR GBL, f. 327/I, k. 22, d. 33 (D. A. Tolstoi, "Kak osushchestvilis' by na praktike predpolozheniia Redaktsionnoi komissii, esli by oni byli utverzhdeny"). See also "Pis'mo D. A. Tolstogo [aprelia 1861 g.]," *RA*, 1905, no. 4: 687–89.

[3] For Tolstoi's background as a "Konstantinovets," see Beyrau, "Von der Niederlage," p. 45, and Kipp, "Grand Duke Konstantin Nikolaevich," p. 2. The mentality of *gosudarstvennik* prevailed to the end of Tolstoi's career; see, for example, his report as minister of interior in the 1880s, summarized in Theodore Taranovsky, "The Politics of Counter-Reform: Autocracy and Bureaucracy in the Reign of Alexander III, 1881–1894" (Ph.D. diss., Harvard University, 1976), pp. 407–33.

of the Russian character are considered, one can idealize the Russian people. But when one sees them up close, in ordinary life, as they exist in reality, this imaginary ideal dissipates like a fog, and before one there arises images that are impossible to love."[4] Though Tolstoi later held such remarks in check,[5] he would not nourish hopes for local initiative, the Special Commission's strategy in the early 1860s. Yet Tolstoi was determined to achieve reform, for he believed it essential that the clergy provide popular education and combat the Catholic menace in Russia's western provinces.[6] From the first, insiders realized that this conservative envisioned major reforms, and Tolstoi's first annual report—published for all to see—put society and Church on notice of his ambitions.[7]

Significantly, Tolstoi embarked on reform with strong episcopal sympathies but soon experienced a change of heart, growing intensely dissatisfied with his principal collaborators in governing the Church. It was a pattern, as we have seen, that constantly recurred in the relationship between the chief procurator and the ranking prelates. Initially, Tolstoi came to his post with the implicit trust of the bishops: his scholarly study of Catholicism in Russia had elicited high praise from prelates and partly explains why Akhmatov recommended him to be chief procurator and why the hierarchs responded so favorably to his appointment.[8] He also gave every promise of heeding the bishops' views, reportedly declaring that "earlier the chief procurator's task was to defend lay interests from encroachment by the Church, but now it is to defend the Church from attacks by secular authorities."[9] He backed those words with action: in late 1865 he supported plans to modify the Church's system of judicial appeals in a fashion that would greatly augment the role of diocesan bishops—much to the consternation of state officials and white

---

[4]OR GBL, f. 231/III, k. 26, d. 22 (Tolstoi to Pogodin, 28.9.1861).

[5]One notorious exception was his declaration that the peasants, given their backwardness and illiteracy, could only be governed through selective use of corporal punishment (quoted in Taranovsky, "Politics of Counter-Reform," p. 189).

[6]See below, pp. 302-8.

[7]"Iz zapisok senatora K. Lebedeva," *RA*, 1911, no. 7: 364. For the report, see *Vsepoddanneishaia dokladnaia zapiska ober-prokurora Sv. Sinoda, gr. D. A. Tolstogo, o deiatel'nosti pravoslavnogo dukhovnogo vedomstva s iiunia 1865 g. po ianvar' 1866 g.* (St. Petersburg, 1866), pp. 41, 49–50, 63–64, 66.

[8]Tolstoi's book originally appeared in French (*Le Catholicisme romain en Russie*, 2 vols. [St. Petersburg, 1863–64]). As he explained to Katkov, his purpose "was to acquaint foreigners with the Latin-Polish question in western Russia and to resurrect historical facts that have been deliberately distorted" (OR GBL, f. 120 [M. N. Katkov], k. 11, d. 17, ll. 2–2 ob. [Tolstoi to Katkov, 9.10.1863]). The volume appeared in Russian translation in 1876 (*Rimskii katolitsizm v Rossii*). For praise of his book, see the letter from Metropolitan Arsenii in 1864 (OR GPB, f. 780 [D. A. Tolstoi], d. 2, l. 1); for the favorable response to his appointment, see the congratulatory letters in TsGIA SSSR, f. 797, op. 35, otd. 1, d. 149.

[9]Beliaev, "Kazanskii i ego perepiska," *BV*, 1911, no. 9: 123.

clergy.[10] But over the next few years Tolstoi, encountering opposition from ranking prelates to his reform plans, underwent a shift in perspective and began to support the parish clergy at the expense of episcopal prerogative. That new attitude, as we shall see, found its fullest expression in the project for judicial reform in the early 1870s.

The burst of reforms in the late 1860s was not due solely to Tolstoi's determination. One important precondition, no doubt, was the death in 1867 of Metropolitan Filaret, a stalwart champion of the old order and a skeptic when it came to change, especially in his later years. Though Tolstoi managed to overcome Filaret's opposition to seminary reform in 1867, the prelate's death later that year greatly facilitated the procurator's task in subsequent reforms. A former procurator, A. P. Tolstoi, had once declared that Filaret "is the last dike—raze it, the water will pour through, roaring in and inundating everything."[11] Dmitrii Tolstoi had precisely the same perception, and on the day of Filaret's funeral he allegedly exclaimed, "[His death is] an enormous loss, but I'll tell you frankly that his death has untied our hands."[12]

The rapid pace of reform also derived from a growing conviction that change was undeferrable, that hasty reform was better than none at all. According to Metropolitan Isidor, Tolstoi conceded basic flaws in the new seminary statute but explained frankly to the emperor that something had to be done immediately.[13] Not only liberal priests but also many bishops shared that conviction. Bishop Nafanail of Arkhangel'sk, for example, wrote Tolstoi that "the needs of our Mother, the Church, are great and ubiquitous," and Archbishop Dmitrii of Kherson noted the mounting impatience of parish clergy: "The clergy awaits with impatience a better order in its material and, especially, moral condition."[14] At the same time, the government appeared more disposed to assist reform, partly because its own fiscal crisis had eased, partly because the assassination attempt on the emperor in 1866 increased the government's desire to bolster the Church and religion. Altogether, the climate was highly favorable to an aggressive procurator. And Tolstoi was just that kind of procurator.

[10]To deal with dissatisfaction over the Synod's review of appeals against diocesan bishops, Tolstoi proposed to distribute the appeals to all diocesan prelates for comment and judgment. Alexander created a special committee to review the proposal, designating the chief procurator, several members of the Synod, and four high-ranking state officials. Within a few months, the committee was deadlocked: a majority (the bishops and Tolstoi) favored the reform; a minority (the state officials and two archpriests of the Synod) vehemently opposed it, evidently because the measure would only augment the bishops' power. OR GPB, f. 573, no. AI.60, ll. 155–57 (Tolstoi to Isidor, 18.10.1865); L'vov, Pis'ma, pp. 651–52.

[11]"Iz zapisok preosv. Leonida," RA, 1907, no. 10: 150 (4.6.1864).

[12]OR GBL, f. 149, d. 20, g. 1871, l. 17 (Leonid's diary, 22.6.1871).

[13]L'vov, Pis'ma, p. 350 (Isidor to Filaret, 3.10.1867).

[14]TsGIA SSSR, f. 797, op. 35, otd. 1, d. 149, ll. 31–31 ob. (Nafanail to Tolstoi, 19.6.1865), 53 ob. (Dmitrii to Tolstoi, 26.6.1865).

Reform and the Special Commission

At Tolstoi's behest, the Special Commission adopted several major reforms in the clergy's system of service, hereditary estate order, and social and economic status. In many respects Tolstoi simply drew heavily upon earlier data, proposals, and draft projects, and brought that work to fruition. His tie to past efforts, moreover, was also apparent in strategy, for Tolstoi made one more attempt to appeal to society for support, this time turning to the zemstvo for aid to the clergy and parish schools. But when that scheme failed, Tolstoi struck out in a new direction, giving an entirely different meaning to the idea of "emancipation of the clergy."

Tolstoi's Appeal to the Zemstvo

By 1865 the old strategy for reform from below had clearly failed. Neither parish councils nor provincial commissions had proved effective in marshaling new resources to aid the clergy. That failure was painfully evident in the procurator's annual reports, which listed instances of local assistance to the clergy; few in number, small in scale, they did nothing to solve the clerical question.[15] As publicists, especially clerical ones, endlessly wrote, the search for local solutions had foundered, primarily on the parishioners' callous indifference to the clergy's needs.[16] The failure was, understandably, a cause of great disappointment. To quote one archpriest: "A great deal has been written and even said about improvements in the material and nonmaterial condition of the clergy (indeed, they still have not stopped writing and talking about this), but so far nothing substantial has been done."[17] The failure to reform evoked dark gloom among the clergy: "With each passing year the rural clergy is losing hope as it waits for the long-sought and urgently required improvement" in its economic condition.[18]

Thus it is all the more surprising that Tolstoi made one last attempt to solicit aid from below. His approach differed from past attempts in that he appealed to the zemstvo, the new organ of self-government established in 1864 to handle various local needs. One such need, public education, pertained directly to the clergy, who had established parish schools in recent

---

[15] *IVO (1866)*, pp. 130–32; *IVO (1867)*, pp. 157–58; *IVO (1868)*, pp. 241–44; *IVO (1869)*, pp. 247–50.

[16] V. Pevnitskii, "Polozhenie voprosa ob uluchshenii byta dukhovenstva v Tambovskoi eparkhii," *PO*, 1866, no. 20: 283–84; A. Zaitsev, "Kak reshaetsia vopros ob uluchshenii byta dukhovenstva," *DV*, 12 (1865): 684–95.

[17] I. Liubomirskii, "K voprosu ob uluchshenii byta pravoslavnogo dukhovenstva v Rossii," *SL*, 1866, no. 1: 5–6.

[18] Ponomarev, "Dvizhenie i sovremennoe polozhenie voprosa ob uluchshenii byta pravoslavnogo dukhovenstva," *RSP*, 1866, no. 1: 18.

years and still hoped to receive assistance (even salaries) for their trouble. Although an appeal to the zemstvos seemed reasonable enough, it was clearly fraught with difficulties. Quite apart from evidence of the zemstvos' indifference, even hostility, toward the clergy,[19] the new organs suffered from serious economic weaknesses and were hard pressed even to meet their statutory obligations. As one journal warned, "there is no reason for the clergy to count heavily on [assistance] from our poor zemstvo. there is no reason to look upon it like a suitcase full of money, passed out to everyone like a pension."[20]

Still, the zemstvo bore responsibility for primary education, and some of its leaders seemed eager to give the clergy a major role in the schoolroom.[21] That idea appealed strongly to Tolstoi, who, mainly for reasons of sheer practicality, sought to give the clergy primary responsibility in popular education. The clergy, he argued, "represent the most readily available teachers, especially in our country (and for a long time to come)." To warnings of "clericalism," Tolstoi replied:

> Unfortunately, we live and are guided by phrases that have been translated from foreign languages. From there our enlighteners have discovered that there is clericalism in Europe, that this clericalism is the enemy of freedom, etc.; but they have not realized that clericalism is only possible where there is ultramontanism. Here everything is reversed; our clergy not only does not attempt to seize control of secular affairs but unfortunately is characterized by apathy and indifference.[22]

Thus Tolstoi hoped that the zemstvo would provide support for clerical participation in primary education and even render direct assistance to the clergy.

At Tolstoi's suggestion the Special Commission turned to the zemstvo for assistance in early 1866. Upon reviewing the opinions of parish clergy and the reports of diocesan authorities in 1863, it concluded that the fundamental weakness of parish schools was inadequate financing and that, "if they continue to exist, it is not because of outside assistance, but primarily because of

---

[19]There were even some attempts to exclude clergy from participating in the zemstvo; see, for example, "Letopis' sovremennoi zhizni," *Nedelia*, 1866, no. 10: 153–54, and I. S. Belliustin, "Dukhovenstvo i zemstvo," *Dukh khristianina*, 4 (1865): 467–84. Interestingly, Metropolitan Filaret opposed clerical participation in the zemstvo, noting (as did many zemstvos subsequently) the contradiction between the clergy's involvement and their tax-exempt status (TsGIA SSSR, f. 796, op. 146, g. 1865, d. 171, ll. 4 ob.–6; Filaret, *Pis'ma Antoniiu*, 4: 453; Filaret, *SMO*, 5: 454–57).

[20]*Glasnyi sud*, 1867, no. 265.

[21]"Uluchshenie byta dukhovenstva," *SL*, 1866, no. 32: 1–2.

[22]OR GBL, f. 120, k. 11, d. 17, l. 5 (Tolstoi to Katkov, 25.3.1866).

the zeal and sacrifices of clergy, whose own material resources—scanty as they are—are insufficient to provide these schools with permanent support."[23] The commission also noted other weaknesses, such as meddling by state officials and peasant indifference, but held up finances as the principal problem. To expand the clergy's role in education, the commission urged that the Church be given a major role in supervising education, that seminaries offer special pedagogical training, and that society provide financial support for parish schools. Here its hopes rested mainly with the zemstvo: "Because the clergy lack the means to support the elementary schools that they have founded, and because it is impossible to demand significant sums from the state treasury, it is necessary to turn to the zemstvo with the proposal [that it]: (a) build schoolhouses, provide heat, light, and maintenance; (b) provide support for the teachers; and (c) provide the means to acquire books and teaching aids for the schools."[24] On behalf of the commission, Tolstoi sent a circular to zemstvo chairmen, stressing the zemstvo's responsibility in education and the potential importance of parish clergy in this task. He noted the extraordinary growth in parish schools, which by 1865 numbered over 21,000 and had an enrollment of some 400,000 pupils. He warned that these schools suffered from woefully insufficient financing and appealed to the zemstvo to ensure their preservation and development.[25]

The replies, however, were immensely disappointing.[26] To be sure, some zemstvos appropriated modest sums (usually several hundred rubles, at most a few thousand rubles), which elicited formal letters of gratitude from the chief procurator. But such appropriations hardly sufficed for a single school, much less the hundreds potentially needed in a diocese. Moreover, some zemstvos refused outright to appropriate funds, asserting that the zemstvo had other, more urgent obligations and that additional taxation on behalf of parish schools was out of the question. For example, the zemstvo chairman in Mirgorod district expressed sympathy for parish schools but declined to provide funds, "because this is linked to significant expenditures that would require an increase in the land tax."[27] The chairman of the zemstvo in Putivl counseled that the zemstvo must wait until more means become available, prompting a vexed Tolstoi to scribble in the margin: "That will be a long

[23]TsGIA SSSR, f. 804, op. 1, r. 1, d. 471, ll. 61 ob.–62 (zhurnal, no. 21).

[24]Ibid., ll. 59–137 ob.; d. 91, ch. 1, ll. 101–10 ob.; PSZ (2), 41: 43053. Simultaneously, to stir zemstvo involvement, the Special Commission authorized provincial commissions to invite zemstvo representatives to their sessions (TsGIA SSSR, f. 804, op. 1, r. 3, d. 471, ll. 139–45 ob. [zhurnal, no. 22]).

[25]TsGIA SSSR, f. 804, op. 1, r. 3, d. 471, ll. 147–52 ob. (draft circular); d. 91, ch. 1, ll. 189–90 (circular, 5.3.1866).

[26]See the overview in Blagovidov, Deiatel'nost', pp. 72–76.

[27]TsGIA SSSR, f. 804, op. 1, r. 1, d. 91, ch. 2, l. 242 ob. See also the materials on Valdai (ll. 183-83 ob.), Tsaritsyn (l. 131), and Lebediansk (l. 223).

wait!"[28] In Ekaterinoslav district the zemstvo chairman proposed to support the parish schools by sequestering parish land, a scheme that infuriated Tolstoi: "I.e., rob the clergy!"[29] Furthermore, some zemstvos challenged Tolstoi's assumption that the clergy should dominate primary education. The zemstvo assembly in Borzna district argued that the clergy might be given responsibility for religious instruction in schools but that the regular "teachers should be found amongst the people themselves: it is easier for them to inspire trust than teachers from other estates, [and] they will more quickly grasp what one needs to teach the people."[30] The district zemstvo in Tim (Kursk province) repeated an oft-cited argument that the clergy lacked the time and training to teach effectively "because they are often distracted by parish duties and because most rural priests have not received the necessary pedagogical training."[31] Such declarations were very disappointing to Tolstoi, who wrote "Very regrettable!" on the report from Kazan, which stated that "the zemstvo shares the view that one can form public schools for the rural population without the clergy."[32] As Tolstoi explained to the emperor in a formal report of 1867, the zemstvos had appropriated 109,929 rubles for education, but almost nothing for parish schools. The procurator observed that, as the data clearly show, "the zemstvos in most provinces are sympathetic to the cause of popular education, but the sums hitherto allotted for this are woefully inadequate, even for the most modest support of the present rural schools." He attributed this disappointing response not to the zemstvos' lack of resources but to their "immaturity," which impelled them to devise grandiose plans for new schools while ignoring a network of parish schools that already existed.[33]

Zemstvos were still less responsive to appeals for direct economic assistance to the clergy. As one observer noted, "in many areas the zemstvo took up the question [of improving the clergy's economic condition] and responded to it with indifference."[34] Indeed, the provincial zemstvo in Kazan implicitly blamed the clergy's economic problems on their own ineffectiveness: "The clergy's poverty does require measures, but in a large degree these measures depend upon the clergy and ecclesiastical authorities, and these should consist of the establishment of direct, vital bonds between parish and clergy

[28] Ibid., ll. 197-97 ob. (Putivl').
[29] Ibid., l. 299 ob. (Ekaterinoslav).
[30] Ibid., ll. 312 ob.–13.
[31] Ibid., l. 214 (Tim); see also l. 49 (Mglinsk).
[32] Ibid., l. 30 ob.
[33] Ibid., r. 1, d. 93, ll. 60–64 ob. Without zemstvo support, parish schools declined rapidly. Between 1866 and 1870 their number decreased from 19,436 to 13,914. For details on individual dioceses, see the appendixes to the annual volumes of *IVO*.
[34] S.P.P., "Eshche neskol'ko slov po voprosu ob uluchshenii byta dukhovenstva," *SL*, 1867, no. 45: 6–7.

(which, unfortunately, are now sundered), without which a proper relationship between the pastor and his flock is inconceivable."[35] Some zemstvos even exuded anticlerical sentiments, as delegates, especially peasants, seized the opportunity to denounce the clergy for solicitation and abuse.[36] There were some exceptions, however. For example, three district zemstvos in one province voted to convert traditional emoluments into a fixed parish tithe.[37] The zemstvo in Riazan also seemed sympathetic to the clergy's needs and showed genuine interest in the proposal of one delegate (an influential priest) that parish land be surrendered to laymen in exchange for a regular salary.[38] But most zemstvos gave little attention to the clerical question or refused outright to put it on the agenda. By 1870 contemporaries judged the effort a clear failure: "When the government invited the zemstvos to seek means to alleviate this evil [clerical poverty], they found no resources for this."[39] In his own convoluted prose Tolstoi admitted the truth of such assessments: "Since the time of the founding of the zemstvo institution, our clergy has not abandoned hope in finding sympathy in the zemstvo for its material needs and active assistance in meeting these. For the time being, this hope is realized in only a few provinces and in small amounts."[40] Indeed, not until the 1890s would the zemstvo become a significant factor in promoting public education. When Tolstoi appealed in 1866, it had neither the means nor the desire to finance the development of parish schools.[41]

Reform in the Western Provinces

Though the Special Commission made provincial boards responsible for easing the lot of most clergy, it continued its work on the western provinces as the emperor had ordered. Despite the sums allocated by the state in 1863–1864 (600,000 rubles) the commission as yet was unable to achieve the long-sought conversion of natural obligations into monetary dues. That task became more urgent with each passing year. The Third Section complained of the clergy's shortcomings and, rather optimistically, declared that "if our

[35] TsGIA SSSR, f. 804, op. 1, r. 1, d. 91, ch. 2, ll. 30 ob.-31.

[36] See A. Drozdov, "Nechto o zemstve," *Saratovskie EV*, 1867, no. 5: 155–67; N. Demert, "Zemstvo i sel'skoe dukhovenstvo," *Nedelia*, 1868, no. 5: 150–153.

[37] TsGIA SSSR, f. 804, op. 1, r. 1, d. 21/a, ll. 149–52, 177–78; f. 796, op. 149, g. 1868, d. 303, ll. 1–8 (Kazan).

[38] Ibid., f. 804, op. 1, r. 1, d. 21/a, ll. 136–46 (Riazan).

[39] "Meropriiatiia 1869 g. po preobrazovaniiu byta dukhovenstva," *Kievskie EV*, 1870, no. 2: 35–36. See also "O noveishikh reformakh dukhovenstva," *Nedelia*, 1868, no. 32: 995.

[40] *IVO (1868)*, pp. 244–45; *IVO (1869)*, pp. 250–53.

[41] The standard account is B. B. Veselovskii, *Istoriia zemstva za sorok let*, 4 vols. (St. Petersburg, 1911), 1:447–592. For an incisive summary, see A. B. Eklof, "Spreading the Word: Primary Education and the Zemstvo in Moscow Province, 1864–1910" (Ph.D. diss., Princeton University, 1977), pp. 160–90.

clergy possessed the proper moral qualities, the number of conversions from Catholicism [to Orthodoxy] would increase significantly."[42] Similarly, the governor-general of Kiev, A. P. Bezak, warned that "the white clergy—almost everywhere, but especially in the rural areas—is devoid of that significance which by right and by calling it should possess." Reciting the clergy's many problems, such as its social dependence and poverty, Bezak stressed that "there is thus an urgent need to improve the clergy's condition and, at the same time, to free the parishioners of the mandatory obligations in kind that bear the character of *barshchina* and give rise to unpleasant conflicts."[43]

Early in 1866, spurred by Bezak's urgent report to the emperor, the Special Commission renewed its work on reform in the western provinces. This time, however, it sought a *gradual* conversion of natural obligations, beginning first with the labor obligation and using the funds already allocated by the state. Such conversion required a further 400,000 rubles, which the commission proposed to raise through a special land tax and diversion of some existing revenues (*protsentnyi sbor*). Though Valuev still insisted that responsibility rested with the community, he too agreed to the necessity of a "temporary exception" in this case.[44] Minister of Finance M. Kh. Reutern proved intractable, however. He warned that the proposed levy "would fall primarily upon the poll-tax classes, which are already burdened with significant direct levies"; hence the levy could hardly achieve its avowed purpose of "establishing good relations between the clergy and parishioners." Instead, he argued, it was far more "desirable that such assessments be established by the parishioners themselves through a voluntary agreement."[45]

The commission stood firm. Though it regarded the cost estimates provided by Bezak as unduly low, it agreed to adopt them as a temporary solution.[46] Its proposal sailed through the State Council, which, no doubt heedful of past failures to elicit "voluntary agreements" and mindful of the emperor's intense concern for the western provinces, ignored Reutern's arguments and levied a land tax to raise the required sum of 400,000 rubles.[47] With the funds available, in 1867 the commission abolished all natural obligations in kind, thereby annulling the parish reform of 1842 for the six southwestern provinces. Two years later it received additional funds to extend the reform

---

[42] TsGAOR, f. 109, op. 223, g. 1866, d. 31, ll. 126–26 ob.

[43] TsGIA SSSR, f. 796, op. 205, d. 349, ll. 73–74 ob. (report to the emperor).

[44] Ibid., f. 804, op. 1, r. 3, d. 471, ll. 188 ob.–94 (note from minister of interior, 18.4.1866).

[45] Ibid., ll. 185–86 ob. (note from minister of finances, 24.3.1866). Bezak, who had first recommended a land tax, ridiculed Reutern's homilies about "voluntary" agreements, noting that few parishes agreed to conclude such commitments and that, when they did, they offered sums as small as 2.50 rubles per year (ibid., ll. 194–203).

[46] Ibid., ll. 156–227 (zhurnal, no. 23).

[47] Ibid., r. 1, d. 92, ll. 2/b–2/c.

to the northwestern provinces as well.[48] The reform significantly increased clerical stipends (from 100–180 rubles to 300 rubles), though at the price of abolishing all the parishioners' obligations in kind—labor, parsonage, firewood, and the like. The new decrees thus terminated a long-festering conflict, but on terms far less favorable to the clergy than any countenanced in the late 1850s. This new order demonstrated not only Tolstoi's effectiveness in autocratic politics but also his willingness to violate clerical interest for the higher benefit of the Church and State.

Abolition of the Clerical Estate

By the mid-1860s most publicists and bureaucrats agreed that the soslovie system, generally deemed harmful to the natural development of a society, had inflicted special harm on the clergy. To authorities, at least, the most obvious dysfunction was the tendency of the soslovie to overproduce candidates, who still numbered in the hundreds in most dioceses in the 1860s. In 1867, for example, reports to the Synod showed 658 "idle youths" in Vladimir, 509 in Kaluga, 733 in Kursk, 800 in Tver, and 770 in Tula—little improvement, if any, over the 1850s.[49] But the principal criticism concerned the social consequences of that hereditary order—the special culture and style that set the clergy apart, the press of family claims that overrode merit in appointment, the routine channeling of sons into the priesthood without regard to commitment and zeal. Whether described by the more conventional term "soslovie" or the more pejorative "caste," the clergy should be transformed into an open social group, with sons free to leave and outsiders free to enter. The main task, believed many, was to demolish entirely the clergy's "casteness."[50]

The soslovie order had its defenders nevertheless. Most significant of all, the parish clergy itself showed far less interest in the elimination of the estate system than did contemporary society. Few rank-and-file clergy, even liberal publicists like Belliustin, demanded systematic abolition of the hereditary order.[51] The most outspoken defense of the soslovie appeared in an anonymous memorandum of 1866 entitled "Is the Orthodox Clergy a Caste?" It complained that "'Levitism,' 'caste order,' 'separateness,' and 'immobility' are the favorite expressions of contemporary Russian publicists" but that in fact the clergy do not constitute a genuine caste: sons of the clergy *do* leave,

[48] Ibid., r. 3, d. 472, ll. 192–203 ob. (zhurnal, no. 33); *PSZ (2)*, 45: 48139.

[49] TsGIA SSSR, f. 796, op. 148, g. 1867, d. 224, ll. 15, 22, 30, 54, 62.

[50] See, for example: *Sovremennye izvestiia*, 1868, no. 213; *Moskovskie vedomosti*, 1867, no. 275; "Iz pisem," *SL*, 1865, no. 23: 4–5.

[51] See above, p. 210.

outsiders *can* enter the clergy (even if few wish to do so). The problem, argued the author, was not the clergy's "casteness" but the "general disinclination" of lay society to enter the clergy, evidently because laymen believed that the priest, "by his very rank, is something of little value, unimportant, insignificant." Indeed, authorities should seek to reinforce, not disband, the clerical estate, not only because of potential shortages of candidates but also because of the soslovie's great service and stability.

> Members of this estate, created by life itself, are directed from childhood toward sacred service, perform it humbly and meekly; [this estate] staunchly preserves the dogma and typicon of the Holy Church; without external glitter, without fanfare, it develops and strengthens the religious feelings and taste of the people, without meddling in matters and the relations of other estates; it supports the principle of state law (which is not apparent to everyone); in spite of indifference and opposition by the very same people whose welfare they seek to secure, they bear the heavy burdens of their service with patience, with the most paltry compensation for their labors, hoping only for generosity from the Lord on High.[52]

Still, most authorities held a contrary view, regularly embodied in the memoranda of high-ranking officials like Valuev or in the bishops' reports to the commission in 1863. All urged abolition of the hereditary soslovie.

That consensus underlay a Synodal resolution of 1867 that summarily abrogated family claims to clerical positions. It noted that such claims, rooted in custom, had obtained legal recognition in the 1823 statute on the clerical poor, which authorized bishops to transfer positions to qualified candidates who married daughters or otherwise agreed to support the previous cleric and his family. Given the Church's lack of pensions, clerical positions had in effect been the only kind of "capital" available for such welfare. As Tolstoi explained in his accompanying note on the Synod's resolution, this kind of welfare entailed a plethora of problems—candidates with family claims demanded precedence over candidates of merit, positions remained vacant until daughters reached marriageable age, new clerics had to share their meager income with sundry in-laws, diocesan authorities had to untangle suits and settle feuds, and, in any event, such "deals are not consistent with the significance of the clerical rank and Church law."[53] Curiously, in contrast to so much reform legislation, this decree did not follow months of deliberation and reams of memoranda. It appeared quite suddenly, reflecting perhaps Tolstoi's decisive influence, since the decree so baldly embodied his general policy of placing the Church's interests before those of the soslovie. But

[52] TsGIA SSSR, f. 832, op. 1, d. 85, ll. 1–18 ob.
[53] Ibid., f. 1149, op. 7, g. 1867, d. 72, ll. 2–7 (Tolstoi to State Council).

the resolution also reflected longstanding criticisms of family claims, which, at least from an institutional perspective, were difficult to justify. Because the 1823 statute had been confirmed by the state, the Synod could not simply promulgate its order but first had to obtain the approval of the State Council and emperor. The Council readily concurred with the reform: "As a form of charity for aged clergy and [after death] their families, the appointment of relatives and children to positions is hereby abolished; in filling vacancies that appear upon death or retirement of clergy from service, [in selecting] among candidates in diocesan jurisdiction, do not consider kinship with the deceased or retired [cleric] as a circumstance giving precedence over other persons." The new decree also attacked the custom of "reserving places" for daughters (whereby "the right of appointment to these positions [belonged to] candidates who marry such girls") and strictly forbade diocesan authorities to enforce such contracts.[54]

That same year the Special Commission began deliberations on the problem of clerical children (especially sons) and their ascription to the clerical soslovie. The Church had long been concerned about the plethora of superfluous candidates and had taken some measures. For example, in 1851 it authorized clergy to educate their sons in secular schools, and in 1865 it empowered bishops to release seminary graduates from Church jurisdiction without Synodal approval.[55] Such measures, however, only loosened the soslovie bonds that still tethered most youths to the Church, as the large number of "idle youths" continued to attest. The Special Commission had made the surfeit of youth one of its principal concerns from the outset and had specifically raised this problem in its diocesan survey of 1863. But in its first years the commission concentrated primarily upon the economic question, turning attention to the soslovie question only in 1867.

The impetus to action—as so often in nineteenth-century Church reform—came from the western provinces, this time in a report from the governor-general of Kiev, A. P. Bezak. With unabashed candor, Bezak raised the issue of reform in the clerical soslovie as something essential for the state, especially in the western provinces. He noted that, even after the 1863 Polish uprising, the bureaucracy in the western region still consisted largely of Catholic Polish nobility. The government's attempts to Russify the personnel in local administration had achieved little thus far. The reason, he explained, was the peculiar social system of the area: the nobility consisted mainly of Poles, the townspeople were Jewish, and the peasantry was unfit for government service. However, the state had hitherto failed to tap one valuable

---

[54]Ibid., ll. 2–7, 11–14; f. 796, op. 148, g. 1867, d. 123; *PSZ (2)*, 42:44610.

[55]TsGIA SSSR, f. 797, op. 35, otd. 1, d. 239, ll. 1–2 (procurator to Alexander II, 29.9.1865); *PSZ (2)*, 40: 42507.

source of manpower, the sons of Orthodox clergy, who were both Russian and qualified. Unfortunately, the clergy's children, locked inside the clerical estate, rarely matriculated in state schools and seldom entered state service. In contrast to Germany and England, where pastors' sons entered "all forms of state service and culture," Russia's clerical sons were blocked from such roles: "In our country (with a few exceptions, due to special circumstances) seminarians who do not receive priests' positions can only become sacristans or become the victims of need and poverty, and from time to time because of their excess numbers, are dispatched *en masse* to military service along with peasants and vagrants." In order to rechannel this wasted talent into state service, Bezak proposed to separate seminarians from the clerical estate and confer upon them a secular legal status, to eliminate legal impediments to careers in civil service, and to offer free education in state schools, especially wherever Catholics constituted a majority.[56] Though in some respects curiously outdated (for example, in the reference to clerical conscriptions, which had long ceased to have meaning), Bezak's memorandum tried to solve the old problem of the state's need for trained manpower in a wholly new way—by dismantling the traditional soslovie order.

The commission reviewed closely both the diocesan survey of 1863 and Bezak's memorandum, and in December 1868 it adopted formal recommendations on the status of clerical children. It recognized the existence of many complex factors, but concluded—like the bishops—that the main barrier to exit from the clerical soslovie was the multitude of legal disabilities, especially those inspiring fear of consignment to the lowly poll-tax population: "Instead of transferring from the ecclesiastical rank to the poll-tax statuses, they regard it as preferable to wait a few years for a position in the ecclesiastical domain than to deprive themselves and their children of the right to exemption from recruitment and poll-tax obligations." The commission therefore recommended that the clergy be given a relatively privileged status, beneath nobility but above commoners—namely, the semiprivileged status of "honored citizen" (*pochetnoe grazhdanstvo*), hereditary for priests' sons, personal for sacristans' sons.[57] This status conferred the right to enter service or to engage in any business without risk of descending into the poll-tax population. In effect, it nullified the discriminatory articles of the *Digest of Laws* that blocked access for clerical sons to state service. To add substance to this new status, the commission also urged the Ministry of Education—Tolstoi's other domain—to grant special tuition exemptions, particularly in

---

[56] TsGIA SSSR, f. 804, op. 1, r. 1, d. 104, ch. 1, ll. 3–22, 25–26 ob.

[57] Isidor insisted that priests' sons have the rank of personal noble, but the commission's lay secretary, I. G. Tersinskii, objected, arguing that one cannot "inherit" personal nobility—which in fact was the very meaning of the status (ibid., ll. 211–12 ob.).

the southwest.[58] The commission then drafted specific legislation proposing twenty-two changes in the *Digest of Laws*, and in January 1869 it transmitted its proposals to that overseer of government law, the State Council, for formal consideration.[59]

Significantly, on this occasion the State Council, which so often torpedoed legislation on Church reform, accepted the draft, even though this proposal directly attacked the foundations of the soslovie order. The Council did raise two questions, however. First, it challenged the commission's plan to bestow the rank of "hereditary honored citizen" on priests' sons, explaining that the Department of Laws had already received numerous complaints about the "undue proliferation" of that rank.[60] To sidestep that controversy, the Council proposed to confer the rank of "personal nobility," a slightly higher status that bequeathed the rank of hereditary honored citizen to children. Curiously, the State Council for once proved more generous than church reformers, if for purely political reasons. Second, the Council voiced fears that transfer would become *too* easy, and it questioned "whether the abolition of laws attaching the clergy's children to the ecclesiastical rank will not cause some difficulties in the staffing of clerical positions." Tolstoi, representing the Special Commission, denied such dangers. He argued that most clergy would still prevail upon their sons to remain in the clergy, that many youths would prefer a free seminary education, and that "no doubt in time, especially after the material condition of the clergy has improved, forces [from other *sosloviia*] will not be slow to appear" and seek entry to the clergy.[61] With that assurance, the State Council approved the reform legislation, and it was signed into law by Alexander on 26 May 1869.[62]

This reform, as Tolstoi exulted in his annual report, will free "the clergy from the shackles of a closed estate order," making it possible for their sons "to choose freely a profession in any area of public life."[63] The explicit focus was on exit, the emancipation of the church from the multitude of "idle youths" that had grown ever more oppressive in the nineteenth century. Curiously, so long accustomed to the surfeit of youths, authorities attached

[58]When in May 1868, before completing its final proposals, the commission inquired at the Ministry of Education about assistance for the clergy's children, a deputy minister rejected blanket tuition exemptions but admitted the possibility of special policies for the western provinces (ibid., ch. 1, ll. 27–32). Within the commission, Tolstoi pronounced himself in favor of sharp increases in tuition exemptions; the commission resolved to leave the matter to Tolstoi's discretion as minister of education (ibid., ll. 289–91).

[59]Ibid., f. 1149, op. 7, g. 1869, d. 12, l. 1 (Tolstoi to State Council, 15.1.1869); the commission's list of changes for the *Svod zakonov* are in ibid., f. 804, op. 1, r. 1, d. 104, ch. 1, ll. 275–88 ob.

[60]Ibid., r. 1, d. 104, ch. 1, ll. 325–26 ob.

[61]Ibid., ll. 319–22.

[62]Ibid., ll. 315–18.

[63]*IVO (1869)*, pp. 243–44.

little significance to warnings that too many would depart, that too few would enter. Fully in the spirit of the Great Reforms, the new measure sought *raskreposhchenie*—the unshackling of vital social forces—with little fear that a new kind of demographic imbalance might result. Pleased with the outcome, Tolstoi wrote exuberantly that the new legislation meant "the elimination of the clergy's structure as a caste," an opinion widely echoed in the contemporary press.[64]

Having reformed the status of clerical children, in 1870–1871 the Special Commission addressed the question of clerical wives and their status.[65] One issue was endogamy, the custom that obliged clergy to marry women from their own estate. After first reviewing the various opinions expressed by diocesan authorities in 1863, the commission accepted the general consensus that the closed marital order was harmful, that the clergy, like the rest of society, should be free to marry women from any social estate. It therefore reaffirmed the "open-estate" policy of the sixties that had shaped the new law on children's status. The commission observed that in fact the bishops no longer had any legal right to require candidates to marry within the clerical estate, since the reform of 26 May 1869 removed the clergy's children from Church jurisdiction and hence beyond the bishops' purview. Since "custom alone" was at stake, the commission saw no need to amend the *Digest of Laws* and merely asked the Synod to distribute an appropriate explanatory circular to diocesan authorities.[66] That reform went one step beyond the Synod's resolution of 1867 abolishing family claims to positions: whereas the resolution eliminated economic imperatives to marry a priest's daughter to obtain his position, the commission's new decree in 1871 explicitly authorized clergy to marry at will. The goals were to draw the clergy closer to society, to give priests full civil rights—even at the expense of the current generation of clerical daughters.

The commission next drafted proposals to improve the legal status of clerical wives. The diocesan reports of 1863 had shown much anxiety about their juridical status, especially those who were widowed early: if they remarried men in the poll-tax population (common townsmen and peasants), they forfeited their own privileged status and acquired that of their new spouses.[67] Interestingly, the bishops were concerned not only about the severe hardships this law entailed but also about the implicit discrimination; since women of

---

[64] TsGIA SSSR, f. 804, op. 1, r. 1, d. 150, ch. 1, l. 1 (Tolstoi to Tersinskii, 16.2.1869).

[65] The commission's staff prepared a report and proposal in 1869, but the commission deferred action until 1870–1871, at Tolstoi's request, to give the State Council time to confirm the proposals on the status of clerical children. The explicit purpose was to obtain a clear precedent for altering the legal status of clerical wives; see ibid., d. 150, ch. 1, ll. 74–75.

[66] Ibid., r. 3, d. 472, ll. 242 ob.–44 ob. (zhurnal, no. 40).

[67] *Svod zakonov Rossiiskoi imperii izdaniia 1857 g.*, 10 vols. (2nd. ed.; St. Petersburg, 1857–1860), vol. 9, pt. 1, arts. 272, 283.

other privileged status groups lost their rank only for committing serious crimes.[68] Hence most diocesan authorities proposed to give clerical wives an inalienable privileged status, independent of the clerical estate, to be retained even if the women became widows and remarried into a lower status group.[69] Accepting this general view, the commission drafted a comprehensive statute in 1871 that formally separated clerical women from the soslovie: like their children, clerical wives should "be listed in their husbands' service records only for the sake of information," and, juridically, they should hold the secular status of personal noble (for priests' wives) or personal honored citizen (for sacristans' wives).[70] That proposal, though seemingly an innocuous extrapolation of the 1869 decree on clerical children, was of great significance, for it razed the last pillar of the soslovie system. Hereafter only clergy, not their dependents, would belong to the "ecclesiastical domain." However, this decisive attack on the soslovie order would encounter stiff opposition in the State Council. As we shall see, government policy on soslovie questions had begun to shift by 1871, jeopardizing the acceptability of this new reform proposal.

Though zealous in abolishing family claims, authorities proved far less thoroughgoing in attacking the underlying cause: the need for pensions for retired clergy and support for widows and orphans. To be sure, in 1866 the state created a pension fund for priests, but the sums and terms were so niggardly that they did little to ease the lot of the overwhelming mass of clergy.[71] Unable or unwilling to assume a greater burden, central authorities merely urged clergy to address their own welfare needs, mainly by encouraging them to form special pension funds (emirital'nye kassy) and to establish special schools for clerical girls. Curiously, even as authorities promulgated laws to dismantle the clerical soslovie, they actively encouraged the clergy to act collectively for its special soslovie interests, even to design the girls' schools such that they prepared "ideal wives" for men of their own soslovie.[72] In practical terms, however, little came of such appeals, which is scarcely surprising, given the clergy's economic difficulties. The clergy in a few dioceses established pension funds and (somewhat more frequently) opened special schools for clerical daughters, but they did so on a scale of little statistical consequence.[73]

---

[68] For the commission's synopsis of diocesan opinion, see "O pravakh dukhovenstva" in TsGIA SSSR, f. 804, op. 1, r. 1, d. 150, ch. 1, ll. 15–15 ob.

[69] Ibid., ll. 24 ob.–25.

[70] Ibid., ll. 24–27; r. 3, d. 472, ll. 242 ob.–44 ob. (zhurnal, no. 40).

[71] PSZ (2), 41: 43970 (providing pensions to those priests who served a minimum of 35 years).

[72] TsGIA SSSR, f. 796, op. 149, g. 1868, d. 282/a, ll. 1-402; PSZ (2), 43: 46271.

[73] Pension funds, though widely discussed in the clerical press and even in some diocesan assemblies, made little headway. The clergy in Samara established the first such fund in 1866, but their peers in other dioceses were slow to emulate that example ("Po delu o sostavlenii

In sum, the Special Commission focused upon the juridical dimensions of the soslovie question, seeking mainly to alter the status of clerical dependents. Its aim was to serve the interests of the institution and the clerics, not the soslovie. As the abolition of family claims in 1867 made clear, the goal was to "emancipate the Church from the soslovie" and rid the Church of supernumerary, uncommitted candidates. That reform violated the vested interests of the soslovie yet offered no substitute or compensation for the old privileges it abrogated. Evidently, authorities thought that, once unshackled from soslovie bonds, the clergy could provide their own welfare and pensions, pooling resources and displaying the initiative that reform sought to evoke. In effect, Tolstoi readdressed Valuev's "invitation" from the community to the parish clergy, summoning clergy to solve their own problems. Paradoxically, this antisoslovie legislation implicitly assumed the persistence of the estate, both to supply an ample number of future recruits and to act collectively in solving welfare needs. Secular reformers—evidently mesmerized by the clergy's caste image and overwhelmed by the data on "idle youths"—put little credence in warnings that the Church would find itself with too few candidates. The presumption of strong soslovie bonds was apparent in Tolstoi's statement to the State Council, even though authorities so far had failed to make *any* improvement in the clergy's material condition. That failure in turn suggests the lack of coordination in soslovie reform, the inability to devise a whole "package" capable of providing alternative welfare and assuring an adequate flow of recruits. Instead, reform was decentralized: some measures appeared as Synod decrees, some as Special Commission orders, some as State Council laws. Reform was also piecemeal, stretching out over several years and gradually enveloping diverse parts of the soslovie order. Although piecemeal legislation was politically simpler (Tolstoi, for example, consciously used the children's reform as a precedent for legislation on wives),[74] it deprived reform of coherence and balance. It also exposed the clergy to extraordinary stress, which, as we shall see, had a profound effect upon the feasibility of reform and the clergy's self-awareness.

The Service Reform of 1869

In 1868–1869 the Special Commission addressed the problems of the clerical service order—its economics, structure, and privileges. The economic

---

pensionnogo kapitala," *SL*, 1865, no. 62: 6–7; *IVO [1867]*, pp. 165–68; *IVO [1868]*, pp. 248–52). The special schools for clerical daughters were more widespread; by 1867 they numbered 39—11 under the wardship of the empress, 28 others operating under diocesan auspices. Yet, because they were dependent mainly upon diocesan clergy for support, they remained small in size, elementary in curriculum, and poor in finances (*IVO [1868]*, p. 190).

[74]TsGIA SSSR, f. 804, op. 1, r. 1, d. 150, ch. 1, ll. 74–75.

problem was most salient and most difficult, as the frustrating attempts to find a local solution had demonstrated earlier. Stymied by the refusal of society to cooperate and by the inability of the state to assume a large financial burden, the commission had achieved little. As a result, the press and some provincial commissions concluded that the only alternative was to reorganize parishes and reduce staffs, thereby raising the ratio of parishioners to clergy. A second problem was the service structure, especially its lack of a graduated hierarchy (seminarians became priests without experience and at a young age) and the presence of the ill-reputed sacristans. These issues, long in gestating, had for decades elicited proposals to require that seminarians serve first as sacristans and that the current generation of sacristans be summarily expelled from the clergy. The third problem concerned the clergy's service rights, which had attracted considerable attention in the 1863 episcopal reports. The bishops, as we have seen, urged steps to facilitate voluntary defrocking, the award of medals for meritorious service, and sundry other privileges and perquisites. All these problems became the subject of a major reform prepared by the commission in early 1869 and signed into law by Alexander on 16 April 1869.[75]

On the question of parish reorganization, the commission ordered provincial commissions to make a systematic reorganization and merge parishes into larger, more viable units. When such parishes were merged, one parish was to be the "main church" (*glavnaia tserkov'*), the other an "attached church" (*pripisnaia tserkov'*). Depending upon the circumstances, such parishes might have a single priest, serving alternately in the two parishes or only in the main church, or two priests, each serving in his respective church. The commission thus showed some flexibility in its plan for reorganization. In effect, the attached church might be closed altogether; it might remain open, but share a single priest with the main church; or it might even have its own priest, existing under the nominal supervision of the main church. Noting that each diocese had its own special needs and circumstances, the commission delegated primary responsibility to the provincial commission in each diocese, which was to draft the "new registries of parishes" (*novye rospisaniia prikhodov*), taking into account population density, distance from the nearest parish, transportation, size of parish, and the "moral-religious" condition of parishioners. It was a complex task, one that would drag on in some dioceses for over a decade.

The second issue, the structure of clerical service, provoked the first radical change in staffing schedules (*shtaty*) since their establishment under Peter the Great in 1722. First, in parishes with more than one priest, the commission devised a new internal hierarchy, with the ranks of *nastoiatel'* (head or

---

[75] Ibid., r. 3, d. 472, ll. 136–90 ob. (zhurnal, no. 32); r. 1, d. 18, ll. 1–109.

rector) and *pomoshchnik* (assistant or curate), thereby establishing clear lines of authority and subordination. The commission also raised the requirements for ordination, demanding that all candidates for priesthood not only possess a seminary degree but also be thirty years old and have prior experience as either sacristan or teacher. It allowed for some exceptions (for example, dioceses with too few graduates could ordain nongraduates as priests), but it strongly enjoined bishops "as far as possible" to observe the new requirements on age, education, and prior experience. Further, the commission virtually eliminated the deaconate (save in city cathedrals) and sharply reduced the number of sacristans (one, rather than the two traditionally allotted each parish). By pruning the lower ranks, the commission hoped to achieve considerable savings without disrupting parishioners' religious life. Finally, the commission envisioned an entirely new kind of sacristan. Although declining to replace sacristans with hired laymen (believing that most rural parishes lacked literate, respectable laymen qualified for this position), it sought to uplift the group by installing seminary graduates as sacristans, thus simultaneously providing the graduates with a valuable apprenticeship before ordination into priesthood. To emphasize the sacristan's new character, the commission created a new term, *psalomshchik* (psalmist), to replace the earlier term *prichetnik* and the more specific rank titles of diachok and ponomar. Finally, the commission left the door to service slightly ajar for uneducated but pious commoners; they might enter the clergy if they were over forty, celibate, and "completely known to diocesan authorities for their zeal toward the Church and for their completely irreproachable lives."

On the third issue, the clergy's service rights, the commission adopted several important changes. It condemned the practice of "involuntary transfers" to new positions, whereby bishops punished clergy for misdeeds. Such transfers, as we have seen, wrought great hardships on the clergy and evoked much discontent. The commission admonished bishops to avoid them, though it admitted that reassignment was still necessary in cases where the cleric had irretrievably compromised himself in the eyes of the parishioners. Moreover, the commission abolished the traditional passport restrictions on clergy, giving them full rights to travel and simplifying procedures for obtaining permission to leave their parishes. The commission also authorized clergy to request retirement before the old minimum age of sixty, primarily to spare clergy the trouble and humiliation of seeking specious medical excuses. On the thorny issue of voluntary defrocking, the commission reaffirmed the Synod's earlier, abortive resolution to eliminate disabilities on clerics voluntarily leaving their rank. As it had done for most priests and bishops, it proposed to give such clergy the right to enter state service after a short waiting period. The commission also devised measures to raise the clergy's service status, primarily through the conferral of various perquisites

(travel expenses and medals) that would put them on the same level as secular officials.[76] Lastly, to stimulate the clergy's religious initiative, the commission dismantled various censorship restrictions, authorizing parish priests
to deliver "public lectures on questions of Christian faith and morality, on
biblical events and Church history and the like," and to publish articles in
the secular press without prior Church censorship.[77] Some of these changes,
such as the rule against coercive transfer, the parish reorganization, and the
new service order, took effect immediately. Others, such as voluntary
defrocking and service perquisites, affected state law and required approval
by the State Council. In the interim the commission promulgated the order
for parish reorganization and for changes in the shtat and instructed diocesan
authorities to proceed with implementation.[78]

The statute of 16 April 1869 radically restructured the system of clerical
service, projecting the first fundamental change in that system since the early
eighteenth century. The principal goal, as in the other Church reforms of
the late sixties, was to serve the institutional interests of the Church—to fashion a new class of parish clergy, adequately supported, experienced, and
dynamic. Thus the new statute tilted the center of gravity toward the priesthood by eliminating deacons and one-half of all sacristans. The statute also
raised the standards for clerical service: priests must be mature and experienced; psalmists must have a full seminary education. Ideally, the new service system would close the gap between priest and psalmist, transform these
ranks from separate social groups into two stages in the same hierarchy, and
raise standards all around, giving a heightened sense of unity and even
mobility. The reform also chartered substantial improvements in the clergy's
legal and social status. Thus state medals, such as the automatic right to the
Order of St. Vladimir, Fourth Degree, which conferred noble status, would
dramatically augment their social standing; the ban on arbitrary transfer
would afford protection from episcopal tyranny; and the new rights of
speech and press would unshackle the clergy's creative forces. Once implemented, the reforms should dramatically improve the clergy's composition,
status, and performance.

But implementation would be no simple matter. Above all, the statute violated a host of vested interests—clergy left idle by reductions, parishioners
deprived of their local church, bishops fearful of weakening the Church's
infrastructure of parishes and clergy. The success of the reform hinged upon

[76]Travel rights, medals, and other service perquisites were matters of great importance to
the clergy; see the commission's synopsis of diocesan opinion (ibid., ll. 167-69).

[77]For a lacerating account of such "censorship," see Belliustin, *Opisanie*, pp. 133–36; see
also the bishops' annual reports of the toils of such censorship committees on sermons (TsGIA
SSSR, f. 796, op. 440, 442).

[78]TsGIA SSSR, f. 804, op. 1, r. 1, d. 18, l. 103 (commission circular).

rigorous implementation; significantly, the more ruthless the implementation, the more resolute the opposition. No doubt aware of these problems—such difficulties had plagued more modest parish reorganization in the 1840s—the Special Commission provided only a blueprint for the new order, leaving the ultimate responsibility for implementation to local authorities. That decentralization, though dictated by the complexity of the task and the diversity of the empire, presumed that diocesan authorities would be effective, enthusiastic agents in implementing reform. It remained to be seen whether the prelates and their administrative apparatus would be willing and able to overcome the entrenched interests of laymen and clergy in the parish.

Educational Reform

Concurrent with soslovie and service reform, Tolstoi and the Synod once more took up the issue of ecclesiastical education.[79] The formal proposal prepared by the first committee of 1860–1862 had foundered on criticism by bishops and seminary boards as unworkable and ill-conceived.[80] Though the committee failed to produce an acceptable reform, its work, in Tolstoi's words, demonstrated "the necessity of immediate, radical transformation of the entire system of ecclesiastical education."[81] Such concerns were reinforced by the apparent links between the seminary and radical nihilism in the sixties. Though greatly exaggerated, such connections had a profound effect upon bureaucratic and public opinion, providing a powerful impetus to radical and immediate reform.[82] Even in the elite academy, complained faculty, discipline seemed to be fast disintegrating. As one professor wrote, academy students "do not go to class, turn in compositions late (or write them poorly), do not live at home, and permit themselves everything with impunity."[83] Meanwhile, old structural weaknesses like finances became ever more acute. The bishop of Riazan, for example, wrote in 1866 that "our ecclesiastical academies, seminaries, and elementary schools—because of a steadily rising inflation on all basic items of necessity—have gradually grown poorer

[79] For details, see Titlinov, *Dukhovnaia shkola*, 2: 300–420.

[80] *Svod mnenii otnositel'no Ustava dukhovnykh seminarii, proektirovannogo komitetom 1860–62 godov* (St. Petersburg, 1866); the original replies are in TsGIA SSSR, f. 797, op. 36, otd. 1, d. 395, ch. 3, ll. 1–714.

[81] *IVO (1866)*, p. 55; *Vsepoddanneishaia dokladnaia zapiska*, pp. 35–41.

[82] Such views, which enjoyed wide currency in the 1860s, elicited a rebuttal from V. Pevnitskii, "Tiazheloe narekanie," *TKDA*, 1866, no. 8: 461–96 (with references to the secular journal *Otechestvennye zapiski*). Church censors endeavored to suppress charges of seminarian nihilism; see, for example, the case in TsGIA SSSR, f. 807, op. 1, d. 1429, ll. 186 ob.–87.

[83] Beliaev, "Kazanskii i ego perepiska," *BV*, 1912, no. 3: 553.

and poorer, and they have at last reached their present condition, which is difficult in the maximum degree."[84] Quite apart from the sheer magnitude of these problems, some hierarchs urged that the Church act promptly to preempt prior measures by the state. Bishop Antonii of Smolensk, who conducted early reform experiments in his seminary, warned that "while we procrastinate and make no decisions, our 'benefactors' will have time to do a good job of ruining everything."[85]

He was right. Tolstoi had every intention of making basic reforms in Church schools. Early in 1866 the emperor approved a private memorandum urging substantial state funds for the seminary, and shortly afterwards he ordered Tolstoi to prepare a formal proposal on reform.[86] Together with the minister of finance, Tolstoi worked out a proposal for a state subsidy of 1.5 million rubles to be introduced gradually over the next five years, explaining that "the present condition of church schools [is] close to breaking down, rendering a correct approach to education impossible."[87] To supplement this aid, Tolstoi revived Archbishop Dmitrii's old scheme to give each diocese control over candle revenues, thereby providing local clergy with real incentive to ensure full delivery of the revenues. The state funds, held Tolstoi, should only serve to augment that incentive; allocations should go first to those dioceses where clergy are most zealous in aiding the schools "by making contributions from their own local resources."[88] The new subsidy in hand, the Synod created a new committee to draft reform, with Metropolitan Arsenii of Kiev as chairman.[89] Though it was different from what he originally envisaged, Tolstoi observed that "the composition of the committee is not bad, and I shall make every effort to see that the [new] statutes for secondary and primary [Church] schools are absolutely finished this year."[90] Tolstoi, who was—wrongly—credited with responsibility for obtaining the large government subsidy, earned high praise from leading hierarchs for his

[84]"Rasporiazheniia eparkhial'nogo nachal'stva," *Riazanskie eparkhial'nye vedomosti* [hereafter *Riazanskie EV*], 1866, no. 11: 142–45.

[85]A. Matseevich, ed., "Pis'ma arkhiepiskopa Antoniia Amfiteatrova," *TKDA*, 1883, no. 7: 530.

[86]The initiative for the state subsidy actually rested with S. P. Shipov, who implored the emperor to grant 3,000,000 rubles to aid Church schools. At the time, few were apprised of Shipov's role, which became public knowledge only in the 1880s. In the interim, Tolstoi deftly exploited "his" apparent achievement to press his views of seminary reform.

[87]TsGIA SSSR, f. 797, op. 36, otd. 1, st. 2, d. 395, ch. 1, l. 5 (Reutern to Alexander II, 14.3.1866), 17–17 ob. (formal expression of Church gratitude).

[88]Ibid., ll. 4–4 ob. (Tolstoi to Alexander II, 14.3.1866).

[89]Tolstoi declared that he would rather throw away the new funds than waste them on the existing Church schools; see his 1867 letter to Katkov in OR GBL, f. 120, k. 11, d. 17, l. 13 ob. See also TsGIA SSSR, f. 797, op. 36, otd. 1, st. 2, d. 395, ch. 1, ll. 9–10 ob. (Tolstoi to Synod), 23–23 ob. (Synod resolution, 17.3.1866), 24–25 ob. (Tolstoi to Alexander II, 19.3.1866).

[90]OR GBL, f. 120, k. 11, d. 17, l. 6 ob. (Tolstoi to Katkov, 25.3.1866).

achievement and evident good intentions. As Filaret wrote, "all of us clergy must be grateful for your memorandum [to the emperor requesting a subsidy]. We ourselves could not write—or even utter aloud—all that you expressed so forcefully in your note."[91]

The astute Tolstoi exploited this gratitude as he pressed demands for immediate, fundamental reform—a goal apparent in his very first communications with the committee. The primary question was the purpose of Church schools: should they aim to serve primarily the needs of the Church or those of the clerical soslovie? The answer given here would affect all other questions on curriculum, enrollment, and social policies.[92] Tolstoi himself favored schools to serve the needs of the Church, not the clerical soslovie, a view exemplified as well in his reforms of the soslovie and parish service. Still, the procurator himself admitted that "if the goal of schools is separate from charity, then by what means can one assist the clergy in the basic preparation of their sons [for other careers]?"[93]

That dilemma caused a major split in the committee: some members advocated Church interests; others defended the needs of the soslovie.[94] After a month of inconclusive debate, in late May the committee finally turned to the Synod to resolve the question, presenting the majority and dissenting opinions for its consideration.[95] The majority opinion, espousing institutional interests, found moral training to be the schools' chief weakness and urged the construction of dormitories to ensure better supervision and to isolate youths from the corrupting influence of townspeople. Though that view reflected the judgment of the earlier committee, this one drew different conclusions: given the limited finances, the Church schools should admit only enough students to satisfy diocesan needs and not attempt to educate all the clergy's sons. The majority also proposed to open Church schools to all estates, a policy that would "gradually free our estate from those criticisms of some kind of isolation (which alienates the sympathy of society) and from those suspicions that perceive zeal and devotion to our Church as [nothing more than] the pursuit of personal or soslovie interests." After analyzing data on appointments for the past decade, the majority found that seminaries need enroll only 9,000 students to meet the Church's annual manpower needs—that is, about one-half the current seminary enrollment of 16,441. To

[91] Quoted in "Iz zapisok S. P. Shipova, 'O dukhovno-uchebnykh zavedeniiakh'" (TsGIA SSSR, f. 797, op. 54, otd. 1, st. 2, d. 40, l. 132).

[92] Ibid., op. 36, otd. 1, st. 2, d. 395, ch. 1, ll. 50–51 (list of questions, with Tolstoi's emandations, dated 12.4.1866).

[93] Ibid., l. 50 (Tolstoi's marginal notation).

[94] Ibid., ch. 6, ll. 1–34 ob. (zhurnal komiteta, nos. 1–5 [April–May 1866]).

[95] Ibid., op. 87, d. 223, ll. 6–19 ob.; op. 36, otd. 1, st. 1, d. 395, ch. 1, ll. 96–107 ob. (Nektarii to Synod, 30.5.1866). See also Tolstoi to Arsenii, 11.5.1866 (ibid., f. 796, op. 205, d. 365, ll. 59–59 ob.).

educate that smaller number in improved seminaries would, according to the majority, consume most of the 1.5 million rubles allotted by the state, leaving just enough to finance one elementary Church school in each diocese, which thus could accept only a small proportion of the clergy's children. To educate the remainder, the clergy itself would have to raise funds, primarily through more efficient collection of candle revenues. The committee majority also envisioned some changes in the curriculum to bring order to the courses, but it did not recommend abandoning the traditional core of classical education.

Some members of the committee sharply dissented from this plan. Metropolitan Arsenii of Kiev, who left the committee to attend to diocesan business, wanted merely to restore the 1814 statute, stripped of Protasov's innovations, and he explicitly opposed the majority's decision "to accept students from all sosloviia and strictly according to [academic] records and conduct, and to give no attention to [such qualities] as poverty, orphan status, and clerical origin."[96] Similarly, Archimandrites Filaret of Kiev and Mikhail of Moscow wanted seminary reform to serve primarily the interests of the clerical soslovie. For example, Mikhail proposed that "ecclesiastical schools, as in the past, be supported and set up on such a scale that all children of the clerical soslovie can receive such a general education that, on a level equal to the gymnasium, they will have the possibility of pursuing any [career]."[97] Curriculum, finances, even moral training might all be designed to serve the interests of soslovie or Church, and the traditional aspiration to serve both still had its adherents. But the Synod upheld the majority view favored by both Tolstoi and the committee's new chairman, Nektarii of Nizhnii Novgorod, and it directed the committee to draft appropriate proposals.[98]

The committee worked steadily over the next few months, and by December 1866 it had completed its draft statute, supplemented by a detailed explanatory memorandum and other supporting documents.[99] In surveying its work, Tolstoi noted that, "as the foundation of the new seminary statute, the committee has adopted the idea that the seminary's purpose is to serve exclusively [the goal] of preparing worthy clergy for our Church." Hence it aspired to attract students "from all sosloviia" and to enroll only enough students to fill "the clerical positions that fall vacant each year."[100] Significantly, however, the committee stopped short of a complete denial of soslovie inter-

[96]"Pis'ma mitropolita kievskogo Arseniia," *RA*, 1892, tom 1: 221 (Arsenii to Platon, 26.7.1866). For Arsenii's statement to the committee, see zhurnal no. 2 (TsGIA SSSR, f. 797, op. 36, otd. 1, st. 2, d. 395, ch. 6, ll. 10–17 ob.).

[97]OR GPB, f. 573, no. AI.82, ll. 197–266.

[98]TsGIA SSSR, f. 797, op. 36, otd. 1, st. 2, d. 395, ch. 1, ll. 108–10 ob. (Tolstoi to Alexander II, 17.6.1866).

[99]Ibid., d. 395, ch. 6, ll. 60–235 (zhurnaly komiteta, nos. 7–21), 382–477 (draft statute for seminaries), 330–81 (draft statute for elementary Church schools).

[100]*IVO (1866)*, p. 61.

ests. Although the number of regular students (with full stipends) was limited, the seminary could add "parallel classes" at the volition and expense of diocesan clergy—a clear, if unmagnanimous, concession to the clerical soslovie. The draft statute also gave new authority to the local bishop, faculty, and diocesan clergy, shifting primary responsibility for such matters as supervision, appointments, and finances from Petersburg to the provinces. The goal was partly to eliminate paperwork, which often caused belated, bungled decisions, and partly to stimulate local initiative, especially among the schools' teachers and parish clergy. As its original statement testifies, the committee sought only modest changes in curriculum: it retained the old classical core and did little more than to reorder and delete a few courses. The decision to maintain the classical core was controversial, but Tolstoi— who also imposed classical studies on secular schools—defended the decision on traditional pedagogical grounds: "As the foundation for a general education, [the committee] adopted classical languages and mathematics, and the importance of studying these for the general, independent development of intellectual abilities of students has been demonstrated by centuries of experience in education in European countries." To that he appended the hierarchs' traditional defense of classicism: "The knowledge of Greek and Latin, in particular, with the vast Church literature of the first nine centuries [being only in those languages], is necessary for a substantial theological education."[101] Tolstoi also pointed out that this curriculum meshed well with that of secular schools, thereby promoting the cause of social mobility: "The education afforded youths in ecclesiastical schools is of the variety that can enable them to pass easily from these schools to [lay] secondary schools." Interestingly, Tolstoi was concerned mainly with outward mobility in order to relieve the surfeit of youths. He was noticeably less sensitive to the question of inward mobility, remaining generally silent on that issue and taking no special steps to encourage the matriculation of outsiders.

In its final version, these proposals represented a trim version of Dmitrii's scheme of 1862, now denuded of its earlier soslovie ambitions. Yet, although the new system satisfied primarily Church interests, it also gave diocesan clergy the opportunity to expand the seminary and district schools at their own expense. In curriculum, too, the schools broadly followed Dmitrii's bifurcated approach: the lower schools, financed primarily by parish clergy, served the soslovie and bore a strong secular emphasis; the advanced seminaries, financed primarily by the state, served the narrower professional needs of the Church. This compromise reflects a vague desire to help the clergy, recognition of the special needs of the soslovie, and perhaps even a tacit wish to ensure the largest possible pool of candidates.

Even as the committee completed drafting these proposals, the scheme

[101] Ibid., pp. 65–66.

came under sharp criticism from Metropolitan Filaret of Moscow. With evident pique he wrote Tolstoi that, although he had not been "invited" to comment on these reform plans, the contemporary press had already done so with abandon, and so he too felt free to express his views on the subject.[102] Apart from some practical objections (why force *all* students to reside in dormitories, when at least some could reside with local kinsmen and receive excellent moral supervision?), Filaret was primarily concerned about the plans for a seminary shtat, a policy that he had opposed for nearly two decades. Implicit was his overriding concern about the quality, not the quantity, of candidates: by depleting the pool of potential recruits, the shtat severely restricted the number of graduates, many of whom—for spiritual or intellectual reasons—might well be unworthy of ordination.[103] Tolstoi sought to smooth the ruffled feathers. Besides reiterating the customary arguments for a shtat, he reassured Filaret that his views would be considered and promised to send him a copy of the committee proposals as soon as they were complete.[104]

Once Filaret had those proposals in hand, he rose to challenge the very foundations of the reform. Most striking of all, he questioned the whole attempt to transform the seminary into an all-class institution. His objections reveal a strong sense of soslovie pride and concern:

> Children of the clerical estate have the advantage that from childhood they follow their fathers into church for services, and, gradually entering upon this service from childhood (beginning with the preparation of censers, removal of candles, and reading), they thus imbibe the spirit of the Church and acquire a predisposition toward Church service and some familiarity with it. Children of other estates will of course enter seminaries without such a favorable predisposition, and one can also fear that some, especially those from the middle and lower estates (particularly, given the present state of morality in our fatherland), will enter the seminary with habits unsuitable for the clerical rank.

That kind of argument derived in part from ideas that had appeared often in eighteenth-century discussions of seminary school policy, but they acquired still greater force amidst the nihilism and materialism of the sixties, as Filaret's reference to "the present state of morality" attests. Therefore,

[102]TsGIA SSSR, f. 797, op. 36, otd. 1, st. 2, d. 395, ch. 1, ll. 204-4 ob. (Filaret to Tolstoi, 2.11.1866); published later as "Zametki i pis'ma Filareta, mitr. moskovskogo," *BV*, 1916, no. 10/12: 231–38.

[103]TsGIA SSSR, f. 797, op. 36, otd. 1, st. 2, d. 395, ch. 6, ll. 251–57 ob. (Filaret, "Ob otnosheniiakh k sviashchenstvu v eparkhii").

[104]Ibid., d. 395, ch. 1, ll. 205–6 (Tolstoi to Filaret, 7.11.1866).

argued Filaret, "in the event of equal merit in examinations, preference should be given to children from the clerical soslovie."[105] Moreover, Filaret was overtly determined to safeguard the needs of the clerical soslovie, declaring that the principle that "clergy's sons be educated at Church expense primarily for Church service ... is just as good and fair in 1867 as it was in 1808." As the final link in his argument, Filaret adduced fears of mass flight, a perenniel concern of hierarchs, heightened now by the relative deterioration in clerical status: "The hereditary disposition toward [service in] the clerical estate is losing its power. The wandering thoughts of the pupil, given the clergy's difficult life and hard service, will flee to the expansive domain of the secular world, where it meets with flattering dreams of advantage and honor." This tendency, he warned "can easily lead to the point where the more capable pupils seek lay careers, leaving the theological seminary and Church services with mainly the mediocre products of the general educational school."[106] A few months later Filaret urged Metropolitan Isidor to raise further objections to the draft statutes, especially the scheme for normative enrollments, and warned that the responsibility imposed on parish clergy to open parallel sections was an intolerable burden.[107]

Filaret was by no means alone in his opposition, and some of his admonitions, especially about flight, proved prophetic. Bishop Makarii also filed a lengthy critique of the proposal, complaining that it failed to address new needs (for example, the training of effective preachers) or even old ones (such as education for all the clergy's sons). Like Filaret, Makarii feared that the shtat would wreak havoc on the clergy. Noting that the norm set for Kiev was some four hundred students, compared with a current enrollment of one thousand, he wrote, "Six hundred therefore will be utterly left without [a secondary] education—this is not, of course, the 'improvement in the clergy's material condition' that the state is so concerned about."[108] Although Makarii conceded the need for clergy's sons to seek non-Church careers, he shared Filaret's abiding fear of a sudden dearth of candidates, especially good ones. Metropolitan Isidor, upon reading Makarii's note, wrote "I agree" in the margin.[109] The same objections came from Bishop Antonii of Kazan, who

[105] Ibid., d. 395, ch. 6, ll. 377–79 ob. (Filaret, "Zamechaniia").

[106] OR GPB, f. 573, no. AI.82, ll. 283–86 ob. ("Zapiska Filareta na proekt preobrazovaniia uchilishchnykh zavedenii dvukh arkhimandritov"). Filaret was commenting upon a proposal from two archimandrites to maintain closed estate schools with a secular curriculum that would facilitate exit into lay careers (for their proposal, see ll. 197–266; also in TsGIA SSSR, f. 797, op. 36, otd. 1, st. 2, d. 395, ch. 6, ll. 258–89 ob.).

[107] Filaret, Pis'ma Filareta, mitropolita moskovskogo i kolomenskogo, k Vysochaishim Osobam i raznym drugim litsam, 2 vols. (Tver, 1888), 1: 26–27.

[108] [Makarii], "Zamechaniia na ustav dukhovnykh seminarii i dukhovnykh uchilishch" (OR GPB, f. 573, no. AI.82, ll. 345 ob.–46).

[109] Ibid., l. 346.

warned that the shtat would cause a shortage of qualified candidates, oblige bishops to lower standards in the appointment of future clergy, and arouse intense discontent among the parish clergy.[110]

After reviewing these comments from selected prelates as well as articles in the contemporary press, the committee reworked its original draft and submitted a final version in March 1867 that contained only minor changes.[111] The Synod devoted three sessions to a meticulous review of the draft and, whatever the reservations of some, approved the new statute in May 1867.[112] In transmitting the proposal to the emperor, Tolstoi stressed that the principal goal was to serve the needs of the Church, not the clerical soslovie: "The seminary exists solely to prepare worthy clergy for the Church, not for the general goal of educating all the clergy's sons, as hitherto has been the case." Thus the new statute ordered the seminary to examine applicants and to admit youths "from all estates without tuition, but [only] in such quantity as necessary for filling clerical positions that may open in each diocese in the course of a year." As in the original draft, the statute authorized parish clergy to establish parallel classes at their own expense. Although nominally giving the bishop more authority (including responsibility to oversee the schools), the statute sought mainly to use the faculty and diocesan clergy as "forces of educational and moral development," giving both a key role as members of the seminary's governing board. Most striking of all was the scheme for diocesan assemblies of clergy at both the district and the provincial level. Elected representatives of parish clergy were to convene each year to discuss the needs of Church schools, check on their condition, seek new funds, and even discuss some other vaguely defined matters of mutual concern.[113] Once Alexander signed the statute on 14 May 1867, the Synod ordered gradual implementation, beginning first with Astrakhan, Riazan, Nizhnii Novgorod, Kostroma, and Samara.[114] Press response to the reform was highly favorable, giving special praise for the plans to integrate the clergy with society through the new social policy.[115]

Even as the Church was putting some final touches on its seminary statute, Tolstoi also took steps to reform ecclesiastical academies. In response to his

[110]TsGIA SSSR, f. 797, op. 36, otd. 1, st. 2, d. 395, ch. 1, ll. 253–61 ob. (Antonii to Tolstoi, 21.1.1867). Tolstoi tried to allay fears, noting that the clergy could open additional sections (through funds they must raise themselves, of course) and that the normative shtat was higher than that set in 1851. See ibid., ll. 249–51 (Tolstoi to Antonii, 12.3.1867).

[111]Ibid., d. 395, ch. 6, ll. 615–19 ob. (Nektarii to Synod, March 1869), 620–99 (proekty).

[112]Ibid., d. 395, ch. 1, ll. 285–86 (Synod resolution, 3.5.1867).

[113]Ibid., ll. 287–96 (Tolstoi to Alexander II, 14.5.1867).

[114]*IVO (1867)*, pp. 105–10.

[115]*Moskovskie vedomosti*, 1867, no. 163; "Preobrazovanie dukhovno-uchebnykh zavedenii," *SL*, 1867, nos. 16–19; "Obozrenie 1867 g.," ibid., 1868, no. 2; *S.-Peterburgskie vedomosti*, 9 June 1867; *Syn otechestva*, 1867, nos. 12, 41, 49, 51–52, 60–61, 72.

request for opinions on desirable changes,[116] all four academies replied by May 1867 with a host of diverse problems, including lack of subject specialization, difficulties in overseeing seminaries, and disorders in internal administration.[117] To analyze these commentaries and prepare a new academy statute, the Synod created a special committee in June under Bishop Nektarii of Nizhnii Novgorod, who had recently chaired the committee for seminary reform.[118] The Academy Committee did not begin work until early 1868,[119] and in the interim Tolstoi permitted the contemporary press to publish the replies of the academy councils, which elicited detailed comments and suggestions.[120] The committee finally began work in January 1868, and six months later it sent a draft to the Synod for consideration.

The committee noted that the academies, as designed in 1808–1814, had a dual purpose: to develop theological scholarship and to train faculty for seminaries and Church schools. However, the schools suffered from too little specialization, a plethora of subjects, maladministration, and weak finance. To remedy these problems, the committee prepared a radical revision of the existing statute. One change was to confer substantial power on the faculty in order to check rectors' misdeeds and "to instill vigor into the activities of academic administration." It thus rejected the earlier "patriarchal form of academic administration" and instead placed power in the hands of a faculty council, which had the authority to appoint seminary officials (even the rector), confer degrees, approve manuscripts for publication, and assign students to fill teaching posts in the seminaries. Second, the committee devised a new curriculum, which included a core of common courses in religious subjects but permitted students to specialize in a particular field (theology, religious history, or philosophy) so that they could become more effective scholars and teachers. Third, the committee opened the academy to all estates, including graduates of the gymnasium, with no prejudice in the distribution of stipends. Finally, the committee raised faculty salaries to make them competitive with the university.[121] Although the committee drew no comparisons, it essentially tried to remodel the academy after the university statute of 1863, especially in its division into faculties and the provision for faculty autonomy.

[116]TsGIA SSSR, f. 797, op. 37, otd. 1, st. 2, d. 1, l. 1 (Tolstoi to academy conference boards, 24.1.1867).

[117]Ibid., ll. 2–25 (St. Petersburg Academy), 27–54 (Moscow Academy), 54–63 (Kiev Academy), 64–106 (Kazan Academy).

[118]Ibid., l. 124 (Synod resolution, 28.6.1867).

[119]Ibid., ll. 150–51 (Tolstoi to Alexander II, 23.1.1868).

[120]Severnaia pochta, 1867, nos. 143–44. For a contrary view, arguing that the academies required only minor adjustments in their statute, see V. Pevnitskii, "Po voprosu o preobrazovanii dukhovnykh akademii," TKDA, 1867, no. 5: 253–91.

[121]Ob"iasnitel'naia zapiska k proektu Ustava dukhovnykh akademii (St. Petersburg, 1868).

This draft elicited strong opposition from leading prelates, mainly for its stress on professional specialization and relative inattention to "spiritual development." Most vehement was Archbishop Antonii of Kazan, who denounced the "secular spirit" of the draft, especially its provision to appoint laymen as inspectors and professors. He pointedly observed that the old academy had been the primary source of educated recruits for monastic orders. The new statute, in his view, was oblivious to such needs; its pervasive secularity appeared certain to discourage recruitment to monasticism. He warned that this bias could lead to an acute dearth of educated monks in the hierarchy—just what the Church's foes wanted most.[122] Metropolitan Arsenii of Kiev complained that the formation of three specialized faculties in the academy was a crude and ill-advised attempt to imitate the university. That imitation, he declared, ignored the distinctive purposes and values of the Church, especially the need for integrated religious education.[123] The new metropolitan of Moscow, Innokentii (Veniaminov), raised similar objections and fiercely attacked the faculty's right to elect its rector: "If a large part of the teachers uphold the principle of endless 'progress,' then they will choose someone who shares those views. Thus the harm will not be limited to the academy, but will spread to the seminaries—and through these to the future pastors of the Church."[124]

Whereas the seminary committee in 1867 blithely ignored criticism and essentially reaffirmed its original proposal, the Academy Committee, facing much more resolute opposition, substantially revised its draft statute.[125] One change, for example, involved its scheme for three fields of specialization; though retaining the basic principle, it replaced philosophy with "practical pastoral activity" as something useful for academic-trained parish priests.[126] It also weakened the faculty's autonomy, most notably by providing that the Synod, not the faculty, choose the rector. The Synod approved the main outlines of this draft, and Alexander signed the new statute into law on 30 May 1869.[127] These changes did not satisfy Innokentii, however. He wrote that "the statute conforms to the wishes of the chief procurator, not us," and complained that "we'll be singing to him."[128] By contrast, the new statute elicited

[122]TsGIA SSSR, f. 797, op. 37, otd. 1, st. 2, d. 1, ll. 173–80 ob. (Antonii, 10.8.1868). Antonii also complained to his fellow prelates; see, for instance, his letter of October 1867 to Gerasim ("Vyderzhki iz moikh vospominanii," *Astrakhanskie eparkhial'nye vedomosti* [hereafter *Astrakhanskie EV*], 1880, no. 18: 283).

[123]TsGIA SSSR, f. 797, op. 37, otd. 1, st. 2, d. 1, ll. 187–214 (Arsenii's memorandum of 14.9.1868).

[124]Ibid., l. 291 ob. (Innokentii, 4.2.1869).

[125]Ibid., ll. 313–14 (Synod resolution, 12.4.1869/13.4.1869).

[126]Ibid., ll. 361–68 ob. (zhurnal, January–February 1869).

[127]Ibid., f. 796, op. 148, g. 1867, d. 779/a, ll. 14–16 ob. (Tolstoi to Synod, 11.4.1869); f. 797, op. 39, otd. 1, st. 2, d. 92, l. 2.

[128]I. P. Barsukov, *Innokentii*, p. 656 (Innokentii to Leonid, 20.5.1869).

favorable comment in the press, along with some stinging criticism of the last-minute changes made to placate episcopal opponents.[129]

The reform statutes significantly recast the social and administrative structure of Church schools. Their primary goal was to serve the Church's needs by supplying only a limited number of priests and by giving academy students more specialized training. The explicit aim was to husband institutional resources, to tie school enrollments to actual recruitment needs. A secondary, yet important, goal was to transcend the soslovie isolation of prereform schools, in part by formally opening admission to outsiders and by drawing the schools closer to secular life (for example, by giving preference to lay specialists over monks). Nevertheless, the reform did make some concessions to the soslovie: in contrast to the prior shtat of 1851, it gave diocesan clergy the option of supplementing the skeletal system with parallel classes at their own expense. Thus, even while giving priority to institutional needs, the reform also encouraged the clergy to show initiative both in overseeing the schools and in raising supplementary funds for them.

The educational reforms, moreover, demonstrated Tolstoi's willingness and capacity to override opposition in the hierarchy. He first disarmed bishops by taking credit for obtaining new funds, thereby earning much gratitude. More important, Tolstoi proved an adept politician: he mobilized public opinion behind reform (as Filaret irritably noted) and made no attempt to survey episcopal opinion, thereby giving the bishops no opportunity to oppose, or even delay, the reform. Though the difference between the seminary and the academy statutes suggested growing difficulties in reform— Tolstoi made no concessions in 1867 but had to make substantial ones in 1869—the chief procurator had masterminded the first radical revision in Church schools since the statutes of 1814. But, thus far, Tolstoi had only rewritten laws. How the new system worked would depend largely upon the cooperation of diocesan authorities and the willingness of parish clergy to solicit additional funds. As in the case of parish reform, the crucial test was not the battle for enactment but the battle for implementation.

Administration, Censorship, and Justice

By the mid-1860s, the dimension of the clerical question discussed least in official, if not private, circles was reform in diocesan administration. Though the contemporary press had given much attention to abuses and injustices, authorities had thus far collected little data, summoned no committees, and drafted no statutes to reform administration, justice, and censorship. Yet it

---

[129]"Po povodu novogo Ustava dukhovnykh akademii," *SL*, 1869, nos. 59–60; "Po povodu novogo Ustava dukhovnykh akademii," *PO*, 1869, no. 7: 128–34.

was in precisely these areas that major changes had been made in parallel government institutions, and thus the Church felt increasing pressure to do likewise, if only for the sake of consistency and symmetry of systems. To be sure, some individual bishops had made tentative experiments (for example, permitting the election of superintendents), but it was not until Tolstoi became procurator that central authorities embarked on broad reform. Because it heightened the bishops' perennial fears of state encroachment, that reform proved exceedingly difficult and elusive, even for one so determined and imperious as Dmitrii Tolstoi.

Diocesan Administration

Liberal demands for reform, apparent already in the early 1860s, became more strident in the second half of the decade. The most sensational statement appeared in yet another foreign publication, this time a two-volume work, *The White and Black Orthodox Clergy.* Its author, D. I. Rostislavov, was a former professor at the St. Petersburg Academy and had earlier published a devastating portrait of ecclesiastical schools that traced most problems to the pernicious role of monks.[130] The new volumes went further, blaming "learned monks" for virtually all the Church's failings and accusing them of tyrannical abuse of the parish clergy. Characteristically, even "good deeds" by bishops bore the taint of despotism; for example, one prelate was so eager to raise funds for the diocesan girls' school that he forced the clergy to give substantial "donations" to receive much-coveted medals and honors. "If one sows but a little," he allegedly declared, "one shall also reap but a little."[131] As before, Rostislavov and liberal clergy believed that the task was not simply to eradicate bribery by such means as raising the salaries of diocesan clerks; rather, they wanted to confer substantial power directly on the parish clergy. Given power to choose superintendents and members of the consistory, it was argued, the clergy could not only defend themselves against episcopal tyranny but also muster their collective forces for more effective pastoral service.

Conservative churchmen, however, envisioned quite different reform. Perhaps best described as the episcopal program, this scheme entailed the devolution of authority from the state to the Church, from the Synod to diocesan bishops. The main idea, which had been circulating since the mid-1850s, was to create episcopal councils (*sobory*), especially at the regional

---

[130] Rostislavov, *O belom i chernom pravoslavnom dukhovenstve;* see also, above, p. 234.

[131] *Penzenskaia eparkhiia; istoriko-statisticheskoe opisanie* (Penza, 1907), pp. 20–21. The "secret section" of the Synodal archive contains some fascinating material on the plight of the bishop of Smolensk, who had evidently wronged a local priest. In letters to Metropolitan Isidor, he describes his "gifts" to the priest to hush up the affair (TsGIA SSSR, f. 796, op. 205, d. 503, ll. 1–11).

level. The leading exponent of the episcopal program was A. N. Murav'ev, who had showered memoranda upon chief procurators about such councils for well over a decade. Still hopeful of convoking an episcopal assembly, in 1867 Murav'ev submitted a new memorandum to Tolstoi that reiterated his old arguments about the plight of the Synod and urged the convocation of episcopal assemblies. The Synod, argued Murav'ev, was unfit to engineer a renewal of Church life: "What is the Synod? That is no council [*sobor*] but a tribunal occupied with current business, [functioning] under the supervision of the chief procurator, and [preoccupied] with only those matters that the chief procurator deigns to present for discussion." Murav'ev believed that only regional assemblies could regenerate the Church, and he proposed that these convene around the three metropolitans (Moscow, Petersburg, and Kiev) and the archbishops of Kazan, Vil'na, Khar'kov, and one Siberian diocese.[132]

Conciliarism did not strike a responsive chord in high places, as Murav'ev soon discovered when he attempted to convene a council on the occasion of the fiftieth anniversary of Filaret's consecration. Its task would be to "discuss church affairs," and Murav'ev hoped that such a gathering might provide the precedent for "future assemblies of bishops" as well.[133] He outlined his proposal in a new memorandum, which he asked a sympathetic prelate to transmit to the procurator and empress, adding, "I do not know whether this will succeed, but I have tried, as carefully as possible, to broach the subject of councils [*sobory*] and, knowing the general distrust [toward this idea], to cloak it in the greatest possible legality, with the presence on this occasion of the chief procurator and all this in the name of His Grace's jubilee."[134] But by early March he was ready to concede failure, writing that, "as is his wont (and with his customary courtesy), I have not received an answer" from Tolstoi.[135] Murav'ev also cast some blame on the bishops, who, he complained, are guilty of "silence and cowardice" and "act only according to orders."[136]

Filaret's succesor, Innokentii, renewed the demand for episcopal councils. Once an advocate of reform, now profoundly disillusioned with its course, especially in ecclesiastical education, Innokentii protested the procurator's dominance in Church policy and declared that only a council had the canonical authority to make fundamental changes in Church institutions and their operation.[137] Though the emperor and Tolstoi endeavored to accommodate

---

[132]OR GPB, f. 498 (A. N. Murav'ev), d. 8, ll. 1–22 (A. N. Murav'ev, draft of "Zapiska oberprokuroru D. A. Tolstomu o nedostatkakh tserkovnogo upravleniia").

[133]OR GBL, f. 149 (uncatalogued letter, Murav'ev to Leonid, 9.2.1867).

[134]Ibid. (uncatalogued letter, Murav'ev to Leonid, 16.2.1867).

[135]Ibid. (uncatalogued letter, Murav'ev to Leonid, 2.3.1867).

[136]*TsOV*, 1877, no. 30; see also Kazanskii's letter to Bishop Platon, 26.11.1867 (Beliaev, "Kazanskii i ego perepiska," *BV*, 1913, no. 5: 133).

[137]Savva, *Vospominaniia o Leonida* (Moscow, 1877), pp. 196–98; "Iz zapisok senatora Lebedeva," *RA*, 1911, no. 11: 343.

Innokentii, the procurator plainly resisted the idea of regional assemblies and argued that only a national council had purpose and justification—probably believing that a gathering in Petersburg would be more amenable to his control.[138] At Tolstoi's request, a trusted bishop, Makarii, drafted a research note on episcopal assemblies in the Byzantine and medieval Russian Church that summarized their prerogatives, competence, and composition. Tolstoi, whom hierarchs increasingly suspected of favoring priests over bishops, asked specifically whether members of the white clergy had been allowed to participate in such councils. Makarii's memorandum showed that the state's role in medieval assemblies had been limited but had included the right to confirm the councils' resolutions. He also contended that white clergy had participated in such councils but had no right to vote.[139] In the end, a quasi-official gathering took place in 1869 to celebrate first the fiftieth anniversary of the Kiev Academy and then the jubilee of Isidor's consecration. But there the experiment ended, not to reappear until the 1880s.[140] Tolstoi fostered some modest decentralization (minor questions were shifted to diocesan administration to eliminate useless paperwork for the Synod),[141] but he had no intention of mobilizing his adversaries in the hierarchy. Though he remained tactful, paying lip service to the notion of enhanced episcopal power, his whole strategy of reform—in diocesan administration as in other issues—was to improve the status of parish clergy and give them a more active role in diocesan affairs.

Unsympathetic to episcopal councils, Tolstoi nonetheless was well aware of the need for administrative reform. He first directed his attention to the old issue of low budgets, which left diocesan clerks underpaid and impelled bishops to tolerate "gifts" as indispensable supplements to the grotesquely inadequate salaries.[142] Such problems were most acute in dioceses relegated to "rank three" in the hierarchy of dioceses established by the state in 1764 as part of its secularization of Church peasants. This division into three classes, Tolstoi observed, "was based neither on the seniority of the dioceses nor on their size, nor on the number of inhabitants there, nor on the relative difficulty of governing diocesan administration." Tolstoi also blamed the evil of frequent episcopal translation on the system of diocesan ranks: "This divi-

[138] A. V. Gorskii, "Neizdannye mesta iz 'Dnevnika' A. V. Gorskogo," *BV*, 1914, no. 10/11: 402–3.

[139] F. I. Titov, ed., "Zapiska o russkikh pomestnykh soborakh," *TKDA*, 1906, no. 2: 305–12.

[140] For the attempts to establish episcopal councils in the 1880s, see below, pp. 444–47.

[141] TsGIA SSSR, f. 797, op. 35, g. 1865, otd. 1, d. 148, ll. 1–126; f. 796, op. 146, g. 1865, d. 1099, ll. 1–338; *PSZ (2)*, 40: 42347-49, 42506-8, 42558-60, 42699-700.

[142] The journalistic attention to such irregularities was immense; see, for example, "Ob otnosheniiakh dukhovenstva k konsistorii," *SL*, 1868, no. 6: 5–6, and "O noveishikh reformakh dukhovenstva," *Nedelia*, 1868, no. 32: 994–95. Significantly, bishops were no less disturbed by the failings and foibles of their secretarial staff; see, for example, Savva's lamentations to Leonid in a letter of 13.4.1868 (OR GBL, f. 149, uncatalogued letter).

sion has had the disadvantage [of impelling] bishops to be transferred from one diocese to another (in a higher class) as a promotion, which does not in the least accord with the dignity of the episcopal office or the canons of Church councils, and which is also contradictory to the interests of [regular] diocesan administration."[143] Despite repeated complaints that diocesan budgets were insufficient and ill-distributed, the government steadfastly refused to provide additional sums for the usual fiscal reasons. As recently as 1862 Alexander had rejected a Synod request for supplementary funds, writing that "despite my desire to assist ecclesiastical administration in its needs, I find this impossible to do at the present time."[144]

Tolstoi resumed the Church's effort to augment diocesan budgets shortly after his appointment as chief procurator. Aware of the state's refusal to grant new monies, he created a special committee to consider the matter and suggested that it explore the possibility of imposing a tax on Church documents (such as birth and marriage certificates).[145] Although that idea had been periodically considered earlier, it had been rejected as unseemly for the Church, difficult to administer, burdensome for clergy, and (one suspects) too vulnerable to peculation.[146] Tolstoi's committee refurbished these plans nevertheless and projected a potential revenue of one-half million rubles per annum.[147] Although the State Council rejected the scheme on the usual grounds that it was unseemly, it authorized Tolstoi to prepare a formal request for state assistance and ultimately approved most of the 700,000 rubles that he sought.[148]

Tolstoi thus achieved a substantial improvement in the salaries of lay clerks, raising hopes that the Church at long last could put an end to extortion and bribery. *The Contemporary Paper*, for example, pronounced the change "a major event in the ecclesiastical domain" that would permit the

---

[143] *IVO (1867)*, p. 160.

[144] Quoted in TsGIA SSSR, f. 796, op. 148, g. 1867, d. 548, l. 20.

[145] Ibid., l. 21; *IVO (1866)*, pp. 151–53.

[146] For an overview, see TsGIA SSSR, f. 796, op. 148, g. 1867, d. 548, ll. 15–25.

[147] Ibid., ll. 21–25; f. 1149, op. 7, g. 1867, d. 104, ll. 1–52. While awaiting action by the State Council, Tolstoi tapped the funds of the defunct Bureau of Ecclesiastical Education (dismantled in the 1867 seminary reform) to augment the salaries of diocesan clerks (*IVO [1867]*, pp. 187–89).

[148] For the State Council's opinion, see TsGIA SSSR, f. 1149, op. 7, g. 1867, d. 104, ll. 92–94 ("Mnenie Gosudarstvennogo soveta," 9.3.1868). Tolstoi's original budget not only abolished the three-class division of dioceses but also prescribed enormous increases in diocesan budgets; the consistory secretary, for instance, would have his salary raised sixfold (from 257 rubles to 1,500 rubles per annum). To finance these increases, Tolstoi proposed to abolish the remaining district boards and to request an additional 490,822 rubles from the state—altogether, providing the 700,000 rubles needed for the reform (ibid., f. 796, op. 148, g. 1867, d. 548, ll. 58–61 ob. [Tolstoi to Synod, 2.8.1868]). The State Council reduced these demands to a total of 600,000 rubles, to be made available through gradual increments over the next several years (ibid., ll. 72–79).

Church to introduce a whole new order of regular, honest government.[149] Tolstoi himself expressed hopes that the new budget would lead to "a change in the relationship between consistories and diocesan clergy, who (for well-known reasons) regarded their organs of diocesan justice and administration with fear and antipathy." He made his sympathies clear when he added the hope that "the consistory can come out of that pathetic, degrading condition in which it has stood in the opinion of clergy and society."[150] Though a few commentators were more skeptical, suggesting reform could succeed only if accompanied by a full-scale purge of the present corps of officials, most foresaw a new era in Church administration.[151]

Such hopes were further buoyed by the increasing tendency to permit clergy to elect their own superintendents, which had been a primary demand in Belliustin's *Description* and in the clerical press ever since. Although only a minority of bishops permitted elections by the mid-sixties, the innovation enjoyed great popularity among journalists and, by all accounts, the rank-and-file clergy as well. Thus one liberal paper, *The Week,* proclaimed the election of superintendents "the most important new reform" in the Church, and even the moderate *Orthodox Review* wrote that "the superiority of the electoral order for the appointment of superintendents is universally recognized."[152] Parish clergy in Poltava made bold to petition their bishops for permission to elect their local superintendents: "Fully appreciating the superiority of the new order for the selection of superintendents, we cannot remain under the old order and can only wish for the maximum possible application of the new order [in our diocese]."[153] A survey conducted by Tolstoi in mid-1866 found that roughly one-third of the dioceses permitted some form of clerical participation and that the election of superintendents was often attended by agreements to provide modest salaries as compensation for their work.[154]

[149]"Po povodu novykh shtatov dukhovnykh konsistorii," *SL*, 1869, no. 32: 1.

[150]*IVO (1869)*, p. 268.

[151]*Syn otechestva*, 1869, no. 99.

[152]"O noveishikh reformakh dukhovenstva," *Nedelia*, 1868, no. 29: 899. See also "[Peredovaia]," *SL*, 1866, no. 2: 2; "Izvestiia i zametki," *PO*, 1869, no. 4: 137–38; "O vyborakh blagochinnykh i blagochinnicheskikh s"ezdakh dukhovenstva," *Litovskie eparkhial'nye vedomosti* [hereafter *Litovskie EV*], 1869, no. 21: 1218–53; "Raznye izvestiia," *PO*, 1866, no. 10, zametki: 99; "O vybore blagochinnykh v nashei eparkhii," *Vladimirskie EV*, 1868, no. 2: 85–96.

[153]"Izvestiia i zametki," *PO*, 1869, no. 4: 137.

[154]TsGIA SSSR, f. 797, op. 36, otd. 4, d. 151; *IVO (1866)*, pp. 108–10. The specific procedures in each diocese varied widely, as bishops established different rules on voting rights (especially for sacristans), tenure, and confirmation by diocesan authorities. For examples of these rules, see the regulations promulgated for Tula (*Tul'skie EV*, 1867, no. 4: 77–86), Vologda (TsGIA SSSR, f. 804, op. 1, r. 1, d. 18, ll. 11–11 ob.), Saratov ("Vybor blagochinnykh," *Saratovskie EV*, 1865, no. 12: 23–28), and Viatka (*Viatskie EV*, 1868, no. 22: 531–36).

But the majority of bishops had *not* introduced the new method, and some emerged as outspoken critics of the change. The most prominent foes included the venerable metropolitan of Moscow, Filaret, who censured his fellow prelates for acceding to the "fashion" and advised that "caution is in order if 'democratic principles' are not to be allowed to penetrate the diocese."[155] Filaret even composed a lengthy memorandum on the subject, in which he dismissed the electoral principle as a shallow imitation of secular policies and warned that it could undermine the very foundations of Church administration. The metropolitan feared that elected superintendents would prevent effective governance by bishops and become a shield for clerical malfeasance: "What will this [new order] mean? Simply that [parish clergy] will choose mainly not the zealous and strict but the tolerant and weak, who will conceal their failings and not inform [authorities] of disorders."[156] In fact, some bishops who had experimented with the election of superintendents confirmed such complaints. The bishop of Chernigov, for example, reported cases "where the election was either accompanied by disputes and arguments among electors, or fell upon persons with a bad record in the consistory's files (and hence, given the regulations in the Statute of Diocesan Consistories, had to be replaced)." The bishop consequently decided to reestablish the old order of appointed superintendents "to avoid useless paperwork."[157]

The new order, however, had its defenders in the hierarchy. One was Archbishop Antonii of Smolensk, who hastened to apply the new principle to his diocese and affirmed his belief that "it is necessary and useful at the present time" to permit such elections, especially since "one cannot deny the clergy what is given to the peasants."[158] In a note to Metropolitan Filaret of Moscow on the election of superintendents, Antonii offered an animated critique of an anonymous memorandum actually written by Filaret himself.[159] Antonii refuted the arguments about imitation of secular practice, noting that the clergy had until recent times elected the clerical elders, and he denied the import of various difficulties that Filaret foresaw. But his principal argument in favor of elected superintendents was the need to improve relations within the clerical domain between the hierarchy and the parish clergy. Although Antonii saw no evidence of dangerous conflict at the moment, he warned that archaic methods of rule "can cause a spirit of dissatisfaction to develop and give rise to just complaints against superiors." In his view, it was far worse for the bishop to designate a bad superintendent

---

[155]TsGIA SSSR, f. 796, op. 205, d. 636, ll. 1–1 ob. (unsigned letter, 30.4.1867).

[156]Ibid., f. 832, op. 1, d. 32, ll. 28–31 ([Filaret], "O vybore blagochinnykh"; published in "Materialy dlia biografii mitr. Filareta," *ChOLDP*, 1868, kn. 5: 168–70).

[157]TsGIA SSSR, f. 797, op. 36, otd. 4, d. 151, ll. 26–26 ob.

[158]OR GBL, f. 149, uncatalogued letter, Antonii to Leonid, 25.1.1866.

[159]TsGIA SSSR, f. 832, op. 1, d. 32, ll. 15–15 ob. (Antonii, 19.2.1866).

than for parish clergy to elect one, for such errors compromised the moral authority of bishops and diocesan government. Even more striking than Antonii's concern about the tensions between white and black clergy was his desire to stimulate corporate initiative in the parish clergy. In his words, "the right of election will awaken the clergy from apathy and unconcern for Church affairs in which it is now buried by the present administrative order (and other unfavorable circumstances of the past), and will give clergy the possibility and incentive to assemble periodically not just for mutual celebrations, but for the discussion of matters pertaining to their service and interests."[160] That concern, in fact, had also impelled some bishops to create superintendents' councils (*blagochinnye sovety*), small boards composed of the superintendent and a few local priests, who gathered regularly to resolve minor administrative and judicial matters.[161]

Although such ideas meshed well with Tolstoi's program of reform and enjoyed his own cautious support,[162] the Synod took no formal action on the question of elected superintendents and left it to the discretion of individual bishops. That policy provoked much tension in dioceses where clergy did not yet enjoy this privilege, but Tolstoi evidently feared to press the hierarchs for a formal resolution of the problem. Opposition seemed so strong among ranking prelates and among diocesan bishops more generally that Tolstoi preferred to concentrate upon two other issues, censorship and justice, where he would chart the most radical reforms of all.

Censorship Reform

The erosion of censorship that had begun in the late 1850s continued unabated throughout the 1860s, gradually depriving the Church of effective con-

[160]Ibid., ll. 16–27 (Antonii, "O vybornom nachale v prilozhenii k blagochinnym").

[161]See, for example, *Chernigovskie eparkhial'nye vedomosti*, 1869, no. 1; for a summary account, see *IVO (1868)*, pp. 128–29; *IVO (1869)*, pp. 100–2.

[162]Tolstoi's official report for 1869, for example, noted the special trust that parish clergy held for elected superintendents (*IVO [1869]*, pp. 102–3). Characteristically, Tolstoi the *gosudarstvennik* primarily saw in the election of superintendents a new device to finance Church administration. From the very first, Tolstoi sought to link elections with the local clergy's willingness to provide remuneration, enabling the superintendent to perform his duties with greater zeal and less peculation. As he wrote in his published report for 1867, "with the acceptance of the elected principle in other [additional] dioceses, one can hope that the superintendents will not be left without [monetary] support" (*IVO [1867]*, p. 170). Tolstoi did more than hope: in 1866 he sent a circular to dioceses with elected superintendents, urging the clergy to provide fair compensation (TsGIA SSSR, f. 797, op. 36, otd. 4, d. 151, ll. 53–53 ob.). Although clergy in some dioceses had already done so (those in Ekaterinoslav and Orel, for example, provided from 50 to 500 rubles), elsewhere the parish clergy or bishop rejected this demand as unwarranted or unfeasible (ibid., ll. 55–56, 58–58 ob., 75–76, 113–14 ob.; *IVO [1866]*, pp. 169–70).

trol over literature about the Church, clergy, and religion. The process markedly accelerated after 1865, partly because of the reform in government censorship (which substituted punitive for preventive censorship in most forms of publication), and partly because of the state's striking leniency toward critical comment on religious matters. Even within its own domain, the Church found it increasingly difficult to regulate comment: the rapid proliferation of ecclesiastical periodicals simply overwhelmed the primitive structure designed by the 1828 statute on Church censorship.[163] Although censors could interdict an occasional piece, and although Petersburg could rebuke local authorities for publishing unseemly articles in diocesan serials, the Church had plainly lost the capacity to muzzle and regulate contemporary journalism.[164]

Nothing so dramatically illustrates this disintegration as the "second Belliustin affair," which involved a strictly religious tract, *The Week of Passion*. First submitted by Belliustin in 1865 and in due course approved for publication by Church censors, the manuscript stirred talk and aroused the interest of Metropolitan Filaret, who arranged for a further review of the work by his suffragan bishop, Savva (Tikhomirov). The latter was horrified to find that Belliustin had drawn explicitly upon Ernest Renan's *Vie de Jésus*, an infamous biography that treated its subject as merely human. On Savva's report, the Synod retracted permission for publication and informed Belliustin that "such a work as his, largely or wholly drawn from the works of Renan, is unworthy of an Orthodox priest."[165]

But the era of Great Reform, if nothing else, had emancipated the spirit. Belliustin, who had quailed in fear in 1858, did not "accept" that judgment

---

[163]Simultaneously, the censorship apparatus had virtually collapsed; see "Zapiski arkhiepiskopa Nikanora," *RA*, 1908, no. 2: 182. On the surging growth of diocesan periodicals, see the summary account in *IVO (1866)*, pp. 121–22.

[164]To be sure, the files of the St. Petersburg censorship committee show that it did interdict some literature. In 1866, for example, it rejected articles for making "false judgments on Church schools," for exhibiting "the excessively acerbic tone of an exposé," and for "ridiculing the system of administration in the Russian Church" ("Zhurnaly S.-Peterburgskogo komiteta dukhovnoi tsenzury," TsGIA SSSR, f. 807, op. 2, d. 1448, l. 121 ob.; d. 1429, ll. 186–87, 250; d. 1482, unpaginated). Though most diocesan periodicals, such as *Moskovskie eparkhial'nye vedomosti*, feared "to publish any bold articles and avoided any polemics" (Beliaev, "Kazanskii i ego perepiska," *BV*, 1916, no. 2: 303), some occasionally slipped from the bishop's grasp and published highly controversial essays. See, for example, the complaint by the minister of interior in 1866 against an article in *Chernigovskie eparkhial'nye vedomosti*, which drew the bitter conclusion that so far the state had done nothing to improve the clergy's lot (TsGIA SSSR, f. 797, op. 36, otd. 1, d. 75, ll. 1–32). At the same time, official complaints did little to temper the tone of *Sovremennyi listok* (sponsored by the St. Petersburg Academy) or, especially, secular newspapers like *Novoe vremia* and *Russkie vedomosti*. See the official complaints on all three in TsGIA SSSR, f. 807, op. 2, d. 1433, l. 5; f. 797, op. 38, otd. 1, st. 1, d. 90; f. 796, op. 149, g. 1868, d. 889.

[165]TsGIA SSSR, f. 807, op. 2, g. 1868, d. 1478, ll. 17–17 ob.

and sent four petitions to the Synod, each more angry than the last, denying that he had borrowed anything more than isolated historical and ethnographic data from Renan.[166] The priest's fourth petition (September 1868) even contained an unveiled threat. He admonished the Synod to act promptly, "before he submits a complaint to the Sovereign for slander against him." Amazingly enough, the Synod retreated, agreeing that Belliustin could resubmit his manuscript after he made the necessary "revisions," which consisted mainly in the elimination of all references to Renan.[167]

Together with the liberals' argument that censorship had shackled Orthodoxy more than its foes, this breakdown of censorship renewed authorities' earlier interest in censorship reform.[168] The prime mover here was Chief Procurator Tolstoi, who made a formal proposal in 1870 to replace the outdated and unworkable 1828 statute with a new order more consistent with Church interests and contemporary practice. He based his argument primarily upon sheer practicality, for the new academy statutes of 1869 had abolished the academy "conference" (konferentsiia), the organ formally responsible for censorship of religious literature. As interested as ever in aligning the Church with the parallel state system, Tolstoi noted that the government itself was currently reviewing its own censorship laws and had already formed a special commission under Prince Urusov. When Tolstoi proposed that the Church form a similar committee, with one member of the Synod, three clerics, and two deputies of the procurator, the Synod agreed. As chairman it designated Archbishop Makarii (Bulgakov) of Lithuania, an outspoken critic of the existing censorship and a close ally of the reforming procurator.[169]

Makarii's committee completed its deliberations within a few months and in May 1870 submitted its proposals for "the necessary changes and improvements" in ecclesiastical censorship.[170] Transcending Tolstoi's narrow "institutional" argument for reform, the committee offered a scathing critique of the arbitrariness so endemic to the present order:

> Quite apart from the fact that [censors] have different levels of education, they sometimes (because of suspiciousness and fears of personal accountability) delay or forbid things that actually contain nothing reprehensible,

[166] Ibid., ll. 17 ob.-23 ob.

[167] Ibid., l. 23. For the emperor's secret order banning Belliustin from visits to St. Petersburg (directing the local bishop, without explanation, to refuse Belliustin the obligatory travel permits), see ibid., f. 797, op. 34, otd. 1, st. 1, d. 89, ll. 1-6.

[168] See above, p. 332.

[169] TsGIA SSSR, f. 797, op. 40, otd. 1, st. 1, d. 7, ll. 3-4 ob. (Tolstoi to Synod, 9.1.1870), 6-7 ob. (Synod resolution, 16.1.1870).

[170] Ibid., f. 796, op. 151, g. 1870, d. 1422, ll. 14-39 ("Soobrazheniia o neobkhodimykh izmeneniiakh i uluchsheniiakh v Ustave dukhovnoi tsenzury"); see also IVO (1870), p. 272.

harmful, or dangerous. Censorship practice provides examples where the censor has forbidden something merely because it is less dangerous for him to prohibit it, even though he himself is not entirely persuaded that, if approved, what he has prohibited would [actually] prove harmful and dangerous.

Worse still, argued the committee, the present censorship had proven incapable of eradicating truly evil publications (such authors could always find ways to circumvent the law) and primarily served to hamstring authors of good intentions. If anything, existing censorship only served to arouse discontent and anger among educated society. The committee also repeated the view of Church liberals that censorship had sapped the intellectual vitality of Orthodoxy, for it "does not permit the slightest growth and development of lively activity of the intellect in the area of theological doctrines, and drains the energy of writers by constantly reminding them not to utter anything excessive or conditionally incorrect." In effect, censorship aimed to stifle controversy, which actually lay at the very heart of discovery and had been characteristic of the first, most fertile centuries of Christian thought. The committee also observed that censorship was a relatively recent phenomenon; it appeared only in the Synodal period and, significantly, coincided with a general stagnation in Orthodox thought.

The committee's proposals to integrate Church censorship fully into the larger system of state censorship followed lines wholly amenable to Tolstoi. Organizationally, that meant the formal merger of secular and ecclesiastical censorship through the formation of a single committee composed mainly of laymen and including one delegate from the Church. The committee also recommended adoption of the new state system of punitive censorship for "all scholarly works of religious content," arguing that "this censorship alone would suffice to reach the goals of ecclesiastical censorship—[namely,] to protect the teachings, traditions, and rites of the Orthodox Church from abuse by the press." Citing with approval the model of lay censorship, the committee expressed the hope that "ecclesiastical literature will be afforded, at least, what was already been given to secular literature." Specifically, the committee proposed to exempt all religious literature (save liturgical texts) from prior censorship and to apply to the Church the "temporary rules" adopted in the government's censorship reform of 1865. As guidelines for censorship, the committee urged drastic revision of the existing rules to replace the vague injunctions of the 1828 statute (which even required evaluation of literary merit) with more precise formulations of punishable offenses, such as blasphemy, "blatant" disrespect for dogma, and subversion of episcopal authority.

The Synod approved these proposals almost in their entirety. It even incorporated the committee's report into its own resolution, with only minor stylistic changes to temper the committee's liberality (for example, it changed the phrase "blatant disrespect of dogma" to mere "disrespect").[171] That the Synod agreed to some kind of reform is hardly surprising: the disintegration of its old machinery, the leniency in state censorship, and the sheer volume of ecclesiastical journalism made reform inevitable if the Church was to exercise any influence on the press. It *is* remarkable, however, that the Synod agreed to entrust ecclesiastical censorship to an overwhelmingly lay committee, given the bishops' longstanding distrust of state authorities. The Synod's acquiescence to Makarii's proposals thus bears eloquent testimony to Tolstoi's enormous influence at the time and, perhaps, its covert hope to reassert *some* influence over the press, lay as well as clerical. Widely praised in the contemporary press,[172] the Synod's proposal went to Urusov's special committee, where it became part of the larger—and ever more complex—politics of reform in the seventies.

Judicial Reform

Church justice had long been the butt of criticism, but its failings became still more obvious after November 1864, when the state adopted a modern judicial system for civil affairs that embraced publicity, jury trials, and the basic elements of modern European jurisprudence. Church justice, by contast, was a bizarre mixture of Byzantine canon law, Muscovite tradition, and Petrine rules—a hybrid that seemed increasingly backward and unenlightened. Its deficiencies affected not only clergy but also laymen, who were vitally concerned about such issues as marriage and divorce. But the parish clergy were the principal victims of ecclesiastical justice in a great variety of service and civil affairs. Beginning in 1865, and for a whole decade thereafter, Tolstoi and Church reformers labored to reconstruct the system of ecclesiastical courts, ultimately devising a plan that would radically change the traditional order.

The Church first explored the question in 1865, shortly after the state established its new system and even before Tolstoi became chief procurator. Aware of the great rift between secular and ecclesiastical justice and cognizant of the urgent need to realign these institutions, Chief Procurator Akhmatov directed his legal counsel Polner to outline the changes required for restoring harmony between the two systems.[173] Polner drafted a preliminary

[171] TsGIA SSSR, f. 796, op. 151, g. 1870, d. 1422, ll. 40–58 (Synod resolution, 20.1.1870/ 1.2.1871).

[172] For a convenient survey of opinion, see "Po voprosu o tsenzure dukhovnykh knig," *PO*, 1870, no. 3: 533–53.

[173] TsGIA SSSR, f. 796, op. 445, d. 408, ll. 1–70 ("Dokladnaia zapiska iuriskonsul'ta pri Sinodal'nom ober-prokurore o soobrazheniiakh na osnovanii koikh nadlezhalo by sostavit' dlia dukhovnykh ustanovlenii instruktsii po povodu sudebnykh ustavov 20-go noiabria 1864 g.").

plan, but it touched upon areas of state law and therefore required joint review by the government agencies involved—the Ministry of Justice, the Ministry of Interior, and the Second Department. In September 1865 the Synod obtained the emperor's permission to form a joint commission on the issue and designated Archbishop Filofei (Uspenskii) of Tver as chairman.[174] The committee's goal was extremely modest: to smooth away differences in matters of jurisdiction and procedure. It was not empowered to draft a comprehensive reform of ecclesiastical justice. News of the committee's formation elicited enthusiastic, but premature, praise.[175] Riddled by sharp internal conflict, the committee could do no more than draft a set of modest proposals that neither removed weaknesses in Church justice nor resolved the sharp discrepancies between ecclesiastical and secular justice.[176]

The failure of the first committee led Tolstoi in May 1869 to renew demands for judicial reform, but this time in a far more radical, systematic fashion. Tolstoi noted that the Church lagged far behind the state in modifying its basic legal system: the state periodically made substantial revisions in the *Digest of Laws*, but the Church had made virtually no changes in the Statute of Diocesan Consistories since its adoption in 1841. Furthermore, noted Tolstoi, the reform of government justice in 1864 had left an immense gap between ecclesiastical and secular courts, which now operated under radically different principles. To avoid encroachment by state courts, to protect the Church from public criticism, and to eliminate the widespread contempt for ecclesiastical justice that was evident even in official pronouncements, not to say the popular press, Tolstoi stressed the urgency of fundamental, radical reform:

> It is impossible to reconcile the Statute of Diocesan Consistories with the new principles [in secular justice] by changing and correcting individual articles [in the Statute]; just to modify a few articles in the Statute, without introducing the principles of the [state's] new judicial statutes into ecclesiastical justice would mean leaving judicial affairs in the Church on a lower level compared with justice in the civil, military, and naval administrations.

[174] Ibid., f. 797, op. 96, d. 35, ll. 2–3 ob. (zhurnaly komiteta).

[175] "Novyi sud," *SL*, 1866, no. 60: 12; "Raznye izvestiia," *PO*, 1866, no. 8, zametki: 177.

[176] On the internal conflicts, see "Zhurnaly vremennogo komiteta" (TsGIA SSSR, f. 797, op. 96, d. 35, ll. 3 ob.-10 ob.); see also the brief account in *IVO (1866)*, p. 154. The archives, unfortunately, contain no documents on the fate of this committee or even its final report; the minutes themselves are in the section of the chief procurator's archive for "miscellaneous materials" (TsGIA SSSR, f. 797, op. 96). Some information on the committee, however, is contained in Tolstoi's report to the Synod in 1869 (ibid., f. 796, op. 150, g. 1869, d. 736/a, ll. 2–3) and in "O soglasovanii tserkovnogo suda s sudebnymi uzakoneniiami 20-ogo noiabria 1864 g.," *SL*, 1869, no. 28.

Tolstoi recommended that the Synod form a special committee to design the reform, and he laid particular stress on the need for strong representation by academy professors specializing in canon law.[177]

In December 1869 the Synod approved his proposal and created a special committee to draft a full set of reform statutes. Though acquiescing in Tolstoi's demand for reform, the Synod evinced less enthusiasm for radical change and instructed the committee to heed "the basic principles of the state's judicial reform" of 1864 only "insofar as this proves possible for the specific character, purposes, and needs of ecclesiastical justice." Nonetheless, the Synod designated Tolstoi's ally, Archbishop Makarii, as chairman, no doubt at the procurator's behest, and also gave white clergy and juridical specialists a numerical preponderance on the committee, which consisted of five white clergy professors, two lay academy professors, the procurator's legal counsel, and eight lay legal specialists.[178] As one might expect, public announcement of the committee's formation evoked enthusiastic praise in the contemporary press, both liberal and conservative, reflecting the broad dissatisfaction with the Church's archaic and inefficient system.[179]

The committee assembled for its first meeting on 30 April 1870 and, over the ensuing two and a half years, held eighty-four sessions, finally concluding its work in early 1873.[180] The complex and controversial issues before it often caused its sessions to dissolve into angry, acrimonious debate. On most issues the committee divided into a liberal majority and conservative minority that reflected the numerical domination of laymen and jurists.[181] By the time the committee completed its work, however, most members, including Makarii, signed the draft proposals, with only three members filing separate dissenting opinions.[182] In February 1873 Makarii submitted to the Synod the fruits of his committee's labors—a draft statute on ecclesiastical justice, together with a detailed explanatory memorandum customary for such proposals.[183]

The committee noted that it was originally convoked for the purpose of

[177]TsGIA SSSR, f. 796, op. 150, g. 1869, d. 736/a, ll. 1–10 (Tolstoi to Synod, 23.5.1869).

[178]Ibid., ll. 12–14 ob. (notes from the metropolitans of Kiev and St. Petersburg, November–December 1869), 15–18 ob. (Synod resolution, 10.12.1869); f. 797, op. 39, otd. 1, st. 1, d. 295, ll. 5–7 (Alexander's approval for the formation of the committee, 12.1.1870).

[179]For vigorous expressions of support, see "Dukhovno-sudebnaia reforma," SL, 1870, no. 38; "Sudebnaia reforma v dukhovnom vedomstve," Golos, 1871, nos. 115–16, 171, 251, 289, 334, 359; "Dukhovno-sudebnaia reforma," Birzhevye vedomosti, 1871, no. 156. The reform also had vociferous foes; see, especially, the essays by a prominent member of the reform committee, A. F. Lavrov: "Novyi vopros v Pravoslavnoi russkoi tserkvi," Prib. TSO, 1871, kn. 2: 328–83; "Vtoraia apologiia po novomu voprosu," ibid., 1871, kn. 4: 677–788.

[180]TsGIA SSSR, f. 796, op. 150, g. 1869, d. 736/a, l. 38.

[181]See Golos, 1872, no. 60, for contemporary comment on this conflict.

[182]TsGIA SSSR, f. 796, op. 150, g. 1869, d. 736/a, ll. 46–47 (Makarii to Synod, 26.5.1873).

[183]The committee's proposals, explanatory memorandum, and other files are in TsGIA SSSR, f. 796, op. 445, d. 409.

reforming the existing institutions, its charge formally defined as "a review of the Statute of Diocesan Consistories." The main impetus for the review, it declared, was widespread concern about slowness and injustice in marital cases, where, "because of the mere absence of one party, the resolution of marriage cases sometimes dragged on for years at a time." But the committee had found limited amendment impossible: procedures for marital cases could not be altered without reforming the larger judicial system. Given authority therefore to redesign the basic structure of Church justice, the committee set as its explicit goal the elimination of shortcomings through the application of modern principles of secular justice. Since that program was likely to conflict with canon law, the committee, with surprising candor, defined its priority clearly: "The committee, [while] constantly having [canon law] in mind, is concerned to support and to preserve this insofar as it appears necessary and also consistent with the contemporary condition of the Russian Church's structure and administration, and also with the order of the state system and the demands of state laws." In other words, the committee intended to seek fundamental changes even at the expense of received tradition and canon law.[184]

The draft statute fully conformed to that declaration, for it charted a truly radical reform in the jurisdiction, structure, and procedures of ecclesiastical justice.[185] To avoid conflicts between secular and Church justice, which had escalated in recent years, the committee proposed to redefine the existing spheres of competence by expanding the Church's jurisdiction over the clergy but surrendering its authority over the laity—most strikingly, by yielding primary responsibility for divorce. This proposal was certain to be anathema to church traditionalists, who had repulsed such attempts in the past, and popular among laymen, especially educated society. To defuse opposition, the committee preserved the bishops' nominal right to oversee divorce cases and argued that the reform would greatly benefit the Church: it would spare bishops the task of investigating sordid cases of adultery and also free "ecclesiastical administration from [the onerous task] of conducting these numerous—and often quite complicated—investigations." Still, as conservative churchmen were sure to realize, secular control would invite liberalization of divorce and even the recognition of schismatic and sectarian marriages.

The committee also discerned major deficiencies in the structure and procedures of Church justice. One problem was the role of bishops, who held both judicial and administrative authority—a combination utterly antitheti-

---

[184] Proekt preobrazovaniia dukhovno-sudebnoi chasti: Ob"iasnitel'naia zapiska (St. Petersburg, 1873; copy in GPB [37.32.1.28/2]).

[185] Kratkaia ob"iasnitel'naia zapiska k proektu polozheniia preobrazovaniia dukhovnosudebnoi chasti (St. Petersburg, 1873; GPB [37.32.1.28/2]).

cal to modern jurisprudence, even if firmly embedded in canon law and Church tradition. Moreover, argued the committee, the judicial authority of the bishop and consistory embraced a broad range of punishments, some of extraordinary severity. Though moderated by the right of appeal to the Synod, this power (often vested in mere administrative orders) seemed arbitrary and incompatible with the values and institutions of postreform Russia. A second problem was the archaic formalism of procedure: borrowed from earlier state law and contrary to modern law, the Church judicial process was secret, even from the accused, and recognized only formal written proof, even when common sense admitted the falsity of such evidence. Finally, the existing system was unduly centralized, burdening diocesan authorities with numerous petty issues best handled at the local level. To overcome these deficiencies, the committee proposed: "(1) to separate judicial authority from accusatory and administrative authority; (2) to found courts [at a lower level], closer to the accused; (3) to replace written procedures with oral ones at public sessions of the courts; and, (4) to abolish the theory of formal proof." It argued that such changes, already adopted in the government's reform of 1864, had earned universal approbation and were no less necessary for ecclesiastical courts.

To apply these principles, the committee had to redesign the whole system of church justice. Separation of powers was the most delicate issue, for it entailed formal encroachments on the bishop's power and the creation of new organs in his stead. The committee argued that the bishop would not "forfeit" but merely "redelegate" his authority, as indeed some prelates had already done when they created superintendents' councils (*blagochinnye sovety*) to process minor disputes. The committee opposed further expansion of such councils, however, arguing that they were too slow and cumbersome to handle the great volume of petty cases that clogged the dockets of ecclesiastical justice. Such cases, in fact, represented 87 percent of all judicial matters in 1867–1869 (15,538 of 17,891). Instead, the committee designed a four-tiered system to streamline, professionalize, and decentralize church justice. The first instance was a new "district court" that would comprise one or more districts (*uezdy*) under an ecclesiastical judge elected by the parish clergy themselves. Such first-instance courts were to resolve petty cases and had no competence to consider more important offenses (for example, those punishable by defrocking), which in recent years had numbered about 780 per annum. To judge these, the committee proposed to create regional (*okruzhnye*) ecclesiastical courts, encompassing several dioceses and composed of a single bishop as chairman and several white clergy elected by their peers. Hence the committee sought to remove judicial matters entirely from diocesan administration, delegating minor cases to the district judge, important ones to regional courts. The regional court, though at first glance similar to the government's regional courts, differed in distribution: the latter appeared in each province; the former covered several provinces or dioceses, thereby leapfrogging the bishop as a judicial instance in the new order. Appeals against the regional court were to be reviewed in a special "judicial subsection" of the Synod and, as a final resort, in a plenary session of the whole Synod. Responsibility for investigating and prosecuting offenders would be transferred from the consistory and bishop to professional lay procurators, who, like procurators in state courts, would have formal legal training and also be subordinate to the chief procurator.

Here indeed was a blueprint for radical reform, one that shifted power from the bishop and consistory to professional jurists, chief procurator, and parish clergy. The draft proposal was an apotheosis of Church reform in the 1860s, reflecting the desire to rationalize institutions (even at the expense of canon law and tradition), to realign the Church with parallel state institutions, and to accord more autonomy and authority to the parish clergy. More than any other single reform, the judicial proposal represented a direct challenge to the traditional privileges and responsibilities of episcopal authorities. And, in contrast to such innovations as "elected superintendents," this reform cited no historical precedents; its explicit justification rested in rationality, modern conceptions of justice, and contemporary dissatisfaction.

That kind of proposal, clearly, put episcopal reformism to a stern test. Though any reform of ecclesiastical courts would inevitably entail some displacement (as it did in Western Europe as well),[186] the committee's scheme would compel the bishops to violate the canons and surrender their own authority. The first hint of how they might react was contained in the Synod's resolution on the proposals: it declined to take immediate action and instead distributed the draft proposal to diocesan authorities for comment and analysis. In other words, it turned the reform over to those who would suffer most from change. Its fate, as we shall see, now rested with them.

The Great Reforms of the late 1860s fundamentally recast the traditional Church order—its educational system, soslovie, service, and some aspects of administration. To tally up briefly what had been achieved by the early 1870s, most significant were the decrees abolishing hereditary family claims to positions (1867), separating children from the clerical estate (1869), setting up a new parish and service order (1869), and rebuilding the system of seminaries (1867) and academies (1869). Drafted, but not yet enacted, were even more far-reaching proposals to change the status of wives, the system of censorship, and the Church's judicial order. To the clerical question raised in the late 1850s, authorities had provided an answer for most, if not all, dimensions.

Yet that answer was substantially different in spirit and conception from

---

[186]See, for example, the problem of reforming ecclesiastical courts in England: *Report of the Commissioners Appointed to Inquire into the Constitution and Working of the Ecclesiastical Courts*, 2 vols. (London, 1883), 1: vii.

the original visions of an "emancipation of the clergy." Initiated under the
banner of "improving the clergy's material condition," reform in the late
1860s came to serve primarily the interests of the institution, not the soslovie.
In effect, Tolstoi's new measures emancipated the Church from the soslovie,
not merely by opening its doors to outsiders, but also by abrogating the main
prerogatives of the soslovie for education, appointment, and welfare. As the
redefinition of children's status showed, authorities drew a new distinction
between cleric and estate. The aim was to promote the interests of more
professional clergymen, even if that meant depriving their peers of positions,
their sons of education, their wives of pensions, their daughters of dowries.
The overarching goal was to reconstitute the clergy into a more dynamic,
more effective, more committed class of pastors—a change intended to serve
primarily the interests of the Church.

The reform was a legal rather than a social revolution: it pulled out the
legal underpinnings of the soslovie order; yet it implicitly assumed that the
clergy's reconstitution would be a gradual, long-term process. Indeed, for the
immediate future, the reform would rely heavily upon the traditional soslovie to supply most of the newer recruits (as Tolstoi frankly admitted) and
to provide financial support for schools, pensions, and special education for
clerical women. In large part that reliance upon the old soslovie was the
product of raw necessity, for the state lacked the resources to provide such
services. The only alternative was to summon the clergy itself to act in its
own interests. That policy was also a significant concession to the hierarchs
who feared a shortage of qualified candidates. And it reaffirmed the earlier
premise of reformers that authorities must overcome the clergy's traditional
inertia and give them an opportunity to assume a more active role in Church
and community. Ultimately, the reform would rebuild the clergy's social
composition, but its primary immediate effects were to alter the clergy's
"caste image" and, possibly, to inspire more initiative and zeal.

Reform, above all, affected the clergy's status within the Church, as Tolstoi
consistently sought to augment the priests' authority and role. The formation
of diocesan assemblies, the election of local superintendents, the right to
speak and write freely on religious subjects—such reforms were designed to
unleash the creative energies of clergy and enable them to play a more active
missionary role. Those concessions, however, brought the procurator increasingly into conflict with ranking prelates, ever fearful of state encroachment,
ever distrustful of procurators. The feeling was mutual. Bruised by conflict
with hierarchs, determined to make the clergy more zealous, Tolstoi grew
increasingly inclined to violate traditional episcopal privilege. As suggested
by his formation of diocesan assemblies and, more striking still, by his hint
that white clergy should participate in a national council, Tolstoi openly
favored the parish clergy's aspirations for a greater voice in Church affairs.
Although these changes aimed primarily to unleash the clergy from their

traditional "inertness," they also threatened the vital interests of the ranking prelates and even the unambiguous canons of the Church.

That kind of reform required its own politics. Above all, it placed a high premium on prompt, sudden action. After decades of memoranda and numerous committees, the landslide legislation in 1867–1869 was almost breathtaking. Here Tolstoi and his committees profited much from the work of predecessors, using the data, proposals, and opinion surveys collected in the early 1860s. The main value of that stockpiled data was not that it facilitated committee labors but that it simplified the politics: claiming to have in hand "diocesan opinion," authorities prepared new drafts with minimal consultation, avoiding the hazards of procrastination and outright opposition. At the same time, Tolstoi adeptly exploited public opinion. When he anticipated support (for example, in the educational or judicial reforms), he published the draft statutes for public consideration; when he did not expect such support (for example, in the parish reform of 1869), he gave no forewarning, and the statutes came like a bolt from the blue. The great exception to this astute politics was administrative reform, and here the results were different. By the early 1870s, without prior opinions and elaborate committee work, Tolstoi had drafted only preliminary proposals and, in the case of judicial reform, still had to run the gauntlet of diocesan commentaries. And prospects were not uniformly bright: even bishops who were committed to institutional over estate interests and had supported the reforms of the late 1860s were far less likely to support schemes to violate episcopal privilege, Church tradition, and canon law.

Thus the Great Reforms, though in large part already enacted, faced a severe challenge in the seventies—quite apart from the increasingly conservative mood in society and state, as difficulties beset the secular reforms. The statutes, as Tolstoi himself would admit, were vulnerable to criticism: hastily drafted and promulgated, they suffered from vast lacunae that would require reams of explanations. Moreover, the committees failed to design an integrated reform. The Synod, Special Commission, and State Council promulgated various reforms at various times and left some important laws unenacted and still under consideration. Yet the Great Reforms had begun to unravel a complex social and institutional order. It was imperative that authorities construct a new system, coordinating and integrating the changes in economics, education, and social policy. Significantly, Tolstoi's reforms rested upon a constituency of future professional pastors; in the interim they seemed likely to provoke opposition from bishops, priests, and parishioners— all of whose interests they had violated. Such opposition was all the more potent because implementation remained primarily a local affair: Petersburg drafted the blueprints, but diocesan authorities and local clergy had to build the new order and make it work. It was here, in implementation, that the ecclesiastical reforms would face their decisive test.

PART · THREE

From Reform
to Revolution

By the late 1870s state officials no less than oppositionist journalists were drawing alarming portraits of conditions in the Russian Empire. Famine on the Volga, strikes in St. Petersburg, disaffection in high society, terrorist acts by the revolutionary intelligentsia—all suggested fundamental problems in the new order created in the sixties. The very agenda of issues in the 1870s and 1880s—the peasant question, local administration, censorship, judiciary, education—revealed a growing belief that the Great Reforms urgently required major changes. *How*, not *whether*, was the essential question debated by officials and journalists, liberals and conservatives. Few contested the need for some kind of action, yet the very scope and gravity of the problems seemed to erode the bureaucrats' faith in their capacity to govern. Like the bureaucrats around him, Alexander too "lost confidence in everything he himself had created, in everything that surrounds him, even in himself."[1] Moreover, the renewal of reformism, as officials knew well, was fraught with great risk. As the emperor's chief minister wrote in 1880, "the countless series of commissions and endless, fruitless correspondence irritated public opinion and satisfied no one."[2] Ultimately, however, authorities addressed these questions anew, laying plans and adopting measures to modify—if not overturn—the Great Reforms of the sixties.

A transitional era of great importance, the 1870s and early 1880s have received relatively little attention. Much historiography concentrates upon the Great Reforms or the Great Revolutions, skipping over the intervening— and decisive—decades in between. Important problems, consequently, have gone virtually unexplored. One such problem is the actual impact of each reform. With the exception of peasant emancipation, most reforms await a more careful reassessment, a systematic inquiry into how and why particular reforms succeeded or failed at the grass roots.[3] Nor do we understand clearly the transition from reform to counter-reform. Though historians have traditionally taken the tsar's assassination in 1881 as a watershed, it is clear that

[1] D. A. Miliutin, *Dnevnik*, 4 vols. (Moscow, 1947–50), 1: 119–20.

[2] "Vsepoddanneishii doklad gr. P. A. Valueva i dokumenty Verkhovnoi rasporiaditel'noi komissii 1880 g. kasatel'no," *RA*, 1915, tom 3: 242 (M. T. Loris-Melikov report, 11.4.1880).

[3] Some reassessments have appeared for such areas as education (Sinel, *The Classroom and the Chancellery*) and the judiciary (W. G. Wagner, "Tsarist Legal Policies at the End of the Nineteenth Century," *SEER*, 54 [1976]: 371–84; J. W. Atwell, "The Russian Jury," ibid., 53 [1975]: 44–61).

reform and counter-reform do not form neat, discrete stages: liberal reformism persisted well after 1881; conservative counter-reform commenced well before that date.[4] The actual politics of counter-reform, moreover, remain a great enigma. Though recent scholarship has revealed the role of bureaucratic interest groups and competing bureaucratic ideologies in blunting counter-reform, it nevertheless remains puzzling that so imperious a ruler as Alexander III had difficulty obtaining counter-reform legislation.[5] Most important, research has focused mainly upon bureaucrats and revolutionaries, so that we know little about the development of other social groups in the seventies and eighties. Yet the dramatic appearance of broad social ferment in the nineties suggests fundamental changes in the preceding decades. It is essential that we explore more fully the evolution of attitudes and aspirations, especially with regard to the regime, the reforms, and each group's own place in the new order.[6]

Part Three seeks to provide the ecclesiastical dimension to these broader problems—the viability of the Great Reforms, the transition from reform to counter-reform, the impact of reform upon interested parties, and the authorities' efforts to amend or replace the Great Reforms. Chapter Eight examines the implementation of reform at the grass roots to see how Tolstoi's new legislation on soslovie, service, and seminaries worked in practice. Important, too, are the reactions of the clergy and, more generally, society to a new order that aimed to rebuild the Church, but at considerable cost and sacrifice for priest and parish. Chapter Nine addresses the politics of reform, the slow transition from Great Reform to counter-reform. Here it is important to see how bishops and bureaucrats assessed the Great Reforms, how they proposed to rectify them, and how these issues exacerbated long-

---

[4]For the policy shift of the mid-1870s, see the cases of the university statute (Alston, *Education and the State*, pp. 107–15; Sinel, *The Classroom and the Chancellery*, pp. 116–29) and local administration (Thomas Pearson, "Ministerial Conflict and Local Self-Government Reform in Russia, 1877–1890" [Ph.D. diss., University of North Carolina, 1977], esp. pp. viii–x). On the other hand, liberal currents survived into the eighties, generating some liberal reform proposals (for example, the Kakhanov plan for local administration and the Pahlen Commission on Jewish policy) and blocking ultraconservative schemes of counter-reform (for example, the judiciary). See Taranovsky, "Politics of Counter-Reform"; P. A. Zaionchkovskii, *Rossiiskoe samoderzhavie v kontse XIX v.* (Moscow, 1970); Heide W. Whelan, *Alexander III and the State Council: Bureaucracy and Counter-Reform in Late Imperial Russia* (New Brunswick, 1982).

[5]Soviet historians have particular difficulty explaining the "contradictions" in state policy; see, for example, the well-informed but awkward treatment of university policy in G. I. Shchetinina, *Universitety v Rossii i Ustav 1884 g.* (Moscow, 1976).

[6]For evidence of major changes in two groups, doctors and the nobility, see Nancy Mandelker Frieden, *Russian Physicians in an Era of Reform and Revolution, 1856–1905* (Princeton, 1981), pp. 129–31, and Roberta Thompson Manning, *The Crisis of the Old Order in Russia: Gentry and Government* (Princeton, 1982), chaps. 1–2.

standing tensions between Church and state. The final chapter addresses the ultimate impact of reform and counter-reform. It examines the condition of the Church at the close of the century, considers the continuities and shifts in the reform process, and weighs the reforms' broader effect upon clerical behavior during the revolutionary upheaval of the early twentieth century.

CHAPTER 8

The Great Reforms:
Implementation and Impact

By 1870 authorities had finally enacted major reform legislation on the Church, aiming to reconstitute the clergy from a moribund hereditary estate into a more dynamic profession of zealous, dedicated pastors. Although the reform made no provision for the sudden replacement of the current generation of clergy, it promised in time to reshape the Church's institutions in many fundamental ways. The new curriculum and structure of schools, the new service order, the merger of parishes, the abolition of hereditary ties—all laid the foundations for an entirely new kind of parish clergy and parish service. Yet these reforms—rationalizing measures designed to serve narrow institutional needs—directly violated the vital interests of bishops, priests, and parishioners. As Tolstoi must have realized, his reforms were certain to stir vociferous debate and determined opposition from below. In this chapter we shall move from the musty chambers of St. Petersburg to the grass roots of the Church, where our primary task is to see how well—or how poorly—the new reforms actually functioned.

Reform in Church Schools

By official accounts, the statutes of 1867 and 1869 that fundamentally redesigned the structure and purpose of Church schools seemed to be working well in the seventies. Admittedly, the reform progressed more slowly than Tolstoi originally predicted: the full implementation that the procurator had expected to see by 1872 was not achieved until 1879.[1] Despite such delays, Tolstoi proclaimed the reform a major success and gave a glowing picture of substantial improvement in his annual reports to the emperor.[2] Most improved in his view were the academies. They now attracted distinguished scholars to professorships, enjoyed rising enrollments, set higher intellectual standards, and even brought laymen to public lectures and dissertation defenses.[3] The seminaries likewise experienced a radical improvement, especially those reformed earlier, which "proved to be generally in very satisfactory condition during inspections."[4] Only in the case of elementary Church schools did Tolstoi admit problems. Yet here, too, he emphasized positive gains: "The conditions are gradually improving, although many of [these schools] still require minor efforts to bring all aspects into full agreement with the norms set in the statute of 1867."[5] Here diocesan clergy bore principal responsibility and, understandably, had great difficulty raising the capital to construct new dormitories and improve conditions.[6] Still, argued Tolstoi, reform had brought palpable improvement at all levels, effacing the ugly image that pervaded the *bursak* literature of the early 1860s.

Beneath the official gloss, however, observers discerned a number of serious shortcomings. One was a high rate of attrition: as in the prereform school, large numbers of students failed to complete the full course of study. In Viatka, for example, only 17 percent of the class entering in 1877 completed the four-year Church school in the allotted time; another 42 percent finished later; and 41 percent failed altogether to complete the school.[7] Moreover, many of those who finished the elementary school proved so ill-prepared that "a great percentage [of them] cannot pass the entrance examinations for the

---

[1] *IVO (1870)*, p. 145; *IVO (1878)*, pp. 165–66.

[2] Tolstoi relied heavily upon the investigations of the central Educational Committee *(U-chebnyi komitet)*, general overseer of Church schools, which dispatched professional educators to inspect each school every few years. Their reports were published and, for the most part, are available in GPB and GBL; see, for example, Uchebnyi komitet, *Otchet po obozreniiu dukhovno-uchebnykh zavedenii Viatskoi eparkhii* (St. Petersburg, 1871), located in GPB (18.225.3.7).

[3] *IVO (1870)*, pp. 142, 145; *IVO (1872)*, pp. 93, 95–97; *IVO (1875)*, pp. 156–57; *IVO (1876)*, pp. 143–50.

[4] *IVO (1878)*, p. 178.

[5] *IVO (1875)*, p. 183.

[6] For graphic descriptions of the persisting problems—poor physical plant, foul air, overcrowding, bad food, and the like—see the published journals of the diocesan educational committees (for example, "Zhurnal pravleniia Shuiskogo dukhovnogo uchilishcha," *Vladimirskie EV*, 1880, no. 7: 194–95; 1883, no. 6: 167).

[7] P. Luppov, *V dukhovnom uchilishche. Viatskoe dukhovnoe uchilishche v nachale poslednei chetverti proshlogo stoletiia* (St. Petersburg, 1913), pp. 29–30.

seminary."[8] In Volhynia, for example, nearly one-third of the applicants in 1876 failed the qualifying examination. The problem was so serious that some dioceses even established special trade schools to aid the dropouts.[9] Though the attrition rate in state schools was as high as or higher than that in elementary Church schools, the latter nevertheless weighed heavily upon public consciousness, offering proof that educational conditions in Church schools were still poor—Tolstoi's reforms notwithstanding.[10]

Official inspections, which were published and available to the public, confirmed such criticism. An inspection of one seminary, for example, revealed that some teachers still required rote memorization, not comprehension: "Those whom I questioned gave literal answers according to their notes, but [in response to] my questions that demanded more precise explanation of what they had just said, they had difficulty answering. In general, the pupils inadequately understood what they had said, had mastered the material for the most part mechanically, and had difficulty expressing their thoughts."[11] Such problems were still more acute in district schools, where one Greek teacher taught poorly "because he is studying the subject himself," and the catechism teacher forbade pupils to "deviate from the text."[12] Fearful of diocesan clergy, who now wielded considerable authority over the schools, teachers gave inflated grades; one instructor in Russian composition, for example, gave high marks to most compositions, with this comment: "Good, but illiterate."[13] Even conscientious teachers had difficulty because classes were still large, because they suddenly had to prepare new subjects, or because the pupils lacked proper background.[14] Reports like these flooded the secular and clerical press, raised serious doubts about the success of reform, and forced many to conclude that it had improved material conditions but not academic standards.[15]

Another rising source of concern was mass flight (*begstvo*) from the schools, as swarms of seminarians transferred to secular schools, especially the university. The reform, to be sure, had deliberately planned for some transfers. To reduce the number of candidates and make room for outsiders,

---

[8] "Normal'no li sostoianie nashikh nisshikh dukhovnykh uchilishch?" *TsOV*, 1876, no. 112: 3.

[9] "Iz Volyni," ibid., 1876, no. 133: 2–3.

[10] Between 1872 and 1889 some 75 percent of all gymnasium students failed to complete the course of study (Sinel, *The Classroom and the Chancellery*, p. 317).

[11] *Reviziia dukhovno-uchebnykh zavedenii Kazanskoi eparkhii v 1877 g.* (St. Petersburg, 1878), pp. 1–2; see also "Zloba dnia dukhovnykh seminarii i uchilishch," *TsOV*, 1878, no. 71.

[12] *Otchet o revizii dukhovno-uchebnykh zavedenii Iaroslavskoi eparkhii* (St. Petersburg, 1877), p. 22.

[13] *Reviziia dukhovno-uchebnykh zavedenii Kazanskoi eparkhii (v 1877 g.)*, p. 23.

[14] P. Rutkevich, *Seminarskie gody* (Kiev, 1912), pp. 1–5.

[15] See the discussion of such claims, primarily in secular journals (such as *Vestnik Evropy* and *Otechestvennye zapiski*), in "Khronika," *Str.*, 1876, no. 4: 97–98.

it coordinated the seminary curriculum with that of state schools and, more important, permitted seminarians to enter the university on privileged terms (namely, to matriculate after just four years' study and without taking the entrance examination). From the first, some critics had forecast mass flight, given the clergy's low social and economic status, and that indeed proved to be the case.[16] Flight was first apparent in the outlying dioceses, which traditionally complained of personnel shortages, but by the mid-1870s even central dioceses began to voice concern.[17] Here, however, the question was quality, not quantity; it was the most gifted who deserted the Church in droves. The conservative suffragan bishop of Moscow complained in 1875 that "the best seminarians [here] are transferring to lay ranks," and even the liberal press concurred that "seminarians—those best in development and ability—shun a theological education and transfer to secular schools of higher learning to complete their education."[18] This "brain drain" greatly alarmed the bishops. As Archbishop Savva wrote, "all the more capable and gifted students left the seminary prior to graduation," whereas "those who complete the seminary are weaker, less capable students who then constitute the main contingent of candidates for the clergy."[19] Another prelate pro-

[16]"K voprosu o preobrazovaniiakh v dukhovno-uchebnom vedomstve," *PO*, 1870, no. 11: 519–56; "Neskol'ko soobrazhenii po voprosam, predstoiashchim Kurskomu eparkhial'nomu s"ezdu," *Kurskie EV*, 1871, no. 21: 1121; A. F. Gusev, "Zhivoi vopros nashei tserkvi," *Grazhdanin*, 1872, nos. 7, 15–17; "Predlozhenie glasnogo sviashchennika Molchanova," *Riazanskie EV*, 1870, no. 10.

[17]For example, the bishop of Orenburg informed the Synod in 1876 that "there is a shortage of priests in this diocese and many parishes remain without priests and earnestly request that these be appointed, but there are no candidates available" (TsGIA SSSR, f. 796, op. 442, d. 642, l. 21 ob.). Similar reports came from bishops in Olonets (d. 641, ll. 30 ob.–31), Samara (d. 652, ll. 17–17 ob.), Ufa (d. 661, ll. 14–14 ob.), Tomsk (d. 630, ll. 21–22), Tobol'sk (d. 658, ll. 18 ob.–19), Astrakhan (d. 616, ll. 24–25 ob.), Poltava (d. 648, ll. 9 ob.–10), and Vladimir (d. 618, ll. 25 ob.–26). Some bishops, however, still had excess candidates, especially in dioceses where the parish reform had been implemented. See, for instance, the annual reports from Iaroslavl and Voronezh (d. 666, ll. 9 ob.–10; d. 621, l. 13 ob.).

[18]OR GBL, f. 149, k. 20, g. 1875 (ianvar'–iiul'), l. 150 (Leonid, "Dnevnik," 16.5.1875); F. Danilov, "Po povodu begstva vospitannikov dukhovnykh seminarii v svetskie vysshie uchebnye zavedeniia," *TsOV*, 1875, no. 133. Likewise, the hard-pressed bishop of Tomsk wrote the next year that "in the last five years the seminary has graduated twenty to twenty-five people, but the most capable have either entered institutions of higher learning or transferred to the civil service" (TsGIA SSSR, f. 796, op. 442, d. 659, l. 7 ob.). See also, on the western diocese of Podolia, "Pis'ma mitropolita moskovskogo Leontiia," *ChOIDR*, 225 (1908), otd. 4: 39. The flight also provoked considerable comment in the contemporary press; see, for example, G. Eliseev, *Begstvo seminaristov* (St. Petersburg, 1876); "K voprosu o dukhovnykh seminariiakh," *TsOV*, 1878, no. 43.

[19]TsGIA SSSR, f. 797, op. 50, otd. 3, st. 5, d. 182, ch. 2, ll. 59–60 ob. (1880 report); see similar reports by the bishops of Kishinev, Nizhnii Novgorod, Orenburg, Khar'kov, Chernigov, Tomsk, Poltava, and Saratov (ibid., ch. 1, ll. 4–5; ch. 2, ll. 2 ob., 5–6, 29–29 ob., 82 ob.–83, 158 ob., 234 ob.–235, 294 ob.–302).

tested that "our [clerical] youth are fleeing to the crossroads of the world, the Church's treasures are being plundered."[20] Though the Church had always suffered such plundering, the reforms introduced losses on an entirely new scale, seriously undermining the intellectual quality of the next clerical generation.

Conservative-minded prelates were even more disturbed by the overt secularity of the new schools. The very attempt to integrate Church education with society and parallel secular schools had, in the judgment of some prelates, led to a dangerous prominence of secular studies, dominance by lay faculty, and disregard for religious training. Such criticisms attended the statutes at their very adoption and won a growing number of adherents over the following years.[21] The most influential was the new metropolitan of Moscow, Innokentii, who vowed that he would seek to have the statutes revised, even at the risk of deposition.[22] In early 1869, less than two years after Alexander signed the statutes into law, Innokentii sent the procurator a letter demanding a formal review, partly because the reforms emasculated the bishops' influence over the schools, but primarily because they fostered a harmful "liberal" spirit: "It is difficult to disagree with those who say that the old statutes had errors and turned the pupils into nihilists. But the new [statutes], without rectifying old errors, make new ones, preparing liberals who are capable of joining every party harmful to our Church and state." Declaring that "I shall not—and I cannot—be calm until the new statutes are reconsidered," Innokentii threatened to confront the sovereign himself "about all that weighs on my heart, whatever the consequences may be."[23] Tolstoi firmly resisted Innokentii's demands, deriding his objections as due to "misunderstandings, inaccuracies and a failure to grasp the meaning of various articles in the statute." Ultimately, he succeeded in deflecting the metropolitan's protests.[24]

---

[20]"Tekushchaia khronika," *Str.*, 1879, no. 1: 139. For the request by the bishop of Tobol'sk to forbid transfers out of the ecclesiastical domain, see "Tekushchaia khronika," ibid., 1878, no. 11: 243. For an effort to discourage exit by publishing the letter of an ex-seminarian about his travails in secular society, see *Astrakhanskie EV*, 1879, no. 17.

[21]L'vov, *Pis'ma*, p. 350 (Isidor to Filaret, 3.10.1867); OR GBL, f. 149, uncatalogued letters, Antonii to Leonid (1.12.1871 and 12.2.1872). See also complaints in Petersburg that Antonii continued to agitate against the new order ("Zapiski arkhiepiskopa Nikanora," *RA*, 1908, no. 2: 181).

[22]Gerasim, "Vyderzhki iz moikh vospominanii," *Astrakhanskie EV*, 1880, no. 15: 283; "Iz zapisok senatora K. Lebedeva," *RA*, 1911, no. 10: 205; Beliaev, "Kazanskii i ego perepiska," *BV*, 1914, no. 4: 711. Significantly, Innokentii had earlier favored radical reform and spoke highly of Belliustin's *Opisanie*; see I. P. Barsukov, *Innokentii*, pp. 414–18, and I. Barsukov, ed., *Pis'ma Innokentiia*, 2: 151, 163–64, 168, 199–200.

[23]TsGIA SSSR, f. 797, op. 87, d. 223, ll. 23–28 (Innokentii, 9.4.1869).

[24]Tolstoi finally agreed to a special secret session of the Synod, which reviewed a memorandum by Innokentii that denounced the new statutes' secular tendencies, denigration of episcopal authority, democratic principles (faculty and clerical domination of the schools), classi-

That outcome did not stifle suspicions and dissatisfaction, which mounted steadily over the next decade amidst growing signs of a new secularity and independent spirit among the students. Typical was the complaint by the bishop of Vladimir: "The Holy Fathers are neglected in the seminaries, [and] everything is taught in accordance with Western theologians." As a result, he concluded, "young people are leaving the seminary as atheists."[25] The secular spirit, noted others, was integrally related to the problem of mass flight. As one critic argued, "only when instruction at the seminary pursues moral development (not just academic goals) will it be possible to hope that the exodus of seminarians to secular schools will abate."[26] The secular spirit also raised problems in the academies, most notably in discouraging students from taking monastic vows. The decline in monks at the academy depleted the number of "learned monks" and thus threatened to undermine the very edifice of the monastic hierarchy and the predominance of learned monasticism in administration and education.[27] Suffragan bishop Leonid, appalled by the secularity of postreform academies, even expressed relief that few graduates took monastic vows: "Alas, where is one to find [true monks]? Not in the academy, from which they have of late ceased to come. But that is good for the clergy's honor—at least it will not be ruined from those quarters."[28] Liberal clergy generally defended this secularity, which they regarded as a means to restore ties between the clergy and laity. Yet even reformers admitted serious problems and the need to reorder and redefine the curriculum.[29]

For the schools' critics, the most telling and politically powerful problem was the emergence of revolutionary radicalism in the seminary. Even in the 1860s, when incidents were uncommon, contemporaries widely regarded the seminary as a hotbed of nihilism, primarily because of the prominence of such ex-seminarians as N. G. Chernyshevskii and N. A. Dobroliubov in the revolutionary intelligentsia.[30] In the seventies ex-seminarians figured much

---

cism, and onerous financial burden on parish clergy (ibid., f. 797, op. 39, otd. 1, st. 2, d. 63, ll.13–46 (Innokentii, "Zamechaniia"). For the Synod's resolution, essentially disregarding Innokentii's objections, see ibid., ll. 48–50 (resolution of 7.5.1869); for Tolstoi's point-by-point rebuttal to Innokentii, see ibid., op. 87, d. 223, ll. 29–34.

[25] Savva, *Khronika*, 6:123–24 (letter of 22.1.1880).

[26] "Tekushchaia khronika," *Str.*, 1878, no. 11: 243.

[27] Savva, *Khronika*, 5: 556 (Savva to N. P. Kireevskaia, 16.6.1877).

[28] OR GBL, f. 149, k. 20, g. 1875 (ianvar'-iiul'), l. 192 (Leonid, "Dnevnik," 26.6.1875).

[29] "Tserkovnoe obozrenie za 1875 g.," *TsOV*, 1876, no. 1; "Neskol'ko slov po povodu peresmotra Ustava dukhovnykh uchilishch," ibid., 1876, no. 112; "Zametki o neobkhodimosti nekotorykh izmenenii v Ustave dukhovnykh seminarii i uchilishch," ibid., 1876, nos. 38–39, 44, 49, 58–62, 70–72, 78–79, 85, 87, 90. Even when rumors of a planned review of the statutes proved groundless, the liberal *Tserkovno-obshchestvennyi vestnik* urged authorities to amend the statute (see "Peresmotr uchebnykh planov dukhovnykh seminarii," ibid., 1877, no. 108).

[30] See, for example, the attempt to refute such notions in Pevnitskii, "Tiazheloe narekanie," *TKDA*, 1866, no. 8: 461–96.

more significantly in the revolutionary movement, constituting some 17 percent of all those arrested. Though that increase primarily reflects the larger number of seminarians in secular schools and especially in the university, most contemporaries tended to place the blame on their earlier education at the seminary.[31] In 1870 the Third Section laid more emphasis upon the role of ex-seminarians in radical circles, a role it attributed to the seminarians' "special philosophical education," their greater maturity (most tended to be several years older than gymnasium students entering the university), and their austere life ("the severity of seminary upbringing develops a concentrated, hardened character quite early").[32]

Though seminarians themselves formed a relatively small proportion of those arrested (less than 5 percent), that rate marked a sharp increase over prereform patterns and did little to ease doubts about the new order.[33] Most of those arrested were guilty of minor offenses, sometimes nothing more serious than reading seditious literature. Yet radical seminarians did share the general outlook of more active revolutionaries.[34] One can imagine Tolstoi's thoughts as he read the file on a seminarian in Arkhangel'sk who had prepared a manuscript journal urging the seminarian *qua* priest to "go to the people" like so many of his generation: "We have to go to the people and teach them. If we were at all familiar with socialist teachings, we could help the peasants with advice, propagate ideas of communal principles. . . . We could do this quietly, because the government would pay no attention to us." His was a utopian dream shared by many young populists of the seventies: "Oh, how good it will be when all are equal, when there is no property, and all is held in common, when there is no government or religious despotism, when in place of this there are free communes. Long live anarchy! Long live freedom!"[35] Nor did such cases inspire much confidence in local school authorities. Thus, when police arrested three former seminarians from Vologda in 1875 for "propagating revolutionary ideas and disseminating anti-

---

[31] V. S. Antonov, "K voprosu o sotsial'nom sostave i chislennosti revoliutsionerov 70-kh godov," *Obshchestvennoe dvizhenie v poreformennoi Rossii* (Moscow, 1965), p. 338. Former seminarians constituted more than one-third of the student population at the university by the late 1870s (see below, 405n).

[32] TsGAOR, f. 109, op. 223, g. 1869, d. 34, ll. 20–20 ob.

[33] Antonov's data on the total arrests for political offenses in the 1870s (5,664 individuals) include 226 students enrolled in ecclesiastical schools (Antonov, "K voprosu," p. 338). Recently published data on pupils expelled for political unreliability show far higher proportions; for example, in 1875 seminarians numbered nearly half of all those expelled (248 of 507) from all schools, lay and clerical (P. S. Tkachenko, *Uchashchaiasia molodezh' v revoliutsionnom dvizhenii 60–70-kh gg. XIX v.* [Moscow, 1978], p. 202).

[34] For example, searches uncovered caches of revolutionary literature in various seminaries; the works included standard fare for the seventies—Proudhon, Blanc, Lavrov, and Tkachev. See reports to the procurator in TsGIA SSSR, f. 797, op. 44, otd. 1, st. 2, d. 8, ll. 290–97 ob.; op. 45, otd. 1, st. 2, d. 17, ll. 3–5 ob.; op, 47, otd. 1, st. 2, d. 8, ll. 33–35 ob.; op. 46, otd. 1, st. 2, d. 9, ll. 64–67, 165–70; op. 49, otd. 1, st. 2, d. 6, ll. 191–91 ob., 197–202, 231–33.

[35] Ibid., op. 44, otd. 1, st. 2, d. 8, ll. 209–10 ob.

government books among the workers and lower ranks of the St. Petersburg garrison," authorities were understandably appalled to learn that all three had been released from the seminary with commendations for "excellent" conduct and morality.[36] To contain such seditious tendencies, authorities not only blacklisted unreliable seminarians but also quarantined unreliable seminaries by forbidding any of their pupils to enter the university, thereby implying that the seminary itself was the source of the revolutionary bacillus.[37]

If bishops and bureaucrats espied much wrong with the seminary, the parish clergy were no less dissatisfied, for the reform had imposed upon them an enormous new responsibility. In a report to Alexander, prepared shortly after the first cases of implementation, Tolstoi admitted a high degree of clerical discontent: "Before the new statutes had reached the dioceses, false rumors about them had succeeded in arousing debates among the clergy in some areas (this bordered on outright [expressions of] dissatisfaction in the diocese of Nizhnii Novgorod) toward the impending reform. Above all, they feared that the great majority of their sons would be left without an education." Tolstoi claimed that "all their doubts vanished upon reading the statute itself in detail," but in fact the clergy remained highly critical of the new system.[38] And not without reason, for it sharply reduced normative enrollments, making the local clergy responsible for financing additional sections and elementary schools. As one embittered priest in Tula wrote, the reform had deprived the clergy's sons of the traditional right to education and served only to extort additional revenues from the hard-pressed priests.[39] Another priest wrote that in his diocese the reform had excluded one-half of the present student body even as it imposed new burdens on the clergy, whose means—given the failure of economic reform—"remain the same as before."[40] Clearly, the terms of reform accorded ill with the hopes for state aid that had soared among the clergy in the early stages of Church reform.

[36] Ibid., op. 45, otd. 1, st. 2, d. 58, ll. 1–1 ob.

[37] For a typical file blacklisting individual students (named on a circular, which prohibited their matriculation or employment in educational institutions), see ibid., f. 797, op. 45, otd. 1, st. 2, d. 15, ll. 26–27. For the quarantines imposed on the seminaries of Saratov in 1869 and Vologda in 1875, see ibid., op. 39, otd. 1, st. 2, d. 94, ll. 1–5; op. 45, otd. 1, st. 2, d. 90, ll. 1–150. For Tolstoi's concern about the problem, see his sharp rebuke to authorities in Arkhangel'sk for concealing disorders (even to the point of destroying evidence), followed by a general demand that seminary rectors report all political cases immediately (ibid., f. 797, op. 45, otd. 1, st. 2, d. 7, ll. 24–25 ob.).

[38] Ibid., f. 797, op. 36, otd. 1, st. 2, d. 395, ch. 1, ll. 343 ob.–44. (Tolstoi to Alexander II, 28.11.1867).

[39] "Ob ustroenii detei dukhovenstva," Tul'skie EV, 1870, no. 17: 147.

[40] F. Vinogradov, "Delo uluchsheniia byta dukhovenstva," SL , 1870, no. 17: 3–4. For evidence of persisting opposition, see also "Sovremennyi vopros," RSP, 1876, no. 17: 507–16; "Zhelanie i zaiavleniia dukhovenstva otnositel'no svoikh novykh uchilishch," Vladimirskie EV, 1870, no. 6: 263–67; "Otkrytie pervogo kursa v seminarii posle preobrazovaniia ee po novomu ustavu," ibid., 1869, no. 22: 1076.

Disillusioning too was the experiment in diocesan assemblies, the new corporate institution of elected deputies summoned to address the needs of Church schools and to consider other common interests of the clergy. The very creation of such assemblies had rankled traditionalists from the first, provoking fears that the clergy, like gentry assemblies or the zemstvos, would exceed their purview and encroach on the rightful prerogatives of bishops.[41] Tolstoi tried to allay such fears in his account of the first wave of assemblies: "Despite some errors in a formal [technical] sense, nowhere did the assemblies exceed their duties or attempt to raise questions beyond their competence. At the same time, the assemblies inspired and reinvigorated the clergy, and to some extent helped to raise their social position."[42] Tolstoi plainly placed great hopes upon the effectiveness of the new assemblies to revitalize the clergy and to finance the reformed schools.

But the assemblies, for the most part, did not perform as expected. The problem was not a usurpation of authority (though there were some instances of that);[43] rather, they failed to aid schools or address the clergy's other needs. Metropolitan Innokentii, for example, castigated the diocesan assemblies in Moscow for their indifference to the schools, and, after reading the assemblies' journals, Tolstoi concurred: "It is clear that the assembly did not want to give a single kopeck to ecclesiastical schools."[44] Educational inspectors from Petersburg brought back similar reports. As one wrote after a visit to Kazan, "diocesan assemblies have been called every year since 1873, but without palpable benefit for the seminaries or Church schools."[45] Significantly, even liberal clergy admitted the predominance of such inertia. A clergyman in Kiev, for example, reported that one recent assembly "was not only indifferent but even hostile to the task [of aiding Church schools], as though it involved a supplementary salary for the emperor of China."[46] Another

[41] TsGIA SSSR, f. 797, op. 39, otd. 1, st. 2, d. 63, ll. 13–46 (Innokentii, "Zamechaniia").

[42] Ibid., op. 36, otd. 1, st. 2, d. 395, ch. 1, l. 345 ob. (Tolstoi to Alexander II, 28.11.1867).

[43] The diocesan assembly in Polotsk, for example, formally accused the bishop of malfeasance and demanded greater authority (ibid., f. 796, op. 154, g. 1873, d. 874, ll. 1–122). See also the infringements of the diocesan assembly in Kursk in 1868 ("Izvestiia i zametki," *PO*, 1869, no. 1: 27–28). Tolstoi himself admitted some problems upon occasion; see *IVO* (1872), pp. 162–63. For continuing problems, see the complaints of the bishop of Kherson in 1878 in "Eparkhial'nye s"ezdy," *TsOV*, 1878, no. 7: 1–2.

[44] TsGIA SSSR, f. 796, op. 154, g. 1873, d. 869, l. 27 (Moscow case). Likewise, the clergy in Vladimir in 1870 declined to construct a new seminary dormitory "until a more favorable time," noting that "even without this the clergy have great needs and inadequate resources" ("Zhurnaly eparkhial'nogo s"ezda dukhovenstva Vladimirskoi eparkhii," *Vladimirskie EV*, 1870, no. 19: 858). Some assemblies showed more initiative; those in Minsk, Saratov, Penza, and several other dioceses opened candle factories to increase revenues for Church schools (TsGIA SSSR, f. 796, op. 442, d. 637, l. 7 ob.; "Eparkhial'noe obozrenie," *TsOV*, 1875, no. 122).

[45] *Reviziia dukhovno-uchebnykh zavedenii Kazanskoi eparkhii (v 1877 g.)*, p. 20.

[46] "Kievskie pis'ma," *TsOV*, 1874, no. 32: 2–3. See also "Khronika," *Str.*, 1876, no. 1: 42; "Nedostatki eparkhial'nykh s"ezdov," *TsOV*, 1878, no. 27: 1–2.

wrote disparagingly that "it is just a waste of time to bother the clergy with these assemblies."[47] Explanations for the assemblies' inertia varied. Liberal journalists, echoing zemstvo ideologues, blamed the failure on insufficient authority and official restraints; conservative bishops discerned a simple refusal to assume financial obligations. Most assemblies rendered *some* aid, and a few proved highly active, but the program as a whole fell far short of the panacea envisioned by Tolstoi in 1867.[48]

Thus the reform gave considerable cause for discontent, first among the bishops and parish clergy, later even among its erstwhile supporters.[49] Though the reform achieved a significant improvement in material conditions and raised scholastic standards at the seminary and academy, it managed to do little at the lower level of Church schools. As ever in prerevolutionary autocracy, it was easier—and cheaper—to reform the top than the bottom, where the sheer costs and magnitude exceeded the regime's capacity to act. Though Tolstoi, like Valuev, looked for aid from below (in this case, the parish clergy), that collaboration proved of little import. The flight of seminarians, the taint of radicalism, and the high attrition rate all gave good grounds for criticism and demands for counter-reform in the seventies and eighties.

Parish and Service Reforms

The parish reform of 16 April 1869 had two principal goals: to improve the clergy's material condition and to raise their standards of service. It aspired to improve their economic status by increasing the proportion of parishioners to clergy through the reorganization of small parishes into larger

---

[47]"Penzenskii obshche-eparkhial'nyi s"ezd dukhovenstva," *TsOV*, 1876, no. 131. Clergy in Tomsk diocese even formally petitioned the Synod to reduce the frequency and size of diocesan assemblies, citing the great costs and time lost, especially for their far-flung Siberian diocese. The Synod, however, categorically rejected the appeal (TsGIA SSSR, f. 796, op. 159, g. 1878, d. 390, ll. 1–20).

[48]For a good picture of the uneven performance of assemblies, see the detailed account for assemblies in Astrakhan, which, though they fell short of original expectations, at times generated substantial aid for diocesan schools ("Deiatel'nost' s"ezdov dukhovenstva Astrakhanskoi eparkhii za pervyi trinadtsatiletnii period [1867–79 gg.]," *Astrakhanskie EV*, 1880, nos. 34–36, 38–43, 45–48, 51–52).

[49]Most critical of the new order were conservative papers, mainly because of its modest application of the electoral principle; see *Moskovskie vedomosti*, 1874, nos. 52, 77; and "*Grazhdanin* i provintsial'noe dukhovenstovo," *Grazhdanin*, 1874, no. 20/21. Even earlier to criticize the new order was the liberal paper *Golos* (1872, no. 195), which cited the numerous emandations to the statute as proof of its weaknesses and failure. Tolstoi's inveterate ally, *Tserkovno-obshchestvennyi vestnik*, which generally regarded the reform as the procurator's greatest achievement, nevertheless admitted the need for revising the statute ("Eshche po povodu peredovoi stat'i pomeshchennoi v no. 52 *Moskovskikh vedomostei*," *TsOV*, 1874, nos. 35, 40, 45–46, 54).

units and through the elimination of some clerical positions. Behind that
scheme lurked the hope that many parishes would volunteer additional revenues to save their local church, thereby assisting the parish clergy without
forcing the Church to dismantle part of its network of parishes. Parish
reform, however, was a staggering enterprise: local authorities had to prepare draft registries for 30,000 parishes in the empire (subject to review and
confirmation by the Special Commission) and then had to apply these, closing parishes and eliminating supernumerary clergy. At the same time, the
reform aspired to raise clerical standards by requiring that future priests possess a full seminary education and that they first serve as psalmists or teachers. Given the complexity of these tasks, the Special Commission set no time-
table and left the procedures for implementation largely to the discretion of
the local authorities. Though that policy was consistent with the spirit of the
sixties (heedful of local peculiarities, open to local initiatives), it remained to
be seen whether it would facilitate implementation or procrastination.

Initial Response to the Parish Statute

Most of the press responded enthusiastically toward the reform. Some journalists were positively exuberant. The Petersburg paper *Son of the Fatherland* exclaimed that "we see in the new decree a great reform for the clergy
that opens the way for a significant uplifting of the clerical rank in the eyes
of society."[50] Similar sentiments appeared in the diocesan paper in Kiev,
which predicted that the reform would lead to gradual, but substantial,
improvements for the clergy—not merely in its material condition, but also
in its service performance and commitment.[51] Most papers offered a more
tempered, though favorable, assessment. Thus *The Contemporary Paper*, a
reformist organ strongly committed to the interests of parish clergy, predicted short-run difficulties, especially in parish reorganization and staff
reductions, but concluded that the proposed measures were rational and certain to yield long-term benefits to both Church and clergy.[52] Another popular
journal for parish clergy anticipated that the reform would raise both income
and service standards among clergy but conceded that "of course it will not
be easy for the clergy to become accustomed to the new order."[53] The journal
of the Moscow Academy also predicted that "transition from the existing
order to the new one (as in other social reforms) may not be easy for the
present staffs of clergy." Yet it heaped praise on the reform, which "so

[50] *Syn otechestva*, 1869, no. 126.
[51] "Reforma prikhodov, sostava prichtov i byta pravoslavnogo dukhovenstva," *Kievskie EV*,
1869, no. 12: 431–38.
[52] "Obozrenie 1869 g.," *SL*, 1870, no. 2.
[53] S. S., "Reformy v bytu dukhovenstva," *RSP*, 1869, no. 30: 453–60.

importantly, so radically, so broadly, and so decisively addresses those aspects of our clerical life that have long demanded reform."[54]

Some periodicals, however, vigorously attacked the reform as harmful to the Church and clergy. The Moscow *Evening Gazette* categorically opposed the reform and warned that the some of its terms, such as the requirement of psalmist service from graduates, would wreak irreparable damage: "It is understandable that this [rule] will distress graduates and force them to find other service—even in another domain—that is more appropriate for their intellectual development and provides better material support than the paltry, unenviable share given a psalmist." The paper also complained that the reform failed to eliminate gratuities, leaving the clergy dependent and weak.[55] Another Moscow paper, *The Contemporary News* (whose editor, N. P. Giliarov-Platonov, was close to Slavophile circles), rejected the reform in principle and declared that parish reorganization would sunder the traditional bond between priest and parish merely to satisfy the selfish interests of clergy.[56] Such expressions of opposition remained rare, however. Most of the press welcomed the reform, even while foreseeing some difficulties in the early transitional period.

But the "public opinion" conveyed in the press bore little resemblance to the mood in society. All the available evidence suggests widespread opposition to the reform—among conservative churchmen, parish clergy, and parish communities—even when the reform was mere statute, its implementation still waiting in the distant, unspecified future. A. N. Murav'ev reported that "the mere rumor [of this reform] has already spread despair, both among the clergy and the people: each fears for his own native church, afraid that it will not meet the conditions needed for its preservation."[57] The suffragan bishop of Moscow, Leonid, who began visitations in his diocese shortly after the law had been promulgated, graphically described the popular response in private letters to the metropolitan: "I appeared in the eyes of Orthodox folk as something like a Tatar *basmach* sent from the Khan with the right to close churches. Some met me with trepidation, like a most ominous appearance, while others fell to my feet, either individually or in whole masses, crying out, 'Reverend Grace, don't seal up our church! Do not turn us into neglected cattle!'" Warning that such discontent could explode into violent disorders, Leonid appealed to the metropolitan to reassure the people

---

[54]"Novaia reforma v bytu dukhovenstva," *PO*, 1869, no. 5: 787–96; no. 6: 895–902; no. 11: 605–11. Such views also filled many diocesan papers: "Pis'mo k sviashchenniku po povodu novoi reformy v byte dukhovenstva," *Moskovskie eparkhial'nye vedomosti* [hereafter *Moskovskie EV*], 1869, no. 30: 6–15; "Neskol'ko slov o novoi reforme v dukhovenstve," *Vladimirskie EV*, 1870, no. 1: 32–33; "Ot redaktsii," *Kurskie EV*, 1871, no. 1: 17–25.

[55] *Vecherniaia gazeta*, 1869, no. 284.

[56]"O reformakh v dukhovnom vedomstve," *Sovremennye izvestiia*, 1870, no. 37.

[57]"Pis'mo A. N. Murav'eva k gr. A. D. Bludovoi," *RA*, 1881, no. 8: 421.

that "all will remain just as it has always been," even if such an act means "not to spare yourself for the benefit and salvation of your flock." Leonid later reported evidence of political overtones in popular discontent and quoted exclamations by angry parishioners:

> What right does the Tsar have to take away our church—it was not his money that built it! We do not touch things belonging to other people— and don't touch ours!
>
> Now there is a tsar for you: he violates the churches, but increases the number of taverns.[58]

Diocesan authorities reported similar problems in many areas, and most could agree wholeheartedly with the commission in Khar'kov that the reform created "an unfavorable impression."[59]

Rank-and-file clergy were no less hostile. Their mood was implicit even in journals anxious to convince priests of the reform's merits.[60] Some priests published articles sharply critical of the reform, declaring that it aided only a select few, inflicted great hardship on many, and left the Church vulnerable to subversion by Old Believers.[61] Embittered priests also complained that the reform failed to abolish the humiliating reliance upon gratuities and extinguished all hope of improvement in their social and economic condition.[62] Suffragan bishop Leonid of Moscow reported that "the clergy are complaining that the government, after demolishing its former unsatisfactory order (which was bad, but something they were accustomed to), gave nothing in return."[63] Clerical agitation even reached the ears of the Third Section, which reported that some clerics "tried to stir up peasants against the new laws, especially in those parishes which, because of the small number of people, could not remain independent." In spite of the clear instructions that the reform be implemented slowly and carefully, "the fear of being deprived of one's livelihood is shared by all the provincial clergy." A superintendent in Orel diocese had allegedly announced at a gathering of nobles

---

[58] OR GBL, f. 214, d. 445/5, l. 8 (Leonid to Innokentii, 17.9.1869).

[59] TsGIA SSSR, f. 804, op. 1, r. 1, d. 18, ll. 246–46 ob.

[60] In fact, much of the proreform literature frankly conceded broad opposition to the new measure; see, for example, "Pis'mo k sviashchenniku po povodu novoi reformy v byte dukhovenstva," *Moskovskie EV*, 1869, no. 30: 6–15.

[61] See, for example, F. Vinogradov, "Delo uluchsheniia byta dukhovenstva," *SL*, 1870, no. 17: 3–4. Some hostile literature was interdicted by censors. Typical was "On the Reduction of Clerical Staffs," an article banned by the St. Petersburg censors because it "speaks of consistory affairs in a tone that is ironic and insulting for an official organ" (TsGIA SSSR, f. 807, op. 2, d. 1301, unpaginated journal, 30.9.1869).

[62] I. Kazanskii, "Nekotorye neotlozhnye mery k uluchsheniiu byta sel'skogo dukhovenstva," *Saratovskie EV*, 1871, no. 12: 285–87. See also I. S. Belliustin, "Chto sdelano po voprosu o dukhovenstve," *Beseda*, 1871, no. 3: 134–57; no. 11: 61–82; 1872, no. 2: 179–210.

[63] OR GBL, f. 214, d. 445/5, l. 10 (Leonid to Innokentii, 17.9.1869).

that "the supreme [state] authorities wish to destroy the religious faith of the people and to transform the clergy into beggars."[64] The Third Section also reported the case of a priest in Vladimir diocese who was overheard to say in a tavern that "the tsar is generous to you, but he's not worth a brass farthing to us: he gave you medals, but he is taking away everything we had left."[65]

To quell discontent among parishioners and priests, Metropolitan Isidor issued a special explanation of the reform on behalf of the Special Commission, seeking to reassure clergy and laity that implementation would be circumspect and gradual. He emphasized that, even apart from the overall aim of improving the clergy's material condition, the Church's first obligation was to provide for the parishioners' spiritual needs. Hence the commission would permit no mergers, even of small parishes, if there were valid reasons to maintain them separately. Isidor also vaguely hinted that the pious laity could always save their parish by guaranteeing to provide supplementary support. To allay the anxieties of clergy, Isidor affirmed that there would be no summary expulsions or forcible relocations, even if one parish were attached to another. The leitmotiv, he emphasized, was caution: "This matter is to be conducted with particular caution, with full attention to the spiritual needs of the parish population, with no oppressive hardships for the present staffs."[66]

The reform also provoked opposition among many prelates: some eagerly embraced the reform, but most sought to evade or subvert its provisions.[67] Bishops in outlying dioceses, predictably, demanded special treatment and in fact obtained various exemptions (for example, from the rule that only seminary graduates over age thirty be ordained).[68] Some went further and pronounced the reform "inapplicable"; the provincial authorities in Vil'na, for example, cited the Uniate problem in that area and flatly declared "any abolition of even underpopulated parishes impossible."[69] More often the opposition was discreet, covert, and devious. One prelate advised a colleague

---

[64] TsGAOR, f. 109, op. 223, g. 1869, d. 34. ll. 83 ob.–84.

[65] Ibid., ll. 36 ob–37.

[66] TsGIA SSSR, f. 804, op. 1, r. 1, d. 18, l. 122/b ob. (circular, 23.8.1869).

[67] Because the commission did not solicit diocesan opinion before promulgating the reform, the bishops gave no systematic comment on their attitudes toward it. Given the lethargy with which many introduced the reform (only one-third filed draft registries within two years; nearly one-quarter still had not filed by 1875), it is clear that they had scant enthusiasm for the new statute.

[68] In June 1869—just two months after the decree was promulgated—the bishop of Minsk successfully petitioned the Synod for permission to ordain seminary graduates under age thirty, citing a lack of candidates for the 19 priestly vacancies in his diocese. Soon Arkhangel'sk, Caucasus, Perm, Olonets, and Kherson dioceses obtained the same exemption (TsGIA SSSR, f. 796, op. 150, 1869, d. 624, ll. 14–15 ob., 17–18 ob., 27–43).

[69] Ibid., f. 804, op. 1, r. 1, d. 18, l. 262 ob.

that "this matter, under a skillful diocesan head and given the good disposition of parishioners, can be arranged perfectly, without any harm to the
Church and without offending the religious sentiments of good parishioners."
Pointing out the significant caveats in the decree, in particular, the need to
consider the moral and religious circumstances in the diocese, he vowed to
"use all the means in my possession to defend small parishes in my diocese."[70]
The bishop of Podolia, in a private letter of 1872, also expressed determination to neutralize the reform and even "to form new parishes and (in some
churches) to double the staff."[71]

Especially hostile to the reform were diocesan authorities in Moscow.
Vicious rumors spread that "Count Tolstoi has fallen under the influence of
some kind of enemy of the fatherland and involuntarily serves him."[72] The
tactic in Moscow was to stall, not confront; in fact, the suffragan bishop procrastinated so long that Metropolitan Innokentii grew uneasy and summoned
him to oppose the reform openly, not covertly. Innokentii complained that
Leonid and other critics had prepared no materials against the reform and
implored him to act decisively: "Again and again I kindly ask you to do all
that you find necessary and essential regarding the new statute on the reduction of parishes. Everyone sees [the problem] and complains, but no one can
help [relieve] this sorrow. But one thing is certain: you can do this in the
name of your [provincial] commission. And may God be your judge if you
do not."[73] But the statute bore the emperor's signature. Few risked overt
sabotage; most preferred Moscow's tactic of silent noncompliance. Yet even
that policy had limits in the face of the Special Commission's demand for
progress reports and a full explanation of "why this matter has come to a
halt."[74]

One prelate, Metropolitan Arsenii of Kiev, formally proposed to revise the
statute. He argued that the attached churches should have their own priests;
otherwise, the priest in the main parish had either to neglect the attached
parish, which in that event was really abolished, or to serve each church
alternately, thus depriving both parishes of regular services. Arsenii also
demanded more flexibility on the "minimum" support, proposing to retain
a parish that offered sufficient support to attract candidates even if that
amount was below the legal minimum. Besides warning that few graduates

---

[70]"Pis'ma mitropolita kievskogo Arseniia," *RA*, 1892, tom 1: 226.

[71]OR GBL, f. 149, uncatalogued letters, Savva to Leonid, 18.7.1872.

[72]Beliaev, "Kazanskii i ego perepiska," *BV*, 1914, no. 9: 69 (Kazanskii to Platon, 26.5.1869).

[73]OR GBL, f. 149, uncatalogued letters, Innokentii to Leonid, 1871. Innokentii added a
telling postscript on his conspiratorial mood: "I do not know whether you can make out what
I have written. I wrote it myself on purpose [rather than use a copyist], because I did not want
anyone to know what I have written you."

[74]TsGIA SSSR, f. 804, op. 1, r. 1, d. 18, ll. 310–11 (Isidor's circular of 2.5.1874).

would willingly become sacristans, Arsenii denounced the provision for a single psalmist, because it would disfigure the beauty of the Orthodox mass, thus dismaying the faithful and heartening foes: "Naturally, in Orthodox hearts there will first come soft, wordless murmurs, but later loud insistent outcries, and finally popular disturbances."[75] On behalf of the Special Commission, Prince Urusov conceded some difficulties with the reform but rejected modification of the statute, so recently approved by the State Council and confirmed by the sovereign. Alluding to the political instability and uncertain mood in Petersburg, Urusov added that "at the present time it is impossible to foresee exactly what might result from a discussion of this subject in the meetings of the Special Commission."[76] Despite popular resistance, the commission was still determined to implement the reform. Like the rest of St. Petersburg, it was becoming more and more apprehensive, fearful of tampering with the statute, sensitive to the new mood in politics, and anxious to turn law into reality.

Preparation of Draft Registries

Preparation of registries (shtaty) to determine which parishes and which positions to eliminate proved exceedingly complex and controversial. Given broad discretion on the compilation of registries, most provincial commissions made some provisions for public participation, but each did so through different organs and at different stages in the administrative process.[77] In some dioceses authorities used old data from the consistory to prepare a draft proposal and then distributed this plan to each district and parish for review, comment, emandation, and counter-proposal. More often, the board ordered that a local organ compile the original draft, usually with the participation of the superintendent, local state officials, parish clergy, and some prominent parishioners. The provincial commission then checked these local drafts against consistory records (for example, on the number of parishioners or distance to the nearest church), examined proposals for mergers and reductions, and then compiled a final draft for the Special Commission. It was a complex enterprise, open to community participation, but ultimately controlled by the provincial commission.

The tactic of community participation had several purposes. One was to

---

[75] Ibid., f. 796, op. 205, d. 355, ll. 3–14 ob. (Arsenii's note, 1871).

[76] Ibid., ll. 1–2 (Urusov to Arsenii).

[77] Ibid., f. 804, op. 1, r. 1, d. 18 (early diocesan reports, indicating procedures used); for a concise overview, see "Svedeniia o khode dela po sokrashcheniiu prikhodov v 1870 g." (d. 153, ll. 5–18).

solicit additional funds—to give underpopulated parishes one last chance to provide minimal support for local clergy. In each case the parish collective had to sign a contract (*akt*) legally binding it to supply specific forms of support—capital endowment, land, tithe, or parsonage. Even at this late date, authorities nourished hopes of parish initiative, if only because of threats to close the churches. Community participation was also intended to defuse popular opposition. Diocesan authorities explicitly instructed local officials to allay the parishioners' fears; in Vladimir, for example, the provincial commission admonished local organs "to conduct this matter with extraordinary caution and, if unfavorable talk is encountered anywhere, attempt to stop it with reasonable measures."[78] Where provincial commissions ignored popular will, they provoked "quite a few petitions, declarations, and resolutions from residents of various settlements."[79] Public involvement, it was believed, would shield the clergy from arbitrary, unfair implementation; given the high stakes and the vested interest of each cleric in protecting positions for himself and his kin, bias and abuses were likely to be rampant.[80]

Such precautions notwithstanding, compilation of draft shtaty proved highly controversial and provoked especially strong opposition from parishioners. The commission in Kursk encountered such a furor that it retreated: "The main reason why underpopulated churches were left independent was to prevent dissatisfied appeals and complaints. Rumors of the attachment of churches aroused dissatisfaction in the people and disgruntlement, which in places threatened to cause a cooling of parishioners toward their own church. . . . Old Believers were not slow to make use of decrees by authorities and, in a distorted fashion, reinforced rumors that the churches were to be closed."[81] The commission in Vladimir, despite its unusual caution, met with determined parish resistance, including this classic statement of traditional sentiment and financial interest: "We humbly request that we be left at our church and not be attached to another that is in need of repair. We will be very sad to leave our completely renovated church [and be obliged] to repair and renovate an alien church. Moreover, our prayers in an alien church will be cold, for we will not see the remains of our close kin there." Dismayed by parish protests, the provincial commission was inclined to make few changes, not "so much because of communications problems as because of the parishioners' attachment to their parish church." It warned that "coerced

[78] Ibid., d. 18, l. 125 (Vladimir).

[79] Ibid., ll. 192–95 (Viatka). Such problems impelled authorities in Kaluga to compile an entirely new draft (*IVO [1869]*, p. 237).

[80] Charges of injustice abound; see, for instance "Iz Chernigovskoi eparkhii," *SL*, 1870, no. 78: 3, and Lavrov, *Avtobiografiia*, p. 50.

[81] TsGIA SSSR, f. 804, op. 1, r. 1, d. 116, l. 14 ob.

reassignment to other parishes will inevitably evoke in them strong grumbling and every kind of dissatisfaction with the new clerical staff."[82]

Where provincial commissions applied the new statute rigorously, the
opposition proved all the more determined. The provincial commission in
Khar'kov, for example, projected sweeping reductions in the number of parishes (28 percent) and clergy (42 percent), eliciting howls of protest from
both clergy and parishioners. Peasants in one parish regarded the reform as
some kind of ecclesiastical serfdom and refused "to assume the obligation for
ourselves and our heirs—either to give an annual fixed sum of money or to
perform certain labor for the staff: in the first case that would be quitrent
[obrok], in the latter corvée labor [barshchina]; that is, freed by the sovereign
from serf obligations toward the nobles, we would become the clergy's
serfs!"[83] In Nizhnii Novgorod, where the provincial board compiled a draft
shtat that drastically reduced parishes and clergy, the laity protested vehemently and vented their anger on the local clergy. The bishop himself wrote
to Petersburg that "the parishioners give [the clergy] neither their former
collections nor the [promised] ruga, but await confirmation of their resolutions." The contemporary press carried accounts of the parishioners'
rebellion:

> Such scenes have occurred that many priests will never forget. The very
> best of the clergy, hitherto loved by their parishioners, have suffered much
> unpleasantness. Parishioners have reproached them on the grounds that
> they allegedly gave petitions to higher authorities (regarding their terrible
> plight), that these priests have become very expensive, and that they [the
> parishioners] will find a less expensive priest.[84]

All commissions, especially those punctilious in implementing the statute,
encountered similar difficulties, as parishioners refused to provide more support or to permit the dismantling of their parishes.

Compilation of draft registries thus proved extremely explosive and difficult, even where provincial commissions exercised caution and afforded
parishioners ample opportunity to question plans or provide supplementary
support. The complexity of the task, the protracted consultation with local

[82] Ibid., d. 18, ll. 123–27; d. 110, ll. 20–22 ob., 24–24 ob., 40–41 (bishop's reports and parish
petitions). To discourage petitions, the provincial commission in Vladimir published an
announcement that no petitions would even be considered unless they provided guarantees of
substantial aid (a tithe of 500 rubles, parsonage, and the like). See "Ot Vladimirskogo gubernskogo prisutstviia po uluchsheniiu byta dukhovenstva," Vladimirskie EV, 1873, no. 6: 156–57.

[83] TsGIA SSSR, f. 804, op. 1, r. 1, d. 18, ll. 246 ob., 252–52 ob.; d. 137, ll. 8–9, 13–13 ob.,
35–36 ob., 37–40.

[84] "Iz Nizhegorodskoi eparkhii," TsOV, 1874, no. 3: 5. See also the archival files for that
diocese: TsGIA SSSR, f. 804, op. 1, r. 1, d. 18, ll. 241–43; d. 123, ll. 15 ob., 47–55 ob.; d. 123,
prilozhenie, ll. 268–387 (zhurnaly gubernskogo prisutstviia).

communities, and the covert opposition of some prelates meant that the provincial commissions proceeded at an extremely slow pace. After eighteen months only eleven of the more than fifty dioceses had submitted preliminary drafts to Petersburg; the rest labored to prepare theirs over the next few years.[85]

Petersburg: Confirmation of the Shtaty

The Special Commission maintained a close supervision of provincial commissions as they compiled registries and insisted upon strict observance of the 1869 statute. In some cases it reproved dioceses that acted too cautiously, insisting that the board make more mergers and eliminate more positions. For example, the Special Commission rejected the Vladimir commission's first draft, which left supplementary clergy at wealthy churches, explaining that "a certain abundance of means should not lead to a burdening of the clerical staff with unneeded numbers."[86] More rarely, the commission intervened to still the ardor of overambitious rationalizers, as in Khar'kov, where it moderated the massive changes originally planned by the provincial commission.[87] Only in the western provinces and Siberia did it tolerate a significant deviation from the statute, requiring only small-scale changes in the existing order.[88]

Faced with delays, the commission elected to "give the parish populations [more] time to express their wishes" and deferred action on the first cluster of draft shtaty.[89] To test the new order, however, it approved a draft registry for Olonets, a small diocese in the northwest, for implementation on an experimental basis.[90] The Olonets commission filed its draft shtat in 1870 after protracted consultations with laity, who had been given ample opportunity to provide supplementary aid to save their church and staff. Although the bishop originally expressed doubts about the feasibility of any mergers, given the low population density and the distances between parishes,[91] the provincial commission finally submitted a draft shtat with a 40 percent reduction in parishes. However, the draft gave most of the "attached parishes" an assistant priest (pomoshchnik), thereby projecting a mere 5 percent reduction in the number of priests. The main force of the shtat struck at the

---

[85] Ibid., d. 153, ll. 5–18 (report on implementation).

[86] Ibid., d. 110, ll. 28–36, 51–67, 146–49 ob. (Vladimir file).

[87] Ibid., d. 137, ll. 37–40 ("Zapiska o novom rospisanii prikhodov i tserkvei Khar'kovskoi eparkhii").

[88] Ibid., dd. 117, 121, 127, 178, 179, 183.

[89] Ibid., d. 153, ll. 22 ob.–23 (data for 1871).

[90] Ibid., r. 3, d. 472, ll. 245–72 (zhurnal, no. 39)

[91] Ibid., r. d, d. 18, ll. 131–131 ob. (Olonets bishop's report, 16.12,1869).

lower ranks of deacon and sacristan (reduced from 423 to 243), achieving a 28 percent decrease in the total number of clerical positions. Hence the registry affected primarily lower clergy, not parishioners: it gave most laymen access to a priest (whether in a "main church" or an "attached church"), had little effect upon priests, and made deacons and sacristans its principal victims.[92] The Special Commission approved the draft shtat without change.[93]

To guide implementation of the shtat in Olonets and later in other dioceses, the Special Commission also clarified some details on the transition from the old registry to the new one. The chief problem was the disposition of "nonregistered" supernumerary clergy, those whose positions vanished under the new shtat. The Commission ruled that such clergy could remain at their present positions until death or relocation, but it added that bishops should "encourage" them to relocate and could ordain no new clergy before eliminating this surplus. The only exception, it declared, should be graduates of theological academies willing to become priests and seminary graduates willing to become psalmists.[94] Though nonregistered clergy continued to receive subsidies if such existed in their dioceses, the income freed as they left their positions was to be distributed to the remaining staff "to increase support for the psalmists who are seminary graduates" and to supplement "the salaries of others, especially those staffs in particular need of improved support."[95] On the disposition of local resources (land and gratuities), the commission rejected the proposal of some prelates that they withhold or decrease the share going to supernumerary clergy, in effect forcing them to relocate.[96] It demanded instead that bishops use only gentle pressure, not coercion, in the process of redistributing clergy and ruled that all clergy, whether regular or supernumerary, should continue to enjoy their present shares of land and income.[97] The commission admitted the possibility of appointing deacons, but only if the parish provided separate funding for their maintenance through a tithe or capital endowment. Finally, to prevent gradual erosion of the new shtat, the commission required that bishops first

[92] Ibid., l. 181 (Olonets bishop's report, 9.5.1870).

[93] Ibid., r. 3, d. 472, ll. 247–50 (zhurnal, no. 39).

[94] Ibid., ll. 250–58.

[95] Ibid., r. 1, d. 146, ll. 2–16 (miscellaneous petitions from Saratov, Kishinev, Riga, and Chernigov), 17–22 (Special Commission to Tolstoi, 2.4.1870); r. 3, d, 472, ll. 273–82 (zhurnal, no. 41/a).

[96] The commission's staff prepared a draft proposal ("Proekt pravil o mestnykh obshchikh sredstvakh soderzhaniia pravoslavnogo prikhodskogo dukhovenstva i o razdele ikh," ibid., r. 1, d. 152, ch. 1). The draft was distributed to diocesan bishops, whose comments on the proposals generally recommended greater power to deal with recalcitrant clergy (ibid., ll. 22–192). The commission's staff then prepared a final report, advocating rather moderate measures to pressure surplus clergy to relocate (ibid., ll. 194–219).

[97] Ibid., r. 3, d. 473, ll. 46–73 (zhurnal, no. 53).

obtain the Synod's permission before establishing new parishes or reopening closed ones.[98]

In 1872–1873 the Special Commission finally promulgated its first cluster of parish registries. After receiving drafts from two dozen dioceses, it appointed a subcommittee to review in detail these cumbersome, complex data.[99] By December of that year the committee filed a general report, reviewed in detail the drafts, and considered the numerous petitions from irate parishioners.[100] In most cases the committee simply confirmed the drafts, making only minor changes in the number of parishes and clergy; in some dioceses, however, it substantially reduced or inflated the shtat, as circumstances seemed to warrant.[101] The committee then prepared a final set of registries of eighteen dioceses, which altogether provided for a 38 percent reduction in registered positions and a 20 percent reduction in parishes.[102] When the commission approved the subcommittee report without alteration in December 1873, it tried to minimize the magnitude of the projected changes.[103] It observed that most of the 14,701 positions that had been eliminated were in the rank of sacristan and deacon and that only 1,263 (9 percent) affected priests. It also assured parishioners in attached churches that they would enjoy regular services: "In rural parishes on Sundays and holidays, services should be [conducted] alternately in the independent and attached churches, [according to a schedule] composed in advance and with the consent of the parish community." Thus, as in the case of Olonets, authorities limited the impact of the reform on parishioners and priests and focused primarily upon reductions among deacons and sacristans.

In 1875 the Special Commission issued new "clarifications" of the statute, concessions intended both to allay popular discontent and to accelerate implementation of the reform. The commission noted that confusion over the terms "main" and "attached" had aroused "fears that the churches built by their fathers or [the parishioners] themselves are intended for abolition at some future time." Because such "unfounded" fears had caused "significant difficulties in [establishing] a parish order correct and appropriate for the support of parish clergy," the commission decided to abolish the terms "attached" and "main" altogether, even while preserving the basic structure of the registries. At the same time, the commission tried to extinguish parish hopes for the restoration of deacons: even if parishes vowed supplementary

[98] Ibid., d. 472, ll. 249–58 (zhurnal, no. 39).

[99] Ibid., d. 473, ll. 7–8 ob. (zhurnal, no. 46).

[100] Ibid., r. 1, d. 110, l. 188.

[101] Thus the commission reinstated 62 parishes in Saratov and 97 in Tambov but increased the number of attached churches in Riazan from 132 to 226 because of the small size of parishes and their close proximity (ibid., ll. 230–41).

[102] IVO (1873), pp. 183–89.

[103] TsGIA SSSR, f. 804, op. 1, r. 1, d. 473, ll. 54–74 (zhurnal, no. 54).

support, the commission admonished bishops not to transmit such requests "under any pretext" and insisted that prelates could only appoint clerics with the conditional title "deacon holding the position of psalmist" (that is, the deacon merely replaced the registered psalmist). Finally, the commission strengthened the bishops' authority to relocate supernumerary clergy. Although it forbade the bishops to use economic pressure (for example, by reducing the income of supernumerary clergy who refused to relocate) the commission declared that "those clergy who prove nonregistered are liable to obligatory relocation to [other] registered positions, and hence it depends upon the judgment of diocesan authorities to reassign such people to registered positions (appropriate to their rank and position)." To spur bishops to make such relocations, the commission strictly forbade them to ordain new priests until all surplus clerics were reassigned.[104] That order was surprising: contradictory to the spirit of the 1869 reform, which condemned forcible transfers, the new decree reflected the mounting concern in Petersburg that the reform show results.

In 1875–1877 the commission promulgated several additional sets of registries, essentially along the lines of those adopted in 1873.[105] For the internal dioceses, it made few changes in parishes or priests but cut a wide swath through the lower ranks of deacon and sacristan. Thus the shtaty approved in 1875 eliminated 32 percent of all clerical positions, mostly in the sacristan rank, with a mere 4 percent decline in the number of priests.[106] By contrast, the commission mandated few mergers and few clerical reductions in the outlying areas of Siberia or the western provinces. For instance, in the registries issued for three western provinces in 1875 the commission eliminated a mere 13 percent of the clerical positions; all reductions were in the lower ranks, and the number of priests actually increased.[107] It pursued similar policies in sparsely populated Siberia: the new shtat eliminated 16 percent of the sacristans but increased the number of priests.[108] By 1878 the commission had approved registries for forty-one of fifty-two dioceses and formally continued work on the remaining areas.[109] Significantly, the reform had yet to

---

[104] Ibid., ll. 135–38 (zhurnal, no. 61).

[105] In December 1875 the commission issued two major sets of registries, one for six internal dioceses (Kazan, Orel, Pskov, Samara, Chernigov, and the Caucasus), the other for three western dioceses (Lithuania, Minsk, and Polotsk). In March 1876 it issued registries for four more internal dioceses (St. Petersburg, Novgorod, Viatka, Iaroslavl) and in March 1877 promulgated its last two clusters of registries, one for internal dioceses (Nizhnii Novgorod, Tver, and Tula), the other for the Siberian dioceses and Turkmenia. See the commission's journals in ibid., r. 3, d. 473, ll.110–48, 162–66, 171–74, 178–86.

[106] Ibid., ll. 126–48.

[107] Ibid., ll. 110–25.

[108] Ibid., ll. 162–66.

[109] In 1878, for example, the Special Commission formed a new subcommittee to continue reviewing draft registries (ibid., ll. 194–95 [zhurnal, no. 69]).

reach such important dioceses as Kiev and Moscow, where episcopal intransigence had delayed the preparation of drafts for nearly a decade.[110] But by the time the commission turned its attention to the remaining areas, the reform was on the verge of collapse.

Application of the New Registries

Predictably, implementation of the new order encountered enormous resistance from parishioners. Some simply declined to attend the new parish and insisted that their old one be declared independent and given a full staff. Others sought to redress grievances through legal channels, inundating local authorities with petitions and protests. In 1875 the bishop of Khar'kov wrote that "almost everyday I receive petitions from various communities to return them to their former parish church or to reestablish their attached church to independent status."[111] The prelate in Vladimir also complained about the multitude of parish petitions, and his diocesan secretary wrote privately that reform "has only spawned thousands of cases for the consistory" to disentangle.[112] Moreover, authorities found that many parishes reneged on their promises of additional support to save their church and ignored Church attempts to obtain compliance.[113] Some parishes vented their anger on clergy, reducing their gratuities or forcibly expelling them. Some dismayed observers concluded that the reform "has placed the parish clergy virtually in an adversary relationship to parishioners."[114] Finally, the reform's initial invitation to lay participation and its invasion of parish rights precipitated a new assertiveness in parishes, galvanizing the laity to defend community interests and even to demand the restoration of old rights, including the power to select clergy. As the bishop of Iaroslavl complained in 1872, "now one does not receive, but is flooded, by letters, requests, resolutions, and even large delegations of petitioners for one or another [candidate]."[115]

[110] Following the death of Arsenii in 1876, authorities in Kiev finally submitted a draft registry, but it changed little: all parishes were left intact, and only 3.3 percent of the clerical positions were eliminated (210 sacristans and deacons were eliminated, but 77 priests were added). The reduction was so negligible that the governor-general of Kiev angrily called the draft an outright evasion of the 1869 statute (ibid., r. 1, d. 179, ll. 36–53 [draft registry], 62–67 [complaint by the governor-general], 79–87 ob. [rejoinder by the provincial commission]).

[111] Savva, *Khronika*, 5: 87.

[112] Ibid., 5: 376.

[113] See, for example, the complaints by authorities in Samara in 1873 (*Samarskie eparkhial'nye vedomosti* [hereafter *Samarskie EV*], 1873, no. 17: 351) and by Isidor in 1884 (TsGIA SSSR, f. 796, op. 154, g. 1873, d. 1178/a, l. 155).

[114] "Voprosy o dukhovenstve," *TsOV*, 1875, no. 117; see also the episcopal commentaries filed in 1880 (below, pp. 421–22).

[115] *Iaroslavskie EV*, 1872, no. 39: 320–21. See also the complaints from authorities in Perm in 1874 (TsGIA SSSR, f. 796, op. 155, g. 1874, d. 1275, ll. 1–10), Tauride in 1875 ("Soob-

The Special Commission reviewed parish protests on behalf of the Synod. Clearly determined to protect the integrity of the new shtaty, it subjected them to close scrutiny. Thus, when diocesan authorities in Vladimir endorsed a request to restore one attached parish to independent status (ingenuously adding that "approval of the peasants' request will spare diocesan authorities the troubles and difficulties that are inevitable should the request be rejected"), the commission flatly denied the petition, insisting that registries could be altered only when the needs were compelling and the resources available.[116] If circumstances warranted and the parish guaranteed substantial new support, the commission would agree to enlarge staffs or reestablish parishes. But such revisions were exceedingly rare before 1880: between 1876 and 1879 the Synod authorized an annual average of four changes in Vladimir, four in Khar'kov, and two in Novgorod, which represented only a handful of the hundreds of parishes in each diocese.[117]

Still more difficult was the task of eliminating redundant clergy, who constituted almost one-third of the existing staffs in the central dioceses. The Special Commission had unceremoniously dumped this nasty problem in the hands of provincial authorities, who, as the Third Section reported in 1876, found it "difficult to designate some clerics as registered, others as supernumerary, in those parishes which have been combined."[118] Prelates were under intense pressure to relocate clergy, for when registered vacancies appeared through retirement or death, the bishop was legally bound to appoint a supernumerary candidate, not a new graduate from the seminary. Naturally, the formidable costs of relocation and the likelihood that transferees would have to sell their houses cheaply and buy dearly made it difficult to induce clergy to transfer. Driven to fill the vacancies, some bishops attempted to force redundant clergy to relocate.[119] In 1877, for example, the bishop of Viatka warned surplus clergy in his diocese that, "in the event they avoid relocating [on their own volition], they shall be transferred by order of diocesan authorities "—by implication to an undesirable position that no one would voluntarily assume.[120] The bishop in Vladimir at first avoided coercive measures, but, frustrated by the clergy's refusal to transfer, in 1878 he ordered that "unregistered members of staffs take care to find themselves a registered position as soon as possible for fear that they shall be transferred

---

shchenie iz Tavricheskoi eparkhii," *TsOV*, 1875, no. 76: 2), and Viatka in 1879 (*Viatskie EV*, 1879, no. 4: 79–80).

[116]TsGIA SSSR, f. 804, op. 1, r. 1, d. 110, ll. 409–12 ob.

[117]Ibid., d. 122, ll. 135–57 ob. (Novgorod file); d. 110, ll. 465–515 (Vladimir file); d. 137, ll. 95–206 ob. (Khar'kov file).

[118]Ibid., f. 1574, op. 2, d. 280, ll. 22–22 ob.

[119]See also the bishops' response to an inquiry on this problem in 1873 (ibid., f. 804, op. 1, r. 1, d. 152, ch. 1, ll. 22–192).

[120]*Viatskie EV*, 1877, no. 2: 34.

to such places at the discretion of diocesan authorities or even be released from active service."[121]

This process ignited a virtual civil war among parish clergy, as registered clerics tried to drive out supernumerary colleagues and to reap the profits of reform. Thus some sent protests—to the commission, to newspapers, to bishops—demanding prompt and full implementation of the reform and at the same time probably subjected hapless peers to harassment and persecution.[122] The bishop of Vladimir, no friend of the parish reform, nevertheless took stern measures to compel clergy to relocate, primarily because of the rampant intraclerical conflict.[123] Such conflict upon occasion turned into violence, as in the case of a Kursk priest who, "wishing to be rid of an unregistered sacristan as soon as possible, one night dispatched him to his grave, after treating him to some tea that was spiked with arsenic."[124] Moreover, the reform aggravated tensions between parish clergy and bishops. Clergy rebuked their superiors for excessive zeal or, more often, for arbitrary implementation of the reform. Liberal clergy in fact blamed the reform's problems primarily upon maladministration, arguing that inattentive bishops and corrupt consistories permitted widespread abuse and bias in compiling and applying the shtat.[125] That animosity was no doubt fueled by the Special Commission's hypocrisy, evident in its public proclamations on the importance of caution and attention to clerical need and its circulars ordering bishops to begin prompt, punctilious implementation.[126]

For all the tumult, the bishops achieved little. Most prelates had no desire to wreak havoc among the parish clergy. They heeded the commission's injunction for caution, and, in any event, they could order transfers only when registered positions fell vacant. As a result, diocesan authorities made only modest reductions in the actual number of clergy. For the whole empire, the total number of clergy fell by 5 percent between 1875 and 1880 (from 98,802 to 92,746 clerics), with the most reductions in the ranks of deacon and sacristan (see table 20). Outlying dioceses like Kherson, long afflicted by shortages in qualified candidates, actually reported increases in the number of priests and only modest declines in the number of deacons and sacristans. The highest rates of decline occurred in central Great Russian dioceses

[121] TsGIA SSSR, f. 796, op. 442, d. 771, l. 24 ob. (Vladimir report, 1878). Similar threats appeared in other dioceses; see, for instance, the decree issued in Novgorod in 1877 (*TsOV*, 1878, no. 1: 5).

[122] See occasional articles in the press from clergy who complained that local authorities failed to implement the reform precisely: "Iz Chernigovskoi eparkhii," *SL*, 1870, no. 78; "Iz Kieva," *TsOV*, 1876, no. 130.

[123] Savva, *Khronika*, 5: 704–5.

[124] Ibid., 5: 725.

[125] "Vopros o dukhovenstve," *TsOV*, 1875, no. 120.

[126] TsGIA SSSR, f. 804, op. 1, r. 1, d. 18, l. 122/b ob.

TABLE 20

Changes in the Number of Clergy, 1875–1880: Empire and
Representative Dioceses

| | Percentage Change in Number of Clerics | | |
Diocese	Priests	Deacons and Sacristans	All Clergy
Iaroslavl	−1.7%	−29.3%	−20.6%
Irkutsk	+21.8	+ 6.2	+12.3
Kaluga	− 2.9	−17.9	−12.6
Nizhnii Novgorod	+ 0.6	−18.5	−11.7
Orel	− 6.6	−14.1	−11.7
Riazan	− 0.8	− 9.8	− 6.7
Saratov	− 2.3	−14.9	−10.0
Tver	+ 0.7	−17.8	−11.3
Vladimir	− 4.6	−19.0	−13.7
EMPIRE	− 1.1%	− 7.6%	− 5.1%

SOURCES: *IVO (1876)*, prilozhenie; *IVO (1881)*, prilozhenie.

like Tambov, which reported a 6 percent decline in priests and a 15 percent
decline among deacons and sacristans. Even so, by 1880 authorities had yet
to reach the ambitious reductions set in the new registries (about one-third
of the clergy in the central dioceses), mute testimony to the force of parish
opposition, the caution of bishops, and the slowness with which vacancies
appeared.[127]

Nor did the reform significantly alter the service standards of parish
clergy. Its requirements that seminary graduates first serve as psalmists and
that only mature graduates become priests proved difficult to enforce. The
greatest failure was the sacristan reform, for few seminarians agreed to
accept the low rank, low salary, and low status of a psalmist. Thus service
records for clergy in 1890 reveal that most priests had some kind of experience prior to ordination but that few served as sacristans; most preferred
instead to teach in public or parish schools.[128] The few who had served as
sacristans found the experience immensely dissatisfying, not only because

[127] *IVO (1876)*, appendix; *IVO (1881)*, appendix.
[128] For example, service registers for 1890 show that only 12 percent of the priests in Kiev
had served as psalmists, 3 percent in Tver, and 9 percent in Kaliazin (TsGIA UkrSSR, f. 127,
op. 119, d. 984; op. 1011, dd. 1175, 1468; GA Kalininskoi obl., f. 160, op. 1, dd. 16303, 16550).

they resented the material want, but also because they lacked training for the psalmists' liturgical role—to the indignation of both priest and parish.[129] Thus the reform left the sacristan question unresolved: it reduced their numbers but did not alter their composition and status.[130] On the other hand, the reform brought positive harm, for it encouraged seminarians to flee into lay professions or to remain idle in hopes of alternative employment.[131] As a result, more and more bishops complained of insufficient candidates, even in areas that once had large surpluses of clerical youths.[132] Some bishops sought permission to ordain seminarians without prior service or to appoint unqualified dropouts as psalmists and even as priests.[133] Hence anachronistic patterns occurred, like that recorded in the file of a sacristan in Kiev: "He did not study in schools and, after learning to read Slavonic Russian in his parents' home, in 1873 he entered the Podolia-Bratskii Monastery as a novice, and in 1875 was installed as psalmist by suffragan bishop Porfirii in the church in the village of Nikulich."[134]

Amidst all these problems and shortcomings, it is hardly surprising that opposition to the reform mounted steadily in the 1870s. As one observer noted in 1878, the parish reform had been the focus of a rising chorus of "complaints in society and in the press."[135] That was no exaggeration. To quote one newspaper's judgment in 1874: "[This reform] has ended in total failure. In some places it produced schism, in others the abandonment of Christianity, everywhere alienation from the clergy, and in the end it did not in the slightest improve the condition of the clergy who remained."[136] Some peasants perceived the reform in the idiom of serfdom and emancipation. A priest in Tula reported wild rumors among local peasants that *all* parishes would be abolished, that peasants would have to "redeem" the

[129]"Zapiski psalomshchika," *Kievskie EV*, 1876, no. 18: 645–60.

[130]The sacristan question triggered an animated debate in *TsOV*, 1875, nos. 38, 143, 146–47.

[131]See, for instance, comments in 1876 by the bishops of Orel and Olonets (TsGIA SSSR, f. 796, op. 442, d. 643, l. 11; d. 641, ll. 21–21 ob.).

[132]For complaints in 1876, see above, note 17. Even the once populous dioceses experienced difficulties; see "Tekushchaia khronika," *Str.*, 1878, no. 11: 241; *Saratovskie EV*, 1878, no. 2: 28; *Samarskie EV*, 1873, no. 8: 26–27.

[133]For the petitions of Kishinev and Arkhangel'sk in 1874, see TsGIA SSSR, f. 796, op. 154, g. 1873, d. 1332; op. 155, g. 1874, d. 1292.

[134]TsGIA UkrSSR, f. 127, op. 1009, d. 984, l. 61 ob.

[135]"Tekushchaia khronika," *Str.*, 1878, no. 8: 253; see also the critical remarks by Giliarov-Platonov in "Sokrashchenie tserkvei," *Sovremennye izvestiia*, 1879, no. 354.

[136]"Ob obespechenii dukhovenstva," *Sovremennye izvestiia*, 1874, no. 106; "O reformakh v dukhovnom vedomstve," ibid., 1870, no. 37. See also the warnings of practical obstacles and scant returns in V. P. Meshcherskii's conservative paper ("Preobrazovanie prikhodov v Rossii," *Grazhdanin*, 1872, no. 17: 583–86). The fullest critique of all was a pamphlet by D. Samarin, who argued that the reform was directly eroding popular religiousness (*Sokrashchenie prikhodov i obespechenie dukhovenstva* [Moscow, 1873]).

churches as they had their land at emancipation: "Just as they made us buy back our land, that's what will happen here too. Yes, they'll take and close our churches, then set up payments over a ten-year period for us peasants to redeem them, and then they will be ours."[137] In 1876 the Third Section brought such discontent to the attention to the emperor, who directed Tolstoi to consider this report:

> Information has been received that in Iaroslavl and other dioceses the implementation of the new parish registries has provoked great difficulties and aroused the concern of parishioners, who submit petitions asking that their parishes remain independent. Alarming ideas have been provoked among the people by changes in the composition of parishes, by reorganizing them, and by depriving the churches of priests.[138]

Though this discontent rarely led to open disorders,[139] reports like these showed that the reform ran contrary to its primary goal of increasing the influence and status of clergy in the village.

Significantly, disenchantment with reform even overtook its former defenders.[140] That shift was most telling in the case of the *Church-Social Messenger*, which published an ever growing number of critical articles and letters from diocesan clergy. In late 1875 its editor, A. Popovitskii, admitted that "the reduction in parishes and staffs, as experience has shown, in many cases has not improved but actually harmed the clergy's material condition," though as yet he placed most responsibility on administrative abuse and callousness.[141] He claimed that the reform was in principle well conceived but that diocesan authorities had conducted parish reorganization "without the circumspection that one would expect and that is necessary if one is not to provoke irrevocable censure."[142] Within a few years Popovitskii abandoned such arguments and frankly conceded that the reform had provoked "protests from clergy, parish communities, individual parishioners, and zemstvos" without palpable result: "Thus the reduction of parishes and staffs, which had well-intentioned goals, proved upon implementation to be laden with many difficulties, provoked a plethora of conflicts, spawned numerous illegal actions, and had a pernicious effect upon the course of religious life in the nation."[143]

Most bishops, skeptical from the outset, gradually became outspoken crit-

[137] N. Tikhvinskii, "Prikhodskaia reforma," *Tul'skie EV*, 1876, no. 5: 175.

[138] TsGIA SSSR, f. 1574, op. 2, d. 280, ll. 22–22 ob.

[139] See Freeze, "Stunted Anticlericalism," for data on the incidence of anticlerical disturbances.

[140] See, for instance, *Golos*, 1871, no. 243.

[141] "Voprosy o dukhovenstve," *TsOV*, 1875, no. 117: 1–2.

[142] "Po delam eparkhial'nykh s"ezdov," ibid., 1877, no. 52.

[143] "Eparkhial'nye otgoloski," ibid., 1880, no. 53.

ics of the reform, even in official reports to the procurator and Synod. Thus the archbishop of Riazan wrote that the reform would have no impact at all until surplus clergy ("of which there are many") had been relocated and that the reform failed to address entirely the clergy's main problem: dependence upon gratuities.[144] The bishop of Vladimir argued that the reform failed to raise service standards, for few seminarians agreed to become psalmists, and, in any event, authorities first had to redistribute the surplus sacristans already in service. Given the great number of surplus clergy, he could discern little improvement in the clergy's material condition: "The reduction in parishes and staffs so far has brought only an extremely insignificant degree of increased support [for the clergy], especially because most staffs still have one, two, or even more supernumerary members."[145] The bishop of Iaroslavl wrote that the reform "has left a depressing impression upon the people and has served as a new incitement for disputes and conflicts between parishioners and clergy."[146] Significantly, when the procurator polled episcopal opinion in 1880–1881, all but a handful pronounced the parish reform abortive and useless, if not positively harmful.[147]

The parish clergy—the reform's purported beneficiaries—confirmed such judgments. Most saw little evidence of economic improvement, noted that reform assisted only those clerics in parishes where surplus clergy had actually departed, and observed that this "progress" came at the expense of the supernumerary clergy.[148] Even where parishioners agreed to give regular support, converting emoluments to a tithe or supplementary aid, the clergy found that they often—at the first opportunity—reneged.[149] Such facts caused one clerical journalist (himself a defender of the reform) to admit that most clergy believed that the reform has "no real significance for improving the clergy's material condition."[150] Another priest, bitter from the whole experience, wrote that the reform "has brought a slight increment for a few of us, but has only whetted the appetites" of the rest.[151] A priest in Nizhnii Novgorod summed up the general attitude well: "What has been the

[144]TsGIA SSSR, f. 796, op. 442, d. 651, ll. 10 ob.–11.

[145]Ibid., d. 618, ll. 21, 23 ob.–24.

[146]Ibid., d. 666, ll. 14–14 ob.

[147]See below, pp. 421-22.

[148]See, for example, the articles of two priests: "O deiatel'nosti nastoiatelei prikhodskikh tserkvei," *TsOV*, 1877, no. 93; "Sposoby uluchsheniia material'nogo byta pravoslavnogo dukhovenstva po vzgliadam *Moskovskikh vedomostei*," *RSP*, 1875, no. 50: 466–67.

[149]See, for example, the official complaint in *Samarskie EV*, 1873, no. 17: 351.

[150]Ia. Novitskii, "K voprosu o material'nom obespechenii pravoslavnogo dukhovenstva," *Kurskie EV*, 1874, no. 14: 722. A priest in Kostroma wrote the next year that "the anticipated improvement in the clergy's material condition has advanced very slowly and unsatisfactorily, and in some places the clergy's material condition is even growing worse" ("Iz Kostromskoi eparkhii," *TsOV*, 1875, no. 85).

[151][Bratets], "Staroe i novoe v zhizni sel'skogo dukhovenstva," *Str.*, 1878, no. 6/7: 55–56.

the result? Nothing good, just a lot of evil—especially in those places where the clergy live under the new order: improvements lie over the horizon, while dissatisfaction between clergy and parish is already at hand."[152]

The failure and pain of reform left behind a great dark cloud of pessimism and disillusionment. As authorities had feared from the first, publicity tended to generate "unrealizable dreams" among parish clergy, and the statute of 1869—even more than Valuev's invitation to society—failed to answer the clergy's aspirations for state recognition and state aid. The ensuing demoralization was aptly summed up by the liberal editor of *Church-Social Messenger* in early 1876: "The endless talk about improving the clergy's material condition, which has not led to any practical results, has only aroused pointless hopes in [the clergy], so as then to thrust them back into disillusionment and virtual despair."[153] Two years later the editor wrote candidly that "many Orthodox priests have grown weary of the futile work on [material improvement for the clergy] and have long ceased not only to write but even to talk about it."[154] The failure to improve and restructure parish economies offered little hope to the clergy for even a gradual improvement in their condition. Little wonder, wrote a priest in Saratov, that "seminarians are fleeing *en masse* into other domains."[155] For those already in holy orders, the prospects were bleak and the mood grim. As one cleric exclaimed, "Hungry, humiliated, downtrodden, insulted at every step, dependent upon parishioners for a piece of bread—the village priest is in no position to be an active 'pastor.'"[156]

An Estate Dismantled?

Reform discussions in the sixties, especially among journalists and bureaucrats, laid great emphasis upon the necessity of abolishing the hereditary estate. Their arguments were many, from a traditional concern about the surfeit of candidates to a growing belief that only open recruitment could attract dedicated professional pastors. The reforms of 1867–1869 had achieved a substantial part of the goal: they formally separated Church ser-

---

[152]"Po povodu novogo rospisaniia prikhodov i prichtov v Nizhegorodskoi eparkhii," *TsOV*, 1878, no. 55. Other clergy complained that the reform had completely failed to address the main issue: dependence upon gratuities. See, for example, I. Kazanskii, "Nekotorye neotlozhnye mery k uluchsheniiu byta sel'skogo dukhovenstva," *Saratovskie EV*, 1871, no. 12; "Dukhovenstvo i obshchestvo," *TsOV*, 1874, no. 109.

[153]"Tserkovnoe obozrenie za 1875 g.," *TsOV*, 1876, no. 1.

[154]"Motiv k voprosu ob uluchshenii byta dukhovenstva," ibid., 1878, no. 10.

[155]N. Vasil'evskii, "Pastyrskaia deiatel'nost' sel'skogo sviashchennika v nastoiashchee vremia," *Saratovskie EV*, 1873, no. 14: 393.

[156]Ibid.

vice from the social estate by eliminating family claims and by giving the clergy's sons a secular legal status. At the same time, Church schools threw open their doors to outsiders, and the parish reform of 1869 permitted the ordination of older, "proven" candidates lacking the requisite formal education. Did the reforms lead to a substantial reconstitution of the clergy?

Reform permitted a great exodus of clerical sons—the so-called flight from the seminaries—but it did not lead to a significant infusion of outside forces into the clergy. As seminary reports from the 1870s and 1880s show, relatively few youths from other social groups matriculated in the elementary Church schools or, especially, in the seminary (see table 21).[157] Nor did many outsiders, with or without a Church education, enter the parish clergy. Right to the end of the century, outsiders remained exceedingly rare in clerical ranks, constituting a significant number only in the outlying dioceses.[158] Though the clergy was no longer a totally hereditary order and permitted sons to leave, the reforms of the late 1860s in practice failed to leaven the clergy with substantial numbers of outsiders.

Indeed, the reform left the Church with the worst of both worlds: clerical sons fled in droves, and few outsiders entered in their place. As some had forewarned, the provisions to ease exit for sons led to a mass exodus. Clerical sons departed in such large numbers that they represented over a third of the university enrollments by the late 1870s.[159] Unable to attract qualified outsiders in their stead, even the central dioceses came to feel the recruitment problems that perennially plagued outlying areas. Though Western churches periodically experienced similar difficulties, such acute and persistent shortages would not appear there until much later—and then not because of an ill-fated experiment in social reform.[160]

Why did the reform fail to entice outsiders or even to hold ample numbers of the clergy's own sons? One major reason, no doubt, was the abortive parish reform: it froze recruitment (superfluous clergy had to be relocated before new ones could be ordained), and, more important, it failed to improve the clergy's social and economic condition. As a priest in Saratov rightly observed, "under the present conditions . . . one not only cannot expect an influx of fresh, vital forces [from the outside], but our own forces [the clergy's sons], the most capable ones, continue to flee and flee into other domains, repulsed by the condition of rural priests."[161] Those qualified by education

[157] Nor were outsiders common at the academy; in 1878 they constituted only 2 percent of the students in all four academies (12 of 627 students). TsGIA SSSR, f. 797, op. 48, otd. 1, st. 2, d. 60.

[158] See below, pp. 453-54, for data at the century's close.

[159] The contingent of former seminarians reached a peak in 1878, when they composed 35 percent of all university students (Shchetinina, *Universitety i ustav 1884 g.*, pp. 71–72).

[160] For the problem of clerical recruitment in the West, see below, pp. 455-57.

[161] I. Kazanskii, "Nekotorye neotlozhnye mery k uluchsheniiu byta dukhovenstva," *Saratovskie EV*, 1871, no. 12: 293–94; see also "Tekushchaia khronika," *Str.*, 1878, no. 11: 242.

TABLE 21

Nonclerical Students in Church Schools, 1880

Diocese	District Schools (total enrollment)		Seminary (new admissions)	
	Students	Outsiders (%)	Students	Outsiders (%)
Kiev	874	42 (4.8%)	99	6 (6.1%)
Novgorod	417	27 (6.5%)	112	9 (8.0%)
Riazan	1,259	174 (13.8%)	140	13 (9.3%)
Viatka	850	31 (3.6%)	101	0 (0.0%)
Vladimir	990	85 (8.6%)	123	11 (8.9%)

SOURCE: TsGIA SSSR, f. 802, op. 1, 1, d. 4, ll. 177 ob.–178, 216 ob., 229, 268, 276, 298 ob.; d. 69, ll. 326 ob., 340 ob.; r. 2, d. 8, ll. 71 ob., 124, 158, 196 ob., 206 ob., 254; d. 15, ll. 344, 363, 382, 396 ob., 406 ob., 417 ob.; d. 41, ll. 161–61 ob., 194 ob., 229 ob., 261, 282, 320.

to receive ordination into holy orders were also part of the dominant youth culture of the day, which was infused with belief in science and materialism, not God, and would hardly find the low status of clergy appealing.

Nor did the reform provide specific mechanisms for the active recruitment of outsiders, especially from lower status groups. That shortcoming was most apparent in the case of Church schools, which had only a limited commitment to social mobility. Outsiders could compete for positions in the seminary, but, as Tolstoi made clear in his statement to the State Council, the clerical estate was expected to continue to provide most seminarians. That expectation pervaded the whole logic of his new system, which made the parish clergy primarily responsible for financing parallel classes at the seminary and for establishing the lower tier of elementary Church schools. Burdened with this sizable financial responsibility, the clergy, quite naturally, opposed the matriculation of outsiders in schools established at their own expense. As the diocesan assembly in Vladimir candidly declared, the admission of nonclerical youths to church schools was "contrary to the interests of the clergy, who maintain [these] schools."[162] Thus Tolstoi's reform contained a strong element of social conservativism: it sought not a sudden reconstitution but only a gradual replenishment, partly perhaps for the sake of gradual change itself, but largely because fiscal necessity forced authorities to rely upon the estate to finance educational reform.

Moreover, bishops still gave covert recognition to family claims, primarily because the Church failed to provide an alternative form of welfare for

[162]"Zhurnaly eparkhial'nogo s"ezda dukhovenstva Vladimirskoi eparkhii," *Vladimirskie EV*, 1870, no. 19: 861.

retired clergy and their families. The lack of pensions[163] and the slow development of special schools for clerical women[164] meant that the welfare needs of the estate remained profoundly acute. As one bishop complained in 1876, "the reduction in clerical positions and the ban against [imposing] obligations on new clergy toward their predecessors have significantly increased the number of those suffering from a lack of support."[165] Especially grim was the plight of daughters, for the abolition of family claims had eliminated their traditional form of dowry, their guarantee of a suitable match in the clerical estate. As a result, wrote the bishop of Simbirsk (himself an ardent supporter of reform), clerical candidates "often marry the daughters of peasants, soldiers, townspeople, and petty officials, while the clergy's daughters are ignored by them, especially if they do not possess a substantial dowry."[166] One priest wrote in despair that "the law [abolishing family control over positions] in itself is marvelous, but what are the consequences? The priest is now obliged to hand over his daughter to the lowliest peasant."[167] Little wonder then, wrote one observer, that the parish clergy "for the most part are

[163] As before, the diocesan welfare boards disbursed pitiably small sums; the board in Orel, for example, dispensed aid to nearly 2,000 individuals in 1875, but in amounts averaging only 2.86 rubles per person for the year (TsGIA SSSR, f. 796, op. 442, d. 643, ll. 1 ob.–2 ob.). Nor did many clergy follow the example in Samara, where clergy established their own pension fund. In most dioceses the issue was raised, but it foundered on opposition among the rank-and-file clergy, primarily because of the costs and long initial period required for capital accumulation. See the drafts and discussions in "Neskol'ko slov ob uchrezhdenii eparkhial'noi emerital'noi kassy," *Vladimirskie EV*, 1873, no. 2: 44–48; "O proekte emerital'noi kassy," *TsOV*, 1876, no. 41: 3–5; "Ob emeriture," *Kurskie EV*, 1876, no. 7: 348–60; TsGIA SSSR, f. 796, op. 160, g. 1879, dd. 686, 817 (Petersburg and Chernigov proposals); "Po delu o sostavlenii pensionnogo kapitala," *SL*, 1865, no. 62; *IVO (1875)*, pp. 258–69; *IVO (1876)*, pp. 274–84. As a result, the only substantial aid was the state pension of 1866, which was limited to priests with 35 years of service and provided only a small sum. *PSZ(2)*, 41:43288.

[164] See, for example, the discouraging assessment of conditions in diocesan girls' schools in 1879 in "Zhurnal Uchebnogo komiteta" (TsGIA SSSR, f. 796, op. 161, g. 1880, d. 379, ll. 3–6). As one priest complained, the Church had discussed the need for such schools for 20 years but so far had done little ("Vopros ob obrazovanii devits sel'skogo dukhovenstva," *RSP*, 1876, no. 12: 364–76). For individual schools, see the list of monographs in a review essay by A. Filofeev, "[Retsenziia]: A. Preobrazhenskii, *Istoriia Vladimirskogo eparkhial'nogo zhenskogo uchilishcha*," in *BV*, 1903, no. 6: 352–71.

[165] TsGIA SSSR, f. 796, op. 442, d. 639, ll. 13 ob–14 (Moscow, 1875 report). For journalistic accounts of the problem, see "Neskol'ko slov ob uchrezhdenii eparkhial'noi emerital'noi kassy," *Vladimirskie EV*, 1873, no. 2: 44–48; M. N., "Blizhaishie mery posobiia vdovam i sirotam dukhovenstva, vozmozhnye so storony samogo dukhovenstva," *Kurskie EV*, 1871, no. 13: 674–95.

[166] TsGIA SSSR, f. 797, op. 50, g. 1880, otd. 3, st. 5, d. 182, ch. 2, l. 71.

[167] F. Vinogradov, "Delo uluchsheniia byta dukhovenstva," *SL*, 1870, no. 17. Similar views voiced by P. Kutepov ("O nedokonchennoi reforme dukhovenstva," *Tul'skie EV*, 1874, no. 14: 62) provoked an official protest from state censors; in their words, Kutepov's article argued that "the reforms undertaken by the government to improve the clergy's condition have in fact improved the condition of only a small segment [of the clergy], while the majority—precisely because of these reforms—have been turned loose to wander like beggars" (TsGIA

hostile to the [soslovie] reforms" that abrogated their rights and gave little in return.[168]

In view of the Church's inability to provide alternative forms of social welfare, some bishops felt obliged to accede tacitly to arrangements that recognized family needs and claims.[169] In fact, the reform of 1867 left the door ajar for family deals: it eliminated the legal right of candidates to demand positions on grounds of welfare or family claims, but it did not forbid the appointment of kinsmen altogether. An informal arrangement, an indulgent bishop—both permitted quiet observance of custom, though less overtly and less systematically than in the past. Thus the bishop of Viatka in 1869 forbade women in the clerical estate to request sons-in-law for their husbands' positions, but he implied that they might arrange this outcome themselves: "Announce in the diocesan paper that the clergy's wives are not to appear before diocesan authorities with such requests [that the bishop designate a seminarian as son-in-law and successor]. It is, however, quite a different matter if a worthy candidate for holy orders himself wishes to marry the daughter of the petitioner."[170] More tactful was the policy of the bishop of Vologda, who "advised" candidates to marry the daughters of clergy—advice tantamount to an order, but supremely discreet.[171] Such deals even appeared on official service records. For example, one priest in Taratsanskii district in 1870 "surrendered his position in the village Sabadakh to his son-in-law Karamskii," and when the latter prematurely died, "in 1874, according to the resolution of Metropolitan Arsenii, he was transferred to his former position in Sabadakh to support the orphans of his son-in-law."[172] The liberal press, moreover, carried recurring complaints that bishops made appointments on the basis of family claims, overriding the merits of other candidates.[173] In 1878 the publicist Belliustin reported that such violations virtually enjoyed official sanction in some quarters.[174] These charges were not the idle fulminations of antiepiscopal liberals. The bishop of Ekaterinoslav, for example, candidly admitted in 1880 that "I have always permitted and now permit the transfer of positions of priests, deacons, and sacristans to children and sons-in-law to support families and household finances where customs permit

---

SSSR, f. 797, op. 44, otd. 2, st. 3, d. 224 [Main Committee on the Press to Tolstoi, 5.11.1874], l.1).

[168] *Sovremennye izvestiia*, 1869, no. 9; also *Golos*, 1871, no. 243.

[169] "Iz iugo-zapadnogo kraia," *TsOV*, 1880, no. 86.

[170] *Viatskie EV*, 1869, no. 14: 269.

[171] "O noveishikh reformakh dukhovenstva," *Nedelia*, 1868, no. 29: 900.

[172] TsGIA UkrSSR, f. 127, op. 1011, d. 1175, l. 277 ob.

[173] "K voprosu o reformakh v dukhovenstve," *SL*, 1869, no. 74; "Po povodu novogo rospisaniia prikhodov i prichtov v Nizhegorodskoi eparkhii," *TsOV*, 1878, no. 55: 3–4; "Iz Iaroslavlia," ibid., 1876, no. 73: 4.

[174] Belliustin, "Progress," *TsOV*, 1878, no. 10; see also "Spravka po povodu 'rekomandovannykh mest' v Pskovskoi eparkhii," ibid., 1878, no. 47.

and the candidate is worthy."[175] In brief, though family claims had lost their dominance, in many areas they continued to play a significant informal role in determining appointments and blocking entrance to outsiders.

Thus the soslovie reform failed to transform the traditional estate into an open social group. From its very inception, in fact, the process of change was bound to be extraordinarily slow, because it applied only to future candidates and future clergy—an extremely slow process of regeneration in any case, but especially so amidst the shtat reductions of the 1870s. As enrollment data in the schools make clear, even the next generation could include but few candidates from other social groups. Contemporaries saw little real change in the clergy's social complexion. As one journalist wrote in 1879, a decade after the reform began, "one can literally count on one's fingers those priests who, from the time of the publication of the law of 26 May 1869, have entered clerical service and belong by birth to the secular classes."[176] These data supported the widespread conviction that reform had utterly failed to abolish the old social order. To quote one disappointed lay observer: "The caste has been abolished by law, but in reality the Russian tribe of Levites remains in its closed circle, just as it was earlier, [and] there is no influx of new elements."[177] The liberal clerical newspaper *Church-Social Messenger* summed up the general view in an editorial in 1879: "[The clergy's] closed estate is sundered, the estate's stamp has been removed from their children (thereby opening before them a path, through rights of birth and education, to all spheres of state activity), access to parish work is opened to members of all estates (except poll-tax members): yet the clergy is still separate, just as it was in all the past centuries of its historical life."[178] Thus, in striking contrast to the Western clergy, which became increasingly "democratized," drawing ever more heavily upon lower status groups for ordinands, the Russian parish clergy remained a rigid hereditary estate.[179]

[175]TsGIA SSSR, f. 797, op. 50, otd. 3, st. 5, d. 182, ch. 2, ll. 44–44 ob.; see below, pp. 453-54.

[176]"Svetskii element prichetnichestva," *TsOV*, 1879, no. 52; see also M. Chel'tsov, "Tsarstvovanie Aleksandra II," *Str.*, 1880, no. 4: 593.

[177]BS, f. Gagarine, X (Russes au Gagarin), unpaginated letter from Prince S. Obolenskii to I. S. Gagarin, 24.12.1876.

[178]"O nravstvennom i material'nom polozhenii dukhovenstva," *TsOV*, 1879, no. 137.

[179]The infusion of lower status groups was most intense in the French clergy. Though nineteenth-century documents are less useful in determining social origin than are earlier records, it is clear that the Catholic Church drew almost exclusively on lower (especially rural) classes for recruits (see Tackett, *Priest and Parish*, pp. 41–71; Hilaire, *Une Chrétienté*, 1: 173–80, 292–96; Marcilhacy, *Le diocèse d'Orléans*, p. 219; Dansette, *Histoire religieuse*, p. 376). For the steady decline in upper status groups, including the clergy itself, and concomitant rise in lower classes as the source of clergy for Protestant churches, see the data on Sweden (Norrman, *Från Prästöverflöd till prästbrist*, p. 210), Norway (Mannsåker, *Det norske presteskapet*, p. 144), Germany (Dahm, *Beruf: Pfarrer*, pp. 86–88; Bormann, "Studien," p. 132; Neher, *Geistlichkeit Württembergs*, p. 36), and England (Robert Towler and A. P. M. Coxon, *The Fate of the Anglican Clergy* [London, 1979], pp. 21–28).

The Emergence of Clerical Liberalism

Though the clergy's social composition had not changed, its *mentalité* had: in growing numbers the diocesan clergy embraced the ideas of clerical liberalism. First articulated in Belliustin's *Description of the Rural Clergy*, that clerical liberalism proved more clerical than liberal. Above all, it expressed the specific interests of the *soslovie* rather than broader social or political concerns. The cutting edge of its liberalism was aimed at the Church, not secular society; clerical "liberalism" was composed primarily of a willingness to violate tradition, custom, and (at times) even canon law. Though parish clergy had little difficulty supporting narrow economic demands (to wit, the ubiquitous cry for salaries in 1863), they were far slower to embrace the more radical demands of journalist Belliustins in the sixties for greater power in Church affairs and greater privilege in society and state. But the abortive reforms of the sixties created a new spirit in the clergy, more independent and self-assertive, distant indeed from the docility and inertia of prereform priesthood.

That new spirit was most evident in the younger clergy, especially those who attended the seminary during the turbulent Great Reforms and experienced the full liberating effect of the postreform school.[180] Young priests were highly self-conscious of their image and, as one wrote, "have begun to regard their office not as a milk cow but as something of high service and a valuable activity."[181] Tolstoi himself boasted that the new generation of seminarians was free of the prereform monkish servility, and bishops—with dismay—concurred.[182] The young clergy's new spirit provoked, for example, this decree from diocesan authorities in Kiev in 1874: "Many young priests of Kiev diocese walk around Kiev in unbuttoned cassocks; some wear shawls and even plaid coats over their cassocks and enter the consistory wearing unbuttoned overcoats, thereby demonstrating their disrespect toward an official residence."[183] Attitudes toward dress, in fact, were laden with great significance. Just as some Western clergy adopted distinctive dress (the "clerical collar" came into fashion about this time in England), Russian parish clergy tried to divest themselves of the distinctive cassock—to the great indignation

---

[180]The reform, not a change in family relationships, seems responsible for the shift in attitudes. Though emancipation may very well have altered the parental-child relationships in the nobility, it had no comparable effect upon clerical families. The priest's homebound service, his direct responsibility for the moral training of sons (a fact regularly noted by the superintendents on the *klirovye vedomosti*), the crucial impact of the seminary as a boarding school—all remained the same, to judge from the memoirs. For the psychological impact of emancipation, see Richard S. Wortman, *The Crisis of Russian Populism* (Chicago, 1967); for the impact of reform on family relationships in the nobility, see Manning, *Crisis of the Old Order*, chap. 2.

[181]"Molodye sviashchenniki i obshchii byt dukhovenstva," *TsOV*, 1875, no. 42.

[182]*IVO (1878)*, p. 200.

[183]"Dukhovnoe vedomstvo," *TsOV*, 1874, no. 88.

of bishops and tradition-minded laymen.[184] These tendencies were so marked among younger clergy that some contemporaries sought to draw a sharp contrast between fathers and sons in the clergy—the former holding firm to old values and conventions, the latter hopelessly corrupted by postreform secularity and even religious indifference.[185]

Though suggestive and in part true, the contrast between fathers and sons is misleading, for it underestimates how much the *mentalité* of the entire clerical estate had evolved under the influence of reform. To be sure, the one hundred thousand clerics manning the parish churches formed a highly complex group, and many priests, especially the holdovers from prereform times, did not share the more liberal, emancipated spirit of recent seminarians. In any event, in the absence of systematic polls of opinion or full democratization of the Church, it is impossible to delineate precisely the numbers of conservatives and liberals in priestly ranks. Perhaps the fairest assessment is that given by one well-informed observer, who wrote that by the late seventies the parish clergy was comprised of three groups: conservative priests with the outlook of prereform clergy, a large ambivalent center, and a powerful liberal minority whose "influence in clerical circles has become all but dominant."[186] Given the relatively low turnover in appointments, especially in the wake of the parish reform of 1869, which greatly restricted the number of new appointments, the cause of this change in attitude must be found less in a new social composition than in a profound disillusionment with the abortive process of reform. As the occasional turbulence in diocesan assemblies suggests, even the majority of respectable diocesan clergy rose in open revolt against the bishops and their policies.

Perhaps the best evidence of the clergy's mood is provided by the phenomenal success of a liberal clerical newspaper, the *Church-Social Messenger*. Established in St. Petersburg in 1874, it bluntly declared that its purpose was to give the white clergy "an organ in which it can freely express its views on questions of concern and defend its vital interests."[187] The paper printed numerous articles by well-known publicists, including Belliustin and Rostislavov, but its principal source of news and contributions was the rank-and-

[184]"Ob odezhdakh dukhovenstva," ibid., 1879, no. 118. See also the complaint of Petersburg authorities in the early 1880s that "the attempts of some clergy to give themselves a secular visage (e.g., by wearing laymen's hats, by making the sleeves [of their cassocks] narrower, by sewing a row of buttons onto their cassocks, by attaching little cuffs or little collars, by trimming their hair, etc.) provokes consternation or perhaps laughter" (*Istoriko-statisticheskie svedeniia S.-Peterburgskoi eparkhii*, 10 vols. [St. Petersburg, 1869–85], 9: 31).

[185]"Veleno priiskivat'," *Vestnik Evropy*, 1877, kn. 9–11; see also "Vzgliady svetskoi literatury na dukhovenstvo," *RSP*, 1882, no. 5, and "Molodye i starye sviashchenniki," ibid., 1877, no. 44: 291–300.

[186]N. V. Elagin, *Beloe dukhovenstvo i ego interesy* (St. Petersburg, 1881), p. 120.

[187]"Dva slova o nashei zadache," *TsOV*, 1875, no. 3: 1. See also the paper's official "program," announced in its application for permission to publish (TsGIA SSSR, f. 797, op. 42, otd. 2, st. 3, d. 148, ll. 7–7 ob.).

file parish clergy. As one provincial priest wrote, the *Messenger* was "the sole clerical organ through which our clergy can freely, without looking around, declare its needs and demands, discuss one or another fact in the social life of the Church, one or another phenomenon in our life, and can combat and expose various kinds of disorders in diocesan life that demand attention."[188] Consequently, the paper was by far the most popular organ among parish clergy, especially when compared with the local diocesan papers, which were subject to the control of local bishops and ridiculed for their innocuous, dull content.[189] Belliustin complained that the *Messenger* paid no honoraria, but he contributed regularly nonetheless, because "it is popular among the provincial priesthood [*popovstvo* (a pejorative term)]."[190] In April 1879 the future procurator, K. P. Pobedonostsev, deplored the paper's popularity among the parish clergy ("to the scandal of respectable people") and added that, "of all forms of liberalism, the most disgusting is the clerical variety, and its organ unfortunately is *Church-Social Messenger*."[191] Another vehement foe of clerical liberalism was N. V. Elagin, who also decried the paper's shocking popularity among clergy and embellished his tirade with a touch of anti-Semitism: "At the same time that other ecclesiastical journals, which do their work honorably, appear in a few hundred copies, while others completely cease to exist because of the shortage of subscribers, *Church-Social Messenger* is flourishing, establishing its own typography, and—in spite of its total vapidity—appears in many thousands of copies. . . . *Church Social-Messenger* is a business [*gesheft*] that many sons of Israel would envy."[192]

Although the main thrust of clerical liberalism was the demand for improvement in the clergy's material and social condition, its message had evolved substantially since the early 1860s, when cries of "Salary!!! Salary!!! Salary!!!" drowned out everything else. Now clerical liberals gave more attention to other issues and, even when dealing with soslovie or material questions, laid new emphasis upon the notion that the clergy themselves must solve their estate needs for pensions, schools, and the like. If that reassessment conformed to Tolstoi's intent to summon the soslovie to handle its own needs, it also reflected a broader reassertion of *soslovnost'*—more legitimate now that the antisoslovie spirit of the sixties had withered away, and more necessary in the face of threatening, punishing reforms.

As clerical liberalism refocused upon noneconomic issues, its most insistent

---

[188] I. Starov [I. V. Skvortsov], *V zashchitu belogo dukhovenstva (po povodu knigi N. Elagina, "Beloe dukhovenstvo i ego interesy")* (St. Petersburg, 1881), p. 219.

[189] See Beliaev, "Kazanskii i ego perepiska," *BV*, 1916, no. 2: 303.

[190] Tsentral'nyi gosudarstvennyi arkhiv literatury i iskusstva [hereafter TsGALI], f. 275 (N. S. Leskov), op. 4, d. 12, ll. 10 ob., 17 (Belliustin to N. S. Leskov, 20.8.1876, 7.10.1876).

[191] OR GBL, f. 230 (K. P. Pobedonostsev), k. 10802, d. 5, ll. 6 (Pobedonostsev to D. A. Tolstoi, 17.4.1879), 7 (zapiska).

[192] Elagin, *Beloe dukhovenstvo*, p. 115 n.

demand by far was for administrative reform in the Church. Here it encountered the least successful part of the Great Reforms. Bishops seemed to grow
increasingly hostile to change and to recognition of the rights of parish
clergy. Liberal clergy noted, for example, that the practice of electing superintendents had ceased to expand and that some bishops had begun to eliminate it. In the words of one journalist, "a premature reaction has set in."[193]
Clerical liberals put the blame for such reaction squarely upon authorities in
St. Petersburg. Because the Synod had failed to promulgate a general rule,
"a new administrative head (or even the same one) can, with a wave of his
pen, deprive the clergy of this privilege [of electing superintendents], which
they hold so dear."[194] Adding insult to injury, some bishops even published
statements explaining why they abolished elections: "The white clergy are
not concerned about the honor of their estate . . . but about [having] the freedom to live with impunity and serve poorly" under a complaisant superintendent.[195] This reaction caused despair among the clergy, expressed well in
this letter from a priest in Iaroslavl:

> In civil society there has been progress everywhere; in the church, by con-
> trast, regression. Fifteen years have passed since the peasant was emanci-
> pated from serfdom, but is [the plight] of clergy now really easier than
> that of a serf? Hierarchs, consistories, superintendents—if they so wish—
> can make themselves despots who are no more bearable than noble
> squires.[196]

Another priest observed bitterly that "the mutual relations between diocesan
authorities and the people subordinate to them have remained virtually
unchanged."[197]

[193] "Nashi dukhovnye voprosy," *TsOV*, 1874, no. 77. For refusals by bishops to extend the
principle to their diocese, see "[Peredovaia]," ibid., 1874, no. 13; "Blagochinnicheskie vybory
v N. eparkhii," *SL*, 1870, nos. 68–69. For the withdrawal of elections, see the cases of Ekaterinoslav in 1874 ("O pravoslavnom dukhovenstve," *TsOV*, 1874, no. 21), Arkhangel'sk in
1875 ("Korrespondentsiia," ibid., 1875, no. 10), and Astrakhan in 1879 ("Iz Astrakhanskoi
eparkhii," ibid., 1879, no. 133). For the corruption and perverse application of the electoral
principle, see the reports on Khar'kov in 1876 ("Iz Khar'kovskoi eparkhii," ibid., 1876, no. 52),
Vladimir in 1879 ("Iz Pereiaslavia-Zalesskogo," ibid., 1879, no. 92), and Simbirsk in 1880 ("Iz
Simbirskoi eparkhii," ibid., 1880, no. 7).

[194] "Vybornoe nachalo v dukhovenstve," *SL*, 1870, no. 37.

[195] Decree of the bishop of Irkutsk of 1877, reprinted in "Dukhovnoe vedomstvo." *TsOV*,
1877, no. 37. Similar was the statement of the bishop of Kishinev, who found it necessary to
"make significant interventions in the elections, either to annul elections or to order new ones,
or to appoint officials (in view of the incorrigible bad faith shown in the elections, and the
selection of those who had only recently been dismissed from service for misconduct)" (TsGIA
SSSR, f. 796, op. 442, d. 634, ll. 5–5 ob. [report to Synod, 1876]).

[196] "Iz Uglicha," *TsOV*, 1876, no. 29.

[197] "O vzaimnykh otnosheniiakh mezhdu eparkhial'noi vlast'iu i belym dukhovenstvom,"
ibid., 1877, no. 8.

Disappointment with reform aggravated the traditional antagonism toward monks and bishops, reflected in the shocking stridency and invective of public discussions in the contemporary press. Indeed, the assault upon the black clergy became a major theme, as *Church-Social Messenger* and other papers endeavored to erode the moral foundations of monastic domination in the Church. Typical was this angry declaration of a rural priest: "The great majority of contemporary monks, given their low level of education or actual illiteracy, know neither Orthodoxy nor Unorthodoxy [*krivoslavie*], and have not the slightest conception of [true] monasticism."[198] The sarcastic assaults that Belliustin had once confided to his diary now became routine in the face of the debilitated, relaxed censorship of the seventies. The theme figured so prominently in *Church-Social Messenger* that one conservative complained that its primary aim was "to disgrace the black clergy and to arouse the white clergy against it," and that this effort "is extremely harmful, for everywhere it is sowing dissension and rebellion."[199] The onslaught was truly staggering. The *Messenger* and other papers castigated bishops for malfeasance, consistories for venality, and monks for immorality and violation of their vows.[200] With greater force and frequency, clerical liberals demanded democratization of the Church—election of superintendents and members of the consistory, even the consecration of white clergy as bishops.[201]

Informing such demands, and in part legitimizing them, was a new definition of priesthood that emphasized liturgical functions less than a broader pastoral role. Above all, that meant more stress on religious and moral instruction, less concern with ritual and sacrament. This attitude, which appeared sporadically in the sixties, found much more frequent and forceful expression in the clerical periodicals of the seventies: "It is becoming more

[198]"Nravstvennyi oblik sovremennogo monashestva," ibid., 1875, no. 86.

[199]OR GBL, f. 230, k. 10802, d. 5, l. 7 (K. P. Pobedonostsev, "Zapiska").

[200]For vitriolic attacks on maladministration (episcopal misfeasance, burdensome visitations, and consistory injustice), see such typical articles as "Neporiadki v nekotorykh eparkhiiakh," *TsOV*, 1874, no. 150; "Eparkhial'noe obozrenie," ibid., 1876, no. 108; "Soobshchenie," ibid., 1875, no. 6; "Arkhiereiskie poezdki po eparkhiiam," ibid., 1876, no. 125. For denunciations of monasticism, see "Podvigi monashestvuiushchikh," ibid., 1876, no. 65; "Dukhovnoe vedomstvo," ibid., 1875, no. 32; "Beloe dukhovenstvo i monashestvo," ibid., 1874, no. 27; and, especially, the celebrated case of an abbess convicted for illegal financial machinations ("Po povodu protsessa igumen'i Mitrofanii," ibid., 1874, no. 128). Of enormous influence too was D. I. Rostislavov's exposé of monastic wealth in *Opyt issledovanii ob imushchestvakh i dokhodakh nashikh monastyrei* (St. Petersburg, 1876).

[201]On the electoral principle, see "Vybornoe nachalo v srede belogo dukhovenstva v Kievskoi eparkhii," *TsOV*, 1874, nos. 121–22; M. Moroshkin, *Vybornoe nachalo v dukhovenstve* (St. Petersburg, 1870), and its rebuttal in [I. U. Palimpsestov], *Pravda o vybornom nachale v dukhovenstve* (St. Petersburg, 1871). On the consecration of white clergy into the episcopate, see *Golos*, 1871, no. 243; "Episkopy i presvitery," *TsOV*, 1875, nos. 65–67, 75–77, 87–99; I. S. Belliustin, "K voprosu ob episkopakh i presviterakh," ibid., 1875, nos. 73, 86.

and more evident that pastoral service cannot—and should not—consist of the administration of rites and liturgy, but a priest should be the leader of the religious and moral life of his flock."[202] Though most clergy were circumspect in criticizing the laity's ritualism and religious ignorance, the more audacious, like Belliustin, attacked ritualism as pernicious, empty "Byzantinism."[203] Indeed, the greatest *cause célèbre* of the seventies—the "third Belliustin affair"—involved his articles on the Old Belief, published in 1879, which depicted the Church and Old Belief as two "parties," both the victims of a blind, ritualistic Byzantinism.[204] These quasi-Protestant attitudes, so hostile to ritual, found unequivocal expression in Belliustin's private correspondence. In one letter to his son, for example, Belliustin declared that Lutheran clergy were far superior to both Catholic and Orthodox priests: "At least they do not conspire to suppress the intellectual development of their flock, and to hoodwink mankind with the miracles of the Madonna, relics, and similar nonsense."[205]

Liberal clergy also showed more interest in social issues, suggesting that a true pastor must be concerned with temporal issues as well as spiritual ones. Such notions had appeared in the 1860s in some diocesan commentaries, where clerical committees asked for greater civil rights in public affairs, and in the 1870s that attitude developed into a clear concern for the social well-being of their flock.[206] To cite one example, an article in *Church-Social Messenger* in 1875 decried the appearance of "a new type" of exploitative land-

---

[202]"Ob otnoshenii eparkhial'nykh vedomostei k mestnomu dukhovenstvu," *Kurskie EV*, 1871, no. 1: 20. One significant concrete index to the change in attitude was the increase in the number of sermons, limited to 2 or 3 per year for most priests in prereform Russia. According to data filed in Vladimir in 1880, the local priests (approximately 1,100) delivered some 44,285 sermons—about 44 each. Though the majority of sermons were still read from printed texts, about one-quarter (11,215) were original sermons (TsGIA SSSR, f. 796, op. 442, d. 920, l. 25).

[203]In the late 1860s Belliustin composed short essays urging major reforms in Church services (replacement of Slavonic with vernacular Russian; abridgment of the overlong liturgy; adoption of more harmonious music) and Sunday readings for the parishioners' edification (see the series "K redaktoru *Russkogo*," OR GBL, f. 231/III, k. 1, dd. 59a, 59; "Voskresnye chteniia," ibid., d. 56). Though such radical ideas did not easily find their way into print, some articles in *Church-Social Messenger* emphasized the need for measures to combat the parishioners' low religious consciousness (for example, N. Runovskii, "Nechto o sel'skom dukhovenstve," *TsOV*, 1874, nos. 78–79).

[204]Belliustin, "K voprosu o raskole," *TsOV*, 1879, nos. 43–44. For the investigation that lasted over a year and nearly ended in Belliustin's defrocking, see TsGIA SSSR, f. 796, op. 160, g. 1879, d. 831.

[205]LOII, f. 115, d. 1220, letter no. 703 (Belliustin to N. I. Belliustin, 12.11.1884).

[206]For the appearance of social activism, limited mainly to clergy in the two capitals and focused upon charity and welfare, see the summary of press accounts in Oswalt, *Kirchliche Gemeinde*, pp. 44–67.

lord, who is "pragmatic, enterprising, often uneducated, . . . and alien to every kind of moral, humane idea."[207] Another cleric likewise summoned his peers "not to be quiet, but to protect the people from abuse, from Jews, landlords, and kulaks."[208] Striking as they are for their indication of broader public concern in the seventies about the onset of an agrarian crisis, such statements were nevertheless relatively rare, even in the liberal *Church-Social Messenger*. In part, that reticence reflects the essentially *clerical* thrust of the priests' liberalism; it also underscores the clergy's distance from gentry liberalism, a separation caused by the survival of prereform hostility to the arrogant squires and by the refusal of gentry-dominated zemstvos to aid the clergy or parish schools.[209] More fundamentally, the blunted social concerns of the parish clergy represent not only the failure to democratize its social composition but also the very reaffirmation of narrower soslovie concerns. And, most important, the relative disregard for the peasant question shows the clergy's ambivalence toward their flock, who proved so indifferent to their pastors' material needs and to the higher spiritual message of the Church.[210]

Though muted and cautiously worded, the liberal message also contained elements of a new attitude toward the state. The naive *étatisme* of the sixties, reflected in simple hopes that the emperor would grant salaries, perished in the wake of the painful reforms of 1867–1869. From the very outset, officials as different as Konstantin Nikolaevich and A. P. Akhmatov warned that the promise of reform would end in acute disappointment, even disaffection. The clerical press, first in the sixties but increasingly in the seventies, provides abundant evidence of such disillusionment. To quote one typical statement: "One can say, without exaggeration, that several thousand proposals, studies, articles, and notes have been written. But where, what are the results of all this scribbling? It did not do a single thing to solve the [clergy's] problems, which remain in the same distorted form that existed before all this intense waving of pens [commenced]."[211] Another rural priest wrote that, despite all the talk about improving the clergy's material condition, "nothing in fact has

---

[207]"Ekonomicheskie usloviia nravstvennogo sostoianiia krest'ianstva," *TsOV*, 1875, no. 40; see also Belliustin, "Gubiteli naroda," ibid., 1878, no. 83.

[208]"Eparkhial'noe obozrenie," ibid., 1876, no. 132.

[209]For clerical attitudes toward the zemstvo, see V. Rubin, "Ob uluchshenii byta dukhovenstva," ibid., 1878, no. 22. Not surprisingly, therefore, the clergy were altogether missing from the ranks of zemstvo liberalism; see N. M. Pirumova, *Zemskoe liberal'noe dvizhenie; sotsial'nye korni i evoliutsiia do nachala XX veka* (Moscow, 1977); K. F. Shatsillo, "O sostave russkogo liberalizma nakanune revoliutsii 1905–07 godov," *Istoriia SSSR*, 1980, no. 1: 62–74.

[210]That attitude was most strikingly apparent in the liberal clergy's lack of sympathy for the parish election of priests; see *TsOV*, 1885, nos. 22, 25.

[211]"Eparkhial'nye otgoloski," *TsOV*, 1880, no. 27.

actually come of this, and now we are totally disillusioned."[212] By the end of
the seventies, even Tolstoi conceded that this in fact was the case.[213]

Disillusionment sometimes turned into outright political disaffection—an
entirely new phenomenon among the white clergy, who had sporadically
become embroiled in peasant disorders but rarely voiced political protests.
Despair over reform precipitated some sensational political cases. Though
these were only random incidents that happened to come to the attention of
the police, they nevertheless hint of much larger disaffection in the wake of
miscarried reform. For example, one priest in Samara diocese, "having
drunk a little, complained that the Sovereign continually promises to
improve the life of the clergy, but in fact he does nothing." He then proceeded to call the emperor a "son-of-a-bitch," whom he secretly curses during each church service.[214] Another priest in the same diocese also denounced
the emperor for plundering the peasants and ended by calling him a
"fool."[215] A sacristan in Viatka diocese, while visiting the local township
office, pointed to the emperor's portrait and "pronounced vulgar words of
abuse," a burst of fury that cost him six months at hard labor.[216] The emper-
or's portrait inspired similar sentiments from a priest in Kursk: "What kind
of tsar is this? This is a —. Today he's the tsar, tomorrow I'll be."[217] As the
revolutionary tide crested in the late 1870s, with repeated assassination
attempts on Alexander, a priest in Penza confidently declared that "they'll
kill the tsar, yes they will, and if they have not done so thus far, it is only
because he is wearing armor or a shirt of mail."[218] Another priest went further, predicting that "sooner or later the house of Romanov will be over-
thrown."[219] Open political protest remained rare, to be sure; nor did the
clergy express collective protest in diocesan assemblies, as educated society
did in some zemstvos in the late 1870s, amidst the "crisis of autocracy."
Nevertheless, the broader currents of discontent and, especially, the profound disappointment in reform combined to loosen the hold of monarchist
and statist sentiments that dominated clerical attitudes in the early 1860s.

The new spirit in the clergy, predictably, evoked intense consternation in
conservative quarters. If bishops in the sixties complained of isolated Belliustins, by the next decade many believed that the whole white clergy had

[212]"Po povodu novogo rospisaniia prikhodov v nizhegorodskoi eparkhii," ibid., 1878, no. 55;
see also "Dukhovenstvo i obshchestvo," ibid., 1874, no. 107; Belliustin, "Po povodu Uchitel'-
skikh izvestii," ibid., 1878, no. 67; "Staryi god," ibid., 1877, no. 1.

[213]See below, 405-7.

[214]TsGIA SSSR, f. 797, op. 44, otd. 3, st. 5, d. 199, l. 8 ob.

[215]Ibid., d. 93/a, ll. 6-8.

[216]Ibid., op. 45, otd. 3, st. 5, d. 116.

[217]Ibid., f. 796, op. 157, g. 1876, d. 1612, ll. 1-1 ob.

[218]Ibid., op. 161, g. 1880, d. 1703, ll. 1-7.

[219]Ibid., op. 159, g. 1878, d. 71, l. 1 ob.

been irretrievably corrupted.[220] Most vituperative were lay conservatives, such as the editor of one newspaper, who called Belliustin a "theological nihilist" and castigated the parish clergy for selfish egotism and antimonastic sentiments.[221] More acerbic still was K. P. Pobedonostsev. Soon after his appointment as chief procurator, he wrote a close acquaintance that "there are terrible priests—priests who are nihilists and propagandists of revolutionary teachings."[222] Though that comment makes unmistakably clear the kind of policies the new procurator would pursue in the eighties, he in fact did not initiate the turn away from the Great Reforms. As we shall see in the next chapter, the drift from reform to counter-reform commenced well before Pobedonostsev took command as chief procurator.

[220] For an early statement, see "Nechto o sovremennykh sviashchennikakh," *Grazhdanin*, 1873, no. 41: 1099–1102.

[221] See the polemical discussion in *TsOV*, 1879, no. 74; 1880, no. 11.

[222] OR GBL, f. 230, k. 4410, d. 1, l. 75 (Pobedonostsev to E. A. Tiutcheva, 22.6.1880).

CHAPTER 9

The Politics and
Quandaries of Counter-Reform

A disheartened liberal wrote at the end of 1873, "what an amazing and lamentable comparison with the situation as it was when I entered the top echelons of government thirteen years ago: then everything surged forward; now everything is sliding backward."[1] Although the state had not yet abjured the Great Reforms and even countenanced some new ones, criticism of the new order mounted steadily in liberal as well as conservative quarters. The result was a gradual disintegration of the reform process. Even the "most modest attempts" to adjust or complete the Great Reforms foundered on "hidden or overt opposition" that often resulted in stalemate. That, wrote the emperor's chief minister in 1880, was "the fate of many questions of cardinal importance, whose solutions had been sanctioned by the sovereign" himself.[2] From the early 1870s onward, the government was a battleground for different groups fighting to reshape and amend the Great Reforms to suit their own special interests or outlooks. Renovation of the Great Reforms, now conventionally termed "counter-reform" in the historiography, was an exceedingly complex process, one that became apparent by the mid-1870s but achieved partial success only toward the end of the next decade. By then, all earlier reliance upon "vital forces" had been abandoned in favor of "the principle of authority," a principle bound to

[1] Miliutin, *Dnevnik*, 1: 119–20.
[2] "Vsepoddanneishii doklad," p. 241 (Loris-Melikov's report, 11.4.1880).

appeal strongly to a bureaucracy at war with revolutionary terrorism and opposition throughout various social strata.

Counter-reform, like Great Reform, was a process subject to procrastination and conflict, requiring many years to reach enactment and leaving much undone. In part, the modest record of counter-reform can be attributed to the government's panic and disorganization from terrorist attacks; symbolically, the new emperor, Alexander III, barricaded himself at the imperial estate at Gatchina after his father's assassination in 1881. Another obstacle to decisive action was the conservative penchant for "gradualness," a distrust of sudden and dramatic changes. But a more important obstacle was the new texture of autocratic politics: despite Alexander III's autocratic visage and spirit, he found it impossible to dominate the bureaucracy as had his grandfather Nicholas or even his father Alexander. In some measure, his weakness derived from the bureaucratic structure, which accorded the State Council a major role in integrating and reviewing new statutes. The Council consisted mainly of top officials removed from office, which in the 1880s meant a predominance of the very same liberal bureaucrats who had designed the Great Reforms in the first place. Not surprisingly, they had no interest in dismantling their own work.[3] More fundamental still, the autocrat simply lacked the time, knowledge, and instruments to mediate the various interests championed by groups that had grown more complex and better organized. It had been one thing to referee ministerial rivalry; it was quite another to reconcile conflicts involving various social and economic groups. Above all, counter-reform could not be simple restoration. It was impossible to return to prereform Russia—to reestablish serfdom, dismantle universities, close factories, and the like. At most, then, the architects of counter-reform could only tinker and modify. They drafted some new legislation, such as the university statute of 1884, the land captain's act of 1889, and the zemstvo and duma laws of 1890, but they left the basic structure of the Great Reforms intact. In the end, counter-reform meant less a change of laws than a change of style: not new statutes, but new policies—tighter censorship, summary political trials, administrative exile—dominated state policy in the 1880s and 1890s.[4]

How did the Church share in this process? It was surely bound to be involved, since its reform had in principle and in conception formed an integral part of the secular Great Reforms. Then, too, as we have seen, its new order suffered from serious difficulties, provoking dissatisfaction among cleric and layman, liberal and conservative. This chapter will examine the transition from ecclesiastical reform to counter-reform, with particular attention to the goals, tensions, and quandaries that this shift in policy entailed.

[3]Taranovsky, "Politics of Counter-Reform," chaps. 3, 5; Whelan, *Autocracy and Bureaucracy*, chaps. 2, 6–8.

[4]See the literature cited in the introduction to Part Three.

Tolstoi: Amending the Great Reforms

By 1871 Tolstoi's Special Commission had largely completed drafting its entire program of reform, but it still had some major pieces of legislation awaiting enactment. That outstanding legislation included plans to improve the clergy's legal status (for example, their right to various medals and the removal of disabilities for voluntary defrocking) and to ease the lot of clerical wives (mainly by giving them a secular legal status like their children).[5] Moreover, the new statutes for ecclesiastical censorship and justice, which would modify the old structure of Church administration, still awaited approval and enactment. Though Tolstoi's influence remained immense, it was by no means clear that he could win approval for such legislation, especially amidst the more conservative political atmosphere of the 1870s and the rising criticism of his earlier reforms.

The change in atmosphere first became evident in 1871. In a dramatic shift away from the antisoslovie policies of the sixties, the State Council rejected the commission's draft statute for improving the status of clerical wives on the specific grounds that it ran contrary to the empire's system of estates. The state's renewed commitment to the soslovie principle, evident as well in the views of such powerful bureaucrats as Petr A. Shuvalov, achieved formal expression in the Council's resolution, a document of extraordinary significance.[6] It admitted that, "because of important reforms of late in the present regime, there have been considerable changes in the mutual relationship between estates and the rights conferred upon each of them, but the [system] of estates remains in all its former force."[7] The 1869 statute on the clergy's children had been such an exception, but the Council refused to accept further changes. Russian law, it held, presumed ascription to one of four estates, a principle that could be violated only for the most pressing reasons. It saw no necessity to do so in the present case, for the main problem—the plight of clerical widows—could be resolved without a sweeping statute on all the clergy's wives. The result was a greatly emasculated piece of legislation that left clerical wives as part of the estate and fixed a new secular status only for those widows who remarried outside the clerical estate.[8] This unequivocal retreat from the antiestate principles of the sixties dealt Tolstoi his first major defeat.

[5] For the draft proposal, see above, pp. 310–13.

[6] For Shuvalov's statement in 1873 that he favored an "all-estate" (vsesoslovnyi) rather than an "antiestate" (vnesoslovnyi) policy, see Chernukha, Vnutrenniaia politika, p. 74. For the recrudescence of the estate principle, see also V. G. Chernukha, "Vsepoddanneishii doklad P. A. Valueva," Vspomogatel'nye istoricheskie distsipliny, 2 (1969): 262–69; Iu. B. Solov'ev, Samoderzhavie i dvorianstvo v kontse XIX v. (Leningrad, 1973), pp. 165–277.

[7] TsGIA SSSR, f. 804, op. 1, r. 1, d. 150, ch. 1, ll. 74 ob–75.

[8] Ibid., ll. 74–84. For a more detailed discussion of the various options and ensuing debate, see Freeze, "Caste and Emancipation," pp. 144–46.

It was not his last. The Special Commission's proposals to raise the clergy's legal status, formally proposed in 1869, also fell by the wayside. In some cases the failure was hardly surprising. State officials, predictably, showed scant enthusiasm for schemes to give parish clergy prestigious medals and honors, especially those that conferred patents of hereditary nobility and could be acquired merely by serving twelve to twenty years without reproach.[9] Most indicative of the new mood in the early 1870s was the defeat of plans to change the law on voluntary defrocking, a reform sponsored by the Synod in 1859 and supported almost universally by bishops and priests alike. Nonetheless, a special committee summoned to consider the matter spurned the proposal, offering no more explanation for its decision than murky allusions to legal and practical "complexities."[10] In practice, authorities resorted to extraordinary rule: rather than revise the statute, they regularly approved special exemptions for individuals to defrock and assume secular status without any special disabilities.[11]

Tolstoi's greatest and most public defeat involved the proposal to reform ecclesiastical justice, which sought to apply the principles of the state's new judicial system to the Church. The proposal, as we have seen, was far-reaching indeed. It fully incorporated modern procedures, created a professional procuracy, virtually eliminated the power of diocesan bishops and consistories, and conferred major new rights upon the parish clergy, including the power to elect local judges.[12] It was certain to cause great controversy in the Church, for it struck at the very heart of episcopal authority and even entailed clear deviation from canon law. When the Synod declined to take immediate action and had the scheme distributed to diocesan authorities for preliminary comment, it was already clear that the reform faced a stiff fight within the Church.[13] Tolstoi, no doubt fearing episcopal opposition and anticipating public support, arranged for the proposal to be published—a curious, yet telling, application of the "publicity" tactic so often used in the Great Reforms of the 1860s.[14]

As Tolstoi rightly surmised, journalistic opinion was almost unanimously

---

[9]TsGIA SSSR, f. 804, op. 1, r. 3, d. 473, ll. 1–5 (zhurnal, no. 45).

[10]On the special committee, see ibid., r. 1, d. 18, ll. 136–54 ob. For continuing demands of reform, see: I. S. Belliustin, "Dukhovno-obshchestvennye voprosy," Sbornik "Nedeli" (St. Petersburg, 1872): 411–17 (a publication of his earlier memorandum of 1857); "O sviashchen-nosluzhiteliakh, slagaiushchikh s sebia sviashchennyi san," TsOV, 1874, nos. 140–41. For an opposing statement, see a memorandum (undated, but composed after 1869) entitled "O slo-zhenii sviashchennogo sana," OR GBL, f. 302, k. 3, d. 13, ll. 1–42.

[11]For example, see "Dukhovnoe vedomstvo," TsOV, 1874, nos. 13, 54.

[12]See above, pp. 342–45, for a synopsis and references.

[13]TsGIA SSSR, f. 796, op. 150, g. 1869, d. 736/a, ll. 39 ob.–41 (Synod resolution, confirmed by Alexander II, 19.5.1873).

[14]The proposals were published not only in central periodicals but in diocesan papers as well (for example, "Novyi proekt dukhovno-sudebnoi reformy," Vladimirskie EV, 1873, nos. 6, 16–20).

favorable. Typical was the enthusiastic reception in *The Voice,* a liberal newspaper in St. Petersburg, which proclaimed the reform to be more important than any adopted so far, but warned ominously of powerful opposition, especially from devotees of "the principles of episcopal omnipotence."[15] Predictably, liberal church organs such as *Church-Social Messenger* and even a moderate academy journal, *The Orthodox Review,* supported the reform proposals. Moreover, archconservative papers such as V. P. Meshcherskii's *The Citizen* at first recommended immediate adoption of the reform.[16] There were, however, some discordant voices. The most strident was that of A. F. Lavrov, a dissenting member of the reform committee who published a two-volume refutation of the reform, affixed with massive citations from canon law and Scripture to show that the entire scheme was uncanonical and antithetical to Orthodoxy.[17]

But the fate of reform rested with the bishops, not the press.[18] Although a few exceptions like Bishop Pavel of Pskov endorsed "all provisions of the committee's project in all its scope and form,"[19] it soon became clear that most prelates, as expected, categorically rejected the scheme. Metropolitan Innokentii of Moscow aphoristically expressed the general mood when he declared privately that "this proposal is straight from Hell and is going right back."[20] His official comment was less colorful but no less adamant. The whole proposal, he wrote, was an ill-advised attempt to "make ecclesiastical justice purely formal, completely similar to secular courts in substance, method, and punishments."[21] Some prelates, like the bishop of Orel, even suspected an evil conspiracy to subvert Orthodoxy: "Everywhere there is

---

[15] *Golos,* 1873, no. 210; see earlier editorials in 1871 (nos. 115–16) and 1872 (no. 60).

[16] "Neskol'ko slov po povodu proekta osnovnykh polozhenii preobrazovaniia dukhovno-sudebnoi chasti," *PO,* 1873, no. 8: 266–76; *TsOV,* 1874, nos. 48–51; *Grazhdanin,* 1873, no. 27. By the following year, however, Meshcherskii was having second thoughts and condemned the proposals as uncanonical (*Grazhdanin,* 1874, no. 20/21).

[17] N. V. Elagin, *Predpolagaemaia reforma tserkovnogo suda,* 2 vols. (St. Petersburg, 1873). On Lavrov's authorship here, see Savva, *Khronika,* 5: 90; V. Lavrskii, "Moi vospominaniia," *BV,* 1905, no. 7/8: 529. For heated rejoinders, see commentaries in a moderate Church journal (N. Nevzorov, "Vzgliad na proekt," *Str.,* 1874, no. 3: 200–19) and the liberal *Messenger* ("Ob osobom proekte dukhovno-sudebnoi reformy," *TsOV,* 1874, nos. 48–51). The impact of the Elagin-Lavrov volume was sometimes decisive. One Kiev journal for parish clergy first favored the reform, then endorsed Lavrov's critique ("Po povodu proekta dukhovno-sudebnoi reformy," *RSP,* no. 1873, no. 34: 491–508; "[Retsenziia]: *O predpolagaemoi reforme,*" ibid., 1874, nos. 1–2, 4, 6).

[18] The original manuscript replies are in TsGIA SSSR, f. 796, op. 445, dd. 410–14; they have been published as *Mneniia preosviashchennykh eparkhial'nykh arkhiereev otnositel'no proekta preobrazovaniia dukhovno-sudebnoi chasti,* 2 vols. (St. Petersburg, 1874–76), and *Mneniia dukhovnykh konsistorii otnositel'no proekta preobrazovaniia dukhovno-sudebnoi chasti,* 2 vols. (St. Petersburg, 1874–78).

[19] *Mneniia arkhiereev,* 1: 111–14.

[20] Savva, *Khronika,* 5: 73 (Archimandrite Simeon to Savva, 1875).

[21] *Mneniia arkhiereev,* 1: 78.

now a desire to be free from the Church's influence, to remove all the authority of monastic bishops, to weaken marital ties bound by holy sacraments, [and] such a desire is fully consistent with the rules of the new judicial proposal."[22] The bishop of Irkutsk questioned the legal validity of the proposal, since it had been compiled not by the Church but by a committee composed primarily of laymen.[23] Archbishop Platon of Kostroma, citing the reduction in the bishops' power, complained that "the [committee's] explanatory note is pervaded with bitterness and hatred for bishops."[24] Metropolitan Arsenii of Kiev, once a leader in Church reform, penned a vituperative commentary that labeled the draft proposals contrary to Church law and Scripture, even "hostile to the spirit of Orthodoxy."[25] The bishop of Ufa questioned the need for reform at all, claiming that demands for change merely represented "the cries of liberal journalists," who certainly "do not comprise public opinion, which is decisively opposed to innovations in the Church and even to the new state courts."[26]

The most influential opinion belonged to the archbishop of Volhynia, Agafangel (Solov'ev), who brazenly published his confidential commentary in the local diocesan paper and helped to set the tone for other responses. Agafangel, a conservative who had exposed the Pavskii lithographs in 1842 and opposed Batiushkov's innovations in 1860, denounced the reform as a crass violation of sacred episcopal authority. Though that argument was routine in the bishop's replies, only Agafangel dared to link this change with the corresponding increase in power for the chief procurator: "The chief procurator of the Synod has enormous power, the likes of which, it seems, are not wielded by a single minister or member of the State Council. But the new proposal concentrates in his hands powers of indictment, justice, legislation, and implementation over the clergy and church, power which belonged to none of the subjects and simply makes the chief procurator the head of the Church." Agafangel also berated the committee for unfair attacks on the existing system and for trying to solve simple problems with a grandiose radical scheme rather than the modest correctives that were more appropriate. Above all, he warned, this scheme violated the very foun-

---

[22] Ibid., 1: 2.

[23] Ibid., 1: 154.

[24] Ibid., 2: 77.

[25] TsGIA SSSR, f. 797, op. 39, otd. 1, st. 1, d. 295, ll. 54–54 ob.

[26] *Mneniia arkhiereev*, 1: 138 (Ufa); see also ibid., 2: 354–61 (Minsk). Many reports defended the bishops' canonical right to govern; see the replies from Astrakhan (1: 57–69), Ekaterinoslav (1: 71), Moscow (1: 72–75), Kaluga (2: 92–93), Tver (2: 323–36), Minsk (2: 354–56), and Olonets (2: 361–92). The bishops also discerned "practical" weaknesses in the committee's proposal, including secular control over marriages (see, for instance, comments by prelates in Viatka, Kaluga, Gurii, Penza, and Tver in ibid., 1: 51–55, 92–111, 313–15; 2: 341–44), the remoteness of regional appellate courts (replies from Riazan, Irkutsk, Kamchatka, and Tambov in ibid., 1: 143–53, 170–71, 176–77; 2: 74–77), and the costliness of numerous district judges (replies from Ufa, Irkutsk, and Podolia in ibid., 1: 114–18, 133–37, 173).

dations of the Orthodox Church: "The proposal for a new judicial order in the clergy (and the attached explanatory note) absolutely must not be implemented, for it perverts the order in the Church established by Church councils and the Holy Fathers." What was needed, he concluded, was the establishment of regional episcopal councils, which alone could revitalize the Church.[27] Agafangel's decision to publish his opinion earned him a formal reproof from the Synod and caustic rejoinders in the contemporary press, but it achieved its main goal of mobilizing the bishops against the reform and stiffening their resolve to resist.[28] Following his example, other bishops wrote more spirited rejoinders and showed new determination to defend episcopal authority.

In the face of this opposition, Tolstoi soon gave way and abandoned the whole effort. The first clue was his decision in March 1874 to disband the committee. Normally, such committees remained in existence to review the diocesan commentaries and make appropriate adjustments in the draft statute.[29] That effort was clearly useless here, since the bishops repudiated the basic principles underlying the draft. Though Tolstoi's decision remained secret, the contemporary press knew of the bishops' opposition and, especially, their purposeful procrastination in submitting replies.[30] One opponent of the reform even speculated that Tolstoi was grateful for the procrastination: "The prime movers behind this proposal are delighted [for the delays], for this will provide them with a specious excuse to retreat or to bury this whole affair, which cannot end successfully for them."[31] By mid-1875, the defeat of reform became public knowledge, as even the most determined liberal organs admitted that the cause was lost.[32]

Yet the attempt was not without consequences, for it significantly sharpened tensions outside the Church. The response of parish clergy was as predictable as it was intense: disappointment and even fury, especially toward the bishops who had sabotaged a reform that seemed so close to enactment. If most diocesan clergy had been skeptical of the liberal attack on bishops in the sixties, they now had abundant and shocking evidence that the bishops did oppose reforms to ease the clergy's lot and raise their status.[33] More strik-

---

[27] Ibid., 1: 227. The suggestion of episcopal councils appeared in a number of reports; see, for example, the responses from Tambov, Vladimir, and Nizhnii Novgorod (ibid., 2: 75, 277, 310–21).

[28] Savva, *Khronika*, 4: 752.

[29] TsGIA SSSR, f. 797, op. 39, otd. 1, st. 1, d. 295, ll. 49–49 ob.

[30] "Kanonicheskie pravila i dukhovno-sudebnaia reforma," *TsOV*, 1874, no. 88.

[31] Savva, *Khronika*, 5: 96 (Lavrov to Savva, 5.4.1875); see also the letter of P. S. Kazanskii, 30.1.1875 (*U Troitsy*, p. 584).

[32] "Dukhovnoe vedomstvo," *TsOV*, 1875, no. 94.

[33] "Po povodu slukhov o priostanovke dukhovno-sudebnoi reformy," *TsOV*, 1875, no. 61; "Tserkovnoe obozrenie za 1875 g.," ibid., 1876, no. 1; "O neobkhodimosti izmeneniia st. 333 Ustava dukhovnykh konsistorii," ibid., 1876, no. 125; "K reforme konsistorskogo suda," ibid., 1878, no. 60; "Dukhovno-sudebnaia reforma," ibid., 1878, no. 16.

ing perhaps was the impact of this reform attempt upon the bishops. It triggered a significant shift in opinion, inspiring a heightened distrust of the state and a determination to defend episcopal prerogative and privilege. That mood was expressed most forcefully in hostility toward Tolstoi, who "bosses everything, directs everything, even does everything that is important."[34] The prelates imputed the most evil designs to the procurator, including a desire to abolish monasticism. Some, significantly, believed that the liberal antimonastic, antiepiscopal *Church-Social Messenger* "is under the special protection of Chief Procurator Tolstoi and serves as his organ for the dissemination of ill-intentioned ideas about monasticism and episcopal authority."[35] Understandably, few bishops would grieve at his fall from power in 1880.[36]

Tolstoi himself was losing faith in the reforms, and, though loath to admit their failure publicly, he prepared to strike out in new directions in the late 1870s. The change of heart was not readily visible to outsiders, though attentive observers could have discerned a new reticence in his annual reports about the reforms' successes and a marked slowdown in the implementation of reform.[37] His first major change came in 1879, when he issued a circular annulling the right of seminarians to enter the university without first passing the entrance examinations.[38] Despite pro forma assurances that the circular merely aimed to establish equality for all applicants, the clergy correctly perceived it as a device to restrict university access for seminarians, partly from concern about the revolutionary proclivities of seminarians, but primarily from a desire to stem the exodus from the clerical estate.[39] The circular had a chilling effect upon the clergy. As one student wrote, the new rule "is equivalent to a complete prohibition on entrance to the university— sad news for our brothers from the clergy."[40]

Perhaps most indicative of Tolstoi's mood was his response to a memorandum from a provincial priest, Ioann Stefanov, in early 1879. The priest deftly

[34]"Zapiski arkhiepiskopa Nikanora," *RA*, 1908, no. 2: 190.

[35]Savva *Khronika*, 5: 563–64.

[36]See below, pp. 408–9.

[37]An undated, unsigned memorandum (evidently compiled in 1880–1881, at the instigation of Pobedonostsev) assembled evidence to demonstrate that Tolstoi ceased to implement the 1869 parish reform and openly conceded its failure. See "Po voprosu o sokrashchenii prichtov i prikhodov" (TsGIA SSSR, f. 797, op. 50, g. 1880, otd. 3, st. 5, d. 182, ch. 2, ll. 406–9 ob.).

[38]For the circular of 20 March 1879, see *TsOV*, 1879, no. 37.

[39]For a denial of discrimination, see "Postanovlenie 20 marta kasatel'no postupleniia seminaristov v universitety i drugie vysshie uchebnye zavedeniia," *Kievskie EV*, 1879, no. 17: 2–9.

[40]"Akademicheskie pis'ma A. V. Martynova k ottsu," *BV*, 1915, no. 10/12: 293. Clerical fears were well grounded: students of clerical origin constituted 35 percent of all university students in 1878, 10 percent in 1885 (Shchetinina, *Universitety*, pp. 72, 199). For the impact on particular universities, showing the decline in absolute as well as relative terms, see G. I. Shchetinina, "Alfavitnye spiski studentov kak istoricheskii istochnik," *Istoriia SSSR*, 1979, no. 5: 123–24.

exploited the government's mounting anxiety about the revolutionary movement, which had launched an escalating wave of attacks on high officials and
the emperor and even threatened to sink its roots into popular aspirations for
radical land reform. Arguing that the state needed an active, zealous clergy
to combat "the revolutionaries and socialists," Stefanov warned that the
clergy were now so demoralized by reform that they were unlikely to provide much support for the regime. Only decisive measures to render real aid,
he concluded, could succeed in turning them into aggressive defenders of
the state.[41] Though Stefanov no doubt overstated the popular influence of the
revolutionary intelligentsia, his point struck a vital nerve. Tolstoi, impressed
by the note, asked for further information about the author as well as copies
of his sermons.[42]

Stefanov's memorandum in fact coincided with new views in high circles,
which—mainly for political reasons—laid greater stress on the clergy's
potential role in promoting social stability. The new emphasis was most
apparent in a shift of opinion about parish schools. Earlier, as we have seen,
state authorities were largely unsympathetic to suggestions that the clergy
hold a dominant position in public education, contending that parish clergy
had neither the time nor the training to teach in schools. In a striking about-
face, the Committee of Ministers in 1879 "expressed the unanimous conviction that the spiritual and moral development of the people, who represent
the foundation of the entire state system, cannot be achieved without giving
the clergy a dominant position in the management of public schools, and in
the earliest possible future it should be set as the goal of efforts coordinated
by the Ministry of Education and the ecclesiastical domain."[43] As a preliminary measure, the ministry distributed a circular asking local officials to seek
ways to augment the clergy's participation, and early in 1880 the emperor
himself voiced support for these proposals.[44] Such talk elicited high hopes
among the clergy, but state finances, as ever, intervened to block action. The
Russo-Turkish War of 1877–1878 had emptied state coffers and, as the minister of finance explained, deprived the state of the means to support the
clergy's participation in schools.[45]

In the wake of that setback, Tolstoi developed a much broader conception

[41] Copies of Stefanov's memorandum are in OR GBL, f. 262 (Savva), op. 1, k. 55, d. 26, ll.
1–9 ob.; TsGIA SSSR, f. 797, op. 49, otd. 1, st. 1, d. 31, ll. 5–14 ob.

[42] OR GBL, f. 262, op. 1, k. 26, d. 58, ll. 27–28 ob.

[43] IVO (1883), pp. 57–58.

[44] Blagovidov, Deiatel'nost', p. 210; "Vsepoddanneishii doklad ot Printsa P. G. Oldenburg-
skogo ot 18 fevralia 1880 g.," RA, 1912, no. 11: 414–17.

[45] For the clergy's enthusiastic response to such reports, see "K voprosu ob uchastii dukhovenstva v dele narodnogo prosveshcheniia," TsOV, 1879, no. 126. For the role of the Ministry
of Finance in burying such schemes, see "Ob"iasnitel'naia zapiska," TsGIA SSSR, f. 796, op.
163, g. 1882, d. 222/a, ll. 16 ob.–17 ob. For the fiscal difficulties that lay behind the ministry's
action (in the face of clear support by the autocrat), see A. P. Pogrebinskii, "Finansovaia politika tsarizma," Istoricheskii arkhiv, 1960, no. 2: 131–44.

of reform, and in February 1880 he petitioned Alexander to form a new commission to deal with the clerical question. Adroitly exploiting the current political "crisis of autocracy," in which the state seemed besieged on all sides by revolutionary attacks and popular opposition, Tolstoi argued (like Stefanov) that the state must uphold the clergy as a crucial stabilizing element. "The tragic events of late," he wrote, alluding to the escalating terrorism, "make it especially necessary to summon the clergy for intensified moral influence upon the people's spiritual inclinations." But, warned Tolstoi, economic hardship and miscarried reform were demoralizing the clergy and causing some to drift toward outright disaffection: "With the extreme rise in prices on all products of late, the clergy's material needs have increased, while their hopes for an improvement in their position (which had been aroused by [past] government decrees) are beginning to give way to a feeling that usually accompanies unrealized expectations." To plot a new course of reform, he proposed to convoke a special conference of high officials, charged with finding ways to assist the clergy and increase their role in secular society, primarily in the area of public education. Alexander formally approved this proposal on 15 February 1880, and three days later Tolstoi dispatched letters of invitation to pertinent ministers.[46]

In preparation for the conference, the Special Commission's staff drew up a general report, "Measures for the Improvement of the Clergy's Condition." It gave a cursory review of attempts in the past century to solve the clergy's economic problems and showed that thus far all steps had done little to ameliorate the plight of the average staff, which still earned only some 300 rubles per annum. The report's basic assumption was the need to provide a full, regular salary; parish reorganization and shtat reductions, which had so manifestly failed in the 1870s, did not even merit discussion. As ever, the problem was means. Setting as its goal a substantial increase in support (600 rubles for priests, 200 rubles for sacristans), the report proposed that the state, not the parish, bear responsibility for this reform, primarily by converting the traditional emoluments into a land tax. In contrast to a levy on individuals, the land tax would weigh most heavily upon the propertied classes. Although preliminary calculations showed that the state must assess an additional 15.7 million rubles to finance this reform, the report claimed that the resulting levies would not appreciably increase the tax bill of each province.[47] Rumors of Tolstoi's new plans soon leaked to the press, generating new hopes that the government was at last ready to tackle the clerical question in earnest.[48]

But two months later, in April 1880, Tolstoi suddenly lost his posts as chief

[46]TsGIA SSSR, f. 804, op. 1, r. 1, d. 175/a, ll. 24–27, 33–37 ob.

[47]O merakh k uluchsheniiu material'nogo obespecheniia pravoslavnogo dukhovenstva (St. Petersburg, 1880); for the statistical data behind these proposals, see TsGIA SSSR, f. 804, op. 1, r. 1, d. 175/a, ll. 74 ob.–86.

[48]"Slukh kasatel'no obespecheniia byta dukhovenstva," Tverskie eparkhial'nye vedomosti, 1880, no. 9: 149–50.

procurator of the Synod and minister of education. Rumors had circulated since early 1880 that Tolstoi would soon forfeit his church position to General A. A. Kireev, a prominent conservative with strong ties to the Church.[49] Though the rumor proved false, it reflected widespread resentment toward Tolstoi in high Church circles and also in lay society, where his policies—especially as minister of education—made him the object of public vexation.[50] His removal was finally engineered by M. T. Loris-Melikov, the new minister of interior, whose "dictatorship of the heart" sought not only to repress revolutionaries but also to reconcile educated society. Both because Tolstoi opposed Loris-Melikov's policies and because he had become the *bête-noire* of educated society, the minister of interior determined to remove his rival from the government. Alexander, however, had a singular attachment to Tolstoi; as one minister noted, "the sovereign stubbornly supports Tolstoi" and resists demands for his removal.[51] Loris-Melikov, however, continued to exploit Tolstoi's unpopularity and his failures in conducting Church reform. In a memorandum to the emperor shortly before Tolstoi's dismissal, Loris-Melikov drew a grim (and exaggerated) picture of problems in the Church: "The clergy has continued, with a few rare exceptions, to stagnate in ignorance and generally has lost the influence it once exercised. It has been systematically removed from everything, parishes have been closed, and seminarians have remained the same coarse *bursaki*."[52] A few days later Tolstoi yielded his position as chief procurator to K. P. Pobedonostsev, a notorious and outspoken conservative who vehemently opposed all the Great Reforms and especially those in the Church. His appointment abruptly terminated Tolstoi's new reform plans, and the preliminary files for the projected conference of high officials were eventually dumped, unused, into the archives.[53]

Tolstoi's removal occasioned a lively debate in the press about the whole era of Church reforms. Despite misgivings, the liberal press generally defended the chief procurator and his reforms, even while admitting the need to revise and, especially, "complete" Tolstoi's measures of the late 1860s. The *Church-Social Messenger* in particular expressed regret over Tolstoi's "resignation" and urged his successor to bring to fruition the reforms begun a decade earlier.[54] But Tolstoi's removal evoked undisguised jubilation

---

[49] OR GBL, f. 126, k. 3, d. 8, l. 2 (A. A. Kireev, "Dnevnik").

[50] Sinel, *The Classroom and the Chancellery*, pp. vii–viii, 252–57.

[51] Miliutin, *Dnevnik*, 3: 243; see also P. A. Valuev, *Dnevnik, 1877–84 gg.* (Petrograd, 1919), pp. 71–87.

[52] "Vsepoddanneishii doklad Valueva," p. 242; "Konstitutsiia gr. Lorisa-Melikova: materialy," *Byloe*, 1918, no. 4/5: 160–61, 181.

[53] TsGIA SSSR, f. 804, op. 1, r. 1, d. 175/a, l. 87.

[54] "Eshche po povodu otstavki gr. D. A. Tolstogo," *TsOV*, 1880, nos. 57–58. A professor of Kazan Academy, A. Gusev, also defended Tolstoi's reforms, especially those on censorship,

in many quarters, even moderately liberal ones. Thus *The Voice*, a liberal paper in Petersburg, welcomed the change in procurators. Tolstoi's parish reform, it declared, "did not improve the clergy's condition," and it concluded that "almost nothing has been done in fourteen years" to ameliorate the clergy's economic status.[55] Commentary was more vitriolic in archconservative papers like *The East*, which unqualifiedly condemned Tolstoi's reforms as harmful.[56] As one bishop noted, with the exception of *The Moscow News* (M. N. Katkov's paper and a staunch ally of Tolstoi) and *Church-Social Messenger* ("the organ of the former chief procurator"), "all other papers unanimously expressed joy on the occasion of Count Tolstoi's resignation."[57] The most untempered attack appeared the following year in a volume edited by N. Elagin, which castigated the effect of the Church reforms and cited them as the cause of a new "evil spirit" among the parish clergy.[58] Elagin distributed copies to all the bishops with this cover note: "The recent reforms in the Church have inflicted so much evil that it is urgently necessary that this be eradicated. This book was published for that purpose."[59] Although the volume provoked sharp rejoinders from moderate journals like *The Orthodox Review* and from the liberal *Church-Social Messenger*, its perspective meshed closely with that of the new chief procurator.[60]

Pobedonostsev: The Theory and Politics of Counter-Reform

K. P. Pobedonostsev's name was virtually synonymous with black reaction in late imperial Russia, and his portrait—deathly pallid, morose, and fearful—seems eerily symbolic of the *ancien régime* in its waning decades.

---

elected superintendents, and abolition of the hereditary estate (*Sovershennoe i ozhidaemoe* [*po povodu otstavki gr. D. A. Tolstogo*] [St. Petersburg, 1880]). Another pamphlet, while conceding the failure to improve the clergy's material condition, argued that the other reforms had had a beneficial effect upon the Church (V. V. Mirotvortsev, *Mery pravitel'stva k preobrazovaniiu byta pravoslavnogo dukhovenstva v tsarstvovanie Gosudaria Aleksandra II* [Kazan, 1880]).

[55] *Golos*, 1880, no. 115; see also "Po povodu naznacheniia novogo ober-prokurora," *Orenburgskie eparkhial'nye vedomosti*, 1880, no. 11: 411.

[56] For a summary of these polemics, see *TsOV*, 1880, nos. 57–58.

[57] Savva, *Khronika*, 6: 150.

[58] Elagin, *Beloe dukhovenstvo*; see also Elagin's acerbic rebuttal to his critics in *Chego nado zhelat' dlia nashei tserkvi*, 2 vols. (St. Petersburg, 1882–85).

[59] Savva, *Khronika*, 6: 366 (Elagin to Savva, 7.1.1881).

[60] See, for example, the devastating review of Elagin's *Beloe dukhovenstvo* in such moderate journals as *Pravoslavnoe obozrenie* (1881, no. 1: 179–96). For a book-length reply to Elagin, denying that the clergy were corrupt or that *Tserkovno-obshchestvennyi vestnik* exercised a pernicious influence, see Skvortsov, *V zashchitu belogo dukhovenstva*.

Although contemporaries grossly exaggerated his influence over secular affairs of state,[61] Pobedonostsev clearly had abundant opportunity to reshape the Church's policies and administration—just as Tolstoi had. As one perceptive observer noted, a change in procurators meant a change in policy, for "we have no system, just people," and a change in the latter meant a change in the former as well.[62] The new procurator clearly intended far-reaching changes in the Church, for shortly after his appointment he wrote a confidant in the clergy that "the more I look around, the more I see that needs to be done."[63]

Pobedonostsev had already earned a reputation as a hardened, uncompromising conservative.[64] Ironically, this bitter foe of the Great Reforms had assisted in preparing the judicial reform of 1864, perhaps the most systematic and liberal reform of all. But Pobedonostsev soon lost his taste for the new reforms, and by the time the judicial reform was promulgated, he wrote a close friend, "You will not believe how much we would like to stop at something stable."[65] Later, as a member of the State Council in the 1870s, he claimed that the reforms had caused indescribable chaos: "All previous [law] is so tangled up that you cannot find the beginning or end."[66] At the same time, Pobedonostsev argued that the present regime itself had provoked the crisis by discarding its own power: "The general, rising dissastisfaction results from the fact that the people do not see or feel a firm government, do not see a unity of authority, will, and direction, and are gradually losing that

---

[61] Pobedonostsev himself denied the popular opinion of his overweening influence; see his autobiographical letter to Nicholas II in K. P. Pobedonostsev, *Pis'ma Pobedonostseva k Aleksandru III*, 2 vols. (Moscow, 1925–26), 2: 330–35. But historians have long sustained his contemporaries' contrary view. Though one Soviet scholar has reaffirmed the traditional view (S. L. Evenchik, "Pobedonostsev i dvoriansko-krepostnicheskaia liniia samoderzhaviia v poreformennoi Rossii," *Uchenye zapiski Moskovskogo gosudarstvennogo pedagogicheskogo instituta im. V. I. Lenina*, 309 [Moscow, 1969]: 76), most treatments now discount a significant role for the procurator, at least after the first few months of power. See, for example, R. F. Byrnes, *Pobedonostsev: His Life and Thought* (Bloomington, 1968), p. 238; Thomas Sorenson, "The End of the Volunteer Fleet," *Slavic Review*, 34 (1975): 131–37. That view, however, has not filtered down to a reassessment of Pobedonostsev's role as procurator; see, for example, Byrnes's account (pp. 165–209) of Pobedonostsev's tenure as "general director of the Synod"; Gerhard Simon, *Konstantin Petrovič Pobedonoscev und die Kirchenpolitik des Heiligen Sinod, 1880–1905* (Göttingen, 1969); Thomas Sorenson, "The Thought and Policies of Konstantin P. Pobedonostsev" (Ph.D. diss., University of Washington, 1977). Though meticulously researched, all three of these works make little or no use of archival sources, especially the working papers of the Synodal and procurator's chancellery.

[62] OR GBL, f. 126, k. 3, d. 8, l. 118 (Kireev, "Dnevnik," 19.3.1880).

[63] Ibid, f. 230, op. 1, k. 9804, d. 2, ll. 4–4 ob. (Pobedonostsev to Amvrosii [Kliucharev], 23.5.1880).

[64] For a summary account of Pobedonostsev's career and views before 1880, see Byrnes, *Pobedonostsev*, pp. 3–138, and, especially, Sorenson, "Thought and Policies," pp. 38–106.

[65] "Pobedonostsev and Alexander III," *Slavonic Review*, 7 (1928–29): 43.

[66] Pobedonostsev, *Pis'ma k Aleksandru III*, 1: 236.

which the people hold most dear—namely, belief in the government."[67] It was essential, he believed, to reassert will and authority, "to bring order into the chaos."[68]

That chaos he blamed on liberal bureaucrats, who had undermined the autocracy so dear to the common people. A consistent, dominant strain in his thinking was a juxtaposition of two Russias, one composed of an elite with perverted ideas, the other nurturing a folk of right-thinking Russians. Typical was his complaint that men in high places "do not have a Russian mind and a Russian heart." He was "sick of officials and educated people, just as though I were in the company of half-wits or perverted apes." To them he contrasted the simple folk, the common peasants he ushered into the sovereign's chamber for refreshing encounters. Here, he declared, was "a great treasury and a great force, which, unfortunately, is not understood by many good people who walk about in gilded uniforms." Thus Pobedonostsev perceived a "false Russia" of Petersburg, which dreamed of "constitution," and a true Russia of the hinterland:

> Petersburg impressions are very depressing and discouraging. It simply rends your soul to live in such a troubled time and see at every step people without real activity, without a clear idea, without a firm decision, preoccupied with the petty interests of their own "I," immersed in the intrigues of their own pride, seeking money and pleasure, engaged in idle babble. Only inside Russia can one get a good impression—somewhere in the countryside, in the rural backwaters. There spring is still real, exuding freshness. From there, not here, comes our salvation.[69]

Precisely because the ruling elite was so corrupt, Pobedonostsev believed that "right-thinking" officials must act slyly, deviously. Though seeming to contradict his demands for "strong will," Pobedonostsev's tactic of political cunning rested on the conviction that only more finesse could overcome the machinations of the governing elite in Petersburg.[70]

This champion of authoritarian principles nonetheless frowned upon radical, precipitous counter-reform. His primary goal was to stiffen the emperor's will, to revitalize "authority" (*vlast'*), not to redesign institutions. As he explained to the emperor in April 1881, when he opposed plans for a so-called national assembly, "now the issue is not the need for new institutions,

---

[67] Ibid., 1: 268.

[68] Ibid., 1: 251.

[69] Ibid., 2: 32–33; 1: 275.

[70] Shortly before his appointment as chief procurator, Pobedonostsev wrote of the problems facing Loris-Melikov: "From the very first day the whole government—in the persons of ministers—met him with mute resistance, and his most important and difficult battle will be with these gentlemen." He observed that "if he knows how first to get around them, then to overcome and discard them, he then has it made" (OR GBL, f. 230, k. 4409, d. 2, ll. 11 ob.–12 (letter to Tiutcheva, 27.2.1880).

but for reestablishing the normal flow of business, the restoration of order, the calming of excited minds."[71] In a memorandum of 1885 he argued that the judicial system of 1864 blatantly contradicted "the people's needs and the conditions of its life," but he warned that "all these [needed] corrections cannot be made simultaneously and suddenly, but must be made gradually and according to a previously thought-out plan."[72] He elaborated this view in a separate memorandum the following year: "The legislation of the past twenty-five years has so confused older institutions and relationships of authority, and has injected so many false principles incompatible with the internal economy of Russian life and our country, that it requires a special ability to make sense of this mess." He concluded that "it is impossible to sever this knot; one has to untie it—and then not all of a sudden, but gradually."[73] His opposition to elaborate statutory counter-reform earned Pobedonostsev the enmity of liberal society and of ranking officials, who regarded him as a bureaucratic nihilist who "meddles in everything but is incapable of creating anything."[74] In Feoktistov's memorable phrase, Pobedonostsev had no solutions but "would only sigh deeply, complain, and raise his hands to the sky (his most beloved gesture)."[75] That assessment, though firmly entrenched in the historiography, is misleading, for the procurator opposed grandiose counter-reform in principle. In contrast to Tolstoi, who looked to a dynamic bureaucracy to refashion institutions, Pobedonostsev at bottom distrusted bureaucracy and, at any event, regarded broad institutional reform as no substitute for awe-inspiring "authority" and slow, incremental change.

That philosophy of state affairs applied no less to the procurator's views on the Church. Here, as in secular society, he believed that the Great Reforms had wrought great harm, and shortly after his appointment he

---

[71] Pobedonostsev, *Pis'ma k Aleksandru III*, 1: 334.

[72] OR GBL, f. 230, k. 4394, d. 3, l. 1 (Pobedonostsev, "Zapiska," 30.10.1885). See also his opposition to radical changes in the university statute of 1884: "Change certain articles, limit the electoral principle, strengthen the authority of administrators, but do not shatter the system of the entire organization at its core . . ." (Pobedonostsev, *Pis'ma k Aleksandru III*, 2: 169–70).

[73] Pobedonostsev, *Pis'ma k Aleksandru III*, 2: 104–6; see also "Iz chernovykh bumag K. P. Pobedonostseva," *KA*, 18 (1926): 204.

[74] Quotation attributed to the empress by state secretary A. A. Polovtsov (*Dnevnik*, 2 vols. [Moscow, 1966], 2: 152). Polovtsov himself subscribed to that judgment; in his view, "Pobedonostsev's mind is purely critical—he has never created anything and never will" ("Iz dnevnika A. A. Polovtsova," *KA*, 33 [1929]: 194). For other examples, see: Kireev, "Dnevnik" (OR GBL, f. 126, k. 10, 1. 167); Alexander III (reported in S. Iu. Witte, *Vospominaniia*, 3 vols. [Moscow, 1960], 1: 369).

[75] E. M. Feoktistov, *Vospominaniia* (Leningrad, 1929), p. 222. For the reflection of such views in the historiography, see Whelan, *Alexander III*, pp. 61–64; Taranovsky, "Politics of Counter-Reform," pp. 343–44; Byrnes, *Pobedonostsev*, pp. 238–81; Shchetinina, *Universitety*, p. 137.

wrote a close friend that "I stand at the summit [of the Church], from which one can see unimaginable scandals, vice, and disorder."[76] In addition to his fundamental belief in gradual change, his fear of episcopal opposition caused the procurator to urge piecemeal counter-reform in the Church. Thus, shortly after his appointment as procurator, he announced his determination to change the parish reform of 1869, but added that "in order to correct this, one must act gradually and cautiously."[77] He expressed similar views on the academy and seminary statutes. Yet such restoration must be gradual: "In our time it is easy to make new reforms but difficult to return to the old way, and thus I intend to arrange this matter carefully, consistently, and as quietly as possible."[78]

In the first instance, gradual counter-reform meant reestablishment of the bishops' "authority," the quality that Pobedonostsev deemed so essential for good order. Though publicly derided as "an accursed clerical," the procurator identified with the upper, not lower, clergy, primarily because of the strong liberal currents so apparent among parish clergy in the 1870s.[79] He complained anxiously of clerical liberalism, and prior to his appointment he implored authorities to curb its primary organ, the *Church-Social Messenger*.[80] Forceful measures, he believed, were urgently needed: "Our [parish] clergy have, unfortunately, badly gone to seed and now, more than ever, an awesome episcopal authority is needed, [and] I, for my part, am trying with all my strength to support this."[81] In this spirit too Pobedonostsev arranged for the publication of the papers of a strong prelate, Metropolitan Filaret, and a memorandum by A. N. Murav'ev, the original architect of the "episcopal program."[82]

More concretely, Pobedonestsev hastened to take steps to dismantle a major liberal concession of the Great Reform era, namely, the right of diocesan clergy to elect their own local superintendents. Introduced into nearly half the dioceses, election of superintendents provoked much debate in the

---

[76]OR GBL, f. 230, k. 4410, d. 1, ll. 74 ob.–75 (Pobedonostsev to Tiutcheva, 22.6.1881). Soon the irascible procurator complained of his enormous workload: "I bear a heavy and great yoke, and just do not know how I shall bear it to the end" (OR GPB, f. 14, d. 658, l. 1 [Pobedonostsev to I. S. Aksakov, 25.11.1880]).

[77]OR GBL, f. 230, k. 4409, d. 2, l. 31 ob. (Pobedonostsev to Tiutcheva, 20.5.1880).

[78]Ibid., l. 71 (letter of 24.9.1880).

[79]See, for example, Polovtsov's characterization of Pobedonostsev as a "sworn clerical" in 1878 ("Iz dnevnika A. A. Polovtsova," *KA*, 33: 194).

[80]See above, p. 391.

[81]"Perepiska K. P. Pobedonostseva s preosv. Nikanorom," *RA*, 1915, no. 4: 463.

[82]Pobedonostsev offered the Murav'ev memorandum ("Zapiska . . . o sostoianii pravoslavnoi tserkvi v Rossii"), found among Filaret's papers, to the editor of *Russkii arkhiv*, with this revealing comment: "It is very curious and worth publishing. It is not completely convenient to do so in ecclesiastical journals—neutral ground is more appropriate, and it seems to me that there is no place more suitable than your [*Russkii*] *arkhiv*" (TsGALI, f. 46 [P. I. Bartenev], op. 1, d. 575, l. 54 [letter of 3.3.1883]).

seventies, and criticism increased sharply after Pobedonostsev's appointment in 1880, no doubt buoyed by his conservative reputation.[83] Ignoring efforts by liberal journals to ward off "reaction," the new procurator engineered the personal intervention of Alexander II to terminate the elections. Confronted with a disturbing report on the number of clerical offenses in 1880, Alexander ordered bishops to increase their vigilance and specifically instructed them to appoint superintendents in accordance with the Statute of Diocesan Consistories—that is, "through personal selection" by the bishops themselves.[84] The order did not explicitly preclude prior nomination by local clergy, and in fact some bishops permitted such nominations into the early 1880s.[85] But most of the contemporary press correctly read the emperor's instruction to mean an end to the election of superintendents.[86] Following Alexander's assassination in March 1881, the liberal *Church-Social Messenger* audaciously suggested that this order, like so many of Alexander's final acts of state, should be reconsidered.[87] It was wishful thinking: Alexander's order fit closely with the views of the chief procurator and in all probability was the direct result of his machinations.

At the same time, Pobedonostsev took steps to tighten Church control over the press. He generally blamed much of the empire's difficulties on the press, a judgment he extended to the Church as well, especially in the case of such newspapers as *Church-Social Messenger*. However, his first priority in 1880 was to thwart the total dismantlement of Church censorship that he foresaw as a result of Loris-Melikov's maneuvers to mollify "public opinion" with new concessions on censorship. Pobedonostsev flatly declared that "the government should not abandon supervision of the press and cast off this burden of responsibility."[88] He became still more alarmed in February 1881, when Loris-Melikov's Commission for the Review of Press Laws raised the issue of reform for Church censorship and gave serious consideration to the Synod's 1870 resolution adumbrating an extremely liberal policy and possible merger with the state's own censorship organs.[89] At Pobedonostsev's insistence, the

[83] P.K.P., "K voprosu o vybore blagochinnykh," *Minskie eparkhial'nye vedomosti*, 1880, no. 10: 255–59.

[84] For the text, see "Rasporiazheniia," *TsOV*, 1881, no. 54.

[85] The decree notwithstanding, the bishop of Tauride abolished the election of superintendents only in 1883 (Germogen, *Tavricheskaia eparkhiia* [Pskov, 1887], pp. 411–12). Likewise, only in 1886 did the bishop of Astrakhan eliminate the electoral order "for undermining proper respect toward [superior] authorities" (I. Savvinskii, *Istoricheskaia zapiska ob Astrakhanskoi eparkhii za trista let ee sushchestvovaniia* [Astrakhan, 1903], p. 293).

[86] See also N. I. Romanskii, "Institut blagochinnykh i vybornoe nachalo v primenenii k russkoi tserkovnoi administratsii," *BV*, 1906, no. 2: 323–44.

[87] "K voprosu ob otmene vybornogo nachala," *TsOV*, 1881, nos. 55–56. For other examples of opposition to the change, see the views summarized in "Mneniia i otzyvy pechati," ibid., 1881, no. 78.

[88] Pobedonostsev, *Pis'ma k Aleksandru III*, 1: 302–3.

[89] See above, pp. 338–40.

Synod reviewed the question and formally repudiated its earlier resolution, warning that it would lead to secular domination ("the voice of Church censors would often remain a voice crying in the wilderness").[90] Within a few months the danger passed: the plan for censorship reform, together with Loris-Melikov's power, disintegrated in the wake of the tsar's assassination in March 1881.[91]

Thereafter Church censors gradually tightened control over the press. In 1881 the St. Petersburg Committee of Ecclesiastical Censorship appointed an additional member, who was to help supervise the dissident *Church-Social Messenger* and keep a tight reign on the press.[92] A year later it even exercised its statutory duty to prevent the publication of poor prose: "This [article decrying the assassination of Alexander II] cannot be approved for publication because it is written rather incoherently; orthography suffers greatly, especially with regard to punctuation."[93] In 1883 the committee forbade the republication of a piece by Nikolai Leskov ("Evfim Botvinkovskii: A New Story about Three Preachers"),[94] and the following year it rejected a manuscript because of its "overt reproof of diocesan authorities" and its "extremely insulting remarks about the Orthodox clergy."[95] Still more ominous was the celebrated case of two academy professors who published a highly controversial volume on Byzantine church history that contained a strong undercurrent of criticism against "externalist religion" and icons. Apprised of the book's harmful "tendencies" from an anonymous denunciation, Pobedonostsev launched an investigation and eventually compelled one of the authors to resign his position.[96]

[90]TsGIA SSSR, f. 796, op. 167, g. 1886, d. 2258, ll. 1–16.

[91]For an overview and references, see Daniel Balmuth, *Censorship in Russia, 1865–1905* (Washington, D.C., 1979) pp. 81–92.

[92]TsGIA SSSR, f. 807, op. 2, d. 1664 (unpaginated resolution of 6.11.1881 in the journals of the Petersburg Committee of Ecclesiastical Censorship).

[93]Ibid., d. 1697, l. 84 (journal, dated 3.9.1882).

[94]Ibid., d. 1694, l. 36 (journal, dated 29.4.1883).

[95]Ibid., d. 1709, l. 59 (journal, dated 3.8.1883).

[96]The volume, *Opyt rukovodstva po tserkovnoi istorii*, part 2: *Grekovostochnaia tserkov' v period vselenskikh soborov* (Kiev, 1883), was the work of two brothers, F. A. Ternovskii (Kiev Academy) and S. A. Ternovskii (Kazan Academy). An anonymous denunciation accused the volume of "Protestant tendencies," primarily because of its disrespect for Church ritual ("Zapiska," TsGIA SSSR, f. 796, op. 164, g. 1883, d. 2345, ll. 1–14 ob.; f. 1574, op. 2, d. 96, ll. 11–23 ob.). Alerted to the matter, Pobedonostsev next obtained a highly negative assessment of F. A. Ternovskii from a very conservative suffragan bishop, Vitalii: "F. Ternovskii is even proud when they openly call him a 'liberal' and 'distorter' [*krivotolk*], and he exercises a negative influence upon the academy" (Vitalii to Pobedonostsev, 30.7.1883, in ibid., f. 1574, op. 2, d. 259, ll. 42–43 ob.). More balanced was the assessment by the archbishop of Warsaw, who criticized the book for its evident denigration of icons yet reaffirmed its intellectual worth. At any rate, he warned, repression would only guarantee "the book's rapid dissemination" (Leontii to Pobedonostsev, 3.8.1883 and 8.8.1883, in ibid., ll. 22a–22b, 21 [sic]). After two months of intense pressure, Pobedonostsev finally hounded F. A. Ternovskii into resigning (ibid., ll. 23–23 ob., 27–28; f. 796, op. 164, g. 1883, d. 2345, ll. 17–17 ob.).

The main subject of more vigorous censorship was *Church-Social Messenger*, long the object of Pobedonostsev's ire.[97] In June 1882 the procurator held conversations with Minister of Interior D. A. Tolstoi about the press and its problems,[98] and in meetings with Metropolitan Isidor Pobedonostsev revealed that his goal was "to subject [*Church-Social Messenger*] to ecclesiastical censorship."[99] Apprised of the looming danger, the paper's editor, A. A. Popovitskii, hastily applied for permission to retitle his paper *The Social Messenger*, that is, deleting "Church" from its masthead while keeping the same program. Disingenuously, Popovitskii explained that he wished to end the inconveniences that resulted "from the perpetual confusion of this publication with ecclesiastical periodicals bearing similar titles."[100] The procurator, without consulting the Synod, sent a negative reply and countered that the *Messenger* dealt mainly with the Church and hence was not an ordinary lay publication.[101] As Isidor later noted in his diary, the procurator found Popovitskii's request "inconvenient" for the simple reason that "otherwise there will be no basis [later] for subjecting [this paper] to [Church] censorship."[102] The day of reckoning drew near in October 1883, when Popovitskii published an essay critical of the hierarchy and provided the Synod with grounds for demanding sole jurisdiction over the paper.[103] Alexander III approved the request, and, when the Synod informed state officials of the change, it noted that "Popovitskii placed in this paper (which is widely disseminated among the clergy) correspondence and news that sowed ideas false and inappropriate for Church decorum and incited a spirit of free-thinking and disobedience toward authorities."[104] That same month the new censorship showed its teeth. Censors rejected "On the Condition of the White

---

[97] Despite repeated attempts by Church authorities to bring action against the *Messenger*, until 1878 the government's Main Committee on the Press declined to take punitive measures; see the Church's complaints of 1874, 1875, and 1877 in TsGIA SSSR, f. 777 (Peterburgskii komitet po delam pechati), op. 2, g. 1873, d. 13, ll. 17–18 ob. 28–29; f. 776, op. 2, d. 17, ll. 199 ob.–201 ob., 293–98). In 1878 an article by Belliustin finally earned a formal warning for the *Messenger* from state censors. The author, alleged the censors, "depicts the activities of higher educational authorities in the most unflattering manner" (ibid., d. 18, ll. 229–31). Far more sensational were two articles by Belliustin the following year. They argued that both the official Church and Old Belief were "parties" and suggesting the need not only for more religious toleration but also for steps to transform the "Byzantinism" of the Church. The affair resulted in a second warning for the *Messenger* and very nearly ended in Belliustin's defrocking (see above, p. 394). For Pobedonostsev's hostility toward the journal, see above, p. 391.

[98] OR GBL, f. 230, k. 10802, d. 5, ll. 9–9 ob. (Pobedonostsev to D. A. Tolstoi, 2.6.1882).

[99] TsGIA SSSR, f. 796, op. 205, d. 450, ll. 134–34 ob. (Isidor, "Dnevnik," 10.6.1882).

[100] Ibid., f. 797, op. 52, otd. 2, st. 3, d. 294, ll. 1–1 ob.

[101] Ibid., ll. 2–2 ob.

[102] Ibid., f. 796, op. 205, d. 451, l. 233 ob. (Isidor, "Dnevnik," 4.10.1883).

[103] Ibid., op. 164, g. 1883, d. 2342, ll. 1–6 (Synod resolution, 19.10.1883).

[104] Ibid., f. 777, op. 2, g. 1883, d. 13, ll. 54–54 ob. (Synod resolution, 7.11.1883).

Clergy" because the article "contains an incorrect view" about the "lack of rights and oppression of the clergy in all respects."[105] In 1885 censors formally closed the paper for two months, and the following year Popovitskii, in the face of such interference, finally shut it down himself.[106]

The shift in policy exemplified by these actions was relatively simple, since it involved nothing more than a change in practice. To revise legislation, on the other hand, required the active support of the bishops. As he set about the task of modifying reform statutes on parishes, schools, and the estate, Pobedonostsev—an avowed defender of episcopal privilege and interests— had every reason to anticipate their approval. To his great surprise and dismay, however, he would encounter determined opposition that effectively delayed and modified his original vision of counter-reform.

Counter-Reform in the Parish

Pobedonostsev, whose reputation as a conservative and a "clerical" was largely responsible for his appointment, had close ties with the Church, and he looked with horror on the reforms in the parish and service order. His first known comment on the subject appears in a private letter of May 1874:

> Please deign to read the attached article from *The Moscow Gazette* [*Moskovskaia gazeta*]. From it you will see how important may be the consequences of a matter undertaken, unfortunately, by the Synodal administration—the closing of churches and reduction of parishes, [which], unfortunately, is now being conducted throughout Russia and arouses general discontent. I took note of this in the State Council, in the presence of the chief procurator, but my voice remained like one crying in the wilderness. This matter makes me indignant: how little they must know Russia, the people's spirits and needs, to have undertaken it.[107]

That concern for the parish church and its flock remained paramount after his appointment in 1880, for Pobedonostsev made revision of this statute one of his primary objectives. In May 1880 he wrote a friend that "I had just assumed my post when I received new registries from four dioceses, already signed by almost all the members [of the Synod]. I did not have the heart to sign [the final decree to implement these], and it has remained lying on my desk."[108] The following month he wrote that "the restoration of churches is

[105] Ibid., f. 807, op. 2, d. 1690, l. 9 (Archimandrite Tikhon to the Petersburg Committee of Ecclesiastical Censorship, 15.11.1883); see also ibid., d. 1694, l. 92 (journal of the Petersburg committee, 15.11.1883).

[106] *TsOV*, 1885, no. 26.

[107] Pobedonostsev, *Pis'ma k Aleksandru III*, 1: 23.

[108] OR GBL, f. 230, k. 4409, d. 2, l. 31 ob. (Pobedonostsev to Tiutcheva, 20.5.1880).

the chief thing on my mind. I have stopped the new registries and reported to the emperor." His tactic, as ever, was not frontal assault but gradual erosion: "Wherever [the new registry] is already in force, we shall facilitate restoration [of individual churches] in every possible way. If only the bishops will help, then there will be no obstacles on our part!"[109] But his goal of revising the statute of 1869 was explicit and well enough known to prompt comment in the contemporary press.[110]

A Design for Counter-Reform

To aid in the task of revision, Pobedonostsev relied upon Amvrosii (Kliucharev), the suffragan bishop of Moscow.[111] In May 1880 Pobedonostsev complained to Amvrosii of the numerous disorders in the Church, but he emphasized that "my main work at first concerns churches and parish staffs." However grave the situation, he saw good prospects for prompt action: "Here at the top I apparently have no opposition whenever we seek to reestablish independent parishes in response to [parish] petitions, [and] perhaps it will also be possible to reestablish deacons as well." It was vital, he declared, that the bishops willingly support such changes, for "the key to this whole affair lies in the diocesan hierarchy—to repeat, [because of them], everything shall stand or fall." Pobedonostsev urged that Amvrosii, in some unspecified way, assist him in rebuilding the Church.[112]

Amvrosii enthusiastically agreed. In a letter saturated with fulsome praise for the procurator, Amvrosii noted that "your concern for the restoration of churches and clergy has already become known everywhere, to the jubilation of the Orthodox faithful." Urging immediate action, the bishop suggested that Pobedonostsev exploit the precedent of the 1840s, when Church officials had closed "excess churches" but eventually had to reestablish them. The prelate reminded Pobedonostsev that autocracy enabled a skillful administrator to neutralize pernicious laws:

> In our fatherland there is a tried and tested, most reliable method for annulling the effect of unsuccessful legislation: exceptions, limitations, explanations, permissions, etc. Utilizing the aforementioned precedent, is it not possible, [even] before the laws of the well-known [Special Commission] are reviewed, to petition the Tsar for permission to allow the hierarchs, in view of the especially important circumstances, to reestablish

---

[109] Ibid., ll. 38 ob.–39 (letter to Tiutcheva, 5.6.1880).

[110] Ibid., k. 10800, d. 2, l. 5 ob. (Amvrosii to Pobedonostsev, 4.6.1880).

[111] Formerly an archpriest in Moscow, famous for his rousing—and conservative—sermons, Amvrosii was widowed at an early age and took monastic vows. After first serving as suffragan bishop in Moscow diocese, he became the archbishop of Khar'kov in 1882.

[112] OR GBL, f. 230, k. 9804, d. 2, ll. 4–4 ob. (Pobedonostsev to Amvrosii, 23.5.1880).

churches and clerical staffs as independent (even with deacons), reporting each such restoration to the Holy Synod.

Amvrosii assured the procurator of the prelates' support for such a restoration: "You will see that the very same hierarchs who so hurriedly embraced the reform—once aware of what kind of wind is blowing and where it is coming from—will fly back to their old places."[113] Encouraged by such statements, Pobedonostsev requested Amvrosii to prepare a formal plan for parish restoration, and by September 1880 the memorandum was in the procurator's hands.[114]

Entitled "On the Reestablishment of Parishes and Parish Staffs," the memorandum began by castigating the whole epoch of Church reform.[115] It claimed that the reform, together with journalism, had corrupted the clergy, for talk of "improving the condition of the clergy" had only stimulated avarice and dissatisfaction.[116] According to Amvrosii, "the press pointed out to the clergy such necessities, which the poorer part [of the clergy] had previously never even dreamed of, and thus aroused exaggerated hopes." Those hopes were never realized, and thus the reform "only made the clergy's existence spiritually more difficult." No less harmful was the seminary reform, which increased the financial burden on parish clergy, substituted pagan classicism for religious studies, and generally failed to produce worthy candidates for the priesthood. Most pernicious of all was the parish reform of 1869, which not only failed to improve the clergy's material condition but also provoked popular animosity toward the clergy: "For the clergy's sake, they have closed a large number of churches, thereby making the clergy detestable to the people, who take revenge on them by reducing [their] income."

Significantly, Amvrosii did not propose mere restoration. It was clear to all that a simple reestablishment of abolished parishes and staffs was impossible, for small and impoverished parishes could not attract candidates, and in many areas both clergy and parishioners might resent the added burdens. To make reestablishment feasible, Amvorsii conceded that each parish must be able to provide a minimum level of support through emoluments or other arrangements. So that parishioners would not find this obligation onerous,

[113] Ibid., k. 10800, d. 2, ll. 5–6 ob. (Amvrosii to Pobedonostsev, 4.6.1880).

[114] Ibid., ll. 9, 19 ob. (letters of 30.7.1880, 25.9.1880).

[115] Copies of the memorandum are in Pobedonostsev's archive (ibid., k. 4410, d. 7, ll. 1–2 ob.) and the Synod's "secret section" (TsGIA SSSR, f. 796, op. 205, d. 646, ll. 2–3 ob.). It was later published in Savva's Khronika (6: 298–304).

[116] Amvrosii was also deprecatory toward the white clergy in his private correspondence. Witness this letter to Pobedonostsev in 1883: "Extraordinary pride, avarice, indifference, and even scorn for the [common] people—such are the things found among the clergy here; it is a miracle that the entire population has not gone over to Stundism or the other sects" (OR GBL, f. 230, k. 10800, d. 8, ll. 7–8 [letter to Pobedonostsev, October 1883]).

Amvrosii recommended a very low norm—300 rubles for priests and 150 rubles for sacristans (about half the sums proposed by Tolstoi's staff in 1880). To supplement that income, he stressed, parish clergy must actively engage in agriculture. He claimed that they had largely abandoned their fields since the 1860s, mainly under the cajoling of liberal journalism, which persuaded them that field labor was beneath their dignity. Neglect of agriculture, however, had caused the clergy to squander their meager monetary income on foodstuffs, needlessly compounding their material want.

Yet even Amvrosii realized that these palliatives were not sufficient to make truly small parishes viable, and he therefore adduced a further list of supplementary devices to use in the case of impoverished parishes. Their common element was the notion that, rather than seek new resources from the laity or state, the Church must appoint "inexpensive" clergy, that is, those with few or no family responsibilities. One such candidate was the young priest: appointed to serve in a poor parish for a mandatory five-year term, he could acquire valuable experience and ably serve the parish while his family, still young and small, required little income. A second type included unmarried seminarians and widowed deacons; having few or no dependents, they would be excellent, inexpensive priests. A third candidate was the retired priest; with his children already grown, he required minimal support, and, because the Church had no meaningful pension system, he would be grateful for the appointment. A fourth candidate was the "uneducated deacon," one who lacked a seminary degree and therefore had no hope of promotion to the priestly rank. Amvrosii argued that such deacons would gladly accept permanent assignment as priests in poor parishes, for such assignments would still represent a significant improvement in their status and income. A fifth type was the clerical "heir," a qualified relative who would inherit a priest's position and property. If the Church annulled its ban on such appointments, the bishop could ordain a priest who would provide for the former priest's family and would not have to purchase a home. Recognition of family rights would also produce a number of retired priests, who, having provided for kinsmen, would be willing and eager to relocate to an impoverished parish. The final kind of new candidate was "the pious commoner," who would be selected by the parish because of his piety and would gladly accept a clerical position in a poor parish. Amvrosii argued that uneducated commoners, for all their deficiencies, would serve more effectively in poor parishes than the current generation of educated, but corrupt, seminarians.

In brief, Amvrosii proposed no mere restoration but felt obliged to deal with the old, seemingly intractable problem of providing support for clergy in small, uneconomic parishes. Some of his ideas were hardly original, such as the ordination of celibate priests; others, such as the ordination of uneducated deacons, were contrary to longstanding Church policy. Perhaps most striking of all was his suggestion to abrogate one of the major reforms of the 1860s by reestablishing family claims. Supported by no statistical data, informed solely by the author's conservative outlook and hostility toward the Great Reforms, Amvrosii's memorandum nevertheless offered a concrete plan for overturning the Church reforms of the sixties.

Response of Diocesan Bishops

In October 1880 Pobedonostsev confidentially distributed Amvrosii's memorandum to diocesan bishops and asked for their views. He did not identify its author, merely stating that it came from "a person who desires to remain anonymous."[117] When Pobedonostsev informed Amvrosii of his plans to circulate the memorandum, the bishop assured him that the overwhelming majority would give their support. Only a few bishops, he wrote, were likely to oppose the plan—mainly those guilty of complicity in framing the reform in the first place.[118] Replies gradually trickled in, the first arriving in October 1880, the last finally reaching St. Petersburg from distant Eniseisk diocese in July 1881.[119]

Most bishops, in fact, did share Amvrosii's negative assessment of the 1869 parish reform.[120] A small conservative faction agreed entirely with Amvrosii that the reform served mainly to weaken popular religiousness, encourage diffusion of the Old Belief, and incite the people against the clergy.[121] Bishop Palladii of Tambov declared that "the people are really indignant with the clergy: they blame the reduction in staffs and attachment of poor parishes entirely upon the clergy and, consequently, take revenge by reducing their emoluments for rites, by filing complaints and accusations, and by making suits against them."[122] More moderate and typical was the view of the bishop of Kishinev, who denied that the reform had alienated the peasantry from

[117]TsGIA SSSR, f. 797, op. 50, otd. 3, st. 5, d. 182, ch. 1, l. 40.

[118]OR GBL, f. 230, k. 10800, d. 2, l. 21 (Amvrosii to Pobedonostsev, 27.9.1880).

[119]The replies varied greatly in length, from the laconic 3-page statement by the bishop of Orenburg to a 30-page line-by-line analysis from the bishop of Kherson.

[120]Moderately critical replies came from the bishops of Nizhnii Novgorod, Orenburg, Olonets, Iaroslavl, Ekaterinoslav, Minsk, Tver, Chernigov, Polotsk, Tambov, Tobol'sk, Tomsk, Ufa, Kaluga, Mogilev, Poltava, Riazan, Viatka, Kazan, Tauride, and Eniseisk dioceses (TsGIA SSSR, f. 797, op. 50, otd. 3, st. 5, d. 182, ch. 2, ll. 1–1 ob., 5–6, 8–8 ob., 12–14, 39–39 ob., 46, 57, 81–82, 103–3 ob., 127, 147 ob., 156–56 ob., 162, 210, 214–15, 228, 238–39, 255–55 ob., 304 ob., 333, 339).

[121]Typical were the comments by the bishops of Tver, Chernigov, and Poltava (ibid., ch. 2, ll. 57, 81–82, 228).

[122]Ibid., ch. 2, l. 127. Similarly, the bishop of Tomsk declared: "More than once I was obliged to hear from some priests that now the parishioners give less payment for performing rites, telling the priests: 'Earlier there were more of you, so we gave more; but now there are fewer of you, so it is necessary to give less'" (ibid., ch. 2, l. 156 ob.).

Orthodoxy. He nevertheless agreed that "it has not improved the clergy's material condition and has aroused the parishioners' hostility toward the clergy."[123] Some bishops confirmed Amvrosii's strictures about the contemporary seminary. The archbishop of Tver joined several others in arguing that it was the very best seminarians who left the Church, thereby lowering significantly the quality of potential applicants and even causing shortages in some areas.[124] For those who remained, the seminary curriculum did little to prepare them for effective priesthood.

Five bishops, however, vigorously defended the reform of 1869, asserting that it had greatly assisted the clergy and had not seriously antagonized the laity.[125] Feognost of Vladimir wrote that "I do not know or have in my possession any factual evidence for the [claim] that the closing of churches has made the people hate the clergy."[126] Similarly the bishop of Simbirsk maintained that the parish reform "has developed and now does not work as poorly and disastrously as some people (who are only slightly and superficially familiar with it) imagine, and who wish to compel others to see it; [the reform] demands further perfecting, not a turn backwards."[127] The bishop of Kherson provided the most meticulous critique of the memorandum, a line-by-line analysis that pinpointed numerous contradictions, fallacies, and unproven assumptions.[128] Still, this faction favorable to reform comprised less than one-sixth of all the bishops who replied.

But, even though a majority shared Amvrosii's negative assessment of the reform, few agreed with his solutions. His proposal for a minimal norm of parish support provoked a mixed reaction. Most bishops favored a guaranteed annual income but considered 300 rubles per priest to be woefully inadequate, perhaps half the sum actually required.[129] Many criticized the idea of depending upon voluntary parish agreements, not only because these were

[123] Ibid., ch. 1, ll. 1/b–2. Similar comments appear in the replies from Nizhnii Novgorod, Khar'kov, Ekaterinoslav, Minsk, Polotsk, and Tobol'sk (ibid., ch. 2, ll. 1–2, 27–27 ob., 39–40, 46 ob., 103–4, 147–47 ob.).

[124] Ibid., ch. 2, ll. 59–60. The bishop of Kishinev, Pavel, similarly noted that "it is definitely becoming impossible to staff all [clerical] positions with students who have completed the seminary" (ibid., ch. 1, ll. 4–5). See also the reports from Nizhnii Novgorod, Orenburg, Khar'kov, Chernigov, Tomsk, Poltava, and Saratov (ch. 2, ll. 2 ob., 5–6, 29–29 ob., 82–83, 158 ob., 234 ob.–35, 294 ob.–302).

[125] The proreform bishops were from Vladimir, Simbirsk, Tula, Saratov, and Kherson (ibid., ch. 2, ll. 20–25, 61–75, 119–25, 263–71, 272–302, 309–32).

[126] Ibid., ch. 2, l. 21.

[127] Ibid., ch. 2, l. 63.

[128] Ibid., ch. 2, ll. 309–22.

[129] For demands about state salaries, see replies from Olonets, Don, and Riazan (ibid., ch. 2, ll. 9, 77, 243–44). In lieu of the 300 rubles proposed by Amvrosii, three prelates (Olonets, Khar'kov, Mogilev) set 500 rubles as a minimum, and two bishops (Kaluga and Eniseisk) set 600 rubles (ch. 2, ll. 9, 33, 216, 211, 339 ob.).

difficult to obtain, but also because parishioners were wont to renege: "Almost everywhere one hears complaints that the salaries are not paid by a single parish that assumed the obligation to make payments to the clergy, notwithstanding the contractual nature of the obligation. The clergy complain and protest, but all in vain."[130] Several bishops objected to the reliance upon emoluments, listed their well-known defects (irregularity, variability, and propensity to cause conflict), and urged that the state provide a fixed salary instead.[131] In opposing Amvrosii's suggestion that priests take up the plough and scythe for their own support, the prelates recited objections heard often from mid-century on—that the land was usually infertile, that priests would do better to devote their attention to souls, not crops.[132]

The hierarchs' strongest criticism was directed at Amvrosii's proposals to send "inexpensive" priests to poor parishes. As several bishops pointed out, the author's purpose was not to aid the clergy but to find cheap priests for undersized parishes.[133] Although proposals such as the appointment of younger priests, widowed deacons, celibate seminarians, and retired priests seemed acceptable in theory, the bishops noted that they already had tried these remedies without success: the number of such candidates was negligible.[134] Moreover, most bishops rejected in principle the idea of appointing uneducated deacons for life tenure to poor parishes. Such deacons might be appointed in exceptional cases, but they should be chosen strictly on merit, not simply because they were willing to remain permanently in an impoverished parish.[135] Nor did most bishops approve Amvrosii's ideas about a partial restoration of family claims. Although several bishops admitted that they sometimes gave preference to a relative who would provide for the former priest and his family,[136] none wanted to reestablish prereform hereditariness

[130] Ibid., ch. 2, l. 91 (Podolia).

[131] Ibid., ch. 2, l. 30 (Khar'kov). See also the replies from Tambov, Tomsk, Mogilev, and Riazan (ll. 140–43, 157, 216–16 ob., 243–45); only the bishop of Ufa upheld the traditional emoluments in principle (ll. 167–68).

[132] For denunciations of clerical agriculture, see the replies from Podolia, Viatka, Saratov, Tauride, and Kherson (ibid., ch. 2, ll. 93–95, 258, 274–76, 333–38, 316–17 ob.). Only the bishops of Iaroslavl, Don, and Polotsk defended agriculture (ll. 12–14, 77–77 ob., 105).

[133] Ibid., ch. 2, ll. 146–55, 214 ob., 273–73 ob. (Tobol'sk, Mogilev, and Saratov).

[134] The bishops of Tver, Chernigov, and Poltava opposed the appointment of unmarried priests for fear of misconduct and popular unrest (ibid., ch. 2, ll. 58–58 ob., 84, 230 ob.). On the lack of such candidates, see replies from Kaluga, Tambov, and Khar'kov (ll. 35–36, 130–30 ob., 211–12).

[135] For example, see the reply from Khar'kov (ibid., ch. 2, ll. 36–36 ob.).

[136] Several bishops admitted that, in limited fashion, they gave preference to candidates with kinship claims; see the replies from Kishinev, Iaroslavl, Ufa, Khar'kov, and Ekaterinoslav (ibid., ch. 1, ll. 13–14; ch. 2, ll. 34, 44–44 ob.). Among those who favored *limited* observance of family claims were the bishops of Iaroslavl, Tver, Simbirsk, Don, Chernigov, Polotsk, Tambov, Ufa, Poltava, Tula, and Kherson (ibid., ch. 2, ll. 17–17 ob., 59–59 ob., 71–71 ob., 84 ob., 113–13 ob., 132–33, 192–93, 231–32, 269–70 ob., 321–22).

with all its abuses—fixed marriages, covert sale of positions, and ubiquitous feuds among clansmen over positions and obligations. For example, bishop Palladii of Olonetsk acknowledged the need to consider the interests of orphans but denounced the prereform hereditary order:

> The grant of priests' positions to brides [as dowry] and sons was justifiably abolished by authorities (especially the former—which was accompanied by great disorders). That was sheer commerce, outside the bishop's power. In most cases, the victors in this commerce were the kind of clerical candidates from seminaries who (because of their record and conduct) would never have dreamed of receiving a priest's position in the usual manner.[137]

Seven bishops categorically opposed the hereditary consideration under any circumstances and evoked the specter of prereform abuses as justification.[138]

The bishops' most vitriolic criticism concerned Amvrosii's proposal to ordain "pious commoners." Of the twenty-nine hierarchs who commented explicitly, none fully endorsed the scheme, eight gave only qualified approval, and twenty-one categorically rejected the idea. Even the bishop of Kishinev, a conservative generally inclined to support the memorandum, declared that such appointments could be made only with the utmost caution, after a close investigation for any Old Believer ties and after training in special seminary classes.[139] The vast majority found the whole idea unacceptable. They argued that if one sought to obtain candidates from outside the clerical estate and perhaps closer to the people, it was better to encourage such outsiders to enroll in Church schools and seminaries than to ordain self-taught holy men.[140] They pointed out that priests must know canon law, must perform numerous duties that presume a higher education, and should be able to teach in parish or public schools—duties that lay beyond the capacity of pious commoners.[141] Some bishops also questioned the orthodoxy of self-taught laymen, fearing that Old Believers would exploit this opportunity to penetrate the parish.[142] The bishop of Vladimir went on to question the political reliability of such candidates: "Can one be sure that these commoner-priests, in times of extraordinary events, will know how to say words of wis-

---

[137] Ibid., ch. 2, l. 9 ob.

[138] Ibid., ll. 52 ob.–53, 98–99, 212, 281–282, 307–7 ob. (Minsk, Podolia, Kaluga, Saratov, Kazan).

[139] Ibid., ch. 1, ll. 14–31. See also the replies from Nizhnii Novgorod, Iaroslavl, Minsk, Ufa, Mogilev, and Eniseisk (ch. 2, ll. 3–3 ob., 18–19, 51–52, 193–208, 218 ob.–20, 340).

[140] Several bishops had indeed already experimented with such appointments, but all were skeptical or even opposed to such measures in the light of their own experience; see the reply from Ekaterinoslav (ibid., ch. 2, ll. 43 ob.–44).

[141] Ibid., ch. 2, ll. 37–38, 135–40 (Khar'kov, Tambov).

[142] Ibid., ch. 2, ll. 137 ob.–38 (Tambov).

dom and act intelligently? In the last century, during the Pugachev Rebellion, very many of the Volga priests recognized Pugachev as the true tsar. This was due to their naiveté and lack of [formal] education."[143]

Thus only a tiny core of prelates supported Amvrosii's proposals. Very roughly, the bishops' replies revealed three main factions: a group of eight archconservatives who condemned the 1869 reform and endorsed most of the memorandum; a group of eighteen moderate conservatives, critical of both the earlier reforms and the solutions advanced by Amvrosii; and a group of five liberals who supported the reforms of the sixties and opposed attempts to dismantle them. A majority thus favored some kind of corrective measures, but not those adumbrated in the memorandum. One critic of the 1869 reform, the bishop of Nizhnii Novgorod, cautioned against any precipitate action or grand design like that proposed by Amvrosii. In the spirit of Pobedonostsev himself, he argued that it was dangerous to change everything at once, that it was better to follow the path of gradual readjustment.[144] Most important, Pobedonostsev failed to obtain a hierarchical consensus for counter-reform, at least in the reform envisioned by Amvrosii.[145]

The procurator transmitted these replies to Amvrosii and asked him to review and summarize their general import. It was no easy task to discover support in the replies, and the ill-tempered prelate occasionally embellished the margins with caustic commentary.[146] Even before all replies were submitted—or perhaps fearing a negative response—Amvrosii badgered the procurator to take immediate action on the memorandum. In December 1880 he tried to determine Pobedonostsev's plans, inquiring about the "purpose" of the requested summary.[147] The following month he volunteered advice on how the procurator should proceed: "One should set up the matter like this: the people are grumbling; the policy of leaving many churches without staffs is strengthening the Old Belief; it is necessary to take measures to restore staffs at the attached churches." He urged the chief procurator to approach the tsar directly for permission to overturn the 1869 statute and to give the bishops a free hand in this question.[148] A few weeks later he repeated his queries about Pobedonostsev's plans and implored the procurator to pre-

[143] Ibid., ch. 2, l. 24.

[144] Ibid., ch. 2, l. 4.

[145] See the assessment by Metropolitan Leontii in the "secret section" of the Synodal archive ("Zapiska mitr. Leontiia o svode mnenii eparkhial'nykh arkhiereev po zapiske ob uluchshenii ustroistva prikhodov i dukhovenstva, predostavlennykh v Sinod v 1880 g.," ibid., f. 796, op. 205, d. 606, ll. 1–15).

[146] For instance, next to the bishop of Minsk's declaration that only seminarians and not ignorant commoners could effectively defend Orthodoxy, Amvrosii querulously wrote, "Are seminarians strong in doing that?" (ibid., f. 797, op. 50, otd. 3, st. 5, d. 182, ch. 2, ll. 50 ob.–51).

[147] OR GBL, f. 230, k. 10800, d. 2, ll. 32–32 ob. (Amvrosii to Pobedonostsev, 12.12.1880).

[148] Ibid., d. 3, ll. 1 ob.–2 (Amvrosii to Pobedonostsev, 10.1.1881).

pare "a report to the tsar with the purpose of requesting permission to open churches, in view of the popular disturbances."[149]

Pobedonostsev, however, recognized the significance of the bishops' replies and refused to take such precipitate action. At least in part, his caution was rooted in the political turmoil of early 1881, when he was locked in battle with Loris-Melikov over the schemes for a consultative assembly and could hardly expect support in the committee of ministers or at the court. Equally important was the evident opposition of the bishops themselves to radical revision of the 1869 statute. He wrote Amvrosii that "you cannot change everything at once, for there is no free will [in favor of it], however necessary it might be." Even less likely was the emperor's support: "What you say about a report to the emperor, you say without knowing the local circumstances—such action would only kill the whole cause immediately." Rather, "it is necessary to act very cautiously at this time, taking one step at a time, according to a plan prepared in advance." Hinting at the strong undercurrent of opposition, he reminded Amvrosii that he had distributed the *mémoire* "in order to learn the views and opinions, to enliven your proposal from various perspectives, to familiarize ourselves with local circumstances and views on this matter and with the experience of prior practices."[150] In effect, Pobedonostsev retreated in the face of the bishops' opposition and refused to take decisive action.

There was a further reason for this retreat: a growing realization that restoration required new financial support, which as yet was simply unavailable. In November 1881 Pobedonostsev wrote a confidante that "it would be quite possible—this very day—[to order the reestablishment], but what would come of it? First one must find the means!" The procurator now believed that mere restoration was impossible, declaring that "you cannot return to what formerly existed." He noted that "where once a landowner dwelt, there now remain only the peasants, and many—like little children—request [reestablishment of their church] .... 'Give us services'—but they do not consider that it is necessary to support the clerical staff; otherwise no one will come [to serve] in the church." But "the people often have nothing; the treasury will give nothing." Still, he wrote, "it is necessary to devise a regular system of support—where is one to obtain this?" Thus, for the present, a parish could reopen its church only if it found the requisite funds. A broader measure was unfeasible: "A general measure to reopen closed churches would not make any sense and would have no practical meaning in reality." Reciting a favorite rationale for delay in the Russian bureaucracy—"Local conditions are so diverse that it is impossible to solve everything with a single abstract measure"—the procurator reaffirmed his belief

---

[149] Ibid., l. 12 (Amvrosii to Pobedonostsev, 9.2.1881).
[150] Ibid., k. 9804, d. 3, ll. 9–9 ob. (Pobedonostsev to Amvrosii, 23.2.1881).

in the need for gradualism: "This matter is very, very difficult, and one can do it only very gradually." He reiterated that, though he had a "plan," the "main thing now is to get the means for this."[151]

A Cautious Counter-Reform

After the assassination of Alexander II in March 1881, the chief procurator renewed his campaign for gradual revision, no doubt expecting the full support of Alexander III. In July 1881 Metropolitan Makarii of Moscow requested permission to reappoint deacons in his diocese; in December the Special Commission, most likely at Pobedonostsev's behest, approved the request and extended it to St. Petersburg diocese as well.[152] In 1881–1882 the Synod modified the service rules of 1869, permitting bishops ("if necessary") to ordain candidates without a seminary degree or a full two years of teaching experience.[153] Eager to press the attack, Pobedonostsev became more insistent that Amvrosii complete his analysis of diocesan replies. By April the prelate finally complied, submitting a blatantly misleading summary that claimed virtually unanimous support.[154] In June 1882 Pobedonostsev raised the issue with Metropolitan Isidor[155] and also wrote to Bishop Nikanor of Ufa, denouncing the parish reform of 1869 for its "demand to have educated

[151] Ibid., k. 4410, d. 1, l. 129 ob. (Pobedonostsev to Tiutcheva, 24.11.1881). In 1883 the chief procurator also opposed a state budget to support Moslem schools on the grounds that the Orthodox Church, despite its status as the official church, lacked sufficient support for essential needs (Pobedonostsev, *Pis'ma k Aleksandru III*, 2: 42–44).

[152] Metropolitan Makarii proposed to reestablish deacons in Moscow diocese because of its "special condition" (TsGIA SSSR, f. 804, op. 1, 3. 1, d. 177, ll. 2–3 ob., 5–8).

[153] Ibid., d. 169, ll. 41–42 (Isidor's circular, 12.12.1881), 46–47 ob. (Synod resolutions, 28.4.1882 and 29.5.1882).

[154] When Amvrosii submitted his analysis of the replies, he made the preposterous claim that the bishops had endorsed his memorandum and that the only opposition concerned his call to ordain "pious commoners." Even this he attributed to a misunderstanding: "I was pleased to see that all the ideas of my memorandum won the attention and met with the sympathy of the larger and better part of our hierarchy. You will see that there is a majority against me only in the case of ordaining self-taught men [*nachetchiki*]. This, it seems to me, resulted when many of them overgeneralized my idea, imagining that the memorandum wished to replace our educated clergy with *muzhiki* [boorish peasants], whereas I suggested this [measure] only for extreme cases" (Amvrosii to Pobedonostsev, 25.4.1882 [OR GBL, f. 230, k. 10800, d. 5, l. 15]). To demonstrate the bishops' purported approval, Amvrosii compiled lists of responses to each of his specific proposals; unless a bishop had categorically protested, the response was entered in the "for" column and qualifications were brushed aside. The result was an apparent endorsement, graphically demonstrated by long lists of supporters and short lists of opponents (see Amvrosii's synopsis in TsGIA SSSR, f. 797, op. 50, otd. 3, st. 5, d. 182, ch. 2, ll. 341–405 ob.). Pobedonostsev, who read the responses before transmitting them to Amvrosii, knew their true import even before obtaining an independent assessment from Metropolitan Leontii ("Zapiska mitr. Leontii," ibid., f. 796, op. 205, d. 606, ll. 1–15).

[155] TsGIA SSSR, f. 796, op. 205, d. 450, l. 134 ob. (Isidor, "Dnevnik," 10.6.1882).

priests (those who have finished the seminary) everywhere." He dismissed this requirement as "simply too extravagant" and claimed that nongraduates could better oppose "the schism, which overwhelms us with its extraordinary simplicity (however coarse) of ordination and its limited requirements." Of course, bishops must exercise care in ordaining nongraduates, but Pobedonostsev concluded that "we cannot get along without lowering the academic demands, especially when you think that the new school develops in us incomprehensible pretensions and not a few artificial, false demands." He bluntly advised Nikanor not to be "shy about opening more parishes—all your representations on this matter will be approved."[156] Reestablishment thus depended wholly upon individual bishops. The bishop of Orel, who favored the 1869 statute, opened only twenty-two parishes between 1880 and 1884; the bishop of Khar'kov reestablished fifty-four.[157]

For all his zeal, Pobedonostsev had to wait two more years before renewing his campaign for counter-reform. Quite apart from the press of other business (the conflict over the volunteer fleet and other Church legislation), Pobedonostsev must have had compelling reasons to delay the program about which he felt so strongly and for which he had the emperor's apparent sympathy. No doubt, one obstacle was Isidor, who chaired both the Synod and the Special Commission and showed little interest in abandoning the 1869 reform.[158] Nor did the procurator yet have the additional resources that he himself recognized as a prerequisite for thoroughgoing restoration. Most important, he lacked the general support of diocesan prelates and interpreted their critical response as an insuperable barrier to a general measure:

> The unfortunate law of 1869 has sown dragons' teeth in our fields. They have put down roots not in the heights but in the marshy places [at the foundation] of the Church. Nevertheless, it has been impossible to abolish [this law] all at once. I hope that I can take up this matter soon, so that all the hierarchs see clearly what one must support.[159]

In the interim he continued to decry the state of the hierarchy ("what a harvest, and there is no one to do the reaping," was his favorite cliché)[160] and to seek gradual restoration of specific parishes. Here he fared well; as one member of the Synod wrote in early 1884, "files on the reestablishment of parishes now pass easily through the Synod."[161]

[156]"Perepiska K. P. Pobedonostseva s preosv. Nikanorom," RA, 1915, no. 1: 469.

[157]TsGIA, SSSR, f. 804, op. 1, r. 1, d. 125, ll. 471–635 (Orel); d. 137, ll. 95–325 (Khar'kov).

[158]In a letter written on the occasion of Isidor's death in 1892, Pobedonostsev paid due respect to the metropolitan, declaring that as presiding member of the Synod "his voice was almost always decisive" (Pobedonostsev, Pis'ma k Aleksandru III, 2: 263–64).

[159]"Perepiska K. P. Pobedonostseva s preosv. Nikanorom," RA, 1915, no. 1: 469.

[160]OR GBL, f. 230, k. 9804, d. 5, ll. 1, 37 (letters to Amvrosii, 13.1.1882 and 16.7.1882).

[161]Savva, Khronika, 7: 161.

More important, Pobedonostsev provided a new justification for more churches and more clergy: the establishment of parish schools.[162] The government itself firmly came to his view in early 1881, in the midst of the terrorist attacks and assassination of Alexander II, and instucted Pobedonostsev to prepare a specific proposal.[163] The procurator relied heavily upon the counsel of Sergei Rachinskii, an educator in Tver province who argued that the peasants would accept education only if it were linked to religion and that "the whole future of education depends upon the universal dissemination and correct construction of parish schools."[164] At the instruction of the Council of Ministers, Pobedonostsev compiled data, collected opinions from local bishops, and began work on a specific proposal.[165] He soon persuaded the minister of education to divert a small sum (55,000 rubles) for parish schools, but his real ambition was a full-scale proposal.[166] In September 1882 he persuaded the Synod to form a special committee on parish schools, under the chairmanship of Archbishop Leontii of Warsaw.[167]

By late April 1883 the committee had designed its proposals, which concentrated on "the moral education of the people" and thus gave priority to religious instruction. That goal, it declared, coincided with the views of the people, who have "always regarded the clergy as their legitimate primary teacher," and with those of the state, which, because of "the tragic events of late and signs of underground agitation in popular schools," has decided "to summon the clergy to this work, from which it has been artificially and temporarily excluded." The committee's draft statute provided for a common curriculum based on religion (whatever the formal jurisdiction of the school), called upon the government to provide finances, and gave a special role to priests and deacons (the latter, once that rank was reestablished, would play a major role).[168] In May 1884 the Synod reworked the committee proposals into a final statute, which the emperor approved, adding the note, "I hope

---

[162] For Pobedonostsev's longstanding interest in parish schools, see his letter to D. A. Tolstoi in 1874 (OR GBL, f. 230, k. 10802, d. 5, l. 2 ob.).

[163] TsGIA SSSR, f. 797, op. 51, otd. 2, st. 3, d. 92/a, ll. 5–5 ob. (Zhurnal Komiteta ministrov, 31.3.1881).

[164] OR GBL, f. 230, k. 4411, d. 2, l. 13 (S. Rachinskii to Pobedonostsev, 17.4.1881); see also Rachinskii's "Zametki o sel'skikh shkolakh," *Rus'*, 1881, nos. 45–53 (reprinted: St. Petersburg, 1883), and his *Sel'skaia shkola* (Moscow, 1891). Rachinskii's private letters to Pobedonostsev deal at length with the needs of parish schools; see, for example, the letter in TsGALI, f. 427 (Rachinskie), op. 1, d. 762, ll. 7–18 ob.

[165] TsGIA SSSR, f. 797, op. 51, otd. 2, st. 3, d. 92/a, ll. 2–11, 13–535.

[166] Ibid., op. 52, otd. 2, st. 3, d. 264, l. 3 (Pobedonostsev to Synod, 7.9.1882).

[167] Ibid., ll. 5–5 ob. (Synod resolution). See also material on the committee in Kireev's diary (OR GBL, f. 126, k. 3, d. 9, l. 153 ob.), Rachinskii's letters to Pobedonostsev (ibid., f. 230, k. 4411, d. 3), and Isidor's diary (TsGIA SSSR, f. 796, op. 205, d. 451, l. 183).

[168] TsGIA SSSR, f. 796, op. 163, g. 1882, d. 222/a, ll. 14–35 ("Ob"iasnitel'naia zapiska"), 8–13 ("Proekt polozheniia o tserkovno-prikhodskikh shkolakh").

that the parish clergy will prove worthy of its high calling in this important matter."[169] Parish schools, which explicitly required deacons and held out the prospect of state salaries, made parish restoration far more attractive and attainable.[170]

In the spring of 1884 the Synod finally took up a formal review of the 1869 statute on parish reorganization. The nominal trigger was a petition from the bishop of Mogilev in March 1884, seeking blanket permission to reestablish closed parishes and to restore the old service system, including deacons.[171] The Synod instructed Metropolitan Makarii of Moscow to prepare a formal report on the matter, and in May it formally endorsed his proposals for revising the 1869 parish statute.[172] Before presenting its resolution to the emperor, however, the Synod decided first to submit it to a council of bishops gathered in Petersburg in November 1884 to celebrate Isidor's fiftieth anniversary as bishop.[173]

The council, attended by Isidor and twenty other prelates, as well as three lay officials from the central Church chancelleries, lasted for two hours and encompassed a detailed discussion of ten propositions in the Synod's resolution on parish restoration. After the procurator's aide read aloud a short synopsis of the main issues, the assembly discussed each point, though not at any great length, provoking one annoyed prelate to complain that "at this great episcopal council [pomestnyi sobor]" most of the prelates "gave themselves up to profound silence."[174] The bishops agreed that individual bishops should be able to reestablish closed churches without seeking the Synod's permission, but they expressed concern about the availability of finances. Parish contracts, Isidor warned, were of little value: "It is difficult to rely upon parish promises: they often promise, but they do not fulfill their obligations." In the case of merged parishes, where the two churches were formally united yet still had separate staffs, the bishops agreed to make each church independent. Some prelates preferred a more stringent policy on small parishes, but most acknowledged that such mergers were mere formalities, that recognition of independence had no effect on small parishes. The bishops also agreed to reestablish the rank of deacon (vital for the new parish schools), thus increasing the standard staff of one priest and one sacristan; though parishes ordinarily had to have 700 male parishioners to qualify for deacons, exceptions were possible in the case of urban or wealthy rural parishes. The assembly also annulled the requirement that seminarians first serve as sacristans or

---

[169]Ibid., ll. 46–53 (Synod resolution, 4.5.1884), 54 (Alexander's notation on the chief procurator's report of 21.6.1884).

[170]See also ibid., f. 797, op. 54, otd. 2, st. 3, d. 167, ll. 22–24 ob. (procurator to Synod, 19.1.1885); op. 52, otd. 2, st. 3, d. 264, l. 21 (Synod resolution, 12.2.1885).

[171]Ibid., f. 796, op. 154, g. 1873, d. 1178/a, ll. 73–77 ob.

[172]Ibid., op. 209, d. 1798, unpaginated resolution of 11.5.1884; Savva, Khronika, 7: 230.

[173]Ibid., op. 165, g. 1884, d. 209, ll. 1–17; d. 232, ll. 2–3 ob.

[174]Savva, Khronika, 7: 345.

teachers, thus permitting direct ordination into the priesthood—a striking retreat from the earlier attempt to seek experienced, older candidates. Finally, the sobor agreed to abolish the Special Commission, disingenuously declaring that it had solved all the problems within its competence and that the Synod could handle the remaining ones.[175] In December the Synod, responding to this sobor, issued a final resolution formally overturning the 1869 statute.[176]

Three months later, in February 1885, Pobedonostsev transmitted this resolution to the emperor for approval. In a covering note the procurator explained that it was the product of several years' deliberation and that it "answered the wish of pious people who appealed from all sides to reestablish the abolished parishes." The procurator further claimed that the parish reform of 1869 had closed parishes just as taverns were opening in every hamlet, and "thus in many places the people became indifferent to the Church and turned instead to the tavern." He also asserted that the reform had been a godsend to schismatics, "who exploited [the closing of churches], especially in isolated areas." Alexander III approved the resolution, adding that "I have read and confirm this report with jubilation."[177]

The new decree encountered a mixed response in the press. Much of the press observed approvingly that the new law served the interests of both laity and clergy and that it provided a much-needed corrective to the 1869 reform, which had indeed long been an object of criticism. For example, a priest in Kostroma wrote that the 1869 decree had been an unfortunate reform that had obliged "an entire soslovie to pay for the improvement in material conditions of a few."[178] Surprisingly, however, some clergy and papers expressed muted dissatisfaction with the new decree. For example, a relatively conservative journal in Kiev that wrote mainly for an audience of parish priests criticized the new policy and warned against an unnecessary and harmful proliferation of deacons.[179] Another journal, *Wanderer*, conceded that such sentiment was widespread: "This dissatisfaction, unfortunately, is heard in the ranks of older priests, whose material condition must now change, with equality in income for assistant priests and with the establishment of deacons."[180]

---

[175]TsGIA SSSR, f. 796, op. 154, g. 1873, d. 1178/a, ll. 143–82 ob. ("Protokol soveshchaniia Oo. chlenov Sv. Sinoda i eparkhial'nykh preosviashchennykh o novykh pravilakh ustroistva prikhodov i prichtov").

[176]Ibid., op. 209, d. 1798, unpaginated resolution (11.5.1884/21.12.1884).

[177]Ibid., f. 797, op. 55, otd. 3, st. 5, d. 31, ll. 21–31. See also Pobedonostsev, *Pis'ma k Aleksandru III*, 2: 69–70.

[178]G. I. Gusev, "Vosstanovlenie uprazdnennykh tserkovnykh prichtov i zashtatnykh tserkovnykh prichtov," *Kostromskie eparkhial'nye vedomosti*, 1885, no. 12: 346–61; idem, "Reorganizatsiia sostava tserkovno-prikhodskikh prichtov," ibid., no. 14: 410–22.

[179]P. Runovskii, "O vosstanovlenii tserkovnykh prikhodov i prichtov, zakrytykh v 1869 g.," *RSP*, 1885, no. 14: 379–80.

[180]"Khronika," *Str.*, 1886, no. 3: 532.

These journalistic reports found confirmation in diocesan records. For example, the bishop of Astrakhan complained that "in many parishes priests try, in every conceivable way, not to permit the appointment of new staffs, however great the need for them. Avarice has taken precedence over the duty to be concerned about the parishioners' needs."[181] The *Church-Social Messenger* also noted strong opposition to the new decree, especially to the increase in staffs, but reassured its readers that bishops were to reopen churches and expand staffs only where resources permitted.[182] In light of the clergy's hostility to reform in the 1870s, this opposition to counter-reform was surprising and unexpected. In essence, however, it reflected the clergy's distrust of Petersburg; it embodied the determination of survivors to preserve the gains of the seventies, achieved at such cost; and it represented the traditional opposition of individual clergy to any overloading of their staff.

Although opposition was muted, the authorities encountered serious difficulties in implementation. Most important, the Synod's decree did not provide clear rules of transition but merely gave bishops carte blanche to restore churches and staffs. As a result, some prelates, like the bishop of Vladimir, felt obliged to promulgate supplementary instructions on the structure and relationships in the newly enlarged staffs.[183] Finally, in response to various complaints, the Synod issued an elaborate decree in 1886 to resolve such problems as the proper distribution of land and income shares among the newly reopened churches.[184] It also put limits on the appointment of nonseminary graduates as deacons: since deacons were intended mainly to help in schools, nonseminary graduates must at least be qualified to teach in parish or elementary public schools.[185] Furthermore, the Synod's resolution of 1885 placed responsibility in the hands of bishops, who faced dissatisfaction among laity if they refused to allow a proliferation of underfinanced parishes and staffs. In Novgorod, for example, the local bishop was accused of violating the new law because he declined to establish staffs in poor parishes.[186] Even when the bishops favored reestablishment, they could not always find enough candidates. Voronezh, for example, once plagued with a superabundance of candidates, found it could fill only 511 of 638 newly established positions because of the dearth of candidates.[187] But most diocesan authorities managed to find sufficient candidates, resulting in a sharp expansion in the

[181] *Astrakhanskie EV*, 1885, no. 13: 225 (published report to Synod).

[182] "Po povodu vosstanovleniia prikhodov i prichtov," *TsOV*, 1885, nos. 31–37.

[183] TsGIA SSSR, f. 796, op. 442, d. 1065, ll. 23–28 (Vladimir).

[184] Ibid., op. 166, g. 1885, d. 1124, ll. 73–74 (Synod resolution, 11.12.1886).

[185] Ibid., op. 154, g. 1873, d. 1178/a, ll. 124–25 ob (Synod resolution, 29.1.1886/27.2.1886).

[186] Ibid., f. 797, op. 55, otd. 3, st. 5, d. 31, ll. 34–36 (anonymous note to chief procurator, October–November 1885).

[187] *Obzor deiatel'nosti vedomstva pravoslavnogo ispovedaniia za vremia tsarstvovaniia imp. Aleksandra III* (St. Petersburg, 1901), pp. 149–50.

number of churches and clergy: between 1880 and 1890 parishes increased by 10 percent, clergy by 11 percent (primarily after the 1885 decree). Significantly, however, the counter-reform continued to regard the sacristan as expendable, even while increasing the number of priests and deacons: sacristans declined by 11 percent, whereas priests and deacons increased by 12 percent and 68 percent, respectively. That structure more effectively addressed the Church's newer goals, particularly in education, yet it reflected a long-term process. Quite apart from counter-reform, the proportion of sacristans in the white clergy steadily declined, continuing a policy pursued since mid-century.[188]

Although the procurator obtained his goal of revising the 1869 statute which led to the restoration of many parishes and clerical positions, he did not achieve the ambitious designs of Amvrosii's original scheme. In effect, the parish counter-reform made the bishops entirely responsible for restoration, rather than mandating automatic reestablishment. Perhaps the most striking element here was the procurator's retreat from full-scale restoration. Consistent with his demand for gradual counter-reform, retreat was also expedient in view of the bishops' determined opposition to wild schemes (like Amvrosii's) that violated principles long dominant in the Church, such as the high priority placed on formal education. It was also an acknowledgment of the intractable financial problem: the Church absolutely lacked the means to reestablish churches and expand staffs.

Counter-Reform in the Seminary

The reform statutes regarding seminaries and academies were a source of keen dissatisfaction for the new procurator. He particularly detested the schools' curriculum, contending that its main goal was outward mobility, not theological training. Shortly after his appointment, Pobedonostsev spoke of preparing a new statute for theological academies to ensure "a strict theological education in the spirit of the Holy Fathers, not in the German scientific spirit."[189] Pobedonostsev also frowned over the academies' failure to produce the learned monks vitally needed for staffing the top positions in education and the hierarchy; indeed, within a few months of his appointment, Pobedonostsev had solicited data on the number of academy students seeking to become monks.[190] Although the press carried rumors that he

---

[188] For data, see below, p. 462.

[189] Savva, *Khronika*, 6: 236 (Kiev professor A. D. Voronov to Savva, 20.7.1880).

[190] In September 1880 Pobedonostsev demanded data on the number of students in the academy planning to enter monasticism (I. V. Vasil'ev to I. A. Nenarokov, 20.9.1880 [TsGIA SSSR, f. 797, op. 50, otd. 1, st. 2, d. 90, ll. 1–1 ob.]).

planned to reestablish the seminarians' right of transfer to the university without examination,[191] Pobedonostsev was more inclined to raise barriers, not lower them. The procurator also expressed concern about the secular spirit of seminaries and, especially, the isolated incidents of political radicalism. Though Church schools were relatively tranquil in the 1880s, there were several sensational episodes in seminaries and even in academies.[192] When dealing with lay authorities, Pobedonostsev preferred to blame outside agitators for such troubles,[193] but he was more candid in his discussions inside the Church itself, placing blame primarily upon the ill-conceived statutes of 1867–1869.[194] Predictably, he especially disliked the institution of diocesan assemblies, a piece of democracy utterly anathema to the new procurator— and one of marginal benefit to the financial needs of the schools. By the fall of 1880 he made clear his intention to change ecclesiastical education, a goal that soon became common knowledge in the contemporary press.[195]

Pobedonostsev first directed his attention to the academy statute. In September 1880 he resorted to the customary tactic of requesting that academy rectors submit formal opinions on the weaknesses inherent in the academy statute of 1869.[196] He did not receive replies from all four academies until the fall of 1881—tardiness, as ever in Church politics, was one discreet form of opposition. Indeed, the reports from Moscow and Petersburg staunchly defended the 1869 statute and even declared that the task was not to dismantle but to expand and amplify the liberal principles of 1869. The response from Kazan was more equivocal, but on the whole moderate. Only the rector of Kiev recommended abrogation of the 1869 reform. Still, all the rectors favored some changes, especially in curriculum, where they proposed

[191]"Raznye izvestiia i zametki," *Str.*, 1880, no. 12: 604–5.

[192]On disorders at the seminary in Voronezh in May 1881 and at the academies of Kiev and Petersburg in 1884, see Isidor's diary (TsGIA SSSR, f. 796, op. 205, d. 450, l. 9; d. 452, ll. 409 ob., 412–12 ob., 415 ob., 426 ob.). For a general overview of continuing discontent in Church schools, see B. V. Titlinov, *Molodezh' i revoliutsiia. Iz istorii revoliutsionnogo dvizheniia sredi uchashcheisia molodezhi dukhovnykh i srednikh uchebnykh zavedenii, 1860–1905 gg.* (Leningrad, 1924).

[193]In July 1882 Pobedonostsev wrote V. K. Plehve that his investigations of disorders in one seminary (Podolia) showed that "here—as everywhere—the main source of rot was agitators who are from outside the seminary, the elimination of which is absolutely necessary for the establishment of order in educational institutions" (TsGAOR, f. 586 [V. K. Plehve], op. 1, d. 1017, ll. 14–14 ob.).

[194]See below, especially notes 208–9.

[195]For example, see "Peresmotr Ustava dukhovno-uchebnykh zavedenii," *Litovskie EV,* 1880, no. 51: 448–49.

[196]TsGIA SSSR, f. 797, op. 50, otd. 1, st. 2, d. 90, ll. 2–2 ob. (request dispatched 2.10.1880). The responses are presented in *Svod mnenii o nedostatkakh nyne deistvuiushchego Ustava dukhovnykh akademii i soobrazhenii o sposobakh ustraneniia etikh nedostatkov* (St. Petersburg, 1881; copy in GPB [18.272.5.6]). The only extant manuscript reply (Petersburg's) is in TsGIA SSSR, f. 797, op. 50, otd. 1, st. 2, d. 90, ll. 37–53).

to merge and divide various courses. Academy administration, with its "democratic principles" providing authority for faculty, elicited few criticisms; only the rector in Kiev complained that he had too little authority. In short, the reports (save that from Kiev) evinced no interest in ambitious counter-reform. No doubt dismayed by such responses, the procurator proceeded cautiously, persuading the Synod to create a special committee to review the reports and prepare formal proposals.[197]

As the committee slowly set about its work, the procurator launched his attack on another innovation of the sixties: the diocesan assembly of clergy. He began by distributing an anonymous "memorandum on clerical assemblies," just as he had done in the case of the parish statute. Once again the author was Amvrosii, who volunteered in October 1880 to compose such a note: "The diocesan assemblies are false and harmful institutions. Your attention to my first *mémoire* has encouraged me: will you permit me to write [a new one] on assemblies as well?"[198] After receiving an affirmative reply, Amvrosii hastily set to work and completed the memorandum by the first of December.[199] This time, however, someone leaked the procurator's designs to the press, which openly discussed the memorandum—much to Pobedonostsev's indignation.[200] The division of opinion followed predictable lines: conservative papers, including *The East* and even the moderate *Wanderer*, sharply attacked the assemblies; liberal organs, such as *Church-Social Messenger* and *The News*, defended them.[201] Characteristically, Pobedonostsev did not demand immediate resolution of the issue but first tested episcopal opinion. Isidor's diary for May 1882 records the procurator's persistent, but circumspect, efforts:

> The procurator and the bishop of Volhynia twice discussed the memorandum on clerical assemblies, allegedly compiled by the vicar-bishop of Moscow, Amvrosii, with comments by the inspector-general of seminaries, Zinchenko. The memorandum recognizes the assemblies as unnecessary, pointless, even harmful. Bishop Tikhon defends the assemblies. The procurator holds that they must be based upon new principles.[202]

Pobedonostsev failed to stir the Synod to take decisive action. Though its members were evidently unsympathetic to a sudden abolition of the assem-

---

[197]TsGIA SSSR, f. 797, op. 50, otd. 1, st. 2, d. 90, ll. 15–15 ob., 18–19; ibid., f. 796, op. 162, g. 1881, d. 734, ll. 1–1 ob. (Pobedonostsev to Synod), 12–156 (Sergei to Synod, 13.12.1883).

[198]OR GBL, f. 230, k. 10800, d. 2, ll. 23–23 ob. (Amvrosii to Pobedonostsev, 3.10.1880).

[199]Ibid., ll. 26, 30 (Amvrosii to Pobedonostsev, 15.11.1880, 1.12.1880).

[200]Ibid., k. 9804, d. 4, l. 29 (Pobedonostsev to Amvrosii, 23.12.1881). For an example of the shock caused by rumors of these plans, see "Slukhi ob otmene s"ezdov dukhovenstva," *TsOV*, 1880, nos. 153–54.

[201]"Vnutrennii tserkovnyi obzor," *Str.*, 1881, no. 3: 474–83.

[202]TsGIA SSSR, f. 796, op. 205, d. 450, l. 119 ob. (Isidor, "Dnevnik," 8.5.1882).

blies,[203] Pobedonostsev did not give up easily. In March 1883 he again raised the issue with Isidor, insisting that "the clerical assemblies on educational matters be abolished, as burdensome for the Church and useless for the schools."[204] Yet all his efforts came to naught: the memorandum failed to mobilize support either among members of the Synod or among the diocesan bishops.

In the fall of 1883 the procurator found a new partner, Bishop Vitalii of Mogilev, who sent the procurator a letter strongly condemning the institution of diocesan assemblies. Vitalii argued that most assemblies rendered scant assistance to the schools and merely became the tools of dissident elements in the parish clergy. He claimed that the clergy were generally indifferent to the assemblies, making it possible for radical minorities to manipulate them for their own personal or political interests. Moreover, the assemblies had a nefarious impact upon the schools' faculty, who positively feared those students whose kin were prominent in the diocesan assembly. Finally, he contended, most clergy regarded the assembly as a useless burden: "The deputies themselves, in spite of fines levied [for absenteeism], are burdened by the trips to the assemblies, uselessly squander significant sums of money for such trips to the city and for support once there, and meanwhile are distracted from their parish duties and business." Vitalii therefore proposed to eliminate regular assemblies and to convoke them only when a specific need arose. The procurator transmitted this note to the Synod for consideration, with implicit approval, but once again failed to obtain any clear response.[205]

Pobedonostsev nonetheless persuaded the Church to make some specific modifications in the statutes, mainly to tighten discipline, for even the academies continued to show disturbing signs of unrest (Kiev Academy, for example, had been the scene of recurrent disorders). The Synod also took measures to eliminate nonresident students and to restrict access by auditors.[206] In June 1882 Pobedonostsev sent a circular to seminaries directing them not to waste library funds on "secular journals and newspapers of a so-called 'liberal' tendency," which merely serve "as transmission belts for various social teachings."[207] Finally, in response to a memorandum describing the low morality of seminarians, the Synod in 1883 ordered the clerical family and local authorities to exercise more control over youths and directed seminary authorities to require church attendance by their pupils.[208]

[203] "O s"ezdakh dukhovenstva," *TsOV*, 1881, nos. 22–23.

[204] TsGIA SSSR, f. 796, op. 205, d. 451, l. 255 (Isidor, "Dnevnik," 7.3.1883).

[205] Ibid., op. 165, g. 1884, d. 522, ll. 26–29 (Vitalii, 15.9.1883).

[206] Ibid., f. 797, op. 53, otd. 1, st. 2, d. 63, ll. 1–23; *PSZ (3)*, 3: 1688.

[207] N. P. Sedykh, *Ocherk istorii Permskoi dukhovnoi seminarii za 1877–1884 gg.* (Perm, 1915), pp. 217–18.

[208] The memorandum castigated modern-day seminarians for immorality and ignorance of Church ritual: "From the reports of inspections in ecclesiastical schools, one can see that in

Finally, in March 1883, the special committee submitted its draft changes for the academy statute. First, it proposed to increase the authority of both the bishop and the rector (the latter described now as the "direct, immediate director [*nachal'nik*] of the academy in all aspects of its administration"). Conversely, it reduced the power of the faculty. Although it denied any intention of "removing the professorial corporation from participation in the governance of academies," the committee increased the power of the academy's executive board (the *pravlenie*, dominated by the rector) and diminished the role of the general faculty conference *(konferentsiia)*. The committee also made substantial changes in curriculum: it abolished field specialization, increased sharply the number of required courses (primarily in religious subjects), and converted the fourth year from full-time research to regular course work. Finally, the committee made the academy responsible for overseeing diocesan seminaries. The minority opinion dissented strongly from the committee's recommendations and favored only minor modifications in the statute of 1869.[209] To resolve these differences, the Synod appointed a special subcommittee; it too suffered from sharp disagreements, but finally completed its review of the draft statute in early 1884. The Synod then approved the draft virtually without discussion; indeed, claimed one vexed bishop, the metropolitans of Moscow and Petersburg never read the text.[210]

Pobedonostsev transmitted the Synod's resolution and draft statute to the emperor with a report listing the proposed changes. He noted that the new statute seeks "to limit significantly the principle of self-rule in the academy,

---

both seminaries and Church schools, pupils in many cases have a poor knowledge of the typicon, prayers, chants, and even Church Slavonic (reflected in an inability to read Slavonic correctly, according to tidle and accent)." It also warned of irreligion, citing "cases where pupils shun church services or display disrespectful conduct when there." As further proof of a weak religious spirit, the memorandum cited the mass exodus of seminarians in the seventies into lay schools. Though that flight had been curtailed of late—solely through "circumstances beyond the seminarians' will"—the new restriction on exit merely burdened the Church with involuntary servitors: "Accepting pastoral duties without inner love for them, against their will and solely out of worldly calculations, [such seminarians] usually perform their [duties] with neglect and indifference . . . like hirelings, who care neither for Christ's flock nor the Church." The archival record does not indicate authorship, but in substance (for example, the stress on ritual) it conforms closely to Pobedonostsev's views. Ibid., f. 796, op. 164, g. 1883, d. 909, ll. 1–13.

[209] *Ob"iasnitel'naia zapiska k proektu izmenenii v Ustave pravoslavnykh akademii* (St. Petersburg, 1883; copy in GBP [18.272.5.7]). Pobedonostsev was far from satisfied with this draft. He was alarmed "at the lack of integrality in the basic idea of the statute and its incompleteness in terms of liquidating the weaknesses of the statute of 1869" (paraphrased by Amvrosii in a letter of 17.10.1883 [OR GBL, f. 230, k. 10800, d. 8, l. 3]). Pobedonostsev then solicited the opinions of selected bishops; see Savva, *Khronika*, 6: 826–30, and the letters from Amvrosii in OR GBL, f. 230, k. 10800, d. 8, ll. 3, 11, 25 ob.

[210] TsGIA SSSR, f. 797, op. 54, otd. 1, st. 2, d. 36, ll. 1–2 ob. (Synod resolution, 27/30.3.1884); Savva, *Khronika*, 7: 153–54.

which was widely applied in the statute of 1869, and at the same time to increase the authority of both the bishop (as trustee) and the rector (as immediate head of the academy) over the administration of these institutions of higher education." The new curriculum, explained Pobedonostsev, no longer contained the three fields of concentration and required that all students devote more time to theology. The new statute also set stricter rules for examination and the award of advanced degrees (master's and doctor's). Like the 1814 statute, the new statute gave the academy responsibility for overseeing subordinate seminaries, with professors obliged to make periodic inspection trips to these lower schools. Finally, the statute provided for a modest increase in academy budgets (from 420,000 to 512,900 rubles), primarily for improvements to the physical plant, libraries, and student scholarships.[211] Alexander III approved the statute and, according to Metropolitan Isidor, added that "I am heartened by every improvement in the order of educational institutions."[212] The emperor's views were phrased more baldly in a note to Pobedonostsev, where he expressed his hope that the new statute would lead "to the strengthening of order and discipline in educational institutions."[213]

Once the emperor approved the new statute, the Synod ordered a formal review of the parallel statutes of seminaries and Church schools in order to bring them into agreement with the new statute for ecclesiastical academies. A special committee under the metropolitan of Moscow, formed in late April 1884,[214] worked with haste and submitted its formal proposals to the Synod a month later, together with a note explaining the suggested changes.[215] The committee listed a host of serious deficiencies in the seminary, including some integral to the spirit of reform in the sixties, such as the bishop's diminished authority and the weakness of elected officials inside the seminary. The committee was especially critical of the curriculum for favoring general education over religious subjects:

> The curriculum, in clear contradiction to the goal of the seminary (viz., to prepare youths for service in the Orthodox Church), gives the dominant position in the complex of courses not to theological subjects but to general education—the former receives fifty lessons per week, the latter eighty;

---

[211]TsGIA SSSR, f. 797, op. 54, otd. 1, st. 2, d. 36, ll. 3–10 (Pobedonostsev to Alexander III, 20.4.1884).

[212]Ibid., f. 796, op. 205, d. 452, l. 419 ob. (Isidor, "Dnevnik," 22.4.1884).

[213]OR GBL, f. 230, k. 10802, d. 2, l. 12 (Pobedonostsev to Alexander III, 19.4.1884, with Alexander's notation).

[214]TsGIA SSSR, f. 796, op. 165, g. 1884, d. 522, ll. 1–1 ob.; f. 797, op. 54, otd. 1, st. 2, d. 40, ll. 1–2 (Synod resolution, 25.4.1884).

[215]For details see "Ob"iasnitel'naia zapiska k proektu Ustava dukhovnykh seminarii" and "Ob"iasnitel'naia zapiska k proektu Ustava dukhovnykh uchilishch" (ibid., f. 796, op. 165, g. 1884, d. 522, ll. 8–18, 19–21).

theological studies are virtually eliminated in the first four [years] of the seminary; Church reading, so essential for the preparation of future Church servitors, is placed outside the regular curriculum, with no designation of the number of lessons, almost as though it were a superfluous subject.

Complaining that the curriculum omitted vital religious subjects (such as biblical history, comparative theology, and critical studies of the schism), the committee claimed that "the excessive dominance of classical languages has even brought harm to Russian literature." It concluded that "a direct result of such a system of study was a decline of the Church spirit among seminarians, a cooling toward the clerical rank." The committee also criticized the neglect of moral development, especially in the Church schools, and insisted upon the need for tighter controls. In one respect, however, the committee clearly broke ranks with the procurator, offering a cautious defense of diocesan assemblies: "In the course of seventeen years of their existence, [the assemblies] have already asserted themselves and made themselves apparent through useful results in seeking out the means to open parallel sections at the seminary and especially in the construction and support of diocesan schools for girls and material support of schools for boys." Although it saw no need for annual sessions, the committee firmly defended the assemblies' usefulness.[216]

The Synod reviewed the committee's proposals in August 1884 and essentially endorsed its recommendations, even incorporating the committee's explanatory note into the formal Synodal resolution.[217] In late August Alexander III approved the new statute, which was to be implemented in two stages: administrative changes took effect immediately; the curricular changes became applicable the following academic year.[218]

The new statutes did not fully satisfy the chief procurator. To be sure, they addressed some of his primary demands, such as strengthening the authority of the bishop and the chief school administrators and expanding religious studies in the schools. Still, the classics remained (if attenuated), diocesan assemblies remained (if weakened), and faculty participation remained (if diminished). Some observers were moved to argue that the new statute was not *that* different from the old one and that it certainly did not represent "a restoration."[219] Curiously, some conservatives also criticized the new statute. Katkov objected to the attack on classical languages, and General Kireev wrote that Pobedonostsev "has committed a great stupidity, having (de facto)

[216]Ibid., ll. 2 ob.–3.

[217]Ibid., l. 6 (Synod resolution, 8.8.1884).

[218]Ibid., f. 797, op. 54, otd. 1, st. 2, d. 40, ll. 5–11 ob. (Pobedonostsev to Alexander III, 22.8.1884), 12–12 ob. (Pobedonostsev to Synod).

[219]M. Kupletskii, "Nachalo dukhovno-sudebnoi reformy," PO, 1884, no. 7: 500–22.

abolished Greek at the academies" by making it no longer obligatory.[220] Others, like the suffragan bishop of Kiev, Vitalii, lauded the new statutes, declaring that they "will place authorities [bishops] at the proper elevation so that they will have the opportunity to act, where necessary, in a decisive, independent fashion."[221] Although the Church slightly modified the new statutes in the late 1880s (primarily in an attempt to restrict the admission of outsiders),[222] the schools remained a continuing source of concern, with faculty disgruntled and students dissident, provoking yet another attempt at reform in the late 1890s.[223]

Pobedonostsev and the Bishops

As the desultory pace of counter-reform indicates, Pobedonostsev was hardly the secular patriarch of the Church that many imagined him to be. Although the procurator began as the spokesman of episcopal interests, and although he at first seemed optimistic about the bishops' collaboration, his first months in office soon disabused him of such notions. Significantly, it was not long before the procurator applied to bishops his unflattering view of bureaucratic elites: the bishops, he came to believe, bore much of the blame for the Church's ills, since it was they who had signed, sponsored, and implemented many of the reforms of the 1860s. Indeed, within a month of his appointment, Pobedonostsev wrote a close friend that "we are lost in a marsh, and this marsh is the indifference and inertia of the bishops." Denouncing the parish reform of 1869 as "that strange and calamitous affair," he noted that "in its final product this is primarily the work of episcopal hands" and that "to correct this matter, one has to wage battle with those very same bishops."[224] The procurator's dissatisfaction extended to the

---

[220] *Moskovskie vedomosti*, 1885, no. 271. See also the response by Nikanor ("O klassitsizme v dukhovno-uchebnykh zavedeniiakh," *Str.*, 1886, no. 7: 288–310) and Katkov's critical remarks in a letter of March 1884 ("Klassitsizm i dukhovnaia shkola; pis'mo M. N. Katkova k vysoko-preosv. Ioannikiiu," *BV*, 1913, no. 1: 6–9). For Kireev's diary (4.9.1884 entry), see OR GBL, f. 126, k. 3, d. 10, ll. 44–44 ob.

[221] TsGIA SSSR, f. 1574, op. 2, d. 259, l. 58 (Vitalii to Pobedonostsev, 10.7.1884).

[222] *PSZ (3)*, 10: 7139; 11: 7884.

[223] See N. A. Glubokovskii, *Po voprosam dukhovnoi shkoly i ob Uchebnom komitete pri Sv. Sinode* (St. Petersburg, 1907), and P. V. Znamenskii's review of this volume in *PS*, 1907, no. 10: 521–46. Significantly, the proportion of political offenders from the clerical estate declined only slightly—from 17 percent of all those arrested in the 1870s to some 14 percent for 1878–1887 (V. S. Antonov, "K voprosu o sotsial'nom sostave i chislennosti revoliutsionerov 70-kh godov," *Obshchestvennoe dvizhenie v poreformennoi Rossii* (Moscow, 1965), p. 338; Andreas Kappeler, "Zur Charakteristik russischen Terroristen [1878–1887]," *JGO*, 27 [1979]: 534–37).

[224] OR GBL, f. 230, k. 4409, d. 2, ll. 31–31 ob. (Pobedonostsev to Tiutcheva, 20.5.1880).

Synod itself, which, he complained, is permeated with "the very same indifference and formalism" that one finds elsewhere in the Church.[225] Although he later conceded Isidor's importance, at first Pobedonostsev derided "Isidor's bureaucratic indifference toward everything that transcends the limits of routine Synodal business."[226]

That apathy was all the more frustrating because Pobedonostsev wanted the hierarchs to help repair the damage caused by the reforms of the 1860s. This goal coincided with his belief in the need to reassert "strong authority," not redesign complex institutions. Bishops must, above all, exercise their traditional authority, and for that one needed good prelates, not more laws. At the same time, Pobedonostsev tacitly recognized the Synod's residual authority, substantially reaffirmed since Protasov's death in 1855. Moreover, the procurator much preferred to avoid personal responsibility. As one contemporary perceptively noted, Pobedonostsev "is extremely fearful; everywhere he seeks to act behind the scenes so that in the event of failure he is not the guilty one."[227] His fear was transparent in an 1881 case, where Pobedonostsev transmitted—with his implicit approval—an Englishman's request to head an English branch of the Orthodox Church, with the power to consecrate churches and ordain clergy. To Pobedonostsev's dismay, the Synod routinely approved his request: "And so the road ahead is smooth. But then I became rather terrified: I myself had assumed responsibility for this complicated, difficult, new, and strange affair! But [the Synod members] did not want to go into details on this: the hands of the clock pointed to the hour fixed [for adjournment], and they would not agree to sit longer and discuss this."[228] Pobedonostsev's theory of "strong authority" and hard political reality necessitated that the bishops support his plans to renovate the Church. The protracted discussions on parish and seminary reform demonstrated, however, that the prelates not only held views different from those of the procurator but also were highly distrustful of his overactive intrusion into Church affairs.

Dissatisfied as he was with the bishops, Pobedonostsev found it very difficult to alter the composition of the hierarchy or the membership of the Synod. The bishops, after all, had received rites of consecration and held virtual life tenure; short of criminal malfeasance or hopeless senility, it was almost impossible to force them into retirement. Even in matters of promotion and transfer, the procurator found that he had to observe the wishes of

[225] Ibid., k. 4410, d. 1, ll. 74 ob.–75 (Pobedonostsev to Tiutcheva, 22.6.1881).

[226] Ibid., f. 126, k. 3, d. 8, ll. 193 (Kireev, "Dnevnik," 30.12.1880, quoting Pobedonostsev). See also Bogdanovich's diary, which records Pobedonostsev's "unflattering remarks about Isidor" (A. V. Bogdanovich, Tri poslednikh samoderzhtsa [Moscow-Petrograd, 1924], p. 44).

[227] Bogdanovich, Tri poslednikh samoderzhtsa, p. 55.

[228] OR GBL, f. 230, k. 4410, d. 1, ll. 84–84 ob. (Pobedonostsev to Tiutcheva, 29.7.1881).

leading hierarchs, especially Metropolitan Isidor, who, despite his advanced age, possessed "an extraordinary clarity of mind" and a strong sense of his own dignity and importance.[229] Pobedonostsev periodically tried to manipulate Isidor, but with little success; though scarcely dynamic, by now half-deaf, and even the object of malicious gossip in lay society,[230] Isidor still dominated proceedings in the Synod and enjoyed the respect of ranking prelates. His obstinate skepticism toward anonymous reports of episcopal misconduct chafed the self-righteous procurator, who exclaimed in 1882 that "unfortunately His Grace [Isidor] defends the old fellows [in the hierarchy] to the end, even if they have utterly outlived their time."[231] Even when a vacancy appeared through death or retirement, Pobedonostsev did not have a free hand in choosing candidates; rather, he had to consult with Isidor, and together they compiled a list of nominees for the emperor to consider. It was especially difficult to influence appointments of metropolitans, where seniority was a major consideration. For example, commenting on Platon's appointment as metropolitan of Kiev in 1882, the procurator wrote that Platon was "better than the rest" but that, in any event, there was little choice: Platon enjoyed the "personal disposition [of the emperor] toward him," and he was "more senior than the rest."[232]

More important, Pobedonostsev found the new generation of candidates even worse than their seniors. The principal reason, he believed, was the disintegration of "learned monasticism," a consequence of the more secular and less monastic spirit in the academies: "Of the younger generation there is no one who could honorably occupy this position [as metropolitan in Kiev]. We have become utterly impoverished [in personnel]. I know that prelates are of prime importance for the Church, but is it easy to summon new forces when the school of learned monasticism has been dissolved? God grant us new people!"[233] In fact, because of the decline in learned monasticism, the Church found itself increasingly obliged to consecrate former white clergy (who, upon widowhood, had taken monastic vows) for elevation into the hierarchy. As a result, widowed clergy, who constituted only 11 percent of

---

[229] Nikanor, "Zametki prisutstvuiushchego v Sv. Prav. Sinode," *RA*, 1906, no. 7: 358.

[230] In 1887 Grand Duke Vladimir Aleksandrovich wrote: "Breakfast at Isidor's was positively atrocious, but no one was poisoned. And, as is his wont, he paid attention to my wife, pressed her arm above the elbow, and peered into places where he shouldn't" (Vladimir Aleksandrovich to A. B. Perovskii, 4.16.1887 [Houghton Archives, Kilgour Collection, bMS, Russian 26, letter no. 55]).

[231] OR GBL, f. 230, k. 9804, d. 5, ll. 22–22 ob. (Pobedonostsev to Amvrosii, 18.5.1882). For investigations of bishops in Kostroma and Orel, see Isidor's diary notations of 19.5.1882 and 3.11.1882 (TsGIA SSSR, f. 796, op. 205, d. 450, ll. 124 ob.–25; d.451, l. 201).

[232] OR GBL, f. 230, k. 4410, d. 2, l. 18 (Pobedonostsev to Tiutcheva, 8.2.1882); such complaints parallel closely his view of the civil service (see above, pp. 410–11).

[233] Ibid.

the hierarchy in 1855, represented more than half (53 percent) by 1895.[234] These facts caused the procurator to complain that "the spirit of the Church [*tserkovnost'*] has weakened" in the hierarchy and even given place to liberal ideas: "You just do not know how many fantasies are roaming through the minds of churchmen."[235]

As these disparaging comments suggest, the procurator quickly developed poor relations with many of the bishops. In the Synod itself he could not violate routine procedures because of Isidor, who insisted upon strict adherence to rules. In 1882, for example, when Pobedonostsev sought the members' signature for a matter that had not been formally considered in the Synod, Isidor refused to sign "because there had been no meeting where it would be possible to achieve general agreement on this."[236] Such conflicts incited Isidor to follow rumors that the procurator had lost favor at court, and his diary gleefully reports Pobedonostsev's difficulties.[237] The metropolitan acidly observed that Pobedonostsev "considers himself the benefactor and savior of all Russia, while even Katkov [an archreactionary] is against him."[238] Nor could Pobedonostsev command obedience from diocesan bishops. A close confidante once requested that he intervene on behalf of a priest in Orel diocese. Though Pobedonostsev promised to try, he did not hold out much hope of success: "These matters are very difficult and do not depend upon me. All that I can do is write the prelate, but bishops have various kinds of temperaments, sometimes being very difficult to deal with (and that is our whole problem). In this case the bishop is extremely obstreperous: the bishop of Orel is stubborn, unreasonable, and capricious. I shall write to him, but I am not very hopeful of succeeding."[239] When the procurator confronted

---

[234]Data analyzed from *Spisok arkhiereev*. In most respects, the hierarchy changed little between 1855 and 1890: nearly all had advanced degrees (88 percent in 1855; 91 percent in 1880; 98 percent in 1890); nearly all had prior experience in Church schools (92 percent in 1855; 94 percent in 1880; 96 percent in 1890); and nearly all came from the clerical estate (100 percent [of those known] in 1855; 98 percent in 1880; 98 percent in 1890). The most striking change was the large number of widowed clergy (27 percent in 1880; 32 percent in 1890; 53 percent in 1895); in addition, many more had served prior apprenticeships as suffragan bishops (57 percent in 1855; 80 percent in 1880; 79 percent in 1890). Finally, although the rate of transfers slowed during the Great Reform era, it accelerated in the eighties. On the average, each bishop had served in 1.9 previous dioceses in 1855, 1.8 in 1880, and 2.3 in 1890.

[235]OR GBL, f. 230, k. 4410, d. 2, l. 18 (Pobedonostsev to Tiutcheva, 8.2.1882).

[236]TsGIA SSSR, f. 796, op. 205, d. 450, l. 126 ob. (Isidor, "Dnevnik," 23.5.1882).

[237]Ibid., ll. 20, 33 ob. (entries of 22.8.1881, 2.11.1881).

[238]Ibid., l. 38 ob. (entry of 16.11.1881). Distrust also informed Isidor's reaction to rumors of secret government negotiations with the Vatican: "There was not a single discussion of this subject in the Synod, and there is not even official information that negotiation of certain matters is taking place. Would the chief procurator, without the Synod's knowledge, agree to such concessions in the name of the Synod? Yes, indeed!" (ibid., ll. 45 ob.–46 [entry of 10.12.1881]).

[239]OR GBL, f. 230, k. 4410, d. 1, ll. 82–82 ob. (Pobedonostsev to Tiutcheva, 18.7.1881).

diocesan bishops with anonymous denunciations, they testily rejected the accusations, sometimes demanding to know the identity of the source.[240] Such clashes did little to endear Pobedonostsev to the hierarchs, and within a year of his appointment the well-informed Kireev reported that "on ne l'aime pas parmi le clergé."[241]

These strained relations were a primary cause of Pobedonostsev's curious ambivalence toward episcopal councils (*pomestnye sobory*). His appointment, together with his close association with conservative Slavophile circles, stirred hopes among some bishops that he would support the conciliar principle, either on a national or a regional level. Demands for episcopal councils had circulated since the 1850s, appearing in the memoranda of Murav'ev and others, and constituted the principal aim in the episcopal program. The idea acquired greater cogency in the wake of Tolstoi's reforms, especially his scheme for Church justice, which reinforced the resolve of bishops to buttress the Synod's authority with regular councils. Within a few months of Pobedonostsev's appointment, in fact, the police reported that "some bishops regard as necessary the establishment of [episcopal] assemblies [s"ezdy] for them to discuss and consider ecclesiastical matters and [to adopt] concerted measures to stop the dissemination of the Old Belief, Stundism, Molokanstvo, skopchestvo, and the like, so that all the measures adopted be subject to [later] rectification at similar assemblies."[242]

The most radical expression of conciliarist ideas was a series of essays by a Moscow priest, A. M. Ivantsov-Platonov, published by a Slavophile paper in 1882.[243] The essays discussed various problems in diocesan administration, and although they denied that the bishop was personally responsible, they conceded the ubiquity of abuse and disorder. Indeed, wrote Ivantsov-Platonov, "There is such a fleecing [in the consistories] that it has become a parable." The author proposed a series of radical solutions, some of which were drawn from the platform of clerical liberalism. Most shocking, no doubt, was his suggestion that parish clergy and laymen share in Church administration and even have the right to select bishops (ultimately from the ranks of white, not just black, clergy). Ivantsov-Platonov also advanced proposals to revitalize and restructure the higher layers of Church administration, urging that

[240] Ibid, f. 262, k. 25, d. 37, ll. 13–14 ob., 21–22 ob. (Savva to Pobedonostsev, 11.2.1889, 26.11.1889). For an analogous case, where the bishop of Ufa wrote a prolix refutation of such accusations, see "Iz zapisok arkhiepiskopa Nikanora," *RA*, 1909, no. 2: 209–76; no. 5: 19–77. Anonymous denunciations in fact form a major part of Pobedonostsev's collection in TsGIA SSSR, f. 1574 (op. 2 includes separate files with such denunciations from each diocese).

[241] OR GBL, f. 126, k. 3, d. 8, l. 259 ob. (Kireev, "Dnevnik," August 1881).

[242] TsGIA SSSR, f. 797, op. 50, otd. 2, st. 3, d. 185, l. 1("zapiska dlia pamiati," 5.8.1880).

[243] A. M. Ivantsov-Platonov, *O russkom tserkovnom upravlenii* (St. Petersburg, 1898), originally published in *Rus'*, 1882, nos. 1–16.

the Synod be reconstituted into a genuine episcopal council insulated from the pretensions of the chief procurator, that "metropolitan regions" (with several dioceses subordinate to a ranking prelate) be formed, and that the patriarchate be reestablished for the sake of Church unity and better relations with the Orthodox East. His scheme was the apotheosis of the conciliar principle (*sobornost'*) favored by conservative bishops, infused by Slavophile dreams of reuniting people and Church into a single harmonious whole.

Such neo-Slavophile fantasies held little charm for the chief procurator, but he did recognize the urgent need to improve Church administration. In 1884, for example, he complained of the excessive bureaucratization of the Church: "It is necessary to change the system of Church administration— this bureaucratism [*kantseliarshchina*] is exhausted by the burden of business and everything is moribund."[244] To improve administration, the procurator promoted a number of specific measures: an increase in the number of suffragan bishops, special inspections of ill-reputed consistories, higher educational standards for diocesan secretaries, and even special apprenticeships for the latter at the Synodal chancellery.[245] Besides devolving more authority onto diocesan bishops, Pobedonostsev, like Ivantsov-Platonov, seemed to favor proposals for metropolitanate regions, which would share some of the Synod's burden "for the simple reason that it is difficult for the Synod to contend with the mass of incoming business and still harder for it to breathe life and action into this." Indeed, he complained, "everything is suffocating under the yoke of bureaucratism."[246] Significantly, Pobedonostsev himself arrranged, confidentially, for the publication of a secret memorandum by Murav'ev that urged *inter alia* the establishment of regional episcopal councils.[247]

On the other hand, Pobedonostsev was skeptical of radical innovation and wary of the hasty application of even those ideas he did favor. Thus, although in principle ready to support episcopal councils, Pobedonostsev wrote one friend in 1882 that such councils were good but not "feasible" at the present time—perhaps referring to the current state of mind in the hierarchy.[248] He may also have feared opening the door to more radical ventures, such as Ivantsov-Platonov's vision of a Church council with bishops, priests, and laymen. In 1881 he wrote apprehensively to a confidante about such schemes: "Our idealists are still preaching the idea of a conciliar administration of the Church through bishops and priests. That would be the same as

---

[244]"Kievskii sobor 1884 goda," *RA*, 1908, no. 9: 111.

[245]For an overview, see *Obzor deiatel'nosti*, pp. 112–18. For legislation, see *PSZ (3)*, 3: 1696; 4: 2137; 5: 2710, 2892; 6: 3550; 7: 4387; 8: 5130; 9: 5821; 11: 7808.

[246]"Kievskii sobor 1884g.," *RA*, 1908, no. 9: 111.

[247]See above, n. 82.

[248]OR GBL, f. 126, k. 2, d. 9, 1. 129 (Kireev, "Dnevnik," 9.8.1882).

the zemstvo and peasant elections, from which came some dream of creating a representative assembly for Russia."[249] The following year he personally helped quash an attempt by neo-Slavophiles, through the minister of interior, to summon a national popular assembly (*zemskii sobor*) in secular affairs, and the procurator certainly had no intention of encouraging such schemes in his own domain. But regional assemblies, convoked to address specific issues and composed entirely of bishops, were a less venturesome matter, and by 1884 the procurator stood ready to sponsor such experiments.

The first regional council convened in Kiev in September 1884. It evidently gathered at the behest of Pobedonostsev, who had grown increasingly concerned about the threat of sectarian influence and at last admitted the need for a special meeting of bishops to confront the problem. To a friend he wrote in June, "I have this idea (and shall write about it in a few days to [the metropolitan of] Kiev): the senior [prelate], metropolitan of Kiev, could gather bishops from other dioceses where Stundism has appeared, for a conciliar discussion [*sobornoe soveshchanie*] on [needed] measures."[250] The metropolitan enthusiastically agreed with the suggestion and in a short time formally obtained the Synod's permission to summon a council of bishops from eight nearby dioceses (Kherson, Kishinev, Podolia, Mogilev, Chernigov, Volhynia, Ekaterinoslav, and Poltava).[251] One prelate strongly urged Pobedonostsev himself to attend and take an active role, claiming that, otherwise, the timid prelates would fear to raise important questions.[252] The procurator demurred, however, insisting that the hierarchs themselves needed to act and to overcome "the sloth that is generally characteristic of the Slavic nature."[253] In the end, Pobedonostsev briefly attended the council, hoping that the assembly itself would be short and to the point. The metropolitan of Kiev, on the other hand, wanted a more protracted gathering, so that Pobedonostsev himself was present only for the initial sessions.[254]

Pobedonostsev received a detailed report on the council from the bishop of Kherson, Nikanor (Brovkovich),[255] whose account was based solely on recollection, since Metropolitan Platon of Kiev refused to permit formal minutes. The assembly discussed not only Stundism but fifteen other issues as well, including the clergy's moral and economic condition, ecclesiastical literature, Catholicism, the Old Belief, and alcoholism. As Nikanor stressed in his letters to Pobedonostsev, the council suffered greatly from disorganization

[249] Ibid., f. 230, k. 4410, d. 1, l. 75 ob. (Pobedonostsev to Tiutcheva, 22.6.1881).

[250] "Kievskii sobor 1884 g.," *RA*, 1908, no. 8: 555.

[251] TsGIA SSSR, f. 796, op. 165. g. 1884, d. 161, ll. 1–2 (Platon, 21.7.1884).

[252] "Kievskii sobor 1884 g.," *RA*, 1908, no. 8: 556–59.

[253] Ibid., no. 8: 561.

[254] Ibid., no. 9: 93, 105; Pobedonostsev, *Pis'ma k Aleksandru III*, 2: 57.

[255] TsGIA SSSR, f. 1574, op. 2, d. 259, ll. 69–85 ob. (Nikanor to Pobedonostsev, 12.12.1884, 14.12.1884); "Kievskii sobor 1884 g.," *RA*, 1908, no. 8: 554–74, no. 9: 86–138.

(it had no agenda) and dissension (for example, all the visiting prelates opposed Platon's proposal to fix an obligatory tithe on behalf of parish clergy). As the sessions dragged on, the bishops grew increasingly restive; anticipating a brief discussion, some even lacked proper clothing when an autumn chill settled upon Kiev. To tactful suggestions of adjournment Metropolitan Platon reacted with surprise and irritation; not until the first of October did he finally consent to adjourn the council.[256] Though the prelates spent three full weeks in Kiev, the only result was a rhetorical proclamation against Stundism.[257] That led I. S. Belliustin, an irreconcilable foe of episcopal power, to exlaim, "This *sborishche* ["mob," a pun on the word for council, *sobor*] has composed an address for distribution to churches, having the purpose of 'reinforcing faith and morality in the people,' as *A New Time* put it. In other words, the mountain gave birth not to a mouse but to a stillborn rodent fetus. As if there were not already enough printed rubbish posted in churches, now it is necessary to add to them the product of this *sborishche* in Kiev."[258]

Nor did the Kiev council—or those that followed in Kazan and St. Petersburg—leave a favorable impression on Pobedonostsev, who allowed the whole experiment to expire quietly.[259] The council, after all, failed to devise concrete or resolute measures to contain the rising sectarian movement. More important, it had spilled over into a discussion of broader issues, without authorization and without effect. But at bottom was the fact that Pobedonostsev rejected the implicit premise for councils—a yearning for greater autonomy from the state. Talk about the reestablishment of the patriarchate was muted but persistent; so too was the demand for greater autonomy and new limits on state influence. The chief procurator categorically rejected such notions, and his relationship to the episcopate—strained from the first—steadily deteriorated over the years that followed. By 1905 the bishops, like virtually all other segments of society, were ready to rebel against the morose and frightened little man ruling from his office on Liteinyi Prospekt.

In retrospect, the retreat from the Great Reforms proved a long, difficult process. As in secular affairs, it began in the early or mid-1870s, as authorities encountered serious shortcomings in the Great Reforms and ever more intense resistance to the adoption of any new reforms. Though Tolstoi himself abandoned reform relatively late (not until the end of the 1870s), he suffered serious reverses long before—first at the hands of the State Council,

[256] TsGIA SSSR, f. 1574, op. 2, d. 96, ll. 34–40 (Nikanor to Pobedonostsev, 11.12.1884).

[257] "Pastyrskoe poslanie k svoim pastvam preosviashchennykh, byvshikh na Kievskom s"ezde v sentiabre istekshego goda," *TKDA*, 1885, no. 1: 3–9.

[258] LOII, f. 115, d. 1219, unpaginated letter, no. 699, l. 1 ob. (I. S. Belliustin to N. I. Belliustin, 1.10.1884).

[259] *Obzor deiatel'nosti*, p. 6.

then, more dramatically, in the bishops' repudiation of his scheme for judicial reform. Yet Tolstoi, too, soon recognized the gravity of problems in his new order. Despite some improvements in seminaries and in the system of parish service, the manifold weaknesses—flight, political turbulence, popular opposition to the abolition of parishes—drove Tolstoi to seek major modifications of policy in his last two years of office.

The primary task of dismantling or modifying the new reforms fell to his successor, K. P. Pobedonostsev. The new procurator achieved much of his aim—abolishing elected superintendents, tightening censorship, amending the seminary statutes, and annulling the parish reform of 1869—but he did so only with great difficulty. It is important to note that Pobedonostsev did have a program. He was not the bureaucratic nihilist usually depicted; rather, he profoundly distrusted radical institutional change, even of a conservative variety. Yet, as the archival sources attest, his slow progress in reform derived less from his gradualism than from opposition in the Church: though bishops shared his dismal assessment of the Great Reforms, they did not endorse his specific program—and, no doubt, liked his personal intrusion still less. The result was a very modest counter-reform—not a full-scale restoration, but only a blunting of the sharper liberal edges that Pobedonostsev found so discomforting. In the end, Pobedonostsev himself realized that simple restoration was impossible: counter-reform could not merely disassemble Tolstoi's system but had to find solutions to the problems that had provoked reform in the first place.

CHAPTER 10

Reform
and Revolution

When we study the reports of the Most Holy Synod,
our attention is drawn to the regularly recurring phenomenon that, even with the agreement of legislative
institutions, the pre-sobor conference, and in part of the
Synod on the necessity of certain reforms, these reforms
have not been realized. These institutions remain as
archaic as before, and the condition of things continues
to be exceedingly unsatisfactory, even hopeless.

State Duma Committee Report, 1915[1]

T he failings of parish clergy, long a concern for both Church and
state, became the object of continuing reform in the nineteenth
century. Nicholas I addressed this problem from the very outset of
his reign, at first focusing upon service and education, eventually shifting
attention to the clergy's estate structure. The Great Reforms redefined the
clerical question still more broadly and ultimately sought to rebuild the
whole Church order—its system of education, administration, parish service,
and the estate itself. After a decade of debate, agitation, and abortive
reforms, authorities finally promulgated a set of major legislation in the late
1860s that aimed to transform parish clergy into more active pastors, primarily in ways that served the interests of the Church, not the estate. Those
reforms, however, pleased almost no one. Like other dimensions of the Great
Reforms, from the early 1870s the new order fell victim to criticism and
gradual modification, conventionally labeled counter-reform. After all that
law making and law retracting, how did the Church and clergy stand at the
end of the century?

[1]John S. Curtiss, *Church and State in Russia: The Last Years of the Empire 1900–1917*
(New York, 1940), p. 318.

Church and Clergy at the End of the Century

By the 1890s the authority that the Synod had reclaimed in the late 1850s had largely disintegrated. Contemporary descriptions of the chief procurator's role show an almost uncanny imitation of the Protasov system—the Synod's lay officials manipulated the agenda, withheld material, and reserved sensitive materials for summer sessions with visiting members of low rank.[2] As the Synod's lay archivist wrote, "it is not the hierarchs who govern the Church, but Synodal officials, and [they do so] not on the basis of canons or even laws, but according to their own wishes and whim."[3] That whim had been held in check until 1892 by Metropolitan Isidor, who remained surprisingly vigorous and assertive right to the very end. His death, however, "untied the hands" of lay officials, who arranged the appointment of a more pliable metropolitan and thereafter enjoyed unfettered reign over Church affairs.[4] Power, interestingly, rested not so much with Pobedonostsev as with his more energetic aide, V. K. Sabler, who dominated the conduct of ecclesiastical affairs until 1905.[5] In contrast to Protasov, who bureaucratized central and local administration, Pobedonostsev and Sabler exalted arbitrariness, not law and order—as the chaos of Church archives, mounds of anonymous reports, and irregular procedures all bore witness.[6] As ever in the imperial system, the structure of power rested not upon law but upon personalities, and, to the great indignation of ranking prelates, it shifted once again. By late 1896 one well-connected diarist reported that "in the Synod they are dissatisfied with Pobedonostsev and Sabler—evidently, the personal pressure put on everything by the thick-headed Pobedonostsev has enraged our prelates."[7]

Nor had nineteenth-century reform achieved much change in diocesan administration. The volume of paperwork steadily rose, reaching staggering dimensions; in 1905 authorities in Kherson calculated that they had to process a new document every four minutes to handle the twenty-odd thousand files that gushed through their offices.[8] Much of this paperwork, complained

---

[2]For the late eighties, see Nikanor, "Zapiski prisutstvuiushchego v. Sv. Sinode," *RA*, 1906, no. 7: 353–90; no. 8: 497–519; no 9: 5–37; no. 10: 161–213; no. 11: 321–57; no. 12: 481–504. See also the informed account on the 1890s in A. N. L'vov, "Kniaz'ia tserkvi," *KA*, 39 (1930): 108–48, 40 (1930): 97–124; and the comments by the bishop of Vladimir in 1905 in *Otzyvy eparkhial'nykh arkhiereev po voprosu o tserkovnoi reforme*, 3 vols. (St. Petersburg, 1906), 1: 219.

[3]L'vov, "Kniaz'ia tserkvi," *KA*, 39: 112.

[4]Ibid., 39: 118.

[5]On Sabler's domination, see ibid., passim; for a bitter attack on Sabler, see the undated denunciation in TsGIA SSSR, f. 1574, op. 2, d. 280, ll. 36–36 ob.

[6]For the disarray in archival materials after 1880, see the Note on Sources.

[7]OR GBL, f. 126, k. 3, d. 12, ll. 98 ob.–99 (Kireev, "Dnevnik," 14.12.1896).

[8]*Otzyvy*, 2: 406–7.

one bishop in 1905, was utterly useless: "In Smolensk diocese about 10,000 papers per year (on the average) come to the bishop for confirmation in the form of journals, reports, estimates, and requests of various kinds. Of this vast quantity of paper, the majority are so insignificant that they could be handled by councils of district priests, the consistories, or other diocesan institutions."[9] Nor had reform managed to eradicate the proverbial abuse and bribery that pervaded Church administration. As one academy professor wrote in the early eighties, "All our official institutions were extremely corrupt, but none more so than the consistory's chancellery. Other official departments were cleansed either partly or completely, but not the consistory's chancelleries."[10] Such bureaucratism, at once inefficient and unjust, seemed all the more reprehensible because it eroded the bishop's "paternalistic role"—a suggestively recurrent complaint by liberal clergy from the 1830s right to 1917.[11] The condition of Church administration also made the consistory an object of popular animosity; as a group of clergy of Tver wrote in 1905, "people invariably speak and write of the consistories with animus, derision, and sometimes scorn."[12] By 1905 the catalogue of grievances could easily have been reprinted from the 1860s—red tape, backwardness of ecclesiastical justice, inaccessibility of bishops, bribery, and high turnover in episcopal appointments.[13]

Furthermore, the chief procurator never succeeded in rebuilding ecclesiastical schools. Although he halted the decline in seminary enrollments (see table 22), the quality of education became ever more unsatisfactory.[14] Hints of trouble in the new statute of 1884 were already evident by the second half of the decade, not only in the continuing occurrence of seminary disorders but also in the heavy flow of "corrective decrees."[15] By the early 1890s this system of schools offered "a picture of total collapse" and impelled the Syn-

---

[9]Ibid., 3: 98.

[10]E. E. Golubinskii, "O reforme v byte russkoi tserkvi," ChOIDR, 246 (1913), issledovaniia: 32. For a complaint that the strict controls on the press helped conceal administrative disorder, see the letters by I. S. Belliustin to his son in LOII, f. 155, d. 220, letters 681/b (13.3.1884) and 686 (13.4.1884).

[11]For example, see the Pokrovskii memorandum of 1836 (above, pp. 32-33), Belliustin's Description of 1858, and the Duma deputies' manifesto of 1915 (Zapiska dumskogo dukhovenstva, podannaia v avguste 1915 g. ober-prokuroru Sv. Sinoda A. D. Samarinu [Petrograd, 1916]; also published as "Pechat' i dukhovenstvo," Missionerskoe obozrenie, 1915, no. 11: 286–98).

[12]Otzyvy, prilozhenie, p. 65.

[13]For a summary account, see Curtiss, Church and State, chaps. 5–6. See also T. V. Barsov, "O sobranii dukhovnykh zakonov," KhCh, 1897, tom 2: 281–319, 754–84; and I. Berdnikov, "K voprosu o preobrazovanii eparkhial'nogo upravleniia," PS, 1906, nos. 1–4.

[14]Enrollment in district schools fell slightly, primarily because of growing competition from public schools.

[15]Beliavskii, O reforme, 1: 154–56.

TABLE 22

Church School Enrollments, 1855–1904

Year	Seminary	District School	Total
1855	13,835	37,180	51,015
1866	16,441	37,933	54,374
1890	17,502	30,236	48,510
1904	19,845	29,741	49,586

SOURCES: *IVO (1855)*, prilozhenie; IVO (1866), prilozhenie; *IVO (1890–91)*, prilozhenie; IVO (1903–04), prilozhenie.

od's archivist to observe that "our ecclesiastical schools now not only lack a positive system but are undergoing some kind of real demoralization in both education and moral training."[16] Most obvious was the breakdown in moral training, evident from widespread reports of pupils' indifference to the faith and school authorities' inability to reestablish order and control.[17] Breakdown at the local level was abetted by maladministration in Petersburg, as Sabler sponsored bad appointments and permitted Tolstoi's effective system of inspections to collapse.[18] Appalled by the failure of counter-reform, in 1896 the Synod once more formed a special committee to draft yet another seminary statute, seeking once again to trim the hours of Latin, to tighten moral control, and to restore logic to the curriculum.[19] Characteristically, that reform plan ran aground on episcopal opposition, and as the barricades went up in 1905, the Synod was still trying to bring the committee's work to fruition.[20] In relative terms, stagnation took a heavy toll: the Church failed to increase substantially its academy graduates (even as university education proliferated among the laity),[21] the seminary failed to keep its students

[16] L'vov, "Kniaz'ia tserkvi," KA, 39: 130; Beliavskii, *O reforme*, 1: 158.

[17] For a sound overview, see Beliavskii, *O reforme*, 1: 160–66. For an account of conditions in the Tula seminary in the 1880s and Vladimir seminary in the mid-1890s, see Evlogii, *Put' moei zhizni* (Paris, 1947), pp. 23–25, 72–74; see also the childhood reminiscences in Sergei Bulgakov, *Avtobiograficheskie zametki* (Paris, 1946), pp. 25–26. For a general overview of seminary radicalism, see Titlinov, *Molodezh' i revoliutsiia*.

[18] Beliavskii, *O reforme*, 1: 160–65; L'vov, "Kniaz'ia tserkvi," KA, 39: 121.

[19] Beliavskii, *O reforme*, 1: 169–94; TsGIA SSSR, f. 796, op. 205, d. 655, ll. 1–8.

[20] Beliavskii, *O reforme*, 1: 172–86.

[21] On the Church's failure to expand the academies at a time when educated society increasingly presumed a higher education, see the declaration by clerical deputies at the Fourth Duma in 1915 ("Pechat' i dukhovenstvo," p. 88).

abreast of modern secular culture,[22] and the fearful Pobedonostsev even prevented theological textbooks from incorporating the recent findings of Church scholarship.[23]

The chief procurator also failed to rebuild a more effective parish order. Even in sheer numbers he failed: although he reopened the merged churches and established some new ones, they did little more than keep pace with the rapid growth in population.[24] More important, Pobedonostsev failed to solve the parish's economic problems. As he himself soon discovered in the early eighties, neither the parishioners nor the state were eager to provide sufficient support. In 1894 he finally persuaded the government to allot more subsidies (the first since 1858), but by 1905 he had obtained financial aid for only two-thirds of the parishes—and in small amounts.[25] As a result, the clergy still depended heavily upon gratuities, a form of support that authorities and clergy had denounced as a scourge for nearly two centuries. Like Kiselev in the 1830s, S. Iu. Witte wrote in 1905 that "the first condition for uplifting pastoral activism must be the discovery of such forms of support for the clergy that would spare the priest the necessity to bargain with parishioners over the performance of rites."[26] Five years later another reform memorandum, prepared by the Synod as authorities once again, in vain, tackled the clergy's economic problem, bemoaned the fact that "to this very day the main resources for the support of most parishes remain the donations received as payment from parishioners for the performance of rites."[27] By 1916, as the nation stood on the precipice of revolution, diocesan bishops wrote in their annual reports that gratuities remained the single greatest impediment to the clergy's effectiveness, the single greatest cause of conflict with parishioners.[28]

Nor did the Church ever attract outsiders to the clergy to refresh and revi-

---

[22] In 1896 the bishop of Perm wrote: "It is a pity to look upon priests, of whom the majority do not even have the slightest notion of the ideas that animate and move contemporary society" (quoted in Beliavskii, O reforme, 1: 173). Early in 1905 S. Iu. Witte similarly complained that "ecclesiastical schools pay little heed to contemporary currents of social thought" (A.R., Istoricheskaia perepiska o sud'bakh pravoslavnoi tserkvi [Moscow, 1912], p. 20).

[23] Beliavskii, O reforme, 1: 159–69.

[24] The number of parish churches increased 1.6 percent between 1860 and 1880 (from 30,956 to 31,456), then rose 10.2 percent in the 1880s (from 31,456 to 34,670), and increased another 10.1 percent between 1890 and 1904 (from 34,670 to 38,188). See the statistical appendixes to IVO (1860), IVO (1880), IVO (1890), and IVO (1903–04).

[25] By 1904 the chief procurator had obtained subsidies for 71 percent of all parishes (26,973 of 38,188), but mainly for those in strategic areas like the western provinces and rarely in substantial amounts. See IVO (1903–04), pp. 120–21.

[26] A.R., Istoricheskaia perepiska, p. 17.

[27] Petrovskii, Istoricheskaia spravka, p. 31.

[28] See, for example, the episcopal reports of 1916 summarized in L. I. Emeliakh, Krest'iane i tserkov' nakanune Oktiabria (Leningrad, 1976), pp. 50–52.

talize it—the dream of the sixties. Although the number of outsiders in Church schools increased, the service files for Tver, Kiev, and even Siberia show that by 1890 few had entered the clergy.[29] Aware that outsiders matriculated solely to obtain a free education, the Synod in 1890 tried to limit the number of outsiders, but with little success.[30] By 1900, in fact, the pool of outsiders had risen to 23 percent, impelling the Synod to fix a 10 percent quota on outsiders and to require an oath that they would become clergy.[31] The number of outsiders did not decline to the prescribed 10 percent but fell to 15 percent by 1909.[32] In the end, the Church lured some recruits from the outside, including some famous historical personages—the radical priest Gapon (son of a Poltava peasant), the black-hundredist bishop Antonii Khrapovitskii (son of a nobleman in Novgorod), and the surly seminarian Djugashvili-Stalin (son of a Georgian peasant turned shoemaker). The rarity of such outsiders, however, evoked an age-old appeal on the eve of the Revolution to "throw open the doors of the ecclesiastical schools to pupils from other sosloviia."[33]

In one respect the reform of the sixties worked only too well: the flight begun in the 1870s continued unabated. The proportion of graduates transferring to secular schools fell slightly in the eighties (from 27 percent to 20 percent), but from the early nineties it rose inexorably.[34] By 1904 the flight had reached staggering proportions, and the chief procurator conceded: "Many of the seminarians shun their goal—to be pastors of the Church. The majority, especially the best, leave the clerical rank and enter various institutions of higher learning; it often happens that of 50 to 60 graduates from the seminary, only 2 or 3 (at most 5) become priests."[35] Even more disturbing than the numbers was the quality; as the bishop of Tambov wrote in 1905, those who remain "are not our best students, but only the poor ones" without

[29]Klirovye vedomosti for Kaliazin district in 1890 show only 1 of 196 clergy coming from nonclerical origins. Tver district had 3 of 274; Kiev district, 6 of 245; Chigirin district, 4 of 196. Only the Siberian files, reflecting the acute pressure for manpower there, show more sizable proportions—for example, 9 percent (11 of 118) in Nizhneudinsk district. GA Kalininskoi obl., f. 160, op. 1, dd. 16303, 16550; GA Irkutskoi obl., f. 50, op. 1, sv. 549, d. 10256; sv. 557, dd. 10344, 10350; sv. 548, d. 10231; sv. 557, d. 10350; sv. 555, d. 10325; TsGIA UkrSSR, f. 120, op. 1009, d. 984; op. 1011, dd. 1175, 1468, 3911, 3959, 4009, 4056.

[30]In October 1890 the Synod set tuition fees for nonclerical youths, but the following June, in response to clamor from below, it admitted exceptions for "poor" outsiders (PSZ [3], 10: 7139; 11: 7884).

[31]See the analysis and references in Simon, Pobedonoscev und die Kirchenpolitik, pp. 128–29.

[32]IVO (1910), p. 202.

[33]See the declaration of clerical deputies in 1915 ("Pechat' i dukhovenstvo," p. 289).

[34]Beliavskii, O reforme, 1: 152.

[35]IVO (1903–04), p. 113.

TABLE 23

Seminary Graduates among Parish Clergy,
1835–1904

Year	Percent Clerics with Seminary Degree			
	Priest	Deacon	Sacristan	All
1835	42.5%	4.2%	0.0%	13.6%
1860	82.6	15.6	0.4	29.2
1880	87.4	12.7	2.0	37.4
1890	88.1	12.1	4.3	37.9
1904	63.8	2.2	1.9	29.4

SOURCES: TsGIA SSSR, f. 796, op. 117, g. 1836, d. 1201, ll. 3–6; op. 142, g. 1861, d. 2379; op. 162, g. 1881, d. 2325; op. 172, g. 1891, d. 2883; *IVO (1903–04)*, p. 112.

the means to leave.[36] The result was a severe shortage of qualified candidates, not only in outlying areas, but even in central dioceses, which led to an astounding decline in the level of clerical education in the last decades before 1905 (see table 23). Indeed, once Tolstoi opened the gates, the exodus could not be stopped, and by 1911 some 73 percent of the seminary graduates abandoned the Church for secular careers.[37] As one observer complained in 1916, seminarians "flee into civil institutions, excise offices, agrarian commissions, railway offices—anywhere except the Church."[38] This was a staggering blow to the Church, a sharp reversal of the progress achieved in the nineteenth century, a "brain drain" that profoundly lowered the clergy's cultural level in absolute as well as relative terms.[39] The liberal press spelled out the full implications for the Church: "As a consequence of some kind of spontaneous flight of the best candidates from the Church into lay society, in recent time the intellectual and moral level of rural clergy is falling."[40]

That recruitment crisis, though similar to problems in Western churches, was considerably more severe in Russia. In England, for example, the Anglican Church had complained of a declining *quality* since the 1860s, but only in the immediate prewar years was the supply of candidates seriously

[36] *Otzyvy*, 3: 299; see also the commentary from Vladimir (ibid., 1: 233).
[37] Curtiss, *Church and State*, p. 310.
[38] Ibid., p. 311.
[39] For earlier warnings against this, see above, pp. 357–58, 422.
[40] "Obozrenie vnutrennei tserkovno-obshchestvennoi zhizni Rossii," *PS*, 1905, no. 1: 156.

depleted.[41] In Germany, where the Lutheran clergy enjoyed high status, authorities did not seriously complain of too few recruits until the early twentieth century; although the proportion of university graduates pursuing clerical careers declined there as elsewhere, the Church still had an ample supply of qualified candidates.[42] The Lutheran Church in Sweden and Norway also experienced the general decline in the numbers and status of recruits, but prior to World War I it found more than enough candidates to fill its ranks.[43] The issue of recruits was most pronounced in France, where public lamentations had been heard since mid-century; yet, in practice, it was not until the immediate prewar years that the Catholic Church experienced a sharp drop in the number of candidates.[44] In fact, it was not until the interwar era or until after World War II that most Western churches at last suffered from a calamitous drop in the number of recruits, at a time when their corps of clergy was growing ever older and feeling great anxiety over their utility

[41] For the first expressions of concern, see T. S. Espin, *Our Want of Clergy, Its Causes and Suggestions for Its Cure* (London, 1863), and *The Official Yearbook of the Church of England, 1883* (London, 1883), p. 1. For overviews and data, see R. Towler and A. P. M. Coxon, *The Fate of the Anglican Clergy* (London, 1979), esp. pp. 21–28; and Russell, *The Clerical Profession*, pp. 233–42.

[42] For the decline in students on theological faculties, see the data in Dahm, *Beruf: Pfarrer*, pp. 49–58. For early complaints, see [W. Bornemann], *Die Unzulänglichkeit des theologischen Studiums des Gegenwart* (2nd ed.; Leipzig, 1886), p. 23; and the official warnings of fewer, less qualified candidates in *Kirchliches Jahrbuch*, 31 [1904]: 345–47, 351. The Catholic Church in Germany experienced similar problems, aggravated by *Kulturkampf*, but rooted primarily in the ineluctable process of secularization (Merkel, "Studien," pp. 36–37, 44; Neher, *Geistlichkeit Württembergs*, p. 5).

[43] For Sweden, see Norrman, *Från Prästöverflöd till prästbrist*, pp. 139–92; for Norway, see Mannsåker, *Det norske prestekapet*, pp. 84–102.

[44] The Catholic Church in France experienced recruitment problems on the very eve of the French Revolution. Once it had recovered from the devastating impact of revolution, however, it was able to attract an ample number of recruits for most of the nineteenth century. The first great cry of warning came in the 1870s, but only in the immediate prewar years did the number of ordinands suddenly and precipitously drop. For the eighteenth-century background, see Timothy Tackett and C. Langlois, "Ecclesiastical Structures and Clerical Geography on the Eve of the French Revolution," *French Historical Studies*, 11 (1980): 355–59, 367. For the most famous warning of shortages, see E. Bougaud, *Le grand péril de l'Église de France au XIXe siècle* (Paris, 1878), who blamed the spot shortages on "l'indifférence religieuse" and called it "[une] veritable question de vie et de mort pour l'Église de France en ce moment" (pp. 1, 21). For the statistical record, see Boulard, *Essor ou déclin*, pp. 75–85, 99–106, 465; Huot-Pleuroux, *Recrutement sacerdotal*, p. 69; and, from the series "Histoire des diocèses de France," such typical volumes as that by A. Poitineau, ed., *Le diocèse de Clermont* (Paris, 1979), pp. 236, 265. For a general discussion suggesting that the nineteenth-century "crisis of recruits" was mainly psychological, not statistical, see Edward T. Gargan and R. Hanneman, "Recruitment to the Clergy in Nineteenth-Century France" *Journal of Interdisciplinary History*, 9 (1978): 275–96.

and station in modern society.[45] That crisis of the clergy came much earlier in Russia, where it was essentially rooted in the failure to devise an alternative to the coercive soslovie system for providing new candidates for the priesthood.

The most eloquent testament to *réforme manquée* was a declaration signed by clerical deputies to the State Duma in August 1915, a manifesto that could easily have been written a century earlier.[46] Like earlier generations of priests, they appealed to authorities to eliminate the baneful gratuities: "So long as the present system of abnormal and humiliating form of support of the clergy exists, the clergy's authority in the eyes of the people will not be raised." The Duma priests, like Belliustin in an earlier day, castigated the present system of Church administration and, especially, the domination by monastic clergy. Monastic rule, they warned, not only corrupted monasticism by enticing men to orders for "careerist" purposes but had also transformed the Church into a lifeless, unfeeling bureaucracy: "Bishops hold themselves too high and far away from their co-workers in church affairs—the parish pastors. The clergy do not see paternal leadership on the part of the prelates; instead, one finds a cold, often bureaucratic relationship based largely on paper." Like their liberal forerunners, they deplored the antiquated Statute of Diocesan Consistories of 1841, specifically demanding new limits on bishops' powers to "transfer without trial and investigation, retire from active service by administrative order, imprison in monasteries without trial, and place on trial without sufficient grounds." The Duma priests also demanded that parish clergy be accorded broader rights of assembly, that authorities permit priests to elect superintendents and consistory members, and that some members of the white clergy be included in the Synod. The deputies further complained of insufficient welfare funds, especially for "widows and orphans," whose existing support was "miserly to a horrendous degree." This long list of unsolved problems also included "the question of voluntary defrocking: the existing law is rather unfair and bears a punitive character, [and] it hardly serves the best interests of the Church to retain people in Church service through coercion." In view of the condition of ecclesiastical schools and the parish clergy, the Duma deputies found it natural that so many youths "are fleeing the seminary to enter lay schools" and that "even bishops who were widowed priests [with children] usually

[45]Towler and Coxon, *Fate of Anglican Clergy*, pp. 25–37, 80–82; Russell, *The Clerical Profession*, pp. 233–42; Norrman, *Från Prästöverflöd till pröstbrist*, pp. 139–92; Johannes Dellepoort, *De Priesterroepingen in Nederland; proeve van een statistisch-sociografische Analyse* ('s Gravenhage, 1955), pp. 305–8; Huot-Pleuroux, *Recrutement sacerdotal*, p. 419; J. Duquesne, *Les prêtres* (Paris, 1965); J. Dellepoort et al., *Die deutsche Priesterfrage* (Mainz, 1961).

[46]"Pechat' i dukhovenstvo," pp. 286–98.

educate their sons in secular schools—the lot of the pastor is anything but sweet."[47]

The ultimate price of misfired reform was the failure to raise the level of religious consciousness among parishioners, who, right to the end of the *ancien régime*, remained largely pious but astonishingly ignorant of the faith. Though irreligious tendencies were apparent among the young generation, especially those working in factories,[48] most bishops found the parishioners as pious—and as ignorant—as ever. Typical was the report from the bishop of Astrakhan, writing on the eve of the 1917 Revolution: "The majority of simple people have yet to master not only the basic dogmas of Orthodoxy, but even the correct pronunciation of the most commonly used prayers."[49] The bishop of Kursk, in his annual report for 1916, voiced similar views: "The peasants have very inadequate knowledge not only of Church canons and decrees, but even of the basic truths of the Faith. . . . They have no clear, precise conception of anything and, moreover, mix various superstitions into their faith."[50] Even Pobedonostsev, who so admired the piety of the "simple Russian soul," admitted the laity's abysmally low level of religious knowledge: "Many who call themselves Christians have no comprehension of Jesus and do not even recognize his image on the icon."[51] In 1917, as the Revolution came to its climax, clergy at a national Church council declared that "you encounter many Orthodox people who do not know the dogmas or history [of the Church], and who do not even know the most common prayers."[52] To read through the bishops' reports for the final prerevolutionary years is eerily familiar: the picture differs little from that found early in the nineteenth century—before the waves of painful, repeated, and ultimately ineffective reforms.

[47] That was no exaggeration: clerical sons, who numbered some 600 in secular gymnasiums in 1863, counted 4,331 in 1904, then 8,519 in 1914. In the university, after the sharp decline of the 1880s and 1890s, their numbers again rose after 1900, and by 1913 they totaled 3,677—compared with 388 in 1864 and with the few hundred in the contemporary academy (Rashin, "Gramotnost'," pp. 72, 74).

[48] Soviet historians, relying almost solely upon the bishops' annual reports, show that, especially in the wake of the 1905 Revolution, the prelates discerned a close relationship between irreligion and the factory. See, for example, the material in Emeliakh, *Istoricheskie predposylki*, chap. 3, and I. Z. Kadson, "Otnoshenie rabochikh razlichnykh raionov Rossii k religii i tserkvi," in *Rabochie Rossii v epokhu kapitalizma* (Rostov-na-Donu, 1972), pp. 208–19.

[49] Quoted in L. I. Emeliakh, "Antiklerikalizm i ateizm krest'ian nakanune Velikoi Oktiabr'skoi sotsialisticheskoi revoliutsii," *Po etapam razvitiia ateizma v SSSR* (Leningrad, 1967), pp. 63–64.

[50] Ibid., p. 64. For similar material, drawn from the contemporary press and mainly the bishops' *otzyvy* for the preliminary council, see P. E. Immekus, *Die Russische-Orthodoxe Landpfarrei zu Beginn des XX. Jahrhunderts nach den Gutachten der Diözesanbischöfe* (Würzburg, 1978), pp. 202–36.

[51] *IVO (1884)*, pp. 92–93.

[52] Quoted in Emeliakh, *Krest'iane*, p. 17.

Réforme manquée

Reform had failed. Although it slightly ameliorated the material condition of a few clergymen, it did not solve the economic problems of the parish, create more effective schools, reshape the estate into a new class of pastors, or even sustain the educational level of ordinands. Despite strong and continuing interest, despite dozens of committees and commissions, despite the clamor of public opinion, reform left the Church little better—if not worse—than it was in 1825. Abortive reform figures prominently in the history of nineteenth-century Russia, but that in the Church was particularly striking and catastrophic. How does one account for this failure of reform?

One cause was the economics of Orthodoxy, where the form of worship imposed a high "clerical overhead." In contrast to the Catholic clergy, who were celibate and required more modest support, the Orthodox clergy were married and needed far greater income to support their families. Moreover, the aesthetics of the liturgy, custom, and the illiteracy of most peasant parishioners required that the parish staff include not only a priest but also other full-time clergy—at least a sacristan as reader, preferably a deacon as well. Hence each church had several clerics, all with families and all requiring substantial support. The ensuing cost, no doubt, accounted for the large size of the Russian parish, where the ratio of parishioners to priests was among the highest in Europe. In theory, the Russian Church might consolidate parishes into ever larger, more populous units and increase that ratio still more; in fact, that strategy had been the main thrust of policy since the mid-nineteenth century, and by the early twentieth Russia had kept pace with the general European tendency to expand a parish's size and, thus, its economic base (see table 24).

Yet parish consolidation had limits and risks. For one thing, it was inhibited by the requirements of Orthodox religious practice, which charged priests to perform numerous sacraments, in contrast to Protestant pastors, whose liturgical duties were few and who could thus serve large numbers of parishioners. Hence the Orthodox priest could attend the needs only of a finite number of parishioners; even the size of the nineteenth-century parish put him at a severe disadvantage compared with the Catholic priest, who served in far smaller parishes. In fact, the Russian Church had begun to reach the outer limits on parish size, as was dramatically evident in the larger parishes, where the priest in the course of a day or two heard confession from hundreds of parishioners, a pro forma exercise that perverted the very meaning of the sacrament. Russian geography also raised formidable obstructions: the low population density and lack of good communications often made it physically impossible to combine parishes into larger, more viable units. And even when merger was possible, it contradicted the very purpose of reform—to strengthen the Church's grip on society. On the contrary, the

TABLE 24

Parishioner-Clergy Ratios in Russia and Europe
(Second Half of the Nineteenth Century)

Church and Area	Mid-19th Century		Early 20th Century	
	Ratio	(Year)	Ratio	(Year)
Catholic				
France	752	(1848)	739	(1904)
Protestant				
Denmark	1,279	(1855)	1,791	(1900)
England	1,054	(1861)	1,800	(1911)
Finland	1,801	(1860)	2,864	(1900)
Germany (entire)	1,429	(1840)	2,273	(1910)
Norway	3,164	(1855)	3,103	(1900)
Prussia	1,729	(1847)	2,166	(1901)
Sweden	1,278	(1860)	1,843	(1900)
Orthodox				
Russia				
(total clergy)	457	(1860)	826	(1904)
(priests only)	1,371	(1860)	1,844	(1904)

SOURCES: Bigler, *Politics of German Protestantism*, pp. 55–56; Boulard, *Essor ou déclin*, p. 40; Chadwick, *The Victorian Church*, 2: 244; Dahm, *Beruf: Pfarrer*, pp. 78–79; *IVO (1861)*, prilozhenie; *IVO (1903–04)*, prilozhenie; Jedin, *Handbuch*, 6 (1): 353; *Kirchliches Jahrbuch*, 31 (1904): 340; Mannsåker, *Det norske presteskapet*, p. 76; Towler and Coxon, *Fate of Anglican Clergy* p. 28.

NOTE: Parishioners include all formal church members, not the total population of a country. Clergy represent full-time clerics who have been formally installed.

formation of large, sprawling parishes only weakened the Church's infrastructure, inviting penetration by such adversaries as Old Believers, sectarians, and other confessions.

More important, society did not *want* this kind of reform—"from below"—at its own expense. As reforms from the 1830s to the 1870s demonstrated, parishioners fiercely resisted changes, flouted demands to switch parishes, and even reduced the emoluments paid for individual rates on the grounds that, with more parishioners, the priest required less from each. In part, these failed reforms testified to the ultimate impotence of formal power under the *ancien régime*. Neither Church nor state could compel parishioners to assume additional burdens; at most, they could only cajole and admonish. The most striking element here is society's lack of interest in religious change, specifically, in transforming the clergy into "professional pastors."

As priests warned and experience confirmed, neither peasants nor other classes showed much desire to help "improve the clergy's material condition." Although laymen usually explained that refusal by their own poverty, their indifference was also due to a host of other interacting motives, including fear of fixed obligations (given the variability of their own income) and reluctance to relinquish economic control over the priest.

The chief reason was their refusal to acknowledge the need for reform, the need to replace liturgical functionaries with more professional pastors fit to preach, catechize, teach, and discharge liturgical duties with more elegance and dignity. Slavophiles in the sixties had complained that the parishioners' indifference only testified to the clergy's failure, and they argued that if the clergy showed more spiritual vitality, the economic problem would solve itself. That advice, however, only underscored the vicious circle of parish reform: the clergy could not raise parishioners' morality and commitment without first serving more effectively and recruiting better priests; yet these goals could not be attained until gratuities were replaced with more substantial, more honorable support. By the century's end, clearly, the Church was losing this battle: the quality of new recruits was falling, and Orthodoxy's grip on a more mobile, literate society was slipping. As the Duma's clerical deputies complained in 1915, "The authority of spiritual pastors is steadily falling, so that even the best, most energetic of them sometimes are powerless and, as if in despair, give up."[53]

Although ranking prelates hoped that the economic question could be solved "from above," through financial actions by central institutions, such hopes remained in the realm of sheer fantasy. The Church itself lacked the means; for secularization of Church properties in 1764 had stripped it of independent wealth and left it dependent upon the state for its budgetary allocations. Nor could the Church levy taxes or impose tithes. It required approval for such schemes from the state, which invariably rejected them, usually with the explanation that the people's tax burden was already excessive and that such assessments would inevitably boomerang and cause popular resentment toward the clergy. The state, although genuinely interested in uplifting the clergy, declined to assume a significant economic burden, primarily because the marginal economy of the *ancien régime*, routinely visited by famine and dearth, hardly sufficed to cover the state's own pressing needs. There was no surplus for a government struggling to improve its army, expand its civil service, and lay the foundations of a modern economic order. Characteristically, the very same Witte who emphasized the "necessity" of changing the parish economy hastened to add that "one must consider more than just an increase in clerical support from the treasury, which cannot be rapidly expanded because of the condition of state finances."[54]

[53] "Pechat' i dukhovenstvo," p. 286.
[54] A.R., *Istoricheskaia perepiska*, p. 17.

TABLE 25

Structure of the Parish Clergy,
1824–1904

Year	Priests	Deacons	Sacristans
1824	31.3%	13.8%	54.9%
1860	33.3	10.9	55.7
1880	39.9	8.2	51.9
1890	42.6	13.1	44.3
1904	44.8	13.8	41.4

SOURCES: TsGIA SSSR, f. 797, op. 96, d. 5, ll. 1 ob.-2; *IVO (1861)*, prilozhenie; *IVO (1881)*, prilozhenie; *IVO (1890–91)*, prilozhenie; *IVO (1903–04)*, prilozhenie. The percentages for 1860, because of rounding, add up to 99.9.

Another major obstacle to reform was the clerical soslovie, a phenomenon unknown in the West. Orthodoxy's special service estate made reform profoundly complex, for authorities had to address not only the clergy but also an immense social estate. Above all, the sheer numbers increased several-fold the magnitude and costs of reform; not only priests but also their sundry kin required pensions and welfare, education, and redefinition of legal status. Moreover, traditional paternalism dissuaded authorities from applying radical, draconian measures: however pressing the need, compassionate authorities directed reform only at *future* clergy, not the present population of clergy and their kin. Even in the case of sacristans, widely regarded as an unmitigated blight, authorities declined to undertake a systematic purge and at most charted plans for slow, long-term transformation. As a result, even after a half-century of reform, the majority of parish clergy still consisted of ill-educated deacons and sacristans (see table 25). Nor had attempts to improve the education of these lower servitors achieved much; by 1904 their level of education had actually regressed to prereform standards. The presence of the soslovie, finally, made the clergy unwilling partners in reform: vested interest, especially concern for their families' welfare, impelled many clergy to oppose reform in their soslovie rights, education, and service. Indeed, once "emancipation of the clergy" came to mean "emancipation of the Church from the clerical soslovie," the clergy's enthusiasm for reform quickly waned.

The politics of change in nineteenth-century Russia were also a major cause of misfired reform. Petrine institutions like the Synod were essentially static mechanisms, clocklike instruments designed to regulate, not reform. Hence they had authority to resolve day-to-day matters and to clarify existing law, but not to change unilaterally the governing statutes, whether it be the Ecclesiastical Regulation of 1721, the Censorship Statute of 1828, or the Statute of Diocesan Consistories of 1841. Such a static institutional order soon lost its effectiveness. What worked in 1721, 1828, or 1841 became disjointed from the rest of the state apparatus, even from current needs and policies. The strain of this static order was most apparent in a fixed budget, which had no provision for regular adjustment (even for inflation). Though less measurable elsewhere, such strain in the Church wrenched its entire apparatus, from censorship norms to relationships with civil authorities. Most important, the Synod's lack of legislative power pointed up the ultimate limitation on its "operational autonomy" in post-Petrine Russia: it could run the system, but not change it. That limitation, moreover, impelled authorities with increasing frequency in the late imperial period to employ extralegal devices, such as "explanatory circulars," to circumvent the complexity and risks of a formal revision in legal statutes and charters.

To resolve structural issues, the *ancien régime* routinely used extrainstitutional devices—the committees and commissions that clutter the bureaucratic landscape from the early nineteenth century. The jurisdiction of these committees was often ambiguous, normally limited to the study of issues and the preparation of preliminary proposals. The reliance upon such extraordinary mechanisms derived in part from the static character of governing institutions, but also from irresistible political utility: special commissions helped both to skirt questions of power and when the committee was packed, to create an artificial consensus. Consequently, implementation of a given reform was a test not merely of its viability but also of its acceptability to vested interests, whether in Petersburg or in the provinces. Here reform often encountered opposition and sabotage, as authorities found abundant reason to defer implementation, to reinterpret rules, and to seek special exemptions. Such opposition from below was in fact not necessarily specious; given the enormous diversity of the empire, reforms that worked for one region might prove inapplicable to another, where traditions and conditions were markedly different. Yet regional peculiarities often became a pretext for procrastination, a device to stall reform. Finally, reform also had to overcome opposition from other segments of the bureaucracy, especially when the issue cut across ministerial lines and violated other priorities and interests. As a result, committee plans at the last minute often ran afoul of other bureaucratic "parties," whether the accountants in the Ministry of Finance or the jurists in the State Council.

Réforme manquée in no small degree also measured the failure of personal autocracy. Striking indeed was the sharp decline in the emperor's personal role in reform. Compared with the massive archives of a Peter the

Great or Catherine the Great, bulging with plans and personal notes, the personal files of nineteenth-century rulers are almost barren, the dynamos of change now scattered throughout the bureaucracy. In Church reform the declining personal role from Nicholas to Alexander III was swift: Nicholas I spasmodically intervened in Church affairs, Alexander II rarely did more than read the documents of reform committees, and Alexander III played no role at all in planning or actively sponsoring counter-reform. Yet the entire system presupposed an active, dynamic emperor as the mainspring of action, as the arbiter of interministerial conflicts, and as the living constitution defining power relationships. Whether from sloth, as in the case of Alexander III, or sheer press of other business, the nineteenth-century emperor failed to play his Petrine role or to create a new structure to do it for him.[55] This failure was in fact central to the crisis of autocracy, provoking a continual struggle from the mid-nineteenth century to create a new supreme organ capable of integrating policy.

Given the lack of resources and the complexity of systemic change, reform often shrivelled to "gradualism"—that is, limited to certain areas or certain problems, or scheduled for piecemeal implementation over an indefinite period. That approach, even when mandated by necessity and hallowed by ideology, had the effect of paralyzing reform and mobilizing its adversaries. Above all, this provisional quality of reform tended to breed opposition, inviting outside scrutiny and criticism, especially by the boisterous press of the 1860s and 1870s. As a result, freshly conceived reform had to withstand searching critiques in early transitional stages, when the costs were high and the returns low. Moreover, the provisional quality of reform gave encouragement to antireformers, raising hopes that changes were not final, that one could yet turn back the clock. Nor did gradual reform fare well amidst the turbulent flux of imperial politics, where it could fall victim to external shifts in policy, as happened, for example, with the soslovie and administrative reforms in the early 1870s. Even reform already enacted was vulnerable to subversion by "explanatory circulars" without formal revision. This fluidity in fact gave reform little opportunity to work. One astute observer noted that Russia had no parties or systems, just men, and each man brought along his own system and schemes, overturning his predecessor's work and starting to build everything afresh.[56] That outlook engendered the notion that reform was ephemeral, pointless; as one priest wrote in response to the parish counter-reform of 1885, "Such is now [our] sick and negative age, that first

[55] For Alexander II's refusal to countenance structural reform, see Chernukha, *Vnutrenniaia politika*, pp. 15–135.

[56] OR GBL, f. 126, k. 3, d. 9, l. 195 ob. (Kireev's diary); see also N. Kh. Bunge's memoir, summarized in Taranovsky, "Politics of Counter-Reform," p. 171.

they demolish the old and establish something new, then once again they demolish that structure and start to build all over again."[57]

Reform stumbled, moreover, on the clergy's own weakness, their failure to form a cohesive "clerical party," for neither bishops nor priests coalesced into organized interest groups capable of pressing their demands upon state and society. In prereform Russia, no social group (the clergy included) formed a unified bloc; all lacked both autonomous institutions and the will to unite and press their demands.[58] After 1855 most groups, including the priests and bishops, attempted to organize and articulate their demands, but they repeatedly found their way blocked by the state, ever suspicious of pressure from below that threatened to undermine its traditional dominance. In the clergy's case, there were also important internal barriers to organization: sharp differences within the soslovie, a conviction that "partisan" politics was inherently bad and harmful, and a sense that naked claims for their own interests were selfish and "worldly." Moreover, bishop as well as priest looked for voluntary concessions from the state, reflecting the traditional *étatisme* of Russian political culture and their pessimism about reliance upon the dark and uncomprehending peasant masses. The state, however, failed to provide an easy solution or to allow the clergy, black or white, to organize; it denied conciliarism to bishops and enhanced power in the diocese to parish clergy. As a result, episcopal and priestly aspirations remained largely journalistic currents and furtive memoranda; they did not evolve into coherent programs with a definite body of organized adherents. As N. P. Rozanov observed, there was "an unsystematic, incoherent quality to the statements by liberals and conservatives in the clergy," who addressed "the problem of renewal in the Church" but failed "to work out a concrete program."[59] Although that amorphousness and disorganization applied in varying degrees to other sosloviia before 1905,[60] it was most pronounced and intense in the clergy, hamstrung by dispersion, ideology, and control from above.

Contrary to what one might expect, ecclesiastical tradition and canon law

[57] P. Runovskii, "O vosstanovlenii tserkovnykh prikhodov i prichtov, zakrytykh v 1869 g.," *RSP*, 1885, no. 14: 380.

[58] For the abortive attempts to create corporate estate institutions for the nobility and townspeople in the eighteenth century, see S. A. Korf, *Dvorianstvo i ego soslovnaia organizatsiia za stoletie, 1762–1855 gg.* (St. Petersburg, 1906), and A. Kizevetter, *Posadskaia obshchina v Rossii v XVIII v.* (Moscow, 1903).

[59] OR GBL, f. 250 (N. P. Rozanov), k. 2, d. 1, ll. 270–71 (N. P. Rozanov's memoir).

[60] For the gradual emergence of social ferment in the late nineteenth century, see the overview in *Obshchestvennoe dvizhenie v Rossii v nachale XX v.*, 4 vols. (St. Petersburg, 1909–11), vol. 1. Much recent research has focused upon the nobility; see: A. P. Korelin, *Dvorianstvo v poreformennoi Rossii, 1861–1904 gg.* (Moscow. 1979); Manning, *Crisis of the Old Order;* Gary Hamburg, "Land, Economy and Society in Tsarist Russia" (Ph.D. diss., Stanford University, 1978).

promoted reform in the earlier phases, becoming a barrier only toward the end of the Great Reforms. As discussions during the Nikolaevan prereforms and the Great Reforms reveal, prelates relegated custom and canons to secondary importance, especially in such ambiguous matters as economic aid for the clergy. Stalwarts like Filaret opposed reforms on strictly canonical grounds (for example, in his defense of gratuities), but even he felt obliged to buttress the argument with an array of practical considerations. More important, "tradition" played a curiously progressive role in legitimizing change in the 1850s and 1860s, for it justified the bishops' demands for the restoration of episcopal councils and the priests' desire for the reestablishment of elected clerical elders. Although authorities and even liberal clergy seldom referred to Western models (in contrast to other Great Reforms), the enormous gap in economic level and status was implicit in much of the reformist thinking of the fifties and sixties (for example, in the memoranda of Batiushkov, Valuev, and Bezak). Significantly, however, it was not aversion to Western models but fear of popular reaction that restricted imitation of the West: popular custom deterred prelates from innovations, even in terminology, that seemed likely to excite peasant agitation or enrich the Old Believers' propaganda (as, for example, parish councils or the ordination of celibate priests). After 1870, when bishops joined to resist priests' demands for greater authority and Tolstoi's schemes for judicial reform, the canonical arguments became ever more salient, and much of the debate in the seventies devolved into a tedious war of citations. Canonical argument, however, only increased the polarization, making compromise difficult and driving liberals to urge overt deviation from the canons.

To summarize, the whole experience from the 1820s to the 1880s showed that society *would* not and that authorities *could* not achieve fundamental reform in the Church. The result was *réforme manquée*—rarely effective and sometimes positively harmful to both the institution and the clergy.

Ineffectual as it was, reform nevertheless had a profound impact upon Church politics, giving rise to two diametrically opposed currents: "episcopal conservatism" and "priestly liberalism." If the Great Reforms failed to rebuild the Church, they nonetheless represented a watershed in social relations, aspirations, and self-consciousness. In the Church, as in society more generally, the reforms had the effect of 1789 in France, altering social relations and triggering major new currents of political and social thought.[61] It should be emphasized that this clerical "conservatism" and "liberalism" represented clusters of ideas, not formal programs, still less cohesive movements. Dispersed across the broken landscape of old Russia, deprived of class or professional organization, subject to local conditions and needs, both bishops and priests in varying proportions could adhere to one or the other current

[61]See Hans Rogger, "Reflections on Russian Conservatism," *JGO*, 14 (1966): 195–212.

of thought. Still, these two currents, summoned primarily by the painful experience of reform, provided the principal force in ecclesiastical politics and gradually polarized bishops and priests into differing, destructively antagonistic political camps.

Bishops had long nourished grievances against the state, but no coherent platform of episcopal conservatism emerged until the Great Reforms. Characteristically for this group, its first spokesman was not even a bishop but the layman A. N. Murav'ev, whose memoranda in the 1850s and 1860s provided the first formulation of episcopal goals and aspirations. The bishops, to be sure, had some inherent inclination toward "conservatism"—to preserve the faith, canon law, Church privilege, and their own prerogatives. Still, until the late 1860s most of them actively collaborated in reform. Aware of the Church's problems, hopeful of government munificence, they believed, like most of their contemporaries, that reform could simultaneously serve the best interests of both Church *and* clergy. As a rule, the most venturesome bishops in the sixties tended to come from the central provinces, where the clerical question was most acute and where anxiety about other confessions did not paralyze their will to countenance radical changes. That spirit of voluntary collaboration, however, began to dissipate in the late sixties, once the state not only denied substantial aid but also imposed sweeping reform with minimal consultation among bishops and often at the expense of both Church and clergy. Significantly, two bishops who had eagerly favored reform in the late 1850s, Metropolitans Arsenii of Kiev and Innokentii of Moscow, joined the ranks of episcopal *frondeurs* seeking to overturn the new statutes. Anxious about the surge of antireligious sentiments in contemporary society, skeptical if not hostile to the seminary and parish reforms, and appalled by the scheme for judicial reform, the great majority of provincial bishops by the mid-1870s united with Arsenii and Innokentii in condemning the reforms. Salient too was a new attitude toward parish clergy and seminarians. Alarmed by a new spirit of insubordination and demands for power, prelates began to revise their image of the "bad cleric"—from inexperienced to corrupt, from uneducated to miseducated, from impoverished to avaricious. Opposed to the pretentions of both priests and bureaucrats, prelates demanded decentralization—the shift of power from Petersburg to the diocese, the formation of regional metropolitanates, and the convocation of periodic episcopal councils, ideally under the mantle of a restored patriarchate.[62]

More public and raucous was the clamor of "priestly liberalism." It was initially confined to a small core of liberal priests who concentrated primarily upon the clergy's economic needs and, like the bishops, looked expectantly to autocracy for a solution to the Church's problems. Their principal goal

[62] For recurring murmurs about the patriarchate (inspired, no doubt, by Ivantsov-Platonov's essays in 1882), see OR GBL, f. 120, k. 3, d. 10, l. 45.

was to improve the white clergy by establishing better schools, providing more abundant and honorable support, and securing a greater role in Church affairs. In the name of social justice and, especially, better pastorship, the clerical liberals sought therefore a dual emancipation—principally from their dependence upon parishioners, but also from material want, poor education, and maladministration. But the failure of reform—indeed, the high cost it exacted upon the clerical estate—eroded the original *étatisme*, precipitating a subtle shift from earlier preoccupation with the state as chief benefactor to self-reliance, even to reassertion of corporate estate action. Ultimately, central organs like *Church-Social Messenger* and *Wanderer* argued that the clergy itself must solve its problems, from educating their sons to finding new modes of welfare. Strangely enough, that aspiration was built into Tolstoi's very tactic of reform, which depended financially upon clerical collaboration, but did so in the name of awakening parish clergy from apathy and inertia. Yet that tactic also sharpened intraclerical tensions, filling priests with hopes of new power in the Church and bishops with fears of uncanonical encroachment by both priests and procurators. In a very rudimentary way, too, the reforms stirred a growing interest among the clergy in lay society. Though most priests looked askance at the involvement of parishioners in Church affairs and joined bishops in opposing the custom of parish election of priests, some showed a growing concern for the laity's social needs, and a few, such as Ivantsov-Platonov, even suggested direct lay participation in Church government. By the early twentieth century, despairing of support from above, parish clergy would embrace a new vision of the laity, seeking an alliance of priests and parishioners in the name of social justice and Church reform.

A Church in Revolution

The dramatic denouement of conflict in the Church came in the first decades of the twentieth century, as the empire gradually drifted toward the abyss of revolution.[63] All of society, not just the clergy, grew increasingly restless from the late 1890s: students rose in protest, nobles joined forces to

---

[63] See Smolitsch, *Geschichte*, pp. 306–30; Simon, *Pobedonoscev und Kirchenpolitik*, pp. 249–64; N. F. Platonov, "Pravoslavnaia tserkov' v bor'be s revoliutsionnym dvizheniem v Rossii (1900–07 gg.)," *Ezhegodnik muzeia istorii religii i ateizma*, 4 (1960): 103–209; E. G. Kopenkin, "Sotsial'no-ekonomicheskaia i ideologicheskaia pereorientatsiia russkoi pravoslavnoi tserkvi v predrevoliutsionnoi Rossii kak faktor evoliutsii pravoslaviia" (Kandidatskaia dissertatsiia, Gosudarstvennyi pedagogicheskii institut im. Gertsena, 1973); B. V. Titlinov, *Tserkov' vo vremia revoliutsii* (Petrograd, 1924); P. N. Zyrianov, "Pravoslavnaia tserkov' v bor'be s pervoi russkoi revoliutsiei," *IZ*, 95 (1975): 314–55; and the still useful monograph by Curtiss, *Church and State*.

fight Witte's industrialization, peasants revolted with demands for more land, and workers struck for more rights and better wages. Between 1900 and 1904 the regime managed to alienate virtually every group in society and faced a broad liberation movement that aspired to emancipate all society from this "oriental despotism." Ferment permeated the Church as well: liberal Church journals raised their voices once more, churchmen reprinted Ivantsov-Platonov's program for radical reform, journalists debated the issue of "parish renewal," and some clergy toyed with ideas of Christian socialism and even helped to organize the workers.[64]

Once Bloody Sunday sounded the start of revolution in 1905, the bishops, like other segments of society, seized the opportunity to demand reform and to reclaim lost privileges. Their leader was the moderate metropolitan of St. Petersburg, Antonii (Vadkovskii), who penned the manifesto of episcopal revolt in February 1905 that inquired "whether now is not the proper time to abolish (or at least to moderate) the constant tutelage and all the vigilant control exercised by secular authorities over the life of the Church and its administrative activities, for this deprives the Church of its independence and initiative."[65] Spurning Pobedonostsev, the Synod in late March appealed to Nicholas II to summon a Church council of bishops to consider the sundry problems of Orthodoxy and, among other things, to deliberate the possible reestablishment of the patriarchate. Although the emperor deferred the council to "more favorable times," he nonetheless in principle approved the Synod's request.[66] In the interim the Synod conducted a survey of opinion among diocesan bishops, who expressed acute dissatisfaction with the state's domination of the Church, urged such administrative reforms as the establishment of regional metropolitanates, and generally supported proposals to restore the patriarchate.[67] Once the revolution subsided, the state shelved all plans for the council and subjected the bishops to the full brunt of the *Rasputinshchina,* so scandalous that it even alienated reactionary black-hundredist bishops like Antonii (Khrapovitskii).[68] By 1917 the bishops stood ready to abandon the *ancien régime.* When the chief procurator appealed

---

[64] See Jutta Scherrer, *Die Petersburger Religiös-Philosophischen Vereinigungen,* Forschungen zur Geschichte Osteuropas, vol. 19 (Berlin, 1973); for the debate about the parish, see the literature reviewed in P. A. Ivanov, *Reforma prikhoda* (Tomsk, 1914).

[65] A.R., *Istoricheskaia perepiska,* pp. 26–31.

[66] I. Smolitsch, "Der Konzilvorbereitungsausschuss des Jahres 1906," *Kirche im Osten,* 7 (1964): 53–93.

[67] These replies have been analyzed many times; see John Meyendorff, "Russian Bishops and Church Reform in 1905," in T. G. Stavrou and R. L. Nichols, eds., *Russian Orthodoxy under the Old Regime* (Minneapolis, 1978), pp. 170–82; James Cunningham, "Reform in the Russian Church, 1900–1906" (Ph.D. diss., University of Minnesota, 1973); Immekus, *Russische-Orthodoxe Landpfarrei;* and N. Sapsai, "Predsobornoe prisutstvie 1906 g." (Kandidatskaia dissertatsiia, Moskovskaia Dukhovnaia Akademiia, 1959).

[68] "V tserkovnykh krugakh pered revoliutsiei," *KA,* 31 (1928): 204–13.

to the Synod on 27 February 1917 for a proclamation in defense of the monarchy, it summarily refused.[69] By fall the Church summoned a national
council, which soon realized a dream long cherished by conservatives: reestablishment of the patriarchate.

The path tread by clerical liberalism was no less dramatic. On the eve of
1905 some priests in St. Petersburg were already drawn into discussions of
Christian socialism, and one of their number, Georgii Gapon, led the workers
on the ill-fated march on Bloody Sunday. Rooted in earlier interest and reinforced by the revolutionary rhetoric of 1905, the views of some parish clergy
drifted steadily leftward, seeking not merely political liberation but social
revolution as well. Especially liberal were the clergy in Petersburg. As one
wrote at the time, "the only solution for the clergy is this: to support the
interests of the peasants, to speak out in defense of their political and economic rights."[70] Even in more conservative Moscow the parish clergy, especially the younger generation, "had very liberal political views and unofficially belonged to the [liberal] Kadet Party."[71] Outside these main urban
centers clerical behavior was less predictable: some priests led rebellions,
some joined the reactionary black-hundredists, but most silently supported
the liberation movement or openly approved the kind of liberal reform
espoused by the Kadets.[72] At the very outset of the revolution even V. I.
Lenin admitted "the presence of a liberal, reformationist movement among
a certain part of the young Russian clergy,"[73] and a reactionary bishop later
complained that, "if not openly sympathetic to the revolution, [the parish
clergy] were either passive or secretly supported it."[74]

The principal focus of clerical liberalism in 1905 was the clergy's own
emancipation—reform to ease their lot, to revitalize the Church, and to shift
power from bishops to priests and laymen. The charter of clerical liberalism
appeared early in a manifesto of March 1905 by a "Group of Thirty-Two St.

[69]See A. V. Kartashev, "Revoliutsiia i sobor 1917–1918 gg.," *Bogoslovskaia mysl'*, 4 (1942):
75–101; R. Rössler, *Kirche und Revolution in Russland* (Cologne, 1969); I. Smolitsch, "Die
Russische Kirche in der Revolutionszeit von März bis Oktober 1917 und das Landeskonzil 1917
bis 1918," *Ostkirchlichen Studien*, 14 (1965): 3–34; J. S. Curtiss, *The Russian Church and
Soviet State* (New York, 1950).

[70]V. Myshtsyn, *Po tserkovno-obshchestvennym voprosam* (Sergiev-Posad, 1906), pt. 2, p.
36.

[71]OR GBL, f. 250, k. 2, d. 1, l. 195 (Rozanov's memoir); see also the close study by John H.
M. Geekie, "The Church and Politics in Russia, 1905–1917: A Study of the Political Behavior
of the Russian Orthodox Clergy in the Reign of Nicholas II" (Ph.D. diss., University of East
Anglia, 1976), esp. pp. 53–174.

[72]For a balanced account, see Curtiss, *Church and State*, pp. 196–207.

[73]V. I. Lenin, *Polnoe sobranie sochinenii*, 55 vols. (5th ed.; Moscow, 1967–70), 9: 211.

[74]Quoted in J. W. Bohon, "Reactionary Politics in Russia, 1905–1909" (Ph.D. diss., University of North Carolina, 1967), p. 145.

Petersburg Priests," all demanding fundamental reform in the Church, primarily through a shift of authority from the episcopate to the white clergy and laity.[75] The "renovationists" (*obnovlentsy*) argued that canon law was not immutable, that ordinary priests could become bishops, that ritual must give way to a faith of higher religious understanding, and that the ritual itself should be changed: "The accessibility and comprehensibility of the language used in religious services is something absolutely necessary, given the very nature of the liturgy as a social-religious act."[76] Although the renovationists' demands appeared first in "Red Petersburg," they were soon echoed across the empire, as diocesan assemblies from areas as diverse as Tver and Ekaterinoslav formulated essentially similar demands. By 1907 a leading Church journal gave this striking picture of the change in outlook effected by the Revolution:

> The movement for Church renewal continues to live and find defenders in that stratum which, earlier, knew it mainly by hearsay. If earlier this movement found support primarily among the clergy in the two capitals, it has now penetrated into remote provinces and found there many supporters, who have openly decided to come out in defense of this movement.[77]

Although authorities eventually suppressed both the Revolution and the renovationist movement in the clergy, driving its more radical leaders from the Church, it was hardly possible to stamp out the movement itself. It lived on in the last prewar years, primarily among the diocesan clergy and the faculties of the ecclesiastical schools.[78]

When revolution erupted anew in 1917, parish clergy made haste to use the revolutionary tumult to press their own demands once again.[79] On 7 March the Petrograd clergy formed an All-Russian Union of Democratic Clergy and Laymen, headed by former leaders of the Group of Thirty-Two St. Petersburg Priests. Theirs was indeed a program of sweeping ecclesiastical

---

[75] Gruppa Peterburgskikh sviashchennikov, *K tserkovnomu soboru* (St. Petersburg, 1906).

[76] Quoted in N. S. Gordienko and P. K. Kurochkin, "Liberal'no-obnovlencheskoe dvizhenie v russkom pravoslavii nachala XX v.," *Voprosy nauchnogo ateizma*, 7 (1969): 325–32.

[77] "Iz periodicheskoi pechati," *BV*, 1907, tom 3: 609.

[78] See Curtiss, *Church and State*, chaps. 5–8; F. Jockwig, "Kirche und Staatsduma: Zur politischen Aktivität der Russisch-Orthodoxen Kirche am Vorabend der Revolution," in *Wegzeichen. Festgabe zum 60. Geburtstag von Prof. Dr. H. M. Biedermann*, Das östliche Christentum, N.F., vol. 25 (Würzburg, 1971), pp. 446–50; and Geekie, "Church and Politics in Russia," pp. 175–272.

[79] In addition to the literature cited above, note 69, see A. Krasnov-Levitin and V. Shavrov, *Ocherki po istorii russkoi tserkovnoi smuty*, 3 pts. (Zurich, 1978), pt. 1; A. A. Shishkin, *Sushchnost' i kriticheskaia otsenka obnovlencheskogo raskola Russkoi pravoslavnoi tserkvi* (Kazan, 1970).

and social change: democratization of the Church and "Christianization of human relations," condemnation of capitalism, redistribution of land to the peasants, profit-sharing for the workers. The leading voice of Petrograd clergy became the *All-Russian Church-Social Messenger*, in spirit and title a direct heir to Popovitskii's liberal paper of the 1870s and 1880s. It propounded not only Church reform but also political revolution and radical social change. Provincial clergy too greeted the Revolution with eager anticipation. Their assemblies approved the overthrow of the monarchy, demanded similar changes in the Church, and sometimes issued resolutions in favor of social revolution.[80] Clergy in a few dioceses summarily deposed unpopular bishops or, as in circumspect Moscow, used pressure to force the prelate to resign.[81] In June 1917 some twelve hundred priests and laymen gathered in Moscow for the All Russian Congress of Clerics and Laymen, where they voted enthusiastically in favor of further democratization of Church and society. By late 1917, however, the priests substantially tempered their radicalism, partly because the Church Council of 1917–1918 answered some of their main aspirations, partly because the deepening political crisis and Bolshevik seizure of power had a sobering effect.[82] For the duration of the Revolution and Civil War (1918–1921) they acquiesced in the authority of the new patriarchate.

The apotheosis of clerical liberalism finally came in the "Living Church" (*Zhivaia tserkov'*) of the early 1920s. Alarmed by the mounting conflict between the patriarchate and the Soviet state, clerical liberals once again rose against episcopal authority, seeking both to avert a direct confrontation with the Bolsheviks and to realize old aspirations. In their "Program of Church Reform," adopted in May 1922, leaders of the Living Church affirmed "the justice of social revolution and world-wide unification of workers to defend the rights of the toiling and the exploited." They also emphasized their desire to purify popular religious consciousness and to eradicate "the superstitions

[80]For example, the diocesan assembly in Voronezh resolved to "support peasant demands: (1) for the abolition of private property of land; (2) for equal land use; and (3) for labor norms" (V. N. Dunaev, "Vystuplenie krest'ian Voronezhskoi gubernii protiv reaktsionnykh deistvii dukhovenstva," *Sbornik rabot aspirantov Voronezhskoi gosudarstvennogo universiteta*, 1 [Voronezh, 1965]: 146).

[81]For example, see the resolution of the diocesan assembly in Vladimir to "remove Archbishop Aleksei . . . as a member of the [black-hundredist] Union of Russian People and because of his connections with Rasputin" ("Zhurnaly Vladimirskogo eparkhial'nogo s"ezda dukhovenstva i mirian," *Vladimirskie EV*, 1917, no 20–21:215).

[82]The Church Council of 1917–1918, besides reestablishing the patriarchate, went far toward recognizing the old demands of parish clergy for diocesan assemblies, greater stress on sermons, and the like, but it also allotted considerable authority for the laity as well. For the import of these changes, see Franz Jockwig, *Der Weg der Laien auf das Landeskonzil der Russischen Orthodoxen Kirche Moskau, 1917–1918* (Würzburg, 1971), esp. pp. 215–18.

and prejudices that have been nourished by popular ignorance and monastic exploitation of the religious feelings of the popular masses." To do that, the Living Church sought to clarify some major theological issues, proposed to simplify the liturgy to "bring it closer to popular understanding," and wanted to make "sermons an integral part of the liturgy." Yet the most striking element in the program was its attack on monasticism; it rejected in principle "the monastic teaching of individual salvation through the denial of the world and natural human needs." To achieve "a final liquidation of episcopal despotism," the Living Church sought both to consecrate married priests as bishops and to restructure power and administration, making the bishop, priests, and parishioners equal partners in the management of Church affairs. Finally, like many generations before them, these priests of the Living Church sought as well "an emancipation of the clergy from the contemporary form of support that is so humiliating, places them under the power of kulak elements, and denigrates their pastoral dignity."[83] For a short time leaders of the Living Church seized control of the Church's apparatus, deposed the patriarch, confirmed the right of priests to remarry, adopted the Gregorian calendar of the West, introduced Russian into Church services (in lieu of Slavonic), and consecrated the first married priests as bishops of the Church. Yet, though broadly popular among the white clergy, the Living Church failed—as had clerical liberalism since the 1860s—to gain a base of support among the laity, and it eventually disintegrated, surrendering its power once more to the patriarchate.

Profound cleavages separating state, episcopacy, and parish clergy neutralized the Church and clergy as an effective political and social force in the waning years of the *ancien régime*. Even as revolution engulfed Russia in 1905, the Group of Thirty-Two Priests complained that the clergy were powerless, lacking either unity or direction, fearful and uncertain of their posture amidst this revolutionary cataclysm.[84] Perhaps the most striking element in ecclesiastical politics was not the clergy's conservatism or liberalism, the black-hundredist tirades of reactionary bishops or the revolutionary harangues by some "red priests"; rather, it was the coexistence of both currents—the inability of churchmen high or low to fight cohesively for the old regime or even for a new one. The backwardness of social groups in 1917 was not unique to the clergy. All others, even the relatively cohesive working class, lacked unity and organization, leaving them vulnerable to manipula-

---

[83]"Programma tserkovnykh reform, namechennykh gruppoi dukhovenstva i mirian *Zhivaia tserkov'* v razvitie svoikh osnovnykh polozhenii, priniatykh na uchreditel'nom sobranii gruppy 16–29 maia 1922 goda," *Zhivaia tserkov'*, 1922, no. 10: 17–18. See also "Ustav gruppy pravoslavnogo belogo dukhovenstva *Zhivaia tserkov'*," ibid., 1922, no. 4/5: 18–19.

[84]Gruppa Peterburgskikh sviashchennikov, *K tserkovnomu soboru*, pp. i-ix.

tion by the various political parties springing to life after the monarchy's fall. Yet, perhaps more than any other group, the Orthodox clergy entered this revolutionary era wholly unprepared for struggle. Neither priests nor bishops had a coherent program, national organization, or recognized leadership. By the time the clergy attempted to create organs and mobilize adherents, their moment was past, for by then far more worldly parties, with far more worldly visions, had taken to the streets to preach a new gospel for the future.

GLOSSARY

academy (*akademiia*)	Institution of advanced ecclesiastical education, formally equivalent to the university
black clergy	Monastic clergy
chief procurator (*ober-prokuror*)	Chief lay official of the Church, appointed by the emperor as his personal overseer.
Church school (*dukhovnaia shkola*)	Collective term for all levels of ecclesiastical schools
consistory (*konsistoriia*)	Diocesan board of clergy assisting the bishop in the conduct of diocesan affairs
diachok	Sacristan rank, with the right to don a surplice
diocese (*eparkhiia*)	Main administrative unit of the Church, directly subordinate to the Synod and usually identical to the province in civil administration
district (*uezd*)	Subdivision of diocese and province
district school (*dukhovnoe uchilishche*)	Four-year elementary school of the Church
episcopal council (*pomestnyi sobor*)	Formal council of bishops, usually embracing a particular region
Old Belief (*staroobriadchestvo*)	Religious movement of Orthodox dissenters who rejected the official Church because of liturgical reforms in the seventeenth century
ordained clergy (*sviashchennosluzhiteli*)	The upper ranks of archpriest, priest, and deacon (all given formal rites of holy ordination)
parish councils (*popechitel'stva*)	Local Church councils, established in 1864
parish school	Elementary school established by local clergy for the children of laity
pomoch'	Parish assistance to local clergy in the cultivation of their land
ponomar	Sacristan rank, lower than diachok and without the right to wear a surplice
provincial commission (*gubernskoe prisutstvie*)	Boards established in 1863 by the Special Commission to oversee Church reforms at the provincial level
psalmist (*psalomshchik*)	New sacristan title, established in 1869

razbor	Conscription of surplus clerical sons and unworthy sacristans
sacristan (*tserkovnosluzhitel'*; also *prichetnik*)	Unordained clergy in the ranks of diachok and ponomar (later, psalmist), without holy ordination or power to administer the sacraments
schism (*raskol*)	Official terminology for the Old Belief
Second Section	Subdivision of the emperor's personal chancellery, charged with overseeing the coordination of changes in state law
seminary (*seminariia*)	Middle stratum of Church schools, formally equivalent to the gymnasium in state education
shtat	Registry of positions; a table of organization, fixing a rough proportion between the number of clerical positions and parish population
soslovie (pl., *sosloviia*)	Estate (*état*; *Stand*)
Special Commission	Chief committee for Church reform, established in 1862 and abolished in 1885
State Council	Chief legislative body of the empire, created in 1810 to examine new laws and statutes
Stundism	Protestant sectarian movement appearing in the second half of the nineteenth century
superintendent (*blagochinnyi*)	Local supervisor of parish clergy
surplice (*stikhar'*)	Outer vestment worn over the cassock by the deacon and diachok during the liturgy
typicon (*tipikon*; also *tserkovnyi ustav*)	Guide to the order and form of the liturgy and other Church services
Uniate Church	Established in 1596; recognized the pope's authority, but retained a Slavonic liturgy and married clergy; formally absorbed into the Russian Orthodox Church in 1839
white clergy	Parish clergy
zemstvo	New units of self-government at the provincial and district level, established in 1864

A NOTE ON SOURCES

The printed sources available for the study of the Russian Church are voluminous and rich. Apart from such well-known collections as the secular law codes (*Polnoe sobranie zakonov*), the Church published its own compendia of decrees and resolutions, many of which did not appear in the secular legal collections.[1] The annual reports of the chief procurator, published almost without interruption from 1836 to 1914, also contain much useful information, in particular, regular statistical material on such matters as the number of churches, clergy, and schools.[2] The Church's internal publications, although rare and generally unavailable in Western libraries, are exceedingly valuable; intended for official use only, they contain a wealth of information on the Church's various institutions, their problems, and authorities' attempts to set things aright.[3]

More interesting still is the ecclesiastical press, which first began to appear in the 1820s but proliferated only after 1855 (much as in fact happened in secular publications). One type was the "thick journal" of the main academies; though comprising primarily religious and philosophical materials, these journals in the Great Reforms began to include substantial sections on contemporary problems, especially those that directly concerned the clerical question.[4] Here, too, appeared much historical material, especially the personal correspondence and papers of leading prelates and Church figures. A new kind of press, the diocesan serials (*eparkhial'nye vedomosti*), appeared only in 1860, gradually spreading, until by the end of the century they existed in most dioceses. Appearing weekly or biweekly, the diocesan serials consisted of two parts: an "official section," with the bishops' resolutions, copies of Synod decrees, and other official announcements; and an "unofficial

[1] For a convenient collection of material, see S. T. Barsov, *Sbornik deistvuiushchikh postanovlenii*, and S. V. Kalashnikov, *Alfavitnyi ukazatel' deistvuiushchikh i rukovodstvennykh kanonicheskikh postanovlenii, ukazov, opredelenii i rasporiazhenii Sv. Prav. Sinoda (1721–1901 gg.)* (3rd ed.; St. Petersburg, 1901).

[2] Although the chief procurator's reports (*IVO*) contain useful appendixes, they rarely disclose much about internal policies or, especially, plans. Even raw data are not beyond reproach. In 1905 the historian Golubinskii urged that these reports be composed such that they "not represent idiotic lies, but depict the true condition of things" ("O reforme v byte russkoi tserkvi," *ChOIDR*, 246 [1913], issloedovaniia: 93).

[3] Both GBL and GPB contain valuable internal publications; to identify these rare, often anonymous works, the call number is given in the more important cases.

[4] For example, *Pravoslavnoe obozrenie, Trudy Kievskoi dukhovnoi akademii, Pravoslavnyi sobesednik, Strannik*, and *Khristianskoe chtenie*.

part," containing articles on Church reform, copies of sermons, essays on pastoral service, and occasional documents or historical studies. Although tightly constricted by censorship, the papers addressed some major issues, especially in the 1860s and upon occasion thereafter.[5] Finally, for one brief period the parish clergy had a "secular newspaper," *Tserkovno-obshchest-vennyi vestnik*, which appeared three times each week for some dozen years (1874–1886). It was secular insofar as, until 1883, it remained under government, not Church, censorship; as a result, it published candid and wide-ranging articles, mostly from the pens of provincial clergy.[6] Other secular organs took some interest in the Church after 1855, occasionally but not often including useful commentaries on the problem of Church reform.

Of the immense stockpiles of neglected archival material, by far the most important is preserved in TsGIA SSSR, which contains the main institutional archives of the Church. Here is Petersburg's official memory—its reports, plans, drafts, and investigations, all recording the capital's perception of the Church's problems and the proper direction of reform. The single largest collection is the Synodal archive (fond 796), an immense preserve with more than one-half million archival units for the whole Synodal period. The primary set of materials remain catalogued in the annual inventories (*opisi*), each including 1,500 to 3,000 files (ranging from vital reform files to petty requests for a pension). Beyond the main annual inventories, this collection also includes a special section for the Synod's resolutions (bound as separate volumes, with the "secret resolutions" in special tomes), a division of diocesan reports (*otchety*, begun in the mid-nineteenth century, with descriptions of the condition of diocesan administration and local clergy and the spiritual complexion of the laity), a "secret section" (opis' 205, preserving material deemed too sensitive for the general staff of Synod clerks to see), and a miscellaneous section (opis' 445, comprising various reform journals and much material uncatalogued from the revolutionary turbulence of 1917.)

The collection of the chief procurator (fond 797) contains relatively little material before 1840 (with just ten opisi for the entire preceding period), but thereafter—parallel with Protasov's rise—it became an important, but by no means main, center of documentation. For the period 1840–1880 the archive collection is well ordered. Each year's annual registry is systematic and indexed; it usually overlaps materials in the Synodal archive, but it also contains original documents not found there. After 1880, characteristic of the

[5] The *eparkhial'nye vedomosti* are of stupendous magnitude, representing a thick volume for each year per diocese (most commenced publication in the 1860s or 1870s). Given the immense quantity, I have been able to read systematically vedomosti for every year from only ten dioceses (Iaroslavl, Irkutsk, Kaluga, Kiev, Kursk, Riazan, Saratov, Tula, Viatka, and Vladimir); for the remaining dioceses, I have read only selected years (1863, 1865, 1869, 1875, 1880, 1885) and the more important articles indexed in the main periodical bibliographies.

[6] For the establishment and juridical status of *TsOV*, see above, pp. 390–95, 415–17.

disintegration of bureaucratic regularity in late imperial Russia, the files are in great disarray; much valuable material in fact ended up in the personal files of the chief procurator, K. P. Pobedonostsev (fond 1574).

The archive of the Special Commission (fond 804) is immensely rich and complex. The first section (razdel 1) includes the working papers of the commission—its own legislative drafts, reports from diocesan authorities and provincial commissions, and correspondence with pertinent state authorities. The second section (razdel 2) contains the commission's printed memoranda, for the most part duplicating materials found in the first section. The third section (razdel 3) contains the commission's original journals (dd. 470–73), each signed by the commission's members and formally confirmed by the emperor. The great bulk of this section consists of the clerical opinions of 1863, more than four hundred volumes of hand-written replies from every parish staff in the empire. Scrawled on dark yellow or deep blue paper, the ink paled and smudged, these documents are a mine of information, not only commenting upon the needs of clergy but often speaking more broadly to the needs of their parishioners as well.

The central archives include a host of other, less important institutional collections. The files of the St. Petersburg Committee for Ecclesiastical Censorship (TsGIA SSSR, fond 807), like church censorship itself, declined steadily in importance in the Great Reforms, never fully recovering its erstwhile control. Still, the files contain much of interest, shedding light not only on the perennial battle between author and censor but also on the mounting strain between secular and ecclesiastical censorship. The various government archives contain some useful information, such as the periodic reports of the Third Section (TsGAOR, f. 109) and the response of ministries and the State Council to questions of clerical reform (TsGIA SSSR, ff. 1275, 1249). Much valuable material is also found in the archive of the St. Petersburg Ecclesiastical Academy (OR GPB, f. 573), which includes a host of major memoranda (in particular, Isidor's collection), diverse materials on reform, and a mass of documentation on academy business.

Of a different character are the clergy's service records—the *klirovye vedomosti*, preserved only in regional and provincial archives. Each file contains a standard set of data on the church (its date of establishment, landholdings, other resources, number and status of parishioners, and support available for local clergy) and on each cleric (age, education, past career, family status, personal conduct, number of sermons, previous record of awards and punishments). In some cases, such as Kiev and Tver, the replies from each district were bound together for a single year; elsewhere authorities sometimes bound all the replies for a single parish over a protracted period. Given the stupendous volume of this material (each district had several hundred clerics in any given year), I have made selective use of these files—for metropolitan Moscow, a north central diocese (Tver), a diocese in the fertile black soil zone (Kursk), one diocese in the western provinces (Kiev), and two dioceses in Siberia (Tomsk and Irkutsk). In the present work, full statistical data are offered for areas in a single diocese (Tver), with briefer summary analyses for the other dioceses, in order to provide a full picture of complexities within a specific area and the broader regional patterns across the empire.

Finally, rich information can also be gleaned from the numerous personal archives of leading churchmen and bureaucrats. Of extraordinary value is the massive archive of Metropolitan Filaret of Moscow, both the main collection in OR GBL (f. 316) and the smaller set of sensitive materials in TsGIA SSSR (f. 832). The main manuscript depositories contain useful material in the archives of some statesmen heavily involved in the question of Church reform, such as P. N. Batiushkov (OR GPB, f. 52), P. A. Valuev (TsGIA SSSR, f. 908), A. P. Tolstoi (OR GBL, f. 302), and K. P. Pobedonostsev (TsGIA SSSR, f. 1574; OR GLB, f. 230). Private materials—diaries, letters, draft proposals—are a vital supplement to the official archives, casting light upon decisions that were deliberately obscured in routine documents. Although some of this private material appeared in prerevolutionary serials (collections of letters and the like), most of it was simply too sensitive to pass the gauntlet of censorship.

SELECTED BIBLIOGRAPHY

The single best guide to sources and secondary literature is Igor Smolitsch, *Geschichte der russischen Kirche* (pp. xv-liii). Additional references can be gleaned from G. V. Florovskii's *Puti russkogo bogosloviia* (pp. 521–74), A. P. Dobroklonskii's *Rukovodstvo po istorii russkoi tserkvi*, and Edward Kasinec, "A Bibliographical Essay," in T. Stavrou and R. L. Nichols, eds., *Russian Orthodoxy under the Old Regime* (Minneapolis, 1978), pp. 205–28. Consult also the library catalogues of the main theological academies: *Katalog sistematicheskii (po distsiplinam) russkikh knig, nakhodiashchikhsia v biblioteke Leningradskoi dukhovnoi akademii*, 3 vols. (Leningrad, 1954); *Sistematicheskii katalog knig v biblioteke Moskovskoi dukhovnoi akademii*, 5 vols. (Moscow, 1881–1910); and *Alfavitnyi ukazatel' knig i rukopisei, nakhodiashchikhsia v biblioteke Peterburgskoi dukhovnoi akademii*, 6 vols. (St. Petersburg, 1886–89). For clerical memoirs and diaries, see P. A. Zaionchkovskii, ed., *Istoriia dorevoliutsionnoi Rossii v dnevnikakh i vospominaniiakh*, 3 vols. to date (Moscow, 1976). For the neglected but invaluable ecclesiastical serials, see the indexes in Iu. I. Masonov et al., *Ukazateli soderzhaniia russkikh zhurnalov i prodolzhaiushchikh izdanii, 1755–1970 gg.* (Moscow, 1970).

Listed below are some of the more important, but little known, works in Church history.

Archival Sources

Gosudarstvennyi arkhiv Irkutskoi oblasti
    f. 50   Irkutskaia dukhovnaia konsistoriia
Gosudarstvennyi arkhiv Kalininskoi oblasti
    f. 103   Tverskaia uchenaia arkhivnaia komissiia
    f. 160   Tverskaia dukhovnaia konsistoriia
Gosudarstvennyi arkhiv Kurskoi oblasti
    f. 20   Kurskaia dukhovnaia konsistoriia
Gosudarstvennyi arkhiv Tomskoi oblasti
    f. 170   Tomskaia dukhovnaia konsistoriia
Institut russkoi literatury (Pushkinskii dom)
    f. 3   Aksakovy
    f. 34   S. O. Burachek
    f. 220   N. S. Leskov

f. 265   Arkhiv zhurnala *Russkaia starina*
f. 274   M. I. Semevskii
f. 293   M. Iu. Stasiulevich
f. 319   P. S. Usov
f. 361   I. M. Snegirev
f. 579   P. A. Pletnev
f. 616   A. D. Zheltukhin
Leningradskoe otdelenie Instituta istorii
f. 115   Kollektsiia rukopisnykh knig
Otdel rukopisei. Gosudarstvennaia biblioteka im. V. I. Lenina
f. 23   S. A. Belokurov
f. 120   M. N. Katkov
f. 126   Kireevy i Novikovy
f. 149   Leonid (Krasnopevkov)
f. 178   Muzeinoe sobranie
f. 201   A. S. Norov
f. 214   Optyna pustyn'
f. 218   Sobranie postuplenii s 1948 g.
f. 230   K. P. Pobedonostsev
f. 231   M. P. Pogodin
f. 250   N. P. Rozanov
f. 262   Savva (Tikhomirov)
f. 302   A. P. Tolstoi
f. 304   Troitse-sergeevskaia lavra (sobranie)
f. 316   Filaret (Drozdov)
f. 327   Cherkasskie
f. 341   Sheremetevy
f. 344   P. P. Shibanov
f. 356   A. B. Derman
Otdel rukopisei. Gosudarstvennaia publichnaia biblioteka im. Saltykova-Shchedrina
f. 14   I. S. Aksakov
f. 15   Aleksandro-nevskaia lavra
f. 37   A. I. Artem'ev
f. 52   Batiushkovy
f. 78   D. N. Bludov
f. 208   A. V. Golovnin
f. 253   A. A. Dmitrievskii
f. 377   I. P. Kornilov
f. 378   F. P. Kornilov
f. 391   A. A. Kraevskii
f. 498   A. N. Murav'ev i M. I. Semenov
f. 531   A. S. Norov

f. 539   V. F. Odoevskii
f. 542   Oleniny
f. 550   Osnovnoe sobranie rukopisnykh knig
f. 573   Sankt-Peterburgskaia dukhovnaia akademiia
f. 692   P. P. Serebrennikov
f. 780   D. A. Tolstoi
f. 000   V. A. Tsee
f. 874   S. N. Shubinskii
f. 1000   Novoe sobranie rukopisnykh knig

Tsentral'nyi gosudarstvennyi arkhiv literatury i iskusstva
f. 46   P. I. Bartenev
f. 194   N. V. Elagin
f. 275   N. S. Leskov
f. 373   M. P. Pogodin
f. 427   S. A. Rachinskii
f. 459   A. S. Suvorin
f. 1348   Sobranie pisem pisatelei, uchenykh i gosudarstvennykh deiatelei

Tsentral'nyi gosudarstvennyi arkhiv Oktiabr'skoi revoliutsii
f. 109   Tret'e otdelenie
f. 586   V. K. Pleve
f. 677   Aleksandr II
f. 678   Aleksandr III
f. 722   Mramornyi dvorets
f. 728   Zimnii dvorets

Tsentral'nyi gosudarstvennyi istoricheskii arkhiv goroda Moskvy
f. 203   Moskovskoe dukhovnoe pravlenie

Tsentral'nyi gosudarstvennyi istoricheskii arkhiv SSSR
f. 675   Makarii (Bulgakov)
f. 776   Glavnoe upravlenie po delam pechati
f. 777   Petrogradskii komitet po delam pechati
f. 779   Tsentral'nyi komitet tsenzury inostrannoi
f. 796   Kantseliariia Sv. Sinoda
f. 797   Kantseliariia Ober-prokurora
f. 799   Khoziaistvennoe upravlenie
f. 802   Komissiia dukhovnykh uchilishch
f. 804   Osoboe prisutstvie po delam pravoslavnogo dukhovenstva
f. 807   S.-Peterburgskii komitet dukhovnoi tsenzury
f. 832   Filaret (Drozdov)
f. 908   P. A. Valuev
f. 1149   Gosudarstvennyi sovet: Departament zakonov
f. 1275   Sovet ministrov
f. 1281   Sovet ministra vnutrennikh del

f. 1282   Kantseliariia ministerstva vnutrennikh del
f. 1284   Ministerstvo vnutrennikh del: Departament obshchikh del
f. 1574   K. P. Pobedonostsev
f. 1604   I. D. Delianov
Tsentral'nyi gosudarstvennyi istoricheskii arkhiv Ukrainskoi SSR
f. 127   Kievskaia dukhovnaia konsistoriia
Houghton Library, Harvard University
    Kilgour Collection
Bibliothèque slave, Paris
    Archives Gagarine

Contemporary Newspapers and Journals

Astrakhanskie eparkhial'nye vedomosti
Birzhevye vedomosti
Bogoslovskii vestnik
Chernigovskie eparkhial'nye vedomosti
Chteniia v Obshchestve liubitelei dukhovnogo prosveshcheniia
Den'
Dukh khristianina
Dukhovnyi dnevnik
Dukhovnyi vestnik
Dushepoleznoe chtenie
Golos
Grazhdanin
Iaroslavskie eparkhial'nye vedomosti
Irkutskie eparkhial'nye vedomosti
Kaluzhskie eparkhial'nye vedomosti
Khersonskie eparkhial'nye vedomosti
Khristianskoe chtenie
Kievskie eparkhial'nye vedomosti
Kostromskie eparkhial'nye vedomosti
Kurskie eparkhial'nye vedomosti
Litovskie eparkhial'nye vedomsti
Minskie eparkhial'nye vedomsti
Moskovskie eparkhial'nye vedomosti
Moskovskie vedomosti
Nedelia
Nizhegorodskie eparkhial'nye vedomosti
Orenburgskie eparkhial'nye vedomosti
Orlovskie eparkhial'nye vedomosti
Penzenskie eparkhial'nye vedomosti

Poltavskie eparkhial'nye vedomosti
Pravoslavnoe obozrenie
Pravoslavnyi sobesednik
Pribavleniia k Tvoreniiam Sviatykh Otets
Riazanskie eparkhial'nye vedomosti
Rukovodstvo dlia sel'skikh pastyrei
Russkie vedomosti
Russkii vestnik
Samarskie eparkhial'nye vedomosti
S.-Peterburgskie vedomosti
Saratovskie eparkhial'nye vedomosti
Smolenskie eparkhial'nye vedomosti
Sovremennye izvestiia
Sovremennyi listok
Strannik
Syn otechestva
Tomskie eparkhial'nye vedomosti
Trudy Kievskoi dukhovnoi akademii
Tserkovno-obshchestvennyi vestnik
Tserkovnye vedomosti
Tul'skie eparkhial'nye vedomosti
Tverskie eparkhial'nye vedomosti
L'Union chrétienne
Vecherniaia gazeta
Vera i razum
Viatskie eparkhial'nye vedomosti
Vladimirskie eparkhial'nye vedomosti
Vologodskie eparkhial'nye vedomosti
Volynskie eparkhial'nye vedomosti

Printed Sources

Arkhangel'skii, S. A. "Iz vospominanii." *Vladimirskie EV*, 1875, nos. 10–14.
Austin, M. R., ed. *The Church in Derbyshire in 1823–24: The Parochial Visitation of the Reverend Samuel Butler*. Derby, 1972.
Barsov, N. I., ed. "K biografii Innokentiia, arkhiepiskopa khersonskogo." *KhCh*, 1883, tom 2: 629–56; 1884, tom 1: 188–224; tom 2: 99–161.
Barsov, S. T. *Sbornik deistvuiushchikh i rukovodstvennykh tserkovnykh i tserkovno-grazhdanskikh postanovlenii po vedomstvu pravoslavnogo ispovedaniia*. St. Petersburg, 1885.
Barsukov, I., ed. *Pis'ma Innokentiia, mitropolita moskovskogo i kolomenskogo*. 2 vols. St. Petersburg, 1897–98.

Beliaev, A. A., ed. "Professor Moskovskoi dukhovnoi akademii P. S. Kazanskii i ego perepiska s arkhiepiskopom Kostromskim Platonom." *BV*, 1903, nos. 1, 5, 7–9, 12; 1904, nos. 3, 5–8; 1905, nos. 7–10, 1910, no 2; 1911, nos. 6, 9. 12; 1912, nos. 3–9; 1913, no 5; 1914, nos. 1–4, 5–9, 12; 1916, nos. 2–4.

[Belliustin, I. S.] *Opisanie sel'skogo dukhovenstva*. Paris [Leipzig], 1858.

Bogdanovich, A. V. *Tri poslednikh samoderzhtsa*. Moscow-Petrograd, 1924.

Bogoslavskii, G. K. *Chernigovskaia seminariia 50 let nazad*. Chernigov, 1915.

Briantsev, I. D. "Vospominaniia." *Smolenskie EV*, 1890, nos. 10, 14, 20.

[Elagin, N. V.] *Beloe dukhovenstvo i ego interesy*. St. Petersburg, 1881.

————. *Chego nado zhelat' dlia nashei tserkvi*. 2 vols. St. Petersburg, 1882–85.

————. *Predpolagaemaia reforma tserkovnogo suda*. 2 vols. St. Petersburg, 1873.

————. *Russkoe dukhovenstvo*. Berlin, 1859.

Filaret (Drozdov). *Mneniia, otzyvy i pis'ma Filareta, mitropolita moskovskogo i kolomenskogo po raznym voprosam 1821–67 gg*. Moscow, 1905.

————. *Perepiska Filareta, mitropolita moskovskogo, s S. D. Nechaevym*. St. Petersburg, 1895.

————. *Pis'ma Filareta, mitropolita moskovskogo i kolomenskogo, k A. N. Murav'evu*. Kiev, 1869.

————. "Pis'ma Filareta, mitropolita moskovskogo i kolomenskogo, k A. V. Gorskomu." *Prib. TSO*, 50 (1882): 541–70; 51 (1882): 55–70, 396–442.

————. *Pis'ma Filareta, mitropolita moskovskogo i kolomenskogo, k Filaretu Gumilevskomu*. Moscow, 1884.

————. *Pis'ma Filareta, mitropolita moskovskogo i kolomenskogo, k namestniku Sv. Troitse-sergievoi lavry arkhimandrita Antoniiu, 1831–67 gg*. 4 vols. Moscow, 1877–84.

————. *Pis'ma Filareta, mitropolita moskovskogo i kolomenskogo, k pokoinomu arkhiepiskopu Alekseiu*. Moscow, 1887.

————. *Pis'ma Filareta, mitropolita moskovskogo i kolomenskogo, k Vitaliiu*. Moscow, 1887.

————. *Pis'ma Filareta, mitropolita moskovskogo i kolomenskogo, k Vysochaishim Osobam i raznym drugim litsam*. 2 vols. Tver, 1888.

————. *Pis'ma kolomenskogo i moskovskogo mitropolita Filareta k Gavriilu, arkhiepiskopu riazanskomu*. Moscow, 1868.

————. *Polnoe sobranie rezoliutsii Filareta, mitropolita moskovskogo i kolomenskogo, po raznym voprosam*. 3 vols. Moscow, 1905.

————. *Sobranie mnenii i otzyvov Filareta, mitropolita moskovskogo i kolomenskogo, po delam pravoslavnoi tserkvi na Vostoke*. St. Petersburg, 1886.

————. *Sobranie mnenii i otzyvov Filareta, mitropolita moskovskogo i kolomenskogo, po uchebnym i tserkovno-gosudarstvennym voprosam.* 6 vols. Moscow, 1885–88.

————. "Zametki i pis'ma Filareta mitr. moskovskogo." *BV*, 1916, no. 10–12.

Germogen (Dobronravin). "Moe proshloe." *Str.*, 1908, nos. 1–11.

Giliarov-Platonov, N. P. *Iz perezhitogo.* 2 vols. Moscow, 1886.

————. *Voprosy very i tserkvi.* 2 vols. Moscow, 1905–06.

Gloriantov, V. I. "Vospominaniia." *RA*, 1906, no 2: 209–20; no. 11: 471–80.

Glubokovskii, F. G. *Perezhitoe i perechuvstvovannoe v Pinskom dukhovnom uchilishche.* Brest, 1899.

Gorskii, A. V. "Dnevnik A. V. Gorskogo." *Prib. TSO*, 1884–85. (Also separate offprint: Moscow, 1885.)

————. "Neizdannye mesta iz 'Dnevnika' A. V. Gorskogo." *BV*, 1914, no. 10/11.

————. "Vospominaniia." *Russkoe obozrenie*, 1896, no. 1.

"Graf A. Kh. Benkendorf o Rossii." *KA*, 37 (1929): 138–74.

Griaznov, E. *Iz shkol'nykh vospominanii byvsh. seminarista.* Vologda, 1903.

Iosif (Semashko). *Zapiski.* 3 vols. St. Petersburg, 1883.

Ismailov, F. F. "Iz vospominanii." *Str.*, 1882, no. 9; 1883, nos. 1–7.

————. "Iz zapisok starogo professora seminarii." *PO*, 1870, no. 7: 94–124.

————. *Vzgliad na sobstvennuiu proshedshuiu zhizn'.* Moscow, 1860.

Ivantsov-Platonov, A. *O russkom tserkovnom upravlenii.* St. Petersburg, 1898. Originally published in *Rus'*, 1882, nos. 1–16.

"Iz biografii Innokentiia." *RA*, 1911, tom 2: 167–90.

"Iz bumag S. D. Nechaeva." *RA*, 1893, nos. 4–5.

"Iz pisem Innokentiia." *RA*, 1907, no. 8: 432–38.

Izvlecheniia iz otcheta po vedomstvu dukhovnykh del pravoslavnogo ispovedaniia. St. Petersburg, 1837–63. New series title: *Izvlecheniia iz vsepoddanneishego otcheta ober-prokurora Sv. Sinoda po vedomstvu pravoslavnogo ispovedaniia.* St. Petersburg, 1866–84. New series title: *Vsepoddanneishii otchet oberprokurora Sv. Sinoda po vedomstvu pravoslavnogo ispovedaniia.* St. Petersburg, 1886–1915.

"Iz zapisok arkhiepiskopa Leonida." *RA*, 1905, nos. 8, 12; 1906, nos. 4–5; 1907, nos. 10, 12; 1908, no. 4.

"Iz zapisok arkhiepiskopa Nikanora." *RA*, 1908, no. 5; 1909, nos. 2, 5.

Katanskii, A. A. *Vospominaniia starogo professora.* St. Petersburg, 1914.

Khranevich, K. N. *Pri starykh poriadkakh.* Kiev, 1896.

"Kievskii sobor 1884 g." *RA*, 1908, nos. 8–9.

Klebanovskii, P. I. *Boguslavskoe dukhovnoe uchilishche.* Kiev, 1894.

Korsunskii, I. N. "Pis'ma mitr. Filareta i Serafima." *RA*, 1899, no. 6.

Kriukovskii, V. Ia. *Okolo bursy.* Sventsiany, 1914.

Lavrov, M. E. *Avtobiografiia sel'skogo sviashchennika.* Vladimir, 1900.

Leontii (Lebedinskii). "Moi zametki i vospominaniia." *BV,* 1913, nos. 9–12; 1914, nos. 1–3.

Listovskii, I. "Filaret, arkhiepiskop chernigovskii." *RA,* 1887, nos. 8–11.

Luppov, P. *V dukhovnom uchilishche. Viatskoe dukhovnoe uchilishche v nachale poslednei chetverti proshlogo stoletiia.* St. Petersburg, 1913.

L'vov, A. N. "Kniaz'ia tserkvi." *KA,* 39 (1930): 108–48; 40 (1930): 97–124.

―――. *Pis'ma dukhovnykh i svetskikh lits k mitropolitu moskovskomu Filaretu* (St. Petersburg, 1900).

M.V. *Shkol'nye i semeinye vospominaniia.* 2 vols. St. Petersburg, 1911–15.

Malein, I. M. *Moi vospominaniia.* Tver, 1910.

"Materialy dlia biografii mitr. Filareta." *ChOLDP,* 1868, kn. 5–6; 1869, kn. 6–9; 1870, kn. 10–12; 1871, nos. 2–4, 6–9, 11–12.

"Materialy dlia istorii russkoi tserkvi." *ChOLDP,* 1874, no. 11; 1875, no. 2; 1876, nos. 5, 8; 1877, no. 12.

Meshcherskii, V. P. *Moi vospominaniia.* 3 vols. St. Petersburg, 1897–1912.

Miliutin, D. A. *Dnevnik.* 4 vols. Moscow, 1947–50.

Mneniia preosviashchennykh eparkhial'nykh arkhiereev otnositel'no proekta preobrazovaniia dukhovno-sudebnoi chasti. 2 vols. St. Petersburg, 1874–76.

[Murav'ev, A. N.] "Zapiska A. N. Murav'eva o sostoianii pravoslavnoi tserkvi v Rossii." *RA,* 1883, no. 3: 175–203.

Nachal'nye narodyne uchilishcha i uchastie v nikh pravoslavnogo dukhovenstva. [St. Petersburg, 1866].

Nikanor (Brovkovich). *Biograficheskie materialy.* Odessa, 1900.

―――. "Pis'ma arkhiepiskopa Nikanora." *RA,* 1909, no. 6.

―――. "Zapiski prisutstvuiushchego v Sv. Sinode." *RA,* 1906, nos. 7–12.

Nikitenko, A. V. *Dnevnik.* 3 vols. Moscow, 1955.

Nikitin, I. S. *Sochineniia.* 4 vols. Moscow, 1960.

Nikodim (Kazantsev). "Zhizn' arkhimandrita Nikodima." *BV,* 1910, nos. 1–3, 11–12.

Nikodim (Krasnoiarskii). "O Filarete." *ChOIDR,* 101 (1877), otd. 2: 1–114.

Ob uchilishchakh devits dukhovnogo zvaniia. St. Petersburg, 1866.

Ob uchilishchakh dlia devits dukhovnogo zvaniia. Moscow. 1866.

Obzor deiatel'nosti vedomstva pravoslavnogo ispovedaniia za vremia tsarstvovaniia imp. Aleksandra III. St. Petersburg, 1901.

Opis' dokumentov i del, khraniashchikhsia v arkhive Sv. Pravitel'stvuiushchego Sinoda. Dela Komissii dukhovnykh uchilishch. St. Petersburg, 1910.

Otzyvy eparkhial'nykh arkhiereev po voprosu o tserkovnoi reforme. 3 vols. St. Petersburg, 1906.

Parkhomovich, A. M. *Stranichka iz zhizni dukhovno-uchebnykh zavedenii Poltavskoi eparkhii v seredine proshlogo XIX st.* Kishinev, 1911.

"Perepiska K. P. Pobedonostseva s preosv. Nikanorom." *RA,* 1915, nos. 5–11.

Petrov, N. I. "Pis'ma preosv. Filareta." *TKDA,* 1915, nos. 6–9; 1916, no. 1.

Pevnitskii, V. *Moi vospominaniia.* 2 vols. Kiev, 1910–11.

———. "Zapiski." *RS,* 123 (1905): 117–69, 314–45, 540–79.

"Pis'ma mitropolita kievskogo Arseniia." *RA,* 1892, tom 1.

Pobedonostsev, K. P. K. P. Pobedonostsev i ego korrespondenty. Pis'ma i *zapiski.* 2 vols. Moscow, 1923.

———. *Pis'ma Pobedonostseva k Aleksandru III.* 2 vols. Moscow, 1925–26.

Polnoe sobranie postanovlenii i rasporiazhenii po vedomstvu pravoslavnogo ispovedaniia. Tsarstvovanie Imp. Nikolaia Pavlovicha. St. Petersburg, 1915.

Polnoe sobranie zakonov Rossiiskoi imperii. 1st ser. 45 vols. St. Petersburg, 1830. 2nd ser. 55 vol. St. Petersburg, 1830–84. 3rd ser. 28 vol. St. Petersburg, 1911.

Polovtsov, A. A. "Iz dnevnika A. A. Polovtsova." *KA,* 33 (1929): 170–203.

Pomyalovsky [Pomialovskii], N. G. *Seminary Sketches.* Ithaca, 1973.

Popov, A. *Vospominaniia prichetnicheskogo syna.* Vologda, 1913.

Putiatin, R. T. "Dnevnik." *Khristianin,* 1909, nos. 1–3, 5–12.

Rostislavov, D. I. *O belom i chernom pravoslavnom dukhovenstve.* 2 vols. Leipzig, 1866.

———. *Ob ustroistve dukhovnykh uchilishch v Rossii.* 2 vols. Leipzig, 1863.

———. "Zapiski." *RS,* 1880–1892.

[Rozanov, A. I.] *Zapiski sel'skogo sviashchennika.* St. Petersburg, 1882.

Satserdotov, M. I. "Iz proshlogo Penzenskoi eparkhii." *Istoricheskii vestnik,* 86 (1901): 654–67.

Savva [Tikhomirov]. *Khronika moei zhizni.* 9 vols. St. Petersburg, 1897–1911.

Sbornik Imperatorskogo russkogo istoricheskogo obshchestva. 148 vols. St. Petersburg, 1866–1916.

Sbornik zakonopolozhenii i rasporiazhenii po dukhovnoi tsenzure vedomstva pravoslavnogo ispovedaniia s 1710 po 1870 god. St. Petersburg, 1870.

Skvortsov, I. V. [pseud. I. Starov]. *V zashchitu belogo dukhovenstva (po povodu knigi N. Elagina "Beloe dukhovenstvo i ego interesy").* St Petersburg, 1881.

Snegirev, I. M. "Dnevnik." *RA,* 1904, nos. 1–11; 1905, nos. 1–5.

Sobranie postanovlenii Sv. Sinoda 1867–74 gg. otnositel'no ustroistva dukhovnykh uchilishch. St. Petersburg, 1875.

Sokolov, V. A. *Gody studenchestva.* Sergiev-Posad, 1916.

Solov'ev, I. A. *Opisanie zhizni I. A. Solov'eva, sostavlennoe im samim.* Tver, 1905.

Spisok arkhiereev i ierarkhov vserossiiskikh i arkheograficheskikh kafedr so vremeni uchrezhdeniia Sv. Sinoda (1721-1895 gg.) St. Petersburg, 1896.

Sychugov, S. I. "Nechto v rode avtobiografii." *Minuvshie gody*, 1916, nos. 1–3.

"Tekushchaia khronika i osobye proizshestviia. Dnevnik V. F. Odoevskogo." *Literaturnoe nasledstvo*, 22–24 (1935): 79–308.

Titov, F. I. "Dva mneniia Makariia Bulgakova." *TKDA*, 1906, nos. 1, 8/9.

————, ed. "Perepiska moskovskogo mitropolita Makariia Bulgakova." *TKDA*, 1907, nos. 1–11; 1908, no. 1.

————. "Zapiska o russkikh pomestnykh soborakh." *TKDA*, 1906, no. 2.

U Troitsy v Akademii, 1814-1914 gg.; iubileinyi sbornik. Sergiev-Posad, 1914.

Valuev, P. A. *Dnevnik.* 2 vols. Moscow, 1961.

————. "Duma russkogo." *RS*, 70 (1891): 349–59.

"Vsepoddanneishii doklad gr. P. A. Valueva i dokumenty Verkhovnoi rasporiaditel'noi komissii 1880 g. kasatel'no." *RA*, 1915, tom 3: 216–48.

Zav'ialov, A. *Tsirkuliarnye ukazy Sv. Prav. Sinoda, 1867-1900 gg.* 2nd ed. St. Petersburg, 1901.

Secondary Sources

Abbott, Robert J. "Police Reform in Russia, 1858–1878." Ph.D. diss., Princeton University, 1971.

Agntsev, D. "Istoricheskii ocherk Riazanskoi dukhovnoi seminarii (1840–67 gg.)." *Riazanskie EV*, 1893, nos. 21–23; 1894, nos. 1–23; 1894, nos. 1–6, 9.

————. *Istoriia Riazanskoi dukhovnoi seminarii.* Riazan, 1889.

Aivazov, I. G. *Tserkovnye voprosy v tsarstvovanie imp. Aleksandra III.* Moscow, 1914.

————. *Zakonodatel'stvo po tserkovnym delam v tsarstvovanie imp. Aleksandra III.* Moscow, 1913.

Alsne, Sten. *Från prästtionden till reglerad lön. Pastoraliekonventionerna i Uppsala Ärkestift 1810-1862.* Uppsala, 1966.

Alston, Patrick L. *Education and the State in Tsarist Russia.* Stanford, 1969.

Andronnikov, N. *Istoricheskaia zapiska o Kostromskoi dukhovnoi seminarii.* Kostroma, 1874.

Balmuth, Daniel. *Censorship in Russia, 1865-1905.* Washington, D.C., 1979.

Barsukov, I. P. *Innokentii, mitropolit moskovskii i kolomenskii.* Moscow, 1883.

Barsukov, N. P. *Zhizn' i trudy M. P. Pogodina.* 22 vols. St. Petersburg, 1888–1906.

Becker, C. B. "The Church School in Tsarist Social and Educational Policy from Peter to the Great Reforms." Ph.D. diss., Harvard University, 1964.

Beliavskii, F. N. *O reforme dukhovnoi shkoly.* 2 vols. St. Petersburg, 1907.

Beyrau, D. "Von der Niederlage zur Agrarreform. Leibeigenschaft und Militärverfassung in Russland nach 1855." *JGO,* 23 (1975): 191–212.

Bigler, R. M. *The Politics of German Protestantism: The Rise of the Protestant Church Elite in Prussia, 1815–1848.* Berkeley, 1972.

———. "The Social Status and Political Role of the Protestant Clergy in Pre-March Prussia." In Hans-Ulrich Wehler, ed., *Sozialgeschichte Heute* (Göttingen, 1974), pp. 175–90.

Blagoveshchenskii, A. A. *Istoriia Kazanskoi dukhovnoi seminarii.* Kazan, 1881.

Blagovidov, F. V. *Deiatel'nost' russkogo dukhovenstva v otnoshenii k narodnomu obrazovaniiu v tsarstvovanie imp. Aleksandra II.* Kazan, 1891.

———. *Ober-prokurory Sv. Sinoda v XVIII i pervoi polovine XIX st.* 2nd ed. Kazan, 1900.

Bligny, B., ed. *Le diocèse de Grenoble.* Paris, 1979.

Bonifield, W. C. "The Economics of the Ministry: An Analysis of the Demand and Supply of Protestant Clergy." Ph.D. diss., University of Minnesota, 1968.

Bormann, Gunther. "Studien zu Berufsbild und Berufswirklichkeit evangelischen Pfarrer in Württemberg: Die Herkunft der Pfarrer." *Social Compass,* 13 (1966): 95–137.

Boulard, F. *Essor ou déclin du clergé français?* Paris, 1950.

Brecht, M. "Herkunft und Ausbildung der protestantischen Geistlichen des Herzogtums Württemberg im 16. Jahrhundert." *Zeitschrift für Kirchengeschichte,* 80 (1969): 163–75.

Bronzov, A. A. *Beloozerskoe dukhovnoe uchilishche za sto let ego sushchestvovaniia, 1809–1909 gg.* Sergiev-Posad, 1909.

Brugerette, J. *Le prêtre française et la société contemporaine.* 3 vols. Paris, 1933–38.

Butkevich, T. "Arkhiepiskop Innokentii Borisov." *VR,* 1884–86.

Butkovskii, A. I. *Istoricheskaia zapiska o Bakhmutskom dukhovnom uchilishche.* Bakhmut, 1893.

Byrnes, R. F. *Pobedonostsev: His Life and Thought.* Bloomington, 1968.

Chadwick, Owen. *The Victorian Church.* 2 vols. London, 1966–70.

Chernukha, V. G. *Vnutrenniaia politika tsarizma s serediny 50-kh do nachala 80-kh gg. XIX v.* Leningrad, 1978.

Chistovich, I. A. *Istoriia S.-Peterburgskoi dukhovnoi akademii.* St. Petersburg, 1857.

———. *Rukovodiashchie deiateli dukhovnogo prosveshcheniia v Rossii v pervoi polovine tekushchego stoletiia.* St. Petersburg, 1894.

————. *S.-Peterburgskaia dukhovnaia akademiia za poslednie 30 let (1858–88)*. St. Petersburg, 1889.

Chizhevskii, I. *Ustroistvo pravoslavnoi tserkvi*. Khar'kov, 1898.

Dahm, Karl W. *Beruf: Pfarrer. Empirische Aspekte*. Munich, 1971.

Dansette, A. *Histoire religieuse de la France contemporaine*. 2nd ed. 2 vols. in 1. Paris, 1965.

Diakonov, K. *Dukhovnye shkoly v tsarstvovanie Nikolaia I-go*. Sergiev-Posad, 1907.

Dibelius, O. *Das Königliche Predigerseminar zu Wittenberg, 1817–1917*. Berlin, [1918].

Dmitriev, S. S. "Pravoslavnaia tserkov' i gosudarstvo v predreformennoi Rossii." *Istoriia SSSR*, 1966, no. 4.

Emeliakh, L. I. *Istoricheskie predposylki preodoleniia religii v sovetskoi derevne*. Leningrad, 1975.

Evenchik, S. L. "Pobedonostsev i dvoriansko-krepostnicheskaia liniia samoderzhaviia v poreformennoi Rossii." *Uchenye zapiski Moskovskogo gosudarstvennogo pedagogicheskogo instituta im. V. I. Lenina*, 309 (Moscow, 1969): 52–338.

Field, Daniel, *The End of Serfdom*. Cambridge, Mass., 1976.

Fischer, Otto. "Bilder aus der Vergangenheit des evangelischen Pfarrhauses." JBKG, 21 (1926): 12–21.

Florovskii, G. V. *Puti russkogo bogosloviia*. Paris, 1937.

Freeze, G. L. "A Case of Stunted Anticlericalism: Clergy and Society in Imperial Russia." *European Studies Review* (forthcoming).

————. "Caste and Emancipation: The Changing Status of Clerical Families in the Great Reforms." In David L. Ransel, ed., *The Family in Imperial Russia* (Urbana, 1978), pp. 124–50.

————. "P. A. Valuyev and the Politics of Church Reform, 1861–62." *SEER*, 56 (1978): 68–87.

————. "Revolt from Below: A Priest's Manifesto on the Crisis in Russian Orthodoxy." In T. G. Stavrou and R. L. Nichols, eds., *Russian Orthodoxy under the Old Regime* (Minneapolis, 1978), pp. 90–124.

————. *The Russian Levites: Parish Clergy in the Eighteenth Century*. Cambridge, 1977.

Geekie, John H. M. "The Church and Politics in Russia, 1905–1917: A Study of the Political Behavior of the Russian Orthodox Clergy in the Reign of Nicholas II." Ph.D. diss., University of East Anglia, 1976.

Grigorovich, N. *Obzor obshchikh zakonopolozhenii o soderzhanii pravoslavnogo prikhodskogo dukhovenstva v Rossii so vremeni vvedeniia shtatov po dukhovnomu vedomstvu 1764–1863*. St. Petersburg, 1867.

Harms, B. "Die örtliche Herkunft der evangelischen und katholischen Geistlichen in Württemberg." In *Festgaben für Friedrich Julius Neumann* (Tübingen, 1905), pp. 357–403.

Hartmann, F. X. "Die zeitliche, örtliche und soziale Herkunft der Geistlichen der Diözese Augsburg von der Sakularisation bis zur Gegenwart,
   1804–1917." Dissertation, University of Erlangen, 1918.
Heeney, Brian. *A Different Kind of Gentleman: Parish Clergy as Professional Men in Early and Mid-Victorian England*. Hamden, Conn.,
   1976.
Hilaire, Yves-Marie. *Une Chrétienté au XIXe siècle? La vie religieuse des
   populations du diocèse d'Arras (1840–1914)*. 2 vols. Paris, 1977.
Horowitz, A. M. "Prussian State and Protestant Church in the Reign of Wil-
   helm II." Ph.D. Diss., Yale University, 1976.
Huot-Pleuroux, P. *Le recrutement sacerdotal dans le diocèse de Besançon
   de 1801 à 1960*. Paris, 1966.
Hutton, L. T. "The Reform of City Government in Russia, 1860–1870."
   Ph.D. diss., University of Illinois, 1972.
Iasnopol'skii, L. N. *Ocherki russkogo biudzhetnogo prava*. Moscow, 1912.
Immekus, P. Erwin. *Die Russische-Orthodoxe Landpfarrei zu Beginn des
   XX. Jahrhunderts nach den Gutachten der Diözesanbischöfe*. Würz-
   burg, 1978.
Jedin, H., ed. *Handbuch der Kirchengeschichte*. 7 vols. Freiburg, 1962–
   1979.
Karpov, S. "Evgenii Bolkhovitinov kak mitropolit kievskii." *TKDA*, 1913,
   nos. 7–9; 1914, nos. 1–10.
Kedrov, N. *Moskovskaia dukhovnaia seminariia, 1814–1889 gg*. Moscow,
   1889.
Keller, E. "Das Priesterseminar Meersburg zur Zeit Wessenbergs (1801–27)."
   FDA, 97 (1977): 108–207; 98 (1978): 353–447.
Kipp, J. W. "The Grand Duke Konstantin Nikolaevich and the Epoch of the
   Great Reforms, 1855–66." Ph.D. diss., Pennsylvania State University,
   1970.
Kolosov, V. *Istoriia Tverskoi dukhovnoi seminarii*. Tver, 1889.
Korelin, A. P. *Dvorianstvo v poreformennoi Rossii, 1861–1904 gg*. Moscow,
   1979.
Kotovich, A. *Dukhovnaia tsenzura v Rossii, 1799–1855 gg*. St. Petersburg,
   1909.
Lagovskii, I. *Istoriia Permskoi dukhovnoi seminarii*. 3 vols. Perm, 1867–77.
Lincoln, W. B. *Nicholas I*. Bloomington, 1978.
McClatchey, Dianna. *Oxfordshire Clergy, 1777–1869*. Oxford, 1960.
McManners, John. *Church and State in France, 1870–1914*. New York,
   1972.
Malitskii, N. *Istoriia Vladimirskoi dukhovnoi seminarii*. 3 vols. Moscow,
   1900–02.
Manning, Roberta Thompson. *The Crisis of the Old Order in Russia: Gen-
   try and Government, 1861–1914*. Princeton, 1982.

Mannsåker, Dagfinn. *Det norske presteskapet i det 19. Hundreåret.* Oslo, 1954.

Marcilhacy, C. *Le diocèse d'Orléans au milieu du XIXe siècle.* Paris, 1964.

Mathes, W. L. "The Struggle for University Autonomy in the Russian Empire during the First Decade of the Reign of Alexander II (1855–66)." Ph.D. diss., Columbia University, 1966.

Merkel, G. "Studien zur Priesternachwuchs der Erzdiözese Freiburg 1870–1914." *FDA,* 94 (1974): 5–269.

Mozharovskii, A. F. *Kratkaia zapiska o Kazanskoi dukhovnoi seminarii za ee polutarovekovoe sushchestvovanie.* Kazan, 1869.

Nadezhdin, A. *Istoriia S.-Peterburgskoi pravoslavnoi dukhovnoi seminarii, 1801–84 gg.* St. Petersburg, 1885.

Neher, A. *Die katholische und evangelische Geistlichkeit Württembergs, 1817–1901.* Ravensburg, 1904.

Nichols, R. L. "Metropolitan Filaret of Moscow and the Awakening of Orthodoxy." Ph.D. diss., University of Washington, 1972.

Nikol'skii, P. *Istoriia Voronezhskoi dukhovnoi seminarii.* 2 vols. Voronezh, 1898–99.

Norrman, Ragnar. *Från prästöverflöd till prästbrist. Prästrykryteringen i Uppsala Ärkestift 1786–1965.* Uppsala, 1970.

Orlovsky, Daniel T. *The Limits of Reform: The Ministry of Interior, 1802–1881.* Cambridge, 1981.

Oswalt, Julia. *Kirchliche Gemeinde und Bauernbefreiung.* Göttingen, 1975.

Papkov, A. A. *Tserkovno-obshchestvennye voprosy v epokhu Tsaria-Osvoboditelia (1855–70 gg.).* St. Petersburg, 1902.

Parkhomovich, I. M. *Dukhovnye uchebnye zavedeniia Kishinevskoi eparkhii.* Kishinev, 1913.

Pearson, T. S. "Ministerial Conflict and Local Self-Government Reform in Russia, 1877–1890." Ph.D. diss., University of North Carolina, 1977.

[Petrovskii, E.] *Istoricheskaia spravka kasatel'no sposobov obespecheniia soderzhaniem pravoslavnogo prikhodskogo dukhovenstva v Rossii za sinodal'nyi period upravleniia russkoiu tserkov'iu.* St. Petersburg, 1910.

Pravdin, E. I. *Istoriia Shuiskogo, Vladimirskoi gubernii, dukhovnogo uchilishcha so vremeni osnovaniia ego v 1816 g. po 1886 g.* Vladimir, 1887.

Preobrazhenskii, I. V. *Otechestvennaia tserkov' po statisticheskim dannym, 1840–1 po 1890–1 gg.* 2nd ed. St. Petersburg, 1901.

Pruett, J. H. *Parish Clergy under the Late Stuarts.* Urbana, 1978.

Radetskii, V. *Kievskaia dukhovnaia seminariia v 1-oi polovine XIX st.* Kiev, 1907.

Rashin, A. G. "Gramotnost' i narodnoe obrazovanie v Rossii v XIX i nachale XX v." *IZ,* 37 (1951): 28–80.

Rieber, Alfred J. "Alexander II: A Revisionist View." *Journal of Modern History,* 43 (1971): 42–58.

Runovskii, N. *Tserkovno-grazhdanskoe zakonopolozhenie otnositel'no pravoslavnogo dukhovenstva v tsarstvovanie imp. Aleksandra II.* Kazan, 1898.

Russell, Anthony. *The Clerical Profession.* London, 1980.

Ruud, C. A. "The Russian Empire's New Censorship Law of 1865." *Canadian-American Slavic Studies,* 3 (1969): 235–45.

Schneider, J. *Die evangelischen Pfarrer der Markgrafschaft Baden-Durlach in der zweiten Hälfte des achtzehnten Jahrhunderts.* Lahr/Baden, 1936.

Sedykh, N. P. *Ocherk istorii Permskoi dukhovnoi seminarii za 1877-1884 gg.* Perm, 1915.

Shchetinina, G. I. *Universitety v Rossii i Ustav 1884 g.* Moscow, 1976.

Simon, G. *Konstantin Petrovič Pobedonoscev und die Kirchenpolitik des Heiligen Sinod, 1880-1905.* Göttingen, 1969.

Sinel, A. *The Classroom and the Chancellery: State Educational Reform in Russia under Count Dmitry Tolstoi.* Cambridge, Mass., 1973.

Smirnov, S. K. *Istoriia Moskovskoi dukhovnoi akademii do ee preobrazovaniia.* Moscow, 1879.

Smolitsch, I. *Geschichte der russischen Kirche, 1700-1917.* Leiden, 1964.

Sorenson, Thomas. "The Thought and Policies of Konstantin P. Pobedonostsev." Ph.D. diss., University of Washington, 1977.

Speranskii, I. *Ocherk istorii Smolenskoi dukhovnoi seminarii.* Smolensk, 1892.

Starr, S. F. *Decentralization and Self-Government in Russia, 1830-70.* Princeton, 1972.

Strel'bitskii, I. *Letopis' Odesskoi dukhovnoi seminarii.* Odessa, 1913.

Stroup, John M. "The Struggle for Identity in the Clerical Estate: Northwest German Protestant Opposition to Absolutist Policy in the Eighteenth Century." Ph.D. diss., Yale University, 1980.

Tackett, Timothy. *Priest and Parish in Eighteenth-Century France.* Princeton, 1977.

Tackett, Timothy, and Langlois, C. "Ecclesiastical Structures and Clerical Geography on the Eve of the French Revolution." *French Historical Studies,* 11 (1980): 352–70.

Taranovsky, Theodore. "The Politics of Counter-Reform: Autocracy and Bureaucracy in the Reign of Alexander III, 1881-1894." Ph.D. diss., Harvard University, 1976.

Teodorovich, F. *Volynskaia dukhovnaia seminariia.* Pochaev, 1901.

Ternovskii, S. A. *Istoricheskaia zapiska o sostoianii Kazanskoi dukhovnoi akademii posle ee preobrazovaniia, 1870-92 gg.* Kazan, 1892.

Titlinov, B. V. *Dukhovnaia shkola v Rossii v XIX st.* 2 vols. Vil'na, 1908-09.

———. *Molodezh' i revoliutsiia. Iz istorii revoliutsionnogo dvizheniia sredi uchashcheisia molodezhi dukhovnykh i srednikh uchebnykh zavedenii, 1860-1905 gg.* Leningrad, 1924.

Titov, F. I. *Makarii Bulgakov, mitropolit moskovskii i kolomenskii*. 2 vols. Kiev, 1895–1903.

Troitskii, A. *Penzenskaia dukhovnaia seminariia za istekshii stoletnii period ee sushchestvovaniia (1800–1900)*. Penza, 1901.

Verkhovskoi, P. V. *Uchrezhdenie dukhovnoi kollegii i dukhovnyi reglament*. 2 vols. Rostov-na-Donu, 1916.

Vinogradov, N. *Istoricheskaia zapiska o Pereiaslavl-Zalesskom dukhovnom uchilishche*. Vladimir, 1888.

Vostokov, N. M. "Innokentii, arkhiepiskop Khersonskii." *RS*, 21 (1878), nos. 2, 4; 23 (1878), no. 11; 24 (1879), no. 4.

Werdermann, H. *Der evangelische Pfarrer in Geschichte und Gegenwart*. Leipzig, 1925.

———. "Pfarrerstand und Pfarramt in Zeitalter der Orthodoxie in der Mark Brandenburg." *JBKG*, 23 (1928): 53–133.

Whelan, Heide W. *Alexander III and the State Council: Bureaucracy and Counter-Reform in Late Imperial Russia*. New Brunswick, 1982.

Wortman, Richard A. *The Development of a Russian Legal Consciousness*. Chicago, 1976.

Zaionchkovskii, P. A. *Rossiiskoe samoderzhavie v kontse XIX v*. Moscow. 1970.

Zelnik, Reginald E. *Labor and Society in Tsarist Russia: The Factory Workers of St. Petersburg, 1855–70*. Stanford, 1971.

Znamenskii, P. V. *Istoriia Kazanskoi dukhovnoi akademii za pervyi (doreformennyi) period ee sushchestvovaniia*. 3 vols. Kazan, 1891–92.

———. *Prikhodskoe dukhovenstvo v Rossii so vremeni Petra Velikogo*. Kazan, 1873.

INDEX

LIBRARY OF CONGRESS CATALOGING IN PUBLICATION DATA

Freeze, Gregory L., 1945–
   The parish clergy in nineteenth-century Russia.

   Bibliography: p.
   Includes index.
   1. Orthodox Eastern Church—Soviet Union—Clergy—History—19th
century.   2. Church renewal—Orthodox Eastern Church—History—19th
century.   3. Soviet Union—Church history.   4. Clergy—Soviet Union—
History—19th century.   I. Title.
BX540.F72 1983   262′.141947   82-61361
ISBN 0-691-05381-2